Hasidic People

Hasidic People

· A Place in the New World ·

Jerome R. Mintz

Harvard University Press
Cambridge, Massachusetts
London, England
1992

This book is printed on acid-free paper, and its binding
materials have been chosen for strength and durability.

Library of Congress Cataloging-in-Publication Data
Mintz, Jerome R.
Hasidic people: a place in the new world /
Jerome R. Mintz.
p.   cm.
Includes bibliographical references and index.
ISBN 0–674–38115–7 (acid-free paper)
1. Hasidim—New York (N.Y.)—Social life and customs.
2. Jews—New York (N.Y.)—Social life and customs.
3. Hasidism—History.   4. Habad.   5. Satmar Hasidim.
6. New York (N.Y.)—Social life and customs.   I. Title.
F128.9.J5M46   1992
974.7'1004924—dc20   92–6573
CIP

For
Betty, Aviva, Aaron, and Paul

Acknowledgments

This work would not have been possible without the cooperation and assistance of a great many persons in the Hasidic community. Those who have helped are among the rank and file as well as the leadership. There are still others who are related to the Hasidic community in one way or another. I am also grateful to the dozen or so Hasidim from various courts who read chapters in manuscript and offered their criticism and comments. It is impossible to name them all here but they all have my thanks and gratitude. Many of those who aided me have diametrically opposed views from each other. Of course they are not responsible for my point of view and analyses.

Israel Friedman was an invaluable guide to the history of the Boyaner Hasidim. I am grateful to the Friedman, Brayer, and Heschel families, without whose cooperation I have could not recorded so much of the history of the Rizhin dynasty. Lubavitcher Hasidim (including Simon Jacobson, Aaron Raskin, Mendel Shemtov, Yehuda Krinsky, Avrom Flint, Barukh Jacobson, and Pinchas Korf among others) offered tremendous help and assistance. I especially thank Simon Jacobson for his critique of several chapters. I am also grateful to a number of Satmar Hasidim and a great many Hasidim from a variety of courts whose identities I must protect. I thank also Rabbi Morris Shmidman and the Council of Jewish Organizations of Borough Park, and Samuel A. Weismandel of the village of New Square. In addition to providing valuable testimony, Dr. Rashi Shapiro read and commented on the chapters on family concerns. Edwin Svigals and Lawrence Fine read the manuscript with great care and made valuable suggestions.

Martin Needelman and Nathan Lewin read and commented on chapters containing legal materials and generously made available to me a variety of legal documents. Terrence L. Olivo reviewed material concerning the Monroe-Woodbury school district. My colleague Henry Fischel helped me countless times with his wisdom and kindness.

The Thrall Library of Middletown, New York, opened its newspaper files to me, and I am grateful to Mattie Gaines, Linda Amumick, and Susan Weekly for forwarding new materials. Stephen Katz advised me on Hebrew orthography. John M. Hollingsworth prepared the map. Elena Fraboschi gave me an entree into some of the more sophisticated uses of the computer, which eased the pain of organizing and editing the manuscript. Michael Morgan and Andrea Singer supplied valuable references. Mildred Mintz, my mother, collected out-of-the-way newspaper clippings and translated out-of-date Yiddish expressions.

I am especially grateful for a senior fellowship year provided by the National Endowment for the Humanities. The Lucius N. Littauer Foundation and the Jewish Studies Program of Indiana University offered additional assistance at critical moments to aid in the completion of this work. My thanks go to William Lee Frost, President of the Littauer Foundation, and to Alvin Rosenfeld, Director of the Jewish Studies Program. Some material on the courts and police action appeared earlier in "Ethnic Activism: The Hasidic Example," *Judaism: A Quarterly Journal of Jewish Life and Thought,* 28, no. 4, Fall 1979.

My wife, Betty, has never before allowed me to thank her in print for her help in thinking through this book and other works. She has been my most demanding and ablest critic.

Contents

Contents

Hasidic People

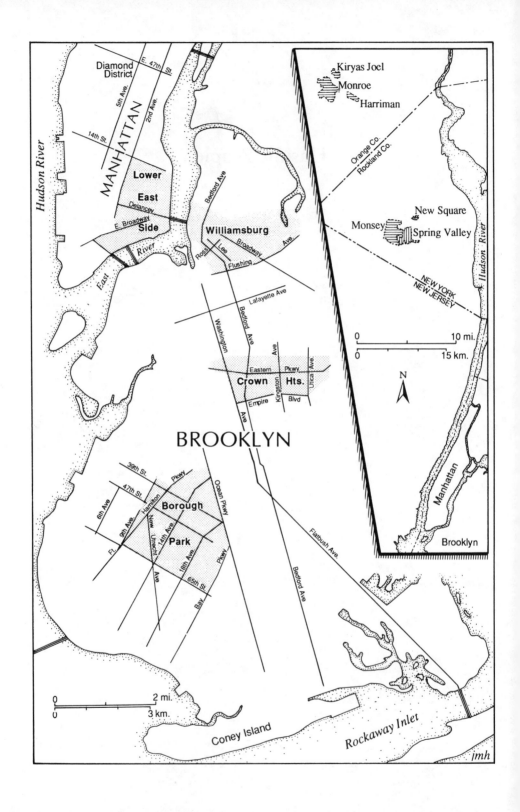

Diamond District
E. 47th St.
5th Ave.
2nd Ave.
14th St.
MANHATTAN
Hudson River
Lower
East
Delancey
E. Broadway
Side
East River
River
Ross
Lee
Bedford Ave
Williamsburg
Broadway
Flushing
Ave.
Lafayette Ave.
Washington
Bedford Ave.
Ave.
Eastern
Pkwy
Utica Ave.
Crown Hts.
Kingston
Empire
Blvd
BROOKLYN
39th St.
Pkwy
47th St.
Hamilton
6th Ave
Borough
Ocean Pkwy
9th Ave
New
14th Ave
Park
Ft.
Utrecht
18th Ave
Pkwy
Ave.
65th St.
Bay
Flatbush Ave.
Bedford Ave.
0   2 mi.
0   3 km.
Coney Island
Rockaway Inlet

Kiryas Joel
Monroe
Harriman
Orange Co.
Rockland Co.
New Square
Monsey
Spring Valley
Hudson River
NEW YORK
NEW JERSEY
0   10 mi.
0   15 km.
N
Manhattan
Brooklyn

jmh

Introduction

Beginning in the latter half of the eighteenth century, the Hasidic movement revitalized Orthodox Jewish belief and ritual in Eastern and Central
Europe. Hasidim share a common history, customs and dress, and language; they are renowned for their fervor in fulfilling the law and for awe
of their Rebbes, who are reputed to have power to bless and to heal. To
casual observers the Hasidic community may appear to possess a seam-
less exterior. Common features and devotion to Orthodox Judaism, however, mask differences between courts as well as factions that develop
within courts during times of stress. Today, rather than a unified sect, the
Hasidim comprise a tenuous alliance of courts and court members, with
some courts on less than amicable terms.

This book is about the Hasidic people in the New York City area. It
concerns family life, social organization, social change, and conflict
within the Hasidic community. It also considers how the Hasidim have
fared in relationships with other ethnic groups, in local-level politics, and
in the American judicial system. This is a social history which examines
the perspectives and cultural values revealed in the context of events and
in life experiences.

The growth of the present community began following the Second
World War with the arrival of the survivors of the Nazi Holocaust. This
remnant of the once populous Hasidic communities of Eastern and Central Europe came to America with a greater sense of social continuity
than had earlier immigrants. They came not as individuals seeking jobs,
wealth, or adventure, but rather as refugees struggling to restore their
communities.

The Hasidim are bound together in a common spiritual enterprise. The
Hebrew word *Hasidim* means *the pious ones*. Like all Orthodox Jews,
the Hasidim are dependent on the Holy Scriptures to govern and guide
them. Their lives are circumscribed by the 613 *mitzvot* (commandments)

which according to rabbinic tradition are found in the Hebrew Bible and elaborated on in the Oral Law and in subsequent teachings and traditions. These laws, great and small, extend to every phase of their lives and include ethical, social, and ritual obligations. They concern diverse matters such as belief in God, observing the *Shabbes* (Sabbath), giving charity, not swearing falsely, eating only *kosher* (ritually pure) food, putting on *tefillin* (phylacteries), nailing a *mezuzah* (small scroll) to the doorpost, as well as laws, such as those governing sacrifices, which can no longer be carried out. The Hasidim, however, are set apart from other Orthodox Jews: they are distinguished by their distinctive social organization centered around Rebbes, by their identification with their unique history, and by the enthusiasm and joy they bring to the punctiliousness of Orthodox Judaism.

The intense piety of the Hasidim, and of many others in the ultra-Orthodox world, is given its impulse by supernatural and social considerations. The fate of the Jewish community is tied to fulfillment of the mitzvot, for in the eyes of the Hasidim, impieties have resulted in exile, delay in the coming of the Messiah, and, according to some, the terrible tragedies of this century. The 613 mitzvot are thought to have a correspondence to the 248 "limbs" of the human body and the 365 days of the year and bear specific consequences for the individual and the community. In kabbalistic terms the mitzvot are tied to the structure of the human soul, and, in the event of failure or error in carrying them out, to the punishment and purification of the soul through various transmigrations.

An ascetic sensibility, as well as a nagging fear, encourages the Hasidim to seek out greater degrees of difficulty in fulfillment of their faith. To protect the community from contaminating offenses, the Hasidim post additional strictures as a protective buffer to the law. These may be precepts regarding clothing, customs, diet, and the separation of the sexes. Each new situation encountered is measured to determine if it is in keeping with the law.

Religious zealousness is softened by Hasidic social values. From their earliest years every Hasid knows what is required in terms of social action and religious ritual: "Torah, worship, and acts of lovingkindness." [1] The first two provide structure, order, and tradition for the Hasidic community. They set the calendar for the day and the year. The third, however, gives each day its special delight. Acts of lovingkindness not only bring satisfaction to the giver and to the receiver but establish a community-wide ambiance of joy and satisfaction. Acts of lovingkindness and charity (*tzedakah*) go hand in hand. [2] When there are pain and inequality in the world, those who practice their piety can help to redress misfortune through the performance of mitzvot.

The Hasidim are divided into twenty-five to thirty separate communities (or courts) ranging in size from 100 to 5,000 and more families, with ties based on affiliation, ideology, and dynastic lines. Each court is bound by faith and loyalty to a particular Rebbe, the term used by the Hasidim to denote their religious leader, and by extension to previous Rebbes in the same lineage. This allegiance is usually a family tradition passed on from father to son. An attachment to a Rebbe may also be formed through attendance at the Rebbe's *yeshivah* (a school for the study of rabbinic literature), or it may come about after a long search for a wise man, a healer, or a father figure. In most instances it is a lifelong relationship that is seldom questioned and rarely altered.

Each Rebbe is believed by his followers to possess remarkable powers because of his holiness, his devotion to the law and to prayer, and his lineage linking him to the great Rebbes of past generations. In Europe each Rebbe had his *hoyf* (court) where the synagogue, the *mikvah* (ritual bath), and the Rebbe's residence were located. Now as then, each Rebbe's point of view concerning spiritual and temporal matters lends his court its philosophy and style, and helps to establish customs, patterns of behavior, and dress.

The followers of a Rebbe customarily visit him at least once a year to receive his blessing. Then and at other visits they may ask for his help in resolving problems. Each such visitor presents a *kvitl* (petition) which contains the name of the petitioner, the problem to be resolved, and the blessings needed. It also lists the name of the petitioner's mother, through whom it is possible to trace the lineage of the petitioner's soul. In this way the Rebbe is able to determine the root of the problem and to pray for its resolution. The Rebbes are thought to move in spheres not understood by ordinary men. It is believed that the Rebbes can, in dire circumstances, intercede on behalf of their followers with the Heavenly Court. Their prayers, unhampered by the gross sins of lesser men, fly upward and are received on high.

The Rebbes customarily are asked for aid in the problematic areas of life—the birth of a child, an illness, or economic difficulty. Often the Rebbe offers a petitioner his blessing and general assurance. At times the Rebbe's diagnosis suggests unusual precision. Misfortune and ill luck are sometimes traced to a ritual object, such as a missing or misshapen letter in tefillin or a mezuzah; a remedy sometimes requires the performance of a neglected ritual, such as going to the ritual bath. Even when a physician is called and modern medicine provides a cure, x-rays, surgery, and antibiotics do not eliminate faith in the power of the Rebbe. Believers inevitably discover that mystical aid was necessary to locate the right doctor and to select the appropriate medicine.

In the Hasidic community there are significant differences between the offices of Rebbe and rabbi. The Rebbes rule the courts. Their social and spiritual authority exceeds that of the rabbis. While the Rebbe assumes the place held by his father as if by natural right, a rabbi is appointed to his post by the *kehillah,* the community, which provides him with a contract and a salary. While the Rebbe inherits his place, rabbis are granted *semikhah,* their rabbinic degree, after a course of study at a yeshivah or with a leading scholar. To be considered a bona fide rabbi, however, one must be the leader of a congregation, or the head of a yeshivah, or a master teacher and scholar—one of those to whom the community turns for knowledge of the law.[3]

The rabbi is not the Rebbe. In his own mind and in the eyes of the other Hasidim, the rabbi does not possess the unique insights and extraordinary powers of the Rebbe. He does not accept *kvitlekh* (petitions) and with them the responsibility for the well-being of his followers. The major province of the rabbi lies in determining the parameters of the law: what conduct is permitted or forbidden under certain circumstances. It can involve matters of personal concern (such as fertility or sexual behavior), the handling of business affairs, or requirements in community matters such as *shehitah,* the ritual slaughtering of animals. In any of these and countless other matters, violations of the laws adversely affect the individual and can contaminate the purity of an entire community. A rabbi also serves as a *dayyan* (judge) to hear and settle civil disputes, either alone or with two other rabbis. He officiates at ceremonies concerning marriage, divorce, and death; he addresses the congregation on occasion; and he may handle a host of other matters that have made the rabbi's role more varied in America than it was in Europe. The rabbi usually addresses the congregation a few times during the year, and individual Hasidim meet with him and ask his advice, usually on matters concerning ritual law.

A chief rabbi of a group in the community compared the roles of the two key figures:

> A rabbi is somebody who has studied more law than other people. When there's a question of what to do I'm able to tell them. Also I can hold sermons, with the help of God, to show them what I believe is the right thing to do. That's as far as it goes. I can convey to them what I feel is right, but I don't profess that I can perceive and that I can expect to know what they actually need.
>
> The Rebbe is someone who recognizes the functions of the soul. He can direct a person, help him, with wisdom and with prayer, to control himself and to guide him in the proper way. The Rebbe can anticipate the problems that everybody encounters in everyday life. He counsels him how to serve his Creator during the course of prayer, the study of Talmud, performing mitzvot. That's what a Rebbe means.   (MW)

The Hasidim, and all Orthodox Jews, are as interested in the workings of the world as are biologists, physicists, and social scientists; but the theories Hasidim believe operative are mystical rather than organic, mechanical, or social and historical. The creation of the universe, the causes of disease, the unfolding of events are thought to be tied to the deity and to the sacred ritual and moral structure. While all events are believed to be preordained by God, good works, obedience to the law, and prayer are believed to control man's fate. The predetermined order of events can be annulled by a *tzaddik* (a righteous man), a Rebbe: "I rule man; who rules Me? [It is] the righteous: for I make a decree and he [may] annul it." [4]

The flexibility required in such a complex system is supplied by belief in *mofsim* (miracles). Reliance on miracles performed by a righteous man, most often a Rebbe, has been a key concept in Hasidism from its inception to the present. Tales of miracles performed, of prophetic foresight, and of medical cures make up the bulk of the continuing corpus of Hasidic tales. At the foundation of every legend and tale is an unshakable faith in the efficacy of prayer. This inherent power available to the righteous is believed to be achieved by concentration, communion with God, and enthusiasm. [5]

> I'll tell you a story which is relevant to this. This is about my father, God bless him. He is an ordinary man, a fine man, but he is far from being a Rebbe. I mean you know my father. He was a *shohet* [ritual slaughterer]. This goes back thirty years or so. I was a small child. We were a household of children. We grew up in Antwerp in Belgium. There was this carpenter who came to fix one of the beds or a piece of furniture. And since my father had a lot of children, he wasn't that rich, so he asked him, "How much do you charge?"
>
> The carpenter says, "I see you don't have money. I'll fix it for you for free."
>
> My father was a *mohel* [circumciser] too. And every night before he makes a *bris* [circumcision] he prepares everything, and it happened that that night he was holding the *mohel messer* [circumcision knife] in his hand, so he said, "You know what? God willing, I hope I could serve you with this mohel messer."
>
> The man, this couple, didn't have children for ten or fifteen years after the wedding. And he said *Amen* with such belief that he started to cry. Because it touched him in his heart. A year after he had a boy and that's the only child that they have had all their lives.
>
> What are you going to say, that my father is a wonder man? It's because the man gave such an Amen with so much belief that it's going to happen that he had a child.   (AS)

Use of the term Orthodox Judaism, of which Hasidism is a part, came into currency in the early nineteenth century following the French Revolution and the period of emancipation. Orthodox Jews were Jews who maintained the traditions of the past and who adhered to the mitzvot; the term was used to contrast them to those Jews influenced by the new Reform movement, begun in Germany, which encouraged the liberalization of religious practices and the integration of Jews into modern society.

At the present time American Jewry is divided into large groupings ranging from pietists to the irreligious. There are Orthodox (including the Hasidim), Conservative, Reform, Reconstructionist, and unaffiliated Jews. Recent estimates indicate that Orthodox Jews represent approximately 8 to 10 percent of American Jews, and the ultra-Orthodox or Hasidim constitute about 5 percent of that number.[6] Within the Orthodox movement, at least three major groups of Orthodox Jews can be cited: the Hasidim and ultra-Orthodox, the strictly Orthodox, and the modern Orthodox, each overlapping with the others and yet distinguished by variations in social organization, dress, attitude, customs, and educational and political agendas.

In Europe differences within the Hasidic community, and between Hasidim and Misnagdim (their Orthodox opponents), though often severe, were usually cushioned by distance and time. National borders, plains, and mountains kept courts well apart, and news, good and bad, could move no faster than a loaded wagon, a packman's horse, or a train ride. In Brooklyn, the courts are only footsteps, or a brief car ride, apart. With telephones in every household and a fax machine in every office, gossip moves at an electronic gallop. Today a dispute may range from Jerusalem to New York, but allies and antagonists are joined instantaneously by wire, satellite, telephone, fax, the daily press and television. As a result the tradition of criticism, gritty gossip, and contention continues with an intensity more than equal to the quarrels of past times.

Before the Second World War and the Hasidim's final emigration from Europe their religious conflicts concerned the forces of enlightenment and acculturation, both considered to be dangers to Orthodoxy. The Zionist movement was also scorned for attempting to preempt God's role in restoring the Jews to the Holy Land. Since 1948 the State of Israel has been the primary flashpoint of contemporary dispute. While all Hasidim oppose the secular orientation of the nation, the most zealous pietists excoriate the new state's very existence for its violation of the Messianic vision. Animosity between Hasidic courts on this point began when some Hasidim moderated their views and accepted relations with the Israeli government. In Israel they participated in parliamentary elections, accepted ministerial posts, and received government funds for education. The argument advances and recedes with the latest newscast and with each court's response to current crises. Attitudes toward the Israeli government often determine conflicts and alliances in the Hasidic community.

In this book I give major attention to the changes that have taken place in the community in recent years. In the mid-1960s the Hasidic population in the New York City area expanded as the new generation began raising families. At the same time there were changes taking place in neighborhood life related to the migration of people to New York from the South and the Caribbean, the tightening of ethnic boundaries, the civil rights movement, and the government's poverty program. The Hasidim were forced to make adjustments in community resources, organization, and leadership. Changing circumstances and the introduction of new concepts were reflected in the social environment and in family life. The Hasidic courts I have chosen for discussion from among the many that make up the Hasidic community are those which exemplify aspects of Hasidic life and the range of social change taking place. Inevitably recent events have called attention to some courts more than to others.

Since this is an account of contemporary times, most of the ideas and information presented are derived from interviews.[7] Some information is drawn from court records and from newspapers. The Hasidim also record the biographies of Rebbes and aspects of their social history in the form of historical accounts, legends, and tales, passed on primarily in oral tradition.[8] These include tales of wisdom and faith, as well as accounts of local events including disputes and quarrels. Still other information derives from the community's wellspring of gossip.

It is forbidden to spread *loshon horah* (gossip, evil speech) even if it is true. It is still more serious to spread slander.[9] Fear of the evil effects of loose talk is related to ancient belief concerning the animosity and jealousy of evil spirits, the angel of death, the evil eye, and plain bad luck. Despite the detailed description of types of gossip and how to avoid it, gossip is a means of disseminating news and is as common in the Orthodox community as it is everywhere in the world. Of course unverified gossip cannot be trusted to provide an accurate account of events. In fact it may confound historical record keeping by providing several versions of the same events, each varying according to the point of view and motivations of the speaker. In some instances it is possible to see a tale evolving from gossip. For our purposes gossip serves primarily to provide a measure of community concerns and reactions. At the very least it indicates subjects that warrant further investigation and study. Gossip, along with legends, tales, and anecdotes, can be seen as a form of oral history and as community fiction. The tales, dramatic dialogues, and pithy commentaries are the creations of people who do not write plays, short stories, or novels, but who enjoy devising other forms of verbal entertainment.

There is little that is simple in the Hasidic world. Religious themes are interwoven with mythic ideas, historical events, disputes, personalities, chance occurrences, carefully plotted strategies, and the range of human emotion. Like all human families, the Hasidim have their admirable ideals and actions as well as a fair share of mortal frailty. I have tried to write objectively about contemporary American Hasidim without either idealizing or demeaning them. My task has been to relate matters as clearly and as accurately as I am able, so that others can see that at this time and at this place this was how matters stood, how events occurred, and how people acted.

· 1 ·

The Dynasty of Reb Dov Ber:
From Mezritch to East Broadway

Reb Dov Ber, the Maggid of Mezritch

Hasidism is a relatively young religious phenomenon, spanning the mid-eighteenth century to the present. The Hasidic movement is traditionally said to have begun with the appearance of Rabbi Israel ben Eliezer, the Baal Shem Tov (the Master of the Good Name, 1700–1760), a pious healer and wonder worker in the Ukranian regions of Podolia and Volhynia whose teachings inspired fervent and joyous fulfillment of the law. The new movement spread rapidly among Eastern European Jewry when leading disciples of the Baal Shem Tov won followers of their own and formed separate communities apart from other Orthodox Jews.

The model for these new communities was established by the court of the Baal Shem Tov's chief disciple, Reb Dov Ber, (1704–1772), the learned and charismatic Maggid (Preacher) of Mezritch, a town in Volhynia. A visit to the court of Rabbi Dov Ber was made by Solomon Maimon, then a curious rabbi and later a skeptical philosopher, who left a memorable picture of the new faith.

> Accordingly, on Sabbath I went to this solemn meal, and there found a large number of respectable men who had gathered together from various quarters. At length the great man appeared, his awe-inspiring figure clothed in white satin. Even his shoes and snuffbox were white, this being among the kabbalists the color of grace. He greeted each newcomer with "Shalom." We sat down to table and during the meal a solemn silence reigned. After the meal was over, the superior struck up a solemn inspiriting melody, held his hand for some time upon his brow, and then began to call out, "Z . . . of H . . ., M . . . of R . . ., S.M. of N . . .," and so on. Each newcomer was thus called by his own name and the name of his residence, which excited no little astonishment. Each as he was called recited some verse of the Holy Scriptures. Thereupon the superior began to deliver a sermon for which the verses recited served as text, so that although they were disconnected verses taken from different parts of Scripture they were combined with as much skill as if

they had formed a single whole. What was still more extraordinary, every one of the newcomers believed that he discovered in that part of the sermon which was founded on his verse something that had special reference to the facts of his own spiritual life. At this we were of course greatly astonished.[1]

The new movement appeared to threaten the stability of the Jewish community. The first Hasidic work, *Toledot Ya'akov Yosef,* written by Jacob Joseph of Polonnoye (d. 1782), challenged the integrity of the religious functionaries—the rabbi, the *shohet* (ritual slaughterer), and the *hazan* (cantor)—for their narrow concerns and their failure to protect the purity of the community.[2] In the new Hasidic congregations the *tzaddik* (righteous man), commonly called the Rebbe, replaced the rabbi as community leader; the role of the hazan as singer and prayer leader was eliminated so that a layman could be called on to chant the prayers. The prayers themselves and the modes of praying were altered in accord with Hasidic mystical perceptions. In self-defense, the learned rabbis, threatened by this new populist movement, argued that Hasidism diminished the place of learning in favor of idolatrous worship of their leaders, and they charged that Hasidic enthusiasm and miracle tales were delusions.

Despite this opposition, Hasidic teachings were carried to communities throughout Eastern and Central Europe by Hasidic disciples who had witnessed the new ways and the new miracles at first hand at the court of Dov Ber and later at the courts of other Rebbes. Hasidic ways of piety, humility, and enthusiasm, infused with kabbalistic insights, transformed religious practices and religious authority. In a generation the social and spiritual powers of the Rebbes became the ascendant feature of Hasidism.[3] As the new movement stabilized, the Rebbe's position as leader was passed on to his sons, and the Rebbes and their congregations of poor but ecstatic Hasidim developed distinctive patterns of prayer, dress, and custom.

Hasidic congregations became dynastic courts, each with a Rebbe as its revered leader. The central structures of the *hoyf* (court) were the house of the Rebbe, the *besmedresh* (*bet ha-midrash:* house of study and synagogue), a yeshivah, and a mikvah. Living nearby were the resident followers of the Rebbe, whose occupations and businesses were based largely on the needs of visitors to the town. Some visitors came because of familial, comradely, and hereditary ties; others were drawn by the fame and reputed prowess of the Rebbe. There was wisdom to be learned at the table of the tzaddik, and his fervent prayers were said to heal the sick and provide nourishment for the poor.

As with all Orthodox Jews the morning began with purificatory rites. The most dedicated Rebbes spent much of the day in learning and prayer. Their perspectives were determined by contacts with a past, part history and part myth, that commanded a greater reality than the broad fields and muddy lanes of Poland, Hungary, and Russia. Their metaphysical journeys in time and space were guided by kabbalistic constellations, so that some could recall their experiences in lives in earlier times.[4] The relationship of Rebbe and Hasid existed on many levels. The Hasidim petitioned their Rebbe to ease the calamities of daily life: to protect or restore their health and to enable them to earn a livelihood. When the Hasidim visited their Rebbe or listened to his *toyre* (teachings), they sensed that they were in the presence of someone with standing in the Heavenly Court. The Rebbe's lineage, purity, and piety would enable him to intercede with the heavenly powers on their behalf. He knew their problems and perceived the past lineage of their souls. While some Rebbes were beloved for their wisdom and their charitable deeds, others became famous for miracles as related by their followers.

The rise of *tzaddikism,* the cult of personality, in which the wonder-working Rebbes became the primary focus of the Hasidic movement, was seen by critics as having debased Hasidism. As the number of Rebbes multiplied, so too did complaints of abuse of their position and power. Some Rebbes acquired notoriety among their opponents for opportunism and materialism. There were competing legends related by supporters and detractors. Conflicts and feuds between the courts became commonplace, so that in religious as well as in "enlightened" circles Hasidism came to be characterized as divisive, shallow, and rooted in superstition.

The person regarded as the epitome of tzaddikism was Israel Friedman of Rizhin, the great-grandson of Dov Ber of Mezritch. During his lifetime (1798–1850), the Rizhiner Rebbe became preeminent among Ukrainian tzaddikim and the most controversial figure in the Hasidic world. Accounts of his life and activities tell of a contradictory mix of mysticism, wit, and extravagant materialism. Visitors to Rizhin and later to Sadagora in Bukovina found the Rebbe seated on a throne, as elegantly dressed as a Russian noble. His hat was laced with gold embroidery. He had a moustache but only a small beard, and his eyes were said to be hypnotic.[5]

Critics of Hasidism frequently cited the lavish customs of the Rebbe of Rizhin and derided his excesses. To his loyal followers, however, the Rizhiner's display of wealth was a symbol of spiritual riches and devout homage. The luxurious carriage and spirited horses, the great house and furnishings, the ornate candelabra and table settings were said to be symbols expressing the nobility of their faith. That majesty was meant to honor not man but the Almighty; and the rich appearance of the Rizhin was reported to conceal his true humility.

Throughout the nineteenth century, Jewish life in Eastern and Central Europe continued to be insular. The common language was Yiddish. Communities were organized according to the religious and ritual tenets of Judaism: there was an internal system of charity, education, loans, burial, and care of the sick. Grievances were redressed in rabbinic courts. Learned rabbis and the well-to-do formed the established religious and social hierarchy. At the same time the Jews were estranged from the outside society by oppressive laws and customs. Within the Pale of Settlement Jews had been prevented from owning land, forbidden to live in the cities, limited by law to a few occupations, and victimized by official policies as well as popular prejudice.

Despite the absolute authority of the tsars, Russian laws were not echoed in the Torah and consequently had no standing in the Jewish community.[6] In general, secular law which had no sanction in Scripture was consigned to a category below that of religious law. The latter is thought to be given to man by God and is immutable; the former is temporal and is the result of interaction between men. Breaking religious law carried the threat of supernatural retribution, not only for the individual involved but often for his family and all his people, and even for the land in which he resided; the secular law could be changed, argued, protested, ignored, and even broken with impunity if it conflicted with religious law.

Like most populations coping with an oppressive government the Jews developed a subsystem of practices to work their way around official statutes. In nineteenth- and early-twentieth-century Russia, in order to evade the proscriptive laws, property in Jewish hands was registered in the name of a gentile, who usually received payment for this service. Since the Jews were excluded from customary markets, business transactions often meant smuggling heavily taxed and prohibited goods. For protection, Jewish smugglers relied on the need for their services and, when called for, bribery, a not uncommon seal of such transactions.[7] In Eastern and Central Europe, smuggling, bribery, and tax evasion were not only commonplace, at times they can be seen as having been acts of protest and even heroism. In the absence of civil justice, one managed by one's wits, often within the framework of a more popular, underground social system. Such businessmen lived nimbly on the balls of their feet, never certain when the ground might slip from under them.

In an atmosphere of moral ambiguity, it could be argued that laws, even those that did not offend sacred doctrine, could be evaded in favor of fulfilling a still higher law. In some instances, however, a religious rationale was needed to support actions contrary to sacred law. The argument supporting such a stand found its way into the first Hasidic book set in print, *Toledot Ya'akov Yosef* (1780), containing the sermons of Jacob Joseph of Polonnoye: "When the Besht's soul ascended to heaven, he saw how Michael, the great protector of Israel, defended Israel by maintaining that any sin committed by Israel may really be a good deed. If Jews cheat a little, it is only to marry their daughters off to talmudic scholars and to have something to give to charity. Whatever they do is from necessity and not because of a wish to sin." [8]

Toward the end of the nineteenth century the Jewish community as a whole slowly broke free from political, economic, and intellectual bondage. The new generation saw the slackening of religious practice and the diminution of the status of the Rebbes. Eastern Europe was threatened by revolutionary social change. The new social movements of Socialism and Zionism attracted the children of the pious with their promise of freedom from exploitation and their hope for the future of mankind. Others were excited by the possibility of emigrating to the New World where there were work, liberty, adventure, and even a chance at wealth. The First World War further uprooted Hasidim in villages and towns along the battle lines and sent them fleeing into the cities, where they were a step closer to the New World. Between the years 1890 and 1924, there was a vast outpouring of population from Europe to America, and some two and a half million Jews, most from Eastern and Central Europe, made the voyage to American shores. It was not until the mid-1920s that restrictive American legislation brought a halt to Jewish immigration. [9]

The major base of Hasidic life, however, remained in Eastern and Central Europe. Most Rebbes stayed in Europe rather than accompany their followers to the New World. Social change among the ultra-Orthodox was barely perceptible until the start of the Second World War.

The Boyaner Rebbe

Reb Israel, the Rizhiner Rebbe, had established one of the great Hasidic family dynasties, first in Rizhin and then in towns such as Sadagora, Husiatin, Tchortkov, Shtefanest, and Leovo as his five sons established courts of their own. It was customary for one son to assume control of his father's court, while the others would strike out for new communities in other towns. In 1845 (after spending twenty-two months in prison, accused of ordering the murder of two Jewish informers, and five years wandering from town to town), the Rizhiner Rebbe received permission from the Austro-Hungarian emperor to settle in the town of Sadagora. When the Rizhiner Rebbe died in 1850, his eldest son, Reb Shalom Joseph, survived him but one year, and his second son, Reb Abraham Jacob, remained in Sadagora and was known as the Sadagora Rebbe. When Reb Abraham Jacob died in 1883, he left two sons, Isaac and Israel. His eldest son, Reb Isaac, decided that Sadagora was too small a town to maintain more than one Hasidic court, and, anxious to avoid a family quarrel, he agreed to let his younger brother continue as the Sadagora Rebbe, while he settled in Boyan, a small town near Chernovtsy, the capital of Bukovina, one of the eastern provinces of the Austro-Hungarian empire. [10]

Isaac's grandson, Israel Friedman, recalls:

Boyan was a small town with no more than five or six hundred Jews and maybe a couple of thousand gentiles. This was a hoyf town. The entire Jewish community existed by hundreds of people coming there to see the Rebbe. There were little inns and little restaurants. One of the businesses was to rent *shtraymlen* [fur hats] for *yontev* [Shabbes and the holidays]. You have to understand that Russian Hasidim do not wear shtraymlen. But my grandfather insisted that in Boyan on yontev everyone was to wear shtraymlen. So some enterprising entrepreneur got himself a couple of shtraymlen, and if I remember, my father jokingly said each consisted of sixteen hairs, and they rented them for a small fee. The town more or less lived from the Hasidic community, which arrived there by the hundreds and by the thousands, especially during the times of the Jewish holidays. (IF)

The dynasty endured no more than one lifetime in Boyan, as the outbreak of the First World War forced townspeople to flee from the area. Boyan, just a few miles from the Russian border, came under immediate attack, and the Boyaner Rebbe and his family and followers fled the war zone for Vienna, then the gathering point for refugees.

When Reb Isaac died in 1917, he was succeeded by his son Reb Mordchei Shlomo Friedman. The youngest of four sons, Reb Mordchei Shlomo remained in Vienna, where he had a *shtibl* (a small house of study and prayer) with a few loyal Hasidim. His social and economic prospects, however, were poor, as he was the youngest of the Rizhin dynasty, with scant hope of attracting greater numbers by outshining his older, better-known brothers and cousins. In 1924, when his followers in America invited him to visit the United States, he accepted in the hope of earning enough to support his family and remain in Europe. After his return to Vienna, however, a sudden illness consumed his earnings.

He had hoped to accumulate some money, and then with the savings he would be able to live. But when the savings evaporated he had two choices: the Hasidim in America wanted him to return, while some Boyaner Hasidim in Galicia wanted him to settle there in Drogobych. My father didn't feel like going to America and be away from the family, but my mother, being more modern, did not feel like being in Drogobych where she would be completely surrounded by an ultra, ultra Hasidic community. This would have given her no freedom whatsoever. It would have been a great strain on her as she wanted to remain in a more Westernized milieu. So he went to the doyen of the Rizhiner dynasty, the Tchortkover Rebbe [the grandson of the Rizhiner Rebbe], who was one of the great figures in Jewish life, and not only in Hasidic circles. He was one of the leaders of Agudat Israel.[11] It took everybody by surprise that the Tchortkover Rebbe advised my father to go to America because he felt that he would be able to accomplish something for *Yiddishkayt* [the observance of mitzvot and the spread of Torah learning]. (IF)

Dire predictions were made for those abandoning Europe for America. The temptations and opportunities available in a pluralistic free society, where both ideas and goods could be displayed openly in the marketplace, were always measured with apprehension by the Orthodox. The most conservative feared that the dream of freedom in the New World could become a nightmare for an unshackled populace. In America, it was said, freedom would accomplish what no tsar had been able to do—separate Jews from Judaism.

In 1926, after receiving another invitation from his American followers, all of them poor and working-class new Americans, the Boyaner Rebbe decided to emigrate permanently to the United States.

I remember before he went to America, my father went to visit his oldest brother in Chernovtsy. Since Boyan is not too far from Chernovtsy he went to Boyan and he could not recognize it. It was completely destroyed.

When we left, the entire family, perhaps forty or fifty people, gathered at the railroad station to bid us goodbye. There were tears galore. Both my mother and my father were the youngest in their families and were very, very beloved, and everyone felt they were going away and who knows when they were going to see them again. They were going to the wild reaches of America where Yiddishkayt was very poor. In general it was felt how could they leave Europe? (IF)[12]

Between the Wars: The Boyaner Rebbe in America

Like most Jewish immigrants from Eastern and Central Europe the Boyaner Rebbe settled on the Lower East Side of Manhattan. A once elegant three-story house at 247 East Broadway became the family home and the center of the Boyaner Hasidim in the New World.

We came there in August of 1927 (my father arrived in 1926) and we actually occupied three floors. The ground floor was a synagogue. The first floor consisted of our kitchen and where my father had an office and where he received people; we had the *tish* [communal meal] there. We lived on the second floor, where we had six rooms. We ate downstairs. The third floor was rented out. But during the depression we realized we could no longer afford to live in the duplex apartment, and so we gave up the second floor and we moved into the first floor where we organized our living quarters. My father's office went to the ground floor where the *shul* [synagogue] was sort of shortened and the part of the shul toward the street was made into a separate room where my father *davened* [prayed] and where he received people. (IF)

The location of the house was in the heart of the immigrant Jewish community. East Broadway, once the seat of the well-to-do, was still a prime street in the neighborhood, wider and with more elegant housing than its neighbors. The poverty of the neighborhood did not diminish its social and intellectual horizons. There were several Yiddish newspapers: just down the block was the *Jewish Daily Forward,* which heralded a Socialist point of view; nearby were the *Day,* a more moderate bourgeois paper, and the *Morning Journal,* which was Orthodox. Next to the *Forward* was the Famous Cafeteria, with a clientele as eager to exchange opinions as to eat; the Cafe Royal, where the literati dined, was at not too distant Second Avenue. Nearby streets such as Rivington, Hester, and Orchard were teeming with tenements, small stores, and pushcarts. Worshipers in the area could find a *minyan* (quorum of ten worshipers) in tenement apartments along the street. These little *shtiblekh* (one-room shuls) often had sawdust strewn on the floor as in the Old World, but here, too, many old customs were slowly swept aside. While the elders were upstairs praying, some of their young sons might be found playing ball in the street, or socializing in their own social-athletic club organized in a tenement basement.

The Boyaner family, the Friedmans, had kept little of the splendor and means of the Rizhiner dynasty. The Boyaner Rebbe and his followers were struggling new immigrants. A few richly ornamented silver candelabra remained as remnants of the family's more luxurious past. Like the silver candelabra, the Friedman family too could be seen as reminders of a more glorious past, when Rebbes and Hasidim celebrated the Shabbes and the holidays with sacred pomp.

The Friedman family retained its prestige despite the loss of its wealth. The place of the Rizhin dynasty was beyond dispute. While the Boyaner Rebbe had forsworn the path of luxury followed by his illustrious forebears, he was nonetheless an elitist.

> My father believed in aristocracy in the best sense of the word. He didn't believe that Hasidism should cater to the lowest common denominator. (IF)

The Boyaner Rebbe's reputation as a man of wisdom, humility, and charity was well known, and visitors and petitioners could always find sympathy and help.

> They came to him because he was a man of God and not because of miracles. They came for compassion and for his blessing. They didn't need miracles. What they are looking for is not someone to give advice, but someone around whom to be unified. They feel at home with one another and want to continue community identity. They need hope. They need someone to look up to or else their kids will move away.

My father did not pay much attention to miracles. He would say that miracles are only in the lands of the Hamites and not in the lands of the Jews.[13] Now when they speak of him they speak of his learning, his kindness, except for a few who tell legends and miracles.

My father studied the Talmud, and he remembered a great deal. I don't think he could be considered the equal of some of the *rosh yeshivot* [yeshivah deans and leading teachers], but he was a very learned person who remembered a great deal and could discuss matters on an equal level with some of the big *talmidim khakhomim* [scholars]. Another rabbi, the Tshebiner Rov, was an expert in *mikvot* [construction of the ritual bath and ritual immersion], which is an intricate and difficult subject, and once my father came to him and happened to speak to him about this problem. My father knew the *halakhah* [legal traditions] inside out. So he was able to speak to the Tshebiner Rov on an almost equal level. Yet when somebody came in, a woman who had just had a problem with her husband, or she was sick, or a person who was a complete *am ha-aretz* [ignoramus], he was able to relate to them, listen to their stories, and calm them.

This was told to me by the man to whom it happened. At that time he was a fifteen-year-old kid. My father's habit was on Friday night after he finished his meal to go down to his room in the synagogue. The Rizhiner way is that the Rebbe does not daven together with the Hasidim but in a separate room. I don't know why that is but that's the way. So he sat down and learned for an hour or two. Other people also came to our shtibl. They weren't necessarily Hasidic people, but were neighbors who knew the synagogue was open. Some people learned, some people learned with somebody else, some said *tehilim* [psalms]. It was my father's habit to go upstairs after he finished his own learning; but before he went upstairs he would come into the synagogue and say a few words to somebody, say hello, good Shabbes, maybe talk to somebody.

This was Friday night. After the meal he went down to the synagogue, and the only person who was in the synagogue was this fifteen-year-old kid. So my father came inside the shtibl, said hello to him, asked him what he was learning, and then went upstairs. At that time my father was no youngster anymore—he must have been in his seventies. Within a few minutes the boy heard footsteps and my father came down again, and he profusely apologized to this young man, a fifteen-year-old kid, for forgetting to say good Shabbes to him.

There's more to that story because it is typical of my father's constant attempts never to hurt anybody. To feel always that maybe by not paying enough attention to him this other person would feel bad. (IF)

Once the Council of Torah Sages of the Agudat Israel [Union of Israel] (of which my father was a member), the most important rabbis of America, came together on some emergency meeting.[14] These were all the biggest rosh yeshivot. They started talking about some Talmudical saying and they didn't remember in which tractate it was. The ocean of the Talmud is so vast that they forgot where it was. And my father said in an offhand way, "It so happened that just this morning I read that Gemara and the Talmudic saying is there and there." Sure enough they looked it up, and it was correct. On the way back one of my father's most devoted friends, also a Rebbe, who was rather brusque, and not afraid of anybody, said, "Come on, Boyaner Rebbe, who are you bluffing? You didn't learn that Gemara today. You probably remembered it."

"I must admit that I said an *umpinktlekhkayt* [not exactly 100 percent true]. But I felt that it would be embarrassing to all these prominent men, these great scholars, that I, just a plain Rebbe, should remember a Talmudical saying, and they not, and so I felt it was permissible to say a white lie." Again the idea is not to hurt anybody, not to make somebody ashamed. (IF)

The Boyaner Rebbe kept himself informed about local and international events by reading all the Yiddish daily newspapers. Although the Rebbe seldom had occasion to speak English, and spoke it haltingly, he had mastered the written language and each day he also read the *New York Times*. In those days such forays into secular knowledge were acceptable by the pious, and in the case of a Rebbe enabled him better to understand the problems faced by his followers. While the Rebbe became more sophisticated about world affairs, at the same time he never relinquished the use of folk cures to aid his Hasidim, often providing a petitioner with a *matbe'a,* a silver coin usually of foreign origin, which he blessed as an aid to cure a malady or to avoid ill luck.

Through the years the spiritual and physical center of the Boyaner court remained at 247 East Broadway. As their circumstances improved, however, the Boyaner Hasidim scattered to various parts of the city, and even elsewhere in the country. They were part of a generation undergoing rapid change and acculturation. In spite of the undermining of the faith they remained loyal to their Rebbe and continued to return to seek his advice and moral support.

As acculturation and assimilation became more widespread, the number of Orthodox believers sharply eroded. Many Jews turned their attention to social and political movements, while others were attracted to more modern forms of Judaism introduced by their German coreligionists a generation earlier. Those who welcomed the new freedom folded their prayer shawls and tefillin and stored them in a bottom drawer. Their children enrolled in public school rather than in the yeshivah. The day, the week, and the month were no longer marked by prayer services at the shul. On the street, among the younger generation, Yiddish gave way to English. Profane activities—business, card games, automobile travel, ball games—marred the Shabbes.

Even among the most faithful followers of the law, some Old World customs slowly slipped away. The elderly retained their beards and their

Shabbes kaftans; but the younger men discarded Old World dress, their beards and *peyes* (earlocks). Even the most esteemed Orthodox families were under continual pressure to adapt to modern practices, at the very least in terms of secular education.

The forces of acculturation affected the family of the Boyaner Rebbe as well. His three children, two sons and a daughter, in addition to their yeshivah education, went on to college.

> My father very much wanted me to wear a beard, and I countered by saying that there were not more than ten young people in all of the United States who at that time (the thirties) were wearing beards and peyes. It was altogether a different climate at that time. I personally, and many, many people with whom I exchanged views, felt they were not too sure of their pride in being Orthodox Jews. They felt they were outsiders. They felt this was not within the mainstream of society. Nobody thought of wearing a *yarmulke* [skullcap] outside the home. Certainly no one who went to City College ever thought of wearing a yarmulke while being in school. I frankly was ashamed. I would never have done it. Neither I nor anybody else. When I had to eat I snuck myself away to the Great Hall in some corner and put on my yarmulke and ate there in the corner so that no one would notice me. (IF)[15]

Nor was much consideration given by the sons of Rebbes to continuing the family tradition. There were other visions of the future.

> At that time [in the 1930s] the rabbinical field was in such disrepute and salaries were so depressed that most people did not ever think of entering the rabbinate. My father and I never discussed the question of becoming a Rebbe because it would only become a reality if the Rebbe were to pass away. He was in the prime of his life and in good health, and there was no question of that ever coming up. It was never discussed realistically.
>
> When I graduated from college I did not initially know what my vocational goal would be. I had unrealistic ambitions of becoming a teacher, not realizing that you needed perfect English pronunciation to pass the teacher's exam and that even a slight accent was cause for failure.
>
> I was leaning toward Social Democratic ideas, with a planned society as its end result. At that time a social vision called Technocracy, started by Stuart Chase and other engineers, believed that a planned society would best be run by engineers, who by their very vocation could run things consistently, exactly, and to the point. I thought I would be able to combine a vocation like an engineer's with my ideals of having a planned society. But I could hardly pass physics, and I did not really understand that engineering was closed to Jews. It was always impossible to enter that field. I finally decided to go into sociology and eventually into social work. At that time there was a Jewish School for Social Work sponsored by the Jewish Federation which I thought I would be able to enter and thus move into that field.

When I said I would go into social work, my father said, "That's the next best thing to being a Rebbe." (IF)

It was the height of the Depression. The first wave of Hasidic immigration to the United States had ended. The most notable Rebbes, fearful of the openness and freedom in America, had remained in Europe, tragically ignoring or misreading the ominous social and political signs.

In America in the following decades, the number of followers of the Rebbes dwindled as Orthodox Judaism declined in influence and authority. The Jewish population shifted from the Lower East Side to Brooklyn, Queens, and the Bronx, and the house and shul of the Boyaner Rebbe appeared like a castle slowly being abandoned by its vassals and householders.

· 2 ·

The M'lochim

The Malach

With the immigration of Jews from Eastern Europe cut off in the mid-1920s by proscriptive legislation, a new religious landscape developed. The percentage of Jews adhering to Orthodox precepts greatly eroded, along with public expression of their faith. Even in those neighborhoods still marked by the immigrant population, few men wore kaftans even on Shabbes, or covered their heads with yarmulkes outside of the synagogue, and even fewer women wore wigs or attended the ritual bath to purify themselves following menstruation.

In this new permissive environment clothing was selected for style and there was less concern for its modesty. There were new foods to taste, and acceptable ways for men to pass the time in the evening and on Shabbes other than at Torah study. The line distinguishing the social behavior of Orthodox and secular Jews also became less distinct. Orthodox Jews and Hasidim attended the theater, and courting couples could go to the movies without stirring community gossip and disapproval.

Despite the general diminution of Orthodox ritual, some who held to the ways of the past were regarded with special reverence. Such a man was Rabbi Chaim Avraham Dov Ber Levine HaCohen, a respected Lubavitcher rabbi and sage who was known as the Malach (Angel). In 1923 he had emigrated to the United States where he received the respect and honor accorded a distinguished Talmudic scholar.[1]

In Europe the Malach had been held in high esteem by Rabbi Sholom Dovber Schneersohn (1860–1920), the fifth Lubavitcher Rebbe. Rabbi Sholom Dovber had selected him to tutor his own son, Joseph Isaac Schneersohn (1880–1950), who was destined to succeed his father as the sixth Lubavitcher Rebbe. As we shall see, the honor brought the Malach disappointment and frustration and led to his estrangement from the Rebbe. Nonetheless, in the New World the Malach initially maintained his ties with Lubavitch. He became the rabbi of a Lubavitcher congregation at Washington Avenue and 169th Street in the Bronx.

As an eminent sage known for his piety and learning, the Malach attracted a great deal of attention. Visitors came to hear him express his thoughts on the conduct required of a religious man; others came to seek his judgment in business disputes or his advice on pressing family matters. The emotional texture of the Malach's advice can be gauged by his written counsel to a distraught father:

> . . . my heart brims with your grief and so I will answer you according to my own poor wisdom, [and] that which I have gathered from learned men, books, and writers. And that is that the father should talk to his son and explain to him to what depths he has sunk, to show his son the terrible abyss into which he has fallen, and then, let the father weep bitter tears for him so that the son should have some mercy on him. Then, certainly, with G-d's help, the son will repent of his evil deeds, and in his heart, the son will decide that from now on, he will leave his wrong ways.[2]

Bernard Sobel, who wrote on the M'lochim in the 1950s, described the anxiety raised when the Malach learned of his own son's secular interests: "The Rabbi, upon discovering that his son had knowledge of biology, suffered a near stroke. He became white and trembled violently, so that his family feared for him, and he made his son promise never to study biology again."[3]

Included among the Malach's admirers was Rabbi Shraga Feivel Mendlowitz, the rosh yeshivah of the Yeshivah Torah Vadaat, the most important Orthodox yeshivah in the United States. Torah Vadaat, which was then located in Williamsburg on Wilson Street, was founded in 1914 by modern Orthodox Jews trying to match their religious beliefs to the demands of the new environment. Rabbi Mendlowitz had arrived in the United States in that same year, 1914. He served as a teacher and principal in Scranton, Pennsylvania, until 1921, when at the age of thirty-four years he was appointed as principal of Torah Vadaat. It was under Rabbi Mendlowitz's leadership that the yeshivah rose to its position of prominence. An innovator and driving force in religious education, he started a *mesifta* (high school) to continue the education of students under his care, and in general helped to upgrade the level of yeshivah learning in the United States. While still a student in Europe, Rabbi Mendlowitz had become a follower of Rabbi Samson Raphael Hirsch, the advocate of the Neo-Orthodox movement in Germany, who welcomed the integration of Western European middle-class culture into Orthodox Judaism. Rabbi Hirsch's philosophy was summed up in the phrase, "Torah with worldly learning."[4]

While Orthodox religious principles were maintained at Torah Vadaat, the yeshivah was intended to enable the students to compete successfully in the professions and in the marketplace. The goal was to eliminate educational barriers to the acceptance of Orthodox Jews as full-fledged American citizens. In keeping with that goal, the Yeshivah Torah Vadaat offered classes not only in traditional religious subjects but also in secular subjects, and the students divided their time between religious and secular spheres.

It was Rabbi Mendlowitz's practice to bring his students into contact with the religious leaders in the community. Each week he escorted a small number of students of the high school to visit the Malach. Although Rabbi Mendlowitz was not a Hasid, he was learned in Hasides (Hasidic philosophy), and he considered the two religious figures most influential in his life to be Rabbi Samson Raphael Hirsch and Rabbi Shneur Zalman, the first Lubavitcher Rebbe. He recalled with pleasure how during his first years in America he had studied Shneur Zalman's work under an oak tree in Scranton: "Under the shade of this tree I spent many, many happy days. Here I went through the entire *Tanya*." [5]

Rabbi Mendlowitz taught a class in *Tanya* himself, and he welcomed the opportunity to hear the Malach's commentary on the holy tracts for his own pleasure as well as for the education of the students. Primarily the visits provided the opportunity to introduce his students, all of whom had been born in the United States, to an example of the "living Torah." Rabbi Meyer Weberman, now chief rabbi of the M'lochim, recalls being one of those students in Torah Vadaat.

> Everybody in Torah Vadaat went to the Malach. He was the spiritual mentor. We started to absorb some of his profound teachings. He would just discuss certain questions. During the week we would go in the afternoon and spend the evening there. We went to his home, which was about a block from the shul. We would sit in his parlor. It wasn't fancy. There was no rug; the floor was covered with linoleum. During the week we would discuss what we had absorbed while we were there.   (MW)

It had not occurred to Rabbi Mendlowitz that the Malach would become a living icon. Although the Malach consistently maintained that he was a rabbi and not a Rebbe, the students soon settled into a master-disciple relationship, and they were eager to carry out the principles and precepts he espoused. They saw the Malach as someone to be emulated as well as admired. His piety and devotion were a revelation to them. They had discovered a living saint, someone who protected himself from the temptations of the world around him and brooked no compromise with desire or assimilation. To the students it appeared that their own licentious desires, and the accompanying sense of guilt, could be expiated by carrying out the highest ideals of conduct and behavior as espoused by the Malach.

He never gave any orders. He just said what he thought would be right. He didn't force anybody. He explained that that would be the right thing to do: various profound questions, divine God-given thoughts, concepts of what the world is, how a person is to live, how a person directs his desires, how a person expresses his desires, how to sublimate the iniquities, wickedness, to channel it into the sublime. If someone has the feeling of lust—direct it into the study of Torah.   (MW)[6]

The counsel of the Malach covered a wide range of activities. Bernard Sobel described:

The boys soon began to repair to the Malach more often and to seek his advice on a wider variety of subjects. He instructed them as to when and what particular field of learning they were ready for, or which particular tract of Talmud should be emphasized. He soon began to exhort them concerning their personal beings, instructing them to allow their beards and peyes to grow longer, to give up wearing ties and other frivolous and gentile attire. He convinced them of the desirability of wearing distinct dress, such as black kapotes [coats] and hats, and of forgetting about secular learning completely.[7]

It was as though a prophet had turned to them and said "Follow me!" and they had at once abandoned their old lives and walked in his footsteps. They proclaimed their Orthodoxy with their black kaftans and prominent sidecurls. Yiddish became their sole language of study and communication. They were absorbed with the requirements of *kashrut* (dietary laws); intense prayer and study were the primary concern of their existence. Their abrupt adherence to Hasidic ways was a revolutionary turn in belief and conduct.

The radical change left Rabbi Mendlowitz in dismay. The student followers of the Malach stood in direct opposition to his philosophy and to the standards of the yeshivah. He worried about their possible effect on the other students in the yeshivah. Rabbi Mendlowitz was noted for the range of his moods. He could dance exuberantly with the students or fall into a deep melancholy. At times, as the students knew, when aroused, he could be sarcastic and blunt. The disciples of the Malach had passed the threshold of his patience and acceptance.[8]

The members of the yeshivah governing board and most of the parents seemed to agree that the ultra-pious students set a dangerous example. They undermined the balance of secular and religious studies, and they contradicted the modern perspective of the yeshivah. Parents feared that their sons too might be influenced to return to the European manners that they or their own parents had so willingly discarded. The M'lochim were an anachronism—American-born boys whose extreme piety was worn like a hairshirt.

It went much further than he [the dean] expected it to go. He lost control. He feared that the school would be converted into an ultra-Hasidishe school, something which was totally foreign and alien at that time. He called together a meeting of the Board of Directors and they decided that those who insisted on continuing to go to the Malach weekly would not be permitted to attend classes. They consented. He had their certification. Some parents complained too, but he was the main motivating force. He didn't approve this type of conduct. This whole dress, the attire, the peyes, the *tzitzit* [fringes]. (MW)

In 1931 the followers of the Malach were expelled from the yeshivah. Cut off from the rest of the community, the expelled students drew still closer to the Malach and formed a tightly knit society of their own.

The original M'lochim were in a certain way outstanding in that they separated from the prevailing group at the time and they assumed practices which were looked down on by the major portion of the public as being fanatic and extreme and not in accordance with what we would consider etiquette. I absorbed from him for a year and a half when I had my adult intelligence. He passed away when I was eighteen. (MW)

The Malach and the Lubavitcher Rebbe

The Malach understood the pain of the separation of his followers from their yeshivah and from the surrounding society. He too had suffered his own personal rebuff from the fifth and sixth Lubavitcher Rebbes, and although he spoke little about it, the students took his hurt to be their own.

Although the Malach considered himself to be a Lubavitcher Hasid, there were strains between him and the sixth Lubavitcher Rebbe, Rabbi Joseph Isaac Schneersohn, who succeeded his father as Rebbe in 1920. The conflict between the two men had its origins from the time that the Malach had served as Joseph Isaac's tutor. Sobel attributes the rupture to the Malach's injured feelings at being slighted by his former student. A Lubavitcher version of the break hints at the misunderstanding that occurred.

At a certain point the Malach told the previous Rebbe's father [Reb Sholom Dovber Schneersohn] something that the son [Reb Joseph Isaac Schneersohn] had done wrong, and his father didn't talk to his son for a couple of days. Then the Rebbe found out that it was a libel and he confronted the Malach and sent him away. (AR)

An account of the same circumstances by a Malach who is a vitriolic opponent of Lubavitch places the blame squarely on the sixth Lubavitcher Rebbe and attempts to raise questions concerning the Rebbe's character.

[The break began when] the Malach dismissed Joseph Schneersohn as a pupil. He caught the Rebbe's son reading books on the Enlightenment and dismissed him as his student. He told his father why. Joseph then denied reading the books. He [the Malach] said, "He's a liar and I don't want to deal with him." (JC)

Gradually the Malach's attachment to the memory of the fifth Rebbe, Rabbi Sholom Dovber, withered, much as did his relationship with Lubavitch. Although the Malach's ties with his Lubavitcher past seemed to be completely severed, he continued to feel the referred pain that often recurs after an amputation. Sobel writes:

> On one occasion, the Malach took down the one photograph [of Rabbi Sholom Dovber] which had adorned his walls for years, explaining to his son that for years he knew he was sinning by keeping this picture, but that he could not bring himself to take down the photo of "der alte Rebbe" who had been his master. "But now," he said, "I'm older. I've learned more and understand more, and I must do it." [9]

Rabbi Chaim Avraham the Malach died in 1938. In the following years the M'lochim continued to revere his memory and maintained themselves as a group of his disciples. In 1940, just before the onset of war, the Lubavitcher Rebbe, Rabbi Joseph Isaac Schneersohn, arrived in the United States and settled in Crown Heights, in Brooklyn, where a place had been prepared for him by his followers. The M'lochim, who felt bound to the earlier teachings of Lubavitch, nonetheless refused to attach themselves to the Lubavitcher Rebbe. They were too conscious of the Malach's sense of rejection from Lubavitch. Instead, new leadership of the M'lochim came from within the group. Rabbi Yankev Schor, one of the early students, was named as rabbi, but he shared the responsibilities of leadership with Rabbi Meyer Weberman. Both men, like the Malach before them, maintained that they were rabbis and not Rebbes.[10]

Before the new immigration of Hasidim following the war, the M'lochim had established strict standards for the dietary laws, mitzvah observance, and religious study. Their influence on others in the community, however, was slight. They insisted on separation from the rest of the community as the means to protect themselves from contamination by the less religious. When they married and had families they declined to teach their children English or any secular subject.

Although they were out of step with their generation, they were attuned to the voice of Malach and they marched smartly to the pious rhythm he had instilled in them. M'lochim attitudes and practices forecast what would be commonly accepted standards among Hasidim who would arrive later. At the time, however, it seemed bizarre to most observers that these young New Yorkers would dress and act as though they had been raised in an Eastern European shtetl.

· 3 ·

Satmar in America

Rabbi Joel Teitelbaum, the Satmar Rebbe

In December 1944 a trainload of Hungarian Jews, ransomed for one thousand dollars for each person, pulled out of the Bergen-Belsen concentration camp. Their number included Rabbi Joel Teitelbaum, the Satmar Rebbe, one of the 1,368 rescued and sent to Switzerland and then to Palestine and the United States.

Hasidism undoubtedly would have continued to be a force in contemporary European life had it not been for the rise of Nazism. Most of the Hasidim of Eastern and Central Europe were among the six million Jews who perished in the Holocaust. The fate of the Jews in each country depended in part on geography and the number of years they were under direct Nazi domination. Those close to the Russian border could flee to the relative safety of the Soviet Union. Time was an essential factor in the survival of those who remained behind. In Hungary, an Axis ally, the worst excesses of the Nazis were delayed until March 1944, when German troops entered the country and the SS assumed full authority. In Hungary "over 450,000 Jews, 70 percent of the Jews of Greater Hungary, were deported, were murdered, or died under German occupation." [1] Negotiations with the Germans to ransom as many Jews as possible—*Blut fuer Ware* (Blood for Goods), R. R. Kasztner's bargain with the Germans—for the most part failed, but the shorter period in the camps under Nazi control helped to save a proportionately larger remnant of the Hasidic population. These twists of fate in the war account for the relatively large percentage of Hungarian Hasidim in New York today, for as terrible as were the losses in Hungary, the situation was still worse in countries that fell early to the Nazis. Poland was defeated in September 1939, and three million Polish Jews (90 percent of Polish Jewry) perished in the six years of starvation and liquidation that followed. Fewer than 300,000 Polish Jews survived the war. [2] Few Hasidim were among them, and there are practically no Hasidim of Polish origin in the New York community.

During his confinement in the Bergen-Belsen concentration camp, the Satmar Rebbe was said to have maintained his austere piety and devoted himself to intense prayer. His companions reported that the Rebbe denied himself food that might not be kosher; on occasion he had traded his food for tissues in order to maintain the cleanliness required to continue his deep prayers.[3]

> One thing for sure is that the Satmar Rebbe had some higher power that I don't think any of today's Rebbes have, because he was a special gift left over from before the war to renew everything that had been destroyed by the Nazis. (AS)

Rabbi Joel Teitelbaum had held the center stage of Hasidic life from his youth at the turn of the century in Hungary. He first attracted followers in 1904, soon after the death of his father, the Szigetter Rov, when Joel was only eighteen and newly married. Joel's elder brother, Rabbi Chaim Hirsch, succeeded their father as the Rebbe and chief rabbi in Sziget— Sziget being one of the Hasidic dynasties where the role of Rebbe and rov (chief rabbi) are joined, giving the Rebbe-rov wide-ranging authority over spiritual, ritual, and organizational matters. Joel Teitelbaum left Sziget to become the leader of a congregation in Satu-Mare, one hundred kilometers distant. The Satu-Mare Jewish community of fifteen to twenty thousand included Hasidim, Misnagdim, more modern Orthodox, and others. Because of the diversity of power in the community the struggle to name Joel as chief rabbi took six years. Joel's religious perspective was clearly defined and controversial: to defend the laws of the Torah from change and to reject any view that was not based on the law. He determined to maintain contemporary Hasidic life as it had existed in the past, and he sharply rejected Zionism and secularism. No idle philosopher, he augmented support for his point of view by appointing religious functionaries who supported and carried out his edicts. When Reb Chaim died in 1926 the rabbinical post in Sziget passed to Reb Jekuthiel Judah, his fourteen-year-old-son, who was also the son-in-law of the Satmar Rebbe.[4] By that time, however, Joel had established a large following of his own. The force of Joel's personality and his unrelenting views, combined with his personal integrity, wit, and charitable deeds, made him a figure who could not be ignored.

Reb Joel's admirers saw in him the exemplification of traditional Orthodox virtues. His followers could recall that in Joel's boyhood his purity was beyond reproach and he was always prepared to study Torah. It was said that even as a child when he went to bed he would sleep with his hands inside his sleeves so that his hands would not touch parts of his body not usually exposed, such as his chest, legs, underarms, private parts, and even the hair under his yarmulke. Such contact would render one *tameh* (ritually impure) and would require washing one's hands before resuming study or prayer, which must be carried out with clean hands.[5] To be fit for prayer he guarded his bodily cleanliness, meticulously evacuating and cleansing his body of fecal matter, and changing his clothing if he saw that it was stained. Others noted that Shabbes was the only day on which he slept in a bed, and that he pursued his Torah studies day and night without sitting down. When he reached maturity, students and visitors were invariably impressed by his mastery of Torah, the ease with which he could expound on a passage in the Gemara and quote from the Midrash. They admired as well his modesty and the way he discounted the miracles attributed to him.[6]

When the Satmar Rebbe arrived in New York City in 1947 (after a stay in Switzerland and then the Land of Israel), he was sixty-one years of age, demonstrably vigorous, and determined to renew Hasidism in America. His vision to defend a Torah-based way of life was now even stronger. He put his enormous prestige to work to preserve every vestige of the past as a rampart of piety.

Hungarian Hasidim in particular flocked to his congregation.

> In the old world, in the *kehillah* [community], everybody voted [for the chief rabbi]. In Europe there were elections and when he was named the Rebbe he had to do what was demanded of him. Here when the old Satmar Rebbe came he built a shul himself and the people came to daven. The old Rebbe had a sharp sense of humor and he told them: "When I was elected I had to do what you told me to. Here I'm not obligated to do anything." He had a great sense of humor.   (YA)

The Community

The shared mission of Hasidic Jewry in New York City was to recreate the world that had existed in prewar Europe. In part this was a debt that they owed to the generation that had been destroyed. It was a way too of affirming victory over those who had tried to annihilate them. Initially the dark record of the past seemed insurmountable. There was the terrible absence of family and friends lost in the war. On the Shabbes nowhere to be seen were the *spodikes,* the high, round fur hats worn by the Polish Hasidim, almost all of whom had perished in the ghettos and camps. But unlike the immigrants of earlier decades who had sought to eliminate differences between themselves and other Americans and to integrate into American life, these new Hasidic arrivals went to extraordinary pains to protect their identity as ultra-Orthodox Jews. Distinctiveness from the American community, rather than acculturation, was the keystone of their social strategy.

The dynastic courts, united by common customs and beliefs and by their adherence to a particular Rebbe, recreated the social honeycomb that had existed in Europe. Like bees unerringly retracing their pathway to a particular hive, the Hasidim congregated according to their linguistic, ethnic, geographic, and religious affiliations. Most of the newcomers settled in Williamsburg, Crown Heights, or Borough Park in Brooklyn. Members of courts that had once sprawled from Bratislava to Odessa were now located a few streets from one another or only a brief car ride apart. Each neighborhood quickly acquired a particular ambiance of its own, as those with common affinities sought apartments on the same streets, formed *minyanim* (quorums of ten men) for daily prayers, and enrolled their children in newly organized yeshivot. Several hundred families allied to the Hungarian court of Satu-Mare (now Satmar) settled close to Rabbi Joel Teitelbaum in Williamsburg, along with courts of twenty to a hundred families each from Klausenberg, Pupa, Tselemer, Skvera, Vizhnitz, Stolin-Karlin, Viener, Belz, Spinka, Munkacs, and Breslov, among others. Russian Lubavitchers moved to Crown Heights, where Rabbi Joseph Isaac Schneersohn had established a base; in time Borough Park welcomed a potpourri mirroring Williamsburg, with Hasidim of Galician, Russian, Romanian, and Hungarian courts.

The surge of activity brought Hasidism back to life. The men needed houses of worship and study; the women required mikvot; the children had to attend yeshivot. The men helped one another to find jobs in shops and factories. A loan association was established for those needing small interest-free loans. New standards were established for the community: meat and other food products had to be not only kosher but *glat* kosher (unquestionably without blemish). A matzah bakery was opened. Modern intrusions into their lives—such as television and movies—were immediately banned.

> There's the Torah, the Talmud, and the 613 mitzvot. If you do more than what's required, that's when one is a Hasid. That's how we understand Hasidism. You can't go to the Rebbe with a question that doesn't follow the laws. With the Satmar Rebbe first you have to be a complete Jew: "Don't ask me anything that transgresses on the 613 mitzvot!" (ZS)

Codes of modesty long ignored in America were reinforced: the heads of married women, shorn at marriage, were covered by a kerchief, wig, or turban. Sheer silk stockings were exchanged for those of an opaque, heavy gauge. Women's clothing was designed with long sleeves and high necks (although styles might range from simple to fashionable, depending on one's taste and pocketbook). Clothing composed of mixed woolen and linen fibers (*shatnez*) was eschewed and a laboratory was opened to inspect fabric under a magnifying glass. Full beards, long kaftans, and black hats distinguished Hasidic men from more acculturated Jews and from non-Jews.[7]

Contrary to the common mode, men's coats were buttoned from right to left; ties were rarely worn or were left unknotted. Some explain these customs as a social response: one does the opposite of what the gentiles do in order to remain separate and distinct. Others relate the placement of buttons to the Hasidic belief that the *Yetser ha-Tov* (the good inclination in man) resides on the right side, while the *Yetser ha-Ra* (the evil inclination in man) resides on the left side. The placement of the buttons expresses the wish that good should cover, or be ascendant over, evil. Similar explanations can be made concerning the long coat, or kaftan; it can also be said to be worn to preserve simple modesty, since the coat covers the lower half of the body, where the sexual and bodily functions are located.

New Leadership

The social situation in which the Hasidim found themselves in New York was far more fluid than that of prewar Europe. If the New World presented fresh problems in the realm of employment, health, and housing, this democratic country also offered amazing opportunities to resolve them in ways that the Hasidim had never before experienced. After centuries of discrimination and persecution in Europe, they were confronted with the possibility of a more open relationship with the larger community and with the government.

The most conservative and traditional Hasidic court, Satmar, was among the first to take up the new social challenges. The question, however, was who would lead the community in this new sphere of activities. The Rebbe, steeped in study and prayer, was expected to conduct relations between heaven and earth, but he could not also be pushed to interpret civil law, raise funds, arrange loans, provide training for high-paying jobs, negotiate with government officials and local politicians, cope with housing needs, and exorcise neighborhood crime. A new level of leadership was required to deal with the secular world. Success in the social areas would be critical to maintaining a viable community.

The first priority was to name men experienced in practical affairs to help guide the court and realize a complicated social agenda. The Satmar Rebbe initially named Rabbi Lipa Friedman, who had been a bank director in Czechoslovakia before the war, as overall community president. From his arrival in New York in 1948 until his death in 1972, Rabbi Friedman had the responsibility for running the affairs of the Satmar court. A quiet, serious man, Rabbi Friedman preferred clear direction to unnecessary dispute. He davened at a small shtibl near his home rather than at the main besmedresh where rumor and gossip were commonplace and where partisans in one controversy or another tended to congregate. With justifiable pride in his choice, the Satmar Rebbe said of Rabbi Fried-man, "He could run a government."

Responsibilities were roughly divided into two parts: the yeshivah and the community (kehillah). In Rabbi Friedman's eyes religious education took precedence over more general community problems, and he concentrated his energy on creating a new yeshivah system, the United Talmudic Academy. Unlike the situation in Hungary (where the appointment of the head of the Jewish community and strict educational requirements were matters involving the state), in New York the Satmar community was presented with the unique opportunity to manage its own schools. Apart from satisfying educational requirements in English and certain secular subjects, and meeting health and fire codes for the building and cafeteria, the curricula and organization of the yeshivah were their responsibility. Municipal school buildings no longer in use were obtained from the city for minimal sums. Two separate staffs were hired to teach the religious and the English curricula. In time the Hasidim created their own textbooks in English, but initially they utilized texts from the city system and on occasion hand-me-down Catholic textbooks, which were acceptable because they did not contain material on evolution and on romantic or sexual relationships. The United Talmudic Academy soon had over five thousand students, and, with the population increasing daily, the promise of still greater expansion in the near future.[8]

The Satmar educational system focused solely on religion. Advanced secular education, college, university, and professional training in science, medicine, and secular law, which were an accepted part of modern Orthodox Jewish life, were not options for Hasidic students. Even visiting a public library was unacceptable and a subject of gossip.

Employment and Individual Enterprise

The Hasidim faced enormous social difficulties in the New World. Young and old had to familiarize themselves with a new language and the unfamiliar charged ambiance of New York—the close contact between men and women on the subway and buses, the long hours at work, the demand for consumer goods, the intrusive values hawked on radio and television and in the streets, and the competition with other minorities for housing and jobs. Their options for jobs were limited by their religious obligations—the need to worship three times each day and to devote the Shabbes to prayer.

Pursuing a career had no significance for the Hasidim, and their beliefs and lack of secular education eliminated all professional possibilities. Most of the men had to acquire additional skills in order to find work that paid a good wage so that they could keep up with higher costs for kosher food, education, and housing. A large percentage of the workforce remained in teaching, the only position for which yeshivah studies prepared them, or served as bus drivers for the school system. Some opened stores providing kosher food or other products related to religious needs. Some continued in traditional employment as tailors, cutters, and sewing machine operators. Others learned new skills as cutters and polishers in the diamond industry, or as electricians, plumbers, painters, and plasterers. Younger Hasidim took courses in the new field of computer programming, or entered the new electronics market as wholesalers and retailers. Others raised the capital for business ventures in real estate, manufacturing, construction, or the diamond industry.

The best-known Hasidic business enterprise was undoubtedly 47th Street Photo, which sold home electronics equipment, cameras, televisions, and jewelry. In 1966, Irving Goldstein, a twenty-year-old newly married Satmar Hasid, opened a modest camera store with the help of his father-in-law, a wholesaler of camera equipment. His stock soon included personal computers and other electronic items. Using discounts, advertising, verve, and enterprise, Goldstein developed the best-known mail-order business for home electronics. Customers learned that the business hours were governed by Orthodox law, and some were aware of the anomaly that one of the largest television retailers in the United States did not watch television or own a television set. By 1987 Goldstein's mail-order business and sales from his four Manhattan retail outlets grossed well over a hundred million dollars, despite the fact that the stores closed early on Friday and remained closed all day Saturday in honor of the Shabbes. In all, 47th Street Photo employed approximately three hundred Hasidic men and women, primarily in sales and office positions.[9]

In addition to providing jobs, business successes proved crucial to the educational and charity support systems of the Hasidic community. The rich provided an important reservoir of funds for ongoing institutions as well as for immediate charity needs, usually setting aside 10 percent of the profits of their businesses for the community. Some gave even more. Support for the court and the various charities for the needy were mitzvot mandatory for everyone. The Rebbe participated in the system of charity by making available the funds of the *pidyen,* the monetary offering made by visitors to the Rebbe. Rebbes customarily used the monies to meet the wants of those who came to them with financial woes—the cost of an operation, a wedding, a new apartment.

The Hasidim had quickly reestablished their own governance. They required little of the city and state to maintain a system of justice, education, and welfare. It had always been so wherever the Jews had settled in their exile. Rabbinical courts handled torts, mediated complaints, and, on rare occasions, settled divorces. As a result of the various charities, poor or infirm persons could survive without government welfare, and those requiring small loans never had to appear before a bank loan officer who would demand collateral and interest. In a pinch additional collections were made by friends and relatives in each shul and shtibl.

The wider community of Williamsburg provided further sources of strength. In 1966 Rabbi Friedman and representatives of other Hasidic courts and Orthodox organizations (such as Young Israel and Agudat Israel) created the United Jewish Organizations of Williamsburg to deal with common community problems such as municipal services and health care. The UJO also concerned itself with community housing problems and economic development. In time it served as a conduit for funding derived from the federal poverty program.[10]

In short order there were weddings in Williamsburg and Borough Park (initially with the older men who had lost their first families in the death camps), and later there were circumcisions. Soon a new generation filled the besmedresh and the yeshivot; the streets became crowded with children and proud parents. Strolling on the Shabbes in holiday garb became a sweet pleasure once more.

Satmar Managers

A variety of new leaders helped Rabbi Friedman to establish and coordinate the various Satmar programs. They served as "culture brokers," mediating between the Hasidim and the surrounding society. These men were not usually to be found among the learned rabbis, whose knowledge of the subtleties of sacred law is often matched by their innocence of secular matters. Rather, they were among those whose experiences had made them more sophisticated concerning secular life than their more cloistered colleagues.[11] Some had started their own businesses or had worked in a variety of jobs. They were usually curious about the outside world and had a bent for mastery of social and cultural problems. They were often younger men who had become familiar with American life and were able to hold their own in negotiations with officials, politicians, landlord-tenant committees, and local school boards.

Some of the new young leaders were American born. A few had been raised on the periphery of the Hasidic community and followed the Rebbe as adults or married into the community.[12] Their advice would be sought on practical matters such as employment, housing, discrimination, and voting. The Rebbe often consulted with such "culture brokers" for their knowledge of hospitals and doctors, so that he could offer more astute counseling to his followers. As a result of their experiences, both inside and outside the community, the new leaders were able to integrate new information into the community. Under their direction the Satmar court organized complex community programs.

> We do, if you will, the blue-collar work, the actual labor of putting people together with opportunities. Matching up people. It's a need that's created and that's dispensed with because the need develops. There was no one else to do it, so I did it. If you want to lead people you have to have a balanced view of the community. The emotional bond blinds you to a lot of things. (ES)

The small group of leaders and so-called troubleshooters quickly established a remarkable series of achievements. During the 1960s the Satmar court raised private capital to provide its community with a new besmedresh. The besmedresh, with room for more than 7,000 people, was ready by Rosh Hashanah in 1968. A new bathhouse for women was also constructed. As is common in most Orthodox communities, the community provides interest-free small loans. Satmar also owns glat kosher butcher shops whose profits are used to support the yeshivot. The community's own employment agency provides job listings. To keep their far-flung membership together they organized a private bus company connecting Borough Park and Williamsburg. A weekly newspaper, *Der Yid*, owned by the community and edited and published by Sender Deutsch, provides the community with local news and information.[13]

After Rabbi Friedman's death in 1972, the community programs continued under the leadership of Leopold Lefkowitz, a wealthy businessman and manufacturer, as president. Sender Deutsch, the editor and publisher of *Der Yid*, was named as vice president. The staff of managers they had developed continued to generate new ideas. In 1974 Satmar won a $300,000 grant through the Department of Commerce to operate a federally funded program of loan assistance for small, minority businesses. To administer the grant the Satmar Hasidim formed the Opportunity Development Association (ODA). Through their continual efforts the ODA soon grew to include a variety of business, medical, health, and vocational programs. It enabled the Hasidim to provide aid to initiate new businesses.

What was done for Jews in danger in the past is also undertaken for individuals today by Hasidic troubleshooters.[14] The injunction to "love a fellow Jew" is extended to individuals prevented from fulfilling their religious obligations, even if they are convicted felons.

Crimes committed against one's fellow man must be punished; however, from the Hasidic point of view punishment should be exacted without endangering the criminal's need to fulfill the mitzvot. On occasion the community has attempted to prevent the arrest of someone accused of bilking members of the Hasidic community out of their savings—because the police came to arrest the culprit on Shabbes. Rather than see a fellow Jew forced to break the religious law by riding in a car on the Shabbes, neighbors attacked the police officers in an effort to have the man's arrest put off until a profane weekday.

> Whatever offense the person may have committed, he is entitled to be helped. Just as in ancient times, when the landowner would evict a person for nonpayment of rent that did not make the person any less worthy of being helped. Although he was remiss in his obligations, it was still required of all Jews to help another Jew in redemption. Today's world is more sophisticated and the occupations are differently structured, but if a person has difficulties and if a person has problems that sometimes may result in [prison] sentences [he must also be helped].   (ES)

For the Hasidim the crime itself is not relevant to the need to aid an Orthodox person to carry out the holy laws. If confinement in prison prevents the religious Jew from eating kosher food, then a way must be found to provide it for him while he is incarcerated.[15]

> Now that's where I became involved. One, there was no kosher food in Allenwood [prison] and it took me a long time to try. I went down for a number of official visits with congressmen, with representatives, and went through all of the motions and could not get them to provide acceptable kosher food there. He was sentenced for a year and a month. [The duration of time was] not too bad, but given the circumstances it was terrible.   (ES)

Zionism

Before the Second World War most Orthodox Jews had opposed Zionism. Agudat Israel, an association and political party with a broad constituency embracing German, Hungarian, Polish, and Lithuanian Jewry, was founded in 1912 with the aim of promoting adherence to the Orthodox laws. Many in the organization would not support the formation of a Jewish state, believing that such an event should come about only through divine means. Faced with the creation of the new State of Israel their hostility wavered. They could not undermine the homeland of their fellow Jews, and most accommodated themselves to the new reality. The State was seen as "the beginning of the redemption" achieved by human hands but awaiting action by God. They opposed, however, the formation of a secular society, asserting that the law of the Torah must be paramount. After the State of Israel was founded in 1948 the Agudat Israel became a political party. Following the elections to the First Knesset in 1949 the Agudat formed a front with other religious parties. Some religious leaders came to regard voting in the national elections as an obligation to ensure the resettlement.[16]

Its unyielding opposition to Zionism set the court of Satmar apart from most other Jews. With the creation of the State of Israel in 1948 the antagonism intensified. Satmar Hasidim and other ultra-Orthodox charged that the existence of the State had delayed the redemption of the Jews. They asserted that the Zionists had violated the vows existing between Israel and God. From their point of view the State should come about only through the Messiah.[17]

> The Satmar said, "If it's against the Torah, as high intentioned and as good spirited as it might have been, it's wrong because it's against the Torah. The Torah says that you can pray but you cannot take any action to bring the Messiah." (AS)

The Satmar Rebbe cited the Israeli government's relentless campaign to undermine religious belief: inducting women into the army, building a swimming pool for both sexes in Jerusalem, desecrating ancient graves in construction sites and in archaeological digs, developing a secular school system, and allowing secular activities to continue during the Shabbes.

> The Satmar Rebbe had said that Zionism makes people irreligious. He maintained that Zionism had had a hand in the Holocaust, and every speech he gave after World War II he blamed everything on Zionism. He felt that it was like a wound in Jewish belief. Belief in Zionism, this is against believing in the Messiah, against believing in certain things that you have to believe, and so he was very strong and very bitter about the idea of Zionism after World War II. (YA)

The Satmar Rebbe referred often in his weekly toyre and his writings *(Vayoel Moshe)* to the danger of heeding false prophets.[18] He frequently cited the Lord's specific injunction:

> If there appears among you a prophet or a dream-diviner and he gives you a sign or a portent, saying, "Let us follow and worship another god"—whom you have not experienced—even if the sign or portent that he named to you comes true, do not heed the words of that prophet or that dream-diviner. For the Lord your God is testing you to see whether you really love the Lord your God with all your heart and soul. Follow none but the Lord your God, and revere none but Him; observe His commandments alone, and heed only His orders; worship none but Him, and hold fast to Him. As for that prophet or dream-diviner, he shall be put to death; for he urged disloyalty to the Lord your God—who freed you from the land of Egypt and who redeemed you from the house of bondage—to make you stray from the path that the Lord your God commanded you to follow. Thus you will sweep out evil from your midst. (Deut. 13:2–6)

The Satmar Rebbe's message was clear: In the past the peril had been associated with false prophets enticing the people of Israel to worship other gods; in the present the danger came from those Rebbes and rabbis who ignored the precepts of the Torah by accepting the State of Israel. Stay clear of them, he warned, for their efforts would help to delay the arrival of the Messiah. Regard other Rebbes with a wry, critical eye. Suspicions should be aroused by any sign of self-aggrandisement. Adherence to the Torah was his sole criterion of judgment. Reputation, personality, popularity carried no weight with him.

> The older Rebbe always discouraged people to believe in any human being. That was one of his main fights: not to believe in any human being—this person is going to be the Messiah, or this person whatever he says that is the truth. You learn the Torah. Whatever the Torah says, that is correct. When a person tells you something, you just don't go by his word, you check it up. You look it up in the Torah. If it's written there, it's okay. If it's not, no matter who he is, no matter who he represents, no matter what he is, it's not okay. That was part of the controversy surrounding the Satmar Rebbe. (AS)

Accommodations to temporal reality were unacceptable to the Satmar Rebbe. His zeal often strained even his long-standing friendships, such as with the Boyaner Rebbe, who had served as president of Agudat Israel and had urged support of Israel.

> The Satmar Rebbe and my father [Reb Mordchei Shlomo, the Boyaner Rebbe] visited each other each year. After an argument when they talked of Israel, the Satmar Rebbe delivered a diatribe. My father proposed to him that he would like to keep up their friendship but that they not talk about Israel. They agreed. They talked about everything under the sun but not Israel. (IF)

The Rebbe and His Followers

The Satmar Hasidim took pride in their Rebbe's uncompromising arguments.

> We have a different way. We are not going with the stream. Because the Rebbe did not mind what the world says. For us what the Torah says is what is important and from the standpoint of the Torah it is unacceptable to establish a government in Israel. So he fought for that. In this case we are against the rest of the world. We are damned for that. (RH)

The Satmar Hasidim carried their Rebbe's views one step further into action. In Israel, Satmar Hasidim organized protest rallies, turned in their identity cards, refused to participate in elections, and would not serve in the armed forces. In the United States, Satmar Hasidim held street demonstrations, picketed embassies, organized boycotts, and argued their case in leaflets and in the press. They badgered those who did not agree with them, and had no tolerance for other Orthodox Jews who defended Israel or who accepted state support for their educational institutions in the Holy Land. In Manhattan mystified onlookers saw thousands of Satmar Hasidim in mass demonstrations against the presence of Israeli officials.[19]

The Satmar Rebbe was proud of the skepticism he had nurtured in his Hasidim, and he joked that they scrutinized him as carefully as any other religious leader.

> The Satmar Rebbe once said, "The difference between me and my *hasides* [teachings] and the others is that if all the [other] Hasidim would see their Rebbe eating ham they're going to say, 'This wasn't a pig, this was a ram.' It's like the animal sacrificed for Jacob, and the slaughterer was Moses the prophet. [But] if they're going to see me eating ham they're going to say, 'You're a *sheygetz* [gentile].'"
>
> You know what that means? That's the way he trained them. Don't fool yourself. Don't be blind. He believed that this was the danger at all times, like Shabbetai Zevi [the false messiah, 1626–1676] and those kind of people who were given a blank check as leaders. As long as the leaders follow the Torah it's all right.   (AS)

Despite these admonitions the followers of the Satmar Rebbe regarded him as a unique, almost otherworldly being. A sign of their esteem could be seen in the new house constructed for him in the late 1960s on Bedford Avenue. Set along a row of mud-colored Williamsburg brownstones, the Rebbe's elegant white house, fronted with classical pillars, had an ethereal look that identified it with another time. It seemed a vision of an ancient meeting place of sages of Torah, or perhaps lent a hint of *Gan Eden* (paradise) itself. The Rebbe's apparent obliviousness to such grandeur made him all the more beloved to his followers.

> The old Satmar Rebbe wrote in his book, *Vayoel Moshe,* that the ways of the Baal Shem Tov have been forgotten. This made other Hasidic Rebbes angry. How could you say such a thing as that? In response, [it is said] he replied, "Listen to me. The Skverer said, 'Nobody follows the right way except me.' The Vizhnitzer says, 'Nobody follows the right way except me.' And the Gerer the same. And I say, nobody has the right way including me. I don't have the right way either."   (YA)

The miraculous powers attributed to Rebbes were scorned by the Satmar Rebbe. What prowess they had belonged to the Almighty.

> I'm going to tell you a marvelous story that the Satmar Rebbe once said. Somebody asked him, "You know that you, Satmar Rebbe, always say that there are a lot of Rebbes who are not so capable and not truly meant to be

Rebbes, and still hundreds of people say that they've seen wonders by them. What's going on here?"

He said, "I'll give you a good example. There was a villager who lived many years in his little village. And he heard that there's a big king in a palace in the city, but he never had a chance to go into the big city to see him. He heard that whoever goes there and asks the king for something is sent home with whatever he needs. So he says, 'If I have to sacrifice my life I'm going to the city.' So he sold off a few things to get carfare, and he shlepped himself there. When he got there he asked for directions to the king's palace, and they told him go this way and that way and at the end you'll see the palace. He goes over there and he never saw such a beautiful sight.

"Outside the palace they were standing guard and one of the soldiers had a big spear and a sword, and he figured that this must be the king. He never saw such a beautiful outfit. He goes over and he says, 'Long life to the king. Please, I live in a village and I have nothing for the cows and I need a new barnyard.'

"This guard that he thinks is the king asks him, 'Where do you live?' He writes this down and he says, 'Don't worry. I'll send you home special delivery whatever you need.'

"'Fine.'

"Upstairs on the porch was standing the real king. He was listening to the whole conversation. He was in a dilemma. What should he do? Should he send what he was asking for? He didn't ask him, the king. He asked this little shnook who was pretending that he was the king. Now if I'm not going to do it because I want to punish my servant, this guy in the village is going to say that the king has no power. Because he doesn't know the difference. So he decided, 'I'm going to send him whatever he was asking, but this guard is going to pay for it.'

"So if a Hasid comes to any Rebbe and has the real faith, he is going to be helped because the miracle comes from HaShem [God], it doesn't come from the Rebbes. The Rebbe is only the intermediary.

"So HaShem says, 'So that the Hasid shouldn't say I was asking HaShem and he didn't give it to me, so I'm going to send it to him. If the Rebbe isn't capable he's going to get it in the world to come.'"

So the Satmar Rebbe said, "I know that if you go to a Rebbe and he gives you a blessing, and you have faith, HaShem sends the miracle and it happens." (AS)

As a counterpoint to his iron demands concerning the law, the Satmar Rebbe's generosity and his open purse were legendary. The pidyen redeemed many Hasidim from debt to a doctor or a grocer, provided many a poor father with means for his child's marriage—the purchase of an apartment, clothing, and the cost of the wedding ceremony. Accounts of his largess are legion:

A man came from Israel needing ten thousand dollars for a couple to be married and he went and poured his heart out to the Satmar Rebbe. The Rebbe gave him the whole ten thousand dollars. (AS)

During the turbulent renaissance of the community, the Rebbe was always present to offer reassurance.

He cared so deeply for every individual in the community that he literally remembered them not by the strength of his memory but by the strength of his love and caring. His heart. If you care for somebody you keep track of them, you remember their childhood and their childhood tribulations. (ZS)

To his followers, the Satmar Rebbe was a demanding but concerned father. Petitioners who brought *kvitlekh* (personal petitions and requests) to the Rebbe knew how he prayed and searched the holy writ for answers to their problems. They in turn responded with the uninhibited affection of loving children. When the Rebbe strolled in the street after prayer, the crowds of worshipers parted ranks in visible awe. On occasion a follower would break through to the Rebbe's side and bend and kiss his hand.

There's not a life in this community that he hasn't touched. In so many different ways. There's not a single person that I know that I come in contact with that did not have at least one incident that would be considered miraculous. With me it happened several times.

I was employed in the same company I'm employed in now. I was there for about a year and I didn't get along with the manager. I was in by the Rebbe and he asked me, and then I was unmarried, I was a young man, and he asked me, "How are things?"

And I said to him, "I'm not too happy because I'm in the job that I'm in and I'm a packer. I used to pack pieces of crystal, wrap them in paper, and the manager, somehow, I think he's picking on me. And he's making life miserable. He's giving me all the rough jobs, and I can't take it anymore. And I want to leave."

He said to me, "The place you're in is a good place, the owners are very good people, and I think it's good for you."

I said, "I'm having a problem with the manager."

He said, "So who said it's eternal?" In other words he insinuated to me that this domination that this manager has over me it's not going to last forever. It's a cycle. So push it through. It'll come out fine. Good. The Rebbe says stay there, so I'll stay there.

About a month later the owner of the company comes into the warehouse and he comes over and he says, "You have a pretty good talent. I remember you write English pretty well. You speak pretty well. We're opening a warehouse on the West Coast and I simply need somebody to keep the records for it."

This was in 1973. And he started giving me more and more work. After a couple of months my position and my status in the company grew incredibly. First of all I had absolutely no contact with that manager any more, and in the eyes of the owner I had even more leverage already and more clout than the manager. I developed a very close personal relationship with the owner.

So I went to the Rebbe the next time, before the holidays, I go in and I give him the kvitl. He reads the kvitl, and he looks up and he smiles at me and he says, "*Nu, nisht geferlekh*,"—It's bearable already, huh?

I was so flabbergasted. I did not communicate to him that I had changed positions. I did not communicate anything. I had no contact with him during that period.

Those things were common. I'm sure that every day there were people who came in and were flabbergasted by such demonstrations. And I attribute that to contact with his people. I don't know how it is transmitted to him but somehow all I can say is he has certain powers. It was incredible. You can't imagine how it made me feel that somebody cares for me.   (ZS)

· 4 ·

Lubavitch

Chabad

The court of Lubavitch is set apart from other contemporary Hasidic courts. Rather than simply protecting its own domain, Lubavitch is concerned with uplifting Jewish consciousness throughout the world. The mission of Lubavitcher Hasidim is to renew the commitment to the laws of the Torah in those who have neglected or forgotten them. Lubavitch is therefore the only present-day court that seeks out other Jews in order to awaken them to their Jewish heritage and bring them into the Orthodox fold.[1] In particular they seek to direct *baltshuves* (*ba'alei teshuvah:* returnees to Orthodoxy) to join the worldwide Lubavitcher circle. In support of this mission Lubavitch is geared to the dissemination of information, the development of educational programs, and fundraising.

The Lubavitcher enclave is in Crown Heights, a middle-class neighborhood of stately houses and apartment buildings in the center of Brooklyn. The heart of the court of Lubavitch is 770 Eastern Parkway, a 1930s mansion.[2] The old mansion now houses the yeshivah, the shul (synagogue), the official library, and the Rebbe's offices. The apartment building adjacent to 770, 788 Eastern Parkway, contains the educational center and publishing arm of Lubavitch, with offices, a print shop, computers, video apparatus, and translation and editorial offices. The two buildings are a caldron of activity. Students, worshipers, and visitors hurry in or out of the besmedresh and the office complex. Small groups linger on the sidewalk in animated conversation. On the eve of Shabbes, a holiday, or a *farbrengen* (a Lubavitcher gathering), the street becomes so crowded that two police cars are posted to direct traffic. As the center for Lubavitcher Hasidim all over the world, and often the host to international visitors, 770 fittingly faces Eastern Parkway, a boulevard almost as broad as the Champs-Elysées.[3] There are six center lanes of fast-moving traffic, two narrow islands of walkway with park benches on each side of the thoroughfare, and separate side lanes for local traffic and parking. The IRT subway line runs underground along Eastern Parkway carrying passengers between Brooklyn and Manhattan, and there is a subway stop at Kingston Avenue just across from Lubavitch headquarters. The narrow cross-street, Kingston Avenue, is the main shopping thoroughfare in the immediate area. It extends southward up the crest of the hill and then down the slope toward Empire Boulevard. There is a thin line of Hasidic-owned stores along the way—small groceries and vegetable stores; a fish market, a butcher shop, a restaurant, a pizza parlor, a delicatessen, specialty food shops, and variety stores.

The Lubavitcher movement is known as *Chabad* (Habad), an acronym for *Hokhmah, Binah, Da'at*—wisdom, understanding, and knowledge—coined by Rabbi Shneur Zalman of Ladi (1745–1813), the first Chabad-Lubavitcher Rebbe.[4] Chabad Hasidism is identified with the small town of Lubavitch in White Russia (Belorussia), which was the center of life for four generations of Chabad Rebbes from the time of Napoleon until the First World War.[5] It is exceptional among the Hasidic courts in that it teaches a particular Hasidic philosophy, or Hasides (spelled Chassidus in Lubavitch circles), so that advanced students divide their time between learning the Talmud and studying Hasides. The Chabad program is complex and far-reaching: they translate, publish, and distribute the Rebbe's talks; they direct the outreach program, which includes maintaining Chabad Houses throughout the world. They send out groups to proselytize to passersby on the streets of New York, and they organize lectures and weekend visits to the Crown Heights community for those interested in understanding Judaism and Torah. Lubavitch intentions are to engender a long-term commitment to Orthodoxy and to Lubavitch.

Rabbi Menachem Mendel Schneerson (b. 1902), the seventh Lubavitcher Rebbe since Rabbi Shneur Zalman (the founder of Chabad), has a radiant presence. His eyes are quick, and he has a perceptive and kindly smile. To his followers and admirers he appears as a wise and gentle authority figure, his virtues and strengths seemingly formed by adherence to the Mosaic laws and ideals. There is purpose too that shapes his words and his ways. Since 1950, when he succeeded his father-in-law as Rebbe, he has concentrated his energies on training young leaders to revitalize Jewish communities throughout the world and to return less religious Jews to the traditional fold. As he has aged, Rabbi Menachem Mendel Schneerson has maintained his vitality in directing the mission of the court even as he has become more saintly in appearance.

Campaigns

Trained as an engineer at the University of Berlin and the Sorbonne before emigrating to the United States in 1941, the Rebbe is familiar with mathematics, machinery, and manpower, a circumstance that occasionally creeps into his talks. Discussing the revelation of God in today's world, the Rebbe uses technology as a metaphor for revelation.

> It is known that telephone lines and radio waves do not carry the actual voice of the person to the receiving end. Rather, the sound waves of the voice cause vibrations in a diaphragm which generates electrical currents. These electrical current fluctuations are transmitted to the distant receivers and there a sound coil reproduces the movements and the diaphragm vibrates and reproduces a sound that mimics and resembles the voice of the speaker.
>
> However, in our case this point is highly instructive. Here the Jew sees the potential to reveal the infinite power of the Unique One of the world right in the physical matter of the world. Here we see that even the inanimate metal coil and foil of the speaker—while remaining inanimate will still adapt and conform itself to reproduce the "word of G-d," matters dealing with Halachah and the future redemption.[6]

The worldly perspective of Menachem Mendel Schneerson leaves its mark elsewhere in his direction of Lubavitch programs. Although the Lubavitcher Rebbe frequently weaves themes from the kabbala into his teachings, he is more of a field general than a mystic seer. The Rebbe sees the task of revitalizing Jewish communities throughout the world as a struggle involving both social and supernatural elements. He speaks in terms of *campaigns,* which he charts and assigns to his soldiers—the students of the yeshivah and his followers of long standing. The Chabad youth group is called the Army of God *(Tzivos HaShem),* and the image of the Hasid as brave soldier has won wide acceptance by Lubavitchers.[7]

> We have hundreds of young fellows all over the U.S. They're all alone in the city and they don't have supervision. The Rebbe holds them together. How do you know when a soldier is good or not? When he is walking down Pennsylvania Avenue dressed in his uniform? You can't tell then. It's only when he's on the front. When he has to shoot—that's when you can tell. (MS)

New Yorkers are accustomed to seeing young, bearded Lubavitcher Hasidim in various neighborhoods throughout New York City. They arrive in rented vans—"Mitzvah tanks against assimilation"—which they park at key intersections where they urge less religious Jews to take up Orthodox practices: to put on tefillin daily, to attach a mezuzah to their doorpost, to keep a charity coin box, and to bring prayer books into their homes. The men of Lubavitch seem less distant than most other Hasidim. Many Lubavitchers wear clothing that is a mixture of European and American styles: they favor the American fedora hat rather than the fur-trimmed shtrayml, and they don kaftans only on the Shabbes, preferring ordinary business suits for everyday wear. Proselytizing is not common to Orthodox Jews, and passersby in diverse neighborhoods from Wall

Street to the Upper West Side are often surprised to be invited into the vans to put on tefillin and recite the accompanying prayers, an act considered a first step toward carrying out the other holy mitzvot.

More enduring contacts are developed at Chabad Houses. To try to restore the lost remnant of secular Jewry to the Orthodox fold, the Chabad-Lubavitch organization sends graduates of their yeshivah to head Chabad houses located throughout the country, usually close to college campuses. The Lubavitchers hold services, celebrate the holidays, and provide literature to students and other interested persons.

Other yeshivah graduates work as teachers, writers, or office workers within the Lubavitch educational system. When the young men finish their studies they visit the Rebbe to receive his blessing and his direction. They know that their mission is to teach and spread Judaism, and they are ready to set aside personal plans and wishes if the Rebbe so decides.

> I asked him what I should do. I said I wanted to become a businessman. He said, "No." He needs me. (AH)

At the outset of the Rebbe's leadership he initiated educational campaigns around the world. In their first campaigns in the early 1960s, the Lubavitcher Hasidim distributed matzah at Passover, and at Hanukkah taught about the meaning of the holiday and other festivals; but the first campaign in which the Rebbe organized his forces and sent them out on the streets concerned real soldiers and was tied to the 1967 war between Israel and Egypt.

> In the 1967 war the Rebbe came out with a campaign to visit the soldiers in the Israeli Defense Force. In addition to trying to build up their spirit, to urge them to put on tefillin every day, or as often as possible. The Rebbe picked this mitzvah because it says that when the enemy sees the tefillin on the head they will fear you.[8]
>
> The Rebbe said at that point, "This mitzvah will be a beginning and will lead on to other mitzvot. As it says in *Ethics of the Fathers*, 'One mitzvah brings forth another mitzvah.'"[9]
>
> We all know the miracles of the 1967 war, how they won the war in just six days. It definitely helped. The mitzvot stand guard over you. The Rebbe gave the example of a helmet. Someone shoots a bullet and the soldier is lucky enough to wear a helmet. If not, God knows what would happen. You can't say whoever doesn't wear a helmet will get killed. It's the same thing: you can't say that if they didn't do the mitzvah, put on the tefillin, that they would have lost the war. The helmet protects, and the mitzvah protects. This was the first campaign. (AR)

In the years following the 1967 war, until 1974, the Chabad movement marched in quick step with a series of mitzvah campaigns that are a litany of the Orthodox faith and practice. The brief list that follows hardly does justice to the depth of belief and feeling that inspired them, or to the drive and energy needed to carry them to fruition. Each campaign underlined a particular article of faith: studying Torah, giving charity, educating one's children in Judaism.[10] Then there was a campaign to encourage the use of a mezuzah, the small scroll attached to the doorpost of a Jewish home.[11] Next came a campaign to increase charity giving. This was followed by a call that every household contain the basic Jewish books—the Bible, a *siddur* (prayer book), and the Psalms—to help educate the family members. Subsequently, women and young girls were exhorted to perform the mitzvah of lighting the Shabbes and holiday candles, and to train children to perform this mitzvah when they reached the age of three.

In the summer of 1975 the Rebbe urged keeping a kosher home and eating only kosher food, and a fund was established to aid those willing to kosher their homes.[12] Next the Rebbe told couples to maintain family purity, with women attending the ritual bath following their menstrual cycle. Two additional campaigns were soon undertaken: the first to ensure that Jewish children receive a Jewish education, and the second, since Jews are charged with the mitzvah "Love your fellow as yourself," to demonstrate love for a fellow Jew.[13] In another campaign focused on education, an organization of children was created called "the army of HaShem." In this army, however, the performance of mitzvot is paramount. Members receive a newsletter with comics, puzzles, and stories; each issue also sets a mission—to visit a sick person in a hospital, or to encourage someone to light candles—that carry points leading to higher rank.[14]

In the next decade the Rebbe continued his task of inspiring Jews to renew their enthusiasm in leading a religious life and in intensifying their commitment to Judaism. In 1985, a decade after the kosher campaign, the Rebbe asked that all congregations adopt the custom of reciting two verses from Leviticus and the Psalms. Before beginning the morning prayer, one should recite: "I take it upon myself to fulfill the mitzvah 'Love your fellow as yourself.'"

No prayer better highlights the difference between the Lubavitcher Hasidim and other Hasidim. It demands an open door and an open heart toward Jews who from the Lubavitcher point of view do not fulfill their religious obligations. It is in effect a signal not to dismiss the less religious Jew, the forgetful Jew, the recalcitrant, and even the rebellious Jew. They must be drawn back to Judaism through persistent effort, kindness, reasoning, and example. Sowing the Orthodox faith among the Jews and respect for moral law among all people will hasten the coming of the Messianic age. The verse recited at the end of the prayers gives voice to Lubavitcher hopes: "Righteous men shall surely praise Your name; the upright shall dwell in Your presence."[15]

Farbrengen

The nature of the Rebbe's contacts with his Hasidim offers an important measure of the Chabad movement. For many years the Lubavitcher Rebbe met individually with his followers and visitors three nights a week, often remaining awake until early morning to hear all the petitions and questions brought to him. The number of requests to see the Rebbe eventually became overwhelming. In recent years, except for special visitors (such as Natan Sharansky after his release from a Soviet prison) private audiences were virtually discontinued. Today few persons ever see the Rebbe alone. Instead the Rebbe increased the number of his public appearances. He speaks to his Hasidim at farbrengens (Lubavitcher gatherings) held on every holiday and on days sacred to the court—the anniversary commemorating the *yortsayt* (death) of a tzaddik or the date of a tzaddik's release from prison. At the close of the farbrengen the Hasidim pass in front of the Rebbe and many present him with a written note requesting a blessing.[16] Every Sunday at his office or home the Rebbe hands out dollar bills to long lines of individuals who pass in front of him (with men and women in separate lines). The purpose is to encourage the giving of charity: the recipient gives the dollar bill to charity and adds money of his own. The lines of people move rapidly, but during this time the Rebbe also receives requests for blessings.

Unlike other Hasidic Rebbes who customarily offer their toyre at the third meal of the Shabbes, the Lubavitcher Rebbe speaks at farbrengens held early Shabbes afternoon. A farbrengen can last anywhere from two to five hours, although in recent times they have tended to be shorter than before. In the course of the farbrengen the Rebbe usually delivers two types of talks: one is called a *sicha*, a talk or lecture; and the other is *ma'amar*, discourse. The sicha is the more informal of the two and is usually a discussion of a particular issue. During the course of a farbrengen the Rebbe presents several *sichot*, each of which is followed by singing and toasting the Rebbe *(l'chaim)* with celebratory glasses of wine.[17] When the Rebbe stops speaking, someone in the crowd will strike up a song, or the Rebbe himself will hum a tune that is taken up in chorus. These pauses between talks and singing give everyone the opportunity to compare notes concerning what the Rebbe has said.[18]

During the course of the evening the Rebbe will signal with a nod that he is about to present a ma'amar. The ma'amar is more esoteric and deeper in intent than the sicha. Hasidim believe that every ma'amar is like the giving of the Torah at Sinai. The sense of holiness intensifies. The Rebbe ties a handkerchief on his fingers to keep his soul bound on the ground. Everyone in the congregation stands, and they continue to stand during the twenty minutes or the hour that the Rebbe speaks. During this time the Rebbe, however, stays seated, and his eyes remain closed as he speaks. The ma'amar is recited in a different tone of voice than the sicha and a different verbal melody is employed. The ma'amar is similar to davening (prayer), but the text may be academic and intellectual and at the same time deeply personal in discussing the struggle of a soul surviving in the material world. When the Rebbe concludes, there are more songs. The Rebbe offers another sicha. There are more songs, and so it continues until the end of the gathering.

The published texts of the Rebbe's sichot and ma'amorim are prepared by a small staff of editors who first transcribe the Rebbe's words from a tape recorder or from memory. They then provide a general translation of the Rebbe's words from Yiddish into English, Hebrew, and Russian, among other languages; they provide appropriate footnotes and references, and then turn it over to the printer down the hall, who prepares the pamphlets to be mailed out to the worldwide list of subscribers.[19]

At the core of the Rebbe's talks is the popularization of Orthodoxy and kabbalistic mysticism in contemporary life. The Rebbe's commentaries move from literal to allegorical study of the text for the week. They frequently shift from emphasizing fulfillment of the daily rituals, to concern with moral philosophy, to current events, and finally to inspired kabbalistic interpretations on a wide range of subjects which appear to explain how the world works.

Rabbi Menachem M. Schneerson: . . . the significance of the number three is associated with the very essence of Torah itself. The Torah, which is comprised of three parts: Torah [the Five Books of Moses], Nevim [Prophets] and Kesuvim [Scriptural Writings], was given to the Jewish nation which is also comprised of three groups—Kohanim, the Levites and Israelites. Furthermore, the Torah was given in the *third* month of the year, the month of Sivan . . .

In advising us how to abstain from sin, the Mishnah uses the Hebrew word "Aveirah" which literally means "transgression." Consequently, one who transgresses is called a "Maavir." The term "Maavir" is also used in a different context in the laws of Shabbos. It describes, one who trespasses from one domain to another—a private domain where spirituality prevails, to a public place, where mundanity prevails. In the light of this interpretation, the Mishnah is telling us that "three things," the concept of *three*, transforms the worldly domain into holiness thus preventing any trespassing from one domain to another. It is a third and higher element in creation which unites the two domains, eliminating the possibility of trespassing from one domain to another.

This may be explained as follows:

On the first day of creation G-d created heaven and earth. The second verse of Genesis describes the earth on the first day of creation as being without form; the heaven and earth existed as one entity . . . on the second day of creation, the concept of divisiveness—two domains—was introduced into the world. The impact of this divisiveness on creation was so great that we find, unlike *all* other days of creation, that G-d does not say "It was good." However, on the third day, the Torah states *twice*, "And G-d saw that it was good." Commentaries explain this to mean that not only did the creation of the third day find favor in the eyes of G-d, but on this day there was an added dimension to creation which rectified the impact of the divisiveness of the second day; the *third* possessed a certain quality which is able to introduce unity in a place which was hitherto in a state of divisiveness.

Thus "one" represents the existence of one domain; "two" represents the existence of two conflicting elements; and "three" reveals a level of unity inherent in both domains, creating a connection and bond between the two on an apparent level.

Returning to our Mishnah, we may understand it as follows. The universe consists initially of two divisive parts, heaven and earth—holiness and secularism—and one must avoid confusing these two realms and trespassing from one to another. Therefore, the Mishnah tells us that in order to avoid this trespass, "reflect upon three things," i.e. introduce the third dimension, the unifying factor that reveals the sanctity of even the mundane world and thus makes it one with the heavens.[20]

Despite their metaphysical bent, Lubavitch programs stress the application of what is commonplace for all Orthodox Jews: to observe the Shabbes, eat only kosher food, put on tefillin daily, educate their children in Jewish law and custom, pray daily, attach a mezuzah to their doorpost, keep a charity coin box, bring prayer books into their homes, and so on through the 613 mitzvot, commandments of the Torah. Underlying Chabad actions is the view that wholesale return by the Jewish community to their religious roots is a necessary requirement for the arrival of the Messiah and the redemption of the Jews.

· 5 ·

Satmar, M'lochim, Lubavitch: The Struggles between the Courts

Contemporary Conflicts

The passionate commitment of Hasidim to their Rebbe, to a shared philosophy, and to common local customs have often led to competition and antagonism between groups of pietists. The history of Hasidism is marked by contention between the Hasidim and their Orthodox opponents, the Misnagdim, and subsequently between Hasidic courts who criticized, quarreled, and issued bans against one another. Letters and leaflets rained down on opposing communities from Pressburg to Sziget and Sadagora to Sanz. At the heart of the matter were usually differing views on how to ensure adherence to religious law and on the control of community life.

Today, in Brooklyn, contention between the two leading Hasidic courts in America, Satmar and Lubavitch, has become commonplace. Sharply different points of view on a number of issues indicate a deep philosophical division between the two courts. Concerning the causes for the tragedy of the Second World War, Joel Teitelbaum, the Satmar Rebbe, declared that the Holocaust had been punishment for the evils of Zionism. Menachem Mendel Schneerson, the Lubavitcher Rebbe, believes that "the tragedy of the Holocaust is an unanswerable question. There is no human rationale whatsoever that can explain such indescribable suffering." [1]

The two polarized courts hold deeply felt beliefs. Satmar, however, appears to seek its controlling vision exclusively in the past, while Lubavitch looks forward to the joy of spreading Yiddishkayt and educating fellow Jews. The two courts are in visible contradiction to each other: Satmar Hasidim dress is an exact replica of Orthodox garb in Hungary a century ago, while Lubavitcher Hasidim follow more contemporary style both during the week and on the Shabbes. The different modes of dress reflect Satmar concern to keep a safe distance between themselves and nonbelievers, and Lubavitch eagerness to interact with and to proselytize secular Jews. Differences between the two courts are rubbed raw when the Lubavitchers elect to extend their mission and hawk their philosophy in other Hasidic courts. Other Hasidim resent Lubavitch assumptions that they need to be lectured to.

> The mitzvah tanks of Lubavitch are sent all over including Williamsburg. It's sending coals to Newcastle. They have loudspeakers; kids go around with leaflets and ask people to put on tefillin. The Hasidim are insulted. (BP)

The geographical proximity of the courts provides good cause for staking out a territorial claim as a form of self-protection and for maintaining other social distinctions.

> Satmar and Lubavitch are the two major superpowers among the Hasidim, and they're only fifteen minutes apart by car. I mean it's about five miles. And in order to ensure that the Satmar Hasidim should keep by themselves, they organize a big difference in belief between Satmar and Lubavitch. This protects Satmar that their people shouldn't be threatened to convert to another type of Hasidism. (YA)

The State of Israel

The quarrels between these groups are sharpened by their opposing attitudes toward Zionism and the State of Israel. While all Hasidim oppose the secular orientation paramount in Israel, the most zealous scorn the very existence of the new state. It is the violation of the Messianic vision that makes the State of Israel the primary flashpoint of contemporary dispute.[2]

Animosity between Hasidic courts was heightened when some courts in Israel decided to moderate their feud with the government. They participated in elections and in the parliamentary government, and they accepted government funds to run their yeshivot.

In contrast to Satmar, the court of Lubavitch actively supports Israel. While the Lubavitcher Rebbe may object to Israeli actions considered profane, the Lubavitcher Hasidim have been a vital link between the government of Israel and the Orthodox community. The Rebbe is a hardliner on refusing to surrender territory for peace with the Arabs, and 770 Eastern Parkway has seen Israeli generals and politicians, including former Prime Minister Begin, pass its portals for an interview with the Rebbe.[3]

The older Satmar Rebbe usually expressed his disapproval of the Lubavitcher Rebbe's point of view in relatively mild terms, but his followers needed little encouragement to demonstrate their rising animus against Lubavitch.

The Satmar Rebbe would say a joke about the Lubavitcher Rebbe and that's about it. He wouldn't organize anything. If they would tell him the Lubavitcher Rebbe said something about Israel, he would say, "He doesn't know what he's talking about," but that's all. He never came out with any directives. In the beginning he had a pretty friendly relationship with the Lubavitcher Rebbe. (YA)

The continual struggle for survival in the Middle East kept the quarrel simmering. Each day's headline provoked a new round of argument.

After the Six Day War the rivalry between the Hasidic groups became very intense, very bitter. The reason was that the Lubavitcher Rebbe spoke about the miracles of the Six Day War. Before the war he said there was nothing to be afraid of, and he persuaded people from leaving. He received questions from parents—should we bring our children home? He said no. The hand of God is there to perform miracles. To Satmar this was totally unacceptable—to them he was taking the depths of evil and building it up. (AF)

The M'lochim

Satmar's ideological ally in the rigorous defense of traditional customs and in the struggle against Israel is the American-based group called the M'lochim. The Satmar and the M'lochim are the largest and one of the smallest Hasidic courts in the United States, with thousands of families in one, and perhaps one to two hundred in the other. Despite the difference in population the M'lochim match Satmar's passion concerning the State of Israel. In addition, the M'lochim hold a particular animosity toward the court of Lubavitch stemming from their deceased leader's difficulties with the fifth and sixth Lubavitcher Rebbes. While Satmar's size and apparent militancy award it greater attention in the press, the small court of the M'lochim has played a unique but little-known role as the point of the bayonet.

By the 1950s the tiny group of American-born disciples of the Malach was made up of married men with families. The Malach, Rabbi Chaim Avraham Dov Ber Levine HaCohen, had died more than a decade earlier, but his followers had remained loyal to his name and to his teachings. Their spartan code had remained intact, seen as necessary protection against the temptations of the secular world. There was of course no television, radio, or newspapers in M'lochim households. Although their extreme pietistic behavior had anticipated the resurgence of Orthodoxy, the M'lochim had no cohort among the new immigrants seeking to join them. Without a Rebbe the group had no magnet to attract new members. On the contrary, the new Rebbes who had arrived drew some of the M'lochim to their Shabbes tables. Through defection and dissension the

M'lochim population shrank by half to approximately 140 men, women, and children.[4]

During the 1950s Lubavitcher Hasidim made repeated visits to the M'lochim shul hoping to draw these orphan followers back to Lubavitch.[5] They seemed to meet with little success and were even asked to leave the shul; however, in 1960 five M'lochim shifted their affiliation to Lubavitch. This was a severe psychological blow to the group considering their scant numbers, and continued proselytizing by Lubavitch presented a threat to their survival as a group. In subsequent years, however, the M'lochim held their own, although they did not share in the expansion enjoyed by other Hasidic courts. To their first historian, Bernard Sobel, it appeared inevitable that their numbers would soon be further eroded by the departure of those attracted to the teachings of newly arrived Rebbes, by the social strain they brought upon themselves, and by the rebellion of their children who, it was assumed, would be attracted to more modern ways. According to Jacob Cohen's more recent estimate, however, by the 1980s the M'lochim numbered 120 to 130 families. These were divided between Williamsburg and suburban communities in Monsey and Monroe. The number of families in the base group in Williamsburg has remained fairly constant with 50 to 60 families.

In Sobel's view, the M'lochim environment held little to attract new adherents. They seemed to present a grim visage when compared to other livelier Hasidic courts:

> among the M'lochim the worship is much more somber, much less expressive and colorful than is the case with most Hasidic groups . . . From the synagogue to the home, the color, the energy, which mark Hasidism as a distinguishing force in Judaism is lacking . . . The M'lochim believe the Biblical injunction against making graven images to extend to practically all forms of decoration. In the synagogue . . . even the traditional symbols woven into the covering of the holy ark were absent and the cloth was merely an unadorned felt cover. Similarly, the home is marked by a lack of photographs as well as of pictures and do-dads.[6]

Sobel found examples of conflict between the women and men of the group concerning the strict codes of behavior:

> The ascetic-like discipline which marks the male members of the group, finds little sympathy among the women and examples of flamboyant breaches of the principles which the men hold dear are evident . . . He has no radio, no television set, is not permitted to read the newspaper, and is forbidden to go to the movies. As she expressed it: "There are times when I just can't stand it any more; I have to do something, so I go to the movies without my husband's knowledge." Her reaction seems not atypical. Another Malach's wife, Mrs. A., reads the newspapers in the corner candy store

while the other women of the neighborhood act as lookouts, warning her if her husband is approaching.[7]

The severity of the M'lochim's doctrines was most apparent in their attitude toward Israel. The M'lochim were numbered among the new state's harshest critics, as Rabbi Meyer Weberman, the rabbi of the M'lochim, explains:

> Our doctrine is that we in no way can compromise with any type of government, whether it be secular or religious, in what was called Palestine and is now Israel, under Jewish administration. No matter what form it would assume: Orthodox, Reform, extreme Orthodox—no government at all. We feel that it is a basic violation of the concept we call Mashiah and *golus* [exile]. Now Lubavitch professes to entertain the same ideas, but at the same time they participate in the government there, they take funds from the government, and they receive government officials. That's the basic difference between Lubavitch and M'lochim. (MW)

It is a debate that has no middle ground. The M'lochim see the world moving first toward catastrophe and only then, happily, toward redemption.

> I can take my position on what the Talmud tells us. I see that everything is crystallizing right now. This is what the Malach told us too. That the moral code of the world has sunk to such a low degree that the basic precepts of society have been cast aside. The world cannot exist, society cannot exist, this way. Humanity cannot exist. It's breaking apart at such a fast rate; it manifests itself in the way that governments are being shaken up. That's just the symptom. It shows something more basic than that. There's nothing to hold the world together any more. There's no loyalty, no morality, no justice, no concept of protecting the innocent from the criminal.
>
> We've seen that happen to a certain extent in the Bible in Sodom and Gomorrah. They had laws which not only condoned but encouraged certain seriously immoral acts. The Tower of Babel, the times of the Flood—those periods passed over and the world got back on its feet again. But now with modern technology everything is going so fast it is a torrent, a tidal wave, that cannot be prevented. And the Talmud tells us that that is the fate, the lot of the world before God will reveal the true light. (MW)

The formation of the State of Israel, however, was considered a rude interruption of that inexorable process toward destruction and renewal. The arrogant Zionists were said to have usurped the role of the Messiah, and the Holy Land itself was now in grave danger.

> It is something which I abhor. I'd rather not discuss it. It's a difficult question because some of our coreligionists live there too. But I seriously hope and pray to our God Almighty to destroy that land without the least harm to the faithful Jews. God can do everything. I don't know how. I don't want that government to exist. Vehemently so. Not in a militant manner. But I can

pray. I can supplicate. Because I feel it is a basic abrogation of what God wants. God put us into diaspora because we deserved it. When he sees it fit, when we deserve it, He will take us back again. To go back before that is catastrophe.   (MW)

The M'lochim became bitter foes of their coreligionists who supported Israel. Their stand on this issue further strained relations between themselves and Lubavitch, which supported the State of Israel. In time the dispute would become tinged with calumny and ridicule, and the struggle between them would be carried into the street and into the courtroom.

Purim

In 1975 during Purim, a holiday touched by a mischievous spirit similar to that of the European carnival, a large crowd of Hasidim gathered at Lee Avenue and Hewes Street in Williamsburg directly in front of the M'lochim shul. On that raucous day they hanged an effigy of the Lubavitcher Rebbe from a telephone pole and for good measure they also burned an Israeli flag. A mitzvah tank caught on Lee Avenue en route to Manhattan was pelted with stones and bricks. Among the hundreds, and perhaps thousands, who milled in the street were a great many young Satmar Hasidim who it seemed had carried their Rebbe's views and his well-known humor over the edge. In point of fact, however, the event had been orchestrated by Jacob Cohen, a slender Malach yeshivah student with a gift for mockery and yeshivah pranks.

It was just to show that the effigy of this man [the Lubavitcher Rebbe] should be hanged. The Lubavitcher Rebbe sold out to the Zionists and we came out against him. I put up posters and gave out leaflets to make sure that people would come. I was not involved in burning the flag. Later some people told me that it wasn't the right thing to do.   (JC)

A leader of the Satmar community, who received the first calls of complaint, knew where the responsibility lay.

Nobody else knows these points and these secrets better than myself because at that Purim I was the person who got the call from Lubavitcher headquarters from Leibel Grunner. Nobody else. He called me up. I didn't know that this is happening. I was sitting with my family at my home. Leibel Grunner is the first secretary of the Lubavitcher Rebbe. I know him well. I was shocked and I sent the *shames* and the secretary to go down and disperse the people and everything was ended. But we were blamed for that. Not only that but Jacobson in the *Algemeiner* [*Journal*] started to publish a series of articles for a whole year, protesting and telling the whole world that Satmar is hanging [an effigy of the Lubavitcher Rebbe] and it's Satmar, Satmar, Satmar. But we cannot even defend ourselves and write in the *Algemeiner* that you are a liar.   (RH)

While it was reported that Satmar officials condemned the hanging (nothing was said about the attack on the Israeli flag), their claim that they had nothing to do with the demonstration was given scant credence. In the meantime, more mischievous sparks were scattered. In Williamsburg the Yiddish weekly newspaper, the *Algemeiner Journal,* sympathetic to Lubavitcher causes, became forbidden reading. Newsdealers carried it at their own risk. Harassing phone calls were made to subscribers, distributors, and advertisers. These pranks took a more dangerous turn when the *Algemeiner's* offices in Borough Park were ransacked and later burned to the ground. A candy store in Williamsburg that carried the newspaper was also razed by fire.

The Satmar Hasidim received most of the blame and the negative publicity associated with the Purim happening. The Lubavitcher Rebbe apparently did not know of Cohen at the time and placed the blame squarely on Satmar. At a Shabbes farbrengen ten days after the events he observed that he had waited ten days for a sign of repentance before speaking out.[8] Responding to the Satmar claim that only children were involved, he cited pictures of the attack on the mitzvah tank in the press showing many older men with long white beards standing by, laughing and smiling.

Conflicts

In midsummer of 1976 differences between Satmar and Lubavitch were sharpened by their responses to events in the Middle East. On June 27 an Air France jet flying from Tel Aviv to Paris with a manifest of approximately 250 passengers and crew was seized by 7 pro-Palestinian guerrillas. After refueling the plane in Libya they forced the crew to fly to the Entebbe airport in Uganda. Claiming to be members of the Popular Front for the Liberation of Palestine, the kidnappers threatened to blow up the plane and kill all of their hostages unless 53 terrorists were freed from prisons in Israel, France, West Germany, Kenya, and Switzerland. The Israelis, 2,300 miles distant, launched a rescue mission on July 3. Under cover of darkness they landed three cargo planes at Entebbe. To confuse the terrorists and delay their initial response one of their number drove up in a Mercedes Benz dressed as Idi Amin, Uganda's head of government. In a lightning assault on the terminal Israeli troops killed all 7 hijackers and saved 103 passengers and crew members (143 passengers had been released earlier through negotiation).[9]

The daring raid was hailed throughout the world as a brilliant rescue and a blow against terrorism. The elated Lubavitcher Rebbe called the event a miracle; the Satmar Rebbe, however, scorned it as a misguided risk.

Relationships deteriorated even further after the raid on Entebbe. Again the Rebbe said it was a miracle. God performed miracles through the Israeli soldier. To the Satmar this was totally unacceptable. He would do anything to destroy what he considered to be the cancer of our generation.   (AF)

The community then waited for the next incident to occur. One's relationship to the Israeli government became the measure used to determine even the sacred obligation of charity.

The Satmar Hasidim give enormous *tzedakah* [charity], but they refuse to give money to any institution which is supported by the Israeli government. Forty-Seventh Street Photo gives but not to supporters of the government. I asked Goldstein for support for our yeshivah in Israel and he said, "I have one question: Do you accept money from the Israeli government?"
I said, "I have to admit that we do."
And he said: "Then I'm sorry but I can't give you anything."   (IA)

Tempers rose the year following Entebbe when the Lubavitcher Hasidim sent their "Mitzvah tanks" into Williamsburg, the heart of Orthodoxy. The Satmar Hasidim considered it an intolerable intrusion. As the trucks turned down Rodney Street, where the Satmar besmedresh is located, they were greeted by flying stones, the police escort notwithstanding.

The Lubavitcher Hasidim could not understand the hostile reaction. A custom had been inaugurated under the previous Lubavitcher Rebbe of visiting places of worship in Williamsburg on the seventh day of Passover to deliver short talks on Lubavitcher philosophy. They remained determined to fulfill their previous Rebbe's program and continue their activities in Williamsburg.

For the past forty years on the seventh day of Passover we've gone to shuln in Williamsburg, Borough Park, and Crown Heights not to antagonize but to increase happiness on the holidays. We always obtain permission in advance from the president or rabbi of each shul. We didn't go to Satmar but to other shuln where we had permission.   (AR)

There were warnings of violence if Lubavitchers continued this practice. The present Lubavitcher Rebbe, however, indicated that he could not stop something that his predecessor (his revered father-in-law) had initiated. This drew a sharp reaction from the leadership of Satmar.

They are not telling the people what they are doing. They came in with troops, with sound trucks, marching here and there in the street. What did they want to dispense here? Hasidism? We have our own Hasidic life. We don't need the Lubavitcher Rebbe to teach us his philosophy. We didn't go to Eastern Parkway to preach there. They look for trouble. Lubavitch had a custom that every Passover they came marching in the hundreds in the street. I called them and I told them, "Don't come to Williamsburg. Why do you need to have controversies? You want we should learn Hasides? We should learn Tanya? We are learning Tanya anyway, and not only Tanya, we are learning from all the other Hasidic books as well. And we are not Lubavitch. What do you want here?" (RH)

On the seventh day of Passover in April 1977, the Lubavitcher Hasidim, en masse, again took a three-mile stroll from Crown Heights to Williamsburg. They contended that this was in the spirit of achieving friendship and unity, but the Satmar Hasidim regarded the march as an outrageous provocation. There was a startling confrontation between the disputants on the streets of Williamsburg. The fists of the righteous knotted. Garbage cans were tossed at the invaders in outrage. Some zealots pummeled one another.

> We were attacked. The Lubavitchers did not hit back. I remember walking down the street and I was spit at in the face. I didn't do anything in return. The Rebbe always farbrengs the last day of Passover. After this happened the Rebbe thanked all of his Hasidim for not fighting back, quoting a verse in the Torah: "HaShem will fight for you and you shall remain silent." (AR)[10]

Despite their irritation, the leaders of Satmar and Lubavitch attempted to move past the crisis and restore a sense of calm that had eluded their followers.

> They insisted they are coming, so there was a fight, and finally they had to go back. We were blamed for that. We didn't want the fight.
> We took in a few of their older people to the old Rebbe and he gave them his hand and he blessed them "Gut yontev!" And [later] the Rebbe said, "I did not need the whole thing that they should come. I didn't need the fight, that we should throw them back, and I didn't need that they should come in so that I should have to give them *sholom-aleykhem*. I didn't need any of it." (RH)

Despite the efforts of the leadership of both courts to restore peace, threats were reportedly made against the life of the Lubavitcher Rebbe and the police arranged twenty-four-hour police car protection outside his home. Since the marches were considered provocative the Lubavitcher Hasidim canceled such plans for the future. They realized the futility of making overtures to the population of Williamsburg. Even the Mitzvah tanks that usually drove down Bedford Avenue on their way to Manhattan were rerouted to avoid Williamsburg. The only ones possibly amused by the whole affair were less-religious Jews. Sometimes offended by Hasidic disdain, they could note the irony of a secular state using its police force to prevent religious pietists from attacking each other.

· 6 ·

Families

Growing Up

Hasidic families appear to be happy. They are typically large, generous, and warm hearted. Religious laws and customs are carried out impeccably, but children are introduced early and gradually to constraints so that compliance is less of a burden than it appears to be to outsiders. While the children are still in their cribs the parents carry out their ablutions and prayers as a joyful game. As soon as their fingers can clench, the children are encouraged to drop coins in the *pushke,* the charity box. These early moments of standing upright, clinging to their parents' fingers, become rhythmic movements for prayer and for dance. Their accomplishments are encouraged by handclapping and praise.

Growing up, children become accustomed to use the besmedresh as their playground. Adults, for their part, are permissive of their tumult, even at hallowed times. Children learn that prayer is joyful, cathartic, and uplifting, and that it is a mitzvah to provide charity and to care for the sick. Steeped in the law, and raised with rigor and affection, children remain wedded to study and to their place in the besmedresh after the years of formal schooling are ended. Progressive steps into adulthood and marriage are relatively simple and are arranged with the support of family and friends. There is a common bond between the generations in fulfillment of the commandments and in allegiance to the community and to the Rebbe.

The present generation has rigorous standards concerning modesty, more stringent than was evident among Hasidim in America in the past. From an early age boys and girls are kept apart. The present generation learned this lesson well and acts on it with more vigor than did its parents and grandparents. Once limited to the most zealous Hasidim, these standards are now fairly widespread among all the courts.

When they were young, boys and girls went together in the bath. Not today. Today they wouldn't do it. Today three-year-olds don't want to go in the same tub. Today it's different. They wouldn't do it. The kids themselves wouldn't do it. Today they put long stockings on girls at three. Before, it was eight or even older. My father, rest in peace, used to say it was okay until twelve. (FH)

From the first class in school (usually at age three) boys and girls attend separate classes with distinctly different curricula. The separation of the sexes does cause some strains, particularly during adolescence. The problems that inevitably arise are better understood today; however, the basic customs remain in vogue, as a Hasidic school counselor observes.

The most crucial time, not just for religious persons alone, but for all human beings, is adolescence. A person is under tremendous stress. It is pre-adulthood. Adolescence is basically a physical thing too. There are bodily changes. Sex is a special problem. There is openness out in the street. I presume that yeshivah boys feel the stress more than in my youth. In my youth there was no choice except to learn, and to live with it. Boys don't socialize with girls. There's no chance even to touch girls. They don't even shake hands. They have guilt feelings. They're thinking while they're davening. He feels that there's something wrong with him, not with religion. I try to give him the sense that his feeling is normal, a part of life.

A boy will have guilt feelings about masturbation. I try to give him the sense that he is only a human being. He should practice self-control within his limits. I don't condone it. I can't condone it. It's not accepted from a religious point of view, but whatever I say to a boy I have to see if it is destructive or constructive. If he comes in feeling like two cents, I must make certain he doesn't go out feeling like one cent. I give practical advice, to play sports. After a while I get him to face the fact that human beings are not angels.

Premarital sex does not come up. If such a situation would exist the person would have different emotional problems because [our] society is so set against it. He would have to seek it out. It's not accepted. In other societies it's different. (BI)

The education of men involves religious learning and ritual obligations but ignores any vocational or career training. The education of women has a more specific focus: the care and upbringing of children. While women are virtually excluded from much of the religious ritual life, they are nonetheless recognized as the mainstays of the values of the family and the faith.

My daughter I sent to study in Israel. Not necessarily because I am of the opinion that daughters need higher education, or better education. My own personal philosophy is that the most important task for any woman is that she raise her family, and everything should be geared toward being able to do that in a better way. In other words I wasn't against her if she wanted to go to school or college provided that she concentrates. What she really needs to know are only those things which would help her become a good mother. I'm a very big male chauvinist in that fashion. I believe very strongly that

everyone has a certain task. I do not think that women are in any way inferior—either intellectually or emotionally or in any way. Because I've spent
much of my life working with youngsters and working with children, I very
strongly believe that. It is the most challenging job. Business is a breeze. You
learn one thing and you do it. The most difficult thing is to raise good kids
which is what my wife did, wonderful kids at the top of everything. I'm
bragging about my children—tops scholastically, tops as far as personality
is concerned, as far as pleasantness and good qualities, good characteristics—and that came about because both my wife and I, especially my wife,
raised the children with warmth, with discipline, with warmth. She has her
head on in the right place on how to raise children.   (SH)

Courtship

Hasidic couples generally marry young. The religious injunction is to
marry and have children. The Hasidim also recognize that sexual desires
can be deferred only so long.[1] When they are in their late teens or early
twenties, with little psychological or social preparation, the Hasidic
youth are introduced to prospective mates. A *shadkhan* (matchmaker),
who may be a friend or a relative or even the Rebbe himself, suggests
someone as a suitable spouse.

> Instead of relying on that blind element, instead of meeting a person ten
> times or going out for a year—instead of doing that, we rely on the mother,
> we rely on the sister. If I'm looking for a wife, I rely on the sister, my sister,
> to help make that selection, rather than on my own experience, because my
> own experience would be a misleading experience. The parents do the re-
> search and they suggest that everything is okay. The kids rely on them.   (ES)

Parents inform themselves, if they do not already know, about the religiousness of the family and the character of the young man or woman.

> For my daughter I want someone who is *frum* and *erlekh*—pious but honest
> in his religion. For my daughter I would consider an *erlekher* family, sincere,
> a religious father, a *talmid khokhem,* a learned man. The parents should get
> along well. I see very often divorces in three generations.   (BI)

> The main thing to look for in a prospective *hasene* [groom] is character. I
> met my husband and we became engaged, and I never thought of anyone
> else after that. We choose by the family. We know the family. We know what
> the people are like. When my daughter grew up I would say to her, should I
> pursue the matter with this one or that one? And she said no plenty of
> times.   (SL)

The list of traits compiled by a young bride-to-be focuses on the groom,
but the particular qualities of the groom's family are still a major concern,
as one newlywed affirmed:

I wanted someone tall, dark, and reasonable looking. I wanted someone
who was smart—that was the most important. He should have a good character. He should not be angry nor stingy. He should come from a fine family
with *yikhes* [pedigree]. The parents should not be beggars in terms of status,
money, learning, or yikhes.   (PS)

When a suitable match is suggested, the two families discuss the matter
and arrange for the young people to meet. In two or three polite encounters the couple sound each other out. If they are in accord, they agree to
become engaged. There is usually more latitude in courting practices in
Lubavitch, where couples are a year or two older when they marry than
in other courts. (Courtship patterns are the same for the children of
Rebbes and rabbis as they are for all Hasidim. In rabbinical families,
however, even greater care is taken to search for families of equal piety
and yikhes, with the result that frequently the children of Rebbes marry
the children of other Rebbes.)

I saw my husband three times. We sat alone together in a separate room for
two to three hours.   (PS)

More often than not the first encounters are unsuccessful, as one Hasid
recalls the matches he rejected:

I didn't find them to be the ones I would want to live with. Knowing myself
who I am, getting to know who they were, they were perfectly okay, but not
for me.   (AG)

There are a host of reasons of why couples decide to accept each other,
as a young bride in Lubavitch indicates:

I waited until I was twenty. I went out on dates. I went out with my present
husband and then we broke up, and then someone presented him as a possible match. I figured, oh well, what's the point of shlepping around for
another year.   (SN)

If the couple is agreeable, details of the match are then worked out—the
date of the wedding, the nature of in-law support, the continuance of the
bridegroom's schooling.

I met my fiance once before we were engaged. Then we saw each other a few
times after. It was enough. He's going to continue studying after we marry.
He'll study and I'll have a teaching job. The Vizhnitzer's daughter is a friend,
and someone asked her how it is that she intends to marry a boy from Israel
whom she has never seen. So she answered: "Thousands of people come to
my father with questions and he tells them what to do. So I shouldn't accept
his advice?"   (CL)

To some extent the customs to be continued after marriage help to
shape the choice of a spouse. Hasidim from different courts are not likely

to marry unless the courts follow similar customs and share common views.

> The groups rarely intermarry. Usually if they're willing to intermarry, for example, a Stoliner with a Bobover, so before they meet there are certain guidelines. Will he wear a *shtrayml?* Stoliners don't wear shtraymlen; the Bobovers do. Will he or won't he? All these great big decisions are made way in advance. Is he the type who's going to sit and learn? Is he the type who's going to go to work? All this is done before the boy meets the girl. A match was suggested for my daughter to a boy from Israel and I turned it down because the boy's background is different. (BI)

Because there are members of the same dynastic court residing in different countries it is possible to marry within the group and at the same time be introduced to a totally unknown set of relatives, as in this instance when a young Satmar Hasid from Williamsburg married a Satmar girl from England.

> You go to a country where you have never been before. You get married over there. There's no one there you can invite to your wedding. All of them are strangers. And you have to adjust yourself to members of the family whom you've never seen before. I hadn't even seen my mother-in-law before I got married, because it was only my father-in-law who came when I got engaged. It was a crash program. You get married and at the same time you get to know your mother-in-law, your sister-in-law, your aunts, your uncles, people of the community, people of the shul, the synagogue. And you have to greet them and meet them and appeal to them. It's a lot of stress. (AG)

Marriage between members of different Hasidic courts usually means an accommodation in custom of one sort or another. Sometimes the change is very minor, but whether or not it is carried out with a good heart depends on the particular marital relationship.

> When a couple marry they usually follow the customs of the husband's family. Skver is similar to Belz. One thing I had to do different. I cover my *sheytl* [wig]. I put on a little hat to cover part of the wig. The Rebbe said the women should cover part of the sheytl. I did it for him and his Rebbe. (SA)

Since the sexes have been separated since childhood the anticipated sexual encounter following the marriage ceremony is a matter of great moment and anxiety. Yet any discussion of sex is put off until close to the time of the wedding. At that point persons in the community known for their understanding and tact are frequently called on to explain the roles of the bride and groom and what they have to look forward to on their wedding night. Women and men frequently attend separate premarital classes to learn of marital duties and responsibilities, although men more often have individual discussions with a teacher, counselor, or other well-informed person. The orientation regarding sex, presented in the context of holiness and Torah, usually emphasizes that the patriarchs, the tzaddikim, their own parents, and even their Rebbe have taken this step before them. Bride and groom are reassured that this is an act both desirable and pious.[2]

In addition to their emotional trepidations, couples are also concerned with ritual demands on their wedding day. The bride must be menstrually clean for seven days before marriage. If the celebration has been badly timed and the bride shows signs that she has entered her menstrual period, some learned advice may be sought. If the signs are correct, sexual relations must then wait until the flow has stopped, seven more days have passed, and the bride has been immersed in the mikvah and is ritually pure.[3] If there are signs of menstrual blood the wedding ceremony will be carried out; however, a chaperon (usually a younger sibling) will remain with the couple until the bride goes to the mikvah.

As a result of these possible calamities, wedding announcements and invitations are delayed until the last possible moment. Often the specific date is not set until the bride has her period. As soon as that occurs wedding invitations are sent out for a wedding to take place ten days to two weeks later. Since nowadays it is often necessary to reserve a reception hall and send out invitations months in advance, long before there is any certainty concerning the bride's condition, it has become common for prospective brides to take birth control pills to control their menstrual cycle up to the date of the marriage ceremony. (This is the only time that Hasidic women are likely to use birth control pills. Many in the community frown on their use in these circumstances because they present a danger to health and familiarize women with their use.)

The morning after the wedding the bride's hair is cut with scissors, barber's clippers, or an electric shaver. Customs concerning the length of a woman's hair vary from court to court. Among the Satmar Hasidim, and Hungarian Hasidim in general, the bride's hair is cut close to the scalp; among the Lubavitchers the haircut is usually less severe and is sometimes simply a short bob.

> My hair was clipped close but my head wasn't shaven. The Lubavitcher Rebbe doesn't really want the women to shave their heads. It's too fanatic. (ZR)

Henceforward when she is at home the wife covers her hair with a kerchief, except perhaps at times when she is alone with her husband. Whenever she steps from her home she covers her hair with a wig, a wig and hat, or a kerchief. In some courts (such as Satmar and Belz) wearing a wig covered by a hat has come to be seen as a higher standard of religiousness than wearing a wig alone. A woman who spurns these practices runs counter to a community custom which has the force of law and is a powerful social fact of life. (In the suburban Satmar community of Kiryas Joel, for example, it is estimated that approximately 90 percent of the women wear both a wig and a hat outside their homes, while the remaining 10 percent wear kerchiefs. Few women appear in public wearing a wig alone.)[4]

Husbands and Wives

The men are the religious and political leaders of the community. Women care for the children and maintain the purity of the marriage and the household. They visit the Rebbe to ask for a blessing. Women help raise funds for the needy, and look in on the sick, shop, and cook meals for them. They light the Shabbes candles and prepare the house for the holy days. In earlier times in some courts, the day before Yom Kippur the ladies' auxiliary would bring in wax, roll it out, and place wicks in the newly made candles. Religious ceremonies in the besmedresh, however, are carried out only by men. The women prepare food for the Rebbe's tish and for the melave-malke, but only the men attend these gatherings. Men crowd the main floor for prayer and study, while a smaller space set off from the main floor, or often a balcony, is reserved for the women. A curtain or a woven wooden lattice shields the women from the men's sight. On holy days some of the women congregate behind the lattice to pray and to watch the activities on the main floor of the besmedresh. In the social as well as the religious spheres men and women remain apart. When families attend a wedding or a bris (circumcision) the men and women celebrate the occasion in separate rooms. There is, however, a clear harmony in ceremonial and ritual occasions. In shul on the fast day of Yom Kippur the women supply the wailing and the tears that augment the cries and moans of the men.

In the religious world there are only distant echoes heard of the revolutionary changes undergone by women in secular society. Hasidic women often take jobs as secretaries, teachers, and bookkeepers, sometimes outside the community, before they have children. Women have less difficulty than men obtaining permission to attend college and study secular subjects.

Usually, the Hasidic young man and young woman marry into families much like their own and begin a new generation. A Hasidic marriage does not have the tension between fulfillment of career aspirations and family needs that is commonplace in nonreligious marriages. Mastery in marriage is always a delicate balance, dependent on the personalities of the individuals involved; nevertheless, among the Hasidim, at least in terms of decisionmaking, it is weighted heavily in the man's favor. The men study the law and their wives defer to their superior knowledge.

Even on a visit to the Rebbe, women are placed in a subservient position. The Rebbe is even more circumspect toward women than are his followers. He will not shake a woman's hand or even look directly at her. The husband is seen as the head of the family.[5]

> If a woman wants to talk to the Rebbe they could feel free to talk to him. My husband has priority. My husband stands in front of the Rebbe and I would be on the side. (SA)[6]

Women's lower station in the religious sphere is considered to be balanced by the respect they receive for their role in the household. The well-matched couple are able to establish an enduring and happy marriage.

> I felt that this was for me. We had the same ideas. It was *bashtimt* [definite], we say. *HaShem* wanted it for me. I'm very proud of my husband and I hope he's proud of me. He's very special—more than nice. He helps me out with the children. He does shopping for me. When I'm preparing for Shabbes he'll take the kids out. Anything he can help out he really tries his best. The Belzer Rebbe lives in Israel and the past two years he's gone to Israel for the holidays for the whole month. This I did for him. Now I want to go to Israel. But I've put it off. I've been planning to use some money that we received at the wedding. (SA)

Shaidl and her husband Yosef and their three small children live in a cramped apartment on the third floor of a private home that has been subdivided into apartments. Like most Hasidim of modest means they do not have a living room. The largest room, where everyone congregates, is the dining room, commanded by a large wooden table weathered by spills and by clattering spoons. The apartment is alive with the noise of a happy family—pots boiling in the kitchen, crib bars rattling, and playful calls for attention and affection.

Although they have been married for five years, Yosef, like many young married men, continues his religious studies at a *kolel,* a seminary for married men, supported by a small stipend and by help from his in-laws and his family. Yosef also tutors two small boys almost nightly. He is a dedicated student but he is anxious to conclude his formal studies and find work as a teacher or principal in a yeshivah. For her part, despite their difficult economic circumstances, Shaidl is proud of her husband's extended education, and she defers to his learning in all matters, including household affairs. "I'm very proud of him. He knows so much I listen to him." She dismisses notions to have Yosef enter the world of business and says, "I want him to find something in education as a teacher."

Most of Yosef's colleagues in the kolel will eventually seek jobs as teachers, or in business, or as skilled workers, perhaps in computer technology or in the diamond industry. There are virtually no professional goals, and work is primarily to provide for one's family and to meet religious responsibilities. A large portion of family earnings pays for yeshivah studies for the children, the expenses of kosher products, and the preparation for the holidays.

Questions related to sexual satisfaction and sexual problems are seldom discussed, even among friends. But it is evident that passion and love need not be diminished by an arranged marriage.

> Love comes after marriage, and then the hardest thing is to stay away from each other during the time when you're not permitted.   (RA)

Children

The major focus of the Hasidic family is to produce, nurture, and educate the children. This is a virtue sustained by law and custom and reinforced by a commonly understood need to replace the generation that vanished.

> After the war the feeling was that more children were needed to compensate for the terrible losses during the war. There may be some birth control, but, judging by the number of *brisn* [circumcisions], not much. The idea is to have as many Jews as possible.   (IF)

Having a large family is a religious mitzvah and a social benefit. It is the expectation of every Hasidic bride to raise a large family.

> The girls here are brought up with this plan. They come from large families. When a girl is ten or eleven years of age she's helping her mother diapering babies. It's not a new concept. She looks forward to it. You never hear a girl who's married say she has time to wait to raise her family or that she can't afford it, or that she thinks of overpopulation or what the secular world thinks about. Everyone wants children and they look forward to it.   (FH)

Every Friday night in the Satmar besmedresh the *shames* (beadle) announces the names of the boys who were born during the week. For the girls born during the week there is a *kiddush* (benediction said over a glass of wine) on Shabbes. There are more than a dozen births celebrated each week in Satmar alone. Hasidic families in the city average six to eight children; and in the suburban settlements at Monsey and Monroe the average is slightly higher.

Most Hasidim are wage earners with modest incomes. In the struggle to provide for one's family, the Hasidim have the advantage of their strong faith.

> We don't make long-range plans. We plan for each day. And God will provide. We believe that God will help us. So we just do what we have to do. We don't say we can't have more children because we can't afford it, or we'll need for the future. We just do it. Each day is its own. God will take care of the rest. We don't plan for the future. We plan for today.   (SL)

Our minds dictate that the One above will provide. For some it's a little harder; for some, a little easier. If God gives the children, there'll be enough to feed and support them. We have to have hope and faith that God will provide for us. We thank God for the breath we breathe and for every drop of water we take in. We give a blessing every time we take bread and water. (KG)

Since most Hasidim do not practice birth control, it is not uncommon to encounter women on the street with three children under three and a half years of age: two babies a year apart in a baby carriage, and a child of three toddling along behind. The larger the family the more impossible the burden appears. Nevertheless, it is clear that the Hasidim delight in the pleasure that children can bring.

My wife had just given birth. We had eight children. It was very hard for her. The child is up all night. So a friend of mine gave me a good idea. He came to me, "Meyer, I have a good idea. In Far Rockaway there's an organization that will take care of the baby for four weeks for free, or for a minimum fee. They take very good care of the baby, with nurses, doctors, so when your wife comes back she can take care of the eight children."

I can't wait for her to come home to tell her the story. They give me the number. I called up and arranged everything for them to take care of the baby for a week after she comes out of the hospital until she could come to herself. I was so happy.

She starts crying. She started crying. I couldn't imagine what's happening. "The baby—this is my best time. You're taking away my best time. Sure you're up all night, but this is the best time. There's no such thing as bad." She was crying like a baby. She couldn't stop crying. (MH)

I was mad at him for suggesting it. (FH)

For the Hasidim the pleasures of a large family continue with the years. Meyer spends every Shabbes afternoon after prayers visiting his children and grandchildren. With eleven children, most of them married and with offspring of their own, it's a full day.

It's my pleasure. I spend a little while at each house playing with my grandchildren. I had such great fun with my kids. You can't buy such pleasure. (MH)

Meyer's wife, Frieda, stays at home because, as she says, "I don't want to interfere."

You know from after the war my husband didn't have a family. His kids mean more to him because he didn't have a family. And he's more lenient because of that. He doesn't care for material things altogether. (FH)

The ties that bind the families remain strong, and with the years the pride in having a large family often increases. As Sarah L. recounts:

I have fourteen children. I feel very proud of my children, my family. For some people two are too many. For others, no. I feel like the queen of the family. I'm very proud of my family. I never felt it was too much work. Some people with two or three it's too much. It is a lot of work. You can't conceive of how much work I did. It's unimaginable. When I think of it, it's impossible. I worked. But I liked it. I lost two other children who were premature. Now sometimes I think I could have had two more. My eldest is twenty-seven years older than my youngest. Now every week there's something—a wedding for a child, a bris for a grandson, a bar mitzvah for another. I'm always busy. And I feel like a queen. I'm the queen of the family and my husband is the king. We always had enough. We're not rich but we had enough. And each child who married got something. Not much, but something. This one will have furniture and help for an apartment in Jerusalem. (SL)

Sarah's outlook gives courage to her children to have large families.

My mother did, so I think I can do it too. (CL)

· 7 ·

Boyan and Kapitshinitz: The Sons of the Rebbes

Rabbinic Succession

The death of a Rebbe is a wrenching experience for the court and for each of the Rebbe's followers. To prevent the dissolution of the court a new leader must be named. The Rebbe's sons are the first to be considered in the line of succession to become Rebbe.

In past times in Eastern and Central Europe, an abundance of candidates for the position of Rebbe often existed, so that while one son continued in his father's place, his siblings, unless they sought other ways of earning a livelihood, customarily established new courts of their own in other towns. The proliferation of Rebbes, according to historians and critics of Hasidism, had the effect of weakening and diluting the Hasidic movement. In the United States, up to the present, the reverse has often been the case. In some courts there have been too few candidates, and not everyone with the lineage and the piety to be named Rebbe is willing to accept that role. Some may already be committed to an alternative career or to a different way of life; some are too modest or uncertain; some are too aware of the demands of the position of Rebbe. Wisdom—even informed fear—prompts some men to shrink from becoming a captain in that sea of humanity.

Boyan and Kapitshinitz

The courts of Boyan and Kapitshinitz were among the earliest Hasidim to settle in America and reorganize their courts here. Both were originally located in the eastern region of the Austro-Hungarian empire, and there were many similarities between them. The Boyaner Rebbe, Reb Mordchei Shlomo Friedman, arrived first in the New World in 1927. In 1939, the year following Hitler's entrance into Austria, Rabbi Abraham Joshua Heschel, the Kapitshinitzer Rebbe, fled with his family to New York and settled on Henry Street in lower Manhattan close to the Boyaner.

My father was the Kapitshinitzer Rebbe. Kapitshinitz is a small town by the Austrian-Russian border, an area where the dominant Hasidic influence stemmed from the Rizhin *rabbeim*, the offspring of the Rizhiner Rebbe—the Kapitshinitzer, the Boyaner, the Husiatiner, the Tchortkover, among others. The towns had small resident populations but there were hundreds if not thousands of Hasidim who flocked to the Rebbes. In many instances it was the presence of the rabbeim that put the towns on the map. Kapitshinitz, I am told, was important enough as a town because the railroad train ran through and even made stops there. Catering to the visitors who came to see the Rebbe was a vital part of the commercial life of the community. Each of the rabbeim had his own court, which was called a hoyf. This consisted primarily of a large shul, part of which was a large room where the Rebbe held his tish. Also there was the Rebbe's house for his family, a study hall where the resident scholars, *batlonim*, supported by the Rebbe, ate, studied, and told Hasidic tales. Each court had its resident scribes, gabbaim, caretakers, and so on—a small army if you wish. People flocked to them in the old days.

All this came to an end with the outbreak of the First World War. Without any warning all the Rizhiner rabbeim had to flee their towns in advance of the onrushing enemy soldiers. Everything was left behind.

Most of the Rizhiner rabbeim from that time, including the Boyaner and the Kapitshinitzer, fled to Vienna where they attempted to establish their hoyfn within the urban environment. My grandfather, Rabbi Isaac Meier Heschel, the first Kapitshinitzer Rebbe, passed away in Vienna on Rosh Hashanah in 1935 and my father immediately succeeded him.

Then Hitler marched into Austria in March 1938. After the annexation, the *Anschluss*, the persecutions of the Jews became daily occurrences. My father and my older brother were badly beaten by the SS and by the local Nazi hoodlums. As the terror mounted everyone thought of escaping, but my father wouldn't hear of it. How could he leave his people behind? He maintained that it was his duty to stay with his Hasidim.

One day, early on, the Nazis herded all the Jews together and one of the highlights of their fun was to shave off the men's peyes and beards. The frightened people were lined up, helpless, terrified. When my father's turn came he held out his index finger and said to the Nazi soldier, "*Bitte*, please cut this off but [pointing to his beard] leave this on." The SS man was taken aback and then, miracle of miracles, burst out laughing and told the other SS men about this dumb Jew. For whatever reason he let my father go without touching his beard.

In retrospect this incident must have saved our lives. Subsequently the Nazis discovered that when they needed a photo event of a Jew being humiliated they had no photogenic subjects anymore. Until someone remembered that there was a bearded Jew left in Vienna. And so nearly every day my father was dragged out of the house and forced to march in front of the jeering Austrian Nazis and made to mop up a freshly painted swastika on the street. Initially my father insisted that he could tolerate the ordeal, that it wasn't that terrible an ordeal. But then they came each Shabbes and the trauma and hurt of having to desecrate the Shabbes or yontev was more painful to him than any torture. So finally he relented on not leaving Vienna. We left in February 1939, almost a year after the annexation. When we left I was nine years old.

My father then was a Rebbe on the Lower East Side of Manhattan, on Henry Street, near the Boyaner. (SH)

The families of Kapitshinitz and Boyan were intertwined by descent and by marriage. Boyan was the direct descendant of the house of Rizhin; the Kapitshinitzer lineage ran to the Apter Rov and, secondarily through marriage, to the Rizhin line as well. The families had intermarried over the generations. Both lines had a common point of view and a shared geographical sphere of influence. They also shared a mutual respect stemming from earlier times.

They tell a story about the Apter Rov [Abraham Joshua Heschel, 1765–1835] who was then fifty years old and the Rizhiner Rebbe who was then seventeen years old. Yet this older Rebbe, the Apter Rov, who was the most important Rebbe in the Ukraine, treated this young man as if he was the greatest of the Rebbes. The story, which is perhaps apocryphal, is that once in the Apter's presence, the *gartl* [silk belt] of the Rizhiner fell down. The Apter Rov allegedly is supposed to have picked up the gartl and put it on the Rizhiner and said, "It's like putting on the *gartl* of the *Sefer Torah* [Torah scroll]." (IF)[1]

At the end of the Second World War, most of the Boyaner and Kapitshinitzer Hasidim, like most of the Lower East Side's Jewish population, religious and secular, moved to more ample apartments and houses in Williamsburg, Borough Park, and other neighborhoods in Brooklyn and on Long Island. While the Boyaner Rebbe remained in Manhattan, the Kapitshinitzer Rebbe settled in Borough Park along with the majority of his followers.

In the 1930s and 1940s the Hasidim then in America lived in two worlds—the Orthodox world of their household and the shul, and the secular environment of school, the street, and work. Extraordinary pressure was placed on the children of the Rebbes to maintain the ways of the old world in the new generation.

I admired my father [the Kapitshinitzer Rebbe] very much. I admired him for the good things that he did—for his unbelievable generosity, for his personality, and so forth. Yet was I my father's Hasid? No. There were too many things that got in the way. He wanted me to be somebody else than I really was, and he made too many demands of me that I couldn't live up to. And so things got in the way. (SH)

The influence of the powerful new American Hasidic community was still a generation away. In the interim, conflict continued between the pull of the religious and the secular worlds.

When we [of Kapitshinitz] came here of course we went to yeshivah. I went to yeshivot which were not really Hasidishe yeshivot. My father was looking for a Hasidishe yeshivah and the Lubavitch yeshivah just opened up. I got *semikhah* [rabbinic ordination] from Torah Vadaat [an Orthodox yeshivah].

It wasn't acceptable then to go to college. Well, let's put it this way. My father was liberal enough. He did not consider that it was proper to give a blank authorization for anybody to go—for a yeshivah boy or a beis yaakov girl—to go to college. The danger as it was perceived then, and as it's perceived now, is twofold. One is the subject matter that you might learn—philosophy and *apikoyres,* which is heresy; the second problem, which is not easily overcome, is the mixing of the sexes, of boys and girls together in the same classroom.

So then, as today, it is frowned upon. In most Hasidic houses it is absolutely forbidden. My father also would not just give blind authority. He did allow and counsel, when someone came to ask him, if he had a specific goal in mind, to learn a specific trade or perform a specific function. I never went to college for the sake of getting, and I didn't get, a degree, a bachelor's or a master's. At that time I wanted to go to college because I had some talent—that's the wrong word—I had a leaning toward creative writing and it was something I wanted to do when I was very young. And so I took some courses in writing. And as I was there I took a course in public speaking, and another course in political science because that was a kosher subject as long as I'm there already.

In the yeshivah I went through the motions of studying, of learning, until I met a friend of mine who had a tremendous influence on me to really put in time at the yeshivah. Eventually I gave up college completely, but not necessarily because I chose one over the other. A combination of factors made me sit down and study hard [at the yeshivah], which is what I did for a couple of years. After that I began to work. I went to work for my brother-in-law. I did office work.   (SH)

The Passing of the Rebbes

The courts of Boyan and Kapitshinitz faced crises of succession within a few years of each other. In 1967 Rabbi Abraham Heschel, the Kapitshinitzer Rebbe, passed away in Borough Park at the age of seventy-nine. After the death of the Kapitshinitzer Rebbe the court first asked the eldest of the Rebbe's three sons, Rabbi Israel (Sruel), to accept his father's post, but he adamantly refused. After a year of waiting, when it became clear that he would stubbornly reject all their pleadings, they turned to the Rebbe's second son, Reb Moshe, who accepted the court's entreaties.[2]

Rabbi Moshe Heschel, the new Kapitshinitzer Rebbe, proved to be universally popular. He had grown up in America and understood American mores. He had been in the business world, and so he was familiar with the environment beyond the yeshivah and besmedresh. The followers of

Kapitshinitzer were few in number but the new Rebbe attracted many from outside his immediate circle. Modern in his outlook, optimistic, and gifted with insight, he was able to deal with the emergence of a rising phenomenon among the Orthodox—marital discord. Young couples experiencing difficulty in their marriage went to be counseled by the young Rebbe.

> My brother had been a highly successful businessman before he accepted the position. He was very much accepted, very much liked by everyone. He possessed a very happy and very jovial nature, a bubbling personality full of humor and wit. Before his bar mitzvah he developed rheumatic fever and was ailing all his life. Many weeks he was confined to his bed. He had constant pains, difficulty in breathing, and a heart condition. Yet, amazingly, it never showed. He always appeared as a warm, gregarious, and humorous man who had everything except his health going for him. He gave up a lot to become the Rebbe. He accepted the position because he felt he had a responsibility to the Hasidim of my father. He didn't do it on account of guilt, although a lot of people used that on him.
>
> Very shortly he attracted many young people who ordinarily would have had no connection with Hasidism, nor have any Hasidic background. They were attracted to him because in him they found someone warm, caring, and one who always had a good or wise word. Before long some of them who had problems with their lifestyles or with their marriage came to confide in him. They came with their wives and made him almost part of their family; they recommended him to their friends and relatives. Before long he developed a following of the many people whom he helped and who admired how he immersed himself in their problems. While there are professional people who advertise themselves as marriage counselors, there was then and there is today no Rebbe who devotes himself to this important work. Before he passed away suddenly, my brother got to the point where he was busy eighteen to twenty hours a day attending to healing such relationships. (SH)

Hasidim in other courts spoke highly of the Kapitshinitzer, as a Stoliner Hasid observed:

> The Kapitshinitzer was born in Vienna. He was young with a heart of gold. His oldest child is not yet bar mitzvahed. He lived in Borough Park. He had a group of American Hasidim. He had businessmen, young Americans. He was easygoing, easy to talk to. People would open up to him and talk. They gave him charity generously. The Kapitshinitzer gave a lot of charity. In Israel fifty widows were receiving money and no one knew it. He ran an orphanage in Israel. The Kapitshinitzer had 150 davening in his shul but he had contacts. He was a rabbi, a therapist, a marriage counselor.
>
> In one other aspect he must be considered as the true inheritor of the mantle of the Kapitshinitzer Rebbe. He was a super generous person. Not only was he unbelievably giving of money, not only did he put himself on the line for others by cosigning or guaranteeing loans (for which he almost

always had to pick up the tab), not only did he work hard for a children's home in Israel, for widows and orphans of the wars in Israel, but he also imbued his newfound Hasidim with this spirit. Namely, that the most wonderful and rewarding thing that they can do for their own life is assume the task of helping someone else. This legacy is still carried on by his Hasidim to this day. The Kapitshinitzer shul in Borough Park has a number of Hasidim of whom it can truly be said that they follow in the footsteps of their Rebbe in kindness and charity. (PR)

Boyan: Weighing the Balance

In 1969, two years after the death of the Kapitshinitzer Rebbe, Reb Mordchei Friedman, the Boyaner Rebbe, suffered a disabling stroke. He died on March 2, 1971, at the age of eighty-one, and was buried in Israel.

For two years following his stroke my father [the Boyaner Rebbe] was out of commission. People still came to him. What didn't my mother do for my father for the first few months of his stroke, and then she had a stroke too. When he passed away they were desolate. Literally hundreds of people in Israel tore keri'ah.[3] They felt he was like a father.

When we sat shivah [mourning], an old man came in. Nobody knew him. From his accent you could determine that he was a Litvak, certainly not a Hasid. He came from about two hours away, from near Haifa someplace. And somebody asked him, "Why did you come? Did you know the Rebbe?"

He says, "I met him only once. But I felt I had to pay him his last respects."

It turns out he was an old-fashioned rabbi who wrote a book, and you know when you write a Talmudical book there are no publishing firms that can sell it or advertise it. You sell it on your own and try to get back the cost of the printing and make a little profit on it.

So he came to America. He didn't know anybody. He was a stranger. He met with a great deal of disdain and rebuff. Somebody said, "Go to the Boyaner Rebbe. The Boyaner Rebbe is known to be a man of charity. I'm sure he'll give you a few dollars which will satisfy you."

He said, "Okay, I'll come and I expect arayn un aroys [in and out]. If I get five dollars I'll be happy and if I get ten dollars I'll be even happier."

"It was a different story altogether. The Boyaner Rebbe realized the troubles I'd been in and what rebuffs I'd had, and how unhappy I was, and how I felt bereft and abandoned by everyone. He sat me down for two hours, and we talked. I talked about my problems. He felt sympathy with me. He gave me a large sum of money. But that wasn't important. The important part was that I was able to talk my heart out, my problems out, and I left like a new mensh [man]. And that's why I came to pay respect at the mourning."

And this attitude of my father's was literally prevalent in all people who met him. He was able to relate to people like a good psychiatrist, like a psychotherapist. You could talk to him. He would listen to you. You could tell him your problems and your progress.   (IF)

The Boyaner Hasidim were now confronted by the dilemma of choosing a new Rebbe. Among the foremost Hasidim of Boyan there was a direct descendant—Israel Friedman, the eldest son of the Rebbe—who might have been expected to assume the leadership of the community. Israel Friedman was the mainstay and chief fundraiser of the Rizhin yeshivah in Jerusalem; he played a key role in all community decisions, and he had close ties with most of the Boyaner Hasidim. He was as well a bibliographer of some note who had amassed an extraordinary collection of Judaica, so that bookcases double-stacked with books commanded every nook and cranny of his large apartment. For more than twenty years he had been cataloguing dissertations that contained information on Jewish topics, and informally providing researchers with pertinent references. He had spent his life in social work and welfare administration rather than in the rabbinate, but in many ways his experience made him uniquely qualified for the post. Initially, however, he was not pressed to become Rebbe.

> The first year after my father's death I was torn between two things: would the Hasidim ask me to be the Rebbe, and how would I react?
> When we returned from my father's funeral in Israel—his three children—no one came to the airport to greet us. After all, I was the son of the Rebbe. It was an old tradition. More than twenty-five thousand people had come to my father's funeral. After the funeral and the shivah I felt so shocked and disappointed.   (IF)

The Boyaner Hasidim too had serious questions to consider. They respected Israel Friedman as the Rebbe's son, as an influential leader and promoter of their yeshivah, and as the community's chief fundraiser. His position of leadership and responsibility in the secular world was of less interest to them. In fact, his knowledge of the secular world and his obvious intellectual capabilities were potential drawbacks to his being named as Rebbe. They wanted someone tightly bound to traditional learning without the distractions of secular knowledge and modern concepts. Since the Boyaner Hasidim were widely dispersed they appeared to need someone who could be unanimously accepted and serve to draw the court together. The majority of Boyaner Hasidim are in Israel, where the Rizhiner yeshivah is located and where other descendants of the Rizhiner Rebbe reside. A relatively small population of a few hundred families live in New York, and their numbers are scattered in four different neighborhoods: they maintain two small synagogues in Manhattan, one on the Lower East Side and one on the Upper West Side, and two in Brooklyn, one in Borough Park and another in Williamsburg. Still others had migrated to cities in the Middle West and only intermittently visited New York.

After a few months of soul-searching they did turn to Israel Friedman, the Rebbe's son.

After the first year or so was over, the Hasidim played around with the idea that I should become the Rebbe. They approached me many times. Not because I am a man who in any way could fill my father's shoes, but for want of another person. They needed somebody. A king is somebody who is the center of social and national responsibility and if he's not such a great ethical man, it's also not so terrible.

The Boyaner Hasidim in Israel asked me to become Rebbe. It gave me a certain pride in myself that they could visualize I was worthy of it. In terms of myself, the question of being a Rebbe was divided into three parts: its American part, its Israeli counterpart, and the part which could be created. My father did not have these problems. My role would be to attract the modern American Jewish person. I could have accomplished this because of who I am. The question of combining these three worlds would have been a difficult one. I would have had to play a different role in each of these three worlds. (IF)

For his part Israel Friedman had been reluctant to put himself forward as a candidate for the post, or even assume that he was the right person to carry out the demanding role spelled out for him by tradition. As the son of a Rebbe he knew the difficulties he would face more clearly than anyone else, and he also realized that his experience in America had given him more liberal views than those of the revitalized contemporary Hasidic community.

They beseeched me and beseeched me and delegations came after me, but obviously for several reasons I couldn't comply with their wishes. Number one, not because I'm such a modest person, but because basically I did not feel that I was ethically and morally capable of carrying on my father's leadership, especially my father's leadership. Second of all, my lifestyle is such that I would be doing them a disservice by acting as their leader. I could not give up all my worldly interests to become somebody who was at the beck and call of a very strict Orthodox community, especially the one in Israel. I couldn't do it and I felt also that I would not be able to fulfill their hopes and wishes. My wife's position [as a sociologist at Columbia University] was also a factor in my consideration. Family considerations came up and they were not willing to make sacrifices. But the other two were so overwhelming that my wife's view was not the only concern to be taken into consideration. It's a tremendous responsibility. You don't live your own private life. You have to dedicate yourself to a life of responsibility, and, at the same time, service. You're at the service of the community in terms of giving advice, in terms of asking for help, in terms of merely acting as a center of attraction to a community of perhaps a thousand people.

Basically they [the Boyaner Hasidim] were in search of continuity. They had respect for me and thought I could change overnight to what they wanted. It obviously was a great temptation, but realistically it would have been impossible. I don't think I would have been able to adjust to the life. I could not have adjusted to their demands on me. Perhaps it would have been possible with the Boyaner Hasidim of twenty years ago. I told them I wouldn't be able to adapt to their demands today. I would see nothing wrong with their kids going to college. Boyan of twenty years ago would have accepted it.   (IF)

The Hasidim had not expected a rejection.

They were desolate. I feel a sense of guilt. It would have been an impossible situation, but I always felt I have a certain knack, even when we discuss individual problems, of developing a mode of handling matters that could have been of help. I would have been helped by my background as a social worker. I could have aided more in terms of advice and moral support. Unlike a social worker, my decisions would have had more weight. That's my only regret. I could have given them strength because of my social work background, but not in bringing their prayers to heaven.

Possibly they enunciated a sigh of relief when I refused. Some are still close to me. In Israel they have respect for me because of what I have been able to do for them. The one thing that kept them together as a community was the yeshivah. The yeshivah is the source of the present Boyaner Hasidim.   (IF)[4]

The Boyaner Hasidim continued to rely on Israel Friedman as their nominal leader. They called on him to keep the community together while they pondered the question of future leadership. For months afterward the Boyaner court was in a quandary as to who would succeed Reb Mordchei. Then the months became years.

I was still asked to make final decisions in the Boyan community. Some people broke away, which, for a while, threatened to split the community. It was a threat because the Hasidim who broke away joined forces with another Rebbe—my uncle—the Sadagerer, in Israel.[5] Our Hasidim exaggerated the importance of the break. It involved only one family, but they became hysterical. I remember that they became so hysterical that they insisted and beseeched me that I must come over. I went over with my brother. In some fashion the speech, which I made to them when the entire Hasidic community was together, was claimed to have strengthened their resolve to stay together as a community and that made them live in the hope of remaining so. They had very dim hopes of somebody succeeding my father, but somehow they hoped that eventually something would happen.   (IF)

The Boyaner Hasidim considered the branches of the Friedman lineage. Israel's sister, Malka Friedman Brayer, had two sons, both highly regarded. They first tentatively suggested the elder son, Yigal, an aerospace engineer, but when that did not work out Israel Friedman suggested

Malka's husband, Menachem M. Brayer, who had a notable lineage of his own. His family were followers of the Rizhin dynasty and his father and his grandfather had both been the Chief Rabbi of the town of Stefanesht in Romania.

Menachem M. Brayer already had an outstanding career in the academic world, but such success worked against him as a candidate to become Rebbe.

> I am too modern in the eyes of the Hasidim. I had academic training. To prove the point, my name is just Reb Menachem to them. Rabbi Menachem. There's never any mention, and correctly so, of doctor, professor. I have a university chair. I have a university chair and two professorships. It's never mentioned, that's fine. I have two doctorates, one in Hebrew Literature in the Biblical Targumic literature and a Ph.D. in Clinical Psychology. These titles are never mentioned. This is the secular image of the person. When I am with Hasidim wearing Hasidic garb, I am a Hasid, period, totally divorced from the outside world. Problems come up with therapists, like this man who just called me now. I answered him to the best of my ability. I am a teacher too. So I feel comfortable not being a Rebbe. I never considered myself as being a Rebbe—far from it. I don't take *kvitlekh* [personal petitions presented to a Rebbe]. I am a practicing psychotherapist.
>
> I have spoken at many gatherings. I speak at every gathering in New York City at the Boyaner Hasidic *tishn* [meals], at every occasion when the Hasidim get together, basically giving them some Hasidic orations with some *mussar* [moral exhortations], with some sense of follow-up behavior, and always reciting and interpreting a piece of toyre of my revered father-in-law the Boyaner Rebbe. I keep the Hasidim together. So does my brother-in-law Israel. (MMB)

Kapitshinitzer

In 1975, seven short years after succeeding his father as Rebbe, Rabbi Moshe Heschel died suddenly at the age of forty-eight. While the passing of elderly leaders is not totally unexpected, the death of a young man who had only recently succeeded his father struck particularly hard. He had seemed to point a way to the future, combining the piety and faith of the Old World with the added aplomb and expertise of the New World.

After the death of Rabbi Moshe Heschel, the Kapitshinitzer Hasidim were in disarray and there was an added sense of urgency to find someone to carry on his work. Attempts then began to convince Syshe Heschel, Moshe's younger brother, to become Rebbe, but he begged off as unequal to the demands of the role. Reb Syshe acted informally to maintain the activities of the court, and he responded as a concerned individual to the problems brought to him; but he insisted that the Hasidim would have to search elsewhere for a new Rebbe.

When my brother died, I accompanied the body for the funeral and the burial in Tiberias next to my father. The Amshinover Rebbe, Reb Meier'l, came to meet the body at the plane and for the few days that I remained in Israel he stayed much of the time with me.

The Rebbe made the most intelligent case why I should become Rebbe. Everyone else was trying to persuade me by telling me, "Don't be so modest . . . you are really good . . . you're perfect for the role . . ." or "you'll grow into the role." That didn't wash well with me. But the Amshinover Rebbe, who was sixty-five or seventy years old at the time and a Rebbe of considerable stature in Israel, turned to me and said: "You say you're not a Rebbe? None of us are Rebbes today. None of us are like the rabbeim of old times. I'm not like my father and I imagine you're not like your father. But the role of a Rebbe has changed today. A Rebbe today is just somebody who binds his people together. He has to strive to keep them together and give them spiritual strength. In their being together they will be better people for it. And that's what I do," he told me, "and that is what you can do."

But I couldn't accept this counsel. I rejected it. Let's assume I'm overly modest. Let's assume that I don't have any feelings of inferiority. Let's assume all these things. I still had to deal with the reality that to be a Rebbe requires you to be a special person, a tzaddik, a wise man and a scholar. I don't see myself as a special person.   (SH)

It was not an easy matter to settle. During the decade following his brother's death Syshe Heschel tried to divest himself of the special authority that he had inherited. The responsibility weighed heavily on him.

Even with my not taking this official position, I still deal with many problems of the Hasidim, though less and less as time goes on. My brother died, it's going to be, it's eleven years now, exactly eleven years ago [1975]. It was eleven years ago this Passover. From the experiences I have had I've become more convinced that I am unable to cope with other people's problems. I'm unable to give them advice or hope or encouragement.

I try. My father, and to an unbelievable extent, my brother, gave of themselves. They gave up their own money, their own time, their own desires. They sacrificed their own needs in the demands of this role. They were very selfless people. With my father, you know, whatever money came in went out to charity right away. In my father's house there was no such thing as holding on to money. The vast majority of the people that came calling on my father came to ask for money.

This is what differentiates me from my father and from my brother. The last two people that called here this evening asked for money. If I had plenty of money, I say to myself, then I could see myself giving and perhaps even love the act of giving. I imagine every person feels the same way. I don't consider myself as being more selfish than the average person. But there's the difference. My father and my brother went out of their way to do good to others. They felt good if they gave up their own needs for the pleasure (yes, pleasure) of having helped someone in need. They searched out to do good to others. It didn't bother them—the encroachment of money, of time, of everything in order to help others. That's what it was to be Kapitshinitzer. Much to my regret and sorrow, that wasn't me. I wasn't up to such standards.   (SH)

It proved difficult to convince the Hasidim of his decision.

This is a story of the Seer, the Lubliner, and of his contemporary, the renowned Rabbi Ezriel, known as the Rosh ha-Barzel, the mind of iron, out of respect for his intellect. He was a big Misnaged. One day the Seer, the Lubliner, met him and complained about how difficult life was for him. People were constantly beleaguering him. Hasidim were constantly showering him with honors, and asking him for advice, for his blessings. It was all too much for him.

"Well," said Reb Ezriel, "the solution is very simple. Next Shabbes when you're in shul, get up on the podium and tell the people that you are unworthy of honor, that you are really not learned and thus not deserving. Ask the people not to come to you any more."

"Good idea," the Lubliner said, and he promised that he would do so.

When they met next Reb Ezriel asked him how it went, and the Seer, the Lubliner, said, "It's worse than ever. No sooner did I make my announcement than the crowd grew larger. Now they say 'Look how modest he is. He must be a great tzaddik.'"

So Reb Ezriel said, "I didn't think of that. But I have a solution. This Shabbes get up on the podium again and tell them how brilliant and saintly you are and they'll run from you."

"Aah, no," the Lubliner said, "that I can't do. That would be lying."

It was like that with me. When I protested that I was unequal to the task of being a Rebbe they said that my modesty was proof that I was worthy, and they wanted me all the more.   (SH)

Boyan: Reb Nahum Dov

A growing number of appeals convinced Menachem Brayer of the need to prepare one of his sons to become the new Boyaner Rebbe.

It so happens that when my revered father-in-law, the Rebbe of Boyan, may his memory be blessed, passed away in 1971, I was called in by the previous Gerer Rebbe, Rebbe Israel of Jerusalem (they called him Bayes Yisrael), and he asked me in very clear language to keep in mind the future of the dynasty and to make sure that my two sons attend the Rizhiner yeshivah in Jerusalem, which is the unique Hasidic yeshivah built by my father-in-law, and which carries the philosophy and perpetuates the tradition of Rizhin. I had no choice but to promise him that I will. And I felt also the obligation, as they say, *noblesse oblige*, that if there are no other descendants who will perpetuate the dynasty of Boyan, Sadager, and Rizhin, which goes back to the Maggid of Mezritch, this would be, God forbid, an extinction of a long chain of traditional leadership of Hasides, and so I felt impelled both by conscience and also by tremendous pressure from all Hasidic and rabbinic authorities—from Rabbi Feinstein, blessed be his memory, to the Lubav-itcher Rebbe, to the Gerer Rebbe, to all the rebbes in Israel, and other rab-beim, that Boyan should be continued. To make it short, my children, my two sons, studied in Jerusalem. My oldest son, Yigal Israel, claimed he is not worthy to sit in his grandfather's chair. He became an aerospace engineer—working for Rockwell for NASA. He studied in Jerusalem and got his rab-binate—a brilliant mind and a humble heart.

The younger one, Nahum Dov, got all the pressure and everyone con-verged on him. I have a tremendous sense of humility, an enormous sense of concern and worry that I have encouraged a young man to undertake a her-culean task which is too much for him. I felt a supreme sense of obligation that in my hands, so to say, humbly, lies the balance between the continua-tion of Boyan, or the extinction of it. I had to make a decision and I made it. (MMB)

Reb Nahum Dov, the younger son, began his studies at the Rizhiner yeshi-vah in Jerusalem with the idea of fulfilling the responsibilities of his legacy.

The Declining Years of the Satmar Rebbe

The Rebbe's Toyre

In his later years the Satmar Rebbe's frail health allowed him to attend only the third Shabbes meal *(shaleshudes)* held late Saturday afternoon, the customary time for the Rebbe's *toyre* (teaching). This meal, concluding the Shabbes, was always attended by a multitude of the Rebbe's followers. Packed tightly in the besmedresh, they watched the Rebbe's every movement in awe as he nibbled uninterestedly at a sumptuous meal of fish prepared for him. The *rebbetsn* (Rebbe's wife), Feiga, appeared to the side and handed the Rebbe's young male attendant the covered dish she had just prepared. She was a thin, taut woman with nervous movements and a quick smile; her head was tightly bound in a scarf. The only other women present were unseen, seated in a balcony screened off from the men's sight.

Despite the crowd present at such meetings with the Rebbe, the besmedresh was always strangely quiet. The room seemed a vacuum with the air locked in the lungs of the onlookers. It was as if one of the patriarchs was dining before them and they watched each gesture searching for holy signs and symbols. It remained hushed until the Rebbe, who had scarcely touched the food, indicated that he was finished eating. The *shirayim*, the remains of his meal, were then divided into small portions and passed out among those present. As the trays and plates were passed overhead by the throng, every scrap of bread and fish, made holy by having been in contact with the Rebbe, was snatched by eager hands.[1] Then the tense silence returned to the besmedresh as the Hasidim listened intently to the Rebbe's toyre, searching for its mystical intent and personal significance.

Rabbi Joel Teitelbaum, the Satmar Rebbe, was the community's anchor to the past. He provided as well their perception of the present and their vision of the future. It seemed impossible to most that it would not always be this way until the coming of the Messiah.

After the war people thought that the Messiah was coming. Because of the war experience, the horrors, the suffering, they expected the Messiah to appear. Then they began a new life, building, reconstructing. Here again there was a target. The Messiah was going to come in the Rebbe's lifetime.   (ES)

The Messiah will come. It's not something we say but something we believe. In the darkest hour the Messiah will come.   (LL)

As he grew older the Rebbe walked with an aide supporting him on each side. Nonetheless the Rebbe's mental vigor survived unchanged until 1968, when he suffered a stroke which at the time seemed certain to end his life.

The Rebbe was even brought back from the dead. The day he took sick it was Shabbes in the morning, before the reading of the Torah. The rebbetsn went to the ark, opened it, and started to sob uncontrolledly and to scream at the people: "Pray! Repent! Bring him back. We are nothing without him." This was the turning point. The cries visibly penetrated all the way up. An eighty-two-year-old man was brought back from the dead.

I was on the phone with the doctor, the neurologist who treated him. "Face it. He's an old man. If he pulls through I'll become a believing Jew." The doctor never became a believer, but the Rebbe came through.   (ES)

Temporary Leadership

The sudden illness marked a great change in the Rebbe's participation in the life of the community. The Rebbe's schedule was greatly reduced and his attendance at the Shabbes meals came to an end. No longer would the Rebbe speak his own toyre. From that point on for the most part he addressed the people through his representatives. To a great extent the major activities of Satmar came under the control of the rebbetsn and Yosef Ashkenazi, the majordomo of the court and the Rebbe's *gabbai* (assistant). (A second gabbai, Ezriel Gluck, joined them to take on some of the added responsibilities.) The Rebbe also relinquished his critical role as rosh yeshivah to Rabbi Nusen Yosef Meisels, who now served as his chief spokesperson.

Rabbi Meisels was a respected religious authority. He was also a phenomenal speaker, and he had the rebbetsn's support. That underlined his authority. He assumed the position of rabbi unofficially, because actually the Rebbe was really Rebbe and rabbi. Rabbi Meisels gave speeches in the yeshivah as rosh yeshivah. He gave speeches as a community leader. He gave talks when they were needed in the shul and he made pronouncements or indicated the kind of strategy that was to be followed in such circumstances as the dispute with Lubavitch, or on school problems, on appeals for funding, and so on. He was an excellent speaker and he was highly respected. He had a very strong voice. He spoke at protests, at demonstrations, at fundraisings, at school openings, at school closings—on every occasion where a speech was required. Sometimes, when there were problems, he gave threatening speeches. He was a great speaker.

Rabbi Meisels acted with the advice of those who in a sense were above him, Gluck and Ashkenazi and the rebbetsn. He was younger than they were, but he had the religious authority and the religious prestige since he was the rosh yeshivah.

Gluck and Ashkenazi were ordinary people, business people. They were not rabbis respected for their opinions, but they were respected because they transmitted the Rebbe's opinions. They spoke on his behalf. If necessary they would bring the Rebbe into the public eye and he would clarify a point or say that they had the authority to do this or that.   (JF)

Despite the Rebbe's visible physical weakness, his uncompromising ideological stands remained strong, particularly concerning the evils of Zionism.

Rabbi Meisels used to say that the Rebbe didn't believe in reading these particular books, or that the Rebbe didn't believe in that, and the people knew that the Rebbe had very strong views and they simply accepted Meisels's statements as fact. The Rebbe always spoke against Zionism and Meisels did too on the Rebbe's behalf. Meisels would say he spoke in the name of the Rebbe, and this strengthened whatever he decided to do. If there was a dispute on anything the Rebbe usually supported Meisels and all his leaders in the community in order to strengthen their hand and to keep things running the way he wanted them to.   (JF)

Although the Rebbe held few public meetings his Hasidim could make an appointment to see him. Despite his precarious health the Rebbe often met individually with his Hasidim when they had pressing problems or needed a blessing.

I'll tell you the most amazing thing. When I was about to get engaged, my older brother, whom you know, went with my father-in-law of sacred memory to tell him about this. The Rebbe was sick already. He had a stroke. He turns around to my brother and he says, "Is this the older one?" So my brother thought the Rebbe you know is not so clear. He thinks that I'm older than him. He says, "No, Rebbe, he's younger than I am." So the Rebbe says, "I know, but from those two who are studying in my yeshivah, is he the older one?"

At that time the yeshivah had at least seven hundred boys. The Rebbe wasn't capable to come anymore to give lectures, and still he remembered that two brothers from this family are in the yeshivah and I'm the older one. You know what that means? It means he carried in his head every *bokher* [youngster] at that time when he was sick. That's amazing.   (PM)

The Rebbe's stroke began a period of great stress for the Satmar population. Since childhood they had regarded the Rebbe as their father, and his close brush with death left them uneasy. Without his strong presence the future seemed cast in deep shadow. Some found the source of their own ills in the diminution of the Rebbe's powers.

> I was outside the community for two years. I have never desecrated a Shabbes, but at fifteen I started getting disillusioned. The Rebbe had a stroke. From a vibrant community where the Rebbe played such an active role, the Rebbe was not active. There was a vacuum. (PM)

With their Rebbe wounded by illness, the Satmar community suffered more than a loss of spirit. They had taken their strong ideological direction from the Rebbe. They were focused on a limited set of issues which they saw as vital for their survival and which brought them into continual conflict with their coreligionists. Accustomed to receiving orders, the community was at a standstill without its commander.

During this period of uncertainty, daily gossip assumed more importance than usual. Every day new rumors were reported, many concerning the rebbetsn, who had assumed such a prominent role in the community and who in the absence of her husband had become the surrogate head of the family. If new tales seemed to lag, then old gossip was revived. Some accounts concerned earlier family struggles; other tales centered on the rebbetsn's frustrated hopes for a child.

The Rebbetsn

The Satmar Rebbe was fifty-one years of age in 1937 in Hungary when he was married for the second time, to Feiga Shapiro, who was then in her twenties. The Rebbe's first wife, Eva Horowitz, had died the year before. She had been plagued by a heart condition which was inherited by her three daughters, two of whom died young. The new rebbetsn's youth held the promise of children.

> It was very important to the Satmar Rebbe to have children. He wanted very badly in his second marriage to have children. From his first wife he had three children but they all had heart problems and they all passed away. (YA)

The new rebbetsn's youth also led some to believe that she could be treated as someone lacking maturity. Both notions proved to be incorrect. The rebbetsn failed to conceive and never bore a child; moreover, despite her youth, the young rebbetsn demonstrated a daunting character. She quickly came into conflict with the surviving daughter of the Rebbe's first marriage over control of the household. Family gossip soon made the rounds of the court.

> The rebbetsn had a fight with the Rebbe's daughter. She didn't get along with the Rebbe's daughter. There was a very famous fight and nobody wants

to admit it. It's not too much to the credit of the Satmar Rebbe. It's a long story.

The Rebbe had three daughters. Two daughters died. The remaining daughter and the [new] rebbetsn did not get along. For one thing she was older than the rebbetsn, and some say that she was smarter.

When the Rebbe married the second time the daughter took advantage of the [new] rebbetsn because she was older and she tried to knock her down. You know, "I have a famous father," while the rebbetsn's father, he was maybe a rabbi in a small town. The daughter didn't give her the authority that a wife should have. In the beginning the rebbetsn was treated badly by the Rebbe's daughter. You know, the daughter felt like, "We'll treat her like another person in the house but we'll keep the authority in the house." The rebbetsn felt she had to stand up for her rights. In the beginning, she had a reason to be angry. In a way it's not right. In the end the daughter lost power. In the end the rebbetsn acted up too much.   (YA)

Some of the tension could be traced to the concern over shifting loyalty and affection. Some conflicts were the result of two women struggling for authority in a kitchen and a household that represented the entire court.

The daughter had taken care of the Rebbe and the whole household before the war, and she ran everything. She was in charge of the shopping, the cooking, the cleaning. It was a completely open household and there were always pots of food available for the poor who came there. It's even said that some people could go to the grocery store when they needed food and charge it to the Rebbe's account. The kitchen was always open. When the rebbetsn came in she made a complete change. She said that she was in charge of everything and that no one could cook and shop and charge anything in the store without her approval. So this started a feud between the two women. The daughter held that that's not the policy of the Rebbe. The Rebbe wanted to have an open house, and this could not be considered to be an open house. What if somebody doesn't have food to eat? It was a difference of opinion. The Rebbe, in order to smooth over this fight between his daughter and his wife, arranged a post for the daughter's husband as rov in Sasov in Hungary.   (JF)

The feud survived the war and accompanied the refugees to New York.

After World War Two they all came to America and the fighting got hotter and stronger, with the rebbetsn trying to attack the Rebbe's daughter with misstatements that the daughter didn't care about her father and that she wouldn't come to visit him. But when she did come she was discouraged and prevented from coming in. They would say that the Rebbe wasn't available, he wasn't around, he was eating, he was sleeping, or whatever, but they had people to bar the door. So in the United States they wouldn't let her in.   (AI)

Other accounts concern the relationship between the Satmar Rebbe and his daughter's husband, the Sasover Rov, who in the past was also considered as a potential successor. That possibility, however, had soured even before the war. One skirmish was said to have begun because the Satmar Rebbe was accustomed to travel for Shabbes to other cities and towns and in his absence the son-in-law led the tish and offered his own toyre. Some of the Rebbe's more irascible followers considered this to be a slight to the Rebbe and a presumptuous grab for power. Not unexpectedly, part of the difficulty between the Satmar Rebbe and his son-in-law was said to concern the State of Israel. True or not, it was an inevitable attribution.

> The Satmar Rebbe refused to recognize or know his daughter, probably because the Sasover was not sufficiently anti-Israel. It might have been for other reasons, even in Europe, because the Satmar Rebbe could not brook any opposition on any subject.   (MF)

In other instances, however, the Satmar Rebbe is said to have encouraged his son-in-law to sit close to him at the tish, belying stories that he was angry with him; still other tales relate that some of the Rebbe's fervent followers, resentful of the son-in-law's special place, unbeknownst to the Rebbe, would try to make his son-in-law uncomfortable at the tish, blocking his way, pushing him, without the son-in-law even catching on. Contradictions in these accounts raise questions about the reliability of court gossip; however, wherever the truth lies it is clear that there were bitter and long-lasting tensions in the Rebbe's family.

Accounts of the early family struggles, muddled as they are, help to explain more recent conflicts between the rebbetsn and the Szigetter Rov, Rabbi Moshe Teitelbaum, who eventually would succeed his uncle as the new Satmar Rebbe. Reb Moshe had been raised in the Rebbe's household from the age of eleven following the death of his father. In the conflicts that followed the Satmar Rebbe's remarriage Reb Moshe had remained loyal to the Rebbe's daughter, his own first cousin, and this brought him into contention with the young rebbetsn.

The primary tension involving the Szigetter Rov and the rebbetsn is said to have concerned her failure to provide a son and successor for the Rebbe, a circumstance that increased the possibility that the Szigetter Rov would succeed his uncle and become the new Satmar Rebbe. This was a matter of central concern not only for the Rebbe and his family but for the entire court. Given the potential of the situation it was inevitable that a dramatic version of events, real or imagined, be told and retold.

> Thirty years ago the Szigetter Rov sent a respected older rabbi to the Satmar Rebbe that obviously the rebbetsn cannot have children and he should consider divorcing her and taking another wife. So he didn't answer him. He said that he should come back tomorrow and he will think about it and give him an answer. The second day that old rabbi came and he knocked on the door and the rebbetsn found out about it and she started yelling at him. And

he was a smart guy. He said, "Satmar rebbetsn, it wouldn't give you too much honor for people to say the Satmar rebbetsn is yelling in the street." So she calmed down.

He went into the house and he came to the Rebbe, and the Rebbe said, "I spoke with Ashkenazi about this and he will give you an answer." And Ashkenazi told him that he doesn't think of divorce. I don't know if he actually told him a reason at this time, but people say that he said that after she struggled with him in World War II he doesn't feel like divorcing her.

So she got mad and she really fought back on this. (YA)

Despite the cross-currents of negative gossip the rebbetsn endeared herself to most of the Rebbe's followers through her generous contributions to charity and the devoted care she extended to the Rebbe. A reasonable excuse if not a just cause could be found for presumed acts of spite and pettiness attributed to her.

The rebbetsn was still trying to protect herself because I guess she felt a little guilty that she doesn't have children. She felt she could be overthrown: "Well, you didn't have children. You're the second wife. The Rebbe had a first wife." You know it's like you're not important around here.

The rebbetsn was criticized a lot. She was too involved and she made a lot of enemies. She didn't get along with the Rebbe's family, especially the Szigetter Rov, because she felt that they were threatening to her position. But the old Rebbe respected her because he said that she suffered a lot for him and he can't deny it. In a certain way the old Rebbe respected her a lot. Whoever she fought with, she did it because she was threatened by them.

In a certain way she was criticized, but she was very respected by most of the people for the good things she did. She gave a lot of charity, an enormous amount of charity she gave to people. She helped the schools a lot and she raised a lot of funds for them. It's very unusual that a rebbetsn should be as active in the social life of the community as she was. Some people would say among other Hasidim, "The Satmar rebbetsn is not a rebbetsn, she's a Rebbe." (YA)

During the Rebbe's illness the influence and power of Feiga Shapiro Teitelbaum, the rebbetsn, grew in the community. Rumors related that she held the power in the small circle who now acted on behalf of the Rebbe.

The rebbetsn had the most authority. If she pushed anyone out, that meant they were out. And if she encouraged someone in, that meant they were in. (YA)

The Death of the Satmar Rebbe

For more than a decade during the Rebbe's illness, the rebbetsn and the Rebbe's gabbaim continued to act on his behalf. The village of Kiryas Joel (Joel's Town) was established in 1974 in Monroe Township in suburban Orange County in New York State. It fulfilled the Rebbe's dream to provide housing for the court's expanding population in a area protected from the influences of the city. The community continued to cope with the usual problems of education, organization, and fundraising. Many considered that the direction of the court would persist in this way until the arrival of the Messiah.

> Ashkenazi and Gluck, the Rebbe's gabbaim, maintained stronger than anyone else that the Rebbe would not die. The Messiah was going to come. (YA)

In the new town of Kiryas Joel plans were initiated to build a new besmedresh and a new house for the Rebbe. The besmedresh was completed in 1978 and the following year the Rebbe's house was ready. The rebbetsn had seen to the Rebbe's every need. Hallways and doorways were wide enough for the Rebbe to pass through with an aide helping him on each side. The rooms were of princely dimension and beautifully appointed, so that, as the rebbetsn said, the Rebbe could welcome the Messiah within when he arrived. The Rebbe, however, never lived in the house. It is told that he visited the house but did not enter it. When he came to the portal he stopped and turned away. Within a few weeks of its completion Rabbi Joel Teitelbaum passed away.

On Sunday, August 20, 1979, at the age of ninety-three, the Satmar Rebbe suffered a fatal heart attack at Mount Sinai Hospital.

> His death was shattering. It was as though he were a young man. He was ninety-three. The trauma of his passing—I, we, never experienced anything like this. I didn't go through the war experience, but this was something for which there is no comparison. There was a sea of humanity. When the coffin was brought into the besmedresh there was a cry to wake the dead. Then there were the eulogies. I've never experienced anything like this. It was as if everything was destroyed and the world had come to an end. The despair was so great. Nobody believed there would be a tomorrow. People tore their clothes. My young son sat on the sidewalk with his jacket torn on both sides. He sat on the sidewalk and ripped his jacket on both sides. People tore their clothes. People sat down for shivah. Grown men broke down completely and sobbed as if the world had come to an end. After living through that nothing else can shake me. Everyone had the same thoughts. It's impossible. It couldn't happen. (ES)

· 9 ·

Lubavitch:
Redeeming Fellow Jews

Proselytizing in the Jewish Community

The overriding concern of the Lubavitcher Hasidim is to reeducate and realign the nonreligious Jewish world—to win Jews back to traditional Torah Judaism. The undertaking to redeem Jewry has mystical as well as social implications, since the positive and negative commandments constitute an interconnected human and supernatural network. The commandments have a direct bearing on human health, on the cosmos, on the perfectibility of the community, and, as a consequence, on the appearance of the Messiah and the end of the exile. These factors lend an air of extraordinary importance to the work of Lubavitch.

Chabad-Lubavitch maintains a network of Chabad houses as its centers for training and revitalization. By the end of 1988 there were 140 Chabad houses in the United States, in addition to others in Israel, Latin America, Europe, and other parts of the world, and new Chabad houses continue to open. They are usually maintained by one or two young couples who are called *shlikhim,* emissaries of the Rebbe. The typical Chabad house is located close to a college, with the aim of attracting thoughtful young people interested in studying interpretations of the Holy Scriptures or "grappling with the riddles of existence"; but the emissaries also seek out school dropouts, troubled youth involved with drugs, and those drawn to non-Jewish proselytizing faiths. The Chabad houses also serve as houses of worship and study. They supply Hebrew books, phylacteries, mezuzot (doorpost scrolls), and other ritual items.[1] In response to community needs the emissaries may initiate a variety of services—religious classes for children, seminars and study groups for students and adults. Each Chabad house is supported by a modest budget allocated by the Brooklyn office and may raise additional funds to support special needs. The level of success (or failure) varies greatly according to the abilities of the particular workers.[2]

The Chabad workers recruit those in the community who express interest in traditional Judaism; they then arrange for them to at least visit the Lubavitcher center in Brooklyn. One who completes the journey and follows the Orthodox laws and customs is called a *baltshuve* (*ba'al teshuvah,* a returnee to Orthodoxy).

The proselytizing fervor of Chabad is regarded with disfavor by other Hasidim, as a less-than-neutral Satmar Hasid explained:

> We wouldn't put tefillin on just anybody. You have to wash your hands before [putting them on], you have to be a religious person. Putting tefillin on a nonreligious person is a desecration of tefillin.
>
> They send out people to give candles to a woman to light candles for the Sabbath. We're not even supposed to mix with women. They are not decently dressed, especially in the summer months. You have the Lubavitchers going around the Rose Bowl parades—all the parades in California. It's way out of place. See, our policy is, even though we are more conservative, we are more liberal. We don't impose our views on other people. We want to live and let live.   (AG)

The Lubavitch response to such disdain is to point out the need to love one's fellow Jew as oneself. "If we know of something we have the responsibility to inform them of it" (SJ). They adhere to the basic principle that a Jew, no matter how he practices his religion, retains an essential spark of Judaism and is worthy of reformation. The value of using the act of donning tefillin to revitalize his faith is a case in point. The Lubavitcher Rebbe, referring to earlier texts, contends that there is no man so wicked that he cannot put on tefillin, adding that there is divine joy when a person dons the tefillin even if he has never done so before.[3]

Hasidim in other courts, less aggressive in their faith than the Lubavitchers, cite the danger of interacting with those less religious and question the possibility of real change for those who were not raised in the Orthodox tradition.

> In the first place it's not a good idea to have contact with such people. It's too risky. In the second place these people are not always well balanced. I mean they're good people but often they're troubled. This is a difficult life and one really has to be born into it. We take in some baltshuves too in Bobov but we don't go looking for it.   (MH)

These concerns, although fairly widespread among Hasidim, are muted outside the Hasidic community. In fact, Lubavitch quickly gained the admiration of a broad range of religious and secular Jews. At long last there appeared to be an ultra-Orthodox group who welcomed their less Orthodox brethren and with whom one could discuss differences in point of view. Lubavitcher eagerness to talk challenged less religious Jews to try to meet them halfway. While only a small number of Jews seemed prepared to adopt Orthodox practices, some were inclined to send their children to study at Orthodox yeshivot, particularly in light of the increasing deterioration of the public school system. Many cherished the memory of traditional practices of the past, even though they had long since rejected them in their own daily lives. They were grateful for the warmth and hospitality of Lubavitch, and they were sympathetic to appeals for financial support. Lubavitch had raised a bridge between the Orthodox and secular worlds, and it promised to carry traffic returning to traditional ways.[4]

Initiation into the ways of Chabad often comes slowly and after a long period of gestation. A small step may result from a lifetime of mulling over religious feelings and group identification without having reached any conclusions or even established social contacts. A spark, a revelation, then ignites the process.

> My religious feeling was mild and not an important part of my life until the revelation of the Holocaust in 1945. That revelation created such rage and fear in my soul, and such grief for my poor brothers and sisters. I could easily have been one of them. My grandparents had come over just forty years before. Providence had put me in the Bronx instead of Babi Yar. That's when being Jewish became very important.
>
> Then three years after, in 1948, on top of all this, the miracle of the humiliated, despised, contemptible Jews, beating back the Arabs and creating Israel, made me accede in my mind at least, that something supernatural was happening in history. God was revealing Himself more clearly than in a long time.
>
> Then I got married in 1956. Yom Kippur 1957 I felt a terrible need to participate in the ritual, but I didn't know what to do. I said to myself that the days of religious observance are gone. Who in his right mind who wasn't superstitious could follow all those rituals—keeping kosher, Yom Kippur and all the rest? Yet I still felt that terrible longing. So *erev* [the evening beginning] Yom Kippur I took a shower. I shaved very carefully. I shined my shoes and dressed up in my best suit, and sat in my living room until it was time to go to sleep. No television, no radio. I just sat and thought. God knows what I was doing. I didn't know what to do.
>
> I didn't act on that impulse in the following years.   (EES)

Lubavitch tries to create the opportunities for seemingly chance encounters between Jews seeking redemption and Lubavitcher emissaries that will germinate latent religious longings. The Mitzvah tanks of Lubavitch, however, are most often manned by yeshivah students of high school and college age serving an apprenticeship as future emissaries. These zealous and inexperienced students are thus often the first Hasidim encountered by interested secular Jews.

> I was a graduate student at NYU and they [Lubavitcher Mitzvah Tanks] were parked in front of the Education building. This was in the early seventies. As I passed by one of those black coats said to me, "Are you Jewish?"

I said, "Of course."

"Did you put on tefillin today?"

I said, "I've never put on tefillin in my life."

He says, "Come into the truck and we'll put on tefillin." He wrapped it around my arm, and put it on my head. I repeated the blessings after him. He gave me a metal candlestick for my daughter and a leaflet about the minimum Jewish library I should have and how to bless the Shabbes candles. Before I was finished with my tefillin a guy came in and just before they were going to wind the straps around his arm, one of them said to the guy, "Are you really Jewish?"

He answered them, "No, but I really want to learn about this stuff."

And they answered, "Get out of this truck." No grace whatsoever.

He said, "But I really want to learn about this stuff."

And they said, "You're not Jewish. Get out of the truck."

This was an emotional dissonance with my American values that sympathized with ecumenical values. On the other hand I liked it that they kicked him out. They were very forthright. They weren't smooth. They had to do mitzvot and not worry about getting along with goyim. I thought it was refreshing. But I also felt bad for the guy. He might have made a good Jew. (EES)

The initial contact may lead to further discussions that will end with a commitment to Orthodoxy or seemingly with nothing at all. The outcome is uncertain but the emissary is convinced that the spark of interest ignited by his efforts will remain alive even in those who do not commit themselves to the Hasidic way of life. The Hasidim believe that there is ample evidence that a single such encounter can have an enduring as well as dramatic effect.

When I had that first experiment with tefillin, it was a powerful experience. I mean the physical binding of the arm—it was like binding on a shield—and then it was a helmet on the head with the box containing the scroll saying, "Thou shalt love the Lord thy God with all thy heart, with all thy soul, with all thy might." It was very powerful. And I said to myself, "Hey, I've got to include this in my life, somehow." (EES)

Nonetheless, despite this common positive reaction, a chasm often exists between the emotional and spiritual perceptions of the novice and those of the often still younger emissary.

But the feeling that I had from the Lubavitcher boy helping me was that he had done his mitzvah for the day, and the actual donning of the tefillin, pulling a blessing into the world, was what interested him, rather than setting me up as someone who might become an observant Jew. He didn't care what happened to me. It was a short-range view. They didn't take my name; they didn't suggest any follow-up. They didn't say where one could buy tefillin, and I didn't know enough to ask. Even if I knew how to buy tefillin, I didn't know how to wind them or take care of them. It really wasn't a learning experience. I was just producing a mitzvah. But it stayed with me anyway. About five years later my father died and I dug up my grandfather's tefillin in the back of a drawer and I took them to a rabbi and he showed me how to put on tefillin and how to wind the straps. That's when I started to become religious. I became religious because of the tefillin. Tefillin is the most exotic, foreign artifact in Judaism. There are no known origins describing the straps and the boxes. (EES)

The Lubavitcher Hasidim are proud of the academic and professional people who have joined their ranks and who support their views on the supremacy of faith over science. In their publications they print their views on the folly of evolution, the warm praise they receive from those who accept their views, and on occasion the irritated reactions of those scientists who reject their overtures.

The Lubavitcher Rebbe is prepared to wrestle for the soul of every Jew. Since the Rebbe has a degree in engineering, one suspects that he enjoys a confrontation with a scientific-minded colleague struggling with his identity and his faith, as indicated by the following excerpt from a letter written by the Rebbe:

> It was quite a surprise to me to learn that you are still troubled by the problem of the age of the world as suggested by various scientific *theories* which cannot be reconciled with the Torah view that the world is 5,722 years old.
>
> I underlined the word *theories,* for it is necessary to bear in mind, first of all, that science formulates and deals with theories and hypotheses, while the Torah deals with absolute truths. These are two different disciplines, where *reconciliation* is entirely out of place ... The Mitzvah of putting on Tefillin every week-day, on the hand—facing the heart, and on the head—the seat of the intellect, indicates among other things, the true Jewish approach: performance first (hand), with sincerity and wholeheartedness, followed by intellectual comprehension (head) ... May this spirit permeate your intellect and arouse your emotive powers and find expression in every aspect of the daily life, for *the essential thing is the deed.*[5]

Lubavitcher Hasidim try to emulate their Rebbe, and some serve as emissaries after their day's work is done. Simon Jacobson, a young Lubavitcher Hasid, meets once a week with a small group in his home. Their number includes a rock musician, a literary agent, a bookkeeper, a rag merchant, and an actor, among others, but they are united in an ardent quest to make Judaism relevant to their lives and to investigate the Orthodox ways.

> These people have careers. They're breaking new ground. I don't know what will happen. I started this four years ago [in 1982]. I did it as a friendly thing, informal. I used to talk to a friend of mine. He brought someone along; then he brought another guy. You can see what happened. I never expected or imagined what's going to happen. These are mature people.

They have their lives to live. I feel a responsibility to say what I have learned. They have to make decisions in their lives. We don't have any statistics to analyze what causes people to become baltshuves. I have no idea what will happen to these people five years from now.   (SJ)

The Lubavitcher Hasidim try to reach out to those exploring their religious and cultural ties to Judaism. Their methods are personal as well as public. The Rebbe's talks at the farbrengen are broadcast worldwide. His words, quickly translated from Yiddish into a variety of languages, are printed and sent off. Those who express interest are directed to a series of programs and meetings.

About four years ago in 1982, Michael said he was coming to Crown Heights to talk to somebody, a rabbi, and I said, "You've got to be insane." A couple of weeks went by and he came here and I said, "It's on my way home. I'll drop you off." And the rabbi was Simon Jacobson. And he was sitting there in the office, talking. I didn't know what he was talking about. But I knew the rest of the week the other places that I went to were sort of not fulfilling in a certain way. And I didn't know what was going on, but I did know that it was something and it drew me back to check out what was going on. I came back a few more times and every time I came back when I left it felt good. I didn't really know what he was talking about, though— the inside, the outside. And then one day I began to get it. I was lucky enough to say I'll do it, or I'll pay attention to this, and I was lucky that one day during the week it kind of validated itself to me in my regular life. That's cool. It worked. But it's a very slow thing and it's very difficult to talk about. You can't tell people that. They look at you like you're out of your mind. Judaism? (KA)

For their part, the Lubavitchers who have contacts with returnees or with those still in the early stages of experimenting with their religious feelings are remarkably tolerant of lapses in behavior. The Rebbe has often urged his followers to treat newcomers gently:

Talk to a fellow Jew with words from the heart about Yiddishkayt, Torah and mitzvot, ethics and fear of G-d; do it in a pleasant and peaceful manner; your efforts cannot fail. If you do not see the result immediately, don't make a hasty judgment based on externalities—your efforts certainly had some effect, but sometimes it may take some reflection or contemplation on his part. It might just need some time. Eventually it will reveal itself.[6]

The Rebbe also urges that a positive attitude is needed in order to influence other Jews:

One should not dwell on the punishment which results from improper behavior. Rather, he should stress awareness that a Jew has a pure soul possessing unfathomable treasure—houses of good which have only to be revealed. Only through awareness of one's strengths will he overwhelm the negative qualities and use all resources to accomplish the desired mission.[7]

The greatest efforts to gather in new Orthodox worshipers are made at the Lubavitch weekend programs, variously called "A Weekend of Jewish Connection" or "A Jewish Self-Discovery Weekend." For a relatively modest fee a couple or an individual is housed with a Lubavitcher family and immersed in a round of activities, including prayer, meditation, song and dance, lectures and seminars. The organizers call it "a total, living Jewish environment." It is one that merges the past and the present.

> It was a great training ground for how to conduct Shabbes. How the day should go. How to handle your kitchen—everything. I had been trying to figure out how to handle Shabbes and I'd get a little advice here and there and I didn't know what I was doing. Now I could see what to do. How to deal with the *blech*.[8] What you do during the morning between davening, between *shaharit* and *minhah* [morning and afternoon prayers].
>
> The Lubavitcher hospitality, and maybe the hospitality of all Hasidim, is extraordinary. It's a good model. It makes it easy to do the same thing and not feel like a sucker, a jerk. You learn the joys of generosity from them.
>
> It was an emotional high. It really raised our spirituality.   (EES)

For some, contact with Chabad signals a profound shift in religious ideas. Ultimately some of these people may ask if the clothing and the ritual are as significant as the ideas they have absorbed.

> I had a funny paradoxical experience before I became religious. I was most comfortable with an impersonal God—transcendent—God as cosmic power which didn't even know I existed. I had forgotten the traditional Jewish idea of an immanent God, the God of my childhood, that God that Pascal had sewn into his cloak—not the philosopher's God but the God of Abraham, Isaac, and Jacob. Paying attention to what the Hasidim were saying brought me to understand what Pascal meant.
>
> The paradox seems to me that what educated, rational, liberal people believe about God is what is incredibly naive. God as an impersonal force? What a worn-out shallow idea that is. And the so-called naive childish idea is confirmed by my life experience for me. This has a funny consequence in my ability to pray. In the past I wanted only to offer thanksgiving. I was really grateful for the life that God gave me, including the trouble. But I couldn't offer prayers of supplication. And now, although it's still difficult, I can ask that God fulfill my silly little needs.   (EES)

There is a natural tie between those who come into contact with images of their family's Orthodox past and the proselytizing Lubavitcher Hasidim. The efforts of Lubavitchers to reawaken Orthodoxy have earned them a strong following among less observant Jews sympathetic to Orthodoxy. But of course not every such experience results in permanent commitment to Chabad or to the Orthodox religious way of life. Some reject the overtures completely. In other instances the result is the establishment of a group of people who are sympathetic to Lubavitch and eager to aid its programs, but who are not prepared to commit themselves completely to the Orthodox way of life.

> The warmth, the sincerity, the kindness, the giving—almost convinced Millie that she should follow the law of family purity—almost, but not quite. She almost decided to take up going to the mikvah, but she couldn't quite do it. My only connection now with Lubavitch is that they send appeals for money and I send money back to them. They receive the largest percentage of my charitable donations. They have the Israeli war heroes fund, and the Lubavitch youth organization. (EES)

Although the Lubavitcher Hasidim appear to be more worldly, and their political stance less abrasive, than the most ultra-Orthodox, nonetheless all Hasidim share the same worldview. Fulfillment of the mitzvot is the central focus of their lives. Their efforts have as their immediate goal the perpetuation of the Orthodox faith in this and in the next generation of Jews. But philosophy without specific mitzvah action is considered to be insufficient. For the Orthodox, the laws must be carried out. "The essential thing is the deed."

> The Rebbe, concerned with the situation of Russian Jewry, gets upset when they quote "Let my people go" in English. Moses told Pharoah, they say, "Let my people go." The Rebbe says they forget to add the words afterward: "Let my people go *to worship Me.*"[9] It's not only to be free but to worship God, to learn about the religion, to learn to be a Jew. It means doing what HaShem wants you to do—to know Him in all your ways. When you're out on the street to know Him and do what He wants you to do at all times. (AR)

The end result of many of these contacts is an unusual tie between Orthodox Hasidim and a small number of secular Jews who share their sense of the uniqueness of the Jewish faith. Only a few complete the task of becoming a fully committed Orthodox Jew and a member of the Lubavitch community. Those few are able to express the sense of fulfillment of the converted.

> When he learned that I was a Lubavitcher Hasid, he asked me: "Born or became?"
> I answered: "I was born when I became a Lubavitcher." (EKT)

· 10 ·

Borough Park

A New Neighborhood for Orthodox Jewry

In the 1940s Brooklyn's Borough Park was an unpretentious neighborhood roughly a mile long and a mile and a half wide that had been built up on flatlands far from the center of the city. It had no distinguishing landmarks or notable buildings, and, despite its name (frequently shortened to Boro Park), no public park. Until the end of the war Borough Park had a stable, middle-class population of Jews and Italians, with the Jews estimated to make up slightly more than 50 percent of the population. It increasingly became a Hasidic enclave beginning in the 1950s when Hasidim newly arrived from Europe and Israel began replacing Italians and less religious Jews who were leaving the neighborhood. The Orthodox population was further expanded by newly married Hasidic couples who could not find housing in Williamsburg, and by Hasidic families who needed more space for their increasing progeny. By the 1960s Borough Park was securely established as a major center of Hasidic and Orthodox Jewry in America.[1]

A number of major and minor Hasidic courts, including Kapitshinitz, Sziget, Belz, Ger, and Stolin, among others, established themselves in the neighborhood. In the mid-1960s the entire court of Bobover Hasidim, frightened by the rising crime rate in Crown Heights, sold their besmedresh and yeshivah, vacated their apartments, and moved to the relatively safe streets of Borough Park. As the neighborhood's Hasidic population grew, the side streets took on a more religious cast. The number of older less Orthodox residents dwindled. Only a single Conservative synagogue remained from the past; and even the modern Orthodox yeshivot lost their clientele. Scores of smaller shtiblekh sprang up so that during the week Hasidim could daven in a minyan conveniently close to their homes. In 1972 Egon Mayer counted 31 yeshivot in Borough Park. The following year police officers at the 66th Precinct estimated that the neighborhood contained roughly 50 yeshivot and 145 shuls and synagogues. In 1979 Marvin Schick estimated that Borough Park "is the home of three hundred or more synagogues, and several dozen yeshivot and day-schools."[2] By 1980 the Jewish population reached 72,500. A survey prepared in 1983 by the Council of Jewish Organizations of Borough Park showed that 90 percent of the (then 83,000) residents of Borough Park were white, and that 85 percent were Jewish.[3]

Despite the increasing number of Orthodox Jews settling in the neighborhood, Borough Park maintained a more cosmopolitan air than Williamsburg, where there was a less diverse Jewish population. In Borough Park no single viewpoint dominated the mood of the streets. While the population soon surpassed that of Williamsburg, Borough Park's smaller homes and less crowded streets encouraged an air of greater freedom. New restaurants and shops, attracted by the large number of new shoppers, added to Borough Park's more liberal ambiance, and some of those who elected to move to Borough Park did so not only to find larger apartments but also to be freer of social pressures to conform. A resident of Williamsburg who wanted to purchase a newspaper held in general disfavor had to go to a newsstand on the periphery of the neighborhood, while in Borough Park such forbidden treats were available on the main avenue.

New housing reflected the neighborhood's economic strength and diversity. As newcomers moved in, real estate prices shot up. Older two-story homes became three- and four-story structures; space for additional apartments was squeezed from garages and lawns. The socioeconomic level of the Borough Park population, however, remained modest. Although the area is referred to as "low crime, high income," in fact, most of the residents of Borough Park were working people of relatively moderate means, with a high percentage of elderly persons on social security. Aside from a line of six-story elevator apartment buildings on both sides of the street on 14th Avenue (from 46th Street to 55th Street) and 15th Avenue (from 49th Street to 55th Street), most residents lived in two-story houses, often semidetached, some of which were divided into apartments.[4]

COJO: The Council of Jewish Organizations of Borough Park

Population and power became divided among several groups of Hasidim and Orthodox Jews in Borough Park. While several Rebbes now lived in the neighborhood, there was no one with the dominating presence, prestige, and authority of the Satmar Rebbe in Williamsburg or the Lubavitcher in Crown Heights. Williamsburg was not only the home of the major Rebbes; from 1966 the older neighborhood also had an organization, the United Jewish Organizations of Williamsburg (UJO), which included all the major Jewish courts and organizations, to deal with community problems. Borough Park had no central authority, no clear leadership, and no spokesperson. Nor was there a central office to negotiate with government agencies, mediate internal social and political conflicts, collect information, or authorize public stands. Each court, shul, and yeshivah was forced to deal separately with the Board of Education requirements regarding secular subjects, government regulations, and the purchase of idle public buildings and vacant properties. When problems in the neighborhood appeared a cacophony of voices arose in response and a variety of contradictory actions were threatened.

A plan for a community organization was set in motion in 1974 by Rabbi Akiva Silverburg, the head of the Gerer yeshivah. (The Gerer Rebbe resided in Israel and had few followers in Brooklyn.) Akiva argued that Borough Park's most important industry was education and that its primary products were schools and shuls. The organization's founding group included representatives from a wide range of Hasidic groups including Satmar, Ger, and Bobov; Orthodox organizations such as Agudat Israel; and yeshivot such as Bais Yaakov. They agreed that the community had common interests that could be represented by a united organization. Before serious discussion could begin, however, they had to agree on what the proposed organization would *not* deal with. Questions concerning the State of Israel were removed from the table. Once that controversial problem was excised from the agenda, nothing stood in the way of organizing the Council of Jewish Organizations of Boro Park (COJO). Acceptance of a single community authority was an echo of the role of the *kahal* (communal governing board) in Eastern Europe.

In 1976, two years after its founding, COJO solidified its structure by hiring Rabbi Morris A. Shmidman as executive director. Shmidman was not allied to any Hasidic group, although he was a brother-in-law of the Spinker Rebbe. Shmidman was both a lawyer and a rabbi, steeped in religious law and in the American tradition of civil rights and due process. By temperament and design he functioned as a mediator seeking consensus; at the same time he held firm views and was not fearful of expressing them.

The Council initiated a range of community services. They organized a job training program, an employment service, a mental health program, help for the aged and for youth, a Russian immigrant office, and other educational and information services.[5]

The Attack on the 66th Precinct

The Hasidim have never been free from petty harassment, and they are frequently cursed and taunted by hecklers in passing cars. During the

1970s there was a perceptible increase in local crime. In 1973 two Hasidim were beaten up by a pair of men wielding two-by-fours. On that occasion as on others the Hasidim gathered at the 66th Precinct House on 16th Avenue to ask for increased police protection. Few tangible results came from such protests. By city standards Borough Park was a peaceful neighborhood, and the police were not about to shift men there from high-crime areas.

An altogether different response to threats from the outside came from one of the more outspoken fringe groups. In 1975 Rabbi Meir Kahane of the Jewish Defense League led 150 supporters on a "march for a safe neighborhood" through the nearby Latino area. A few days later, in what appeared to be a counter-move, two synagogues and the homes of two rabbis were firebombed, and a search of nearby rooftops uncovered twenty-six other firebombs primed for use. The neighborhood population became increasingly apprehensive, waiting for the next attack.

At one A.M. on December 2, 1978, an elderly man was robbed and stabbed to death by unknown assailants. The man had worshiped earlier at the Friday evening services at the Bobov besmedresh, although he was not a member of the Bobov community. News of the murder spread by word of mouth, and by eleven o'clock on Saturday morning groups of men and women, most of them Hasidim, gathered in front of the 66th Precinct to protest the death and to demand increased police protection. The four officers on duty were surprised by the sudden appearance of two hundred protesters who entered the station house while another two thousand gathered outside. Included among those inside were a number who were more closely identified with the Jewish Defense League than with the Hasidim. According to a few witnesses some of these men were "out to make trouble." The sergeant at the desk reported that "It got filled wall to wall with people . . . We were literally fighting for our existence." The sergeant called for assistance and 170 policemen from a number of precincts responded to "patrolmen in trouble." [6]

The Hasidim maintain that the protest was orderly until the police reinforcements arrived. As one Hasid described: "They came swinging their clubs, and one guy had a smile on his face while he was hitting people." As the blows rained down, they tried to shield their heads and then reacted angrily. In the ensuing thirty minutes, 72 persons were reported injured, including 62 policemen, a count regarded with skepticism by the Hasidim present. Assemblyman Samuel Hirsch, his aide, and a mayoral aide, there to urge calm, were bloodied by policemen. One Hasid had a heart attack at the scene and later died at the hospital. The station house showed the marks of the riot: windows were wrecked, the outer doors of the station house were torn off, and filing cabinets were broken and their contents scattered on the floor. The following day, Sunday, the *New York Times* headline read ". . . Hasidim Storm a Police Station."

The Council of Jewish Organizations suddenly found itself at the center between the community, the police, city officials, and news reporters.

As soon as an event takes place in the religious community it becomes a media event, and obviously so because we look, the community looks, different, and so naturally it becomes sensational. Plus the fact that you create a sensational issue: Jews who are supposed to be docile, calm, and never take any exaggerated steps, suddenly become very aggressive. It seems to be so out of character with the Jewish nature that it becomes an object of attention and sensation.

The night the incidents were reported we met with the individuals involved, with the police officials; we met with the rabbis. The thing we try to teach the community at all times is that if there is an issue that is important to the community then it must be done through the community itself. It has to come through the rabbinic leadership and the lay leadership of the community.

There were an awful lot of people including public officials taking advantage of the situation. I'm not saying that they were 100 percent wrong, but certainly they did not act in a way we felt to be responsible. And we disassociated ourselves from them. We spoke with the police. We spoke with the mayor's office. We were on television on this issue on several occasions to explain it. The Council tried to quiet the temper and the nerves over that particular issue, and I think it succeeded very well.   (MS)

Handling the situation with directness and calm, and speaking with one voice, was seen as a measure of the maturity of the community.

Shmidman made them realize that they had to sit down, they had to restructure their reactions, they had to teach the community different ways to respond. He spread the word in the community.   (JS)

It proved to be difficult for the courts to assign blame in the few individual cases that came to public attention. Assemblyman Hirsch pressed a complaint against the officer who had clubbed him, only to find himself arrested along with four others and charged with assaulting two policemen. He was later released on the grounds of mistaken identity. It was generally accepted that some police had behaved in the way police are often expected to behave, while some protesters, Hasidim included, had behaved in ways Orthodox Jews are *not* expected to behave. Exchanging blows with policemen inside a police station would be unthinkable not only to their Russian, Polish, and Galician forebears but to almost all groups in the nation. It was a measure of how far the Hasidim had traveled since they arrived in the New World as dispersed and cowed survivors.

In the weeks following the riot, Hasidim strolling in the streets of Borough Park observed that the police were suddenly more visible and that they responded promptly to calls for assistance. Even more noticeable were the reduced number of curses and taunts the Hasidim received from passing cars. Are the drivers thinking, some Hasidim speculated, that maybe we can fight back?

There was another, more surprising development in the neighborhood: Jewish and non-Jewish women of Borough Park formed a civilian patrol to monitor the streets during the midday hours to prevent crime. The patrols consisted of a driver and a radio operator equipped with a walkie-talkie connected to a home receiver monitored by a third woman. If an emergency arose, the woman at home was prepared to telephone the police. The ethnic diversity of the patrols helped to avert any animosity, and since the women did not imply any physical threat, they served to lessen tension in the neighborhood.

New Battle Lines in Borough Park

It soon became clear that prejudice was not confined to a single group in Borough Park. A year after the murder and riot, in December 1979, the neighborhood learned of another outrage, the desecration of Temple Emanu-El, the only Conservative synagogue in Borough Park. A swastika and anti-Semitic remarks were spray-painted on the exterior of the building. Credit for the desecration was claimed not by an anti-Semitic organization but rather by a representative of a so-called ultra-Orthodox group named TORAH (Tough Orthodox Rabbis and Hasidim). The group castigated the synagogue for not separating men and women at prayers and for not observing the Shabbes according to the Orthodox law, among other complaints. The outraged rabbi of the temple declined to remove the offensive scrawls for a time, preferring to have them serve as a reminder of the offenses committed against the Jews in the past, a point not lost on the survivors of the Holocaust living in Borough Park. The rabbi dismissed the claim that the perpetrators represented an organized group, and he was supported in this view by Rabbi Shmidman, who also decried the rumor that they were tied to Satmar.[7]

Another small ad hoc group appeared on the scene a few months later, when in March 1980 Waldbaum's supermarket on 13th Avenue was picketed for remaining open for business during Shabbes. The group "The Jewish Guardians of the Sabbath" called for a boycott of the supermarket. Pressuring stores to close for the Shabbes is commonplace in neighborhoods with a developing religious population. The storekeepers, however, frequently do not know which way to jump. They may have a substantial clientele who would find Orthodox criteria to be inconvenient. While the majority of Waldbaum's customers were Jewish, very few of them were identified as Hasidic. Moreover, there was no guarantee that Orthodox customers would patronize the store even if their wishes were granted. Nor could the managers ignore the preference of other customers, in this instance Italians and Puerto Ricans, who comprised roughly 30 percent of the store's customers. It was even reported that the Italian-American Civil Rights League was planning a counter-demonstration.

The most telling move was made by COJO, which in effect issued a rabbinical order telling Jews not to take part in any demonstrations against the store. Rabbi Shmidman, speaking for the Council, said: "While every conscientious Jew deplores the desecration of the Sabbath, and hopes that people will strengthen their religious observances, at the same time, we do not feel that these objectives are best served by street demonstrations at this time."

> The Waldbaum's store was on the major shopping street, and staying open on Shabbes represented an offense to the community. But we had to balance that with the fact that the neighborhood is made up not only of Jews. If you don't want to patronize the store, you don't patronize the store. But if other people want to shop, it's not something we should interfere with.
>
> The protest concerns a substantive issue; but a more fundamental question is whether protest should be held in the street. We hold that no self-organized protest should take place without prior consultation with senior rabbis. It should have rabbinic sanction—four or five recognized rabbis should approve of the action. (MS)

The question was whether everyone in the community would follow the order of the Council. Rabbi Shmidman appeared confident: "Certainly, anyone who would violate such a thing would not be held in any esteem by the community. No normal, responsible person would dare violate the clear expression of his Hasidic Rebbe or teacher."

The demonstrators, thwarted by the Council, disagreed that the order was binding. One of the demonstrators declared: "There is no such thing. The council is split, the rabbis are split . . . we are going to be demonstrating Saturday. This is largely a Jewish community. If it were the other way around, all the stores would be closed on Sunday. We expect them to be closed on Saturday." [8] Despite such threats the matter quickly died down. The issue was finally put to rest five years or so later when Waldbaum's, dissatisfied with the volume of business, closed its doors. The property was sold and the Dime Savings Bank opened a branch in its place.

A more serious threat to the community emerged when a spurt of violent crime occurred in late April and early May of 1980. On his way to religious services, a sixty-five-year-old Hasid was wounded in the neck and back by two shotgun blasts fired from a passing car. A few mornings later a seventy-two-year-old Hasid was hit in the arm by gunfire from a car. In an apparently unrelated incident a thirty-year-old Hasid was cut in the face when three teenagers shoved him into a metal fence. Two other incidents on the periphery of the neighborhood added to the sense of a community under siege: a seventeen-year-old Hasid was attacked by three young men and beaten with a baseball bat; a few days later a young man on his way home from Friday night religious services was stabbed in the back when he could not satisfy his two attackers' demands for money.

The community mood shifted rapidly to anger and indignation. The Jewish Council advocated hiring a patrol service to guard the streets, with funds provided by taxing each family $52 per year. Noach Dear, then district manager of the community board, urged additional police and block patrols. At a street rally representatives of a group named JACOB (Jewish Athletic Club of Brooklyn) presented an alternative solution. They urged Jews to arm themselves: "A .22 for every Jew." Their response to the call for a paid patrol was to move the rally down several streets to COJO headquarters where they chanted: "Down with the Jewish Council." Members of the crowd complained that the Council had received government funds for patrols but had failed to provide them. The charge was denied by Rabbi Shmidman.[9]

Some members of the Jewish community could not readily distinguish between indiscriminate assaults and deliberate anti-Semitism. Prior experience and their own concerns made it difficult to think otherwise: the governing principle in social life was to separate themselves from others; their distinctive dress set them apart and often made them a target of abuse.

> We had an incident not long ago in which some windows were broken of merchants on 13th Avenue. And of course the first temptation of irresponsible people is to scream anti-Semitism, you know, Nazi attacks. Some times that may be a fact, but it has to be determined first. You can't just let a community get up in arms and make all sorts of accusations against police or individuals when it has no basis in fact, when you find out afterwards it was either the act of some crazy individual, as it was in this one case, but it had no origin in any anti-Semitism by any means. This happened about a year ago in 1985. On the anniversary of Kristallnacht someone threw rocks through the store windows on 13th Avenue. They caught him. It was not an anti-Semitic attack by some individual from another ethnic group. But you can see the potential when you reach the next day's paper—store windows broken. And if somebody would jump on the bandwagon and say this was anti-Semitism and call the whole thing—. If it's not necessary to do that it's not necessary to do that. You must reserve your use of these terms for when it's an accurate description. (MS)

New Social Concerns

By 1983 the neighborhood of Borough Park had the highest density of Orthodox Jews in New York City. As the Hasidim settled in, others, including Modern Orthodox families, left the neighborhood. Etz Chaim, one of the first Modern Orthodox yeshivot in Borough Park, founded in 1917, closed its doors in 1979 when falling enrollments made clear that its constituency had moved elsewhere.

There were changes in the commercial streets of the neighborhood, 13th, 16th, and 18th Avenues, to match the growing population. Along the main shopping street, 13th Avenue, there was an air of a boom town, and restaurants and shops seemed to pop up suddenly like targets at a fair. After being vacant for some time, the buildings on the street where yeshivah Etz Chaim had stood were redone with a new line of stores. The stores and restaurants attracted large numbers of women shoppers, who usually arrived with an escort of baby carriages for infants and strollers for toddlers.

In 1987 two of the most popular stores on 13th Avenue opened between 50th and 51st Streets: Echler's Bookstore and the Kosher Castle Dairy Cafeteria. The interested reader can thread through the narrow aisles of Echler's and find neatly organized stacks of the latest works of Jewish interest as well as religious art objects. The doors of the Kosher Castle, on the other hand, are wide enough for women to wheel in twin-sized baby carriages and park them inside in the aisles. The tables are of picnic dimensions, with enough room for pocketbooks, shopping bags, toys, and trays of food. For service, customers move up and down the food counter asking the Latino countermen to dip into the row of stainless steel hotplates for generous portions of fish, barley and vegetable soup, vegetable cutlets, kashe (groats), slices of pizza, noodles, kugel (pudding with potatoes or noodles), and knishes (dumplings) with potatoes, cheese, spinach, and kashe.

Stores press tightly against one another on both sides of the street. Between 50th and 51st Streets on 13th Avenue there are a dry goods store, a health food store, a gift shop, a flower shop, a travel agency, a bakery, a furniture store, a discount stockbroker's agency, a drug store, a boutique, a shoe store, an electronics store, a grocery, a clothing store, a carpet store, a card and gift shop, and a bank, besides the cafeteria and the bookstore. Another bookstore lies around the corner from Echler's. Across on the side street is a bank of busy outside telephones; opposite the phones is a small candy store where pinball and video games draw the less disciplined yeshivah students. Further down between 49th and 50th Streets are stores much like those on 50th to 51st Street, so every culinary, household, and fashion need can be satisfied twice over. New storekeepers on the street—Sephardim, Russians, and Israelis—provide imported goods and computer technology. More than half a dozen languages can be heard in the space of a block: Yiddish, Hebrew, Russian, Hungarian, Spanish, Urdu, and even English.

The bustling commercial street life continues down 13th Avenue. The congestion on the sidewalk is matched by gridlock on the streets. Cars and trucks double-park on the narrow streets leading to 13th Avenue and sometimes even on 13th Avenue itself, at times narrowing the busy street to one or at most two lanes. The bulky city buses are locked in. Intersections are tied up. Everyone is delayed, impatient, frustrated. The drivers race a few feet, hit the brakes, and lean on their car horns.

Advertisements in the *Boro Park Voice*, a publication of the Council of Jewish Organizations of Borough Park, illustrate the range of culinary, commercial, and social interests on the street:

> *Dagim Home Style Gefilte Fish Balls: Tastes so good your guests will be sure it's Homemade . . . The latest European styles in Juvenile Furniture on special for the new season (strollers, cribs, playpens, high chairs, bumpers and quilt sets) . . . Gelt* [money] *funding for the best mortgage deal in town: refinancing, no income verification . . . Cosmetic and preventive dentistry for children and adults: emergencies treated promptly.*

These commercial ads are more than matched with notices expressing social concerns:

> *Have you ever experienced a Shabbes without challah from your favorite bakery? . . . There are unfortunately hundreds of families that can't afford foods for Shabbes. Thanks to the support of countless individuals who donate money to Tomche Shabbes* [supporters of Shabbes], *arrange luncheons, or volunteer time to assemble and distribute packages, Tomche Shabbes is able to help over 600 poor families . . . We wish to inform our communities that HRA-MAP has increased our Home Care case allotment from 600 to 800 cases . . . Mobilization call from the leading Rabbis Admorim and Roshei yeshivah in Eretz Isroel to support the five million dollar campaign for farmers of 13 kibbutzim and moshavim* [collective farms and cooperatives] *in Israel.*

Despite its air of opulence and good feeling, there are increasing complaints over behavior in the streets of Borough Park. Some assert that since this has become the home of a religious community, greater social responsibility and more courtesy are to be expected in public. One political leader asserts:

> Yiddishkayt is not only between man and God but between man and man. The way people behave to each other in the street is what it's supposed to be all about. The community is overcrowded and there's no solution in sight— the high number of cars, the high number of people. The community is not clean; it's not well kept. *Agudah* magazine did an article the way they drive in the community. They disregard the regulations—they cross against the red light. There's something wrong that has to be addressed. We have to relate learning to everyday affairs because it's not being done. There's too much traffic. There's too much dirt. Borough Park should be on a higher

level. In a certain way it is on a higher level. Crime is extremely low. The streets are safe. But I'm not satisfied. I want relationships to be improved. (DH)

Social tension created by religious intolerance has also come in for its share of criticism. Even Orthodox Jews drawn to the religious ambiance of Borough Park find themselves feeling unwelcome.

Borough Park is becoming more and more Hasidic and there's resentment from the rest of the community—from the Modern Orthodox. The followers of Young Israel, who've been here forty or fifty years, resent the Hasidim. They see the change not for the better. They have the feeling that the Hasidim sometimes lack interest in those laws concerning the relationship between man and man. They lack the sensitivity for people who are different. They must realize that other people are a little different than you are and should be treated in a proper way. Maybe someone doesn't wear a sheytl and they receive verbal abuse. I've seen it. Little kids—five, six, seven years old—yell at them: "Nisht kein Yid [You're not a Jew]." (DH)

It is evident that Orthodox Jews feel slighted by the Hasidim, and their disappointment is deepening. Some who were drawn by the increasing religiousness of Borough Park are now leaving for the same reason.

I need a yeshivah for myself and my family. I need a kosher butcher, a kosher bakery, a mikvah, and a synogogue. And they are all available in great numbers here in Borough Park. This is paradise for an Orthodox Jew. But there is one thing that is lacking—socialization. My children were playing and the neighbors, Hasidic neighbors, came out and told their children, "Don't play with the goyim." I don't think myself, my wife, my kids can socialize in this community. They'll say hello to you, and that's all. We don't get together Saturday night. There's no socialization. That's why I left. There are a lot more people like myself who are still here, but that's how I feel about it. I feel different. They may feel superior, but I don't feel inferior. (JS)

Conflicts are not confined to religious ideals, nor are they contained within the boundaries of the Hasidic community. As the Hasidim expand into neighborhoods beyond Borough Park, such as Bensonhurst and Flatbush, they come in contact with Jewish communities who resent their intrusion and the new standards some zealots attempt to mandate.

People look at them and they think that all Jews are like that. They act like Nazis. They move in and then they push their ways. They're aggressive. They go to the avenue storekeepers and tell them they have to close on the Shabbes or they won't buy from them. They buy houses and then immediately start to enlarge them. They ignore the zoning regulations and build without permits. They tear out the back of the house and build too far in the back. They build out in the front. We have to call in the authorities. They don't pay any attention to the laws. (MB)

Ironically, for many of the most pious, Borough Park provides too liberal an environment. Some steeped in the atmosphere of more traditional Williamsburg see the freer atmosphere of Borough Park as a threat to the stability of the family.

I wouldn't want to move to Borough Park because the various other people over there are not as traditional as Williamsburg. In every sense. Over here [in Williamsburg] it's closer to the past than over there. Over there it's taken on more qualities of what you would say are Western qualities. Here it's more European. In Borough Park you have more women driving cars. I'm just giving you one example. Over here women wouldn't drive cars. Over here kids would have their peyes suspended; over there I suppose they would probably be around their ears or in any other way [tied in the back or under their hats], right? Over here the kids would speak mainly Yiddish—not mainly but *only* Yiddish; over there you will hear kids speaking English. In other words the barriers between Jews and the secular people are much greater over here than over there. Over there the barriers are broken here and there. It's more a mixed community. Over there you see more Western attitudes than you would see over here in Williamsburg. What I mean is women are more outgoing over there. There's more shopping, more restaurants. Over here the women are more modest. They're housewives. They're more housewives over here. The whole community is smaller than over there probably. I prefer these values over here. I want to raise my kids in the values here in Williamsburg rather than those in Borough Park.   (AG)

· 11 ·

Two Courts in Borough Park:
Bobov and Stolin

Choosing a New Stoliner Rebbe

Two distinct Hasidic courts—Stolin and Bobov—exemplify the range and the development of Hasidic social organization in Borough Park. The Stolin-Karlin Hasidim were one of several small Hasidic courts of less than a hundred families. At the core of the court were the American-born sons of Stoliner Hasidim who had emigrated from Europe before the Second World War. Hasidim of the Stolin and Karlin dynasty were always noted for their shouted and table-thumping prayers. Though almost all of the Stoliner Hasidim were American-born young men, they were as devout, as merry, and as enthusiastic as if they had spent their childhood in a Russian shtetl.

In the 1940s the Stoliner Hasidim consisted of elderly and middle-aged men, and some children. Most of the young men between the ages of twenty and thirty-five whose parents were from Stolin had drifted away from Hasidism. They had either attended an Orthodox yeshivah or left Orthodoxy altogether. Many had moved elsewhere. There were very few women in attendance, and those who participated in the activities were middle-aged.

The dynasty of Stolin had almost been extinguished in the war. Four of the six sons of Reb Israel of Karlin[1] had been killed by the Nazis in Stolin, Karlin, and Warsaw. (Another son, Reb Yaakov, had immigrated to the United States in 1929, but he had died in 1946.) Reb Yohanan, the last remaining son, had survived the death camps and settled in Israel. When the Stoliner Hasidim in America learned of his whereabouts they sent a delegation to Israel to convince him to return with them to America. In 1948, Reb Yohanan, then forty-eight years of age, arrived with his daughter and settled in Williamsburg as the Rebbe of a small band of exuberant followers.

When the Rebbe arrived he emphasized the need for Stolin to have its own yeshivah. The identity of Stolin, as of every other court, was built around the boys and young men. To ensure the continued life of the court efforts were made first to establish a yeshivah for the boys. It was assumed that a school for girls could wait for the future, and in the meanwhile the girls could attend one of the Orthodox schools such as Bais Yaakov, then located on South 8th Street in Williamsburg. This focus provided an unforeseen and undesired consequence for the young men of Stolin: when they matured and sought brides they found that the girls preferred to find a husband among the young men attending the Orthodox yeshivot. Many prospective brides were unwilling to consider boys from Hasidic yeshivot, who seemed more fanatical in their appearance and less in touch with modern times. As a result, when they married the young men of Stolin had to introduce their brides to Hasidism.

The Williamsburg shul had two stories, and so the women could watch the activities of the men on the lower floor from a gallery that circled the room. Although the sexes were separated, the shul was small and there were times during charity appeals when the men would shout up to the ladies in the gallery to ask if they wanted to contribute to one charity or another. When the court moved from Williamsburg to Borough Park and converted two stores on 16th Avenue into a shul, a small section in one of the two rooms was designated for women to worship. Subsequently the ceiling of the first floor was cut open and a gallery for women was constructed on the second floor. (Still later, when a third store was purchased and the shul rebuilt, a more ample gallery was provided.)

Reb Yohanan's intellectual gifts were said to be modest: he did not say toyre on the Shabbes and so offered no teachings or governing philosophy. He preferred to speak instead to his followers individually in brief private visits. On the other hand, the Stolin Hasidim regarded Reb Yohanan as a "miracle rebbe." They extolled his powers in curing the sick, foretelling the future, and providing a livelihood (*parnose*) for his followers. Tales of the miracles performed were somewhat encouraged by the Rebbe's own dramatic and emotional accounts.

> The Rebbe told us how he had predicted the war. He said that after traveling in the Sudetenland in the 1920s he had said it couldn't last and there's going to be a war. People didn't believe him.

> Often the Rebbe said, "When I give a blessing I take responsibility."

> When he was asked to give a blessing for someone who was ill, if he said "Okay," if he asked, "How is he doing?" I knew that that person is going to be all right. If he ignored mentioning the person the prognosis was poor. A man came to the Rebbe saying, "My daughter is ill. Save her." He tried to give the Rebbe money but the Rebbe refused it. The man chased after him but the Rebbe wouldn't take the money. Later the Rebbe said, "Now he comes when it's too late."

When you talked to the Rebbe you felt he was reading your mind.

Once a man came to the Rebbe and the Rebbe asked him, "How is your parnose?" And the man said, "Okay." Later we said to him, "Why didn't you ask the Rebbe for parnose?" To this day he doesn't have a decent job.

Once when the Rebbe was sick someone rang the bell and the person taking care of him answered it. He said the Rebbe couldn't see anyone because he was sick. The visitor said, "He'll see me." He said his name was Avrom Z. He had been with the Rebbe in the concentration camp. The Rebbe's attendant went up and told the Rebbe who he was and the Rebbe remembered him but he said he couldn't come up because he was sick and to ask him what he needed. The man said his wife wasn't well. She had cancer on her foot and the next day they were going to amputate her foot. He needed a blessing that everything would be all right. When the Rebbe heard this he said, "It's nothing. Tell him to call up tomorrow."

That night around three in the morning the Rebbe was up with pain. His shoulder was rheumatic and his follower who was his attendant had to rub it. The Rebbe was in pain and he kept groaning, "For Avrom's wife I have to suffer." He had a terrible night. The next day the phone rings. The doctor said there was a mistake in the diagnosis. She was fine. The Rebbe cried, "What don't we do for a Jew?"

The ending of the story I learned just last month. Thirty years have passed. Avrom Z. died and his son became a doctor. One of his patients visited him and reminded him of what had happened. He said he knew the story of how the Rebbe's blessing had saved his mother. It turned out that she had had a melanoma and they thought they would have to amputate her leg at the knee. Six different experts looked at it and they could not have made up this diagnosis. The next day she was found to be absolutely clean of cancer. His mother lived 22 years longer and died of something totally different. (PR)

Perhaps even more important to strengthening the ties between the old Rebbe and his Hasidim was the Rebbe's role as confidant.

We saw him as a close, dear friend. The supernatural powers that he seemed to have were second to his magnetic personality. He showed us a tremendous amount of concern and love. Whenever he was asked something he would mull it over and show concern.

I saw a man come over to the Rebbe in shul and whisper to him and I knew the guy has no parnose. He was unemployed. After shul the Rebbe was walking home and he was mumbling to himself. "How do we go home and make *kiddush* [blessing over wine] when there's someone walking around without a job." He kept repeating this to himself. (PR)

In 1953, the next-to-last year of his life, the Stoliner Rebbe began to present his toyre to a small group at the beginning of every month. The talks took place in Williamsburg at the home of one of his followers who was also the Rebbe's landlord. The Rebbe rented the apartment on the second floor; his accommodating Hasid lived on the floor below where the davening and the talks took place.

> Each month he would discuss a different subject. If it was the month before Purim he would discuss Purim and what one should get out of that holiday. If it was Pesach he would talk about that. He discussed current events and religious current events. He was often dramatic and very emotional. He would cry and get agitated. He told us we have to be prepared to work for Yiddishkayt, that we can see what happened in Europe. He spoke about getting ready for Shabbes. He said once how interesting it would be if we could take a picture of how a person hurries around on Shabbes eve. If we had a picture of ourselves then we could say: "This is what you look like before Shabbes. You are unprepared for Shabbes. You don't look like you're becoming prepared for the holy day." (PR)

Unfortunately, Reb Yohanan's life was cut short after only eight years in America. He passed away after an extended illness, devotedly cared for by one of his closest Hasidim. Despite his relatively brief stay in the United States, by the time of his death Reb Yohanan had left a lasting mark on his followers. Tales of his piety and his miraculous powers recall the fiery and extravagant Stolin-Karlin tradition.[2]

In death the Stoliner Rebbe continued to astound his followers. A dispute arose as to whether the Rebbe's body should remain in America or be transferred to Israel. Lots were thrown three times, and they fell in favor of moving the body to the Holy Land; but others argued that the Rebbe himself had purchased the cemetery lot in New Jersey only the year before. Moreover, in the past Stoliner Rebbes had been buried in the country in which they resided at the time of their death. Although the matter would go to a rabbinical court, it was essentially settled in May 1955 when the Rebbe's daughter Feige had a dream in which her father appeared and spoke to her: "Why are they holding me up?" he asked. In 1956 the wrangling ended when two of the three rabbis of the bet din decided that the body should be removed to Israel. One of the judges recalled that in Israel many years earlier the Stoliner Rebbe had told him: "Even if you can't live here, it's a wonderful place to be buried." And the Rebbe had added without a further word of explanation: "Some day I'm going to need a favor from you"(PR).

Fifteen or twenty of the Rebbe's followers went to the cemetery in New Jersey to disinter the Rebbe's remains for shipment. Fifteen months had passed and the Hasidim were worried about the condition of the body. The coffin had been constructed of wood from the tables in the shul. In accordance with the law no metal nails had been used and the boards were held together with pegs. There had been space between the boards. "We didn't know what to expect. It was winter when we buried him and the ground was muddy" (PR). The Hasidim found that the wooden boards had split and the shape of the Rebbe's body, entwined in a shroud and a *talit* (prayer shawl), was visible. The form, however, had remained intact. The shroud was torn at the bottom and the Rebbe's big toe was visible, and, to their amazement, it appeared as well formed as if the body had been buried the day before. In the journey from New Jersey to Tiberias the Rebbe's body suffered innumerable insults but it remained unchanged. When the body, still in its shroud, was removed from the broken box and carried on a stretcher all the observers were said to have commented to the effect: "If I had not known I would have thought he had just died."

The coffin itself still smelled fresh, but the following day when they returned they found the coffin was a pile of rotting wood. It was said to have totally disintegrated and to have had a terrible odor. The Hasidim present cut splinters from the coffin, which were used in subsequent years under the pillows of the sick or worn on a band around the wrist to prevent illness or to cure some malady.

After the Rebbe's death in 1955, the Stoliner Hasidim were in a quandary. They had enjoyed the sense of unity and devotion that the Rebbe had brought. There was no direct male descendant of mature age to take his place. His son-in-law, Ezra Sochet, a lay person who wore no beard or peyes and who had never been on intimate terms with the Stoliner Hasidim, was not considered suitable to succeed him. The only direct heir was the Rebbe's grandson, Barukh Meir Yaakov Sochet, then still a baby in his mother's arms. The Stoliner Hasidim had to decide whether to align themselves to a different Hasidic dynasty or to carry on the Stolin tradition themselves while waiting for the grandson to mature. It was a perilous choice. To switch allegiance would signal a break with the past and end their own separate identity; to wait for the child to mature was equally risky, since at the end of a long course of years the grandson might fail to live up to their expectations or might reject their offer to become Rebbe. There was a precedent for waiting: in 1872 the Stoliner Hasidim had elected Reb Israel, the Frankfurter, who was also called Yanuka (Child) because he was only four years of age at the time.

In his will the Rebbe had assigned title to the Stoliner shuln and yeshivot to two of the elders in Israel, Feivel Auerbach and Berel Friedman. Both were businessmen rather than rabbis: Feivel Auerbach had a restaurant in Haifa; Berel Friedman, who was beardless, owned a hotel in Haifa. Both men were considered by their fellow Hasidim to be capable and above reproach. For seven years they kept the various factions together until finally some of the Israeli Hasidim who had been followers of Reb Avrom Elimelekh Perlow, the Karliner, chafing under this unwanted authority, broke away and shifted their loyalty to the Lelever

Rebbe, who had been a disciple of the Karliner. Then began a protracted struggle to determine the ownership of the court's properties.

The two elders administered the Brooklyn community as well as the Israeli, and Feivel Auerbach, freed of his business responsibilities in Haifa by his sons, lived in Brooklyn from 1955 to 1960 in order to oversee Stolin affairs. He was responsible for bringing the Stolin yeshivah from Williamsburg to Borough Park, and it was at his insistence that the members moved out of the basement shul in Borough Park and bought the stores on 16th Avenue for use as a shul and yeshivah. "Look here," he said, "you've got to start expanding." An executive committee composed of seven or so of the local Brooklyn members handled the administrative tasks of running the shul and yeshivah, but they brought all matters requiring a decision to Feivel Auerbach. The number of students soon expanded, and a garage and automobile agency on 54th Street were reconstructed for use as a yeshivah.

The New Stoliner Rebbe

For almost twenty years—from the death of their Rebbe in 1955 until his grandson reached maturity—Stolin was directed by the two elders designated in the Rebbe's will and an elected committee. During those years the Stoliner Hasidim demonstrated that while the role of the Rebbe is integral to Hasidism, on occasion a group can survive for an extended period with only a managerial committee in charge. The memory of the deceased Rebbe served as the court's lifeline to the past, while the Rebbe's young grandson served as the magnetic center for renewal in the future.

> My grandfather died when I was one year old. I learned gradually about what was expected of me. It wasn't a specific thing that it began with. When I was young they spoke about my becoming Rebbe. I was able to understand it. I always received special attention. People came to me to ask for a blessing when I was four or five. (BM)

In 1967, just before the Rebbe turned thirteen years of age, Feivel Auerbach and Berel Friedman signed over all the properties entrusted to them by Reb Yohanan to his grandson, the new Rebbe.

The Rebbe's grandson was never formally crowned as Rebbe; instead he gradually laid claim to the prerogatives and the duties of the position.

> There was no fixed time but he slowly began to assume leadership. From his teenage years he began to shoulder responsibility. He would voice his opinion and we would accept it. We allowed him to determine how much responsibility he would accept. If a decision was to be made we would discuss it with him. (PR)

During the new Rebbe's early days, when people came to consult him his father, Ezra Sochet, remained close by so that his young son could turn to him for whispered advice.

> I've not neglected my duty as far as being a father goes. I've no interest in developing a following. I'm opposed to Madison Avenue techniques. I've been exposed to this for some time. You're in the public eye a good deal. There's the awareness of living in a fishbowl—whether in Israel or here. You have to be more careful. You can't be carefree.
>
> The tradition goes back a few hundred years. The line will continue until the Messiah comes. The decision for him to become Rebbe was not for me to make. The meaning of the power of the Rebbe is a question that we can't answer, any more than we can answer why so many millions were killed in the war.
>
> I don't think any Stoliner Rebbe ever looked forward to his position and the responsibilities that go with it. I imagine that you have a responsibility to so many people that you can't turn your back on it. It's a heavy responsibility. People come for advice in every area of human existence.   (EZ)

After more than twenty years of squabbling over ownership of the court's properties, the issue went to a rabbinical court. Reb Barukh Meir, Reb Yohanan's grandson, was judged to be the owner of the court's assets, and the Stolin-Karlin Hasidim were the de facto inheritors of the dynasty. Henceforward the dissidents would have to designate themselves as the Pinsk-Karlin branch of the dynasty.

The crisis period of succession had ended. Feivel Auerbach and Berel Friedman had passed away, but the court was now secure. The Stoliner Hasidim had a new Rebbe. Barukh Meir had a stable group of supporters and a yeshivah and besmedresh in Borough Park as well as in Israel.

The Rebbe's family moved to solidify the dynasty by arranging a match for him with his first cousin Rivka Sochet, his father's brother's daughter.[3] The Rebbe's uncle, who lived in Los Angeles, discussed the match with his daughter, who felt that she would be able to handle the responsibility. The wedding was held in March 1975. The groom was then twenty-one years old and the bride seventeen. A year later a child was born to the couple. Unfortunately, the marriage ended in divorce in 1977.

The divorce harmed the Rebbe's reputation. It made public the domestic disharmony of the court's leading family and it raised questions about the Rebbe's mastery over his own affairs. When the Stoliner Rebbe and his first cousin sought a divorce settlement they turned to an American court rather than to a bet din to decide the terms of the settlement. Bypassing the traditional venue added to the embarrassment. The choice of secular or religious court was particularly significant because the Rebbe's divorce could affect the Stoliner dynasty in the next generation. Since a child had been born from the Rebbe's marriage, questions were raised concerning the Rebbe's (and indeed the Stoliner Hasidim's) role in the boy's upbringing and his association with Stolin.

In the divorce settlement mandated in the New York State Supreme Court in March 1977, Justice Louis B. Heller ruled that the mother should retain custody of the couple's son, David Joshua, then thirteen months of age. The Court decreed, however, that from the age of three the child's education should be under the supervision of the father. Although it was planned that the boy would live with his mother in Los Angeles, the decisions concerning his schooling would be made by his father. Any conflict stemming from this arrangement, the judge ruled, would be settled by the rabbinical court, the bet din. In his decision, "Justice Heller also ruled that if the child was inclined to assume the leadership of the movement before reaching the age of thirteen, the father would prepare him for his role, but if the mother believed the child was too immature to make the decision on his own, the matter would go before the bet din." The *New York Times* reported that the Stoliner Hasidim praised the secular judge for having "the wisdom of Solomon," a view disputed by some in the community.[4]

The young Stoliner Rebbe has not become one of the celebrated contemporary Rebbes, and the Stoliner court has not grown as rapidly as some other courts. The Rebbe does not speak at any of the Shabbes meals, and so he has never won a reputation for scholarship or insight into the holy writings. More serious, however, were a number of controversial decisions which are said to have diminished the Rebbe's position.

Most of the Stoliner Hasidim appear to have agreed that the court lacked the financial resources to develop two centers, and in the course of time they focused their attention on the newer neighborhood of Borough Park. In Williamsburg their three-story building on Rodney Street, which had been used as the yeshivah, became the offices for Stoliner yeshivot in Israel, and was eventually sold in the 1970s. The court also owned the two-story building next door, which housed the men's shul, a long narrow room on the first floor crammed with wooden benches and study tables; a side entrance opened on a stairway that led to the women's shul on the second floor. Now that most of the court was settled in Borough Park less than a minyan of ten worshipers from Stolin remained on Rodney Street. The shul was utilized primarily by worshipers from outside their group, and in 1981 it was proposed that the building be sold.

The majority in Borough Park promised that they would find a smaller shul for the Williamsburg membership after the sale, but the few Stolin families remaining in the old neighborhood considered the proposed sale to be a death blow to their community. They contested the young Rebbe's ownership of the building and challenged his legal authority to accomplish the sale. The case went to a secular court; however, the secular judge ruled that a religious court would first have to determine the ownership of the building. The bet din that heard the complaint decided that the Rebbe was the sole owner, although it also ruled that the remaining families had the right to continue to utilize the shul. The building was then sold to a minyan of worshipers associated with the Nitra yeshivah in Westchester County who needed a place to daven together in Williamsburg. In the minds of most observers it was perceived as a necessary retrenchment.

The Rebbe's luster was further tarnished by the financial crisis facing the yeshivah. In order to meet its bills the school was forced to reduce its staff and close down half its classes. Since that time, however, the yeshivah has undertaken a successful rebuilding program.

In recent years the Stoliner Rebbe's reputation has improved. He has become known as a collector of rare Talmudic commentaries, and he has arranged for the publication of some texts in Israel. As he has matured the Rebbe has become more closely involved in the Stolin kolel, the school attended by married students, assigning them sections of the Shulhan Arukh (Code of Jewish Law) and testing their knowledge himself. His work with Russian Jewry has brought him further attention. He has aided in the resettlement of Russian Jews in Israel and has established ties with those remaining in the Soviet Union. At the present time a Stoliner Hasid in Kiev is considered the chief rabbi of Ukraine.

Most problematic for the future of Stolin in America, however, was the Rebbe's decision to make his primary residence in Israel beginning in 1991.[5] He plans to return to Borough Park for short visits twice a year. According to the most optimistic Stoliner Hasidim the Rebbe is only a phone call away. Many of his American followers, however, plan to follow him to Israel.

The Rebbe remarried in 1978, a year after his divorce, and by 1992 at age thirty-six he had ten children from his new marriage.[6] Although his first wife had remarried and moved back east to nearby Rockaway, the Rebbe's followers believed him to be frozen out of any substantial role in educating his eldest son. It was said that the Rebbe declined to pursue his rights in court. In 1990, when the young man was fourteen, he joined his father in Israel and remained with him for a year before deciding to return to Rockaway. It now seems certain that the future of the dynasty will depend on the children of the Rebbe's second marriage.

The Growth of Bobov

The Bobover Hasidim became one of the chief beneficiaries of the growth of Borough Park. The court had no sooner left Crown Heights to settle in Borough Park in the early 1960s than its numbers increased dramatically, first in yeshivah enrollment and then in general membership. This reflected the increasing interest in Orthodox Judaism in general, but was also due in part to the popularity of the Bobover Rebbe, Rabbi Shlomo Halberstamm (b. 1905), who hewed his teachings to traditional themes and carefully avoided controversy. The young Jewish families, heretofore not Hasidic and perhaps not even Orthodox, were wary of establishing ties with courts known for their extremist points of view. They felt at ease with Rabbi Halberstamm's lack of pretension and his *heymlekh* (home-like) approach to Yiddishkayt.

[The essence of Bobov is] Shalom—peace. Peace with everybody—friendly with everyone. Everyone has his own way for his own reasons. We don't have any political stance whatsoever. Satmar is anti-Israel and another group is pro-Israel, but we understand them. Bobov does not support the Israeli government because it is antireligious, but we don't go out screaming. Satmar has its back up against Israel and Lubavitch. Here we're on good terms with Satmar, Lubavitch, Ger, Belz. (RP)[7]

The Bobover Rebbe arrived in America with his eldest son, Naftali, soon after the war, his family and his followers having been almost completely wiped out in the Nazi death camps. The Rebbe married again, started a new family, and began to rebuild the court. He aided displaced persons to join him in America, and when they arrived he helped to arrange job training in watch repair and in the diamond industry. Others were encouraged to enter the business world. The Bobov community continued to increase in number from internal growth and by attracting new students to the yeshivah. Parents looking for a yeshivah to which to send their children were attracted to the moderate and peaceful court of Bobov. It was a place where one rejoiced in the holidays and in Yiddishkayt, and that was sufficient. In great measure the rise in yeshivah attendance came about as faith in the public school system declined. The Bobover yeshivah soon became the most populous religious school in Borough Park. By 1986 there were 1,500 boys in the elementary school and a similar number of girls. Many of those who came to study at the Bobov yeshivah had no family ties there initially, but they developed strong friendships and associations at the yeshivah and they remained attached to Bobov after their studies were completed.

My family, on my father's side, were from Gorlic in Galicia. The Rebbe of Gorlic was a son of the Sanzer. I studied in the Bobov yeshivah. When I was young I started to go here. My father didn't have where to send me. I lived near Satmar. They were the closest, but he wouldn't send me there. Because I was educated in the Bobover yeshivah I became attached here. Boys who learned in the yeshivah who had no other attachment landed here and that's it.

I feel that he's my Rebbe and I have nothing to see anywhere else. In Israel I went to see the Belzer Rebbe—like people go sightseeing to museums. You learn here, you grow up here, and it comes automatically—if you have no reason to go away. (JF)

Through the years the Rebbe has vigorously presided over the Shabbes activities like a proud father. More down to earth and less awe inspiring than the Satmar and Lubavitcher Rebbes, the Bobover Rebbe customarily helps to arrange decorations at holiday time; at festive meals he cuts and serves food to his followers and their children.

The Bobov community grew in financial strength to match Borough Park's new opulence. Bobov has become the richest and most populous court in Borough Park, with satellite communities in other countries. Financial donors, whether for religious motives or for tax purposes, have helped to construct a new besmedresh, a new yeshivah and dormitory; the congregation also owns a catering hall for weddings, and it has purchased apartment buildings and real estate in a neighborhood development plan.

> We started in Crown Heights. Now we're here in Borough Park, and in London, Antwerp, Montreal, Toronto, and in Israel. We have three institutions in Israel and a settlement. We have a little bit of everything.
>
> Compared with Satmar and Lubavitch, we're still small. We have two thousand families in Borough Park and Flatbush. In London there are four hundred; in Antwerp one hundred to one hundred and twenty; Toronto, one hundred. In Israel we have one thousand families in Jerusalem and Bene Brak. We have a yeshivah in Bene Brak with 250 boys. In Kirat-Bobov there are 150 families, and ten minutes from Tel Aviv we have a yeshivah. (JF)

Continuing one's studies in the kolel after marriage has become a norm in the Hasidic community. The Bobov kolel began in 1971 with 15 in attendance; by 1986 there were over 150 students who were doing advanced studies or were registered in the kolel. Tenure varies from a token year or two to several years of intense study. Those who remain the longest often intend to work in yeshivah education or to serve as rabbis. Many struggle along for five and even ten years after marriage on a modest weekly wage (between $100 and $120 in 1986) for those who continue beyond the first year of study.[8]

> The men are married, and they get raises. It depends on the number of children and on their talent. If you want him to stay, you give him more. The top would be $250 if he's been there six to seven years and you don't want him to leave. The kolel students have two holiday bonuses of about $100 for Pesach and another $100 for Rosh Hashanah, depending on the size of the families and who the person is. (JF)

Running the yeshivah requires most of the court's energy and resources.

> The fees for tuition do not cover all our expenses. A family pays anywhere from zero to $110 a month for each child [in 1986]. Sometimes a person

pays $20 a child. We've never refused a child for nonpayment. We raise money at an annual *melave-malke*. And we send out letters. We have a butcher store at 18th Avenue, between 48th and 49th Streets. The profit from the store goes to the organization. There are four or five who work in the butcher shop and we have one person who *shekhts* [slaughters] in New Jersey. (JF)

The growth of Bobov has benefited from the Bobover Rebbe's refusal to take a strict ideological stand. Because Bobov represents a moderate way, many parents on the edge between the Orthodox and the less religious world have sent their children to the Bobover yeshivah. This sometimes means the yeshivah must insist that the family maintain a completely Orthodox home.

We might refuse a child if he doesn't fit in—if he's not religious. We can't accept a boy who then goes home and doesn't keep kosher or observe Shabbes. We have to be sure they'll abide by the laws. (JF)

The Bobover's liberal attitudes carry over after graduation from the yeshivah. While the Rebbe does not encourage secular studies, he has never cut off any students if they choose to continue beyond the yeshivah and attend college. As a result, many of the young men who attended the yeshivah but have since made their way in the secular world and in the professions have kept their close ties with Bobov and now help to support Bobov programs.

In our congregation in Borough Park we have professional people, business people, working people, rabbinical students. We have professional people, doctors, several lawyers, accountants. Some of them learned in the yeshivah and then went off to secular school. The Rebbe will not say no [deny permission] to some boy who will go to secular school anyway. (JF)

The cost of running the court is high.[9] Everyone must pay their fair share to maintain the yeshivah and besmedresh. The expenses of the educational system, underwriting the fees of poorer students in the yeshivah and the salaries of students in the kolel, depend on tuition and on contributions. Support is also needed for the Rebbe and his family and for the charity they must offer to petitioners. Each person on the court's list of subscribers is asked for an amount in accord with his income. Some of the businessmen who have accumulated great wealth provide major support for continuance of the entire system.

At the besmedresh rich and poor have sat side by side at the same wooden benches since childhood. They are matched by their desire to give charity, and by the satisfaction and sense of honor that it brings. It would be misleading, however, to deny the existence of distinctions based on wealth and a nascent class structure. The rich do live better than the poor. The signs of wealth are seen in obvious ways—size of house and its furnishings, make of automobile, possibility of a summer home. Commonplace opulence is visible in draperies, lighting fixtures, furniture, and sideboards lined with silver cups and candelabra. It can be seen as well in the kitchen, where the well-to-do not only have two sets of dishes, silverware, and cooking utensils, but also install two separate sinks, two stoves, two refrigerators, and, space permitting, two separate cooking areas.

Success and comfort are also expressed in the festivities surrounding the special stages of life—birth, confirmation, and marriage—which sometimes become contests testifying to wealth and position. Celebrations frequently undertaken by Rebbes at the marriage of a son or daughter, or even a grandchild, provide a model for opulence. At a wedding involving a Rebbe's family the entire court is invited, along with families and guests from other courts, and thousands of people may attend. Preparing the meals and arranging for buses and other transportation takes on the dimensions of quartering an army battalion. The Bobover Rebbe, however, in keeping with his court's moderate demeanor, has put a ceiling on exactly what is permitted for celebrations among his Hasidim.

> The [Bobover] Rebbe says you shouldn't overspend. For a bar mitzvah invite only grandparents, parents, brothers and sisters, aunts and uncles. No first cousins should be invited. There are exceptions of course. If there are fewer brothers, then invite the closest relatives. But no halls, no music, no professional pictures. If not, the first celebration is in the Lowell, the second in a bigger hall, and the third is in the Waldorf Astoria.
>
> The Rebbe is trying to set guidelines to go by for weddings. The Rebbe says to do only as much as you can afford. Don't outdo anyone else and don't outdo yourself. With a bar mitzvah because it's for one family the Rebbe can say, if there's a hall, don't do it. With a wedding there are two people, two families, and it's more difficult. The other family may not be from Bobov. One can't make guidelines. It's more difficult. Families usually share expenses for a wedding.   (JF)

The Future of Bobov

The Rebbe organized the court in the traditional European manner by settling his children in positions of responsibility and authority. Although it is not a subject for discussion, it is clear that the succession of the court is secure. The Rebbe's eldest son, Naftali (now middle-aged, and the only surviving child from the Rebbe's first family) is the Rebbe's deputy and heir apparent.

> Naftali is the practical one in charge. They consult with him on curriculum and financial matters. The principal can't go to the Rebbe and discuss what passage to learn, or if there's a problem with one of the teachers. The principal has to discuss it with someone—he doesn't have the final word. He

must discuss it with Naftali. Or, on another matter, should we take a loan or not.   (JF)

Others in the Rebbe's family also play key roles in the organization of the court, the yeshivah, and the kolel. The family's influence extends to Bobov settlements in Israel and in London, where the Rebbe's sons-in-law are ensconced.[10]

Disputes are mediated through a rabbinical court composed of Bobover rabbis. Rabbi Haim J. Tauber has been the judge for close to two decades deciding on matters of ritual law. Rabbi Tauber and other judges, however, in keeping with the Bobov disinclination to stir controversy, rarely sit as a court in judgment concerning two rival petitioners.

> If one has a ritual or a legal question Rabbi Tauber will answer you, but he doesn't sit as a judge. He will mediate but that's all. Naftali will also mediate but he won't sit as a judge in court. If it's a local thing, either one would help, but people don't like the decisions. Satmar is the only one that has a court ready to sit. If it's a local thing either Rabbi Tauber or Naftali would help, but people don't like decisions and therefore they won't sit as judges.   (JF)

Although the Rebbe tells legends and miracle tales of past Rebbes at the melave-malke held every Saturday night, the Bobover Hasidim tend to downplay contemporary tales of miracles, even those concerning their own Rebbe.

> We don't talk about miracles when we see something happen. We tell stories about the Sandzer Rov or the Baal Shem Tov—how they got someone out of the army or somehow had a baby. We want to learn something out of it. Every saint did the same thing—health and business. The Hasid had what he had because of help from the Rebbe. Our Rebbe is a tzaddik whether or not he'll show me what he did. He'll do something privately [to help someone] in sickness or in business.   (JF)

The growth of the court from its first days after the war can most easily be measured at the end of services on Shabbes. The giant new besmedresh, still being decorated within, is crowded with worshipers. As always the Rebbe greets each of his followers in the besmedresh as they file past to exchange good wishes, but his Hasidim are now so numerous that even the most cursory greeting to each follower requires a thousand nods of his head. The intimacy that existed in the court in its earlier years in Brooklyn is now mocked by the line of men attired in shtraymlen and kaftans swirling past the old Rebbe.

· 12 ·

The Succession in Satmar

The Council of Elders

A month after the death of Rabbi Joel Teitelbaum in August 1979, the thirteen members of the Council of Elders of Satmar met to name his successor. The Council is an elected body, with elections normally held every three or four years (although no vote had been held since the Rebbe's stroke eleven years earlier). The president of the Council was Leo Lefkowitz, the secular leader of the community; the executive vice president was Sender Deutsch, the publisher and editor of *Der Yid*, a Yiddish newspaper sometimes referred to by its opponents as the *Pravda* of the Satmar community.

As is customary there were no preparations for succession made in advance of the Rebbe's death. Although the need for rabbinic succession has weighed heavily in every dynastic court since the inception of Hasidism, no true follower of a Rebbe would discuss the possibility of his Rebbe's dying before the coming of the Messiah. The pattern of succession is clear: the new Rebbe chosen is almost always the son of the deceased Rebbe. Possibilities for a power struggle exist, particularly if the Rebbe has many sons or no sons at all so that the court must look to a son-in-law, a relative, or an outstanding disciple. The situations surrounding the succession of a Rebbe have been as varied and as complex as family life itself, and decisions have turned on struggles within rabbinic families and between court factions, and on emotions as generous as love and willingness to sacrifice, or as onerous as jealousy and avarice.

Perhaps to a very few it seemed that the Satmar court could continue as it had during the Rebbe's illness, with the Rebbe's representatives in charge and with the memory of the deceased Rebbe kept in sharp focus. The Bratslaver Hasidim never selected a new leader after the death of their Rebbe in 1810. But they are known as the "Dead Hasidim," and their prestige and influence have declined with each *yortsayt* (anniversary of death).[1] The Satmar Hasidim revered their Rebbe as much as the Bratslavers, but it was clear that the presence of a Rebbe was needed to ensure their way of life and the vitality of the community's institutions and practices. The yeshivah, the besmedresh, the mikvah could not long remain financially solvent without a leader. Contributors were reluctant to pledge money for the coming year without a Rebbe in control and able to mark their efforts.

> When they tried to call in rich people with their steady donations, everybody answered: "Let me first see a Rebbe and then we'll talk about money." So they realized something had to be done.   (TP)

Since the deceased Satmar Rebbe had no surviving children, the most logical successor for the Council to consider was his nephew, Rabbi Moshe Teitelbaum, the Szigetter Rov, then sixty-six years of age. The Szigetter Rov was the son and grandson of distinguished Rebbes. He was reputed to be intelligent and energetic, a scholar, and an interesting and effective speaker. He had lost his first wife and their children in the concentration camps in 1944, but he had married again soon after the war and had raised a new family of six children. As a child in Hungary, following the death of his father, Moshe Teitelbaum had gone to live in the Satmar Rebbe's household. Now he was a Rebbe in his own right, with his father's title and a small congregation in Borough Park, and about to be invited to assume his revered uncle's place. There was some uneasiness over committing the leadership to someone who in recent years had had only limited contact with the court. But there was no one else who could match his lineage and his stature. The community leaders were said to be in agreement on the choice. It seemed only natural that the Szigetter Rov should become the Satmar Rebbe.

The pervasive memory of Rabbi Joel Teitelbaum would make complete acceptance of a new Rebbe by the Hasidim difficult. His followers were heirs to his powerful ideals and absolutist traditions, and all other Rebbes seemed to stand in his shadow.

For Reb Moshe the position of Rebbe promised overwhelming responsibility and controversy. He knew the weight his new duties would bring. He could simply refuse the offer and continue as the Szigetter Rov, content with his own small congregation. To become the leader of Satmar, however, offered many enticements: many more thousands of followers, power, prestige, and a world stage on which to act. This was also the chance to reunite two dynastic lines and to exalt his place in the lineage. To be considered too were the immediate and enduring opportunities that would be opened for his children. As both Rebbe and chief rabbi, he would have limitless possibilities to make appointments of power and responsibility throughout the Satmar empire in Brooklyn, England, Canada, and Israel.

Within the inner sanctum of the court, the coming succession of the new Rebbe was greeted with a sense of inevitability but not with unanimous joy. It was said that the rebbetsn, Feiga Teitelbaum, found it difficult to accept a successor to her late husband. Her unhappiness was attributed to her failure to provide an heir as well as to her displacement from the center of court life. The family history was recalled and retold, and rumors of a long-standing dispute between the rebbetsn and the Szigetter Rov resurfaced to give the succession a bitter edge.[2]

During the interim weeks after her husband's death, the rebbetsn was seen as a disruptive player in court politics. She held the emotional sentiment of the court, as well as properties now deeded in her name following the death of her husband. Some claimed that the rebbetsn made efforts to sidetrack the choice of the Szigetter Rov by proposing a distant relative of the Rebbe as an alternate candidate. Even if true, another candidacy was considered only token resistance to the certain choice of the Szigetter Rov, but the tales emphasized the depth of her loss of power.

> From her point of view she wouldn't lose anything even if there wouldn't be any successor. She would be stronger. She would have some authority. The schools would be run by whoever runs them, and she doesn't care too much about that. But she didn't really fight that much. As far as it looks to me, the rebbetsn realized that there is no other choice besides the Szigetter, but she tried whatever she can do. She tried in a way to say: "I helped the old Rebbe a lot in his ways and I don't want it to go into different hands." (TP)

Naming the New Rebbe

Negotiations between community leaders and Reb Moshe, the Szigetter Rov, began soon after the older Rebbe passed away. In contrast to the uncertain circumstances that had existed when the Hasidim had first arrived and the court had to be created anew, this was an ongoing, populous court with schools and other institutions in place. The negotiations continued for three weeks. During that time the Szigetter Rov was informed in great detail about the organization of the court.

> The only thing to negotiate was the timing and how he will move here and how to go over the boards of the leading people of our institutions. Then we had to decide when and how to have the crowning ceremony. (RH)

The new Rebbe was reported to have won unqualified support from the Council, and most in the court sensed that the new Rebbe had virtually ruled from the outset.

> Within the three weeks people realized that there are no two ways about it: he's the successor, he's the closest to him. Over the years people had looked

on him as probably the only person who could be appointed after the Satmar Rebbe dies.

There was no voting. There was unanimous agreement. There was no second choice, and most of the people realized, even if quietly in their heart, everybody knew he would be the successor. The public did not support anybody against him. (TP)

The entire congregation learned that the selection of the new Rebbe was official when they were summoned to a public meeting.

First they called with one day's notice that people should come to the big shul on Rodney Street. Sender Deutsch gave his little speech. Deutsch is in the office of the yeshivah and he runs *Der Yid*. He made a nice speech for four or five minutes. He said that after the Rebbe passed away, we sat together and we realized that he's the one person in the family. He's our best chance, and thank God that he survived World War II. He said all this kind of stuff, you know as a speaker. Thank God for this and thank God for that, and we have the honor and the privilege and this and that. The Szigetter Rov was not there. (TP)

As a mark of respect for his uncle, the Szigetter Rov did not want to assume the responsibilities of Rebbe until after the first yortsayt. The death of the old Rebbe, who had been like a father to him, signaled a period of personal bereavement. The community too needed a period of mourning and adjustment. In the meanwhile, a residence was prepared for the new Rebbe on the site of the previous yeshivah in Williamsburg, now cleared for urban renewal. (Across the street on Bedford Avenue was the house of the old Rebbe, where the old rebbetsn continued to stay when she was in Williamsburg and which was also used as a shul for a small congregation.) For the time being Reb Moshe continued to reside in Borough Park where the Sziget congregation is located. Formal recognition of the succession came a year later when the Szigetter Rov was crowned as the new Satmar Rebbe.

The year after the Rebbe died they made an official inauguration for him in the new settlement of Kiryas Joel in Monroe [Township]. That was called the *atorah* [crowning]. They crowned him. That was a very big event and it was a nice experience. It was a big ceremony in Monroe. And there were big speakers there. They made a declaration and in a very nice way they crowned him with titles and more titles. They went into the family history and they had great speakers speaking there. He also gave a speech and it was an interesting speech. He said: "Listen, nobody can replace my uncle. Nobody can do it. But schools have to be run and shuls have to be run. You know there is a community. We'll try to do what we can. Don't expect from me what you had from my uncle. All together we can do something." He spoke very firmly. He didn't exaggerate. He's not the kind of guy to exaggerate. (TP)

Change: Structure

The succession of the Rebbe brought about change in the immediate circle around the Rebbe. The old rebbetsn was no longer at the center of power. She was displaced not by the new rebbetsn but by the Rebbe himself. Nonetheless she still played an important role in court life and she still held title to certain properties in the community that had been turned over to the old Rebbe. Her presence was championed particularly by those whose own places were jeopardized or who could not accept the transformation of the court. In spite of their problems past and present, the rebbetsn made an effort to accommodate the new Rebbe and to make him welcome. The strain between them, however, persisted.

When this present Rebbe became the Rebbe I was negotiating with the older rebbetsn. We had meetings with her at the house of Leibish Lefkowitz. It's true that the relationship was not a perfect relationship, but in the first years the Rebbe went to Monroe she made the Shabbes. But it's family things and it's natural that there's a strained relationship.

In every community and in every family you have problems. But if I have disagreements between my children it's my problem, but here if you have disagreements it goes into newspapers, and it's discussed everywhere, and a whole fuss is made of it. It's not only that they're public figures. Some enemies are looking for it and digging it up and bringing it up in public to discredit this person or that person, and it brings frictions. It's true it brings frictions. There are people who have their own interests: this one wants to be the president, this one wants to be a contractor, and they're interested to build up an opposition. (RH)

Some of the old Rebbe's aides and spokesmen were quickly displaced or given different responsibilities.

When the Rebbe passed away, they no longer looked to Rabbi Meisels. Before this he had been the spokesman for the Rebbe, and whenever he had spoken it had been in the name of the Rebbe. The Rebbe wants this and the Rebbe wants that, and it was automatically accepted. He realized that when the Rebbe passed away that he was out. His title as rosh yeshivah existed only because the Rebbe was ill. Otherwise, the Rebbe is the rosh yeshivah. He realized that the new Rebbe, the Szigetter Rov, will be the rosh yeshivah. So there was no position left for him. In addition, he was no longer the spokesman for the community. Before he had had full authority in the eyes of the people. At that time he was about age fifty-five. (TP)

A storytelling version recorded the change in dramatic form.

Meisels came to the new Rebbe and he said that the old Rebbe had given him the keys to the schools—meaning that I know his ways, how the schools have to be run, and I understand him and nobody else does.

The new Rebbe answered him: "If you really have the keys, I'll have to change the locks"—meaning that the old Rebbe had his ways and I have mine.

In order to placate him and also to get rid of him, they made him the rov in London and in that way moved him out.[3]

The Rebbe was now the rosh yeshivah of the principal yeshivah located at Kiryas Joel, but he soon named his eldest son, Reb Aaron, to be rosh yeshivah in his place. He also designated Reb Aaron as the rov (chief rabbi) of Kiryas Joel. Many saw this as an inevitable move, although they did not then realize its consequences.

Criticism

Criticism of Rabbi Moshe Teitelbaum's conduct began the moment he was offered the post as the Satmar Rebbe. Little was known of the content of the discussions between the Council and the Rebbe, and a bevy of rumors took flight in the unstable atmosphere of the court.

> They can't accuse the Satmar Rebbe of eating *treyf* [unkosher food] or that he breaks the Shabbes, so they say he's doing other things. He never negotiated for a salary because in a Rebbe's position there is no such thing about salary. I think that nobody even knows it. I was the person who was negotiating with him to be Rebbe. We made up a salary for the Rebbe. Even today the old rebbetsn has twice the salary that he has. But we also gave the Rebbe a salary as dean of the yeshivah. The issue came up: the Rebbe wants some salary—not because he needs the salary, because he has his own funds from what people give him. And he sent back the check: "Since I'm not full time in the yeshivah, I won't take a salary from the yeshivah."
>
> It's a ridiculous thing to think not only with our Rebbe but with any Rebbe, if you want to give him such a position, that the money factor should at all be mentioned. It's like you negotiated with President Bush or Truman or Eisenhower about the salary of the presidency. It's ridiculous.   (RH)

It was said that the new Rebbe listed a number of specific requirements concerning his salary, the number of days he would be available, fees for the High Holidays, and the title to certain properties—rumors that were vehemently denied as untrue by the Satmar leadership. But the gossip persisted.

> He's interested in fees. He negotiated a salary for himself as Rebbe and a special fee for leading the High Holiday services. It was a shock the first year. Now we're no longer shocked. Before we had a Rebbe who was an idealist. We were spoiled.   (YA)

Whether they bore any truth or not, such tales put the Rebbe's supporters on the defensive. Some argued that the supposed points of negotiation
were understandable and acceptable.

> That's something that makes a lot of sense. He was to an extent hired by the
> Satmar community to be their rabbi, to be their leader. He was hired with a
> contract. So obviously when you're hired with a contract you negotiate a
> salary. It's not like the previous Satmar Rebbe who is the one who created
> this community. This was much different. There was a community and the
> community chose him and they took him with a contract. So in that sense
> they had to give him a salary.   (AG)

The charge that the Rebbe takes a fee for conducting the High Holidays was also vigorously denied by pointing out that the Hasidim have
an established system for providing the Rebbe with extra income, either
by giving him a gift of money (pidyen) when they go to see him for a
blessing, or by offering a gift at a special occasion, often to help defray
the cost of the event.

> You know what we do. If he marries off a grandchild there are enormous
> costs. Naturally people go in, one gives $1,000, another gives $5,000. Then
> the community gives a check to contribute for the wedding or whatever.
> Two or three months ago we had a wedding in Monroe. The Rebbe's grand-
> child was married and we had a party and there were some expenses, small
> expenses that might amount to $2,500. So the people came over to me and
> said: "What's with these expenses? Give it to me and I'll take care of
> it."   (RH)

One of the most persistent and damaging rumors pictured the new
Rebbe as a sharp businessman. Since some members of his congregation
in Borough Park were involved in real estate, it was suggested that they
had promoted his interest in investments. While a reputation for having
a taste for business can be a neutral observation, when made about a
Rebbe it serves to demean his concern with piety and prayer.

> There is no real estate. The house where he lives—usually we turn it over to
> the Rebbe that it's a personal thing.[4] This deed is in the name of the congre-
> gation. He doesn't own it. Absolutely. He didn't want to own it. He has no
> real estate anywhere. He built a yeshivah in Borough Park six years ago and
> then the yeshivah dissolved. His son Aaron is now the rosh yeshivah in our
> yeshivah. Aaron sold that building and with the money he built another
> building in Monroe and turned it over to the yeshivah in Monroe. He built
> it there in his father's name but on the deed is the name of Kiryas Joel of
> Monroe.   (RH)

Still another rumor emphasized the Rebbe's supposed concern with the
stock market. Some reported that the Rebbe had even had a tickertape in

his house in Borough Park, gossip that infuriated the Rebbe's supporters as "stupid nonsense."

> I don't have to tell you that I've been in the home of the Rebbe and he's never had a tickertape. It's silly. It has no validity. But they keep spreading these things and people read it and it's no wonder that they start to believe it. If you read in the *Algemeiner* that the Satmar Rebbe has real estate, that he has nursing homes, that he has a tickertape, then you think that something must be there.[5] It's such a lie. None of it is true. (RH)

Change: Style and Substance

In the months that followed, the Rebbe's new followers closely observed his actions. What changes would the Rebbe bring about in the community? How would he lead the services? What teachings would he emphasize in his toyre? Eventually the differences, small and great, became apparent.

The community was impressed by the new Rebbe's sense of reality.

> He speaks very clearly. That's the good thing about him. With some of the rabbis, it's always "I see in heaven." He doesn't go for this kind of stuff. If somebody would come, a person is sick in the family, all the rabbis would take the person's hand and so on. He would say, "Go to a doctor. What can I do?" He's very straight. (TP)

> The new Rebbe has continued the old customs. On Friday night he still has a *tish* [communal meal]. His style is somewhat different in that he is not given to idle gestures. The older Satmar Rebbe used to gesture with his hand, or shake his head while praying, or [during Sukkot] gesture in the *sukkah* [ritual hut] with the *lulav* [palm branch], and the people would wonder why. We could not understand. This Rebbe has a practical purpose and is not given to the creation of a mysticism surrounding him. He is very plain. What he does, he does in front of you. Now people begin to feel a sense of awe in front of him. Every *shaleshudes* [the third meal of the Shabbes] in the afternoon, every week, he gives a lengthy discourse. The new Rebbe is committed to the retention of the old. "We must not blaze new trails," he says. "We must study the teachings of my uncle." The Satmar Rebbe was his teacher. No one has left Satmar. (AS)

The difference in the generations was marked as well.

> The new rabbi who is much younger obviously picked up much more from the present generation. It's automatic that he knows more of the present times; he's more involved in the present times. He's more interested in politics than the old one. The old one was like an international figure.
> He talks about Yiddishkayt. How to do mitzvot more, to learn Torah more. He talks more about Zionism than other Hasidic leaders do. But in contrast to the old rabbi who was so powerful and so stormy on anything that had to do with Zionism, obviously he's not that strong. (AG)

To some the relaxation on the question of Israel was a welcome relief.

He talks about Zionism a little bit. The old Rebbe talked about it so much it can't be talked about any more. Zionism was in every speech he gave from the time of World War II. This is not the main issue that had to be taught to young children—day and night, Zionism, Zionism, Zionism. There's probably more important things in life. But he felt that it's a very important issue. Some people say Zionism doesn't have as much effect in the religious community as it did when the old Rebbe was here. At that time some of the Orthodox people believed that Zionism had a certain kind of significance in religious life. Now it's a political party and a political movement, and everybody knows Israel is a state like other states.   (TP)

There were disappointing reports of the dispensing of the monies given to the new Rebbe as gifts. Traditionally those funds are distributed as charity by the Rebbe to the needy who come to him asking for help. The amount of charity dispensed by the new Satmar Rebbe, however, was slighted by his critics. Sharp comparisons were made between the largess of the older Rebbe and the allegedly more restrained manner of his successor.

It was commonly said that "With the old Satmar Rebbe whatever money came in went out just as fast" (PM). The charitable activities of the old rebbetsn too remain a reminder of the difference between the past and the present regimes. Although she has no official role, people still give the rebbetsn funds to dispense to the needy, and she has earned fame for her beneficence, as on one trip to Israel when she reportedly carried with her some three million dollars to distribute for charity.

Tales circulated marking the comparisons of the old and the new styles.

Before Rosh Hashanah some go to shul to ask money for many people for charity. One fellow wanted to marry off a child and he needed $10,000. He went to the new Rebbe, and the Rebbe listened to him and gave him $20. Then the fellow went to see the old rebbetsn, the widow of the Rebbe, and she said, "Now that my husband is not around I don't have as much to give. The askers come to me but not the givers." She said she'll send him a contribution. Later a man came to him with an envelope. Inside was $1,000 from the old rebbetsn.   (AI)

Others more sympathetic to the new Rebbe, while acknowledging the difference in the charity dispensed, offered a broader and more sympathetic view of the differences between the past and the present.

This whole way of looking at it is incorrect. The previous Rebbe was known to be that great person, that wonder person, that miracle maker, so people would pour money out to him. He had much more money, and so he gave much more *tzedakah* [charity]. This Rebbe is like a relatively new Rebbe and he doesn't have the fame of the previous Rebbe. The money that comes to him is nothing compared to the money that came to the old one. I remember when he became Rebbe he made a joke that: "I'm not so sure how many people accepted me as Rebbe, but for sure the *shnorers* [beggars] accepted me right away." Before he even had any money to give they were coming to him and asking for money.   (AG)

A similar call for understanding is urged by one of the leaders of the community.

The old Rebbe could take in money and a lady would come in and say her child is sick or whatever and she has no money, and he would take all the money on the table and give it away. He didn't need anything for himself he was such a tzaddik. But it does not mean that the present Rebbe is not giving tzedakah. We're building a school, a project of six to seven million dollars, and this Rebbe donated $100,000 from his pocket. He gave me a check for $25,000.   (RH)

Satmar and Belz

While the new Satmar Rebbe was struggling to find his footing, a long-standing feud with Belz rattled the court and threatened the power and prestige of Satmar in Israel.

Between the years 1979 and 1981, a rift worsened between Satmar and Belz in Israel. In the mid-1950s the old Belzer Rebbe, Rabbi Aaron Rokeah, had sanctioned the Israeli elections and thereby identified the future of his court with Israel.[6] Relationships deteriorated when in the late 1970s Reb Aaron's successor as Belzer Rebbe, Rabbi Issahar Dov Rokeah, seeking power in his own right, decided to challenge Satmar authority in community affairs in Israel.

At the time Satmar named the community rabbis and maintained the religious court to settle torts, divorces, and disputes; Satmar also set the standards for *kashrut* (dietary laws) and designated the shohatim to slaughter animals. Apart from their religious and ritual prestige, these prerogatives represented an economic cornerstone of the Satmar community. Community authority for appointing religious functionaries meant jobs for the Rebbe's followers, while the profits from the retail butcher stores provided revenue to run the Satmar yeshivot. It came as a shock, therefore, when Reb Issahar of Belz decided to go his own way in these ritual and economic matters. He named members of a new bet din as well as a new religious board to supervise kashrut, both independent of Satmar. This represented a serious threat to Satmar's religious and economic leadership.

The new Belzer Rebbe drifted away from the previous line of Belz. This was criticized by us. And he took a step which we could not tolerate. This was that he wanted to create in Jerusalem another rabbinate, a separate rabbinate. This broke the old rabbinate. So naturally then came shohatim, then came rabbis, and everything. (RH)

Antagonism between Satmar and Belz leaped from Israel to Brooklyn, and soon there were sporadic skirmishes between followers of the two courts in the United States, where the Belzer Hasidim are at a distinct numerical disadvantage, outnumbered (in 1979) by Satmar by an estimated 30,000 to 1,500 in Williamsburg alone. The weakness of their numbers was apparent one Sunday night just two months after the death of the old Satmar Rebbe, when a hundred or so Satmar students invaded a Belz shtibl on Ross Street. As reported in the press, the group were armed with rocks, sticks, and bottles. Witnesses recounted that they mauled the dozen or so men who were at class in the synagogue, and then did extensive damage to the interior, smashing windows, tearing out fixtures, and breaking the lectern.[7]

While the major field of contention remained in Israel, the visit of the Belzer Rebbe to the United States two years later, in March 1981, revived the antagonism here. On the eve of the Rebbe's visit, some five hundred men smashed eggs and bottles against the Belz shtibl in Williamsburg. There were provocative leaflets circulated in the various Hasidic neighborhoods, and balloons were distributed which featured a portrait of Rabbi Issahar, the Belzer Rebbe, and the words "Bust me." On the corner of Lee Avenue and Ross Street a commanding caricature of the Belzer Rebbe was chalked in the center of the busy street and an ominous curse scrawled across the crude image of the Rebbe: "May his name be erased."[8]

During the Belzer Rebbe's visit in the United States he was given police protection. After his departure, however, the level of antagonism diminished, leaving only moments of awkward embarrassment when less truculent Satmar and Belzer Hasidim would encounter each other on their way to shul, and silently wonder how things had reached such a state. Besides, in no time at all Satmar tempers were taken up again with other antagonists in the United States.

Comparisons

No matter what efforts he made, the new Satmar Rebbe had one insurmountable problem: he was not the old Rebbe. No one could match Reb Joel Teitelbaum's influence, intensity of purpose, and uncompromising piety.

> At the tish it's just that the old Rebbe had much more to him. It's as simple as that. His wealth of knowledge in Torah was much greater and so therefore everything was different. There's obviously a little bit less enthusiasm than there was at that time. It's still quite something. You still find the shul

packed. You still find the people getting *shirayim* from him. But again the old Satmar Rebbe was something that . . . he was considered like a holy person, like an angel, not like humankind. (AG)

One of the more enduring criticisms of the new Rebbe concerned the placement of his sons and sons-in-law in key positions in the community. Of course, Reb Moshe, the new Satmar Rebbe, did not introduce nepotism into Hasidic life. Naming one's children to posts of responsibility is commonplace in Hasidic society, just as *yikhes,* family lineage, is a crucial factor in becoming Rebbe.

The Rebbe named his eldest son, Aaron, to be head of the community of Kiryas Joel and dean of the yeshivah there. The second son, Zalman Leib, inherited his father's post as the Szigetter Rov. Other sons and sons-in-law were named to head various shuls in Borough Park and elsewhere.[9] While nepotism is usually accepted without complaint as a method of governance, in this instance the new Rebbe exercised his prerogative before his children had set down deep roots in the community and before he himself was established as unchallenged leader and father figure. He still stood in the shadow of the old Rebbe.

Take the most simple example: somebody fathers ten or twelve children and he passes away and there is a stepfather. The stepfather tries but he's not going to have the real fatherly love with the children. He's a very good stepfather, but he still cannot gain the love of the children. (MS)

While Reb Moshe had won the respect and support of most Satmar Hasidim, he had not yet been able to win their complete affection and loyalty.

It was hard to accept the Rebbe. It took him a year to ease into the role. For a year there was no Rebbe. It was hard to accept. We had a king before and now we have an ordinary man. (AFF)

There was another circumstance that cast a shadow into the future. Reb Moshe's son, Reb Aaron, named as rov and rosh yeshivah of Kiryas Joel, was married to Sasha Hager, the daughter of Rabbi Moses Joshua Hager, the Vizhnitzer Rebbe. Some could not forget that Rabbi Hager had not agreed with Rabbi Joel Teitelbaum, the older Satmar Rebbe, on the question of accepting the State of Israel. The Vizhnitzer was one of those who had made his peace with the government, and his followers voted in the elections for the Knesset, the Israeli legislature. Even more striking, the Vizhnitzer Rebbe delivered his weekly toyre in modern Hebrew rather than Yiddish, thereby profaning, from the Satmar point of view, the sacred tongue. These actions contradicted the proscriptions intimated from the Torah concerning the arrival of the Messiah.

The old Rebbe was against the *shidukh* [matrimonial match of Reb Aaron and Sasha]. No one was allowed to go to the wedding. The old Rebbe was angry. At Pesach time the Rebbe said, "Let him come to the *seder* [the festive meal the first night of Passover], but seat him someplace where I don't have to look on his face." (JW)

Twenty-five years had passed since the wedding, but the story was retold by those who relished gossip. And others recalled the old Rebbe's warnings to be on guard against false prophets.

· 13 ·

Politics and Race in
Crown Heights

Neighborhood Change

The Lubavitcher settlement in Crown Heights began in 1925 when Israel Jacobson, a wise and warmhearted Lubavitcher teacher, arrived in the United States from Russia and set about building a following for Chabad Hasidism. Fifteen years later in the spring of 1940, he was joined by his Rebbe, Joseph I. Schneersohn, the sixth Lubavitcher Rebbe, who fled from Poland (where he had lived the previous six years) a few scant months before the Nazis sealed off the Warsaw Ghetto. Due to Rabbi Jacobson's efforts Rabbi Schneersohn found a small but dedicated group of disciples waiting for him. For the most part the Jewish population in Crown Heights was secular or moderately religious. Synagogues were Conservative rather than Orthodox. News that the Rebbe had settled in Crown Heights attracted Lubavitcher Hasidim and other Orthodox Jews who had fled Europe. Soon there was a small but growing Hasidic and Orthodox community.

In the 1940s Crown Heights contained a population of a variety of ethnic origins: Jews, Irish, Germans, Scandinavians, Italians, and blacks. The ethnic composition of Crown Heights, however, was undergoing enormous social change. In the aftermath of the Second World War the more affluent white residents were leaving the city for new housing in the suburbs; their places in the city were being taken by an expanding black and Latino population. A mass migration was taking place in the country: ten million southern blacks, displaced from land and jobs, were encouraged to make the trek to the more prosperous cities of the north. Their numbers were swelled by a million Puerto Ricans anxious to try their luck in New York and by another million or so blacks immigrating to the United States from the West Indies. The large black population of Brooklyn's Bedford-Stuyvesant, strained to its limits, expanded southward toward Eastern Parkway and south Crown Heights. In 1950 whites constituted 85 percent of the population of Crown Heights; ten years later in 1960 the white population had fallen to 70 percent. During the decade of the sixties, three-quarters of the white residents of Crown Heights moved out and the neighborhood shifted from 70 percent white to 70 percent black. Every sign indicated that it would continue to tip still further.

The stampede to leave Brooklyn was exacerbated during the 1950s and 1960s by the disruptive social phenomenon then called *blockbusting*. A black tenant would be introduced into a house or an apartment building and the white homeowners and tenants on the block would panic for fear that the racial composition of the street was changing. Homeowners, frightened that the neighborhood would become unsafe and that their properties would plummet in value, would sell their homes to the first buyer and move to what they believed to be more stable white areas, usually far from Brooklyn. The "blockbuster" would pick up the properties for less than their real value and resell them for an inflated price. A similar fate awaited apartment house tenants who were protected by rent control laws. Harassed by the landlords' discontinuation of services, and frightened by the social disequilibrium, tenants would flee as quickly as they could. New tenants would be shuffled in and out of the buildings, and each time the rents would be raised.

As the white population moved out, financial institutions redlined the neighborhood. Banks withdrew support and declined to issue or renew mortgages. During the 1960s the city began to place families on public assistance in the older buildings where vacancies were frequent, encouraging landlords' acceptance by offering incentive payments. As the poorer tenants moved in, the departure of the older tenants was accelerated. Service to the tenants then declined and the houses deteriorated. Instances of arson increased as some owners tried a final scheme to collect on a dying building.[1]

The neighborhoods were changing. The minute a few blacks came in everyone ran and abandoned the communities. This happened in Bedford-Stuyvesant. They abandoned the shuls and the institutions. In Brownsville they abandoned two hundred shuls. This is the way it was all over the United States. I remember going to my brother's in Detroit, and there was a beautiful Young Israel being put up. The walls weren't finished yet and they were already selling it to a church. This was just the style.

At this time the blacks started moving into Crown Heights and everyone started running. The obvious thing to do was to run out and leave all the institutions. Of course you're leaving a lot of older people who cannot move, and some people who don't have the means to move, and they're stranded. We make a lot of noise about five hundred Jews left over in an Arab country, and yet we have Jews left over in our neighborhoods who are prisoners in their houses. If everyone moves and they don't have the means to move, or they've become accustomed to the apartment, they're just abandoned. (MS)

An increasing crime rate accelerated the departure of white residents. In 1964, after a number of yeshivah students were beaten and a rabbi's wife was attacked, there was rising concern about safety. The Bobover Hasidim who lived in the blocks north of Eastern Parkway went to their Rebbe and suggested asking for police protection when they left the besmedresh at night to return home. The Rebbe told them that, in his father's day, an anti-Semite had thrown a rock through their window; afterward, the anti-Semite contracted blood poisoning and had to have his hand amputated. "This is better than police protection," advised the Rebbe. Soon after, however, the Bobover Hasidim sold their besmedresh and yeshivah and moved en masse to Borough Park.

A few streets away, on the south side of Eastern Parkway, the Lubavitcher Rebbe spoke on the need to defend one's life. In response, a young follower, Rabbi Samuel Schrage, organized a group called the Maccabees to patrol the streets from midnight until five A.M. They were unarmed and in the event of trouble their intention was to notify the police by keeping in radio contact with a central office, or, in more immediate, desperate circumstances, to overwhelm a suspect with their numbers.

For the Hasidim, in contrast to other white residents, the decision of whether or not to flee the changing neighborhood was largely a communal one. While other whites could simply give up their apartments and take up new ones in suburbia, the Hasidim had to consider the enormous social and economic investments which they had made collectively in the neighborhood. After a decade of destruction and dislocation in Europe, their need to remain rooted and close together weighed upon them. The private school systems and religious institutions that they had recently constructed had to be maintained.

As Crown Heights emptied of its white residents, a good measure of the shifting Orthodox population moved to Borough Park. When the Bobover Hasidim decided to sell everything and move, the stage was set for the Lubavitcher Hasidim to follow. The Lubavitcher Rebbe's response, therefore, came as a surprise.

> The Rebbe came out with the call not to move at a farbrengen. "Here we stop." This was the Rebbe's call, and obviously the Hasidim listened to him and didn't move. Really this is not his business to mix into these things, but being no one else is doing this, he said, "No moving!" It was a tremendous undertaking because everyone was laughing at us. There was no such thing in all America. Everyone in Detroit and all over knew that as soon as the blacks move in the whites move out. The neighborhoods keep changing.
>
> The Rebbe was the first one who came up with: "We're not moving. We're staying here." At that time it was as if the Rebbe would say that we

should go to Russia and Communism is going to disappear in two years. Would you think of such a thing? (MS)

As testimony to their determination to remain in Crown Heights the Lubavitcher Hasidim undertook an expensive renovation and expansion of their besmedresh. Now that other Jewish groups had abandoned the neighborhood, the Jewish Community Council of Crown Heights fell into Lubavitcher control, and they used it to organize their economic and social campaign to maintain the stability of the neighborhood. They were for a time the only effective neighborhood organization able to take advantage of government loan programs initiated to fight urban decay.

One of the Hasidim who emerged as a secular leader of the Lubavitcher community was Mendel Shemtov, an energetic and intelligent businessman who had a gift for bringing people together. After spending his youth in the Soviet Union engaged in sub rosa capitalist enterprise, he had emigrated to America where he built up a manufacturing plant producing inexpensive plastic cases, notebooks, and other articles. As his business grew he devoted more and more of his time, and a considerable amount of his profit, to community affairs.

The Jewish Community Council started disappearing because all the others moved out. So the Council became controlled 99 percent by Lubavitch. This is when the Council started influencing people not to move, when it started buying houses from people who ran away, and seeing that there should be a balance in the community and it shouldn't be abandoned.

If we knew that someone was running away and wants to sell his house we would buy the house to preserve it and then resell it, most of the time at a loss. If we heard of a rabbi who wants to make money and sell the shul for a church, we used to put pressure on him. We used to do everything possible—even go to court to fight and tell them that the shul belongs to the people who live here and as long as there is a minyan there he's not the owner of the shul. Out of the whole community only one of them succeeded in selling the shul. Let's say that only ten people cannot afford to keep up the shul, or they want to sell the shul and give the money to Israel. We wouldn't allow this.

We started fighting that a shul should not be sold to a church. Of the forty shuls in our community only one was sold to a church. In another community all forty would have gone. This is where the Council started working. It was such an obvious thing to do. If we dealt with the Farband, the Labor Zionist Organization, we went to Shazar; if we dealt with Young Israel we went to the National Council of Young Israel and told them, "How could you do such a thing? You're going to bring a church in here?" Then someone wants money, and we have to raise money and buy it off. The Farband had a building right across on the other side of Kingston Avenue, and they were about to sell it to a black club. So we went to them and said, "How could you sell it to a club?" And they said, "We know you're going to sell it anyway in another half-year." But Shazar was president then and we used some influence. They agreed to sell it to us for $65,000 instead of $80,000 to the club, but they put into the contract that when we sell it the profit over $65,000 would go to them. They were so convinced we would leave in six months.   (MS)

Tension continued in the streets of Crown Heights, in part because of crime, in part because of the presence of the Maccabees, the Hasidic patrol, which blacks felt was directed against them. Some blacks complained of harassment by Hasidic vigilantes. For their part, the Hasidim maintained that they sought to have interracial patrols, particularly on Friday nights when the Shabbes prohibitions prevented them from driving automobiles. They did not attack anyone, but, rather, informed the police of suspicious persons. They pointed to the high crime rate, and to the many attacks against Hasidic individuals, as proof of the need for the patrols.

A number of tragic incidents supported their view. On a Friday night in September 1975, Israel Turner, an Orthodox Jew, was murdered by a holdup man just as he had reached his home on Empire Boulevard at 11:30 at night. Turner, fifty-four years of age, had just celebrated the Shabbes and the Sukkot holiday at the Lubavitch besmedresh. He tried to explain to the robber that he carried no money because of the religious holiday, and he called up to his wife who was in their first floor apartment. Turner's wife came to the window and pleaded with the robber: "Leave him alone, he has no money." As she ran to the door she heard two shots, and when she reached her husband he was dying from a chest wound. As reported in the *New York Times,* "a neighbor said Mrs. Turner was composed, even though she saw her husband fall before her. 'She told me that she and her husband had been inmates in the Auschwitz concentration camp, had seen members of their family tortured and had learned to have strength for things like this.'" [2]

There was a racial incident on the following Sunday when the funeral procession made a stop at the police station on Empire Boulevard. While the five hundred mourners were listening to a rabbi demand increased police protection, they were suddenly taunted by shouts of "Heil Hitler" and "Hitler was right" from bystanders on the steps of a junior high school across the street from the police station. The Hasidim turned from their procession and grabbed a young man and woman. Police intervened and separated the couple from the Hasidim but the enraged Hasidim broke through the police guard and the couple had to be rescued again and hurried into an apartment building. The children watching from the school windows picked up the offensive Nazi cry and continued to taunt the crowd of mourners.[3]

Differing ethnic mores and patterns of behavior separated the two groups, but misperceptions divided the population still further. The black minister of the First Baptist Church of Crown Heights, the Reverend Clarence Norman, Sr., observed: "The Jews think the blacks are all muggers and rapists. And the blacks see the Jews as white people, as symbols of oppression. Tension could be removed by dialogue." [4]

Black spokesmen voiced resentment of alleged favored treatment for Hasidim in employment, government loans to small businesses, and political clout. The police patrol car then stationed in front of Lubavitcher headquarters at 770 Eastern Parkway, seen by the Hasidim as a mark of honor befitting the worldwide leadership of the Lubavitcher Rebbe, was a constant reminder to the blacks of their own lack of influence in the corridors of city hall and the state house.

Blacks controlled the local Community Board, however, which allocated funds for community projects. They had rejected a Hasidic plan to open a drug abuse center, but Hasidim were now opting to participate more fully on the Community Board itself. The Hasidim were learning about American politics. A Hasid won election to the board of the local antipoverty agency, another Hasid sat as a member of the local school board, and there was a publicly funded daycare center run by Hasidim. The voting strength of the Hasidim, however, was limited, and they had very little discernible political power.

The total area of Crown Heights runs from Empire Boulevard in the south to Atlantic Avenue in the north. The two sections of Crown Heights were known to city demographers as District H.[5] Socially, however, Crown Heights is subdivided in the middle by Eastern Parkway, and the two areas are usually referred to as North Crown Heights and South Crown Heights. North Crown Heights, from Eastern Parkway to Atlantic Avenue, includes part of downtown Brooklyn, with blocks of abandoned factories and housing. The small white population in this area includes few if any Hasidim.[6]

The Hasidic population is concentrated in South Crown Heights in a strip three to four blocks wide running from Eastern Parkway south to Empire Boulevard. A high percentage of the black population in this section are non-Hispanic immigrants from the West Indies—Haiti, Jamaica, Guyana, Trinidad, and Grenada—most of whom have arrived since 1965.

In 1976, when the Board of Estimate of the city came to redefine the city's community districts, the Lubavitcher Hasidim saw an opportunity to consolidate their voting strength, a move which sharpened their disagreement with some of the leaders of the black community. The Hasidim petitioned to have the southern portion of District H declared a separate community district so that they could have a greater voice in matters affecting their immediate neighborhood. The proposed area had the required 100,000 in population, and blacks would still constitute an overwhelming majority of the residents. In December 1976 the Board of Estimate voted to cut the district in half. The area north of Eastern Parkway, Crown Heights North, became Community Board 8. Crown Heights South, where the Hasidim lived, became Community Board 9. Black leaders immediately asked for an injunction in federal court to halt the Board of Estimate's action, but the injunction was denied. By 1980, as whites continued to leave the neighborhood, the percentage of blacks in Community Board 9 was even higher than it had been when the two districts were joined. (The population was 78.4 percent black, 9.5 percent Latino, 9.4 percent white, and 2.7 percent Asian.) Nonetheless, the division of District H left some of the black leadership in a bitter, frustrated mood.

One of the chief antagonists to the Hasidic community in Crown Heights South was the Reverend Heron A. Sam, the rector of St. Mark's Episcopal Church. Rev. Sam was a native of Guyana, and his three-thousand-member congregation was half West Indian and half native black American. It was representative of the well-to-do black community, with a large number of professional people—doctors, dentists, teachers, businesspeople, and clergymen. Rev. Sam was concerned with his own congregation's need to expand. The Hasidic population seemed to be growing at an alarming rate, and he was angered by their increasing influence and power in the blocks south of Eastern Parkway. In a letter published in the *Amsterdam News,* Rev. Sam warned of "Zionist expansion." [7]

For their part the Hasidim were frustrated in their efforts to win concessions from City Hall for needed housing and for police protection, and they had been largely unable to convince householders other than their own Hasidim to remain in the neighborhood. Of special concern to the Hasidim at this time was the safety of the Rebbe, who had received death threats, allegedly from members of a rival Hasidic court. After a request had been made to Mayor John Lindsay a police car had been placed on twenty-four-hour duty in front of 770 Eastern Parkway. The special attention irritated Rev. Sam and other blacks. It came up again in the election of 1977 when Edward Koch, then a congressman from Manhattan, decided to run for mayor.

> When Koch ran in 1977 I went to Koch to support him. I went to his apartment in the Village and I asked him if he was going to keep the car there after the election, and he said, "I'll keep it."
>
> I asked, "And what if Rev. Sam comes and asks you?"
>
> He said, "I'll give him also a car."
>
> I wish I would have had a tape. The minute he was elected he kicked the car out. (MS)

Rev. Sam tells roughly the same sequence of events—from another perspective:

> The Hasidic community is so vocal and maybe politically influential, with police protection and closing off streets. We complained to Mayor Koch and he said the police are not there to babysit any group.   (HS)

Although the police guard was removed the charge of special privilege remained. In subsequent years even the presence of a patrol car when crowds left after prayers, a commonplace service afforded to all religious communities, served to reinforce the charge of special police privileges accorded the Hasidim.

Social tension in the streets of Crown Heights rose sharply in June 1978, when Victor Rhodes, a sixteen-year-old black youth, after reportedly striking an elderly man with a stick, according to one account, or taunting some younger Hasidim, according to another, was beaten senseless by a large group of young Hasidim. Fortunately, Rhodes recovered after five weeks of semiconsciousness. Some blacks saw the incident with Rhodes as an example of intimidation by the Hasidic neighborhood patrols; the Hasidim argued that a group of students had been returning from a wedding and had "overreacted" to the provocation. Two Hasidim from Canada, both in their early twenties, were arrested and charged with attempted murder and assault. Other Hasidim protested their arrest, arguing that the two men had just been driving past the scene and were innocent. The police reportedly replied: "Give us the right ones and we'll let them go." [8] None of the assailants volunteered themselves as the guilty parties, and the police were left with two questionable suspects.

To head off neighborhood confrontations, Mayor Koch named a high-level committee on intergroup relations to study and recommend ways to reduce tensions. One of the irritants cited was the Hasidic patrols that stopped and questioned blacks. The Hasidim responded that the thirty-five volunteers who patrolled the streets were interracial and included ten blacks and two or three Latinos. All the volunteers were interested in having a safe neighborhood.

The incidents brought new black leaders to the fore. In addition to the Reverend Heron Sam there was the Reverend Herbert Daughtry, the minister of the House of the Lord Pentecostal Church on Atlantic Avenue in downtown Brooklyn. Although his church was some distance away from Crown Heights, Rev. Daughtry's fiery attacks on the Hasidim propelled him into a position of leadership in the neighborhood.[9] One of his proposals was to organize a Black Citizens' Patrol: "When the people of the long black coats meet our men, let us see what will happen." [10] Another black spokesman was Dr. Vernal Cave, a long-time resident of Crown Heights, who was disturbed by Hasidic inroads in local housing and by what he perceived as municipal favoritism. The insularity of the Hasidim further offended him: "The Hasidim act as if they don't even know us," he complained. "Years ago, the Jews who lived here were friendly and we conversed regularly, but now, only two houses separate my house from some Hasidim property and they don't even nod toward me." [11]

Rev. Daughtry and Dr. Cave were among the founders of the Black United Front, organized in July 1978 to counter both the police and the Hasidim.[12] Within a few days the Black United Front held a rally opposite Lubavitcher headquarters to protest police brutality and Hasidic influence, and to express their wider resentment at the absence of black voices in city affairs.[13] During the rally the two thousand blacks present heard the Hasidim characterized as "terrorists" and "oppressors."

While the antagonism between the Hasidim and the blacks remained in the news during the summer, the violent rhetoric heard at the rally was never translated into an organized hostile action. There are a number of reasons suggested for the more tempered response. The black community itself is not a single entity and is divided in opinion. Many blacks oppose the call to prejudice and violence. Many prefer to live in an integrated community, and they want to get along with the Hasidim, whom they do not see as a threat. (Twenty-four black Baptist ministers had publicly dissociated themselves from any anti-Semitism expressed at the black rally as well as from any organization expressing anti-Semitism.)

The diversity of viewpoints within the black community also reflected a range of social classes and ethnic groups. Middle-class blacks, many of them West Indians, had moved into the stately mansions near Eastern Parkway and into the surrounding brownstones and small apartment houses. Both whites and blacks expressed similar concerns about property values, integration, and crime statistics. Middle-class blacks in South Crown Heights were wary of being used by agitators from outside the immediate community. Moreover, as George Vecsey, a *New York Times* reporter, discovered, "the long-range problem in Crown Heights may be lack of deep contact rather than a readiness in two camps to fight." Walking in the neighborhood streets a week after the rally, he found that blacks did not consider there to be trouble between the Hasidim and the blacks. As one young black man noted, "I've never seen these Hasidim look for a fight. I'll tell you the truth—if they beat up on somebody, I'll bet they were provoked." [14]

The Hasidim presented an equally complex picture. Because they all dressed alike and to outsiders seemed to look alike, it was easy to assume that they all thought the same way. Negative actions by one Hasid reflected on the entire community—just as the antisocial actions of one black were frequently seen as representative of all blacks. Some Hasidim were open-minded concerning race while others were prejudiced. There were also a very small number of Hasidim who were exploitive landlords or who were among the blockbusters whose actions everyone, Jews and gentiles alike, feared. A devout Lubavitcher Hasid, commenting on one known blockbuster from another Hasidic court, observed: "Not everyone who wears a kaftan and a shtrayml is a Hasid." The negative work of a few selfish entrepreneurs and exploitive businessmen, some Jewish, some non-Jewish white, and some black, made it difficult to preserve the stability and peace of the neighborhood.

While the concern that the Hasidim were contesting for housing in the neighborhood was based on an accurate assumption, the accusation that the Hasidim represented a menace to a fearful black community was termed "an inversion of reality" in a *Commentary* article.[15] Street crime consisted overwhelmingly of assaults by blacks on blacks and Jews. Blacks, however, resented the Hasidic security patrols which were the Hasidic response to the need to control crime. While recognizing that individual Hasidim were no danger, blacks maintained that groups of Hasidim cruising the streets on patrol posed a real threat.

The principal problem, however, as Rev. Sam realized, remained competition for housing.

> There are no points of contention that are generated by us. The problems are the result of the paucity of resources, particularly housing. There is minimum housing for a growing Hasidic community and a burgeoning black community. Everything else is peripheral and inconsequential. The Hasidim seem to be getting a bigger part of housing now and this is an irritant to the black community. Their need for housing has raised prices and put it out of reach of even some black professionals. We should be able to get a piece of the action, be able to be accommodated. Our church has been there for 150 years. It's not about to roll over and die.   (HS)

The housing situation had now come full circle. In the late 1960s and 1970s, with neighborhoods suffering from the threat of decay and abandonment, a number of government-sponsored programs were designed to encourage reinvestment and rebuilding. The Hasidic community organized to apply for government programs in housing rehabilitation and increased community services.

The need for direct support and loans in the development of housing highlighted a dilemma: separateness is crucial to Hasidic ethnicity, but the use of public funds automatically bars any hint of exclusivity that can be interpreted as discriminatory. In this instance the problem was exacerbated by charges that various Hasidic individuals in charge of the programs had used public funds in pursuit of personal gain.

The Chevra Machazikei Hashcunah Inc., the Lubavitcher nonprofit organization, had purchased a number of four- and five-story walk-up apartment buildings, which it now undertook to renovate for Hasidic families, utilizing a variety of loans and subsidies, primarily from federal sources. Chevra had won a number of contracts for programs designed to improve social conditions and rebuild decaying neighborhoods. There were funds to hire security guards and for an escort service to assist older residents to do shopping and other errands; a small homemaker project funded ten workers to do household chores for 150 elderly persons; another more substantial grant of a million dollars went for a summer lunch program for children. Chevra had also been awarded several CETA (Comprehensive Employment and Training Act) contracts to aid the unemployed by providing handyman training in a variety of skills in construction and maintenance to be gained by working on Chevra-owned housing (for tenants below the poverty level). The Participation Loan Program (PLP) provided roughly half of a loan at very low interest rates to encourage building rehabilitation by owners; Section 8 rent subsidies were available for low-income tenants.[16]

The range of government programs that Chevra had succeeded in reaching is testimony to the expertise acquired by Chevra organizers. According to the report of the City Council in 1978, however, Chevra managers had frequently ignored federal guidelines. Some accusations went beyond possible oversight: it was alleged that repairs made by trainees were not on Chevra-owned houses but on private property owned by Chevra board members or their families, or by allied profit-making corporations. In fact, more than half the buildings that utilized the trainees supported by public funds turned out to be privately owned.[17]

Renovation in Chevra-owned housing resulted in further controversy between landlords and tenants. Most of the tenants in the buildings being renovated were black and Hispanic, although one large apartment building held primarily older Jews who were not Hasidic. The breakdown of services (water and heating) and the renovation of existing walls and floors forced out most tenants. Typically, an apartment building of forty apartments would dwindle down to perhaps a dozen tenants who would refuse offers to be relocated elsewhere. As the complaints appeared to go unheard the remaining tenants organized rent strikes, refusing to pay their rent until full services were restored. One building on Carroll Street was being renovated for use as a hotel for visitors who came to see the Rebbe. Renovation was slow, however, since the banks in the area were skeptical of the need for a hotel in a borough where hotels had completely vanished and they declined to provide loans for the project. Half the building was occupied by tenants frustrated by the lack of repairs and services. Meanwhile, some of the empty apartments were already being used to house visitors who came to see the Rebbe.

A series of tenant strikes in 1978 in a number of Chevra-owned buildings led to a broad investigation of tenants' charges: failure to provide basic services in the buildings in order to force tenants to leave, discrimination and unfair practices by failing to inform other minorities of housing opportunities, and monopolizing funds in the Weatherization Program to improve older housing. There were also "allegations of harassment and racial discrimination" in properties owned by Rabbi Fischer, a board member of Chevra, brought by the city's Bureau of Rent Control. Fischer was the president or secretary-treasurer of almost a dozen different realty companies. The address of one of his realty companies was the same as that of a senior citizens' escort service which paid rent for the entire building.

The Hasidic community lost some standing in local politics when it backed Assembly Speaker Stanley Steingut in a struggle for leadership against City Councilman Theodore Silverman. As a result of Silverman's victory Mendel Shemtov lost his appointment to the Community Board of District 9. Mendel Shemtov commented: "We supported Steingut and Silverman said that if we lost I'd be off the community board. He's a man of his word. I'm off." [18] The board, which influences the disbursement of city funds and services, also voted to replace its chairman, Rabbi Samuel Fogelman, with a black man, Edward S. Hightower. This change did not still the dialogue between some neighborhood groups. The victory came only after several ballots, and a rabbi was elected as first vice-chairman and a Catholic priest as second vice-chairman. Hightower, a moderate, expressed a desire to work for unity and peace in the neighborhood; however, while his election was taking place Rev. Daughtry fired a crowd to march to the Lubavitcher center at 770 Eastern Parkway to support the complaint of Ronald Holt, a black who claimed to have been attacked by a number of Hasidic men. The Hasidim in turn accused Holt of tampering with an electric cord being used to charge the battery of a Jewish ambulance. It was a measure of neighborhood tension that a minor dispute could result in a police investigation, protest marches, and angry charges.

The chairman of the Jewish Community Council, Mendel Shemtov, saw the need for cooperation between all ethnic groups in the community. At the same time Rev. Norman and Rev. Sam, pastors of two of the largest black congregations in the neighborhood, also concluded that it was time to talk. After a series of meetings in the spring of 1979 a coalition committee of twenty-two members, chaired by Rev. Sam and Mendel Shemtov, issued a statement of conciliation and cooperation: "Convinced that the atmosphere of trust necessary for the stability and growth of the community can be achieved only by mutual cooperation, we have banded together jointly to build our community." [19] They set up a hotline and an ombudsman's office in order to avert a repetition of the tensions that had disturbed Crown Heights the previous summer. The meetings helped to ease tensions and to reduce Rev. Sam's suspicions of the Hasidim. For their part the Hasidim learned that Rev. Sam was not an intractable opponent. Rev. Sam, however, expressed a common complaint concerning Hasidic social indifference and avoidance which the Hasidim have never addressed: "When I passed Hasidim in the street they didn't say hello to me. I thought they hated me." Rabbi Rosenfeld's response—"They don't say hello to each other. They're busy running back and forth to shul"—acknowledged the reality of the complaint but at the same time excused Hasidic social indifference with reference to their devotion.

Relations with Rev. Sam and Rev. Norman would improve and decline over the years depending on issues and circumstances, but clearly discussions with them had reached a new plane. In time the Hasidim proved willing to help Rev. Norman cut through red tape in constructing his housing development for senior citizens; the Hasidim would also lend their support at Community Board meetings for the development of a parochial school promoted by Rev. Sam, although at the time the project would fail to garner sufficient votes for community approval.

Rev. Sam took credit for the positive turn in relations between the Hasidim and the black community:

> Things are peaceful due to the fact that I decided to deal with matters as two religious organizations—to have a peaceful coalition. We ought to have some common groups. The other route would have been to have strife and bloodshed. This way was urged on me by some of my colleagues. I did go to confrontation at first, but I realized that it would destroy us.   (HS)

Not everyone agreed with the accord. Rev. Daughtry had not been included in the negotiations, and he now called the agreement "a farce, a sellout." He warned: "The situation in Crown Heights is simmering, and this doesn't help it any. The blacks who negotiated have given in to the Hasidim's terms and meanwhile, this area is destined to explode." The tenants' union also scorned the agreement, charging that some of the Jewish leaders involved were associated with Chevra and were seeking to gain "an air of respectability." In a subsequent tenants' meeting, Rev. Sam backtracked a bit by saying he had "misjudged" the amount of property owned by Hasidim and their responsibility in tenant abuse.[20]

There was no question that the relatively small Hasidic population enjoyed greater strength as the result of weak and diffuse leadership in the black community. Each of several black leaders widely known in the community had a separate constituency and a list of particular complaints, be it housing, patrols, parking, street closings, or local politics. Each had as well an agenda for dealing with the issues. The new chairman of Community Board 9, Edward S. Hightower, saw the efforts of the Hasidic community to organize politically and to renovate housing as models to be emulated: "While we are fighting, they are building." He urged all sides in the community to work together.[21]

The Jewish community was soon confronted by a new tragic incident. In October 1979, Rabbi David Okunov, a sixty-eight-year-old recent emigré from the Soviet Union, was shot to death while on his way to early morning prayers. His embroidered prayer shawl was stolen. A thousand Hasidic Jews marched in the funeral procession. Members of the community coalition sought to aid police in their efforts to catch the murderer. Five weeks later a nineteen-year-old unemployed black man was arrested for the crime. There were no neighborhood incidents, but there was a sense of bitterness and frustration at the senseless killing and the never-ending threat of crime and violence.

The hearings and the trial of the two Hasidim accused of the assault and attempted murder of Victor Rhodes dragged on through the fall and winter of 1979. Each day some thirty Hasidic men from Crown Heights would arrive and take seats in the courtroom. Seated nearby would be representatives of the Black United Front, who came from a variety of Brooklyn neighborhoods. While both groups were there to lend support for their causes, the Hasidim were present as part of a defense strategy. Defense counsel had waived the rights of the accused to be present before the bench and had seated the defendants in the audience among the other Hasidim, thereby complicating identification of the accused.

The trial ended in an acquittal on February 27, 1980. The jury that found the two Hasidim innocent was composed of five whites, six blacks, and a Latino foreman. None of the jurors was Jewish. It was revealed subsequently that the two accused Hasidim, who had denied the assault charges, had passed lie detector tests. City Councilwoman Mary Pinkett, however, criticized the seating of the Hasidim in the audience. Rev. Daughtry, the chairman of the Black United Front, protested what he termed "a clear miscarriage of justice." Noting that the jury had six black jurors, he added that there was greater need for education for "race consciousness" and "self respect." [22] For all purposes, however, practical and propagandistic, the incident was over.

To a great extent the coalition committee had been successful in keeping the neighborhood calm. "We have been able to defuse any kind of negative dynamic," observed Rev. Sam. He added that the committee had expanded its mandate by applying for federal housing funds and had agreed to integrate street patrols. An important step in community relations had been taken, and it appeared that community crises would be easier to handle in the future. But no coalition could wipe out crime or reverse long-standing social conditions, and everyone recognized that the problems were far from over. Not everyone in the black community favored Rev. Sam's policy of peace. Accusations concerning favored treatment for Hasidim were repeated by some with renewed passion. For a time a new Black Citizens' Patrol was formed. Black frustration invariably focused on "the people in long coats."

The report issued by City Council President Carol Bellamy at the end of 1978 had created a stir with allegations of financial irregularities and misuse of public funds by Chevra. Some programs were terminated.[23] The official follow-up on the charges, however, dissolved into vague suggestions. Bellamy turned the matter over to the city's Investigation Commissioner, and called upon other agencies to evaluate the charges and impose sanctions. In the end, however, no criminal charges were filed by any local or federal agency.

In 1980, Rabbi Fischer was forced to bow out of one extensive project and surrender responsibility to the Crown Heights Jewish Community Council. The finding of a hearing concerning a building on Montgomery Street determined that Fischer and others were "callous and disruptive influences." A $1,000 fine was levied against Fischer and his agent, Joseph Blizinsky (who was also on the board of the Crown Heights Jewish Community Council) for a variety of charges involving tenant harassment.[24] The controversy surrounding Chevra and the actions of several board members left a bitter legacy that would prove difficult to erase.[25]

· 14 ·

Satmar and Lubavitch
in Conflict

Disciples

Shifting allegiance from one court to another may realize an individual's search for an ideal Rebbe, a satisfying lifestyle, or a more demanding piety. If, as is often the case, the individual is a yeshivah student a new social identity is drawn. The student not only is attached to a new Rebbe but davens in a different shul, has a new circle of comrades, and possibly establishes ties with a set of in-laws. In the tightly knit and committed atmosphere of a Hasidic court such change has wide-ranging consequences. It often entails an ordeal for the student's family, who may find themselves at odds with and even cut off from their son. They may be regarded with sympathy or suspicion in their own community. If several students are involved and the problems reverberate in still wider circles, it becomes a matter of serious concern for the morale of the court, whose very stability may appear to be challenged.

For these reasons, the proselytizing zeal of Lubavitch frequently poses a direct threat to other Hasidic courts. Their competition for the minds and hearts of young students is a major cause of the angry reactions against Lubavitch. Satmar Hasidim, who have always looked askance at Lubavitcher efforts to proselytize irreligious Jews and to redeem Jews who are under the influence of drugs, become alarmed and enraged when they discover Lubavitcher Hasidim, covertly or not, courting their own young students. For their part, the Lubavitcher Hasidim assert that they are being responsive to the request of Satmar students to study Hasides (Hasidic philosophy), in particular the *Tanya* of the first Lubavitcher Rebbe, Rabbi Shneur Zalman. Satmar Hasidim, however, consider this to be a red herring. It is community allegiance rather than philosophy that is at the heart of the dispute. Rabbi Shneur Zalman is venerated throughout the Hasidic world (having provided all Hasidim with a new guide for observance, a Hasidic prayer book, and a key to the kabbala); however, when his teachings are presented by a Lubavitcher it augurs an attempt to win converts for the Lubavitcher community.

Satmar and Lubavitch in Conflict

The increasing concern in Williamsburg over Lubavitcher influence and educational activity recognized a slight weakening of the iron bands of allegiance in the Satmar community. The community had been emotionally drained by the older Satmar Rebbe's long illness and finally his death in 1979. His demise brought a lessening of religious authority and a sense of faltering in the court's unified purpose. Spurred by curiosity, and by the heightened prestige of the Lubavitcher Rebbe, who was by then the survivor of the older generation of great Rebbes, some Satmar yeshivah students were drawn to the excitement and spirit at the court of Lubavitch.

> Lubavitch is strong all across the world, and yet during all these years until lately he didn't catch even one Satmar to him. But now it's a little different. The Lubavitcher Rebbe is the oldest Rebbe in the world now and he's considered the most respected one. There's always some young kids who feel they have to get the right Rebbe, and they conclude that he's the right Rebbe. When the Satmar Rebbe was alive it wasn't really too much of a danger for Satmar because the Satmar Rebbe was so highly respected that they were in effect equal with Lubavitch, but even then it was quite healthy for Satmar to have a little struggle with Lubavitch in order that nobody should think to go over to them. They should realize that the Lubavitcher Rebbe's a *sheygetz* [gentile] and that's it.   (YA)

While the court of Satmar as a whole was not threatened by Lubavitch emissaries, individual families worried over the religious speculations of their young sons. Satmar Hasidim point to the consequences of the case of Rabbi Mendel Wechter, who had been raised as a Satmar Hasid but who was slowly won over to the Lubavitcher cause. As it turned out, the reactions to his new allegiance by his students and subsequently by court zealots had serious personal and community-wide consequences.

Rabbi Mendel Wechter was considered to be a *talmid khokhem,* one of the elite among the pious. Wechter had come to Williamsburg in his teenage years, having been born in Hungary and raised in Toronto, where his father was a respected rabbi. In Hasidic and Orthodox circles Mendel Wechter was known for his yikhes, his deep knowledge of Torah, and his ethical character. It was said that he practiced what he preached and that he made continual efforts to strengthen his character. When he started a yeshivah around 1969 he immediately attracted students, from various Hasidic courts, who were beyond their bar mitzvah (fourteen- and fifteen-year-olds). He selected a dozen or so of the most gifted to continue their studies with him. Because it was soon considered to be a top yeshivah in Williamsburg, with a limited enrollment, some parents eagerly sought to enroll less accomplished sons in order to improve their education.

The texts studied in class were frequently the classics of Chabad Hasidism, the works of the first five generations of Lubavitcher Rebbes—from Rabbi Shneur Zalman (d. 1813) to Reb Sholem Ber, the fifth Rebbe

· 155 ·

(d. 1920). The primary work was the *Tanya,* the common fare for students of Hasidic philosophy.[1] Mendel Wechter was a convincing speaker, but students who attended the yeshivah at that time feel certain that he did not study the works of Chabad with the intention of proselytizing his students. Nor in those first years was Mendel Wechter himself bound to Lubavitch. Over the course of time, however, he found his perspectives influenced by the talks of Menachem Mendel Schneerson, the present Lubavitcher Rebbe, and by the writings of the older Lubavitcher Rebbes. His assumptions about contemporary Lubavitchers were swayed by his increasing contacts with members of their court.

> I was at the yeshivah from 1975 on. The youngest student was fourteen, and most were fifteen and sixteen years old. We learned Chabad Hasidism throughout our years in Mendel Wechter's yeshivah. We were taught *Tanya* and we studied writings of the other Lubavitcher Rebbes.
>
> In the first years when he taught me he was not a Lubavitcher. He studied Chabad Hasides and he needed to know more and more. He got in touch with people [of Lubavitch] and increasingly the barriers fell away. He found that the Lubavitchers were God-fearing people, pious and elite, and that what he had been taught about them was unfounded. (SV)

Rabbi Wechter kept his inner thoughts to himself. Tension between the two courts was high and the followers of the Satmar Rebbe would be impatient with anyone seen as a backslider. There were practical matters to be considered. Mendel Wechter's livelihood as a rosh yeshivah depended on his prestige in the community. His wife's position as a teacher employed in the Satmar school system could also be easily compromised.

The question of loyalty to the prevailing doctrine, however, soon came to a head as a result of a debate that took place in class.

> There was a devout Satmar Hasid who lived upstairs in the same building as our yeshivah. At night he studied privately with boys of the yeshivah. At that time we were studying a book of Rabbi Joel [Teitelbaum's].[2] In keeping with the mood everything that the neighbor mentioned was not only anti-Zionist but anti-Lubavitch. And he cursed the present Lubavitcher Rebbe.
>
> The next morning while we were studying in the yeshivah one of the boys told Mendel Wechter of the session of the previous night and of the curse against the Lubavitcher Rebbe. And Mendel Wechter, though he had been silent until then, could not tolerate this cursing of the Lubavitcher Rebbe. He argued that no one has the right to curse someone with whom he disagrees and that the Lubavitcher Rebbe has a right to his own view. The discussion lasted for six hours and it became very heated. During that time certain opinions that Mendel Wechter had been protecting slipped out. (SV)

The controversial issue raised in the classroom discussion soon moved out into the street. Mendel Wechter's refusal to curse the Lubavitcher

Rebbe and his defense of the Rebbe's right to express his own views became widely known throughout Williamsburg. In a community as tightly bound as Satmar, Mendel Wechter's stand was seen as a sign of heresy and an indication of his shifting allegiance. The boys in the yeshivah too sensed that a change had taken place in Mendel Wechter's thinking.

> People started to demand: "Did you become a Lubavitcher?" And he had to take a low profile. People took sides in the community at that point. He didn't say anything so terrible—he only advocated someone's right to his opinion. He didn't deny what he said, but he had to play it down and say it didn't indicate he was a Lubavitcher. (SV)

Because Mendel Wechter had a unique relationship with the young people of the community as a rosh yeshivah, the matter did not die. His views continued to be given careful scrutiny, particularly by the parents of his students. Had he said anything heretical? Even the notion that each person is entitled to respect for his own opinions was a significant departure on issues considered to be irrevocably closed to dissent. Such liberality hinted that he had something to hide, and soon there were demands that he demonstrate his allegiance to Satmar. He could do that only by openly condemning the principal enemy of the community—the Lubavitcher Rebbe.

> They pushed him to the wall that he had to recant and attack the Lubavitcher Rebbe to show his faith in Satmar, and he refused to do that. As a result the parents took their boys out of the yeshivah. The boys still learned there in 1980 and 1981. Then the yeshivah closed. (SV)

After twelve years of operation the doors of Mendel Wechter's yeshivah were shut. His wife, Rachel, was dismissed from her position as a teacher at a Satmar girls' school. Frightened by the hostility evident in the community, the Wechters moved from Williamsburg to Borough Park.

Although the community seemed to have accepted these actions as the price of stifling dissent, the closing of the yeshivah and the departure of Mendel Wechter marked the radicalization of the students. For a time things were quiet. The boys went off to other yeshivot, but they were quietly measuring the actions of their elders against those of a favorite mentor. The results were far from what the people in Williamsburg expected. In the following months, despite the stiff penalties that threatened them, one by one a number of the students became increasingly attached to Lubavitch.

> Mendel Wechter had planted a seed and we began to think on our own. Mendel Wechter brought us closer to the idea of the Lubavitcher way of thinking but he did not bring us to Lubavitch. All the students realized that he was a Lubavitcher. The boys really loved him. Some of us had disputes at home about Lubavitch. We began to go to Lubavitch on our own. I studied

Hasides and my mind was opened to Chabad Hasides, but I never dreamed of becoming a Lubavitcher Hasid. The yeshivah closed and ten or fifteen remained with him in spirit. Those who stayed with him became Lubavitchers during the next five years.   (SV)

By 1983, two years after the yeshivah had closed, a number of Rabbi Wechter's students had become affiliated with the Lubavitch community. The change from Satmar to Lubavitch appeared to be a measured spiritual and social voyage that lasted several years. The slow pace of change was largely the result of the students' wish to protect their families from further pain. Many of the students gained strength as their new allegiance became public knowledge. Some moved away but retained their old ties; some fled without looking back; and others drifted back to Satmar under the weight of familial and public pressure.

> I never connected our studies to Lubavitch, which was a separate world apart from ours. It wasn't until years later that I became a Lubavitcher Hasid. At first we denied our affiliation and finally over the years we came to admit it. At first we denied it to our parents. Finally we said we're Lubavitch.   (SV)

The tale of shattered loyalty was only the beginning of the problems faced by the families whose sons had shifted from Satmar to Lubavitch. The changes threatened the web of familial ties. The future of the students now belonged elsewhere. Some of the young men were already married; if not, there was scant possibility of arranging marriages within their old court. Moreover, doubts might be raised about the trustworthiness of other members of the family and threaten their marriage prospects as well.

Ranged on one side were the community and the individual families, on the other side the wayward sons now tied to the court of Lubavitch. Each family hoped to win its son back into the fold, but what if the new Lubavitcher convert were to follow the proselytizing tradition and try to influence his brothers to join him? The other children had to be protected even if it meant breaking family ties. It was a time of painful decision, for it placed in conflict basic loyalties: to follow one's Rebbe and to pursue a new ideal or to remain loyal to one's court and to honor one's father and mother. In such instances families could conceivably hold funeral rites for their apostate sons. Actually this never took place in Williamsburg. Although the families were extremely upset, no one sat shivah, the seven days of mourning the dead.

> Each individual had his own problems. My parents disagreed with me. But not one of the parents sat shivah. Not one of the boys was banned from the families. Five or six were married and maybe a father-in-law banned his

son-in-law and wanted his daughter to divorce her husband, but none did. (SV)

The wives of the married students too had been kept in the dark about the change of heart experienced by their husbands. Now they too had to acknowledge and accept their husbands' radical move. In some instances their traditional submissive role helped to resolve the question: "I trusted my husband. I know he's more scholarly than I am" (LO).

Wives as well as husbands had to stand up to familial and community pressure.

> My brothers and sisters were angry with me because they said I was hurting our parents. At first we told my parents that we would change. We didn't want to hurt them. My parents were upset and they hinted that maybe I should get a divorce. They didn't say it directly but they indicated that some people are happier after being divorced. We didn't have any children then. (LO)

In Lubavitch circles Rabbi Wechter was praised as an inspiring teacher whose students had been won over in a just crusade. In Williamsburg, however, there was a great outcry of contempt and anger toward the instigator of the apostasy of ten youths. The general gossip repeated in Williamsburg portrayed a deceptive teacher who used his position to draw students to Lubavitch. The details of this cautionary account were adjusted to enhance the themes of deceit and guile: the age of the students was slightly lowered (to thirteen and fourteen); rather than gifted and astute students they were presented as those who had fallen behind in their yeshivah studies and needed tutoring; rather than using well-known Chabad texts it was now bruited about that unknown to the parents he had used Lubavitcher tracts. The parents were portrayed as innocent dupes who had supported Rabbi Wechter's enterprise because classes were small and each student could receive individual attention. It was said that they never realized until too late that the teacher's main purpose was to win the boys over to Lubavitch.

> He didn't tell the parents that he's going to instill in them the doctrines of Lubavitch. But he did it, until a period of time the parents noticed that the kids have changed. Their whole beliefs have changed. Their values have changed. And you obviously can understand how upsetting that is in this type of religious community when you give your whole life and your whole blood for raising your kids and all of a sudden comes another person and does like missionary work. So it was actually parents of these children that tried to get him out of the community and stop him doing what he did. And even if he gave up the yeshivah he still continued doing this in hiding. He would have people coming to him in his house and he would speak with them and he would continue his work. (AG)

Rumors of family conflicts also described the worst possible scenarios. It was told that some sons were banned from their parents' households and that in the strictest families prayers for the dead were chanted and a period of mourning carried out. As it turned out none of these stories were true. Although most families were unhappy with the turnabout in affiliation, no family cut themselves off from their sons and daughters.[3]

It was impossible to respond to all the unfounded charges. For a time Mendel Wechter found respite in the more cosmopolitan streets of Borough Park. This move, however, could not ensure his safety. None of the parents involved appeared to have plotted reprisals against him, but there were others impatient to act against someone who had so offended community mores.

Rabbi Pinchas Korf's Beard

It was only a matter of time before the example of Mendel Wechter's students would be emulated by others. Several young men of Satmar began visiting the Lubavitcher center at 770 Eastern Parkway. It came as no surprise to Rabbi Pinchas Korf, a well-known Lubavitcher teacher, when David Kohn, an eighteen-year-old Satmar Hasid who had been a student of Mendel Wechter, approached him and asked to study the *Tanya* with him. Rabbi Korf was a popular teacher and considered to be a man of learning, piety, and goodwill. He was modest and retiring in appearance and in action, and even Satmar Hasidim who knew him testified to Rabbi Korf's good nature. (Albert Friedman, then a reporter for the Satmar newspaper *Der Yid*, observed: "It's a pity. He was one of the nicest people in Lubavitch. They took the top of the cream to send to Williamsburg to teach. They didn't want to send any of those missionary types who just go out and put on tefillin. They wanted to get somebody who people could look up to.") Rabbi Korf was then forty-six. He had come to New York thirty years earlier in 1953 from the city of Kharkov in the Ukraine. He was considered particularly gifted in conveying the religious philosophy of Lubavitch.

David Kohn had already decided to leave the Satmar yeshivah. In deference to his father's wishes, however, he would study at a relative's yeshivah in Borough Park. In exchange he could learn the *Tanya* from a Lubavitcher rabbi. The father asked only that his son not go to Lubavitch. "Let him come here." The two could meet in his frame shop, which was located in an industrial area on the periphery of the Satmar community, at Broadway and Union Street. Its proximity to Satmar made Rabbi Korf somewhat uneasy, but in keeping with his mission he agreed to go.

> I teach Hasides everywhere. If someone wants me to teach him Hasides I teach him Hasides. The boy asked me to teach him. He came here to 770.

He had Satmar friends who had become Lubavitchers. There is a group of boys who became Lubavitcher Hasidim. They were friendly with him and they knew him. But he asked me by myself. He came to me to ask to teach him. I taught only him. I made a date with him to teach him every Friday. He said his father will allow me to teach him but only in his store and no-where else. We met only two times in his father's store. His father was there listening. (PK)

The first lesson went smoothly. Rabbi Korf began to discuss the second part of the *Tanya,* the first chapter in part two, which is central to Luba-vitch conceptions.

It speaks about the way that the Baal Shem Tov taught the belief that God is one. The way the Baal Shem Tov taught it is different than the way that others explain it. He explains that God is one. He is only one and there is nothing besides Him. Not only there is only one God, there is no other God, but the meaning is that there is nothing in the whole world besides him. He's the only existence in the whole world. All human beings and everything that there is in the whole world are like the rays contained in the sun. The sun's rays in the sun are invisible. God gives his strength to everything He created. Everything is always within Him, in God's power. What He created are like the rays contained within the sun. Existence is within God's power in every-thing, and since it is always there, the power is the power of the Creator. There is only One and there is nothing else besides Him. (PK)[4]

Lubavitcher Hasidim see their interest in Hasidic philosophy as distin-guishing them from those who follow the religion by rote.

All Hasidim come from the Baal Shem Tov, from the students of the Baal Shem Tov, and all have the same foundation, but not all Hasidim know about these things because not all Hasidim have this way to learn, to under-stand, to have knowledge, to have deep knowledge, to explain the deep things of Hasides. Not all Hasidim know about this even though they have the same basis. (PK)

In Williamsburg the lesson was seen in a different light.

What he [Korf] comes to tell you is not the point. The point is that he wants you to become a Lubavitcher. His idea of coming here and telling you how to be Jewish is not his intention. He is covering up his motives. It's not an issue of religion; it's an issue of the technique and what they stand for. Why does he have to come and teach *Tanya?* Was *Tanya* his message? What's the reason that he has to come to a basement in a Williamsburg factory to teach *Tanya?* Why? *Tanya* is taught everywhere. Everyone knows *Tanya* as good as Korf. The message behind it was more important than the *Tanya.* Come to Crown Heights! (JC)

A month after their first meeting, at the young man's request, Rabbi Korf agreed to study with him again. They met as before in the father's frame shop.

I was teaching him that everyone has something inside that enables him to exist. Not that God created everything at one time and it exists by itself. No. The power of God is always there in every creation. That is the base. That is the beginning.   (PK)

This time, however, a few minutes after the discussion began, five men suddenly entered the room.

They ran into the room and threw me down on the floor. I think there were five of them but I'm not sure. They didn't beat me up and they even said they wouldn't beat me up. They were on top of me. When I saw they had a scissors, I asked, "What are you going to do?" They said, "We're going to cut your beard." In the beginning I had my hands free and I held my beard. I told them in the middle, "You're not allowed to cut the beard. You're not allowed to do it."[5] They said that a hundred rabbis give them permission to do it. It's an expression. I was angry, frightened. I had scissor cuts on my face. They told me I shouldn't tell anyone who did it. They asked if I'll tell and I said no. They said if I'll come back to Williamsburg . . . they threatened me. Not cutting one's beard is very important. Our people in Russia went to jail for not cutting their beards.   (PK)

Since both groups hold the *Tanya* in the highest esteem, this was a social rather than an ideological struggle. The Satmar Hasidim saw the lessons as a threat to their families. They were angered and fearful over the possible loss of their children to another community. To the Satmar Hasidim, the cause and effect seemed simple. A parent was apprised of his son's interest in Lubavitch, and a trap was baited.[6]

If you raise a child for eighteen years, sacrifice and sweat blood, and someone comes along and tries to influence them in a different way from yours, what would you do? Cutting a beard is not so terrible under the circumstances. Our community is built on religion. You can't understand it with your mind. It's more important than any other thing.   (JH)

Outside of Satmar, however, the attack on Rabbi Pinchas Korf became a cause célèbre. Since the attack took place late Friday afternoon, on the eve of Shabbes, the Lubavitchers could not respond until Saturday night. When the Shabbes ended, their actions spoke directly to the Satmar community: all kosher foods prepared under the rabbinical supervision of Satmar were banned. Israel Shemtov of Lubavitch expressed Lubavitcher irritation to the press: "How can we trust them to supervise food when they cannot supervise their own people."[7]
Satmar Hasidim believed that they had been unfairly maligned.

People didn't know what the story was. There were rumors circulating that on Shabbes that some Lubavitcher got his beard cut. He was chased out of Williamsburg and warned that he shouldn't come back again. Nobody knew the exact facts. However, that Saturday night Lubavitch had a meeting. They were up in arms at a meeting on the Saturday night. Their rabbinate gave a prohibition against any products which have a *hekhsher,* a certificate of *kashrut* from anybody affiliated with Satmar. All those products are no longer kosher. People should not use them, not eat them, not drink those products. In other words, before Satmar even knew for a fact what happened, all of Satmar was already prejudged to be outcasts. The Rebbe instructed his rabbinate to do it.   (AF)

Satmar leaders condemned the violence done to Rabbi Korf, while at the same time they criticized Lubavitcher provocations.

> It wasn't coming from our circles. I did my investigation because I wanted to punish them, not the Lubavitchers, I wanted to punish them. And I spoke out at that time against these things. We had a general meeting. We had a few thousand people in the synagogue and I told only the truth there about what happened. I condemned these people that did it that they didn't do harm to Lubavitch, they did harm to us. But at the same time I condemned Lubavitch. Why are they coming in our community? We are not going there.   (RH)[8]

It was also evident that when disputes move from the besmedresh to the streets the Rebbes and other leaders are not consulted beforehand. The beard cutting, however, could not be explained away. It was reminiscent of the painful humiliations endured by pious Jews under the Nazis. To try to minimize the damage done to their image, some Satmar Hasidim defended the action as being slight compared to the offense of proselytizing minors.

The Satmar air of innocence did not sit well with Lubavitch. The identity of at least one of the perpetrators was believed to be known to the Lubavitchers. The Satmar community may have known still more. It was not the sort of thing that could be kept hidden indefinitely. The Lubavitchers soon had a list of ten suspects most active in combatting Lubavitch, and they demanded an arrest.

> They wanted to make a police case out of it. Eventually they picked on somebody, Jacob Cohen, who was an activist. He was a deprogrammer. He is a Satmar young man. He davens in Satmar. But some parents spoke to him and they used him to teach their children that they should not be Lubavitch. He also was a rosh yeshivah in one of those yeshivot for *baltshuves,* you know, for Jews who want to become religious. So he had experience in dealing with people. So they picked on him. He was the most vocal anti-Lubavitcher. They made a story that he was the one in that group who let those vandals cut the beard.   (AFF)

The Satmar Hasidim reacted to the Lubavitch ban on their products by waxing a little indignant on their own.

> Satmar condemned it strongly, this act of cutting somebody's beard. There's no justification for violence. There was a general meeting here in the syn-

agogue where, "We'll find out and we'll take the proper steps." But of course after Lubavitch issued their prohibition against Satmar there was a backlash against Lubavitch so there was no way that the Satmar leadership could find out who did anything. You couldn't even start investigating people. "What? You're investigating? What are you doing? Look what they're doing—Nazi tactics, boycotts."

There were some Satmar businessmen who wanted to fire all the Lubavitchers in retaliation, but the Satmar leadership said, "No, we can't do that. It's irresponsible. They should not suffer for the sins of their leaders. We're big enough, we'll survive. Those few businesses will survive. Nobody will be hurt irreparably because of it."   (AFF)

Many in the community soon realized that the attack had not originated with the Satmar leadership; rather, it had been carried out by a small number of extremists, probably both from the M'lochim and from Satmar who resisted any restraints over themselves. One Satmar leader identified them as being M'lochim.

> The young men who did this were from the M'lochim. Rabbi Weberman [the rabbi of the M'lochim] didn't know. Rabbi Weberman is a nice person, he has his philosophy, he knows what he wants, and he is not in this group. But there are elements and you have no control over them. You cannot know who was doing it. And one of them was a disciple of Lubavitch. He came in from Hungary at the time of the revolution and he was in the circles of Lubavitch and somehow he was disappointed. I don't know what happened, why he wanted revenge on them. In such a thing you can not find out exactly what happened, but I did my investigation and I found out it was not our people.   (RH)

The Attack on Rabbi Wechter

The standoff bore bitter fruit. While the Grand Jury considered indictments in the Korf incident, assailants had their eyes on another target— Rabbi Mendel Wechter. Although he had moved from Williamsburg to Borough Park, Wechter was not out of reach. Unlike Rabbi Korf, who was a Lubavitcher, Rabbi Wechter had been raised as a Satmar Hasid and had been won over to Lubavitch. Even worse from the Satmar point of view, he had connived to convince others to join him, and he had succeeded. In their eyes he was not an idealist and a scholar but a turncoat and a deceiver. Rabbi Wechter was considered more dangerous than Rabbi Korf and more deserving of a stinging rebuke.

Early in the morning on Monday, June 20, 1983, a few weeks after the incident with Rabbi Korf, as Rabbi Wechter was leaving his home on 54th Street for morning prayer services, five men, their faces covered by masks, grabbed him and shoved him into a van. In the course of the struggle the rabbi's left ankle was fractured. The men beat him, cut off his beard, and, as an added humiliation, left him on the street wearing only his underwear.

While the Grand Jury considered the Korf case, there were charges and countercharges aired on the streets and in the press concerning Rabbi Wechter. Lubavitcher spokesmen again were quick to hold Satmar responsible for the new incident, as Rabbi Yehuda Krisky of Lubavitch observed: "Their record of terrorism goes back fifty years. They seem to thrive on it." A Satmar spokesman, Rabbi Efroim Stein, denied the attack and at the same time appeared to justify it on the grounds of extreme provocation: "Satmar does not teach violence . . . We resent the missionary activities of Lubavitch as much as we would resent the Hare Krishna or Reverend Moon." [9]

For a time settlement of the issue in a rabbinic court appeared possible. Calling the violence "un-Jewish," Rabbi Chaim Stauber of Satmar's United Jewish Organizations of Williamsburg expressed his willingness to meet with Lubavitch leaders to resolve the issue. Rabbi Stein of Satmar added: "We will meet with anyone, day, night, or evening, on this matter, but we do not know who did these things. We cannot expel these people without proof."

In response, Mendel Shemtov of the Lubavitcher-led Crown Heights Jewish Community Council agreed to a meeting, but the sticking point was the apprehension of the guilty parties: "We are officially agreeing to let a neutral rabbinical court judge these people. We anxiously want this to happen but we will not let up for one minute on pressure on the police and other authorities to apprehend the guilty persons until we are informed that the guilty parties have been made known to a neutral rabbinical court." [10]

From photos the police had taken of likely suspects, Rabbi Korf had been able to identify one of his assailants, Jacob Cohen, who was employed in the Satmar office in charge of financial aid for students. No other persons were identified and no further arrests or confessions were made. The Grand Jury indicted Jacob Cohen for simple assault, and everyone waited to hear the evidence presented in the jury trial.

Blame for the incident had fallen on Satmar, and other less obvious possibilities were ignored. The issues were clearly more complex than was immediately apparent. Historical factors, as well as ideology and family concerns, appeared to be at work in the dispute between the two great courts. The general assumption was that the attack was the work of Satmar Hasidim and that Jacob Cohen was a Satmar Hasid. But was he? Who was Jacob Cohen and how had he become such a central figure in the case?

· 15 ·

The Struggles between the Courts Continue

Jacob Cohen's Writ of Complaint

The court of Satmar has frequently been accused of supporting and even masterminding the activities of Jacob Cohen, the unrelenting opponent of Lubavitch. By his own description, however, Jacob Cohen is not a Satmar Hasid. According to him he did not study at the Satmar yeshivah, he is not a follower of the present Rebbe, and he does not daven at a Satmar shtibl.

Many inside and outside of Satmar scoff at the description and accuse Cohen of dissembling. Arguably, Cohen's ties to Satmar are close: his job is in the office of financial aid for students in the Satmar yeshivah; his wife is from a Satmar family; and his children, because he is allowed free tuition, attend Satmar schools. An admirer of the old Satmar Rebbe, Cohen agrees with most Satmar positions on religious and political matters. Nonetheless, Cohen's actions do not appear to be controlled by the Satmar community. He acts in accord with his own views and standards of conduct, and he maintains that his closest ties are with the M'lochim. Jacob Cohen says he has davened in the M'lochim shul at 205 Hewes Street for the last eighteen years. In sum it can be said that Jacob Cohen has been a Malach and now has close ties with the Satmar community through marriage and employment.

Lubavitcher Hasidim dismiss Cohen's points as mere semantics, and they see little difference between Satmar and the M'lochim. There is, however, a curious anomaly here caused by a twist in the history of the courts. In terms of present-day actions, ideology, dress, and physical location, the line between the Satmar and the M'lochim is difficult to distinguish. In terms of lineage, however, the M'lochim are more closely related to Lubavitch than to Satmar. If their righteous leader the Malach had not quarreled with Rabbi Joseph Schneersohn, the sixth Lubavitcher Rebbe, the M'lochim would have developed a significantly different perspective, or might have been absorbed into Lubavitch altogether.

· 166 ·

Regardless of any historical or social ties Cohen's identity has been established by a singlemindedness: he seems to see the reflection of the Lubavitcher Rebbe's face in every rain puddle. Virtually possessed by his crusade, he is continually on the attack, arguing his case against the Lubavitcher Rebbe in letters, interviews, and public pranks. He has organized a group, CULTA (Coalition Unmasking Lubavitch Tactics Anonymous), which sends a sharply focused newsletter to influential rabbis.[1]

Like the Malach, Cohen traces his own early religious associations to Lubavitch.[2]

> I used to go to Lubavitch to learn. From the ages eleven to thirteen [in 1965–1967] I used to go every day to daven there, and I had a Hasides class there. Pinchas Korf taught the class. That's how Pinchas Korf knew me. I was in his house many times. I learned with him.   (JC)

A Satmar leader corroborates Cohen's account of his religious legacy:

> He was originally a Lubavitcher Hasid. He was disappointed in Lubavitch. There were a few like him, young people, they were impressed by the Lubavitcher, and they went there, and then finally they were very disappointed because here there is a branch of Lubavitchers, the M'lochim, and they are in a fight with the Lubavitcher. So they were attached to that group and they became enemies of the Lubavitcher. So if they are enemies of the Lubavitcher they came to us.
>
> Today I consider Cohen to be a Satmar Hasid. He davens here. He is considered one of us. But what do you mean by a Satmar Hasid? Satmar is not a sect like Lubavitch. Satmar is broader. You can have people who come in and out of our besmedresh that never had to do with Satmar but they are followers, they sympathize with us, and they have their children here. In Lubavitch there is no such a thing that somebody should be a Lubavitcher Hasid and he should not keep his Rebbe as a saint. Here it is more liberal.   (RH)

By Hasidic standards Cohen's beliefs and his conduct as a Hasid are atypical. According to him he rarely goes to a Rebbe to seek a blessing or advice. He appears to shun the intimate relationship of master and disciple that often exists between Rebbe and Hasid. Cohen mocks some supernatural aspects of the faith, scorning, for example, the visits of the Lubavitcher Rebbe to the cemetery to pray at the grave of his predecessor and receive his counsel.

> I don't want my children should be fooled that a person comes from a graveyard every day and tries to fool people that he [the Lubavitcher Rebbe] spoke to his father-in-law. This is idiocy and plain thievery.   (JC)

He denies himself the supernatural and social support of a Rebbe.

> I don't give anyone pidyen. My Rebbe is Rabbi Meyer Weberman [the rabbi of the M'lochim]. I go for a blessing once a year. I don't believe in these

things. I'm out of this. I try not to believe in those things. I went often to the older Satmar Rebbe, but he was not my Rebbe.   (JC)

Cohen does not offer any immediate explanation for his visceral quarrel with Lubavitch. He says he has no particular philosophy to oppose that of Lubavitch other than his beliefs as a pious Jew.

I'm nothing. I have no philosophy. I have no opinions. I am just a normal Jew. I was born into it. It's a birth defect. I'm not qualified to speak on other subjects. To observe the 613 mitzvot and to live a kosher and religious lifestyle. I'm a normal practicing Jew. That's what everyone in the community stands for. I have no special philosophy. I'm just a normal practicing Jew.   (JC)

Yet Jacob Cohen's charges against Lubavitch seem to echo the disappointment and sense of betrayal felt earlier by the Malach.

Something where I belong is transformed into a phony business. Basically it's a cult with a cult personality leader. It's Jewish televangelism. It's a Jewish Jimmy Bakker. Chabad a hundred years ago meant self-discipline and worship of God, and it's been transformed into a fundraising company. He tries to pretend that he's a saint but he's a plain thief.

The main thing about Lubavitch is that it's a Jewish version of a televangelist movement. There is no doctrine. The doctrine is that money surpasses everything.

Basically they try to promote the Rebbe, try to promote him as above the law, above everything. He can't be questioned and he can do anything he wants. He is dying for power. This man is sick about having his picture all over, like a dictator. He transformed a small religious congregation into a big powerhouse where he is the central figure. And he married for that purpose.

The main thing they're doing is raising funds trying to make themselves richer and richer. They take *tzedakah* [funds for charity]; they're not known for giving tzedakah. They take tzedakah. They're very good in collecting money. The work they do is minimal compared to the amount of money they collect.   (JC)

Lubavitchers acknowledge that funds are collected for education and expansion of their services and that as a result they do not dispense much monetary charity.

In Satmar 80 percent of the people are business people. By us only 10 percent are business people. In my family of six brothers, four are working in Lubavitch education and two are in business. So only two are giving tzedakah and four are taking it. If you are teaching in a Chabad house you have to take tzedakah, not give it. By us only a few are in business; the rest have to collect.   (MS)

Some of Cohen's other criticisms express complaints heard about Lubavitch in other courts. The ubiquitous photographs and paintings of the

Rebbe that are in every Lubavitcher home and are for sale in shops on Kingston Avenue and elsewhere are irritants to many Hasidim in other courts, either appearing to them as promotional placards or jarring deeply based convictions against sculptured images and idol worship.[3]

> They put a picture of the [Lubavitcher] Rebbe up there at every bris. They put his picture behind the bed when the person is sick. They do as idol worshipers do. (JC)

A Record of Distortion

It is difficult to weigh Cohen's criticisms since he frequently overstates his case with a mix of fact and fantasy. He is eager to discover evil in every circumstance, and he is prepared to shift his point of view depending on whom he is trying to convince.[4] Discussing one of the Lubavitcher yeshivot, for example, he asserts that Oholei Torah in Crown Heights is "the only yeshivah in the country from kindergarten to twelfth grade that doesn't teach any English classes." He has to be reminded that his own yeshivah has the same policy and he very much supports it.

Speaking of the beard-cutting incident, he offers an unacceptable alternative explanation: "Mendel Schneerson [the Lubavitcher Rebbe] told Lubavitchers to cut his beard to prepare a blood libel just like the Christians used to do. They planted this whole affair. I have no other way to explain it."

Unfortunately for Cohen, his tactics undermine any legitimacy his arguments may have. Besides the outright distortions he insinuates unsubstantiated charges reminiscent of the "dirty tricks" of political campaigns. In one brief paragraph in his newsletter he suggests dark deeds done and others to be expected. At the same time he asserts that the Lubavitcher Rebbe and his staff are at serious odds: "To put it plainly, the Rebbe seems to fear that if he had a named successor, he would not survive too long . . . Now that his wife Rebbetzin Chaya Mushka, is dead and some details of her death have never been adequately explained, the Rebbe at 87 seems to feel even more pressed to stay in the public eye in order to avoid liquidation by his own 'friends.'"[5] In short, Cohen wants it both ways: the Rebbe's followers consider him to be the Messiah; the Rebbe's followers want to assassinate him.

In recent years Cohen's major goal appears to have been to attack the Lubavitcher Rebbe for alleged violations of the laws of modesty. Cohen purports that the Rebbe has broken the code that keeps the sexes apart. To prove his argument he displays a handful of color photographs which show the Rebbe handing out dollar bills (or manilla envelopes with promotional and educational material) to women who pass in long lines before him. The photos were taken by Lubavitcher Hasidim, are considered by them to be totally innocuous, and are readily available in Crown Heights and other locales for purchase as mementos of the Rebbe. They are part of the growing memorabilia of the people paying homage to the Rebbe. Cohen, however, has carefully selected photographs in which the eyes of the elderly Rebbe appear to meet the eyes of the women who pause to greet him and accept a dollar bill given to encourage charity.

Cohen acknowledges that he himself speaks with women face to face and meets their eyes, but he holds the Rebbe to a higher standard.

> That's what Hasidism is all about. More piety. He is breaking a law, Hasidic law and even Orthodox law. Does it have to say it in the 613 mitzvot? In Hasidic life it is always known that men and women don't interact. He modernized, he secularized the Lubavitcher community.
>
> Lubavitch has a very modern lifestyle. In talking about Hasidic lifestyle let's make it straight. The division between the sexes is very strictly observed in the Hasidic community—except in Lubavitch. In what way? Lubavitchers do get together, men and women, in one room. The Rebbe does it. He spends hours looking at women. The Rebbe gives hands with ladies, he talks with ladies.[6] Basically they're separate here but go out in the States you'll find them mixing. Even here. Nice fundraising affairs—mixed seating. Not only outsiders, even Lubavitchers. They give him their hand and look into his face. That's not Hasidic rules. And that's a mixed gathering inside 770. That would never happen in any other Hasidic place.
>
> Elsewhere they wouldn't put something in his hand. They couldn't even get close to the Satmar Rebbe. At the end of the room they can come. With the Vizhnitzer Rebbe there's no such thing as letting a lady come in to his room. There's no such thing as coming into his room. And any other Rebbe. This is real modernism and in Hasidic terms it's called a sex maniac. To look for hours on ladies it's called pure sex maniac. Under no circumstances has this ever happened in a Hasidic place that a Rebbe should hand something out to a lady. It's a plain manila envelope with something in it. I have pictures where he touches them on the hands but I don't have them right now. I gave them away. Hasidic doctrine is no looking, no giving over hands, no standing in one room. He's a plain modern rotten person in concerns of Hasidic lifestyle. This thing that you see doesn't happen even in a modern religious circle. To stand hours and gaze at women. That's his personality. (JC)

Lubavitcher Hasidim find such charges against their elderly leader to be ridiculous.

> Imagine! In front of ten thousand people. It's so stupid. (MS)

The Lubavitchers contend that the Rebbe gives women a blessing and provides them with dollar bills for charity, but he never offers them his hand. To point out how misunderstanding grows when one looks for something evil, Lubavitchers relate the tale of a student of the Vilna Gaon (the early opponent of Hasidism in the eighteenth century):

The student reported to his teacher that he saw a Hasid dancing with a girl on Tish be-Av [the day commemorating the destruction of the Temple]. It was a double sin: first, dancing with a girl, and second, celebrating on a day of mourning, the day the Temple was destroyed. The Vilna Gaon later found out the truth from witnesses: A wife had given birth to a daughter on Tish be-Av which happened to fall on Shabbes. This meant that the fast was held on Sunday instead of Shabbes. The man was cradling his newborn daughter and dancing. So while the facts in the story were true the report was false. (AR)

Despite such explanations, a Satmar leader more temperate than Cohen observes:

Lubavitch has a different way which Hasidim cannot conceive. There is no-where in the world a Hasidic Rebbe should talk to a woman or should hand dollar bills to a woman. He ceases to be a Rebbe when he does that. (RH)

Cohen has taken his picture show on the road to Hasidic centers in Israel, London, and Montreal. He says he had his greatest success speaking to Rabbi Eliezer Schach of Bnei Brak in Israel, the ultra-right-wing leader of the non-Hasidic Orthodox Jews. In Israel, Cohen can use the Lubavitcher Rebbe's good standing with the government as a second line of attack.[7]

When I met with Reb Schach and told him all about Lubavitch I felt I've done the right thing. He made a split with the Orthodox Jewish community against Lubavitch. I spoke to many of his *talmidim* [students] and tried to educate them. He doesn't have to hang effigies to get his point across. He has hundreds, thousands, of followers who run the yeshivot. Schach was already convinced, but certain things pressed him to go out in the public. He sent out a letter against Lubavitch. He met with me and I had to prove it to him with some pictures. His opinion was somewhat close to mine but he needed some hard evidence. He also brought up some people to testify what they saw about Lubavitch. He's the rosh yeshivah of the biggest yeshivah in Israel. He has carried out a holy war against Lubavitch. He has excommun-icated them. (JC)

Cohen paints his portrait of the Lubavitcher Rebbe in crude brush strokes and raw colors. On his palette he mixes politics, family matters, rumor, gossip, and innuendo. A special target is the Rebbe's wife, now deceased.[8]

Reb Schach was the turning point for a lot of people against Lubavitch. I contributed to that quite a lot by showing pictures and evidence and testi-mony by a few people who know that the Lubavitcher rebbetsn never cov-ered her hair. In Talmud it says whoever permits his wife to go uncovered is considered an evil person. He knew his wife wasn't religious. I told Rabbi Schach that she wasn't observant, that they have a television in his house. There's such a thing as desecrating the Shabbes in public and in private. I wouldn't say she did things in public because she tried to protect her husband, but she didn't observe the Shabbes. She would put on the lights on Shabbes. I have people who knew her and were close associates that testified. She wasn't religious whatsoever. That was my biggest achievement.[9]

I also told about his lifestyle, that he had mingled with girls [before his marriage]. I had some evidence on that, that he had girlfriends. It was a very un-Jewish lifestyle before he became Rebbe. I'm not attacking him. I'm just telling the truth. He's trying to polish himself as the most righteous person in the world and I'm just telling that it's not so. He wasn't righteous then and he isn't righteous now. He's just trying to cash in on an idea and to make a franchise about this certain Hasidic congregation. He franchises out Jewish projects like McDonald franchised the burgers.   (JC)

The Trial

A year after the assault on Rabbi Korf, the case against Jacob Cohen was heard at the Criminal Court Building, 120 Schermerhorn Street, in Brooklyn. The sixth floor, where Judge Sam Lebowitz once tyrannized lawyers and defendants with harsh sermons and tough sentences, now had an exuberant mood. The courtroom and the corridor were packed with yeshivah students from both sides who were brought to the courthouse to lend moral support and to provide any influence their numbers might merit. Satmar was on the defensive in the courtroom but not in the corridors. Excitement was high and Satmar's youthful adherents appeared to relish the reprieve from yeshivah study for the day. The Lubavitchers tried to make up for their slighter numbers by encouraging the district attorney to put on tefillin. The case had earned some notoriety, and lawyers in the building when not on call often attended the proceedings, in part puzzled by the violence practiced by members of a religious group.[10]

Cohen had been identified by Korf from a series of police photos. Korf's student David Kohn, however, looking uncomfortable, would not cite Cohen as one of the assailants. Disappointed observers theorized that Kohn was under pressure from his family and the community to protect Cohen; others speculated that the young man had been assured that lying in a secular court was of no significance compared to the damage his testimony would do to the religious community. When it comes to saving one's community, it can be argued that all manner of sins are forgiven. Cohen's defense was strengthened by the testimony of his wife, mother, and father that he had been at home.

Rabbi Korf's positive identification was critical to the case, but the philosophical rabbi proved to be an ineffectual witness in court. His air of uncertainty was not completely unexpected of a man who is positive only of the existence of God.

Rabbi Korf is the type of person who if at three o'clock in the afternoon you ask him if it's day or night, he would say I first have to go outside and look; and it being a little cloudy outside, and not seeing the sun, he cannot be sure that it's day, and not seeing the moon he can't say that it's night.   (IS)

Jacob Cohen was also frustrated by the trial. Although he knew that he had a skillful advocate in his attorney, Edward Rappaport, he complained that the lawyer would pay attention only to the business at hand. "He would not let me get my message across. He wanted strictly the case."

Nor would Cohen accept the underlying seriousness of the charge. He turned it into a new attack on the Lubavitcher Rebbe. As in other types of criminal defense, the victim was saddled with cause and effect.

Cutting the beard was just to degrade him. It's against the law but not in the case of a Lubavitch. The Lubavitcher Rebbe cut his beard before he became Rebbe. Pinchas Korf can still become Rebbe.   (JC)

As an ancillary tactic, Cohen argues that Lubavitch committed a still graver sin by bringing a Jewish problem to a secular court for remedy. In rebuttal the Lubavitchers point out that the Shulhan Arukh (Code of Jewish Law) allows a case to proceed to a secular court if the litigants will not abide by the bet din, the religious court. In point of fact the Shulhan Arukh provides evidence for both sides of the argument. It forbids cases to be tried "before heathen judges" *except* where the litigant refuses to appear in the Jewish court thereby preventing the claimant from obtaining relief.[11]

Without a positive identification, the charges against Cohen were dismissed by the jury. Little remained that was certain. The injustice done to Pinchas Korf is in limbo. Despite his acquittal, Jacob Cohen remains uneasy and carefully screens visitors to his apartment in Williamsburg.

Aftermath

The ban against food products bearing the Satmar rabbinic label proved to be as inconclusive as the trial. There was a good deal of publicity but little was changed.

Lubavitch at that time thought that the whole Jewish community would be up in arms against Satmar because Satmar is hated in the Zionist world. Not too many people like Satmar. But to their amazement they found out that not too many people like Lubavitch either. The general Jewish community has an attitude, you know, wish them both luck. They were disinterested. Nobody participated in the boycott against Satmar. The boycott is still our problem, but nobody cares. Big deal. It's true, they won't use any Satmar products. But there's no Satmar food company that went bankrupt because of that.   (AF)

In Satmar the general feeling of antagonism remained. As Satmar spokesmen revealed, some Satmar Hasidim regard the Lubavitchers with the fear that many middle-class Americans have for the Hare Krishnas or followers of Rev. Moon: those sects threaten to divorce children from their families and from their native community. On another level, the disputes have the nature of a town rivalry. Ideology aside, it is a contest between two disputants who somehow need each other in order to sharpen their own positions:

> I met that summer Rabbi Bernard Levi. He was in Los Angeles. He has an okay kashrut organization. He's a Lubavitcher. He tells me, "Friedman, this time Satmar's going to lose. You'll lose badly."
> "What do you mean, lose badly?"
> "Hundreds of young people will desert Satmar and become Lubavitchers."
> So I asked him, "Rabbi Levi, you're an intelligent person. What do you mean desert Satmar. Who's going to go away from Satmar? People who are not satisfied with Satmar, let them go. *Gesundheit* [Be well]. They're just going to cause problems if they stay with Satmar. Let them go. If they're troublemakers let them go and make trouble by you." (AFF)

The Aftermath of the Mendel Wechter Case

The tumult between the two courts eventually quieted down. While they are not completely at peace with each other, they are far from war. In midtown Manhattan, Lubavitch and Satmar Hasidim still work together in the same shops, although back in Brooklyn no one is arranging any weddings between their young people. Many Hasidim are less committed to extreme positions and would welcome a period of peace between the courts.[12]

For Mendel Wechter himself the conflict has brought permanent scars. His assailants were never formally identified and brought to trial. Fearful of what might befall him and his family, Mendel Wechter moved to a Lubavitcher community in Israel. Today his name is rarely mentioned in Williamsburg. The question of whether or not violence against him was justified is not considered at all. In Satmar circles Mendel Wechter bears the blame for what was done to him.

> Mendel Wechter was one of the really celebrated students in our system and then he went wrong. What did him in was his ego. He wasn't getting his due here and he saw that he would never be among the leadership. (MR)

Years after leaving Satmar for Lubavitch, one of Mendel Wechter's former students had a different view.

> It changed my perspective on life. I have a totally different conception of my way of life. It's not an individual issue. It's a question of reaching out. Other

groups of Hasidim are afraid to mingle with others. You might sin. They have a valid argument. Lubavitch says we're not scared by those contacts. We think of the Jewish nation as a whole. It's not what I'm going to gain personally. It's not that I'm going to gain *Gan Eden* [Paradise]. All right it's difficult to reach some Jews so we have to go to them. We're a historical people. We're not a sect. It's not this group or that group. We're the Jewish people. (SV)

The wives as well as the husbands found the change from Satmar to Lubavitch to be liberating.

In Satmar they don't believe a woman has to learn. There it's basically what they learn in school and then they're finished. Then it's into baking and cooking without learning. In Lubavitch a woman should know about godly things. In Lubavitch they believe that a person should learn more, that a person's mind should constantly be aware of HaShem's presence. (LV)

In time the students who followed Rabbi Mendel Wechter from Satmar to Lubavitch established new ties to Lubavitch families and worked out their relationships with their own families. Some of the young men became emissaries of the Lubavitcher Rebbe and are directors of Chabad houses. A few established marital ties in the Lubavitch community. Some carried their old customs into Lubavitch: two of the boys from the Pupa Hasidim who attended the Lubavitch yeshivah and married into Lubavitch families continue to wear shtraymlen on the Shabbes and holidays.[13] At those times their fur hats appear in the crowd of black fedoras like exotic migratory birds that have strayed from their familiar route and are nesting in a strange land.

· 16 ·

Family Problems

New Families

Of course there are unhappy as well as happy Hasidic families. While the *shidukh* (arranged marriage) is the accepted way of uniting the sexes in marriage, not even the most experienced matchmaker can foresee all the difficulties that marriage may bring. Little thought is given to the innocence arising from the lifelong separation of the sexes, the scant time that the couple know each other before marriage, and their limited sexual knowledge and understanding. Nor is it often considered that an ostensible strength—the close familial, religious, and communal ties—can also create intrafamily conflicts.

From the outset, a new marriage is tightly integrated into the larger family unit. In the first years of marriage the young Hasidic couple are heavily dependent on social and economic support from the extended family. Every Shabbes will likely find the newlyweds eating dinner with one set of parents or the other, and this may be repeated often during the week as well. It sometimes appears that marriage is but a half-step away from one's family and still a half-step distant from an independent life. The young couple have to cope with the intensity of Jewish family relations at the same time as they are establishing their own household and exploring a new relationship. They are often no match for a persistent mother or father at his or her accustomed station in the kitchen or the dining room, and they frequently find themselves at odds with their families, or with their spouses, over questions of custom, conduct, and privacy. Ruben, a husband in his late twenties, complains:

> One of the basic disputes between me and my in-laws was that I give too much freedom to my wife. Basically [they said] a husband has to be strict in the house. You have to have control of where she goes and where she comes from, what she wears and what she doesn't wear. I told them at the beginning, "You told me to check her stockings, but I'm not familiar with women's stockings, and I don't know how to check it."[1] That was the basic dis-

pute because my mother-in-law told me, "You see, a husband has to be strict in the house. You have to be tough." So I told her, "If you want, you should be the boss in my house and use me as the broom. If you want me to be boss in the house then I'll be boss my way." But the basic dispute was that they felt that I give too much liberty, and that's not religious.   (RB)

The view of his wife, Esther, is even more emphatic.

They have these chauvinistic opinions. My husband should be the ruler of the house. He should be king. What he says you should do. "Your husband should know where you are at all times, all day and all night." But at the same time, your husband shouldn't go out with you anywhere because it's not Jewish to go to the movies or go out to eat.   (EB)

Esther has to cope with the intensity of Jewish family relations as a powerful negative force.

I tell my father, "I'm twenty-eight. Tell me how much longer you're going to tell me what to do. Until I'm thirty? Then I know I have two more years to go. Until I'm thirty-five? Then I have seven more years to go." But he'll tell me what to do forever.   (EB)

Much of the blame for family tension falls on Esther's father, who persists in intruding into his daughter's household. For the time being his attention is focused on her hair covering. He insists first that she wear a kerchief rather than a wig; failing to convince his daughter of that, he next demands that if she wears a wig she also wear a hat. This added touch would be an absolute assurance of ultra-Orthodoxy and would still the murmur of neighbors' tongues. In his eyes anything less would be sacrilegious and an affront to the respect he merits. For her part, Esther despises the wig; and now, freed from her parents' home, she wages war with the parent who insists that she wear it. Since she is married, her father cannot threaten her with punishment. Instead, he warns her that in not wearing a hat over her wig she risks placing her loved ones in jeopardy (through supernatural punishment).[2] His tactics infuriate Esther and fan the flames of her rebellion.

The only thing he ever talks about is why you wear your own hair. It's such a sin, everything that's happening to you, you should know that it's coming from your hair. And do you know what a responsibility that is? That if anything happens to your kid, or if anything happens to your husband, or if anything happens to your household, you should know it's coming because of the sin of your not cutting your hair? Do I want to hear this? I cover it, which I hate to do. I'm doing that and he tells me, well, in the next world, da, da, da, da, you're going to get rewards. I'm not going to get rewarded. Are you kidding me? I'm taking off the wig right now. Are you kidding? I expect so much reward, you have no idea. I'm miserable wearing it. I'm doing it because I'm married to my husband and he's a religious guy.   (EB)

Ruben, her husband, is made uncomfortable by the conflict, but he respects her wishes, and he wants peace in the house. He spurns his father-in-law's wishes and supports his wife's point of view.

> Wearing a wig without covering it was a big revolution in his opinion. But I saw at that time that I had to live with her. So I had to adjust. The wig didn't bother me but the fighting did. The real *frum* [pious] way is just a kerchief covering the head completely without any form at all. The old rebbetsn wore only a black kerchief, nothing else—no form, no hair, no nothing. Most women wear wigs, and some cover the wigs with a kerchief or a hat. There's a higher level in religion that they cover their wig with a hat. If it were left open some people might think it's real hair.   (RB)

The issue continues to aggravate Esther, not only because she finds the wig burdensome and the hat foolish, but also because her wishes run counter to a still more important law she must obey—"Honor your father and your mother." When Esther steps outside her door she wears both wig and hat and stifles her smoldering resentment.

Other Irritants

It seems inevitable that Hasidic laws, mores, and customs, like form-fitting but imperfectly tailored garments, would sometimes chafe and irritate some of those forced to wear them. Sylvia, a young wife with two young children, is rebellious and at odds with her parents and with the customs of her community. She can be considered an atypical Hasidic housewife whose problems reflect her own specific unhappiness and the particular circumstances of her family background. To some degree, however, her complaints reveal the scope and depth of reactions to community and familial demands that only infrequently find direct and open expression.

Sylvia lives in a cramped four-room apartment in Borough Park with her husband and two children. Hers is a far smaller family than those of most of her neighbors. Because of her distaste for household chores, Sylvia cooks as little as possible. The family therefore usually forgoes the common fare of a well-nourished Borough Park household (chicken soup, fish stew, potato pancakes, noodles and cheese), and at mealtimes they nibble on prepared foods, packaged and pickled snacks, and potato chips. Sylvia despises too the ritual of attending the mikvah, the ritual bath, as unsanitary, and she considers the search for stains and spotting from menstrual blood as demeaning and senseless. Attentive toward her children's education, she is dissatisfied with the yeshivah curriculum; she is particularly concerned about improving their English, which suffers from total immersion in Yiddish and Hebrew in the early school years.

Her husband, Israel, is concerned about the children's future training.

He is frustrated that after so many years of intense yeshivah learning he finds himself ill prepared to cope with the vocational demands of the everyday world.

> Some schools have more education in secular life and some have less. A lot of schools at least give the students a high school diploma, so you can go out and qualify for any decent job and make a couple of hundred dollars a week.
>
> Basically, when you don't get what you need in order to keep up your family, you can't really work on your religion. To be religious you're required to make money. I mean you have to have money to send your kids to school, a religious school. You have to have money to buy all these religious articles, and if you don't have the money you get depressed and you rebel against everything.
>
> You have to wake up. If you tell a student, just by sitting and learning you'll be able to be a good Jew, and you don't tell him the real truth, how will he be able to succeed in life and at least be able to support the minimum-sized family? You're cheating him and he won't be successful, not in regular life and not in religious life.   (IP)

Israel daydreams of life at a yeshivah with a farming kibbutz nearby, as was once envisioned for a site in upstate New York.

> Rabbi Weisbaum opened a yeshivah near Mount Kisco and he wanted to make a farm next to the yeshivah. He wanted to create a town. All the students can buy an apartment or rent an apartment and there will be a farm and they can work a couple of hours a day if they want, and there will be some food growing there and milk from the cows and so on. And for the extras maybe they will get some support from others. Somehow it didn't work out because he passed away. He was a sick man, you know.   (IP)

Despite their disagreements and her own deep dissatisfaction, Sylvia is fond of her husband and hopes that her restlessness will not hurt him.

> He didn't know what I was like. It was an arranged marriage. We spoke to each other three times. We talked about general stuff—politics, a little bit about my schooling. Nothing really personal because we hardly got to know each other. He was the best one I met. He was the second one. My father was pushing. It's true that I wanted to get married. Every person should get married. I don't think I'm the kind of person who should get married. I can't cater to my husband. He's not happy.   (SP)

She is also aware of his failings, and, from her friends, of the similarities he bears to other young Hasidic husbands.

> It's sort of hard, when they get married at twenty-one, to start to teach them what to do. They have no experience. Not that I had any experience. When do you think they find out before they do anything? I'm not kidding you. Everybody's about the same pretty much. They want more from their husbands. Sexually! Not just affection, but good love, good sex.   (SP)

Unhappy examples of those who follow community and familial norms are everywhere she turns.

Look at my next door neighbor. You saw that little kid that was here? She has five kids. She does not walk out of the house sometimes even for months. She just had a baby, her fifth one. The baby cannot be more than two months old. She lives in a three-room apartment. Her kids are wild. She doesn't have room to put stuff. She's moving out to Flatbush but she can't move into her apartment yet. She doesn't go out of the house very often and she's becoming miserable. She was telling me she was having a hard time and she started to cry because she wasn't out of the house for four months because she had nothing to wear. Because she's so fat. She's always pregnant. And even if she's not pregnant she has only a stretch of two months or three months free, right? (SP)

Sylvia recognizes that her views run counter to general norms.

There are women who stay at home and cook all day and then the husband comes home and they serve him. They're happy with what they're doing. I talked to some people that I know and they do it every single day, and they are busy with just that and they never have time for themselves. I find it unbelievable. And they're happy. They are genuinely happy. My husband he thinks that I'm different. I'm never going to deny that. I'm not the typical Borough Park and Williamsburg wife and mother. I'm not. And I told him not to expect it, because I'm not that type of person. I'm not. I could never, and I mean never, ever, ever sit home and have five kids, cook and bake and mend and wash laundry all day, and then my husband comes home at six or seven o'clock from a day's work and smile at him and serve him a beautiful three- or four-course meal and still smile. I'd throw the food in his face. I'd be miserable. To sit down with a smile and listen to what he did all day and be encouraging and you know be so loving? What about me? What did I do all day? I'd feel like a slave. There is nothing to talk about my day. What did I do? Mend, wash laundry, clean the house, diaper three kids, cook. Forget it. I could never do that even though my friends all do it. (SP)

The Outside World

For Sylvia, marriage was an important step toward greater personal freedom. For the first time she was able to determine her own behavior.

I came here from Y. There my parents wouldn't let me out of the house. Everything was suppressed. Then I came here to be married and I was free. I didn't know about such a place as SoHo or the Village or the museums. I was like Columbus discovering America.

I never realized how much I would appreciate the art that I saw. When I went to SoHo and checked out galleries and I took books out of the library, a whole new world opened up. I learned something about myself. I love art and I had never seen myself as somebody like that. All of a sudden I was staring at art works and seeing things into them. I started to listen to the radio. I was nineteen or twenty and it was the first time I had a radio. I started flipping stations. (Television didn't come around for a long time.) I would listen to music, and I would listen to the country music station and that's where I first heard Kenny Rogers, Barbra Streisand, and Crystal Gale. I started buying tapes. And then all of a sudden John Lennon was killed, in 1981. And they had this big thing on the radio and I didn't know who he was. They had tributes to him and I heard Beatles music for the first time, and I started buying their albums.

It was this process that led me to at least read more and want to know more, and I realized I had to go back to school and do something with my life. (SP)

Few Hasidim believe the internal tensions of Hasidic family life to be the cause of problems. Instead they see the danger to the family as emanating from outside the community. The righteous believers have always been fearful that the environment of the New World would undermine the traditional belief structure through secular education, social interaction with nonbelievers, and myriad distractions and temptations. The threats are both intellectual and material. There are so many fronts on which to mount a watch that each day provides a minor skirmish in a protracted war.

In recent times, an increasing number of Hasidic women have found employment outside the community as secretaries, teachers, or clerks and in a variety of jobs in the fashion industry. Many more Hasidic women have jobs today than ever before, at least until the birth of their first baby. Some acquire a taste for having a life outside of the home and continue to work on a part-time basis after their family has increased in size. Ruth has a part-time job in Manhattan, much to the dismay of her older sister, who believes a Jewish mother should be home with her kids. Ruth herself has mixed feelings about leaving her family on their own for the day.

I work in Manhattan three days a week. It's a part-time job. I like to go out, but I feel guilty because of the kids. I have four children, two boys and two girls. I don't like to sit at home and do housework. I enjoy working. All the girls leave school in the eleventh grade. People don't want them to be out working in offices. When I was a girl my father wouldn't let me be a salesgirl. It's true you get to know more people. You talk more to men, you go out to a restaurant. Once in a while you see a movie. If I go I do it so not everybody should know. I'll go with Millie. My husband doesn't do it. (RM)

The contacts they establish allow the women to hear voices that are discordant from those in their own society.

Certain people I meet everyday. Well, let me tell you about one of them. I am with her almost every day. We usually talk about work, and then in general she talks about her boyfriend, or she tells me about her brother, her family, her parents. I explained to her some of my religion, what I may and may not do, and she finds it not at all fascinating. She finds it stupid. She really does. She finds no sense in it. Absolutely none.

I'm not the kind of person that gets affected by what somebody else tells me, because all these ideas and all these things which I want to change in myself or something I don't agree with, all this was known before. It was going on before. It's not something new. When I discuss it I get feedback. It's like a sounding board. You're telling somebody something and the person is expressing their view. You find yourself agreeing and then you say that was my view before too. I'm not the only one thinking that way. It's others too. But she's not Jewish so it's not the same.

There is someone here living across from my apartment and she's Jewish, but whatever she likes in the Jewish tradition she does, and whatever she doesn't like she doesn't do. Like she lights candles, but she rides on the Sabbath. She turns on the TV or takes a bath. Because you can't turn on the hot water [on the Sabbath]. Once you turn on the hot water, you have to use the system of heating. So you take the bath Friday afternoon, and then you can take one Saturday night.   (EM)

Within the neighborhoods the community has greater control over the influences of the outside world.

In Williamsburg women generally do not read magazines and go to movies. There's not even a shop that sells an English-language magazine or newspaper. In Borough Park there's a newsstand on every corner. There's a local Hebrew magazine, Jewish newspapers. You're not suppose to read books or magazines that are not written by a Jewish person.   (RM)

Even in Williamsburg, however, not everyone is in accord with the various forms of censorship that exist, and ways are found around them.

On Wednesdays when the *Algemeine Zeitung* [the Yiddish newspaper with ties to Lubavitch] comes out people go down to Broadway to buy it. Everybody ducks out of their car and then ducks back in.   (RM)

Although television is forbidden in many families, it nonetheless manages to surface in community life in one way or another. One evening in the G. family apartment, the eldest son, Yankel, slips off to a neighbor's flat to watch television. His mother is glad to have him entertained, and his father has just hurried away. The cause of his father's hasty departure, however, is his desire to watch President Reagan's press conference on television. In the past the father kept a small TV in the bedroom, and he and his wife would watch it late at night and then push the set under the bed so that it wouldn't be discovered. In a short time, however, Yankel found the TV. He spent so much time watching it that his parents got rid of it. This evening, hopeful that he has maintained the correct religious posture for his son, Yankel's father has rushed off to his brother's house in Borough Park. His brother does not have a TV set either, but the two of them are going down the street to a friend who keeps a set hidden in his house. The friend worries that his mother-in-law will discover it during one of her frequent visits. Meanwhile, with her husband and son both out of the house, Yankel's mother takes out the miniature TV that she has hidden in an empty space in her bureau. The location is covered with a false front so that neither her husband nor her son knows about it. She usually takes it out to watch only when the children are at school and her husband is at work.

In these explorations into the secular world, community mores and standards are stretched and sometimes broken; however, these lapses do not appear to call into question religious faith and acceptance of the Hasidic worldview. Despite Sylvia's rebellious attitudes, for example, she accepts the belief that God dictated the Torah to Moses and that the mythic tales of creation are an exact account of the beginnings of the world.

> Man was created in one day, the sixth day. Evolution? No, never. I don't believe that, ever. It doesn't make sense and I don't believe it. (SP)[3]

Intellectual rejection of Hasidic beliefs represents another dimension of thought still rare in Williamsburg, even among the community's few disenchanted. The most troubling matters focus on practical concerns rather than on spiritual or supernatural concerns.

> One friend of mine uses birth control. She told me this and I was shocked. I mean she's very religious. She wears black stockings. She doesn't wear a wig; she wears only a kerchief. And she has four kids. But she has permission. She gets very dehydrated when she's pregnant. She sits in the hospital for three or four months. I practice birth control. What do you think, this is a miracle? My husband doesn't like that either. He knows about it. I would never do anything behind his back. He knows about it, and every time we have a fight guess what gets thrown at me, right? I don't need anybody's permission. I don't ask. I don't want to get no for an answer. I don't want to. Let me put it this way, I don't care. He doesn't like it. He's not too crazy about having more kids, but he wants to do the right thing. (SP)

Since women's tenure at work is usually short, often lasting only until the birth of the first child, contact with the outside environment is limited. Thereafter, the women's view of the world scene is gleaned for the most part from magazines and, at times, from television.

> The women don't work too many months, and after a kid or two that's it. So what if you read a magazine? What of it? You look at the patterns. Big deal. Or you go shopping and look at the styles.
>
> My friend Yetta has a library card. Her husband knows. But she wears a kerchief and people would talk. Here in Williamsburg it's not accepted to go

to the library, and so I'll get it for her—romances, mysteries, novels by Sidney Sheldon. In Borough Park everybody has what they want.   (EM)

Hasidic men and women have contact with the outside world to markedly different degrees. Hasidic men have more freedom, and, because of their employment, move beyond the community's borders on a daily basis. They appear more likely to feel the pressures of the outside world and to respond to change. A few may succumb to the worst temptations offered by the outside world.

Satmar dress does not change the interior of the person. I'm sure there are Satmar people going to prostitutes dressed as anybody else—I'm sure of that. I just hope and pray that they do it in private and they're not caught because it would cast a shadow on the whole community and they would be thrown out of the community. The people wouldn't talk to them anymore. They would be ostracized, you know, "How dare you do such a thing!" There wouldn't have to be anything official. People would be ashamed just to talk to them—because it would be guilt by association, you're friends with the guy. There are some people who go to Atlantic City. Yes there are some Hasidim who have got the gambling bug, and I wouldn't talk to them. I would be ashamed to talk to such a person—even though I never caught them, just the rumor that they go to Atlantic City. They're not comfortable. In other words, they know they would be hard pressed to find whom to socialize with. They would probably have another couple of bums who would be their friends.

There are some people who deviate from the Satmar way of life and there will be people talking to them trying to put them straight again. If they are still at the stage where they can be saved then they will not be publicized. But if they are bums then people just don't. They're outcasts—finished. We would not physically throw them out of the community. We would not excommunicate them, but they are out. In other words they are not Satmar. Even though they may still put on their shtrayml, but they're not Satmar. People will not look at them as Satmar. Only the outsiders will look at them as Satmar.   (AFF)

Occasionally a Hasidic couple curious to explore the titillations of the outside world do so during vacation time on a trip to the Caribbean or through pay cable television in a motel. They sometimes encounter more than they can handle.

The first time I told my friend about oral sex, she has four kids, she flipped in and out, under and over. And she told me I'm out of my mind, that I flew off Mars. She said, "What are you talking about?" She didn't believe me, so I loaned her a book on it and she still was very skeptical. So then I told her to go to a motel and watch some of those dirty movies. I happen to have seen it once.   (AI)

The Hasidim are well aware that women today are more sophisticated than they were a generation ago and that a new balance has to be struck between couples. The range of responses corresponds to individual points of view as well as to general attitudes held by different courts. Some acknowledge that changes are taking place. A Boyaner Hasid observes: "Women are more liberated but at the same time no one talks about it." But others deny that the traditional roles are being reexamined by women.

> Woman's Lib? We didn't need it. They were never enslaved. Women know that they're going to have a family and children and they don't look for other jobs. (AFF)

An account related by a Lubavitcher Hasid, however, reveals that there are different attitudes advanced in each court. In Lubavitch the chief rabbi not only recognizes that change has taken place but subtly advances the wife's cause in a domestic dispute over sharing household tasks:

> A *baltshuve* [returnee to the faith] came to our rov, Rabbi Dworkin, with his wife, and they wanted a divorce. And the wife is complaining bitterly on her husband: "He doesn't help." He has four or five children and he doesn't help her. So the rabbi asks why. "He comes home, he watches television, and he doesn't help me."[4]
> So he asks the husband, "What's happening?"
> "Listen, I'm working all day. Then I have *shi'ur* [time of learning] for an hour, an hour and a half, I'm learning. Then I'm so tired I can't work. So I watch television. I can't help any more. I'm working for eight or nine hours, I'm learning for an hour and a half, and then I come home and I do watch television. I can't pick myself up."
> So what should the rabbi tell him? What is this television? What are you crazy? Help your wife.
> No. Instead, he told him: "Stop your *shi'ur* and help your wife. Stop your learning and help your wife."
> So you'll ask, did the rabbi do the right thing or not? The man was shocked. Stop learning? If he tells the man not to watch television after working for nine hours, he's not going to listen to him. But if the rabbi tells him it's so important to even stop learning, he feels that it's really important. He'll either stop watching television or he'll help. (MS)

Divorce

The strengths and weaknesses of the Hasidic marital system are difficult for non-Hasidic observers to appreciate, in part because the system is so different from Western models, and in part because there is scant comparative data. To judge primarily by appearances, Hasidic arranged marriages more rarely result in divorce and appear to be more durable than marriages in the nonreligious Jewish world and in the non-Jewish world. The extent of their domestic problems has become more evident only recently.[5]

Maintenance of the Orthodox faith sustains traditional ways and slows social change. Nonetheless, by Hasidic standards there has been a divorce explosion.[6] While it is easier for couples to separate today than in past times, divorce is still seen as a drastic option.[7]

A divorce sets a solemn boundary for the parties involved. One cannot marry in innocence twice, and divorced people are almost always bound to marry other divorcés.

> She's remarried and is very happy. He's divorced again. This time he married somebody very pious who had a kid from a previous marriage. Around here when you're divorced there's like a stigma attached to you. You're sort of an outcast. You're not considered part of everybody else. You're different. (TP)

One of the great dangers seen in divorce is that it poses a threat to the well-being of the children and to the status of the husband in determining the education of his children.

> I have a brother who is divorced after eleven years of marriage. He's in jail because he kidnapped his kids and shipped them off to Israel. Then they came back, and afterward he was put in jail. (BF)

A similar case demanded greater ingenuity.

> My brother-in-law who is separated from my sister snatched a child. It's very unusual in our community but . . . She has eight. He took the youngest. The boy was seven years old. It was a year ago. It was right before the High Holidays. There was a dispute and he went to the rabbinical court trying to get the children to come to him for the Holidays. The children refused because they have a tremendous dislike of him. He was very abusive. So he decided, with the advice of somebody or whatever, and he grabbed the youngest child out of school and he was hiding out here somewhere and I personally chased him. I didn't see him but I kept on following clues as to where he might be, following his trail, and I guess it was getting too hot. A cousin of his, actually a nephew of his, somehow got a passport for this kid. What he did is he took the birth certificate of another child and he made a new passport for this kid and they took off for Israel. I found out about it and I made contact there. I got in touch with some people there. And with the help of friends and what not I grabbed him back, put him on a plane and brought him back to my sister.
>
> I got the passport out of my brother-in-law's pocket. I was very lucky, thank God. He was staying by somebody and I found out who he was staying with and I used somebody who was actually in contact with him whom he trusted. He was staying in the same place, and for a sum of money—it was not done for free—he snuck the passport out of his pocket, and as soon

as he had the passport I had people grab the child, put him on an airplane and he came home. We got a court order after that so that he can't come close to the child anymore.   (AI)

Divorce also poses a threat to the marriage possibilities of other members of the family. Any suggestion of instability or conflict within the family may alarm a potential suitor.

When it was understood that she wants a divorce, her father-in-law came here to this house, and talked to her one time about it. And she said, yes, she had no intention of living with him. And they asked her only to wait because another brother of his was getting married. "So wait until after Hanukkah." This was summertime. She said fine and that was it. After the brother's wedding they got in touch with each other and they went for a divorce.   (BP)

What may appear remarkable to those outside Hasidic society is that couples in arranged marriages show no less empathy and loyalty than couples who have known each other for extended periods of time before marriage. Equally striking are examples of support when divorce seems to be the only alternative.

I had a personal experience with divorce. My younger daughter was divorced. A very tragic situation. It was two weeks after they were married that he had a nervous breakdown. He was not eighteen and she was not yet eighteen. And there was no advance warning at all. And my daughter still wanted to try to stay with him to see if he'd get better. We tried everything. It was a very slow and painful process. He was on medication for a long time, and then about close to a year later he had another breakdown. He had never really recovered from the first one. He had another incident while under a doctor's care. We changed doctors and medications and everything, and while he was still on medication, close to a year after that, he had the third breakdown. My daughter was already suffering. Had she been with him for a longer time after they married and before they had the baby and before he had the breakdown, she might have developed a better relationship with him. But her relationship with him was entirely based on after he became sick. So she never really developed any kind of meaningful relationship with him. And given the nature of his illness, they weren't able to function, because she was always afraid of antagonizing him. Anything that would be against his wishes or against his feelings, or anything at all, she was afraid would trigger a reaction. He was not violent, but he was very strong-willed and she suffered very much.
 I didn't want to interfere. During the whole time the only thing I ever told her was, "You've got where to come home to." After the first one I told her, "The choice is yours. I'm not going to tell you what to do. Whatever you want to do I will always support you, but you should know that you have a home to come home to. You should never feel lost or stranded. You can always come home." After the third she called me up and she told me, "Save me, help me." I took her home. And we got her a divorce.   (ET)

No matter how badly the marriage turns out, it is not usually acknowledged that it would have been wiser for the couple to spend more time together before deciding on marriage.

Let us take any situation between a boy and girl. When they go out, or when they meet, when they sit and talk, what personality does a person put forward when they meet with an intended or a proposed? You always put forward your best character, and a misleading character at that. No one is going to present the kind of character that wakes up at six o'clock in the morning after having been up half the night with the baby, rocking the baby to sleep. I mean that's not the character that you meet. If you go out for a year's time, you still wouldn't see that person.   (ET)

· 17 ·

Before the Supreme Court

Reapportionment

Hasidim feel on more familiar ground in the courtroom than do most recent immigrants. Study of the law has always been part of the Jewish ethos; and Orthodox Jews have customarily resolved differences among themselves using their own legal system. As a result the Hasidim have welcomed the opportunity to litigate as free citizens in secular courts on matters ranging from voting rights to the separation of church and state. Two cases, one brought by Satmar and the other by Lubavitch, reached the highest court in the land.[1]

In the mid-1960s social change taking place throughout the country drew the Hasidim into the turbulence of local politics. Greater community participation was encouraged by the passage of antipoverty legislation, the civil rights movement, and the development of local boards to administer funds provided by government programs. By the end of the decade the Hasidim were recognized as a small but potent voting bloc.

In Williamsburg the Satmar Hasidim relished their participation in the democratic system, but in elections they were content to limit their activities to supporting candidates from outside the community who would best represent their point of view. If the community received word that the Rebbe urged the election of one candidate or another then its complete support was assured.

> Lubavitch runs their own candidate in the district they're in. It's a different policy. We at Satmar feel it's better not to antagonize. We're more comfortable having a non-Jew work for us than having a Jew work for non-Jews. If the non-Jewish guy, or the non-religious guy who is in office, if he's responsive to our needs, fine, he'll get our support continuously. (AF)

In Williamsburg the Hasidic leadership was satisfied that Congressman John Rooney was sensitive to Hasidic concerns. In his position as chairman of the House Subcommittee on Appropriations for the Departments of State, Justice, and Commerce, he helped bring relatives and fellow townsmen of the Hasidim into the country. His conservative views also mirrored Hasidic perspectives: he was opposed to abortion, he was anti-communist and supported the Vietnam war, and he was in favor of increased aid to religious schools. The ties that Rooney, a Catholic, had established with the Hasidic leadership encouraged them to support him even when the opposing candidate was Jewish.[2]

In 1972 Allard K. Lowenstein, one of the principal figures in the "dump Johnson" movement of four years earlier, faced off against Congressman Rooney.[3] Lowenstein's activist political goals, his anti–Vietnam war position, and his charismatic style appealed more to Puerto Rican voters in Williamsburg than to the Hasidim. Lowenstein lost by a slight margin in the June primary, but evidence of voters being turned away at the polls made the primary results so suspect that a new primary election was ordered to be held in September 1972.

Rooney faced two opponents, Lowenstein and Irving Gross of the 14th District. (Gross had earned a token place in the runoff election by garnering 1,817 out of the 29,652 votes cast in the June election.) Both Lowenstein and Gross were Jewish. Rooney, however, had the support of the Hasidic leadership. The day before the special primary was Yom Kippur, and the four thousand worshipers in the Satmar besmedresh were advised by the beadle to vote for John Rooney. Lowenstein lost the election by 2,000 votes, a greater margin than before, and the difference could be measured in the Hasidic community: Rooney, 2,384; Lowenstein, 480; Gross, 48.[4]

Encouraged by their success at the polls, the Satmar made plans for greater participation in state and city contests. Although they were relatively few in number compared to other ethnic groups such as the Latinos and blacks, they derived much of their political strength from their unity and by virtue of being located in one Assembly district.[5] The Hasidim launched a full-scale voter registration drive in preparation for the 1974 elections. In May of that year, however, Hasidic hopes for political influence suffered when the New York State Legislature reapportioned State Senate and Assembly districts in Kings, New York, and Bronx Counties.

The redrawing of the legislative map was the result of a court decision that held New York's 1972 apportionment in violation of the Civil Rights Act of 1964. In Kings County the districts affected included Bedford-Stuyvesant, the largest black ghetto in Brooklyn, and the adjoining neighborhood of Williamsburg, with some thirty-five thousand Hasidic Jews. Complaints had been made that the perimeter of Bedford-Stuyvesant had been broken up into small sections to fit into majority white districts, thereby blunting nonwhite voting strength. As a remedy, the Department of Justice stipulated that new districts be created with 65 percent nonwhite majorities in order to ensure the election of nonwhite State Senators and Assemblymen. To meet this requirement, rather than curtail the power of other contiguous white districts the Joint Legislative Committee split the Hasidic population between two districts, 20,000 in one and 15,000 in the other. They were divided between Assembly districts 56 and 57 (with nonwhite populations of 88.1 percent and 65.0 percent) and into two Senate districts (the 23rd and 25th) with nonwhite percentages of 71.1 percent and 34.7 percent. The Hasidic community would remain in a single congressional district, but their local strength was shattered.

The Hasidim protested the division of their community, and they brought the case to federal court, contending that the arbitrary change diluted their voting strength and deprived them of their rights under the Fourteenth and Fifteenth Amendments. In his argument in federal court, Nathan Lewin, counsel for the United Jewish Organizations of Williamsburg, raised two constitutional issues: first, whether under the Fourteenth and Fifteenth Amendments state officials could be directed by the federal government to establish nonwhite majorities of 65 percent where there was no past discrimination; and, second, whether racial distinctions and racial advantages in the electoral process were permissible under the Fifteenth Amendment when they were "not designed to 'correct a wrong.'" Since racial consideration to correct a prior wrong had already been established in earlier litigation (it had been upheld that pupils could be assigned on the basis of race; and the use of race was sanctioned to end discrimination in housing and in preferential hiring), Lewin's strategy was to separate the Hasidic redistricting from those cases with "overt" past discrimination and to underline the reverse bias of using racial quotas in voting.

The judgment of July 25, 1974, by Senior United States District Judge Walter Bruchhausen, however, affirmed the legitimacy of racial consideration to right a wrong in apportioning voting districts. He decided that the Hasidim had standing in court as white voters but not as a separate ethnic group, and he observed that white voters were adequately represented since the total white population of Kings County was 64.9 percent. The Court of Appeals affirmed the lower court's ruling in a two-to-one decision, and in the fall of 1976 the case reached the Supreme Court. The American Jewish Congress, the Anti-Defamation League, and the Jewish Labor Committee, alarmed at the use of racial quotas in voting, filed "Amici" briefs.

On March 1, 1977, in a seven-to-one decision, the Supreme Court ruled against the Hasidim. But despite the near unanimity of the vote, the arguments of the Justices reflected the great diversity of view regarding the central issues. Justice White, joined by Stevens and in part by Brennan, Blackmun, and Rehnquist, delivered the opinion of the uneasy majority. He asserted that voters belonging to a race in the minority are "similar to that of the Democratic or Republican minority that is submerged year after year by the adherents to the majority party who tend to vote a straight party line."

Chief Justice Burger, the lone dissenter in the decision (Justice Marshall took no part in the case), attacked the reasoning on a wide front, arguing for reapportionment along neutral lines and against the use of racial quotas, noting the absence of neutral standards, and the loss of the ideal of the "melting pot."

While Justice Brennan sided with the majority of the Court, he felt called upon to explain his vote

> because this case carries us further down the road of race-centered remedial devices than we have heretofore traveled—with the serious questions of fairness that attend such matters . . . This impression of injustice may be heightened by the natural consequence of our governing processes that the most "discrete and insular" of whites often will be called upon to bear the immediate, direct costs of benign discrimination . . . [T]he impression of unfairness is magnified when a coherent group like the Hasidim disproportionately bears the adverse consequences of a race assignment policy.[6]

The Hasidim were disappointed with the decision, but they were not defeated in their activist pursuits. "We will fight for our rights any place, any time," commented Rabbi Lefkowitz to the press, adding, "We will not hesitate at any time in the future to resort to the courts if the need should arise."[7] Nor were the Hasidim to be completely ignored in the political arena. Despite their numerical weakness, they had an estimated 80 percent voter turnout and offered lively support for any candidate, a point the Hasidim quickly made in the 23rd State Senate district. A spirited campaign was organized by Albert Friedman, the enterprising son of Liepa Friedman, the former Satmar community leader.[8]

> When we were split four of our election districts went to Bedford-Stuyvesant. I put up a candidate for assembly in the black part of Williamsburg. It was four out of some sixty districts and the Hasidic candidate lost by about 250 votes in the primary. I promised him he'd lose. We didn't pull the vote. I just wanted to make a point that, you know, you cannot get a black assembly just by reapportionment. There were four candidates who split the vote and the guy almost walked in, in spite of our non-efforts. We lost but we gave them a good scare.   (AF)

The message was not lost on the local Democratic politicians, who were intent on consolidating power in a number of districts and who saw the misstep of having a Hasidic Jew represent a black assembly district. In the next reapportionment in 1982 (following the census results of 1980), the districts were gerrymandered once more so that the Hasidim of Williamsburg regained their unity in the new 57th Assembly District and no longer represented a danger to contiguous districts. In addition to recapturing their state assembly district, the Hasidim in Williamsburg and Borough Park were united in the 13th Congressional District.

> This time the community's back together already. You know they realized it's better not to fight with us. Not only that but now in the congressional district Williamsburg's together with Borough Park. They made a gerrymander along the river front so the line from Williamsburg goes down all the way to Flatbush, Coney Island, Borough Park, like a real Jewish congressional district. (AF)

Lubavitch and the Hanukkah Menorah

The midwinter festival of Hanukkah celebrates the victory of the Maccabees over the Greeks in 165 B.C.E. It signifies as well the dedication of the new altar in the Temple to replace the altar profaned by sacrifices to heathen gods. The festival lasts eight days, to commemorate the popular tale of the victors finding one small flask of oil bearing the seal of the High Priest which miraculously burned for eight days. The symbol of the holiday is the eight-branched candelabra (menorah) which by law and custom is shown in order to publicize the miracle.

The Lubavitcher Hasidim have increasingly turned to displaying the eight-branched menorah in public places, as the Lubavitcher Rebbe has mandated.

> A Jew should not be content with merely spreading the light of Torah and Mitzvot in his own home, but it is part of his obligation and privilege to spread the light of Yiddishkayt, Torah, and Mitzvot, also outside his home, to lighten up the outside, the street, the whole environment.[9]

It is a Lubavitcher hope that the menorah will ignite sparks of memory and allegiance in the Jewish people who see it. From their point of view if Jews are reminded of the holiday and the miracle associated with it they may be inclined to take other steps toward traditional Judaism—to put on tefillin and to contemplate the works of HaShem. In keeping with the Hasidic premise of intensifying one's performance of the mitzvot the Lubavitcher Hasidim have erected giant menorahs for public display. This raises the question of where to station these monuments. In a time of year already crowded with Christmas trees and Santa Claus there is a sense that "If anybody else can display whatever they want to, why do we have to be shy?"

In 1986, as part of a nationwide campaign and with the approval of the city, Chabad placed a 16-foot-high menorah in a public park in Burlington, Vermont. The menorah was accompanied by a sign reading "Happy Hanukkah." Two years later the rabbi of a Reform Temple, a retired Unitarian minister, and an attorney for the American Civil Liberties Union mounted a challenge to the stationing of the menorah on public grounds. Permission to display the menorah was granted by the U.S. District Court in Vermont. The case continued on to the U.S. Court of Appeals for the Second Circuit in New York.

In 1986 in Pittsburgh as well the Lubavitcher Hasidim exhibited an 18-foot-tall menorah before the Pittsburgh City Hall. The menorah was set next to a 45-foot-tall Christmas tree. At the same time a Nativity scene was arranged inside the Pittsburgh county courthouse. The presence of the two displays aroused the ire of members of the local chapter of the American Civil Liberties Union, which brought suit to prohibit the use of religious symbols on government property. The case was brought just before Christmas in 1986. The suit slowly made its way through the courts to the Supreme Court, and it moved past the Burlington suit, which was still on the docket in the Court of Appeals.

On July 3, 1989, the Supreme Court disallowed the display of a Nativity scene in the county courthouse, ruling five to four that "Government may celebrate Christmas in some manner and form, but not in a way that endorses Christian doctrine." At the same time by a margin of six to three the Court upheld the legality of displaying on government property the 18-foot-high Hanukkah menorah and the 45-foot tall Christmas tree. In his opinion for the majority Justice Blackmun carefully threaded his way through the issues in the somewhat similar cases: "our present task is to determine whether the display of the crèche and the menorah, in their respective particular physical settings, has the effect of endorsing or disapproving religious beliefs." [10] Blackmun found that "The crèche in this lawsuit uses words, as well as the picture of the Nativity scene, to make its religious meaning unmistakably clear . . . The county sends an unmistakable message that it supports and promotes the Christian praise to God that is the crèche's religious message."

The display of the Hanukkah menorah offered Blackmun a more complex constitutional question.

> The menorah, one must recognize, is a religious symbol . . . But the menorah's message is not exclusively religious. The menorah is the primary visual symbol for a holiday that, like Christmas, has both religious and secular dimensions. Moreover, the menorah here stands next to a Christmas tree and a sign saluting liberty . . . The display of the menorah is not an endorsement of religious faith but simply a recognition of cultural diversity . . . [and] conveying the city's secular recognition of different traditions for celebrating the winter holiday season. [11]

Most American Jewish groups, tempered by knowledge of the historical danger of uniting government and religion, and aware of the need to protect the rights of a minority faith, were disturbed by the Court's decision on the menorah.[12] They would have preferred to have all religious symbols and scenes excluded from government property, including the menorah. From their point of view, in its attempt to be sympathetic, the Court had divorced the menorah from its religious significance.

The menorah is a symbol which expresses religious and political ambiguity. In its placement of menorahs in public places around the country Chabad has emphasized their political content. Alongside the menorah in Pittsburgh was a sign that reflected the wishes of Chabad: "Salute to Liberty. During this holiday season the city of Pittsburgh salutes liberty. Let these festive lights remind us that we are the keepers of the flame of liberty and our legacy of freedom."

The issue was not settled to anyone's complete satisfaction. While secular opponents wanted to prevent any tie between religion and the state, the Lubavitcher Hasidim wanted a carte blanche right to post menorahs on the doorway of every city like mezuzot. When the holiday season came again the Lubavitcher Hasidim took the additional step of placing a menorah on the steps of the City-County Building alongside the Christmas tree. The City of Pittsburgh made an emergency request for the authority to remove the menorah. City officials had objected on the grounds that "the Jewish group should not have the power to determine what will be displayed on the steps of a public building, and that the area is not a 'public forum.'" In December 1989, however, the Court rejected the City's request by a vote of six to three.[13]

Placement of menorahs was deemed constitutional; however, using the specific requirements cited in the July case in Pittsburgh, the U.S. Court of Appeals for the Second Circuit of New York overturned the ruling of the District Court which had upheld the displaying of the 16-foot menorah in Burlington, Vermont. In Pittsburgh the menorah in front of a government building had been placed next to a Christmas tree, thereby establishing it as part of a secular scene. The Burlington menorah lacked a Christmas tree as a companion and was therefore seen apart as a religious symbol. Although the city hastily sought to move the menorah close to a tree strung with holiday lights, the placement of the Burlington menorah was derailed in the 1990 session of the Supreme Court when the Court refused to hear the appeal of the city of Burlington. The menorah remained banned from public property.

Since 1986 hundreds of menorahs have been placed in prominent public places across America and elsewhere, including Fifth Avenue and 59th Street in New York City, Daley Plaza in Chicago, Rome's Piazza Barberini, near one of the mountain tunnels in Rio de Janeiro, and Hong Kong's Chater Garden Central.[14] There have also been a number of challenges to the placement of particular menorahs, including cases in Chicago, Los

Angeles, Des Moines, and Cincinnati. At times the Hasidim have acted in conjunction with city officials and at other times they have brought suit to force city officials to permit the placement of a menorah on public property. Observers of past cases agree that the Supreme Court decision regarding Pittsburgh was a narrow one and that individual circumstances will determine the outcome of each case. Given the number of new appointments to the Court, a new rationale for such decisionmaking is likely in major rulings to come. If American history is a guide, however, no final rapprochement between church and state is likely.[15]

Having established a legal precedent to permit Hanukkah menorahs on public property, Nathan Lewin and his staff engaged in a mopping-up operation, exercising their prerogatives in as many locales as possible and extending their rights to new legal domains. Writing in the *Jewish Week,* Lewin observed: "Today's constitutional issue being litigated across the country is whether cities must allow private menorahs to be exhibited in 'public forums'—that is, locations where private speeches and exhibits on various subjects have traditionally been permitted." He cited a recent case concerning Cincinnati's Fountain Square: "The court of appeals ruled that religious speech could not constitutionally be discriminated against. If a square or a park is thrown open for private speech on secular subjects it cannot be closed to religious speech." And he insisted:

> Contrary to the protestations of organizations such as the American Jewish Congress, Lubavitch has consistently represented the menorah to be a religious symbol that, when erected in a public square, has the constitutional protection of religious expression ... Banishing menorahs from public places means derogating religion and denying to Jews the equal access to public forums that are available to secular organizations, gospel groups and evangelical meetings.

Opponents of the placement of menorahs, Lewin concluded, are "prisoners of their own misconceptions, prejudices and ignorance."[16]

Others, however, such as Allan Nadler, the director of research at the YIVO Institute for Jewish Research in New York, expressed the view that Lubavitch had forced the country to take a backward step in the struggle for religious liberty for all. Nadler was among those who feared additional Lubavitcher victories: "The kindling of huge menorahs in public places across America opens a dangerous can of worms. It can very easily backfire on the Jewish community by undermining the principle of freedom *from* [italics added] established religion, which has always been such a blessing for American Jewry." "In celebration of a holiday that champions religious freedom as no other does, these menorahs have contributed to the most widespread breach of the 'wall of separation' between religion and affairs of state that guarantees Americans of all faiths—not the least Jews—complete religious freedom."[17]

To substantiate his perception of a broad retreat in the face of advo-cates of a religious presence throughout the public domain, Nadler pointed to other elements of the Lubavitcher philosophy—advocating prayer in public schools and supporting anti-abortion legislation—which were also part of the agenda of the Catholic League and other Christian activist groups. The reintroduction of nativity scenes on city and state property and within government buildings, he contended, had been built on Lubavitcher victories in court. "How ironic," he wrote, that the menorah, "the great Jewish symbol of religious freedom," "has of late become the vehicle for a grossly public and widespread violation of precisely that amendment to the American constitution that was for-mulated to prevent the 'establishment of religion' and thereby protect minorities from the tyranny of religious subjugation." [18]

On another front, Nadler argued that "there is absolutely no source in Jewish law or tradition that mandates the kind of aggressive exhibition-ism in which the Lubavitchers are now engaged." [19] In this argument he had the support of other Hasidic courts. In the Hasidic world Lubavitch stood alone on this issue. Other Hasidic courts dissociated themselves from the placement of menorahs. Satmar leaders were at best uninter-ested in the results of the rulings, as well as scornful of the entire concept.

> It's not a Jewish issue at all. It doesn't help the Jewish faith. It may bring out friction between the non-Jews and Jews for no reason. What if we light a menorah in that city? What does it do for the Jewish faith? What do we gain from that? What does it mean to us? The propaganda is good for Lubavitch-ers. The flag is a symbol for patriotism, but this is not even a symbol for patriotism. If half an hour before Shabbes, Shemtov [a leader in Lubavitch] goes to Fifth Avenue and lights a candle and comes back with a helicopter, what did he accomplish? [Mayor] Dinkins is lighting the menorah and he comes back with a helicopter to Crown Heights before Shabbes. What did they accomplish to light a menorah? It's not kosher. It's only a hocus pocus. What does it prove? It doesn't bring anything to the Jewish faith. (RH)

· 18 ·

New Square:
Shtetl and Suburb

New Square

Soon after their arrival in the United States, Hasidim in every court considered how they might best protect themselves and their children from dangers to their Orthodox way of life. Initially all were concerned with strengthening the neighborhood communities, but as they became more familiar with the diversity of the new environment, some looked to the rural areas outside the city as the best buffer against outside influences. In the rural areas, some reasoned, they could establish a self-governing Torah-true community. Television, with its promotion of romantic and sexual illusions, could be completely eliminated, along with other blatant impieties, such as the sight of automobiles desecrating the Shabbes. The plan stirred nostalgia for the Old World shtetl. The old rhythm of religious life would be restored: adults would work and pray; children would study and then marry and settle near their parents. As their families increased the yeshivah would grow and become the center of their lives.

In 1954, after considerable discussion and research, Rabbi Yaakov Yosef Twersky, the Skverer Rebbe, and a small group of his followers purchased 130 acres of a former dairy farm two miles from Spring Valley, New York. Many of these first settlers were survivors of the death camps; a few were American-born Hasidim. None had previously been followers of the Skverer Rebbe, and for that matter some had not been attached to any other Rebbe.[1] The new immigrants who had lost their families and the Americans searching for a spiritual refuge sought to establish new ties that would restore their past and reassure them concerning the future. They were united in the dream of the new community and in their faith in the sincerity and piety of the Skverer Rebbe. The settlement was to be called New Square after the Ukrainian town of Skvira where the Rebbe had once had his court.

The richly wooded countryside along Route 45 with its lush stands of pine and maple seemed to provide a thick curtain shielding the old farm from the distant city. Even so the site was little more than an hour's drive from Manhattan, well within commuting distance. Socially they could develop a self-contained ultra-Orthodox community while their economic ties to the city continued intact. They were urban workers and not farmers, and for the time being at least they would commute to their jobs and businesses. In the future, it was hoped, light industry would develop within the community or nearby and more of the men would have employment close to home.

Spring Valley was not an altogether alien environment for a religious Jewish community. Jews had settled in numbers in Rockland County since the turn of the century, and there were shops and kosher hotels for summer visitors. The number of permanent Jewish settlers had increased beginning in 1941 when Rabbi Shraga Mendlowitz, the dean of Williamsburg's Orthodox Yeshivah Torah Vadaat, had established a yeshivah in Spring Valley and another in nearby Monsey. The growth of yeshivot in the rural setting had served as a magnet for religious Jews with a wide range of affiliation, and there were Orthodox, Conservative, and Reform congregations.

The Hasidim of New Square had a more sharply focused vision than other Jews in Rockland County, but they were ill-prepared to cope with the challenges of development and organization. Naive and idealistic, they were also easily duped. Construction of houses began in 1956, but a series of blunders during the winter season left few foundation walls intact by spring. Costs escalated as construction materials disappeared. Local farmers employed as construction workers noted obvious discrepancies, felt sympathy for the plight of the newcomers, but kept silent. For many of the settlers the first sign of calamity was a financial default, and the resulting accusations and disputes drove out the first community president.

By 1958 sixty-eight houses were finished and occupied by Orthodox families. The community purchased an old bus for a daily round trip to the city. They set a curtain down the center to separate the men from the women. To make good use of their travel time they brought in a small ark that would enable them to daven the morning prayers during the journey.

Each of the early years brought a new round of difficulties for the settlement. The villagers were beset by a lien placed on the property which prevented them from selling additional plots to prospective settlers. Zoning regulations established by the surrounding Township of Ramapo, which had administrative jurisdiction over the settlement, forbade the construction of two-family homes and other multiple dwellings, and denied the use of home basements for stores and shops. There were few newcomers from the city who could afford the purchase of a single-family home, and development came to a standstill. Without new settlers community funds dried up and the school building could not be completed.

As in Williamsburg and Crown Heights, the Hasidim found themselves pitted against their neighbors. In rural Rockland County, however, their neighbors were not members of other struggling minority groups but rather middle-class homeowners concerned with property values, taxes, sewage, and control of local schools. Local residents, accustomed to well-delineated single-family homes, were concerned that New Square would introduce a crowded and disorganized urban sprawl. The opposition came from Jews as well as gentiles.

A struggle over zoning regulations began between the village of New Square and the Ramapo Town Board. The Board cringed when they found that New Square had a synagogue operating in the basement of one Cape Cod house, and a grocery-bakery, a fish store, a print shop, and an engraver's shop located in the basements of other small private houses. They discovered two and three families living in houses zoned for single-family occupancy, and although the householders claimed they were extended families comprising parents and married children, Board members believed that in some instances the houses were simply split between two or more unrelated families. The matter boiled over in 1961 when the community requested a building permit to expand their basement synagogue. The town attorney asked that the entire settlement be condemned, arguing that the houses threatened existing sewer lines. In response, the Hasidim in New Square presented a petition asking that the settlement be incorporated as a village. In July 1961, the State Supreme Court ruled in favor of the move to incorporate the Hasidic settlement. New Square became a village.[2]

With the incorporation of the village, New Square was able to establish its own building codes and zoning regulations. The existing housing units were suddenly legalized. The lien was lifted, lots were sold, and new houses were added to the village (seven by 1963, another ten by 1967), with some designed for three families. Stores and shops that had operated more or less discreetly in house basements could now sell their wares without fear of a court summons. New stores and craft industries began (in basements as usual), including a watch assembly plant and a cap manufacturer. Three knitting mills also started operations, usually taking special orders from larger outside firms. In time, as a final urban touch, a member of the community opened a used car lot.[3]

The New Square community suffered a severe shock when the older Skverer Rebbe died in 1968, but the Rebbe's son, Rabbi David Twersky, was immediately named as his successor and religious life continued without disruption. The Hasidim of New Square and the rabbinic dynasty were now bound together through generations. As a sign of their respect and symbolic familial ties a high percentage of the children born after the death of the older Rebbe were given his name. In one class with twenty-three boys, twenty-two of them were named Yaakov Yosef, and the teacher had to call on his students by their family names.

Some long-range plans did not come to fruition. The development of private industry remained stunted, and most of the men continued to work in the city. In 1970 the community purchased the financially troubled Ramapo General Hospital, located on the border of the village, but their efforts to revive the hospital were unsuccessful. Nine years later the hospital could not meet its full payroll; it was reported to be close to a million dollars in debt to the Internal Revenue Service for back taxes covering withholding taxes and social security.[4] The building was subsequently converted into a yeshivah and administrative offices.

Unpaid local taxes presented another time bomb. In 1969, with funds from the Small Business Administration, the community built a small shopping center with seven units (six stores on the first level and a diamond-polishing operation above). After five years of unpaid taxes to the township, however, the county assumed ownership of the center. Despite this, a local company led by Mates Friesel, the mayor of New Square, continued to administer the shopping center. By the end of 1979 the unpaid taxes amounted to $131,000, plus an additional $50,000 in penalties. It was reported that the rents collected on the property had gone to repay the federal loan, but that only three of the seven stores paid any rent at all (one of the stores being the community grocery owned by the village congregation). It was not clear who had ownership of the money which had been used to cover property taxes and insurance costs. The county finally settled the problem by selling the property back to the original operators in New Square, who were ordered to pay off the debt in monthly installments. The interest and penalties accrued were forgiven.[5]

As New Square became a religious stronghold more Hasidim and other Orthodox Jews were attracted to the general area. The Vizhnitzer Rebbe, Rabbi Mordchei Hager, moved to nearby Monsey in 1972. The Hager and Twersky dynasties already had family ties and further marriages would soon be arranged between them. Families from the Belz and Ger dynasties arrived as well as a few Lubavitcher Hasidim; a few years later there was a contingent of Satmar Hasidim. By the end of the decade there were more than fifty shuln in Monsey alone. A few families from New Square were attracted by the more varied ambiance in Monsey and moved there as well.

Relations between the settlers in New Square and their neighbors in the Ramapo township presented a continual dilemma. Many residents feared the religious community's views on local taxation, school transportation, and athletics. In 1978 the local school board debated closing and then selling one of the school buildings, always a contested and emotional issue for the parents and children concerned. While the township school population was contracting and shifting location, the number of students in New Square was rapidly multiplying, and New Square vied with others to influence the selection of a building adjacent to their community, for which they presented an offer of purchase. For parents and children facing a school closure it was a deeply emotional issue bound to stir resentment. Moreover, the presence of so many bearded and identically clothed men at a public hearing alarmed some in the township who feared their coming influence. Although the Hasidim did not win the vote on the school building, their increasing numbers seemed to augur badly for the secular members of the community, Jew and gentile, whose interests were so radically different.[6]

Despite its problems, New Square developed as an integrated village with its social conscience intact. The village built up an interest-free loan fund for those in need of moderate assistance. It also maintained a society to visit the sick in hospitals and to provide help to the aged and the infirm. There were financial and organizational achievements as well in the form of federal grants and loans.[7] Finally, after New Square was denied permission by the Ramapo Town Board to annex land for further expansion, the scales tipped in favor of the Hasidic community. In March 1982, after a delay of six years, New Square won the right to expand on 95 acres of land adjacent to their community. By 1986 there were 140 one-, two-, and three-family houses and 45 units in a low-rent housing complex.

Because of the limited size of New Square, demographic changes are more readily discernible there than in the larger urban community. The population curve moved in a steady upward climb as the original 68 families who arrived in 1958 grew to 85 families in 1963 (with a population of 620) and 126 in 1967 (with a population of 812). In 1967 10 marriages were celebrated in the community. The 1970 census counted a population of 1,156, with 57 percent under the age of 18. From 1971 to 1986 there was a yearly average of a hundred births, usually evenly divided between boys and girls.[8] Each year, in keeping with the birth rate, fifty or so boys were bar mitzvahed. By 1986 there were more than 450 families in New Square, with an average of 7 to 8 children per family. The population was over 2,100.[9]

The 1970 census revealed that New Square had the lowest per capita income in New York State.[10] The village retained its hold on this statistic in 1980.[11] The increase in the number of children strained the financial resources of the families. This led to a change in attitude toward acceptance of aid from government assistance programs. In 1963 four persons were on welfare for periods of time because of illness. In 1975 there were a dozen people receiving welfare payments, and, according to the village administrator, two-thirds of the families were receiving Medicaid and food stamps.

Marriage in New Square

With so many young people available it is relatively easy to arrange a match: the two or three local *shadkhanim* (matchmakers) know who is available; siblings attending the yeshivah bring back notice of the temperament and character of desirable prospects. Reports on possible candidates from outside the village come from other friends and relatives. The average age of marriage in New Square is between 17 and 20. It is customary for girls to graduate from school in the twelfth grade at age 17 and then marry; the young grooms are usually a year or two older.

Village customs concerning marriage reflect the Skverer Rebbe's desire for harmony and consensus in all matters. A few of the young women of New Square who married men from other Hasidic courts had tried to remain and raise their families in New Square. Eventually, however, the attraction of their husbands to their own Rebbes and to the ambiance of their old courts caused them to leave. It was also a concern that a young man who had studied elsewhere who decided to remain might perpetuate a sense of alienation. As a result it became the custom that a village girl who marries a young man from another court who has not studied in the yeshivah of New Square must leave the community. Village men, on the other hand, whether they wed a local girl or someone from the city, are encouraged to remain and raise their families in New Square.

By deciding to consider someone from the outside, a young woman makes a conscious choice to settle elsewhere. The departure of young brides has at times caused sorrow to families who do not wish to be separated; on the other hand, the practice provides the means for a young woman to leave the community if she so desires. Despite the close ties to family and friends it is clear that the tightly knit life in New Square is not for everyone. Although they express love for their native community, some prefer the more highly charged atmosphere of Borough Park, or even Monsey, where there are a variety of stores, a wider selection of yeshivot for their children, more open expression of diverse opinions, and fewer close neighbors.

During 1985 there were thirty marriages: twenty-five were of men who had lived or studied in New Square (with local girls or with girls from outside). They would remain in the village. Five girls married men from outside of New Square and then set up housekeeping in Monsey or

Brooklyn. During that year there was but one divorce, of a couple with three children who had been married for six years; both partners had been married before.[12]

Before marriage and during the first year, or until a child is born, the young brides take teaching jobs, or find employment as secretaries or bookkeepers. Some work the cash registers or serve as clerks in the small shopping center. Even after bearing several children some women continue to work part time at home as bookkeepers. The young men settle into jobs locally as teachers, bus drivers, deliverymen, or clerks in the stores; some work in the city as computer programmers, others in the diamond industry as craftsmen or entrepreneurs.

Many young men remain in the kolel, the yeshivah for married men. The married students customarily receive a weekly stipend to enable them to maintain their families. It is said to have been the older Rebbe's wish that young men continue their religious studies for at least two years after marriage. He did not want to see young men moving immediately into the business world, and he expressed the view that they should begin their new households with learning as a way of life. The kolel was introduced in New Square in 1963, and by the time of the Rebbe's death in 1968 there were twenty young men receiving stipends of thirty to forty dollars a week.[13]

By 1986 there were approximately 150 married men in the New Square kolel, some full time, some part time. They earned stipends of between fifty and eighty dollars a week, depending in great measure on the number of children in their families. Many continue in the kolel for several years, dependent for their support on their modest stipend, aid from their wives and families, wages from teaching part time or tutoring, food stamps, and whatever other aid they can muster.

> My husband has been studying in the kolel for the past seventeen years. He receives a scholarship. They give him a partner and he helps him out [with his studies]. He's knowledgeable and he helps out the weaker students. (FP)

The early marriages and the high number of children per family have brought a quick march of generations.

> The grandparents are sitting back having *nakhes* [pleasure] that they've achieved that. My father, who is sixty-three, has a grandchild getting married. At my father's age some of the men are great-grandfathers already. I have a girlfriend who is thirty-six who is a grandmother already. (KG)

Community Organization

The administration of the village has in the main followed a typical American pattern. There are a mayor, a board of trustees, and a village clerk. The mayor's assistant, Samuel Weismandel, handles most of the administrative matters for the village. While there is no crime within the village, there is a justice of the peace (a lawyer who practices in New York City but resides in Monsey) to handle cases of harassment from occasional visitors bent on causing mischief.

New Square's religious perceptions, however, distinguish the organization of this Hasidic village from American communities of like size. Even the bus, with its separate sections for men and women and its ark containing the holy scrolls, has rules of propriety and order that establish the religious focus of the community.[14]

> I was reading the *Algemeine Zeitung,* an Orthodox Yiddish newspaper. It's not exactly the *New York Post* with naked women in it. I was reading it and somebody came over to me and said very politely—he knew me and maybe if he hadn't known me he would have been a little more vigorous in telling me what to do and what not to do. He said, "Reb Srudikel," calling me by my first name, "in our place we don't read newspapers in the bus. Everybody should be learning, learning a bit of Mishnah, or saying *tehilim* [psalms], but we don't read newspapers." It's so part and parcel of their upbringing that they don't feel it's nerve. In fact they feel it's nerve of me to transgress their code of behavior.   (IF)

The rhythm of the religious life has remained constant since the village was founded. Each day visitors to the Rebbe arrive by car or on the bus returning after carrying the men to work in the city. Apart from times of special need, the villagers pay a visit to the Rebbe just before Rosh Hashanah. The Rebbe's gabbai writes each visitor's kvitl (petition containing the family name and individual names) and presents it to the Rebbe.

> The Rebbe will ask how the family is, how my husband is, how I am feeling, and if there are any problems. If anything is needed we can discuss it with the Rebbe. When I needed medical advice I went to the Rebbe on whether I should listen to this doctor or that doctor. He's well versed in these matters and his secretary has a whole file of doctors listed by their specialties. The Rebbe usually remembers the doctors by name, and if not he'll tell you to ask the gabbai. He usually knows the names by heart of the doctors and their specialties.   (KG)

While New Square has not achieved its financial and industrial goals, it has become an island of security in a turbulent modern world.

> The whole purpose of the community was not to expose children to outside influences. Thank God we've achieved that. Unfortunately, there's too much in the outside world that corrupts them and the future. Here there's no TV. They don't go to movies. They don't even know about it.   (KG)

· 19 ·

Satmar's Kiryas Joel

The New Settlement

In the early 1970s, more than a decade after the establishment of New Square, the Satmar Hasidim moved to create a similar suburban community. The older Satmar Rebbe had long harbored a dream of founding a community a safe distance from the city which would be governed by ultra-Orthodox religious tenets. The isolated and remote location strengthened by the invisible barriers of culture and language would shield residents from outside forces. In this traditional environment the children would grow up safe from drugs and crime and free of heretical influences. There were equally compelling practical reasons for founding a satellite community. Satmar's growing population could no longer be contained in Williamsburg. Efforts to create new housing in the neighborhood had been stymied, and they were in desperate need of room for their community to expand.

As with New Square they sought land within commuting distance of the city and with the possibility of developing light industry nearby. Over the course of time the community discreetly purchased property fifty miles from New York City in Monroe township in Orange County, a region of heavily wooded, rolling hills. Once both a farming and vacation area (much of the land had been the private estate of W. Averell Harriman), in recent years it had become more heavily populated by year-round suburbanites, in great measure because of the development of the New York State Thruway. It still required a formidable drive of more than an hour to reach New York City, and the Satmar leadership hoped that plants would open in the surrounding area and provide employment for the settlers.[1]

The Satmar community contracted for the construction of twenty-five single-family houses and eighty garden apartments. The housing was especially designed for Hasidic living, with twin kitchen sinks and stoves to ensure separation of meat and dairy foods. Construction was still under way in 1974 when families began to move in. One of the first pioneers was Leibush Lefkowitz, the organizer of the village and the president of the Satmar community. A spacious residence was planned for the Rebbe, who would live there part of the time. The village was named for him— Kiryas Joel, the village of Joel.

As had occurred at Spring Valley, the purchase of the land and the arrival of these strangely garbed pioneers raised some fears in the local community. Long-time residents felt uneasy with the sudden presence of a pietistic religious community in their midst, and many feared that the value of their property would plummet. After learning of the reservations expressed, Leibush Lefkowitz observed: "People don't like living with strange people, but after two years they will find out what a good element we are. Monroe will find that a lot of benefits will come from us." [2]

The youthful Hasidic families that arrived were struck by the beauty of the wooded area. There was a sense of security that they had never before experienced: the children could come and go freely without fear; city traffic, drugs, crime, pornography, and social tensions suddenly vanished. As families arrived, and as the number of births increased, the countryside seemed to bloom with young children.

The first concerns of the adults were to provide classrooms and teachers for the children, to arrange for the availability of kosher food, and to encourage others to settle there and help to share the costs of construction and development. Their experience repeated what had taken place at New Square when initial makeshift plans conflicted with local custom and law. Two years after the first families moved in, the Monroe Town Board accused the Hasidim of violating the local housing code. The dismayed authorities had discovered that the basements of eight garden apartments were being used as schools and shuln; a commercial food store was also located in one basement, and its operator was arrested. Worse still, it was found that eighteen single-family houses had been converted to multiple-family units. The Town Board ordered further construction halted until the existing violations could be corrected.

Rabbi Lefkowitz chastised the township for its lack of hospitality, and countered the Town Board's request for an injunction with the same offer that had been tendered by the village of New Square to the Town Board of Ramapo: to incorporate the Satmar housing as a separate village of some 450 acres. The compromise settlement that was reached in federal court in October 1976 clearly gave the Hasidim the better of the argument, allowing them to incorporate in an area of potentially 340 acres where they could establish their own regulations regarding houses, stores, schools, shuln, and apartments.

Speaking with the patience of one long accustomed to reconciling tradition and modernity, Rabbi Lefkowitz observed: "We believe we are complying with the law. Our family units are large and closely knit, leaving understandable doubt by those who do not know us and our customs." [3]

Some of the long-time residents in the area, fearing financial loss, sold their houses to the first buyer. Those who chose to wait came in for a financial windfall as Hasidim scrambled for houses near the settlement. Prices for land and houses soon skyrocketed.

Growth and Change

Kiryas Joel continued to grow at the rate of one hundred families a year—some as the result of new arrivals, others from marriages of the village's young people. With the growth of the population, the basement shuln and yeshivot gave way to the construction of an imposing besmedresh and schools for the boys (United Talmudical Academy) and the girls (Bais Rachel). The principal besmedresh serves as a yeshivah for the older students, and as the center for study and prayer. The language of the home, school, and street is Yiddish. Hebrew studies begin at age three, and before they take classes in the first grade at age six, few children know any English at all. Young teenagers at the yeshivah are still generally innocent of the world outside the village. They approach visitors with the awkwardness and curiosity of yearling colts.

Local industries have been slow to develop, and most of the men commute to jobs in the city, driving their own cars or riding on community-owned buses. The range of occupations mirrors that of the city population, and for many it is a struggle to make housing payments, meet the fees of the yeshivah, and cover the cost of the special food and clothing that are required. [4]

As had occurred at New Square, many of Kiryas Joel's problems with the township were eased when the village became incorporated. The community then set its own rules and established its own housing codes. Expansion was accelerated and the task of organizing the construction of new housing was surrendered to contractors. The housing went up in waves, as the different strands of architectural style will testify. The community now sells the land and private arrangements are made between contractor and homeowner. A few of the residents have ventured into this relatively new field of home building.

Kiryas Joel does not have the placid, contained atmosphere of New Square. It has more than three times the population and encompasses roughly twice the acreage. [5] The larger village is more animated. There is an air of urban tension and excitement that is at odds with the tranquil rural setting. The center of the village is the besmedresh, a spacious building with a span of stairs as broad as those of a federal courthouse. At prayer time, morning and evening, the parking spaces around the besmed-resh, the streets, alleyways, and driveways are jammed with cars. Prayer time brings urban gridlock. Although these are country lanes, walking is done by children, women, and a few men without driver's licenses.

Land was set aside for a simple shopping mall. An acre was paved with asphalt and a row of family-owned shops opened, including a grocery and a bakery. A sign at the entrance warns visitors that only those with proper attire will be welcome—no shorts permitted. Other land was provided for a medical center to attract doctors to Kiryas Joel. The village rents space to a pediatrician, a gynecologist, and a dentist. The community does not provide health insurance or a health plan. Villagers pay privately for medical services, but if anyone is in need there are many charities that can provide assistance. The community monitors the scale of charges, and doctors are aware that exorbitant fees can result in their being denied use of the medical facility.

With incorporation came greater political organization. There are now a mayor and four board members. A town clerk keeps community records. There is a free ambulance service manned by volunteers. The village is still dependent on outside agencies, however, for other essential municipal services: fire protection is provided by Monroe township, and a private company contracts for garbage collection. The community also relies on the state police for protection from outside harassment. The Hasidim maintain a night patrol to check on incoming cars, and during the Shabbes, when driving is prohibited, a private agency provides two patrol cars. The village of Kiryas Joel has no police force. There is no crime. Robbery or hooliganism by any residents or their children would be proof that the community had failed.

The New Rov

Kiryas Joel is the showplace of Satmar and its forecast of the future. It offers living space and an alternative style of life to the population in Williamsburg and Borough Park. The yeshivah at Kiryas Joel enrolls all of the advanced students of the Satmar communities above the age of eighteen (those students seventeen and younger study at the Satmar yeshivah in Williamsburg). Every young man at Satmar therefore has at least a taste of the village's way of life. Any change in Kiryas Joel would soon be reflected in the community at large.

Soon after his appointment as Satmar Rebbe in 1979, Reb Moshe Teitelbaum named his eldest son, Reb Aaron, as rov (chief rabbi and head of the community) of Kiryas Joel and as rosh yeshivah (dean of the yeshivah). These two posts are crucial to the present and future fortunes of the Satmar community. As both rov and rosh yeshivah, Rabbi Aaron Teitelbaum has authority over all activities in the Kiryas Joel community. He is the linchpin in decisions concerning religious learning for the children as well as for the advanced students. It is also clear that Reb Aaron, as Reb Moshe's eldest son, is being groomed to succeed his father as Rebbe. Even at present he is the Rebbe's representative in all the activities of the community in the city and in the suburbs, and when Reb Moshe leaves on a trip or goes on vacation Reb Aaron assumes his responsibilities.

At the time of Reb Aaron's arrival in Kiryas Joel the village had been in operation for six years. The first settlers had established an ambiance of their own. They expected and needed no more than a *dayyan*, a judge to settle matters of law and ritual, rather than a rov to rule over them. The appointment of the Rebbe's son as rov, while in keeping with the nepotism familiar in Hasidic tradition, created some resentment, particularly among those who had been involved in the development and maintenance of the village.

> The first people out here were like pioneers. To have him imposed on us was terrible. We didn't know him. He didn't go to our yeshivah. He had no contact with us and all of a sudden he was our boss. We fought, trying to convince his father that it's not fair to impose a leader on us. Let us decide. He said absolutely not. (MR)

The acrimony intensified in the following months as grievances accumulated. The villagers' frustration appears to have been fueled by their disillusionment concerning the new Rebbe ("If the older Rebbe had wanted him to become Rebbe why didn't he leave word that Reb Moshe should be in charge?"). They were equally disenchanted with Reb Aaron, the Rebbe's son. There were complaints about his actions and his personality. Some even went so far as to assert that the rov was not sufficiently anti-Zionist, and they reminded skeptics of his marriage to Sasha Hager, a daughter of the Vizhnitzer Rebbe, who was reported to be sympathetic to the Israeli government. In short, Reb Moshe was not considered by some to be the right person to serve as Rebbe and even less was thought of his son Reb Aaron's merit to inherit the dynasty in the future.

The new rov's style in carrying out his responsibilities created additional sources of friction.

> The Rebbe's son is the leader. He leads the services. He controls the functions—weddings, a bris, a bar mitzvah—and he receives a fee for each. He officiates at every wedding. He has to officiate. A large number of weddings are held outside the community because people don't want him to officiate. He shows up at your son's bar mitzvah and you put a fifty-dollar bill in his hand. It's funny how some things begin as an honor, like giving the Rebbe money, and end up being enforced. A lot of traditions begin out of affection and then become enforced. It used to be traditional. (MR)

The Rebbe named the gabbai and exercised his power to have his own people in positions elected by the community: the president (a secular post) and the board of directors.

> After the last election [prior to 1986] the Rebbe didn't like the results and so he nullified them and put in his own people. Now it's "You go your way and I'll go mine." It's up to the individual to decide how much authority he has over you . . . if you accept him.   (MR)

The high hopeful spirit of the village had received a jolt from the new leadership.

> The Rebbe is losing the respect of the people. The community works like a well-established business. There's not an atmosphere of revolt, but there's not the respect of a Hasid for his Rebbe.   (YA)

The smoldering dissent is evident inside the besmedresh when Reb Aaron gives a talk with sixty or seventy of the villagers—some paying attention and some not—seated at the tables around him. This is a sharp comparison to the crowds of Hasidim who in the past gathered to hear the older Rebbe speak and who pondered his every word and gesture. Even more noticeable is the group of Hasidim who ignore the meeting inside the besmedresh and gather outside to converse on matters of their own.

The responsibilities of being dean of the yeshivah hold some inherent liabilities as well.

> There's another handicap that he has, at least a lot of people consider it so and I personally consider it a tremendous handicap, and that is that his father made him the dean of the school system. And being the dean of the school system means that automatically there are parents that may not be happy with the way their son is learning. Being dean of the yeshivah automatically creates five hundred enemies for him.   (MR)

The Old Rebbetsn

Feiga Teitelbaum, the widow of the old Rebbe, lives most of the time in Kiryas Joel. She is still considered the rebbetsn and her presence is a continual reminder of the greatness of past times during Reb Joel's reign as the Rebbe of Satmar. She continues to be the rallying point for those dissatisfied with the present leadership. One form of protest has been to emphasize their commitment to the deceased Rebbe by venerating his widow and by accusing the new Rebbe of mistreating her.

> His treatment of the older rebbetsn is unforgivable. He excluded her and he blamed her for every problem. If someone was angry at him he blamed the rebbetsn.   (MR)

The house that had been built for the older Rebbe stands on a hill overlooking Kiryas Joel. The outside of the house is relatively modest and gives no clue to the sweeping dimensions of the rooms and corridors. Spacious and richly decorated, the interior seems akin to a summer palace of an Oriental prince. Since the Rebbe's death the rebbetsn has transformed the residence into a postnatal care center, and its splendor is now enjoyed by the women who come to the house for a brief convalescence. A few women in bathrobes stroll through the sitting rooms and corridors. In a sumptuous setting nearby the newborn infants are cared for by nurses and staff. The women pay a Beverly Hills price tag for their days of leisure here, although fees slide downward for the less-well-to-do; those with a demonstrable need and with lesser means can register here as well.

Outside the house there is a small cemetery where the Rebbe lies buried. It is quiet and isolated there except on the anniversary of the Rebbe's death in late August when thousands of Hasidim climb the hill to the cemetery to visit his grave. Women enter the cemetery the day before the yortsayt; the day of the yortsayt itself is reserved for the men.

Rich and Poor

The points of contention in most communities often turn on problems concerning wealth and class, but the common religious concerns of the Hasidim and the emphasis on giving charity seem to override economic disparities. This is not to say that the rich are not at times deferred to: a wealthy man known for piety and generosity has a special place in community affairs and may bask in the admiration of his comrades. Nonetheless, even though signs of wealth and financial status are readily apparent, it would be difficult to divide the community on the basis of class.

The size and architectural style of the houses reflect both the tremendous economic diversity of the community and homogeneity of their other interests and concerns. Just as rich and poor stand shoulder to shoulder in the besmedresh, so too are their houses set side by side on the street. A row of modest duplex houses is occasionally interrupted by an expansive and swirling stairway entrance to a home of more than modest means. An expensive car in the driveway may emphasize the point. A winter and a summer home are tangible expressions of wealth; the rooms boast luxurious furnishings and the traditional sideboard is overflowing with silver. In search of added prestige the well-to-do may send their children to study abroad in a yeshivah in Israel or Switzerland.

Away from their homes and possessions, however, in the besmedresh and on the street, it is difficult to distinguish between rich and poor. Only a clothing maven could discriminate between the cloth and cut of one black suit from another. Though perhaps in vastly different economic brackets, yeshivah comrades still meet for a few minutes after prayer to exchange news and political views. They often find themselves on the same side in controversies that riffle through the community.

But wealth itself does not bring a Hasid respect unless his riches are utilized in behalf of the community. The rich must do more than others to maintain the yeshivah and besmedresh, provide jobs, and help those in need. Charity distinguishes rich and poor at least by degree: the rich man, with his greater wealth, has more opportunities to perform mitzvot of consequence and to garner the respect that his deeds merit.

Consider, for example, one of Kiryas Joel's most affluent residents, who learned from one of his less well-to-do neighbors that a betrothed couple in Israel, orphans, lacked money for their wedding and all that that event implies: the ceremony, clothing, an apartment, furniture. Could he help out with a gift? In a fashion worthy of a tale by Peretz, the rich man agreed to furnish everything, an amount said to exceed sixty-five thousand dollars, for people he had never seen. He had but one demand: that the couple marry on the same day as the date set for his own daughter's wedding, to focus, one can assume, the merit of his gift. And, as in a storyteller's ending, the rich man also provided his fellow villager with two plane tickets to Israel to enjoy the wedding, in gratitude for his having given him the opportunity to perform such a mitzvah.

As in all Hasidic communities, there are a host of voluntary actions which help to establish a sense of camaraderie. Visits are made to the house-bound and to those sick in hospitals. At prayer services volunteers collect for a friend out of work or in need of aid to cover medical expenses. Some small acts of service are acts of general friendship and devotion: each morning in Kiryas Joel two schoolteachers voluntarily prepare one hundred gallons of coffee for the throng of worshipers. The two volunteers also collect contributions to pay for the cost of the coffee and the three cases of milk.[6]

Female Bus Drivers

The community continued to have legal struggles. The district school system owns and operates its own bus service to carry the students to school. For nine years, until 1984, male bus drivers were assigned by the district to transport the boys to and from school. In 1984 the female bus drivers, who had more seniority than the men, won a grievance that they were being denied assignment to the longer and therefore better-paying routes because of sex discrimination. The schoolboys, however, in order to maintain the separation of the sexes (outside of the home), refused to ride on school buses with women drivers. (Schoolgirls could ride buses driven by either men or women.) Their parents went to court in Orange County to obtain relief from having women bus drivers transport the boys to school. The thirty-two women who drove the buses then filed a human rights suit in federal court.[7]

The federal court then found itself in a dilemma: on the one hand assigning male bus drivers could be seen as endorsement of religion by the state; on the other hand assigning women bus drivers on the basis of seniority would infringe on the rights of the Hasidim by insisting that they alter their beliefs in order to obtain free transportation. In 1987 the court decided that the state's essential need was to guard the distinction between church and state. The court held that the rights of the women bus drivers superseded the religious strictures affecting the separation of the sexes.

Although the women had won the right to drive the longer routes ferrying the Hasidic boys, it soon proved to be a hollow victory. The Hasidim sacrificed the free bus service for boys and continued to arrange their own transportation to school at considerable expense and inconvenience. The women bus drivers were denied back pay; moreover, there was a reduction in the number of jobs available. The school district of course had to dip into its budget to cover legal fees.[8] The Hasidic community had demonstrated its determination to maintain its traditions.

> It's not a question of law. It's a question of a whole social attitude based on *halakhah* considerations of course, and a desire to maintain a certain lifestyle which has no intrusions upon it. It's worth it for a community to assert its basic rights.   (MSS)

Families

By 1990 the year-round population of Kiryas Joel was over 8,000. In the summer the population expands when those who have summer homes come to the community to escape the heat. There are also over a thousand Satmar Hasidim living in the area surrounding the official boundary of the village. They are subject to the zoning laws of the township rather than the village, and they are also more immune to the social pressures of the village—a tradeoff for those who enjoy the Hasidic ambiance but not the close scrutiny of their neighbors.

Concern over children dominates life in Kiryas Joel. The village is a young community with an unusually high birth rate. In 1986 the size of an average household was 6.6; one-quarter of the residents were under the age of five; many families had eight to twelve children. That year children made up 65 percent of the population. In every corner there are children at play—the boys racing out from under their yarmulkes, their earlocks and *tzitzit* (fringes) flying, and the girls, playing separately, skipping a bit more sedately in their long-sleeved dresses and long stockings.

With such large families it would seem impossible for women to have any free time outside the home; however, since the schools run all day until five o'clock, there is a lively social life for women. Most conversations are carried on by telephone, with a long cord that extends from the wall to the stove, to the table, and to the washing machine. Women meet in each other's homes, or, in nice weather, find occasions to chat on street-corners. Many women do charity work and make hospital visits. They take turns running fundraising parties for the schools and for needy families. An organizer calls up her friends, who divide the responsibilities for the party—baking, collecting, or purchasing cakes and cookies, preparing *nosh* [snack] foods, and printing raffle tickets for a charity drawing. A few women with older children manage to work in a variety of business positions. One woman with six children leaves her youngest son with a babysitter and works from nine to three as a bookkeeper. As for the rest of women's activities: "We cook up a storm, we bake up a storm, we sew up a storm."

After returning home from work outside the village, L is greeted in the house by his five children, with each of whom he exchanges a hug and a kiss. Showing off for the visitor, he asks the children their ages: "I'm six!" one of the smaller children cries. His father laughs and assures him that he's still five, but the boy insists, amid laughter, that he is six. His father reaches into his wallet for a card where he has carefully written the names and birthdates of his children. The boy proves to be precisely correct. "Yankel! Today is your birthday."

Later, after supper, the father exclaims: "I love this place. I really love it here. There's so much goodness. There's so much giving."

· 20 ·

Family Problems:
Views of the Therapists

The Etiology of Mental Affliction

In the recent past children and adults who suffered from developmental and psychological difficulties were kept behind closed doors and were not acknowledged by the community. Families kept secret such afflictions as mental retardation, autism, and Down's syndrome, as well as mental illnesses such as schizophrenia, depression, phobia, and neurosis. Families were marked by the affliction of their child, by the pain of the situation, and by self-imposed isolation.

In some instances involving mental illness not even the rabbi was consulted unless the circumstances became unmanageable. Each family kept its own secrets.

> In Europe they wouldn't come to us [the rabbis] with such a problem, because the worst thing that any person could say to another person in our culture was *er iz meshugeh* [he's crazy]. That was the end. There was nothing as stigmatized and as bad as mental illness. If the person deteriorated to such an extent that they could no longer keep them, so they put them away in some kind of a sanitarium or mental institution, or you had, and still have today, people roaming the streets. In Europe it was unheard of for people to seek help. (CS)

In past times the affliction of mental illness was a powerful negative force affecting everyone in the family in practical and spiritual terms, possibly for generations. If but one member of a family was mentally ill, then everyone in the family lived under the shadow of the illness. The developmentally disabled and the emotionally troubled were rarely seen on the streets, except at night.[1]

> Nobody was supposed to know about it. There are documented cases of families where they used to walk the mentally ill in the middle of the night, like you'd walk a pet, for fear of being seen. (CS)

In the past it was a stigma. Somehow the whole family would feel guilty. They would feel embarrassed. They would feel that there was something wrong with them. It would affect the whole family, because of the fact that you have to hide something—it couldn't be open, you couldn't take your sick kid out on the street and go to places with her. You were bound, locked into your house. You couldn't go anywhere. You had to hide something from your neighbors. You were always living in a certain kind of fear. (AG)

Unwanted notoriety was related in great measure to the need to protect the family and the future marital prospects of other offspring. Given the close ties of the Hasidic community, the relatively small pool of eligible mates, and the swiftness with which gossip can diminish reputation, an apparent predisposition to such illnesses would severely limit the marital desirability of all the siblings in the family.

They kept these kids at home because they were worried about the marriages they would have to do with the rest of the children. They were afraid it will affect them in the sense that people feel that if you have a sick kid at home, the children you would have would be the same, or even without that fear, the fact that something is going wrong with your home. There's a stigma. In other words, even if it's not hereditary, let's say you would have a sick child because of an accident that happened, it would still affect and hurt you. (AG)

Since the world is thought to be under the unerring control of the Almighty, physical or mental impairment is often seen as an aberration and as a punishment for sin: *Pain and death come only because of our sins.*[2] Attitudes toward unexplained illnesses have been shaped in part by this belief, and misfortune is thus made still more painful by feelings of guilt and shame.

"Being mentally ill implies a degree of abandonment by G-d," Dr. Yehuda Nir, a psychoanalyst with Hasidic patients, has observed; "[it signifies] being possibly deficient in one's observance, in one's devotion, having sinned."[3]

If the problem had a religious cause it was possible to reason that religious figures could find a remedy within the established doctrine. In a 1971–1972 study Dr. Harvey Kranzler observed a common perspective on the etiology of mental illness held by Hasidic Rebbes in Israel. It can be regarded as representative of the thinking of the past European epoch.

... it was clear then that those Rebbes interviewed felt that mental illness had a religious etiology, was within the purview of their own expertise and referrals were made for outside psychiatric help only when the patients were very disruptive in order to obtain medication from the "nervim doctor" who would return the patient to them for the therapy provided by religious guidance, observance, and communal support.[4]

The folk etiology of mental illness also incorporated belief in the supernatural, the hosts of demons and devils, and the spirits of the dead. As a Satmar rabbi observed, "Years ago they used to sometimes attribute mental illness to a *dybbuk* [wandering soul of the dead]" (CS).

A tale related about the Satmar Rebbe during his stay in Israel in 1946 provides a capsule account of the shifting tides of belief following the Second World War.

... when the Satmar Rebbe was in Israel a Yemenite from Yemen came with his daughter ... He claimed that a dybbuk entered into her and he's bothering her, and she has pains, and she talks with a strange voice ... So he went to the Belzer Rebbe and ... the Belzer Rebbe commanded the dybbuk to leave the person alone and to go. But anyhow, she didn't feel any better, and she came to the Satmar Rebbe. So they thought that the Satmar Rebbe will do some miracles there, say something and the dybbuk will disappear. So the Satmar Rebbe said, "I think it's a mental case. Better go to a good psychiatrist and leave me alone."[5]

This tale, which was told by Satmar Hasidim in New York City in the 1950s, requires some words of explanation: by the mid-1950s the Belzer Rebbe and the Satmar Rebbe had become bitter opponents concerning the State of Israel, and so the more ignorant position concerning dybbuks is attributed to the Belzer Rebbe; the Yemenite Jews, one of whom brings the girl to the Rebbe for consultation, were considered to be the most backward of all the children of Israel returning to the Holy Land. The tale supports the view that the Satmar Rebbe, as unbending as he was on issues of law and tradition, was also up-to-date in his thinking. Finally, the message was that the Hasidic community in America had become more sophisticated concerning mental illness and previously accepted folk beliefs.

While the disappearance of belief in the dybbuk in America can be attributed to the influence of modern ideas, Hasidim continue to explain the change of thinking in mystical terms.

This community today doesn't talk about, doesn't believe in a dybbuk, because we are in such a spiritual decline in this world that it is not only in the sacred parts but even the impure—the Satanic side—the other side, the dark side—[is diminished]. It says clearly in the scriptures, in Zohar, that these are balances. If one declines then the other declines. You can see we don't have the prophets. We don't have the kabbalists, the mystics, we don't have the Baal Shem Tov, so therefore we know that there is also decline in the other side. So there are no dybbukim today as there used to be. If you have the illness then you have to have the cure and the doctor. Obviously we don't have those spiritual healers that we used to. So we don't believe and we have long since discarded those [ideas]. (CS)

Today, however, the only ones likely to use the notion of a dybbuk as a cause of mental illness are the sufferers, the mentally ill, as Dr. Allen Manovitz points out:

> The belief system of the Hasidic inpatient is one that is well out of the mainstream of Western culture. Often Hasidic inpatients will express beliefs in dybbuks, demons, exorcism, and the evil eye that are syntonic with their community's beliefs, but often appear quite psychotic in a larger cultural context.[6]

A Change of Perspective

In very recent times modern concepts of medicine have permeated the general consciousness of the community and a significant intellectual and conceptual shift has occurred. This change matches the movement throughout American society to extend rights to the handicapped. In every Hasidic neighborhood, community leaders respected for their knowledge and their piety have encouraged new attitudes toward physical disability, mental retardation, and mental illness. This growing awareness finds support in Jewish tradition: "Righteousness saves from death!"[7]

In Williamsburg, the most conservative Hasidic stronghold, Rabbi Chaim Stauber of Satmar led the way in 1982 in founding Pesach Tikvah (Door of Hope) to provide clinical facilities and workshops for the acutely ill. Rabbi Stauber's first task was to educate the community. Initially the clinic encountered serious opposition: "When we first opened, we were picketed and there were some threats . . . There were many who denounced me as a heretic."[8] Soon, however, Pesach Tikvah had a clinic for outpatients requiring psychotherapy, a day program consisting of a sheltered workshop and vocational rehabilitation, and a community residence with twenty-four beds for mentally retarded and autistic women.

> There has been a major turning point in ushering in modern psychiatry into this community with the full blessing and tacit approval of all of the big Rebbes. What I've done is convince the people that there's no sense hiding and pretending that nobody sees when in fact you are being seen and you're just being very foolish by not availing yourself [of help]. It's in the Torah that Almighty God wants us to seek the help of doctors. (CS)

In the Lubavitch community new ideas on mental health were also introduced by baltshuves, the returnees to the faith, who often included men and women who had already graduated from college and had careers in the professions. In the early 1980s, for example, a psychologist would offer Lubavitch workshops for those who like himself felt drawn to Orthodox Judaism. Professional people who became baltshuves were a prize catch for Lubavitch and they often became an important resource in attracting and training other returnees. It was inevitable that through them modern concepts concerning mental health would percolate through the community.

At the same time, as individual Hasidim were seeking avenues to the fields of psychology, mental health, and retardation, professionals in those fields were eager to introduce their healing skills into the Hasidic community. Contacts with Hasidic community leaders were carefully nurtured:

> . . . about five years ago [1985] we began to work with a rabbi in the Satmar community [Chaim Stauber]. He sat in on at least 150 clinical interviews. Over the years he has become increasingly sophisticated in descriptive psychopathology. He is highly skilled in prioritizing the psychiatric needs of his community as the closest psychiatric equivalent to the model of a surgeon's assistant or a physician's assistant we have seen to date.[9]

The community was initially reluctant to attend to the new concepts.

> The general rule is that anything that can be dealt with within the community by either teachers, elders, or wise lay members of the community, or the Rebbe or his assistants, is not referred outside the community for professional evaluation and help. My experience has been the pediatricians and neurologists are usually consulted before the psychiatrist even in cases of overt psychosis, in the hope that the symptoms might fit a medical rather than a psychiatric diagnosis.[10]

It became increasingly clear, however, that the rabbis were often faced with dilemmas beyond their ken, and that their counsel, though well meaning, was often ineffectual. Those rabbis who continued to offer counseling without being trained in individual and group psychology were no longer regarded as unquestioned authorities.

> You came to a rov and he says, "What's wrong? You have a problem? I'll tell you what, you separate for a few weeks and we'll see how you'll get along." Of course that never works, but the rabbanim are not attuned to counseling, marriage counseling. (BI)

While wholehearted approval was slow in forthcoming, the new methods moved steadily through the community.

> Counseling is first becoming accepted in Orthodox society—that there could be something emotionally wrong with a person that could be cured with counseling. It was very difficult before we could even break into marriage counseling, and show the people there was a need for counseling, that counseling could help. (BI)

Rabbi Stauber gives major credit for the increased acceptance of modern ideas to the Rebbes. Once the Rebbe was won over the remainder of the court was soon to follow. In time Rebbes and their assistants came to keep a list of psychiatrists and therapists to recommend to families and individuals who came to them for help. In a highly organized community like Satmar, referrals to psychiatrists became another carefully controlled healing option.

> [In Satmar] in order to treat the Hasidic patient, the psychiatrist has to be approved by the Rebbe or his associate. In the case of the Satmar there is a special medical unit, the MRA (Medical Referral Association) that arranges referrals to all physicians including psychiatrists. It is operated by medically skilled rabbis who make diagnostic assessments over the phone, then give the patient the name of the physician. Often, if a specialist is needed the referral can be out of town, be it the Mayo Clinic or Beth Israel Hospital in Boston. If the patient cannot afford the fee the expenses are covered by one of the Bikur Holim [Visiting the Sick] organizations. In the case of a psychiatric referral the rabbi does not ask for the name of the patient in order to maintain confidentiality.[11]

The Rebbe's approval fosters faith in psychological treatment and in the efficacy of individual practitioners. On this point Dr. Allen Manovitz notes:

> The patient's attitude towards the rabbi, both consciously and unconsciously determined, has an influence on the patient's initial reaction to the physician. Therefore, we have observed that when a Hasidic Rebbe endorses a physician, the physician is usually imbued with immediate and direct positive feelings because of the synergy of conscious and unconscious determinants which we call fleeting transference.[12]

Although he is a scientist, the physician is seen to have supernatural forces working on his behalf, as Dr. Nir observes:

> As a Hasidic Jew sees physicians in general as God's messengers, *shlikhim,* they experience the relief of symptoms as forgiveness and thank the physician for being the right messenger.[13]

These new sources of aid sometimes require staying in a residence. This poses a threat to the religious life of individual patients even if the treatment has the support of their Rebbes. When one of Williamsburg's few drug addicts admitted himself to a rehabilitation clinic, his family was concerned about the range of social options open to him there (an ironic situation considering the self-destructive experimentation already undertaken):

> My family was afraid the whole time. This place was a very free place. They tell you you can do anything you want to do in life. Just don't do drugs. The

reasoning goes that it's certain conditioning we have in us that makes us quite human. My mother and brother went to a big Rebbe, the Spinker, in Williamsburg. "Should we still support him there? His mind is back. Should we still keep him there in such an open, free society?"

And the Rebbe answered, "Yes. Not only are you allowed to, you must." (AI)[14]

The family, however, may consult with the Rebbe more than once on the course of treatment, as Dr. Kranzler reports:

By the time the child or adolescent arrives in my office it is usually with the blessing of the Rebbe. And in many ways the Rebbe is an invisible but significant presence in my session with the child and the family. I personally have never had a case in which a Rebbe did not permit a treatment strategy or the use of medication but I have heard from colleagues that Rebbes have on occasion advised the cessation of medication when they felt it was not efficacious. I suspect that occurs when the Rebbe detects a real ambivalence on the part of the family about the use of medication. But I do think it is rare.[15]

Throughout the Hasidic community ties have been established with mental health practitioners who have helped to make clinical facilities, personnel, and training available. In addition to Pesach Tikvah in Williamsburg there are many other clinics now in operation. In Borough Park, Ohel Children's Home and Family Services provides a residence for children who are developmentally and emotionally disabled, a home for retarded adults, and a family counseling and therapy unit. Maimonides Hospital in Borough Park offers outpatient services at the hospital and at smaller inconspicuous centers in the heart of the community. Tikvah Program New Hope Guild Center in Flatbush provides a range of therapeutic services for patients. There are other hospitals and institutional centers providing similar services, and of course there are now many private consultants in the city and in the suburban areas of settlement.

The Therapists

In Williamsburg and Borough Park, where clinics and programs for the mentally and physically disabled have opened, there are a growing number of Hasidim being trained in counseling and therapy.

The first therapists to treat Hasidic patients were rarely Orthodox, and some were not Jewish. For many in the community it was essential to have the Orthodox point of view represented, and in a relatively short time the number of Orthodox psychologists, social workers, therapists, and counselors greatly increased.[16]

Of course they're not going to send somebody to someone who's not Orthodox. They're afraid to send people to a nonreligious psychologist or psychiatrist. So we had to get together people who are religious who would be accepted in the society, and thank goodness it's beginning to move. (BI)[17]

Counselors and aides were in immediate demand. Initially, in order to increase Hasidic participation in the programs, various types of practical training were arranged.

I didn't go to a formal college or university, but there was a professor, Dr. F, who was a very big psychiatrist, and he began teaching groups. He felt that a layman could learn enough about psychology to be very helpful, and eventually he wanted to turn this into a kind of a layman type of counseling. What I'm doing I don't have to be licensed. I'm a counselor, I'm counseling. It's called religious counseling. So I tell the people in advance that I have no license. I'm just trying to help them and advise them. But I have to be attuned. If there's one of them is a nut, I've got to know that they're nuts, and I've got to know where to send them and so on. (BI)

In some instances Hasidim are brought into an agency and trained to aid the professional staff and to provide custodial service.

I had forty hours' training from the New York State Office of Mental Health in the area of community residence. I went to Manhattan where they taught people from many community residence homes. They gave some basic training, and from there on it was experience mostly. They taught us about the nature of the problems of these people, how to deal with them, what kind of help they need, and what a community residence home is supposed to be, what it's supposed to serve, the whole structure of it, and those kinds of things.

The work is very rewarding, because when you work with people and you help them and you see that they're being helped, that's very rewarding. We have cases of schizophrenia, paranoia. The home in itself, the whole milieu, is a therapeutic one. The mere fact of living over there, the support they get from the staff, the counseling they get from the staff, the reassurance, and the structure they get, relieves a lot of burdens and tensions from them, and in time they get better and better. With some people you see a lot of progress, with some people, less; with some people you don't see any progress. Eventually they move on: some people go home, some people move on to a less supervised home. (AG)

The demand for psychological assistance has carried over into the school system. The yeshivot now have school counselors to help young students work through problems in truancy and behavior. It has become a learning experience for the Hasidic teachers who have become counselors as well as for the students they advise.

I'm the counselor in school and I've become sensitive to people's emotions. I deal with problems not only in religion but in all sorts of things in the surroundings. If there is a religious problem then it is usually a deeper emotional problem with the father. I talk to him, but not about religion but about his background and his family. If necessary I then try to convince the family that they should try to seek some professional counseling. Whether one is religious or not, emotional problems exist just like in other societies.   (BI)

The newly trained counselors and paraprofessionals serve as brokers for the rest of the community, circulating and authenticating the new knowledge. They help to raise the general level of sophistication and understanding regarding heretofore hidden problems.

The most significant reservoir of therapists and counselors promises to be the older married women who have returned to school after raising their families. Even the most traditional Rebbes have come to rely on Orthodox women therapists even when both have to cope with the taboos of a Rebbe addressing a woman:

> We had a number of the Rebbe's Hasidim as patients, and when the office closed I went to see him to see what we could do about it. When we came in my husband (who is not a therapist) sat at the desk next to the Rebbe. I sat on the other side of the room where the women usually sit. At the beginning he wasn't talking to me at all. When he realized who I was he invited me to come forward and sit on the side at a table. At our second visit we sat in the same places as before but now his conversation was directed at me. He asked me a good many questions and was very sophisticated. Since then he has recommended patients to me.   (BH)

In Borough Park in 1986 thirty-five social workers and counselors (thirty women and five men) established a telephone hotline to honor Yitti Liebel, a much admired social worker who had passed away at the age of forty-three. As a measure of the social acceptance of psychology, by 1991 all of the workers had completed an academic degree in counseling or psychology. Volunteers had telephones installed in their homes; each week they donate one hour to respond to calls for help and advice. (The scheduling is on a computer so that the calls are referred automatically to the person on duty at the time.)[18] In four years the volunteers have fielded more than five thousand calls, often from those who prefer not to appear in person at a clinic. Most of the callers are women. Marital problems are the major concern, followed by parent-child relationships, but there is a wide range of problems including child abuse and suicide. Serious problems and repeat callers are referred to clinics and mental health centers.

As word of the Yitti Liebel Help Line has spread, calls have come from an increasingly wide geographic circle, including Israel. There is now a trunk line to Chicago so that callers in that city can reach the help line with a local call. The annual budget of approximately $50,000 includes the cost of two paid members of the group, the director and the coordinator. The funds are raised through an annual luncheon, home brunches, and donations. The group holds a clinical meeting every three months at which problems are discussed and role-playing is done to practice coping with a variety of situations.

The Scope of Psychological Problems

Psychologists who hold a variety of personal religious views describe the problems affecting their Hasidic patients in similar terms. Dr. Menachem M. Brayer has the perspectives of both psychologist and Hasid.

> There is a psycho-religious syndrome. The problems of the Hasidim are very similar or equal to secular problems, but they have a religious component. The superego—the guilt complex—weighs heavily on their shoulders. It's the sin problem. If they are involved in illicit relations or gambling or whatever, their guilt is more intense because they have to account to a Supreme Being. Their problems are more intense. (MMB)

Psychologists note that some problems have specific historical and social roots.

> Parents with survivor background [from the concentration camps] cannot relate to trivia, and their kids feel guilty. Or the survivor can relate up to the age when he or she was put in the camp. Teenagers get upset and parents can't relate to it because it seems so trivial—for instance, a daughter might feel she's not pretty or she doesn't have a pretty dress. The parents may be very depressed.
>
> Patients say that most of the parents in America are European born and they hear from their parents that things were freer—that life was not so terribly rigid. So they're angry with them and have an image of parents as harder than they really are. They usually see parents as very authoritarian and very rule-bound. They resent the rules but feel guilty if they don't do what their parents say. (JA)

Virtually every therapist who treats Hasidic patients finds the struggle for independence to be a common problem.

> Most of my Hasidic patients have been women. They feel that their mothers treat them as if they were five. The mothers come over, they cook, take care of the kids. (JA)

> The mothers put a lot of energy into their kids. Most Hasidishe women don't have a conflict of roles. The family comes first. There's not a conflict where I first have to find myself, and I have to do my own thing, and I have to be successful at work. Their success is measured by their kids. They do spend a lot of time making the kids feel good about themselves. They have clear goals. They want their kids to be religious and to marry and have kids. They want their kids to have lives like they've had. They're not interested in other experiences. (EA)

A number of analysts with wide experience in the Hasidic community have observed the negative side of intense family and in-law relations. Dr. Rashi Schapiro observed:

> There's more potential for interpersonal stresses because you have more people involved here. The mothers-in-law are there and promote tensions. I'd say a Jewish problem is family enmeshment and overengagement rather than distance and isolation. There's a lot of pettiness going on all the time. "Your mother said this and my mother said that." You can have a very intrusive parent or parent-in-law, very intrusive, who wants the couple to live with them or wants to come into the couple's house every night to make dinner, and that is a cultural thing as well as a personality issue.
>
> I first have to help them evaluate how much they want this parent or parent-in-law in, because again as issues they get involved with the religious aspect—honor thy father and mother. Jewish love requires me to respect my mother who wants to come in every night, and that sort of thing, and I have to help them decide. In the long run we have a dispute about the religious issue and I say "Go ask your rabbi" to see if "Honor your father and mother" requires you to have the mother there every night. Then when they check it out—sometimes they don't check it out—they say that they really know that it doesn't require Mom to be in every night. So I say, "If you know that, what are you going to do about it?" Then they have a dispute about what to do until they work things out. Generally these patients are not psychotic. We're not talking about crazies now. We're talking about normals and neurotics whose behavior is not clearly pathological and where I could say, "What you're doing is crazy." Having Mom in every night is not crazy. It's socially approved in Hasidic circles. And so then I have to say, "Is that what you want? Do you want her there every night? Do you want her there once a week? Do you want her there once a year?" (RS)

Dr. Menachem Brayer observed the danger of the continuing dependence of new couples on family and in-laws.

> Either you deal with immature male personalities who are still dependent on their mother figure and are mama's babies and never mature, or financially they are dependent on their fathers and they feel guilty to rebel or fight them again. And in most cases it is in-laws on both sides who would like to dictate the lifestyle of their children. It's a carryover I think from the common mode of living in the shtetl when two or three generations lived together and everyone knew what was cooking in the other one's pot.
>
> Basically it is the woman who is subjugated. It is the woman who rebels against her mother-in-law. The mother-in-law is more of a problem almost classically speaking more than the father-in-law. (MMB)

While women have less contact with the outside world than do men, because of their inexperience and innocence, the effects of change among Hasidic women appear to be the sharper and more painful.

You realize that they don't tell you the truth. The women are very much into presenting a happy facade. I think that's a strong feature of the Hasidic community that they do not admit problems to each other. There's a lot more jealousy and protection of the family unit as an individual unit than there is in secular society.

The woman is much more sheltered than the man is. Women in most cases do not work. They stay in a very limited, enclosed environment, in the immediate neighborhood, so their temptations are far less. What this promotes is a discrepancy in the personal growth or the interests or the styles of men versus women. Some of the Hasidic women have had enough exposure to the world to know that they're missing something. They experience a jealousy between the fact that their husbands are really out there and they're not. Some women are intellectual and intelligent and have a need for or curiosity for more stimulation than they're getting. Some women have a dissatisfaction with just being mothers. Then there's a sense that in some cases, the Hasidic man who is really immersed in self-fulfillment either from a religious point of view—let's say he's studying in yeshivah all day—that sort of thing can lead to a pursuit of individual growth on his part and the woman might feel abandoned or left behind. She will feel a little lonely. (RS)

A female therapist picked up similar clues from her patients.

There are sad things going on. Women watch TV or pick up magazines and see this freedom that's supposed to exist and they think they're really missing something. They're terribly naive and think it would operate according to the ideals portrayed. They think—if they could only go dancing! They have a fascination that something wonderful is out there, and [in truth] it's the seediest part of our society and that's sad.

The women have thoughts of liberalizing certain things—not wanting to wear a sheytl. Or they want to go to a nonkosher resort—they would eat kosher, but they want some other experience. (JA)

Clients and Patients

Inpatient admission for serious cases follows a standard procedure. A family contacts a rabbi concerning a troubled family member or the rabbi learns of the problem from others. The rabbi then refers the family to a psychiatrist or therapist known to him. As practitioners reported at the 1990 meetings of the American Psychiatric Association, there are a variety of deceptions sometimes employed by the patient or the family to avoid being diagnosed as being mentally ill. Dr. Allen Manovitz noted:

. . . it is not at all uncommon for a patient to (a) present with 3 to 7 years of untreated major psychopathology including hallucinations, delusions, manic behavior that has been essentially absorbed into the community. Or (b) for a patient to present on multiple medications regimens and psychotropic medications prescribed by multiple doctors, often not psychiatrists, often not in communication with each other. And for families and patients to be not compliant with these medications because patients and families do not want to see aberrant behavior viewed as psychiatric.[19]

There was, however, a corresponding rise in the expectation that a cure must be sought.

It is important to note, however, that in the last two years we have seen a dramatic drop in the community's and family's tolerance of untreated mental illness and psychopathology, factors that we believe are important and integral are psycho-education as described, liaison with leaders of the community by psychiatrists and an increased communication between members of the community who have been treated psychiatrically. Thus rabbis, families and patients are seeking earlier intervention.[20]

As in American society in general, there is a wide range of patients being treated, as Dr. Harvey Kranzler described.

There is an increasing effort at early detection, treating and providing services to those children who have what are viewed as biological symptoms, such as autism, varying developmental disabilities, mental retardation, psychoses, major affective disorder and even learning disabilities.[21]

Up to this point in time there is little hard data to establish any divergences from the general norm in the types of illnesses treated. Kranzler noted that "There is no data available as to the prevalence of psychiatric illness in children and adolescents in the Hasidic population, but my assumption is that the prevalence is no different than in the general population."[22]

A summary of psychiatric disorders was presented by Dr. Yehuda Nir to his colleagues:

From a diagnostic point of view the majority of my Hasidic patients suffer from either bi-polar or depressive disorders. While depressive disorders are easily recognizable, the patients with bi-polar disorders present a diagnostic challenge. Most of them arrive during the manic stage, in an acute psychotic state when it is difficult to make the differential diagnosis between bi-polar or schizophrenic disorder. It is only with growing experience, after having seen over 100 Hasidic patients that I was able to diagnose the manic phase correctly and with a great degree of certainty. The primary symptoms are usually delusions that have to do with being the Messiah when the patient is a male, or having information about the coming of the Messiah when the patient is female. It is usually accompanied by auditory hallucination, long hours of praying day and night and occasionally ritualistic obsessive compulsive behavior of a bizarre nature, not uncommonly a psychotic parody of a religious ceremony. While initially I would treat those patients with large doses of anti-psychotic medication, I now use, without exception, lithium carbonate augmented initially by small doses of tranquilizers.

Among the patients suffering from depressive disorders the majority are holocaust survivors, their children, and in some cases grandchildren. While Shoah is rarely discussed at home, there is among the survivors a discernible lifestyle centered around sadness. Its theme is often a silent non-verbal commemoration of the departed parent or sibling taking place on every holiday, often on every Sabbath. The second generation does not comprehend the nature of this intense grief and is deeply influenced by this non-verbal affective climate. The survivor's children are often named after a family member who was murdered by the Germans and this adds to the burden.

Post-partum depression is another common entity but I have no epidemiological information as compared to the general population. Post-partum depression has however a specific aspect in this community, namely the issue of contraception. The Hasidic woman is not allowed to use contraception unless the pregnancy can be hazardous to the woman's or the new-born's health. The use of psychotropic medication, in this case anti-depressants, gives the woman permission to use contraceptive devices. Following a positive response to the medication there is a reluctance on the part of the patient to stop treatment as it might imply an immediate pregnancy. It is not uncommon therefore, for the patient to request to stay on medication longer than medically indicated in order to be allowed to continue to use contraception. This request is occasionally motivated by a phobic anticipation that the next pregnancy will precipitate another depression.[23]

Dr. Allen Manovitz provided a preliminary review of the inpatient population over the last five years at one New York hospital.

> . . . a majority of our patients are Satmar, though not exclusively, a 70 to 30 ratio. There are equal numbers of male and female patients with ages ranging from the teens until the seventies, with a majority of the patients in their twenties and thirties. Eighty percent of these admissions are with acute psychosis with 50% of those admissions with psychosis having a diagnosis of bipolar disorder manic episodes, 25% with schizophrenia and 25% with schizo-affective. 10% of the admissions are with major depression and less than 10% of the admissions involve other diagnoses including personality disorder and substance abuse.[24]

The specter of having an individual or family problem known to the entire community means that special precautions are taken in scheduling outpatient treatment. Appointments for patients from the same Hasidic group must be carefully spaced. One practitioner enters Hasidic appointments in red ink to ensure that they do not meet in the office. At times initial appointments are listed under a pseudonym.

Registering a Hasid as an inpatient in a hospital seems even more fraught with social peril. Families sometimes attempt to register admission as medical rather than psychiatric with the result of needless tests and x-rays until the appropriate diagnosis is made and the patient is transferred to the appropriate unit. Hasidic inpatients present additional special problems, as Dr. Manovitz recounted.

Hasidic patients are uniquely socially isolated. As a direct result of their mental illness, they are isolated from their families . . . the need for hospitalization is often shrouded in what is perceived by their family as necessary secrecy leading to further isolation from their community. Often patients choose to isolate themselves in hospitals where they think they will not be found by members of their community. Raised to view the non-Hasidic world as alien, they are isolated from the support of co-patients experiencing similar mental difficulties. Dressed in traditional garb and spending their days in highly regimented religious practices and observances, they often are isolated from the staff on the other unit who cannot fathom their mysterious appearance and behavior. Speaking English as a second or third language further estranges them from their therapist, who is more likely to misinterpret their discourses as peculiar, idiosyncratic, and even psychotic. Even routine unit activities and schedules are often in conflict with the religious practices of a Hasidic inpatient.

Manovitz further noted, "Because psychiatric illnesses are associated with a higher level of stigma in this community, this communal distrust of one another when it comes to matters of mental illness, is often difficult to distinguish from overt paranoia."[25]

Psychology and Religious Law

Orthodox psychologists and counselors who work with the Hasidim frequently encounter special problems that challenge both their professional skills and their religious commitment. The norms of Hasidic culture generate particular conflicts, and it is a clear advantage to understand the dimensions of the law and the customs that surround them. Orthodox therapists, however, are held in the same tight vise of religious law as are their patients. As Dr. Rashi Schapiro recounts, the Orthodox therapist must balance his or her own religious obligations and those of the client, as well as the client's therapeutic needs.

When the Hasidic restricted and sheltered environment collides with the rest of secular society, it promotes unresolved internal intrapsychic conflict that they have to face and deal with. Some of the therapy focuses just on that. I've treated a Hasidic patient who wants to go to college, and for a girl in the Williamsburg community to want to go to college is viewed as almost heretical. Certainly it's not within their norms. So she experiences conflict. Her family calls her a little crazy and she has doubts about herself. Is she really crazy? Or is she just pursuing a goal different from their orientation? She's not sure. As a religious therapist I have to be cautious because my goal is not to advocate any one style of life as ideal. So I'm not going to tell her that she definitely should go to college or she definitely shouldn't go to college. But I'm going to help her explore her own feelings and needs to find out if it's crazy or not.

Consider the woman who says, "I don't want any more children." What should the therapist's response be? What should he respond to the rabbi who says, "Don't use birth control"? How should he handle a woman who comes in and wants an abortion? What about people who have a conflict over the laws of Shabbes? All of the things that we've been talking about are issues that require the Orthodox psychotherapist to evaluate and say, "What is my job here, first of all as a psychotherapist, second of all as an Orthodox Jew, and third of all as an integration of both." And that's a real tough job and there are never any easy answers. (RS)

Not every therapist, however, is so sensitive to the sometimes contradictory demands of faith and psychology.

> Some of the Orthodox therapists give them a hard time. They act like rabbis and not very kindly rabbis. As soon as a woman says she's not going to the mikvah, they're very harsh and say the reason they're having problems is that they're not following the religion properly. Then they get a lot of advice what to do, but they got that from their parents and they already know it.
> For their part, Orthodox therapists would rather have nonreligious patients than religious patients because it sets up a conflict. (JA)

For similar reasons on occasion an Orthodox patient finds it to be an advantage to see a non-Jewish therapist.

> Their reactions to me [as a non-Jewish therapist] vary. One is glad I'm not Jewish so that I talk about the particular problem and not about religion; others say you can't understand. Sometimes I say, "Maybe you should go to see someone who's Jewish." But they don't go. It's easier to come to me because I'm neutral and I'm not judging them. (JA)

At times therapy is the primary outlet they have to express repressed feelings and thoughts which collide with religious requirements. After considering the range of reactions among his own patients, Dr. Schapiro observed:

> I have found a real dichotomy in styles of the Hasidim. There are some Hasidim who almost take therapy as a license to be unusually descriptive and explicit in a way that seems very odd for the generally restrictive style, almost like, "I've been dying to tell someone about this for years and here's my chance. I can talk dirty or say whatever I want." And there are other Hasidim who are extremely restrictive. They take the religious law as being modest to the extreme, saying, "We can't talk about that," or "We're not going to talk about that," and as a sensitive therapist I have to respect their defensiveness about those issues, hoping that at some point in the therapy they'll realize that they have a real problem here and they should be able to talk about it for the betterment of the marriage, which is a big mitzvah. (RS)

Because of their tie to the law, and their feelings of guilt, individuals sometimes act contrary to their own best interests.

That's a real philosophical problem, because if you really believe in Jewish law, if you're a true believer in Yiddishkayt, then you believe that whatever God suggested is in your own best interest even if it doesn't feel that way. There are times when a woman will say, "I can't believe God wants me to have another child . . . I can't believe I have to have a ninth kid. I can't take it," the woman will say. Or the husband . . . husbands usually find ways of reconciling Jewish law with their own needs.   (RS)

Knowledge of the law and its nuances can itself become a source of conflict in marital relations, since it enables a husband to be the arbiter of domestic problems.

The man believes he's the authority because he's the one who studies the Torah, he's the one who knows the law, he's the one who earns the bread. So he has the last word on everything. The women have the sense that "I run the household, and don't tell me what to do." You know, "This is my domain." So that conflict of whose domain is the home really is an issue depending on what these young couples saw in their own homes where they were raised. But in the long run the husband is the one who makes the final decisions. Any type of decision. What school the kids go to. How the house is to be run. What kind of reading materials are to come into the home. What kind of speech is allowed or disallowed.

One interesting problem is patients who use religion as ways of establishing control in the marital relationship, or in the family. Usually, the husband will be quoting *halakhah,* Jewish law, and saying you have to do this and that, and the woman feels disadvantaged because she hasn't studied as much and she's not sure if she's being taken advantage of, or whether he's correct and just in quoting the Jewish law.

What we have to do is explore what the law says. I often send them back to their rabbi, because first of all they're not interested in hearing any religious decisions from a therapist, and it would be inappropriate for a therapist to offer religious information. So sometimes I say, "Why don't you ask your rabbi what he says." But that doesn't preclude my job of helping them recognize the dynamics of their interaction and helping them see that what they're doing is not helping each other. You know they're hurting each other and ruining their marriage and ruining their relationship with the children. They have to find other ways of establishing control.   (RS)

Sexual Concerns

At first glance Hasidic demands for sexual satisfaction seem more modest than in general American society and more subordinated to familial concerns. The desire for satisfaction and experimentation in the sexual relationship may vary greatly in different marriages as well as between the marriage partners.[26] Greater contact with the outside world seems to suggest a corollary rise in interest in sexual experimentation. Matched against this, however, is the drive to be Hasidic—the most punctilious and demanding of religious practitioners. In such areas of conflict the yeshivah background of the therapist provides critical perspective.

> There are Jewish laws about modesty, and depending on how strictly the Hasidic family wants to subscribe to Jewish law, that's how modest they are. There are what we call *chumros*, strict interpretations which are increased beyond the letter of the law. Some people are pursuing higher levels of purity.
>
> I do discuss what their belief of the law is. I do present to them their own conflicts about the law and then I suggest they go back to their rabbi and ask him. Sometimes a husband says something like oral sex is permissible. I'm not going to be the one to say that it's so or it's not so, and I'll say, "Well, why don't you discuss it with your rabbi?" Sometimes they can't discuss it with their rabbi. The point is they're bringing it up as a therapeutic issue, and yet if he's not willing to discuss it with his rabbi it means that he has some doubts or guilt about it, because generally in Jewish law, in Talmudic discussion, any topic is open for discussion and regulation.
>
> Sometimes they're seeking approval. Often they're coming to a therapist rather than a rabbi because they have an intuitive sense that a therapist is going to be more lenient. I send them back to the rabbi for the decision. Then they come back, the rabbi said yes or no and I say, "Okay, let's work with that."
>
> In that case [concerning oral sex] he went to the rabbi and the rabbi said no, and he did come back and we discussed again how he felt about it . . . his frustration . . . and at this point I started seeing him individually. This is one of the cases where he had obviously learned of oral sex from secular society and probably he did see it in an X-rated movie. It is questionable according to the Jewish law whether he should have gone in the first place, but now that he went his expectations and demands became higher. And now he has a conflict in his marriage. The wife wants to pursue a life that she believed was religiously sincere and pure, and she felt that he was breaking the rules. (RS)

Divorce

There are far fewer divorces in the Hasidic community than in American society in general.

> The marriage lasts because no one wants to get divorced. One might see it as a negative. American society places high value on the pursuit of individual happiness, whereas Hasidic society probably places emphasis on the pursuit of family structure, which provides a certain kind of happiness. They're forced to work at it more because they see their alternatives as more limited. (RS)

In recent years, however, psychologists and therapists as well as rabbis have verified what most lay people in the community have already noted:

the rising numbers of couples who are unable to cope with their marital problems and who decide to divorce.

The most prevalent problem is the divorce problem. We're still dealing with a small segment of the population, as compared to Conservative and Reform. But compared to the previous statistics of the Orthodox people this is the highest percentage ever reached within the Orthodox circles. The divorce rate is very, very high. I can't tell you exactly what it is. The only thing I can tell you is that the several Jewish courts are quite busy. This tells you a lot. I came across at least fifteen, sixteen cases this past year alone, most of them in their early thirties. With children. I had two cases and each one had five children, and both asked for a divorce. Two different families with five children. I also heard of several cases of men and women in their fifties being fed up with each other just trying to get out and gain freedom. This is a new phenomenon which was unheard of in the shtetl. Unheard of.   (MMB)

My wife and I both counsel, and divorce has become a big problem. Of course it doesn't compare to the gentile world but it's gotten to epidemic proportions. There are no real statistics, but if you speak to rabbis who write divorces, they are very busy—very busy. Those rabbis who have reached out to the more modern person because they want to make sure that they get a kosher *get* [divorce decree] to avoid complications later on are busy. They're writing six days a week.   (BI)

Even a fractional rise in family breakups poses a serious threat to the community, and analysis points to a wide range of causes.

The major causes are financial instability, emotional unreadiness of the young couples marrying very young without being at all prepared as to the responsibilities and daily vicissitudes that marriage requires, lack of information, lack of marital and sexual education. You get young people with lack of compatibility, conjugal problems, and sexual inadequacy, which is definitely a result of poor training and lack of sex education. They have no training at all. They only know how to have children, mechanically, routine-wise, but they don't know how to make love. And they don't know exactly how to satisfy and fulfill each other emotionally, sexually.
  Economic dependence is commonplace for young couples, basically men, who are occasionally ignorant and unprepared professionally for a job and must depend to a great degree at least for the first few years on their parents or in-laws. After a few years the parents tell them to be on their own, and in most cases they're not prepared for a job. They didn't go to school.
  Another cause I come across in a number of divorces is because of in-law problems, parental involvement in their private life, unusual financial dependence on the parents.
  But basically the fear of divorce and the stigma of divorce has disappeared now in the Jewish street because it's not a disgrace anymore. People aren't afraid anymore to be called divorced. In fact they ask today, "Is it your second one or your third one?"   (MMB)

One Hasidic marriage counselor noted the crucial change that has occurred with regard to financial support after divorce—a fact that makes divorce possible for the poor as well as the well-to-do.

> Today, number one, there's financial independence. If you get divorced you get out and you can make money. The government gives you money. Thanks to the United States government, if she gets custody of the kids, the government will give her quite a bit of money. The welfare system in the United States, especially in New York, promotes divorce. It helps it along. Women are more financially independent. So very often why should she suffer? Why should she suffer for the rest of her life? Maybe there will be better opportunities. (BI)

Since marriages are arranged and the standards of family purity and pedigree have remained for centuries as the principal measures of compatibility, most Hasidim believe that the crisis must be due to new and different factors. The major share of the blame for the increase in divorces therefore most often falls on the assimilation of new ideas from outside the community. Blame is placed at the door of social change. For the Orthodox in particular, social change is seen not as the opportunity to redress long-repressed problems, but rather as the harbinger of the social ills of the dominant outside community. Religious therapists find that the Orthodox world is under siege.

> There are tremendous conflicts with the acculturation process that the traditional Jew is facing these days in America. You're dealing with island people, who are somehow geographically separated from the outside world and still going to work, passing a newsstand, passing a movie, watching the street, no matter how much you close your eyes you're exposed to the secular, what you would call, the real orgiastic, materialistic world from which one would like to insulate oneself as much as possible. So the escape back into the enclosed walls of the American modern ghetto isn't enough because there's too much exposure outside these walls. So there is social intercourse, whether you like it or not, between the traditional Jew and the outside world which is very hard to escape. You need strong roots within your traditional life in order to be able to survive and not to become acculturated. It's one of the reasons why they marry at an early age. (MMB)

· 21 ·

Political Change in
Crown Heights

A Coalition of Blacks and Whites

Despite their organization and supposed political support, at the outset of the 1980s the Lubavitcher Hasidim believed themselves to be a vulnerable minority ignored by city politicians. By 1980 the black population had reached 80 percent of the neighborhood, a radical increase from the 20 percent in 1960, and the Hasidic community appeared to have been swallowed up by the larger ethnic group. In the redistricting that took place in 1982, the 43rd Assembly District, which included Crown Heights, had been gerrymandered into the shape of a dog, with its head in Bedford-Stuyvesant and its tail in Flatbush. The new lines separated the Hasidim from the racially mixed neighborhood of Flatbush and linked them to Bedford-Stuyvesant, which had become a predominantly black community. Customarily, when the political map is redrawn, grievances and complaints are considered; however, votes are the coin of the realm and the political mapmakers considered that the Hasidic community of Crown Heights had little to offer. Mendel Shemtov, the Lubavitcher political savant, was frozen out of decisionmaking.

> One of the leaders of the Democrats came in and we asked them for a favor when they made the reapportionment in the neighborhood. And he asked, "Who are they? They're 400 votes?"
>
> So I said, "It's not true. We'll show you. We'll have our own district leader. Let's run a person against the Democratic party for district leader, and this will excite our people to come out and vote." (MS)[1]

By 1980 the Lubavitcher Hasidim had grown from a core of 150 families to about 1,500 families, with a total population of roughly 12,000–15,000. They were a relatively small percentage of the 96,892 persons living in South Crown Heights (and an even smaller percentage of the 185,846 in both North and South Crown Heights). To increase their numerical strength the Hasidim sought to join forces with blacks in South

Crown Heights who were disenchanted with the local leadership. Together they would create their own political club, the Rainbow Coalition, and present their own slate of candidates for election.

One of the first blacks contacted to join with the Hasidim was Joan Gil, a forty-six-year-old clerk at the Second Circuit Court of Appeals. In the previous election Joan Gil had failed in her first try at politics to win election as a State Committeewoman in a nearby district.

> The Lubavitchers started calling me in June 1982 to join their slate. It was the reapportionment year. You could run from anywhere and then move over. September was the election. When I looked at the district, [I realized that] my family lived here, and my husband's family. There were a lot of registered voters who would come out and vote for my team. (JG)

Joan Gil was accustomed to interacting with people from various ethnic backgrounds. She worked with Jews at the court, and her husband was employed at the United Jewish Appeal managing their audiovisual equipment. The Hasidim, however, were more insulated than most other Jews, and initially Joan Gil had the task of educating her allies to understand black perspectives.

> When I first met those basically close-knit groups, in the beginning I would tell them how to get along with the black community. They said they were willing to give it a try. As we talked about black issues they would openly discuss them and say how they perceive the problem. I told them they would have to wear two hats and be one way in the synagogue and one way in politics. [Rabbi Yisroel] Rosenfeld has a very jolly personality and we were a good team. (JG)

Joan Gil had no illusions about the positions of blacks and whites in society. Unlike many who argued for increased black power, however, she contended that it was only by uniting with whites that blacks would be able to gain political leverage at City Hall.

> When you talk to a lot of blacks who have arrived with regard to material things—education, jobs, housing—they tend to believe that they are equal in our society. But as long as the color of your skin is darker and your hair kinky you are not equal. So the purpose of my getting involved is to bring more of my people over into the mainstream. Once you get a little something, sometimes you tend to become a little intimidated. When the white man says something we tend to stay in our own little world and not reach back and pull the lower class up. I want to work with the Lubavitchers to share in the same benefits. (JG)

Joan Gil also pointed to economic as well as political benefits that could accrue to black homeowners in the neighborhood as property values rose with Hasidic investment and settlement. Despite her arguments, few other local black political leaders saw an advantage in leading a movement for cooperation with the Hasidim.

Assemblyman Clarence Norman, Jr., who had been elected to the State Assembly in 1982, viewed the Hasidim's entry into politics with suspicion. Norman was then thirty-one years old. He had been a trial attorney in the District Attorney's office for five years, but he was best known in the neighborhood as the son of the Reverend Clarence Norman, Sr., the pastor of the First Baptist Church at Eastern Parkway and Rogers Avenue. He is described by some as intimidating.

Despite the flight of almost the entire white population other than the Lubavitcher Hasidim from Crown Heights, Norman saw Hasidic housing rehabilitation efforts as threats to the racial proportions in the neighborhood. He would also require of the Hasidim that they share equally with the black community all their efforts to develop housing, whether it was done with public or with private funding.

> When they do housing, they only do housing for the Jewish people. The blacks and the Hispanic community need housing too. They don't provide information where to apply. They do a lot of private development. They buy buildings. Buildings go into disrepair, they're abandoned, and then they apply for a J51—buildings to be rehabilitated. The apartments then go to Lubavitchers but not to the people who earlier lived in them. The Hasidim are discriminatory. They're putting up fifty housing units, displacing blacks. They raise money and put up not two houses but fifty two-story houses. They should open up those houses to everyone. They're changing the neighborhood. (CN)

Joan Gil challenged Norman to exercise his leadership and to develop programs for blacks similar to those organized by the Hasidim.

> Would Norman put up fifty houses and offer them to the Lubavitchers? You have professional blacks. Let them put in their resources and do the same. We can do some of the same things. We can't do all of it because of prejudice in our society, but we can do some of it.[2] What kind of leadership are you [Norman] giving? Down Nostrand Avenue, outside of Orientals with fruit stores, there are no businesses that you want to patronize. You need to get small business loans for these people. You need to get people to learn how to run businesses. We want respect and we want money to get businesses back into the community. State Senator Marty Markowitz sponsored a bill to bring in money to fight crime. Not one black organization has applied for funds. The funds were made available last year. I said to Norman, "Why don't you organize the way the Lubavitchers do?" (JG)

The two black leaders disagreed on the need for cooperation between the races to increase black power. Norman took a dim view of a Hasid representing Crown Heights, where blacks are in the majority. He wanted a black district run by black leadership. Joan Gil maintained that other tactics were required.

> By limiting the neighborhood to black leadership we could get only so much from the power brokers. But by joining with a white group, who would receive more power, we could gain that much more and do more for our people. I had thought earlier that they were missing the boat and losing the neighborhood. (JG)

When the election results were counted the Rainbow Coalition had held its own against two opposing slates. Clarence Norman, Jr., won his bid for a seat in the State Assembly; but Joan Gil ran ahead of the ticket for her post as District Leader (officially State Committeewoman). The other race for District Leader, in which Rabbi Rosenfeld ran against two black opponents, was so close that a new election was ordered by the court for February 1983. In the runoff Rabbi Rosenfeld was elected. Clarence Norman, Jr., blamed his own candidate's loss on the weather (fifteen inches of snow) and on superior Hasidic organization.

Rabbi Rosenfeld proved to be an energetic spokesman. He was quick to see signs of anti-Semitism in random neighborhood violence, and his voice often had a ring of alarm, but he was active and outspoken, and he quickly developed political antennae. Two years later, in the elections of 1984, Rosenfeld and Joan Gil proved their success had been no fluke when they both won reelection. Rosenfeld again ran against two black candidates, and he garnered roughly 4,000 votes as opposed to the combined tally of 4,700 for his two opponents.

During the two terms following the 1982 reapportionment, Norman built up resentment against the Hasidic community in general and Rabbi Rosenfeld in particular. Norman considered Rabbi Rosenfeld to be unconcerned about litmus-test issues such as affirmative action and boycotting South Africa. Police protection for the Hasidim was a special point of irritation to Norman. "On Friday night, two police cars come down and stand guard when the Hasidim begin their prayers. Why two? That's four policemen and a sergeant. They block traffic on the side island. One car is enough." Norman's agenda included complaints against the Maccabees, the unarmed Crown Heights Jewish Community Patrol: "There are allegations of their assaulting blacks."

The Laws of Noah

The Lubavitcher Rebbe had his own insights—based on Torah—into some of the social ills plaguing the community. In 1983, disturbed about the rising crime rate and the increase in civil disorder in Crown Heights and many other neighborhoods, the Rebbe pointed to the source of the problem—the ignorance of many residents of their basic responsibilities as human beings in God's world. The solutions to the problems in the streets from Kingston to Utica Avenue and in similar neighborhoods across the country were to be found in abiding by the laws stipulated in the so-called Noahchide laws in the Torah. These were the laws derived from the commentaries on the story of Noah, who had in patriarchal times preserved mankind and every other species of bird, beast, and creeping thing through the Lord's angry deluge of forty days and forty nights.

In the reckoning following the flood the Lord enjoined man not to eat "flesh with its life-blood in it" and warned that "Whoever sheds the blood of man by man shall his blood be shed." The commentaries on Noah note seven laws which demanded obedience in the pre-Mosaic world: (1) the establishment of law courts, and the prohibitions against (2) blasphemy, (3) idolatry, (4) sexual immorality, (5) bloodshed, (6) theft, and (7) eating a limb torn from a living animal.[3] The Rebbe now reminded his listeners that while the Jewish people and converts must accept the 613 laws stipulated in the Torah, "every Jew is responsible to encourage the *non-Jewish* denizens of the world to act in accordance with the Seven Noahchide Commandments."

> The Rebbe said we're living in a time when we think we're living in a jungle. For that reason if we would teach, starting with the seven Noahchide laws, that there is such a thing as a God who sees and hears all, who judges our behavior in compliance with His laws, it will definitely help to get us out of the jungle, out of the mess. He said that in past times Jews could not speak out freely. Today, he said, we're living in America and we're more free to speak out publicly.   (AR)

The Rebbe's emissaries threw their strength into a worldwide effort to disseminate knowledge of the seven Noahchide commandments. Many secular Jews feared that the Rebbe's notions concerning separate, simpler rules for gentiles deriving from Noah would be considered to be both patronizing and naive. Hasidim in other courts were also puzzled as to the Lubavitcher Rebbe's new tack, as one Satmar Hasid explained.

> We're mainly concerned about our own. We're not concerned about the secular world, about the goyim, what they should do or not do. It sounds very strange to us, extremely strange, because throughout Jewish history we don't recall anything like that the Jewish leaders be concerned that the goyim follow the seven commandments or not. So many ideas of his are strange—like sending out people on Fifth Avenue. His ideas on Zionism are strange to us. To us it [the laws of Noah] doesn't make sense at all.   (AG)

The Rebbe's prescription for improving social conditions was heralded by his emissaries. Outside of the Lubavitch community, however, the concept continued to have a mixed reception.[4]

Growth in Crown Heights

After several years of what had appeared to be fruitless struggle, the Hasidic community in Crown Heights began to grow. Between the years 1977 and 1985 the Crown Heights Jewish Community Council helped to renovate approximately six hundred apartments in fifteen buildings.[5] Since the Republicans had taken the White House in 1980, however, there had been few starts in housing and little for competing groups to quarrel over. Rabbi Rosenfeld, who was continually searching for loans and grants for Crown Heights in general and the Hasidic community in particular, was stymied:

> The Reagan administration cut out Section 8 housing. We asked for 2,000 units and we got 200. We asked for 65 percent of 200 apartments to be given over to members of our community, and the mayor denied it. They have to be chosen by lottery.

A sign of the activity taking place in the Hasidic community was their need for hotel space for followers, relatives, guests, baltshuves, and dignitaries visiting the community or waiting to see the Rebbe. One of the community's striking achievements was the conversion of 1365 Carroll Street into the Crown Palace Hotel, the first hotel to open in Brooklyn in many years. Like the other community renovations, the building was financed by a corporation established by the Jewish Community Council of Crown Heights.[6]

By the middle 1980s the Hasidim constituted only 6 percent of the overall population of Crown Heights; however, in the narrow band of streets on both sides of Kingston Avenue the percentage of Hasidim and other whites reached between 20 and 30 percent. Long-standing community centers were kept intact, although their purposes were adjusted to meet new needs: the Young Israel building became a Senior Citizens Center, and the Jewish Center was turned into a yeshivah for boys.

> Around 1981 it stabilized. Now it came the other way. There's no such thing as running away. People are looking for houses to buy. But we don't have any. The problem was that when people were running away we had houses and apartments and we didn't have anyone to fill into them. Then it filled in. Now the problem has changed and a lot of people are moving in, building, enlarging houses, building condominiums. We bought back houses and now it's the only neighborhood where the blacks and whites live together. We have other organizations and a planning board together with blacks, and the organizations work together.   (MS)

Defeat at the Polls

In the election of 1986 Clarence Norman, Jr., decided to run for both District Leader and Assemblyman. He won his Assembly seat and he also defeated Rabbi Rosenfeld for the post of District Leader. In his defeat the rabbi was particularly galled that blacks had been told it was a shame to have a white man representing them. "Who believes in integration?" Rabbi Rosenfeld asked in frustration. "Was this Martin Luther King's dream that a black politician should say a white can not hold a position of leadership in this area?"[7]

Despite the loss the Rainbow Coalition remained an influential political group with a voice in community affairs with seats on the Community Board which allocates funds for the various groups. It has, however, been an enduring and demanding struggle for blacks and whites who want to work together. Although she is a successful and popular local leader, Joan Gil has been subjected to abuse and harassment for forming an alliance with the Hasidim.

> Since I've gotten involved I've lost a lot of my friends.[8] They're afraid. I don't think they could get another black to do this. I've had threats. They'd call the house. "We're going to get you!" For what? The phone would ring at two or three in the morning. They almost had me, but then I regrouped and they couldn't bother me. The only one thing I worry about is my son. I tell him just be careful around election time.   (JG)

Mendel Shemtov decided it was time to step down from his leadership role in the Community Council. Toward the end of 1986 he had determined to offer his time and energy to the Chabad movement, which was then rapidly expanding its number of Chabad houses.[9] It was a good time to take stock of what had been accomplished by the Community Council. Shemtov had participated in the development of the Council's political and social organization and had helped to develop the community's social programs.

> We participate in elections and we're on the school board. We have candidates and delegates. We have a whole line of programs: Medicaid, Medicare, weatherization to fix windows. We have all the social services for poor people. (MS)

Interethnic Meetings

The high crime rate in Crown Heights remained the source of a good deal of community friction. In 1985 and 1986 in the 71st Precinct of South Crown Heights there were 2,458 and 2,309 burglaries, 1,253 and 1,498 robberies, 821 and 904 auto thefts, 93 and 86 rapes, and 18 and 30 crimes of murder and manslaughter.[10] The Hasidic safety patrols offended some blacks in the neighborhood who felt that the surveillance was directed against them exclusively and that all black men returning home late at night were targeted as possible suspects.

In midsummer of 1986 two violent murders shocked the community.

On the evening of July 2, a gang of black youths allegedly carrying pipes and wooden staves defied the subway clerk at the Kingston Avenue subway station and jumped the turnstiles. Shortly after, Israel Rosen, an Australian national who had come to visit his son, a yeshivah student, was found in a coma on the subway platform of the station. No money had been taken from his pockets but he had been severely beaten over the head. Rosen never awoke from the coma, and he died at the end of December 1986.

A second deadly assault was committed in Crown Heights at summer's end. In September, Shlomo Fisher was stabbed to death while walking in the streets at three A.M. Fisher was a homeless man who had been drawn to the Lubavitcher community in an attempt to rehabilitate himself. His nocturnal wanderings had placed him in harm's way.

The Hasidim were frustrated by the lack of progress in the investigations of both deaths. No witnesses appeared, no arrests were made, and the cases disappeared from the newspapers and from general concern. (The media's interest was focused on the Bernard Goetz case in Manhattan in which a white man shot four blacks who had accosted him on a subway car, and on the clash at Howard Beach in which three black men were beaten by a white gang and one of the black men was killed by a car while trying to escape from his pursuers.) Frustrated by the lack of progress and by official and media indifference, the Jewish Community Council called a conference for March 3, 1987, on interethnic concerns, to which they invited representatives of the black community, national black organizations, civil rights groups, national Jewish organizations, representatives of the police and the Justice Department, the mayor's office, and members of the press. Rabbi Yisroel Rosenfeld, speaking as an executive director of the Jewish Community Council, explained that the call for the meeting was a reflection of the public clamor over racial violence. Why, he wondered, wasn't the same attention given to Israel Rosen and to Shlomo Fisher as had been awarded to the victims in Howard Beach. "In Crown Heights, there's trouble every day . . . We are the victims in Crown Heights, and the entire world is silent." [11]

The interethnic meeting was held in midafternoon at the Oholei Torah Center on Eastern Parkway. In the course of the meeting it became apparent that many black leaders held views not usually depicted in the press. Blacks at the meeting expressed the desire to join with the Hasidim in attacking common social problems. Leaders of both ethnic groups said they wished to develop an integrated citizens' patrol for the neighborhood but had been rebuffed by the police. It was clear that these two groups had to bear the responsibility for resolving social problems that were not of their own making. As Rabbi Rosenfeld exulted: "We live integration twenty-four hours a day seven days a week."

Between luncheon courses, Rabbi Rosenfeld laid out the litany of Lubavitcher complaints to the forty or so people present. Observing that Crown Heights was the only integrated community in New York, he also noted that no one came to aid the community. "Do you want a Jewish community to stay in Crown Heights? Do you want Martin Luther King's dream to work? Why don't you join hands with us," he implored. Rabbi Rosenfeld cited the failure of the mayor's office to provide the community's fair share of public housing proposed for the area. He asked for sensitivity training in the schools to educate the children and eliminate prejudice. He cited anti-Semitic remarks made by local police officers and by sanitation men, and, in reference to his own recent political defeat for district leader, the pejorative prediction that a white man could not hold a position of leadership in the area. "Where are the civil rights leaders?" he queried.

The community black leaders present at the luncheon responded with expressions of support. "We need to talk to one another," Councilman Enoch Williams began. "We are on a collision course. It seems that the press keeps fanning things. Certain elements keep fanning things. We've got to get together and see whether we can stop this before it happens. If we don't take hold and reach out and talk to people then everybody is going to misunderstand each other and we're going to have chaos."

Rabbi Rosenfeld and City Councilwoman Mary Pinkett, an eloquent spokeswoman for the black community, expressed Jewish and black indignation. To Rabbi Rosenfeld's accounts of anti-Semitic harassment in Galicia, Hungary, Russia, and now Crown Heights, Councilwoman Pinkett supplied parallel evidence in equally strong tones: "My family came from South Carolina. They know what lynching is about. They have smelled burning flesh and so have your people. They have been denied jobs, education, and opportunity. What am I saying? . . . It is easy to inflame, it is easy to hate, it is easy to send the wrong message. But the right message must be sent. And the right message is that in this world we must live and work together. That is the message. That is the message. And there is no other message that is greater than that message."

There were other forces in the black community that did not want to participate in a cooperative relationship with the Hasidim or with any other whites. Virtually any incident could be seen as symbolic of white oppression of blacks. A fire had been set on February 26 at about 1:30 in the morning in the basement of the home of a black woman on Carroll Street, close to Lubavitch headquarters on Kingston Avenue. Police found a can with petroleum. In short order neighborhood gossip linked the fire to the Hasidim. The motive for the incident, which had been widely covered in the press, was supplied by the homeowner, who recalled turning down offers from Hasidic Jews to purchase the house. Some neighbors speculated that Hasidic Jews had set the fire in an effort to force the land-lady from the neighborhood. One witness said one of the two men seen running in the darkness was dressed in a long black coat such as those worn by the Hasidim. Identification of the perpetrators as Hasidim was suspect, however, since the fire was set on a weeknight and the Luba-vitcher Hasidim wear long coats (kaftans) only on the Shabbes. There were, moreover, other reports in the neighborhood that the fire was re-lated to the sale of drugs. No arrests were made.

In mid-April a rally and march by militant blacks along Eastern Park-way shook the fragile tranquillity that existed in the neighborhood after the interethnic meetings of the leadership. The rally had as its cause local discrimination and abuse, but some leaders made serious efforts to tie the Hasidim of Crown Heights to the whites of South Africa and to invoke a mood of hatred. Reporters covering the events for the *Amsterdam News* equated problems in Crown Heights with apartheid in South Africa. In their account matters became so entangled that the reader had to discover for himself which country was being discussed.[12]

The *Amsterdam News* also expressed outrage against Mayor Koch for sending two thousand police to shepherd an estimated six hundred protesters through the neighborhood. Koch and Benjamin Ward, the black police commissioner, were intent on limiting the march to a dem-onstration and not providing any opening for a riot to develop. As added precautions, access to the local streets and the subway stop had been curtailed and pedestrians entering the area were carefully monitored.[13] The newspaper once more accused the police of adopting a double stan-dard toward blacks and whites in Crown Heights.[14]

It soon became clear that the only way to overcome black objections to a Hasidic patrol was to form a single racially integrated group. On May 22, 1987, blacks and Lubavitcher Hasidim agreed to operate an inte-grated unit to monitor the streets. They were to have a hotline to the station house of the 71st Precinct.[15] The civilian patrols were suddenly less of a problem, at least with some sections of the community, and Rev. Sam was able to testify to a victory for common sense.

> We put an end to separate patrols [in 1987] when we made joint patrols. People get training with the police. Cars are put at our disposal, or people use their own cars, and patrols are out every night. We've cooperated in civilian observation patrols. (HS)

The Lubavitchers took practical steps to ensure their future in Crown Heights. In September 1988 they broke ground for a new synagogue and expanded headquarters in the building 784–788 which was adjacent to

770.[16] A small but lively band of Hasidic musicians set a happy beat for the thousands of followers gathered on the street. The Lubavitcher Rebbe was present to dig the first shovelful of earth to initiate the project.

> By 5:00 P.M., a dais had been erected in the yard in front of 770. The Rebbe spoke, referring to the significance of "groundbreaking"—breaking the hold of the gross material and dedicating it for a higher, spiritual purpose. Every Jewish building has to be based on the concept of breaking down the appearance of the material as an entity to itself, negating any possibility of false pride or sense of self-accomplishment without the Divine help that gives it power.
>
> After the Rebbe's words, Mr. [David] Chase spoke. At his grandfather's side, forty-five years before, he had watched the Germans burn down the shul in his native Polish town and shoot the young children. It had seemed like the end of Yiddishkeit, G-d forbid. Now he was overjoyed to be present at the ground breaking for a new shul that is a true world center of Yiddishkeit. "And it's wonderful to see the thousands of *Yiddishe kinderlech* here for whom love for Yiddishkeit comes so naturally."
>
> No one in the world, he said, has affected his life as deeply as the Rebbe has. "I am trying hard to remember some Yiddish words as I agreed," he continued. The only words Mr. Chase could recall were: "Rebbe, I love you very much." Behind him a banner hung from the windows of the apartment building: "We want Moshiach [Messiah] now!"
>
> Then the Rebbe descended from his dais and proceeded to dig a hole and place inside it a large rock lying nearby—the "cornerstone." [17]

Some time after the groundbreaking ceremonies, however, the Rebbe decided that the first priority of the community was to complete two new yeshivot for boys and a school for girls. Building plans for the expanded headquarters were temporarily set aside. The staff continued as usual, working around the temporary alterations and construction debris until additional funding could be found.[18]

In March 1989 an incident took place which showed that people of all ethnic groups could unite in an emergency situation. An assembly of black, Puerto Rican, and Hasidic neighbors rescued a Hasidic woman and her twenty-year-old son from an alleged mugger, a black man, wielding a razor. A passerby, also a black man, who had seen the attack, leaped from his car to help the victim and to stem her bleeding. Other blacks had joined in to help the son and to assault his attacker.[19] In the aftermath there were the countercharges that inevitably follow an arrest. The alleged mugger claimed to have been attacked by whites and accused a Lubavitcher Hasid and his son in the crowd of having beaten him. The Grand Jury subsequently rejected the charge and refused to indict the Hasidim. Blacks and whites had acted according to their own sense of justice, and it seemed clear that left on their own the people of Crown Heights would ignore ethnic differences and protect each other.

With a sense of relief Rev. Sam saw that tension in the neighborhood had subsided.

> That's the way it should be. We've been loving and hating each other. My style has moved from confrontation to negotiation to confrontation. Now we're in negotiation. We're never going to be kissing buddies, but we have to learn to co-exist.   (HS)

The mayoralty election of 1989 showed that when it came to politics the Hasidim had things on their mind other than religion and race. Despite his identity as a Jew, Mayor Edward Koch could not claim the allegiance of the Hasidim. Most Hasidim in Williamsburg, Borough Park, and Crown Heights voted in the primary for David Dinkins, a black man. Koch had done few favors for the Hasidim and they were not inclined to go to the polls on his behalf. Dinkins, moreover, seemed to be a politician in the traditional sense. Little change was foreseen in the general election between Republicans and Democrats. As a Hasid in Williamsburg expressed it: "Dinkins is not anti-Semitic and we have as much access to him as anyone. And he's going to be more concerned that the garbage is picked up on Lee Avenue than is Giuliani [the Republican candidate]."

The Crown Heights Rainbow Coalition suffered serious losses in the election. Joan Gil, frustrated by Clarence Norman, Jr.'s power over committeemen, gave up her position as District Leader to confront Norman directly in the election for Assemblyman. Although both candidates were black, Joan Gil saw the campaign being viewed on completely racial terms. To her irritation Gail Collins in *Newsday* reportedly portrayed the difference between the two candidates as "She's black and he's a black black." Clarence Norman, Jr., won reelection as Assemblyman and as District Leader. The Rainbow Coalition also lost strength on the Area Policy Board, which allocates funds for local social programs. With the support of the Democratic party leadership Norman also became Democratic party leader in Kings County, a post of considerable power and influence.

The old team of the Rainbow Coalition was broken up. By this time Rabbi Rosenfeld had a position in Queens and was less involved in local community affairs. Rabbi Joseph Spielman became the chairman of the Jewish Community Council in Crown Heights and the political spokesman for Lubavitch. Although she was temporarily out of political power, Joan Gil continued her relationship with the Hasidim and began working on other community projects. She took a job with an attorney and quietly made plans to run for the State Assembly again in 1992.

· 22 ·

The Housing Labyrinth
in Williamsburg

Housing in Williamsburg

In order to maintain the Hasidic way of life it is necessary for the Hasidim to live in close proximity to one another and to their religious institutions, the besmedresh, the yeshivah, and the mikvah, as well as to kosher food stores. Providing housing to maintain this essential propinquity is a heartfelt emotional issue in Williamsburg. The Hasidic effort to preserve and increase the housing available to them has put their community in conflict with other ethnic groups equally anxious to protect their turf and their way of life.

Williamsburg is a neighborhood of crowded, aging brownstones intercut with a few towering housing projects. Before the turn of the century, Bedford Avenue, the principal through street, boasted mansions, clubs, and churches of the affluent. By the time of the First World War, however, the neighborhood had attracted the growing Jewish population of Brooklyn. An Orthodox non-Hasidic Jewish community developed in Williamsburg in the early 1920s, and by the end of that decade a few Hasidim from Galicia and Poland settled there as well. The great wave of Hasidic settlement took place after the Second World War in the 1940s and 1950s when the surviving remnant arrived in the United States.[1] To serve the religious needs of the new arrivals some of the old larger mansions, badly weathered, were converted into synagogues and shuls. With the increase of the ultra-religious Jewish population, Williamsburg's growth as a center of Orthodox Jewry seemed assured. By 1970, through immigration and internal growth, the Hasidim had become the neighborhood's second largest ethnic group (approximately half the size of the Puerto Rican population).

Puerto Ricans, who by 1970 constituted the majority of the residents of Williamsburg, had migrated to the mainland as Puerto Rico's expanding population had swamped the impoverished economy of the island. Puerto Ricans came to the United States in large numbers during the First

World War. As citizens of the United States (since the island was annexed in 1898), the Puerto Ricans were not deterred by immigration laws, and they became an important presence in Brooklyn in the 1920s. After the Second World War inexpensive air travel further eased the journey. Having extended families on the island and on the mainland aided in a migratory cycle of people who moved back and forth between the two locations. The large number of Puerto Ricans who settled in Williamsburg replaced Italians, Poles, and Irish residents in the Catholic parishes. Subsequently, Latino migrants arrived from other Caribbean islands. By 1970 there were some 74,560 Latinos in Williamsburg (and of these 62,852 had been born in Puerto Rico or were of Puerto Rican ancestry).[2]

The Hasidic population of some thirty-five thousand is located in the southwestern section of Williamsburg. They live primarily on the streets that crosscut Lee Avenue, the principal shopping street, which runs the length of the neighborhood and is laced by a string of family-owned stores catering to Hasidic needs. In those streets the Hasidim comprise 70 percent of the population. With their striking physical presence, they set the primary tone for the central core of South Williamsburg, a triangle of blocks jutting south from the Williamsburg bridge. This area is edged by Broadway on one side and by Flushing Avenue on the other. The western end of the triangle is bounded by Kent Avenue, a decaying industrial strip that runs along the curve of the East River to the Navy Yard. The neighborhood is hemmed in physically on one side by the East River and socially on the other side by Bedford-Stuyvesant, the largest African-American ghetto in the United States.

Hasidic and Latino families share the neighborhood. Latino residents live primarily near the Bridge Plaza, and down Broadway and Flushing Avenue, streets that mark the borders of the Hasidic enclave. Many Hasidim and Latinos live in the same apartment houses, and in the projects, and they share the streets. Some Latinos in the neighborhood are employed in Hasidic stores and factories. Despite their proximity in the streets, in shops, in apartment house lobbies and hallways, rather than interacting, Hasidim and Latinos often appear to slide past each other seemingly without recognition. Friendship and mutual respect between individuals develop at times, but for the most part contacts are sharply limited.

The two societies appear as far apart as winter and summer. Each culture has its own language that takes precedence over English. Each has clearly defined mores regarding marriage and intermarriage, work, and education. In religious affairs the traditions of Orthodox Judaism stand against Catholicism and Pentecostalism. Musical traditions, rather than serving as bridges, underline cultural differences.

While incidents of violence received a great deal of attention in the local press in the 1970s, they were relatively rare. A very few open clashes on the street were precipitated by a robbery or a purse snatching. Hasidim, responding to a cry for help, confronted the accused offender, often in overpowering numbers, and administered a severe beating. Some Latinos complained that the Hasidim overreacted in such instances and dangerously took the law into their own hands. Father (subsequently Monsignor) Matthew Bryan Karvelis, pastor of the Transfiguration Roman Catholic Church, related his disagreement with Hasidic methods. He was bewildered at Hasidic anger over what he considers a commonplace circumstance: being robbed.

> The worst problem has nothing to do with housing and employment but is the vigilantes. They blow whistles and shout *ganef,* thief, and in seconds there are two hundred people there. When they catch someone they act as judge and jury and beat the individual bloody. They are paranoid about being robbed. Their houses are like bird cages with bars on all the windows.

He also described his own response:

> We don't keep poor boxes any more. They were all robbed. I get robbed regularly but it's not the end of the world.

In 1973 Father Karvelis accused the police of ignoring numerous Hasidic "mob beatings" of Latinos in the neighborhood. The police maintain that few such incidents had taken place, but they did acknowledge five in the space of a few months. The police chief explained to the *New York Times:* "The Hasidim are a tightly knit community with a long distrust of the police in Europe and America. Their tradition is not to report to authorities when they are victimized by a thief or assaulted, but to take matters into their own hands, administering a beating to the suspect and then releasing him." [3]

The failure of Hasidim and Latinos to establish close ties has made it difficult to work together to resolve common problems in housing, education, job training, and business loans. Relationships between community leaders and activists in the two camps have been contentious, and disputes move rapidly from the street and the meeting hall to the courtroom.

Lacking the strictly defined social network of the Hasidim, the Latinos have a less formal leadership structure. Leaders, sometimes from outside the community, appear in response to one issue or another, and few have a large established following. There is no Latino leader who can speak with the same authority as that of a spokesman of the Hasidic community. Hasidic leaders therefore find it frustrating that they cannot identify one or two leaders with whom they can broker an agreement that will be acceptable to the entire Latino community.

Public Housing

In the 1950s the number of available apartments in the neighborhood was reduced when a wide belt of housing was torn out for the construction of the Brooklyn-Queens Expressway. A submerged six-lane highway, the expressway plows through the heart of the neighborhood, passing under Lee and Bedford Avenues, the principal through streets. The construction displaced an estimated five to ten thousand persons. This disaster to the neighborhood met with very little opposition at the time. New Yorkers had come to accept as inevitable plans proposed and carried out by Robert Moses, an innovative and forceful public official who held a variety of city posts and was responsible for the development of new highways. The Hasidim were then newcomers to the neighborhood and to the country, in the process of organizing their community and still unfamiliar with the ways of politics and local government. Longtime residents who watched the blocks being cleared for the new highway frequently heard of plans to construct apartment house projects on the leveled land, but for the most part attempts to replace the lost housing were stymied.

In succeeding decades competition between Hasidim and Latinos for space in the same streets and the same buildings intensified, and the two ethnic groups at the bottom of the social scale who suffer identical problems were reduced to fighting each other for every apartment and every square foot of open space.

Most of the remaining older houses contained small apartments that were soon overwhelmed by the large families of the Hasidim and the Latinos.

> The existing older housing apartments are small and are inadequate for the large Orthodox families. There are people living in three-room apartments with twelve and thirteen children and they haven't got the room to live decently. And the political leadership is ignoring these problems. (ES)

Hasidic complaints concerning housing were echoed by Catholic spokesmen of the Latino community in South Williamsburg, such as Father Karvelis.

> Housing in the neighborhood was built before the turn of the century and it's crumbling. There has been no new public housing since the start of the Reagan administration, other than what was started before he took office. The situation is horrendous. No one has sufficient housing, neither the Hasidim nor the Latinos. Latino families will rent a three-room apartment for $500 to $600 a month. In order to pay that rent everyone in the family has to go to work, and then they take in boarders. So it's not unusual to find ten or eleven people living in three rooms. New housing is out of reach without a federal subsidy.

In the four decades following the razing of streets to make room for the highway, five housing projects were constructed, two in 1964 and three in the mid-1970s. They provided approximately three thousand affordable new apartments, far from the number needed to meet the needs of a neighborhood with deteriorating housing and an exploding population. The few projects completed intensified the competition to control the major share of available space. The local Democratic organization, the Seneca Club, assumed a position of leadership regarding housing, principally to protect its own interests.

The Seneca Club had had an unblemished record for winning elections and managing local affairs since the turn of the century. Its membership included the neighborhood's Italians, Irish, and Jews, and precinct captains kept tabs on every church, synagogue, and social club in the neighborhood. After the Second World War the Democratic politicians had watched the Italian and Irish population move from the neighborhood and be replaced by Hasidim and Puerto Ricans. They were reluctant to include more than a few token Puerto Ricans in the club, in great measure because they feared the newcomers would have their own agenda and compete for roles in the political leadership.[4] Instead, to maintain their numbers they first sought to enroll Orthodox Jews other than Hasidim. In 1964 they tried to convert one of the new projects into a middle-income cooperative to encourage mainstream Orthodox Jews to remain in the neighborhood. When that failed and it was clear that Orthodox Jews would continue to depart they turned to the Hasidim as a new source of support. They saw that the Hasidim were not interested in presenting their own candidates in elections and unlike the Latinos seemed to pose no future conflicts of interest.

In 1964 the Seneca Club sought to settle the Hasidim in the two new housing projects (Jonathan Williams Plaza with 576 units and Independence Towers with 726 units). The Club arranged with the New York City Housing Authority to maintain guidelines of 75 percent white, 20 percent Latino, and 5 percent black in the Williamsburg projects. Since applicants for the projects had to go through the Club, it could easily control the ratio.[5]

Initially the Hasidim were reluctant to take apartments in the towering and impersonal new projects. They feared for their personal security, and they worried over the religious acceptability of the "Shabbes elevators" which automatically stopped on every floor from Friday night to Saturday night (so that the Hasidim would not have to break the Shabbes law by pressing a button to start the electricity). One Housing Authority official visited the Satmar Rebbe to urge his approval of the Shabbes elevator.

I explained to him that there was no increase in the flow of electricity when someone stepped in. The Rebbe felt that using the elevators on Shabbes would look like one was doing a job on a weekday. He thought that people would see the Hasidim riding elevators on Shabbes. But he agreed not to give out an *issur* [ban or edict] prohibiting use of the elevator. Rabbi Joseph Henkin [a recognized Talmudic authority] had said that it was permissible to use the Shabbes elevators.[6]

Housing Authority officials, the Seneca Club, and Orthodox community leaders urged quick acceptance of the apartments. To encourage rentals whenever possible housing officials assigned apartments on the lower floors to Shabbes observers so that they could walk upstairs if they chose to. If a Satmar Hasid was given rooms on an upper floor a phone call was made to the Satmar Rebbe to receive his blessing for the apartment. A housing official also provided a choice apartment in the Jonathan Williams project to one of the Rebbe's chief assistants as a sign that the project was a desirable location. In the face of these inducements Hasidic resistance evaporated, and soon Hasidim were vying for space in the project, particularly on the lower floors, as the housing official recounts.

> The Hasidim wanted the lower floors because they wouldn't use the elevators on Shabbes. They all came in with doctors' notes. All the husbands had hernias and the wives had varicose veins. I called [Rabbi Liepa] Friedman and told him not to give out doctors' notes indiscriminately . . . A few of the Orthodox Jews and Hasidim offered bribes. I told Weinberger and Friedman to announce in shul that anyone who offered a bribe would be sent to jail.[7]

What was an unusual situation soon became accepted as the norm. One aspect of the present dilemma of the Hasidim lies in their desire to be insulated from other cultures and their need to cooperate in public programs. Under the Civil Rights Act of 1964, use of public monies automatically bars any hint of exclusiveness or discrimination based on race, sex, religion, or place of national origin. Moreover, since the passage of the law government agencies have actively sought out instances of discrimination.

The Hasidim argued that the occupation of public housing should reflect the neighborhood's existing ethnic mix. Since they now comprised a majority of the population in their triangle in South Williamsburg, they insisted that they were entitled to a like percentage in all new housing.

The Latinos soon found their voice. Until the mid-1960s Puerto Ricans were poorly represented in the polls. Those who attempted to register to vote were required to pass an English literacy test, and workers at the polling places found excuses to exclude them because their registration card was misplaced or their name (usually two surnames representing the father's and the mother's families) was misfiled. The situation greatly improved beginning with the Voting Rights Act of 1965. Proof of literacy could be established by certification of a sixth-grade education in the United States or in Puerto Rico (providing that English was the primary language of classroom instruction). In 1970 literacy requirements and use of the English language were dismissed altogether. Puerto Ricans could register with less hindrance, and their larger numbers at the polls were soon reflected in a spurt in influence in party circles.[8]

President Lyndon Johnson's antipoverty programs began to be felt in Williamsburg in the mid-1960s. There was a network of seven Community Action Programs. In addition, there was a group of approximately fifteen VISTA volunteers who did a variety of tasks in the community in education, housing, economic development, and daycare organization. Some became involved in the struggle to increase student, parent, and community power in the local schools.[9] Brooklyn Legal Services Corporation A was formed in 1968 as part of a national legal services network. In 1972 the Puerto Rican Legal Defense and Education Fund, Inc., a national civil rights organization, was created. That same year, with the aid of two local Catholic churches, Puerto Ricans on the Southside of Williamsburg formed Los Sures, an organization to rehabilitate housing and protect tenants. When efforts to gain control of the schools were stymied in 1973 by the creation of citywide school board elections, many of the activists and VISTA volunteers turned their attention to housing issues to aid the Latino community.

The Hasidic community soon discovered that their legal adversaries in housing development were likely to be Jewish lawyers with greater devotion to civil rights than to the needs and prerogatives of their coreligionists. In representing the Latino community, Martin Needelman, the counsel of Brooklyn Legal Services Corporation A, saw himself as a defender of the underdog. Needelman, a native of East New York in Brooklyn, had been a VISTA legal volunteer from 1969 to 1971, the year he joined the Williamsburg office of Brooklyn Legal Services. (In 1984 he was named director and chief counsel.) Although he had worked with the Latino community for a number of years, Needelman's European roots were similar to those of many Hasidim, one generation removed. Both sets of his grandparents were Orthodox Jews who emigrated from Poland and Russia around the year 1905, and Needelman was not detached from the passion to maintain an Orthodox Jewish community. In recent years he had become increasingly observant of Orthodox practices. His children attended an Orthodox yeshivah in Manhattan. Nonetheless, he was committed to his role as an advocate for the Latino community: "As a Jew . . . I feel that it is especially important that we be consistently on the right side on principle, and not just when quotas and church-state separation are specifically harmful to Jewish interests. We cannot change sides when wholly inappropriate tactics and tools are used to support our friends or co-religionists."[10]

The Puerto Rican community would no longer be satisfied with a token percentage of apartments. In response to the Hasidic arguments for priority, the Puerto Ricans contended that 50 percent of those displaced by urban renewal were Latino and black and therefore they should be awarded 50 percent of all new public housing. They argued further that new assignments should be drawn from borough-wide lists, on which the overwhelming number of applicants are nonwhite.

There was Latino opposition to new plans involving the Hasidim that were already under way. The city was able to offer cleared and condemned properties at a reduced cost, and low-cost loans could be obtained from federal and state agencies. These advantages encouraged the Hasidim to plan for the development of community service projects (old age facilities and educational institutions) and for middle-class housing where the costs would be borne by those who would invest in their own co-op apartments.

The division of apartments had to be decided for three new housing projects (the Taylor-Wythe Houses with 532 units, the Jewish-sponsored Bedford Gardens with 639 units, and the Catholic-sponsored Roberto Clemente Plaza with 532 units). The Hasidic leadership was divided on how best to negotiate with the Housing Authority and the Latino community. Stephen Price recorded the account of a Hasidic leader which illustrates the planning developed by secular leaders of Satmar and the unifying role played by the Rebbe even when he took little part in practical decisionmaking.

> In 1975, there was disagreement in the Hasidic community as to how to proceed with Bedford Gardens and Clemente. Some wanted Bedford at 75-25 [75 percent white, 25 percent nonwhite] and deal with Clemente later. Others said no, let's get an agreement now [on the entire urban renewal area] while we still have good leverage. I felt the decision should come from the Satmarer Rebbe . . . We got an appointment to see the Rebbe . . . The Rebbe made no decision, but the people felt that his decision was to take the 75-25 at Bedford and wait on Clemente.[11]

The following year, 1976, a lawsuit by representatives of the Latino community alleged discrimination in assigning apartments in the neighborhood's five existing housing projects, which had been built in 1964 and 1976. In the course of the lawsuit it was established that the city had been using strict numerical quotas which characteristically favored the Hasidim and severely limited nonwhites.[12] Future construction and distribution of apartments would require Consent Decrees—agreements that govern future allocation of housing—once prior discrimination was proven. The law stipulates that renewal land cannot be sold, leased, or occupied if in any way there is discrimination on the basis of race, religion, or national origin. Work cannot proceed unless the parties involved stipulate to a Consent Decree that they are not damaged by the project.

A Consent Decree concerning existing housing, worked out during 1977 and signed in 1978, recognized the new reality of the growing strength of the Latino community. Its terms reduced the percentages of white families in housing projects in the neighborhood and set guidelines for renting apartments as they were vacated in order to reach those percentages. In the two projects built in 1964, the percentage of nonwhites would be raised from 25 percent to 32 percent. While the newer Bedford Gardens was 75 percent Hasidic and 25 percent nonwhite, it was projected to reach a temporary percentage of 35 percent nonwhite. To accomplish the changes a larger percentage of units vacated would be allocated to nonwhite families (three out of five in some instances; two out of three in other cases). After these intermediary quotas were met, *all subsequent rentals were to be allocated on a completely nonracial basis.* All quotas were to be lifted immediately at the Taylor-Wythe project (which was then at 60 percent white and 40 percent nonwhite). The not-yet-completed Roberto Clemente Plaza, the centerpiece of the agreement, would consist of 51 percent nonwhite families and 49 percent white families at the time of the initial rental, after which all subsequent rentals would be on a nonracial basis.[13]

Interethnic debate intensified in other areas where the Latino community saw favoritism toward the Hasidim. They were angered at the city's renting vacated municipal buildings to the Hasidim, asserting that they were used for religious purposes.[14] Latino leaders routinely opposed requests for measures that would aid the Hasidim if they appeared to provide unequal benefits.

In the years following the 1978 Consent Decree, negotiations continued in the hope that an agreement would stimulate new housing through private development. The Hasidim were represented by the United Jewish Organizations of Williamsburg (UJO), while the Latino position was presented by the Epiphany Roman Catholic Church, the Anti-Redlining Committee, and later by the Ad Hoc Committee for the Southside Triangle, assisted by Catholic Charities, Los Sures, and Brooklyn Legal Services. For some time there were no tangible results. Every negotiated settlement to release the land from eminent domain was stymied, and there was a deep sense of frustration within both communities.

Like the Hasidim, Latino families want to live in a neighborhood that reflects their own culture. Latino complainants who were offered housing in projects outside of South Williamsburg frequently rejected them for fear of being a very small racial and cultural minority in mostly black projects, or on the grounds that the apartments would take them away from family, friends, and local churches and community centers. Latino residents preferred to stay in South Williamsburg, since it had a significant Latino population. They were fearful that new Hasidic projects would diminish the Latino presence in the neighborhood.

New Social Enterprise

Despite the contention taking place in other levels of neighborhood life, the managers responsible for Satmar secular affairs continued to roll up an enviable list of accomplishments. In 1980, Satmar's Opportunity Development Association (ODA) established a local medical center in affiliation with Manhattan's Beth Israel Hospital. In addition to the medical and dental clinics, the Satmar Hasidim began a pharmacy and an ambulance service. Soon they also handled the WIC program (Women, Infants, Children), which provides nutritional care for mothers and infants, and other programs as well.[15] After the national elections of 1984, the Hasidim were granted minority status by the Department of Commerce. This expanded the scope of programs open to them and enabled them to apply for contracts to provide opportunities for minority business enterprises. They also won funds to retrain unemployed Hasidim in a variety of skilled jobs.[16] A principal goal for the present community is to continue to merit minority status, with all the attendant opportunities for funds for training, education, health, and business loans. Hasidic spokesmen argue that Hasidic unemployment is among the highest in the nation, that the Hasidim are a disadvantaged group like the blacks, Latinos, Native Americans, and others who have suffered economically because of discrimination.[17]

Plans Gone Astray

During John Lindsay's mayoral administration (1966–1973), the Hasidim had won approval to build a medical center, a school, and a nursing home on lands marked for renewal. Unexpected delays and changing circumstances caused the Hasidim to reframe the project. The revised plans were approved by the Board of Estimate in 1983, and they were also passed by the local board. Ultimately the plans called for a 6,000-seat synagogue, a yeshivah with fifty-five classrooms to educate some 1,300 boys, and thirty-four three- and four-bedroom apartments for members of the faculty and their families.

> Mayor Lindsay gave us this block [on Bedford Avenue] to build three projects: a nursing home, a medical center, and a school. But afterwards the investigations into problems with the nursing homes came out. We decided that we don't want to go into the nursing home business at all. We gave it up. So we figured, instead of building a nursing home, we will build a medi-

cal center, a school, and a shul, a big synagogue. After changing these plans with the Board of Estimate and the local board, we divided that block in three parts again. One part, the front [facing Bedford Avenue] will be a synagogue, the end of it [on Wythe Avenue] will be a school, and the middle of it will be faculty housing. Meanwhile, the older Rebbe passed away. We needed an apartment for the new Rebbe. So we figured we will take away a little part of the synagogue and build the Rebbe's house. We had to give a bond of $100,000 to the city that the house will be built and then the synagogue. We paid $142,000 for this part for the synagogue. For the whole program we paid $780,000 from Bedford Avenue to Wythe Avenue, from Rodney to Ross [one city block]. We paid almost a million dollars for this block. (RH)

The redesigned project, with its emphasis on religious education, provided the rationale for a home for the school's dean—the rosh yeshivah. The dean, of course, turned out to be the new Rebbe, Rabbi Moshe Teitelbaum, whose home sat as the only completed structure on the renewal site.

Hasidic efforts in favor of religious education and their Rebbe cost them dearly in negative publicity. Those outside the Hasidic community saw their attempts to expand in the neighborhood as autocratic and prejudiced. Critics assailed "deals" between Satmar and the city's Housing Preservation and Development Agency.[18]

Satmar leaders complained that the charges were false and misleading.

It's not true. The vacant land on this block was given to us from the Lindsay administration. We got this block, parcel 4. It was designated for us. And actually the block was ours [before the land was cleared]. There were no blacks and Latinos on this block. The city grabbed it away from us. All this was ours. Our synagogue was here. They paid us $70,000 for the whole synagogue and we had to pay back a million dollars [for the land]. Koch did not help us at all. (RH)

In the face of public criticism, however, city officials quickly backed away from the project and any hint of patronage; aid to provide publicly owned land was terminated. This new snag engendered suspicion and irritation in the Hasidic community. There were expressions of increasing disillusionment with the leadership that had allowed the enterprise to go astray.

From Quota to Cross-Subsidy

Two years later in 1985 a new agreement was reached between representatives of the Hasidic and the Latino communities. The Hasidim had the organization and the means to develop sites for their exclusive units. There were no Latino developers with sufficient economic strength to make offers for land and then develop that land for private use. Representatives of the two communities agreed to a "cross-subsidy" fund to unlock public land for development. (Some Latinos would later charge that their representatives were hand-picked by city officials and did not reflect the position of the majority of Latino groups in the area.) The city would sell land to the Hasidim, thereby enabling them to develop houses and condominiums using private financing; the money from the sale of the land ($3,500,000) would be deposited in a fund to be used by the Epiphany Church and its affiliates for the Latino community, and to a lesser extent by the Hasidic community, to subsidize low-cost affordable housing. The agreement was negotiated by Father (subsequently Monsignor) Matthew Foley, Pastor of the Epiphany Catholic Church, representing the Latino organizations, and Leopold Lefkowitz and various spokesmen for the United Jewish Organization of Williamsburg.[19] The church and its affiliates agreed not to oppose or obstruct the sale of the property.

The agreement appeared to have the virtue of allowing each community to determine its own needs: the Hasidim could develop their overall educational and housing plans; the Latino community would have the funds for low-cost housing units. Both groups had to reduce their expectations, but the plan appeared to satisfy the concerns of both communities. It was commonly considered to be "a trade-off in dollars versus land."

In all, the cross-subsidy agreement contemplated by the parties would have provided for the construction of 600 units, 300 to be developed under the aegis of the United Jewish Organizations of Williamsburg for lower-middle- and middle-class families, and another 300 to consist of condominiums and rental apartments for lower-income Latino families. The Hasidic development was known as Brooklyn Villas.[20] The Hasidim would receive at least 300 apartment condos with three and four bedrooms. The housing would be built with private funds and without government loans.[21] Of the 300 units designated for Latino families, the Epiphany Church was to develop 150 units, and another 150 were to be built by the New York City Housing Authority.[22] The Department of Housing Preservation and Development would have limited legal control of the funds generated from the sale of the land and from funds generated by the auction of additional lands, and would act only with the approval of the United Jewish Organization and the Epiphany Church.

The Hasidim assumed that completion of the apartments and condos and their ambitious synagogue and school project were in sight. Since they had negotiated the agreement with Father Foley of the Epiphany Church, they did not expect to face another legal barricade set up by the Latino community. As matters developed, however, Father Foley's point of view did not have the complete support of the Latino community. Father Foley had been chosen by city officials as the person who could speak for Latino interests and move the project forward; for his part, Father Foley had been assured that Latino needs would be satisfied. During the next three years, however, as the terms of the agreement were discussed in households and at meetings, it was charged that Father Foley and the city had ignored other influential voices in the Latino community, such as those of the pastors of adjoining parishes and persons affiliated with the Ad Hoc Committee for the Southside Triangle, Brooklyn Legal Services, and Los Sures. These individuals and organizations now joined together to express their opposition to the agreement Father Foley had made.

Community Differences

The difficulty in resolving the housing issue was tied to other community differences. Latinos are keenly aware of the suspicion and hostility they arouse in the Hasidim, and they are angered by the Hasidic security patrols, which they claim have harassed and even beaten innocent Latinos.

If the Latinos needed a rallying cry to unite their community they found it in Hasidic attempts to obtain special privileges in the local schools. In 1985 a Supreme Court ruling reaffirmed that children in private schools are entitled to receive remedial lessons provided by public schools as mandated in Chapter I of the federal law. The Court held, however, that in keeping with the principle of the separation of church and state, public school authorities are not permitted to offer classes on the premises of the private school. The New York City Board of Education attempted to provide remedial lessons for lower-income children from private schools by either providing buses to take the children to sites leased for the purpose, or having the children attend classes at the public schools.

The following year, in accordance with the mandate of the Supreme Court, the local school superintendent agreed to offer remedial lessons to Hasidic girls at Public School 16 in Williamsburg, which is 95 percent nonwhite. In order to fulfill their religious code concerning the separation of the sexes, the Hasidim insisted that the classes be given by female teachers in a section partitioned off from the remainder of the school. The local public school officials agreed to their conditions and had partitions and doors set in place.

Already antagonized by disputes concerning housing, vigilante justice, and police protection, Hispanic parents in Williamsburg were determined to oppose any special advantages offered to the Hasidic community. They were insulted and outraged at this new example of the special privileges they saw afforded the Hasidim and the corresponding lack of respect they felt was granted to them by public school officials. The intrusion of Hasidic religious prerogatives into the public schools confirmed the worst fears of the Latinos: that Hasidic demands knew no bounds and that city officials were quick to acquiesce to their requests no matter how much it offended Latino sensibilities. The insult was sharpened by the fact that the people involved were neighbors—they lived on the same streets and passed one another in building hallways and on the sidewalks. Now their children would be artificially separated from each other by a "wall" that they viewed as suggesting that their children were inferior. They further argued that to create space for the Hasidic girls the district-wide program for handicapped children had been displaced and plans made to relocate those children to other schools. Sensitive to any encroachment of the law by the Hasidim, they were now armed with legal teams of their own, the Brooklyn Legal Services Corporation A and the Puerto Rican Legal Defense and Education Fund.

The dispute was carried on in the street and in the courthouse. Most of the Latino children refused to attend classes. At the same time their legal representatives argued in court that providing special facilities for religious children in a secular school was unconstitutional and violated the separation of church and state. The Federal District Court in Brooklyn initially found for the Hasidim, but the Federal Appeals Court unanimously overruled the lower court and decided against the partition plan. The Board of Education abandoned the idea and the case never went further up the court ladder.[23] Following the court's decision, attorney Needelman stated the dual results stemming from his Latino clients' determination: "It stopped an unconstitutional plan and gave a community that was feeling increasingly powerless a sense of empowerment." The success of the Latino parents of Public School 16 in defending the rights of the larger Latino community renewed their confidence and gave them assurance that they could win in court.

Tensions between the two groups continued on the streets. Latino men resented the refusal of the Hasidim to speak to them or to recognize their presence. Some of the younger Latino women complained that the few men who spoke to them made a sexual assumption and only asked, "How much?"

Latinos soon voiced their resentment at what they considered to be bias on the part of the police in the 90th Precinct in making arrests and in issuing parking summonses. First, there was an incident in July 1990 at Roberto Clemente Plaza involving a Hasid with a history of mental problems who was accused of fondling a Latino tenant in the laundry room. The woman and Latino leaders complained that officers from the 90th Precinct were reluctant to arrest the Hasid without clearing it with a higher officer.[24] Matters came to a head when another young woman charged a Hasid with making improper advances to her on an elevator.

An editorial in the *New York Post* noted that "the accuser had a history of advancing parallel allegations against other Hasidim and against blacks" and stated that the charges were probably bogus.[25] When the accused Hasid was placed under arrest, some three hundred of his comrades demonstrated at the police station during a rainstorm on October 23, 1990. The precinct house's windows were broken and the demonstrators forced their way inside. In the tumult that took place forty-six police officers claimed to have been injured.[26] Latinos were outraged when only a single protester was arrested, arguing that if Latinos had acted up at the police station many more would have been taken into custody.

In the City Council Public Safety Committee hearing to investigate the disturbance, Hector Ariza, a Hispanic police officer, charged that "Members of the Hasidim have the run of the 90th Precinct and my fellow officers are powerless to act because there is an unwritten policy at the 90th Precinct of looking the other way when members of the Hasidim commit crimes." [27] Police Commissioner Lee Brown expressed concern at the perception of favoritism but reported that a review of arrests and summonses revealed no such evidence; similarly, examination of the pattern of the almost 77,000 parking summonses issued showed no significant differences in the number of tickets written for violations in the two communities. Councilman Abraham Gerges saw beyond the petty irritations on the street to the central issue in Williamsburg: "There is a tinderbox in Williamsburg, but it has nothing to do with the police but with the extraordinary need for housing." [28]

There was one very tangible result for the Latino community. The sense of unity that they had developed would come into play again in appeals of discrimination in housing and in protests against the expansion of the Hasidic community.

Latino Protest in Housing

Meanwhile Hasidic construction plans had moved forward. The Rebbe's house had been built on Bedford Avenue, and the foundation for the school was poured. The synagogue would soon follow. While the Hasidim rejoiced, some in the Latino population regarded the prospect of a large new synagogue as ominous news. It forecast an even greater Hasidic presence in the area, with still more residents seeking housing and a street ambiance reflecting Hasidic ways.

In the summer of 1989 Latino residents who had expressed dissatisfaction with the agreement negotiated by Father Foley formed the Southside Fair Housing Committee, a coalition of Puerto Ricans, other Latinos, and blacks. Many of the leaders of the old Ad Hoc Committee were part of the new group. The Southside Fair Housing Committee took a sharply different view from that of Father Foley and sounded a harsher rhetoric.

> We were angered by the fact that while the Hasidics were to get 300 units of housing we would get only 105. In Urban Renewal Area 1 all the parcels of land for institutional use were sold exclusively to the Hasidics. A message to us from the City of New York: "Latinos, blacks and non-Hasidic whites would be forced to move out to allow for an exclusive 'Holy City' to be built in Williamsburg."[29]

The Brooklyn Legal Services Corporation A and the Puerto Rican Legal Defense and Education Fund brought a class action lawsuit in the United States District Court on behalf of the Southside Fair Housing Committee.[30] The suit accused the city and federal governments, the Hasidim and their organizations, and private corporations of continuing bias in the administration of the projects completed in the past and in the proposed new plans.[31] The class action suit charged that the defendants "are engaged in a concerted effort to discriminate against Latinos and African-Americans that has significantly increased the percentage of white households living in the area and that has significantly decreased the percentage of Latino and African-American households living in the area." The New York City Department of Housing Preservation and Development (HPD), it contended, "has discriminated against Latinos and African-Americans and is promoting a Hasidic enclave and thus the establishment of religion."

The depositions filed by the Latino complainants detailed the assertions that a pattern of discrimination existed in favor of the Hasidim. They alleged that a higher percentage of Hasidic tenants lived in public housing projects than would have been the case had there been no discrimination against nonwhites. It also asserted that when apartments became available borough-wide priority waiting lists (which had a 93 percent nonwhite ratio) were ignored in favor of local lists that favored the acceptance of Hasidic tenants. The witnesses also asserted that there was a continuing use of racial quotas maintaining a fixed and inappropriately high percentage of Hasidim and a correspondingly low percentage of nonwhites.

Similar complaints were made concerning the new condominium apartments in Brooklyn Villas. The developer was accused of failing to dispense information so that few outside the Hasidic community knew that the apartments were for sale: minuscule public notice of the apartments was printed in the classified columns in the *New York Times* and *New York Newsday*, while two full-page ads were printed in Yiddish in *Der Zeitung*, a weekly Yiddish language newspaper.[32] Potential buyers had only two weeks to obtain and file an application and deposit. Information packets were printed only in Yiddish. The charges were under-lined by the reality of the spread of the applications: twelve hundred Hasidic applications had been taken, while only two nonwhites filed the necessary forms.

Objections were also raised against the plan to favor extra-large fami-lies, arguing that it was discriminatory in that the Hasidim had the largest families. Rules for the lottery to select the new householders would have allowed families with more than eight members to draw three times; fam-ilies with six or seven members to draw twice; and families with five or fewer to have one chance. Latino complainants also objected to the de-sign of the apartments, which featured double sinks (desired by the Ha-sidim to keep meat and dairy dishes separate), and large terraces (used by the Hasidim to build a sukkah, a wooden booth covered with branches, to celebrate Sukkot, the Feast of Tabernacles).[33]

The lottery for Brooklyn Villas had been carried out, but the results were now held in abeyance. City officials had previously stopped the lot-tery for "affordable housing," requiring the developer to make changes that would make that housing more available to the public at large. A temporary restraining order for the project was requested and the com-plainants asked that the distribution of existing apartments be halted un-til it could be carried out without the alleged discrimination against the Latinos. The judge did not grant the restraining order, but he set an early date for a hearing. In the interim, the two sides began to renegotiate their positions. All the same, Brooklyn Villas signed contracts with Hasidim for 207 of the available apartments. A federal mediator was called in.

In a complex accord covering the five government-subsidized housing developments, an agreement was proposed to do away with offending procedures and to increase housing for nonwhites. The finding fell heav-ily against the Hasidim, in great measure because of the city's and the community's failure to abide by previous court rulings. It was estimated that because of failure to follow the stipulations of the earlier Consent Decree, between the years 1979 and 1989 nonwhites had lost 276 apart-ments (238 in public housing and 38 in two privately owned but publicly subsidized housing operations). The remedy proposed for two of the de-velopments was to skip temporarily over the first 38 otherwise eligible white applicants on the waiting list. In the three public housing projects the next 190 vacancies would be filled exclusively by nonwhites who had been denied the opportunity to apply for apartments during the relevant period.[34]

After present needs were satisfied, the borough-wide priority list would be employed in the future to select new householders. For the privately built proposed housing, Brooklyn Villas, the results of the weighted lot-tery in favor of large families were withdrawn. Marketing the apartments would be redirected through large advertisements to be run for several days in the *New York Daily News,* then the newspaper with the largest circulation. The remaining 22 more-expensive condominium apartments, with an average price of $175,000 each, and 40 out of the 59 less-expensive apartments, to be sold at $81,000 or $87,000 each, would be reserved for nonwhites who could afford them.

It remains to be seen how much change the new agreement will bring about. Only about 160 nonwhite applications were received for even the 40 less-expensive apartments. The more costly privately developed apartments are out of the reach of most local residents.

The whirligig of private and public activities has obscured the needs of the poorest and least able of the Hasidic community as well. Buried in a catchall column in the *New York Times* (for September 29, 1990) was the story of a homeless young Hasidic couple who had been offered an apartment in one of the projects in Bedford-Stuyvesant, the neighborhood adjacent to Williamsburg. The young woman, pregnant with a second child; and her husband, a yeshivah student from Iran, refused the apartment.

> For Hasidic Jews living in Williamsburg . . . that might as well have been on Mars. Synagogue, yeshivot, kosher food—everything that defines their strictly ordered life—would have been hopelessly distant.
>
> "We refused it because we are Jews," said the woman. "Nothing is there for us."
>
> So the two landed on an upper floor of a Williamsburg synagogue in a room barely large enough for two torn mattresses. A dozen other homeless people live in the temple. The place is dirty, dark and smells bad. Flies buzz. There is one toilet. The shower is for men only, meaning the young woman must go to a ritual bath and pay $5: big money for welfare recipients.[35]

Rabbi Chaim Stauber, who had alerted the community to its need for mental health facilities, sounded the alarm on the growing tragedy of homelessness. "This is a community literally bursting at its seams because of the lack of affordable housing." [36]

It was apparent that the Hasidim had learned something from the struggles with the Latino community and the negative fallout over the incident at the 90th Precinct. The Satmar leaders had advised against the demonstration, but their words had been ignored. As a result there were changes made to strengthen the administration of the United Jewish Organizations of Williamsburg. The Rebbe asked Rabbi Moshe David Niederman, who had already demonstrated his leadership abilities as founder and director of Rav Tov, an immigration and rescue agency, to become Executive Director of UJO. Rabbi Niederman made it clear that while he would not intrude in the economic and social areas overseen by Sender Deutsch and Chaim Stauber he intended to establish policy in other areas. The first shot fired let those who had demonstrated know that if they did not heed the wishes of the leadership they would be frozen out of the decisionmaking process, and to emphasize that point he excluded the previous executive director, who was also the director of the Williamsburg Federation of Tenants in Public Housing, and others from a meeting he held with the police.

Rabbi Niederman took an enlightened view of other problems in the community as well. In the past when there had been complaints concerning the misdeeds of one or another housing slumlord the United Jewish Organizations had not taken a stand against him. Now Niederman argued that for the greater good of the community he would actively oppose the slumlords. He began looking into the complaints of tenants and the responses of landlords. He also took steps to join with the Latino community in opposing the environmental hazards in the neighborhood and the threatened toxic waste dump that had been proposed for the adjoining Navy Yard area.

Although the attorneys for the Latinos had won considerable concessions from the Hasidim in the negotiations, and had satisfied their most immediate concerns, some in the Latino community continued to be dissatisfied with the agreement. To a large extent they had negotiated on housing that remained out of the reach of many because of the high costs involved. They still lacked low-cost housing, and the financing for those units remained hostage to the lack of federal, state, and city involvement. Despite their victories in the negotiations, they were left with a sense of frustration.

For their part, the Hasidim were eager to resolve the Hasidic-Latino dispute so that they could complete their plans for the area adjacent to the Rebbe's house at Bedford and Ross Streets: to erect a large synagogue capable of seating six thousand, a yeshivah, and apartments for their faculty. The major threat to Satmar housing plans came from the single remaining portion of the suit by Hispanic groups to contest the sale of the land and halt construction of the project. The plaintiffs' brief charged that Housing Preservation and Development had sold land to the Hasidim "at below market price through a privately negotiated agreement." [37] The city and the Hasidim were accused of attempting to prepare a religious enclave in violation of the First and Fourteenth Amendments ensuring the separation of church and state. The development of the Satmar project, they charged, worked to the detriment of the Hispanic community.

The Hasidim maintained that they had paid a high price for the land and had no apologies to make.

For the cross-subsidy we pay $3,500,000 for the land to satisfy the Puerto Ricans and the blacks. In the Bronx and everywhere the city gives away lands ten times larger for nothing at all. Even in Williamsburg, for the Puerto Ricans in the Southside and Northside, the city gives away the same land for nothing. Here, on the other side of Broadway, so we should not have frictions with the Puerto Ricans, we have to pay $3,500,000 to satisfy the Puerto Ricans and the blacks. And after that the *Village Voice* says we are getting the land for nothing.   (RH)

The city denied the charges made by the Latinos. It was pointed out that the Review Procedure Committee of the Community Board had held public meetings on the proposal and the consensus of those in attendance had been favorable. They had found that the integrity of the community surrounding the project area would not be undermined. There would be no increase in traffic since those attending the synagogue on the Sabbath would have to walk there, and since the housing to be constructed would be limited to faculty employed at the yeshivah. For the Hasidim, the complainants' request for an injunction meant the possibility of another unreasonable delay. The main objective of the Hasidim remained to vitalize their own community with new housing, new schools, and a large new besmedresh. They maintained that they had already made unusual financial concessions to the Latino community. It was also pointed out that land had been offered to both communities. Nonetheless the plaintiffs maintained that their civil rights under the Equal Protection and Due Process clauses had been violated by the sale, which had been made "with intent to discriminate against Latinos and African-Americans."

On November 2, 1990, U.S. District Court Judge Eugene Nickerson ruled that there was no direct evidence that the city had willfully discriminated against Latinos or had violated their constitutional rights. The court noted that in the several years since 1977 when development plans had been approved, no one had made a charge of discrimination at planning meetings and public hearings. Nor had any group or developer offered alternative proposals. Judge Nickerson also confirmed the legality of the sale of land by the city for use as synagogues and churches, and he recalled that one site "was tentatively designated for development by an Hispanic Pentecostal Church with a congregation of about 500" but that the church had decided to locate elsewhere.[38]

In April 1991 the Federal Appeals Court forcefully concurred with Judge Nickerson's opinion, and injunctive relief was denied to the Latino complainants. Within the limitations prescribed in other cases concerning the allocation of public housing, the way was open for the Satmar Hasidim to strengthen and solidify their community in South Williamsburg.

Eyes quickly turned to a potential source of new housing in the Brooklyn Navy Yard, adjacent to Williamsburg. Hasidic leaders had long regarded the property, which was soon to be relinquished by the federal government, as a base for future development. The potential use of the Navy Yard for additional housing was uncertain for Hasidim and Latinos alike. The area was divided into three parts: one section was occupied as

an industrial park; one area was designated for future use as an incinera-
tor (a use opposed by both Hasidim and Latinos and the one issue on
which they had fully cooperated with each other); and one part consisting
of forty-four acres was used by the Navy and had been declared surplus
property. If no federal agency claimed it for use, then it could be sold to
the municipality (for very little if it was to be used in some civic capacity,
say as a jail or a school, or at market value if a commercial building was
to be constructed on the site). The cost of the land therefore would to a
great extent influence the capital that could be attracted and the kind of
housing likely to be constructed. In addition to these hurdles there were
some physical obstacles that might prevent or delay use of the land for
development. It remained to be seen whether the Navy Yard could be
equitably developed and whether the Hasidim and Latinos could unite to
protect the area from being used as a dump for toxic waste—or if the two
groups would continue their battle there in the next century.

A New Boyaner Rebbe
Is Named

Preparation

More than a decade had passed since the old Boyaner Rebbe's death in 1971, and the Boyaner Hasidim were still without a Rebbe. At last it appeared that a successor could be named. Among those most delighted by the news was the deceased Rebbe's son, Israel Friedman.

> These young people and the old people needed someone to sustain them, to be a living example of what a holy man is supposed to be—a man who they think, and hopefully he does too, leads a life which is full of Torah and service to God and service to the community.
>
> They persuaded my [brother-in-law] Menachem to send [his younger son] Reb Nahum Dov to our yeshivah [in Israel], and he adjusted beautifully there. I think Reb Nahum Dov felt a certain obligation, which he already had felt as a child, somehow not to let the tradition die away. He learned in the yeshivah like everyone else, but somehow the most important rabbis, the most learned Hasidim, took him under their wing, learned with him, taught him some of the inside traditions of the Rizhiner Rebbe, of my father, and of their behavior patterns. All the other relatives encouraged him. He himself felt, even at the age of sixteen and seventeen, that somehow his mission would be to carry on the family tradition. But it took a long time before he was able to take the plunge.   (IF)

It was now only a matter of time until the young man would believe himself equal to the task, or until the Boyaner Hasidim would wear him down with their demands that he accept the role, ready or not.

> Without exaggeration, although I'm subjectively involved as a father, I think my son's training was unique. He not only studied in the yeshivah, but he was trained privately by Hasidic authorities, without mentioning names, in Jerusalem in the intricacies of Hasidic lore, plus Talmudic and rabbinic studies, and kabbalistic background.
>
> The stress [in Rizhin] is mainly on the humaneness of Hasidic law, on the *menschlekhkayt*. The basic gestalt is that there should always be a combi-

nation of reverence in the heart but acted out behaviorwise, that theory without application and practice has no value. To be a Hasid does not mean to *khap shirayim* [grab the remains of the Rebbe's meal] or to follow the Rebbe or to just dance and sing and hop, but rather to act like one in terms of the old tradition of the Rizhiner and the Maggid, whereby the inner soul becomes inflamed by the revelation and proximity of God by actualizing God's will within your daily life—not just talking about it but carrying it out. There are innumerable stories of the Rizhiner, of the Friedman dynasty in general, that show the ascent of *avoda shebalev,* covert [inward] worship.

The old Rebbe, my father-in-law, blessed be his memory, never allowed any tape recordings or writing down whatever he said at the *tishn* [communal meals at which the Rebbe gives his *toyre,* discourses]. After I got married in 1952 to his daughter Malka I decided for historicity that I'm going to break tradition, I'm going to write whatever I possibly can during the weekdays. So I invariably carried a pad with me and under the table I always took notes. I have now hundreds of notes which I'm preparing now for publication for whatever is left over. Now my son the Rebbe *shlita* [may he live long] knows almost every toyre, every oration, verbatim.   (MMB)

Choosing the Rebbetsn

The ties between the courts of Boyan and Kapitshinitzer had always been close both in Europe and in America. Now the families became more tightly linked. Syshe Heschel, son and brother of Kapitshinitzer Rebbes, tells the story:

In 1979 my daughter Shoshana went to study in the seminary in Jerusalem. About six months later she wrote us a very serious letter, how after thinking very seriously about it she decided that she would like to marry and spend her life in Israel. "This place," she said, "is the only place to live, the only place to raise children."

Upon reading this letter I sat down and wrote her: "No thank you. Absolutely, positively not." I went into great detail. "You want to marry and live in Israel? Fine, come home, marry someone here and then if you and your husband decide that you want to move to Israel, great."

So I'll tell you what she did. For the next three months, that girl tested herself, trying to prove to herself that she could subsist on the bare minimum. She gave away her spending money. She did not buy any extra food, or clothing, or anything but the barest of necessities. She had to prove to herself that she could do it. We had told her that life in Israel is hard. She tested herself. Could she do it? Yes she could. She still wants to do it and it still is worth it.

In the meantime, a nephew of mine had met my [future] son-in-law [Reb Nahum Dov]. He got to know him, recognized his potential, and he felt that this would be a wonderful match. Their characters were very suited for each other. They're both quiet, gentle people, both are super intelligent; they both have the same desires, and both shared strong feelings about wanting to settle in Israel.

In addition, the Boyaner Rebbe and my father [the Kapitshinitzer Rebbe] were very close personal friends.

It wasn't just my nephew who had the idea. Many people suggested it. Well, one day my daughter calls from Israel in a panic and tells me that my nephew called her up at the school dorm and told her that she has to pack her bags and return home at once. He didn't tell her why because if he had told her she wouldn't have gone home. It turned out that my future son-in-law had also arrived in the States. My nephew was afraid that some other match would reach him first. If my daughter were to have stayed in Israel and the boy was here, there wouldn't be a chance in the world for the match to go through.

We discussed the matter with my daughter and we asked my nephew to explore the issue "with the other side." After receiving word of their interest I called my future son-in-law's father [Menachem M. Brayer] and made arrangements for the two young people to meet. They met once and they said, "We'll meet once again."

Twice they met each other. This was in the summer. Menachem has a summer house on Sackett Lake. So we went over there and we stayed in one room while the young people talked to each other for about half an hour. And they came out and they said they liked each other. I mean they didn't say so in front of each other. She said it to me and he must have said the same to his parents. After the second time it was a foregone conclusion. Shoshana was nineteen at the time; Nahum Dov was twenty. They were married about eight months later, in June 1980.

He asked to make a condition with the Hasidim that before becoming Rebbe he would be allowed to learn Torah for a year after the wedding without being disturbed, without being bothered. So they said, "Well, all right, for a year fine, but no longer than a year." And when the year ended they came to him and reminded him.

And he begged them, "A little bit longer."

And they said, "No. The Hasidim have been without a Rebbe now for ten, eleven years. If you don't take up the mantle right now everybody's going to go away. You're going to lose the people."

And so he assured them, "I promise you they're not going to go away. I promise you that they'll wait. But please give me some more time." So he stretched it out up until Hanukkah, at the end of 1984. (SH)

The New Rebbe

In December 1984, the elder members of the Boyaner community, about ninety American Hasidim including some wives, flew to Jerusalem to crown Reb Nahum Dov as the new Boyaner Rebbe. They carried with them a *kvitl* (petition) containing hundreds of names, which had been signed by every Boyaner and Rizhiner Hasid in New York. At the same time a second still longer kvitl, signed by every Boyaner Hasid in Israel, was also brought to the Rebbe. When the Rebbe accepted the *kvitlekh*, he acknowledged his leadership of the Boyaner Hasidim. He was thus officially "crowned" as the new Boyaner Rebbe. No one was prouder than the new Rebbe's father, Menachem M. Brayer.

I'm emotionally swept up. By the way he behaves, by the way he lives his Hasidic life. He lives it. There's a statement in the Talmud saying those foolish Babylonian Jews stand up when the Torah is being carried past them, but they don't stand up when the *talmid khokhem* [learned man] passes. The talmid khokhem is the living Torah. When I look at him I see a living Torah. He actually practices what he preaches.

To him to be Rebbe means a tremendous burden. He says to me over and over again, "I wish I can get out of it and just sit and learn the whole day. I haven't got the *koakh*, the strength, to take on so many *tsores* [troubles] on my mind. Every day people come with kvitlekh. This one is sick, and this one's wife has to give birth, this operation requires a surgeon, this one's in the hospital, this one has passed away, this one has cancer. Over and over again he says to me, "I wish they could find someone else, it wouldn't have to be me. I have a tremendous burden to worry about all the Jews who come to me." (MMB)

Despite his doubts and misgivings, Reb Nahum Dov felt compelled to become the new Boyaner Rebbe.

As a grandson of a Rebbe, since there was no one else able to take over in the family, it was my responsibility to see to it to continue it in the family. It was put to me officially when I was eighteen or nineteen. I'm now twenty-seven [1986]. I felt I had to do it even though it wasn't my type of plan. I was thinking of staying in learning and education, to teach Talmudic studies in the yeshivah.

Since I was in Israel ten years before I was married, and after, I developed close relationships with the Rebbes of the Rizhin dynasty: the Buhusher Rebbe in Tel Aviv, the Sadagerer Rebbe in Tel Aviv, and the Medzbizher Rebbe, who was first in New York and then in Haifa. (He passed away one year ago.) I learned the ways of the Rizhiner Rebbes—their qualities and the traits: kindness and goodness toward people. My grandfather would give away as much as possible to help other people spiritually and materially— giving time and thought.

Giving advice and help is a big part of being Rebbe. Besides giving counsel, it means trying to contact other people who could help. Usually I discuss with the person the way he should proceed, trying to clarify for the person what he should do. There are medical, financial, spiritual problems—looking for a *derekh*—a way, a path forward.

The Rizhin way of royalty was continued by his children and grandchildren. The great-grandchildren discontinued it. They didn't live that way but kept it inside. I try to keep up my grandfather's *derekh* [way]—his humbleness, his helping people, his righteousness.

There's a story of my great-grandfather, the Sadagerer, the son of the Ri-zhiner. He once met a Rebbe, and the Rebbe asked him to say toyre. "Toyre I should say? We see that the Torah begins with the book of *bereshit* [Gene-sis]. Even though there are no laws and are only stories of the patriarchs, our forefathers, their everyday life was so holy that it itself was considered Torah." And he quoted the Midrash called *Tanah Elohim,* that "every per-son should ask himself, when will my deeds reach [match] the deeds of my forefathers?" How can a person say he should reach the deeds of his fore-fathers? How can a person attain such spiritual heights? To reach also means to touch. Even a person who can't reach such spiritual heights as his fore-fathers—his deeds should at least touch them. He can't reach them but he should follow them and strive to reach them.

HaShem rules the world through the tzaddik. It's as if there was a partner-ship. My grandfather had to know about the world. I'm not at that degree. I have to reach. I realize that it's not my righteousness. My grandfather used to say that the holiness of the grandparents helps, and the community gives strength as well.   (ND)

The First Tish in Israel

In 1984 Israel Friedman, the Rebbe's uncle, went to Israel to share in the first tish presided over by the new Rebbe.

I felt an emotional reaction when Reb Nahum Dov conducted the first tish . . . Both I and my brother felt memories coming back. Above all, I felt the absence of my father. I also felt a sense of jealousy that my father never had as many Hasidim as Reb Nahum Dov did. My father had a tremendously large circle of people who revered him and who knew him, but real Hasidim in terms of people who would walk miles to come to a tish, or to stay over, of that type of people who were there, he didn't have as many. In America my father never had a tish with more than a hundred people. The first time my father came to Israel there was a tremendous outpouring, around eight or nine hundred people. But later on, two or three hundred people would be there. He didn't have that many Hasidim.[1]

This coming together [at a tish] is important to strengthen the ties be-tween him and the community, to strengthen the ties between the people themselves. They'll be living through that feeling of exhilaration for a long time.

Obviously I won't deny that instinctively I also felt that here but for the grace of God go I, knowing full well I couldn't do it. I couldn't do it and I wouldn't do it. I don't think so. It needs a certain knowledge of Torah in the larger sense. I'm not as great a talmudist as my nephew. Again that's honesty, not pure modesty. Frankly, I think that perhaps in my day-to-day dealings with the Hasidim, because of my worldly background, because I believe I'm not exactly the biggest moron in the world, I might be able to give better advice in terms of day-to-day living than this young man who's only twenty-seven years old. I mean, after all, I'm seventy and I've had lots of experience and a social work background. So I felt that perhaps in that sense I would have been a better purveyor of knowledge and comfort. That was a feeling too that occurred. But mostly I felt the tremendous outpouring of people. It was so unexpected and so tremendous and so awe-inspiring, and he did such a beautiful job, which I never expected. I was in awe, in awe of remembrance, in awe of recalling old times.

Just sitting down and presenting himself, and the way he made *kiddush* [benediction over wine], and the way he acted. He acts regally. He acts regally, literally regally. He knows what to do; he knows how to do it. He doesn't fool around; he acts majestically in a sense. It's a complete difference between the way he talked to you and the way he acted, and this was not made up. When he came to us for a visit he carried his kid in his hands and he acted like a regular person. When he's with his Hasidim he also acts naturally. But when he's at the tish he feels that the tish is something which transcends the day-to-day activities. A tish is something which demands a certain intention, a certain ability to transmit values, whatever these values are, and therefore deserves a certain mode of behavior which is on a higher level. In Jewish terms it's a sense of *kedushah* [holiness].

He talks constantly that this shtibl on East Broadway, which was the home of my father for forty years, is a place which was sanctified by somebody's presence. And that person who was there was somebody who was, in terms of behavior patterns, in terms of his relationship of man to God, someone who could be considered a tzaddik. What is a tzaddik? Someone who is a saint who leads a life of service to God and learning, which makes him somewhat on a higher level ethically and morally than the average person.

I would say that Reb Nahum Dov now is attracting a number of people who are not Boyaner Hasidim because of his youthfulness, because of the reputation he's getting as a man of ethical values, because of his modesty, and because of a certain aura of respectability. They come to him in Israel and here in America too. All I know is that while he was here in America quite a number of people came to him because they felt that something new, a new product has arisen, something which seems important to find out about, to get to know. Whether they will remain I have no way of knowing. (IF)

Justifiable family pride was also expressed by Syshe Heschel, the Rebbe's father-in-law. At the same time he was reminded of the gap left by the demise of his father and brother and the impossibility of his assuming responsibility for all the affairs of the Kapitshinitzer court.

I am overwhelmed by the affection that this boy has from his followers. Nearly every Rebbe has the admiration of his Hasidim. They think he's wonderful, they think he's great, he's the brightest, he's brilliant, and so forth. But a genuine love is something that my son-in-law has—to see how they look at him, how they don't take their eyes off him. I don't know if you noticed, in that tremendous heat they stood at attention when he came in.

Before that it was a madhouse, but when he came in they stood quietly, watched his every move, and listened to every sound.

Some people who don't have anyone that they feel close enough to go to, to this day they still call me, they still ask me, they still bother me, with specific problems. Not that I should take the title [of Rebbe]. And I'm just overwhelmed by the burden of it. People call me I should make decisions for them and I can't. I talk to them and I discuss this with them and we try to deal with it, you know, discuss the situation in a logical fashion. What's the logical thing he should do and so forth. But there's a tremendous gap between what to do and the logical thing to do. Do you take risks? Do you take chances? I talk with these people. I try to send some people to someone, but you know the people that still bother me are those people that somehow can't find anywhere else to go to. They have no attachment to anyone else and they just see me as the personification of what my father and my brother were. I get business questions, health questions, divorce questions, marriage questions—typical questions for a Rebbe.

As time goes on more and more I am in contact with this group that still hangs on to Kapitshinitzer. More and more I meet people who have problems, and more and more I see what a wonderful thing it is that the Hasid has a Rebbe. And I don't mean it in a blind sense—the Hasid has a Rebbe and follows everything that the Rebbe says. So many people are troubled. This is such a complex world today. Of course everybody would like a Rebbe to give them the answers, but even today people want a little bit more than that, you know. Sure they would like a miracle man and they would want somebody to offer them the miracle and to give them that *berakha* [blessing] that would bring them a miracle. That hasn't changed because human nature wants miracles. But they do want to lean on somebody. They want to be able to feel that they have a friend who they can talk with, and just in the act of talking out they want to hear what insight the person has into their problems. There's a terrible need today for someone that people can feel close with. The yeshivot today don't have the rabbis who have the ability to influence their students. I think every person—whether it's a Hasid and a Rebbe, or even a good yeshivah boy and his rosh yeshivah—everybody needs to be inspired by somebody. Somebody has to give them inspiration, leadership, guidance. And that's missing today. And I think that the need is tremendous today. "I need somebody to talk to." "I've got problems." "I've got decisions to make." "I don't know where I'm headed." "I don't know what's happening." "I haven't anybody to talk to."   (SH)

The Tish at East Broadway

In April 1986 Reb Nahum Brayer, the Boyaner Rebbe, now a permanent resident of Israel, returned for a month-long visit to New York City to see his followers there. At the end of his stay he presided at a tish at 247 East Broadway, the building that was once the home of his grandfather and still serves as the court's principal shul and the Rizhin yeshivah office.

The tish, held on May 17 just prior to the Rebbe's departure to the Holy Land, would celebrate the third meal of the Shabbes *(shaleshudes)*.[2] This was to be the highlight of his brief visit to the United States.

Only a few families still live close by in Lower Manhattan, and since the tish was on Shabbes afternoon when travel by automobile is forbidden, the Hasidim had to make arrangements to stay over Friday night in the neighborhood or else plan to take a six or seven mile hike on Saturday from the Upper West Side in Manhattan or an equally distant walk over the bridge from Borough Park and Bensonhurst in Brooklyn. May 17 turned out to be a warm Shabbes afternoon, and the sun would make the long walk still more fatiguing.

Number 247 East Broadway was no longer the home that had received such care when the Friedman family lived there. It was now a ramshackle shul and study hall. Israel Friedman's former bedroom had been converted into a kitchen for the congregation. There were huge sacks of bread on the table to be used for the tish. Upstairs in the bathroom the pipes were leaking. There were papers strewn everywhere.

The tish was scheduled to be held in the smaller of two large rooms on the first floor. This was the back room in which in earlier days Reb Mordchei Shlomo, the old Boyaner Rebbe, had held the court's communal meals and had offered his toyre. But the number of Boyaner followers had been fewer then. There was one tiny window set high in the corner of the room. It held a small air conditioner which was already overwhelmed by the humid air. The room could contain only forty or so people comfortably, but there were already more than one hundred Hasidim crowded together, standing on the tops of chairs, benches, and tables. Others continued to press into the room, prompting the young students in back to move to still higher points in order to look over those in front.

No sooner was everyone settled in his place than it was decided to move the tish into the larger front room, the shtibl, where the congregation prays. The extra space would help to accommodate the crowd, and there was an air conditioner which had cooled off the room when it was empty and gave the false promise of greater comfort.

Once the change was announced there was a rush to grab new places. For the moment the room was barren of furniture, since all the tables and chairs had been moved into the other room to set up the tish. Before anyone could be seated, the furniture had to be moved back. So while the crowd was pushing its way in, tables, benches, and chairs were also being carried in over their heads and dropped down. As each bench was passed overhead and then set down the crowd parted and then reassembled, as though stones had been tossed into a lake. Finally, the main table was dropped down. The sudden change of rooms and feats of furniture moving had set some of the older Hasidim to muttering in irritation.

The main table was quickly covered with a white tablecloth, and two giant loaves of Shabbes challah and twelve smaller loaves were set down where the Rebbe would sit. The seats at a long narrow wooden table in the center of the room were reserved for the more prestigious members of the community, the family of the Rebbe, rabbis, and respected older Hasidim. The rest of the men were densely packed around those seated at the table, and the students were behind them, scaled upward on chairs and benches piled on tables set close to the walls. Perched topmost close to the high ceiling, seeking a better view of where the Rebbe would sit, were the most daring teenagers of the group, some of whom clung to door and window frames and bits of wall decoration for balance and support. The Hasidim were sweating in their kaftans. Cups of water were passed hand to hand. One man became faint from the heat and had to be helped from the room. The poor man had walked all the way from Borough Park. Since everyone was packed in so tightly it proved difficult to move him outside into the air.

The Rebbe appeared in the room suddenly. He was a thin young man, the narrowness of his face emphasized by the large shtrayml set on his head. He was much taller than any of his followers. Dignified but appearing somewhat strained, he sat down quickly at the head of the table and began preparations for the tish. The gabbai carried in water in a metal basin and the Rebbe ceremonially washed his hands, pouring water over one hand and then the other. Next the Rebbe broke off a piece of challah and recited the blessing. Even with his head stooping forward in prayer, the tall and slender Rebbe still towered over those seated nearby. Meanwhile, the rest of the challah was quickly divided and passed out among the Hasidim.

A large platter of gefilte fish was then carried in. Again the Rebbe took a small piece for himself and the remainder was divided into small pieces and passed out to the Hasidim on plastic plates. Everyone was too impatient to wait for the plastic forks to be distributed. This was the custom of *shirayim,* sharing the remains of the Rebbe's meal. In this way the Hasidim touch the powerful forces surrounding the Rebbe and emanating from him.

The tish was interrupted frequently by fervent communal singing of Shabbes songs. Small bottles of wine were opened. An announcement had been made that the Rebbe was providing the first three bottles of wine as a gift; after that the names of various Hasidim were called out, indicating who was paying for the bottles of wine. Bearing the cost of the wine was an honor, and calling out their names brought them to the attention of the Rebbe. As the wine was sipped, the Rebbe met each Hasid's eyes to bless each with *l'chaim* (to life), and was blessed himself in return. This lengthy procedure was not complete until each Hasid had been saluted. Later, pears were passed out and the Rebbe recited the blessing over fruit.

The Rebbe gave his toyre in a soft, quiet voice. He stressed that attention should be paid not only to the major commandments that everyone follows—such as observing the Shabbes—but also to the so-called lesser commandments, such as honesty, ethical behavior, and consideration for one's fellow men. As the Rebbe spoke, the half of the table nearest to him pressed closer, straining to hear his words over the rustle of the crowd and the hum of the air conditioner. The Hasidim leaned on one another, climbed on one another, trying to listen. The attention of those out of range of his voice—at the lower end of the table and in the back— quickly diminished, as they realized they would have to wait to hear summaries of what the Rebbe had said from others who were closer.

The tish ended with the Rebbe reciting grace. Afterward the *ma'ariv* services (evening prayers) were conducted. Following the evening prayers the congregation broke up to go outside and recite the prayer for the sanctification of the half-moon. A generation or so earlier the streets would have been crowded with worshipers from immigrant Jewish families living in the surrounding tenements. Now automobile and truck traffic had taken command of the streets and a police car arrived to protect the worshipers. The Hasidim picked their way across the street through the stop-and-start traffic. The moon too was dodging clouds above the tenements.

The congregation returned inside for the ceremony of the *havdalah*, signifying the ending of the Shabbes and the beginning of the week. The Rebbe blessed the wine. He inhaled the aroma of spices contained in a little box and it was passed on for each Hasid to sniff. The Rebbe then recited the blessing over the braided twin-wicked candle, cupping his hand to signify the light changing to dark. In this way the Shabbes was ended and the profane week was ushered in.

The Hasidim chanted:

> He who marks the holy from the profane,
> May he also pardon our transgressions;
> May he multiply our seed as the sand,
> And as the stars that appear in the night.

With the closing of the Shabbes, the atmosphere suddenly became relaxed. Cameras appeared and some of the more audacious young Hasidim snapped pictures of the Rebbe—to his obvious displeasure. The men hurriedly left to find their cars to drive home and join families waiting for their return. The cars were packed, sometimes with as many as twelve people squeezed into one sedan. The Hasidim saluted one another as they passed in their cars on their way back to Borough Park, Williamsburg, Belle Harbor, uptown or downtown.

The Rebbe's uncle, Israel Friedman, was pleased by what he had witnessed.

Tonight, during the tish he constantly stressed this important aspect of Hasidism—that one should not think that the worship of God and adherence to Orthodox Judaism merely consists of obeying only the most important mitzvot, like Shabbes and kashrut. Man and God—you listen, you obey. You obey the mitzvot and Torah. He didn't mention Shabbes and kashrut but that is what he meant. There are also *mitzvot kalot,* the so-called slighter mitzvot of the relationship between man and man, as compared to the relationship between man and God. The mitzvot concerning man and man means you have to be honest, to be truthful, to be honest in business dealings. These are ethical values which all too often are considered minor matters. They are transgressed, but they are just as important as the other more important mitzvot. You would never think of not eating kosher food or transgressing the laws of the Shabbes, but some think that in business you could steal a little bit, you could cheat a little bit, and Reb Nahum Dov constantly stressed fulfilling these laws. He brings in sayings of different Rebbes or Talmudical sayings in his own interpretation. That is the main idea which he stressed again and again.

He mentioned also that the home on East Broadway where my father lived, and which was the center of so much holiness and service, that we should keep up the minyan there. Those are little side issues because there are problems among some of the Hasidim as to whether to keep the minyan. And I think he said it very beautifully, and very succinctly. I told him many times to speak a little louder.

People will go to Israel to see him. Five people will go for this yontev; five people will go for Rosh Hashanah; ten people will go at other times. But they hope that now that the ice is broken that he will come here on a regular basis, once a year maybe. If you want to invest in AT&T stock, it's a good bet because his telephone is constantly busy from here. People constantly call him.

Several people have told me that they felt revitalized in their memories of my father and felt that somehow this young man is continuing the traditions in the very same high standard that my father did.

And the singing! Everyone is singing together. Did you like that *nigun* [melody], the first one? That's an old, old nigun of the Rizhiner.   (IF)

Menachem M. Brayer, the father of the new Rebbe, also felt satisfied that the past and the future of Boyan had been joined.

Izzy [Israel Friedman] told me today that the new Rebbe knows his father [the old Boyaner Rebbe] and behaves like his father and identifies with his father more than he himself ever did, although the new Rebbe barely knew his grandfather. In the sense that he follows the tradition ad litteram, verbatim, speaking in the same manner, behaving in the same manner, giving his orations in the same genre, in essence stressing interpersonal behavior of the Hasidim based on warmth, on love for each other, on the importance of respect for each other, love of the land of Israel without exception, and reverence and respect for one's fellow Jew and gentile alike—that everyone is born in the image of God—that all of us are children of God no matter how far removed we are from tradition. And no one should be ignored.

When you're a public figure you have to pay a price that you cannot devote too much time to your family. His main concern was, he told me before he left at the airport yesterday, "I didn't have enough time to teach my sons." He has young children. He didn't have enough time to learn with them. "I'll have to make it up in Jerusalem when I come back." Because the Hasidim devoured him. They flocked to him from all around, and each one with his own problems.

There are certain things which belong to the dynasty of Boyan. Meron near Safad is a place where Rebbe Shimon ben Yohai, the founder of the kabbala, the author of the Zohar, is buried. And on Lag ba-Omer, traditionally about a quarter of a million Jews, basically Sephardim, flock there and spend the night in prayer.[3] Now, the main feature of the entire ceremony is that at night after evening prayers you light a gigantic torch on the rabbi's burial place. Then comes fantastic dancing and singing for hours and hours. The right for this privilege was given to the Rizhiner, the Sadagerer, and thereafter the Boyaner. My son left yesterday because he didn't want to miss the tradition of lighting the first torch on Lag ba-Omer night in Meron where thousands and thousands of Jews come. It's his right; it comes to him by genealogical tradition. This is the reason why he left.

The other Rebbes look at Boyan now not just as a descendant of the Rizhiner but as a certain image of the Maggid, the founder of Hasidism after the Baal Shem Tov. All the Rebbes, even the older ones, love him, so they say. There's a certain devotion, a certain affinity, a certain personal emotional sentimental touch to Boyan because they feel this is the direct descendancy of the Maggid.

I'm in reverence myself. I must admit that I became a Hasid of my own son. I see a metamorphosis in my own relationship to him. Besides the paternal filial relationship I see also a relationship of respect almost close to awe on my part, seeing that white-bearded Jews from Jerusalem, learned scholars, and young people attend a tish and are in reverence and full of respect of every word that the young Rebbe says. And he's talking with his eyes closed. You saw him, humble, honest. I am extremely proud of him.

The Hasidim love him, because after fifteen years of interruption of the Hasidic chain of rebbes, they finally got a Rebbe. And the most remarkable part is that he's an American product who appeals to the stringent, most demanding requirements of Jerusalem Hasidic life.   (MMB)

· 24 ·

Lubavitch: Days of Trial, Days of Celebration

The Lubavitcher Library

In November 1985, Judge Charles P. Sifton of the United States District Court of the Eastern District of New York determined that a nonjury trial should be held to resolve the ownership of the library housed at Lubavitch headquarters at 770 Eastern Parkway. The court would decide if at the time of his death in 1950 the library had been the personal property of Rabbi Joseph Isaac Schneersohn, the sixth Lubavitcher Rebbe, and his heirs (his two daughters, Hanna and Chaya, and Hanna's son, Barry Gourary), or whether it belonged to the Agudas Chabad, the organization of the Lubavitch community.[1] The plaintiff in the case was the Agudas Chabad. The defendant was Barry Gourary, the grandson of Rabbi Joseph I. Schneersohn. At issue were some four hundred books taken from the library by Barry Gourary in the fall of 1984 and the winter of 1985 and the funds received from their sale. (The counterclaim by defendant Gourary asserted that the four hundred books, and half of the remaining books and manuscripts, belonged to Barry Gourary and to his mother, Hanna Gourary, and half to his aunt Chaya, the wife of Rabbi Menachem Mendel Schneerson, the present Lubavitcher Rebbe, through inheritance from Rabbi Joseph I. Schneersohn.)

The library in question consists of more than forty thousand volumes that Rabbi Joseph I. Schneersohn purchased in 1925 to replace the library of his father, Rabbi Sholom Dovber (1860–1920), the fifth Lubavitcher Rebbe, which had been confiscated by the Bolsheviks early in the Russian Revolution.[2]

Until the time it was confiscated the library of the Lubavitcher Rebbes had been inherited from one Rebbe to another since the beginning of the movement. The fifth Lubavitcher Rebbe had stipulated that the library was the inheritance of his son, Joseph Isaac Schneersohn, the sixth Lubavitcher Rebbe. Rabbi Joseph Schneersohn, however, could not recover his father's library, either because the Soviet authorities refused to return it or because it was impossible to meet the high price they set. To replace the lost volumes and provide necessary research and reference materials for the Rebbe, a personal library was purchased in Leningrad in 1925. Funds for the purchase of the library came largely from the contributions of Lubavitcher Hasidim in the United States. These contributions are called *ma'amad*, "a personal gift . . . from disciples to master in order to create that bond of souls between them."[3]

Included in the library, and their fate to be determined by the lawsuit, were the *ksovim* of the Lubavitch dynasty, manuscripts recording the teachings of the several Rebbes and often written in their own handwriting. These manuscripts were considered precious by the family and the Rebbes' followers, and their possession was often contested by the several sons of the Rebbes. For the most part the ksovim had been kept intact through the generations and had been saved from Soviet hands at great financial cost. In court Hanna Gourary testified to their importance:

> When my father was arrested and imprisoned he said you must save lives and the *ksovim*. Nothing else mattered to him. And that's the way it was when he had to leave Russia, when we had to escape from Warsaw.
>
> *Ksovim* should remain with the family. Even my great-grandfather [the Maharash Reb Shmuel (1834–1882), the fourth Lubavitcher Rebbe], when they were burning the towns around, had horses ready 24 hours around the clock in case it would be necessary to flee to save the *ksovim*.[4]

The outbreak of World War II separated the Rebbe from his new library. The library was left behind in September 1939 in Otwock, Poland, when the Lubavitcher Rebbe fled from there to Warsaw. At the end of the year the Rebbe moved to Riga, in Latvia, and the following year continued on to the United States. The Rebbe's efforts notwithstanding, the library remained in Poland for the remainder of the war. In 1946, when the Rebbe was settled in Brooklyn, he sought the help of the U.S. government in having the library shipped to America. The 120 crates of books finally found their way to Lubavitcher headquarters at 770 Eastern Parkway, where they were catalogued and shelved. The library remained at 770 after the death of Rabbi Joseph I. Schneersohn in 1950 and the appointment of his son-in-law (and distant relative), Menachem Mendel Schneerson, as the new Rebbe.

In the fall of 1984, however, Barry Gourary, the late Rebbe's sixty-two-year-old grandson, a management consultant living in Montclair, New Jersey, took four hundred of the books, including some rare volumes, and sold one-third of them, earning a profit of $186,000. This act raised the question of the legal ownership of the library and the rights of the possible heirs.

The Family Competition

The dispute over the library reopened old wounds that had existed since the death of the old Rebbe in 1950. Joseph Isaac Schneersohn had no direct male heir, but his two daughters were married to men who were considered worthy candidates to succeed him as Rebbe. The older daughter, Hanna, was married to Rabbi Samarious Gourary, who had played a major role in the development of the United Lubavitch Yeshivah and was then chairman of its executive committee. Chaya Moussia, two years younger than her sister, had wed Menachem Mendel Schneerson, who was trained as an engineer. The couple arrived in America in 1941, a year after the Rebbe had settled in Crown Heights. After his arrival in America Menachem Mendel continued to work as an engineer, but he also headed the Kehot Publication Society for Chabad, publishing books and the talks of the Rebbe, and he maintained an extensive correspondence with the followers of the Rebbe, instructing and encouraging them in the spread of Yiddishkayt. He gave up working as an engineer in 1948 when his responsibilities for Chabad demanded more of his time. After the death of his father-in-law in 1950 the leaders of the Chabad, among them Rabbi Israel Jacobson, the doyen of the Lubavitcher Hasidim, supported him as successor to his father-in-law. Menachem Mendel was named the new Rebbe.

> The majority of the older Hasidim sent him a letter binding them together: "We the undersigned accept you as leader and are ready to obey what you ask of us. We want you to teach us hasides." The Rebbe reportedly did not want to take the leadership of Chabad and before he assented he went to the cemetery to talk to the older Rebbe. But the Rebbe did not accept the leadership until the first yortsayt. He said then: "The way of Chabad is that the Rebbe tries to help the Hasidim but they must not rely on him completely. We will all work together to bring the Messiah." (AR)

Barry Gourary counts the beginning of the feud from Menachem Mendel's selection as the new Rebbe. Like his uncle, Barry had a scientific background and was trained in physics. His rabbinical degree was from Torah Vadaat rather than the Lubavitch yeshivah. Nonetheless, Barry considered himself a candidate for his grandfather's post, and in any event, since his father too was being seriously considered, he became emotionally enmeshed in the selection process.

> At the time of my grandfather's death some people were banking on me over my uncle and my father. I was twenty-seven at the time. I was not interested. I'm more of a private person, a researcher, not a public person. So it didn't fit my goals.
> I came here [to the United States] when I was seventeen in 1940 with my

grandfather. By education I am a physicist. I went to Brooklyn College in physics and then to Columbia. Before I finished my Ph.D. thesis my grandfather died. Someone else published my dissertation idea before I did. So I went to the Bureau of Standards.

In 1950 my grandfather died and I supported my father. I was actually closer to my uncle than to my father. We both had a technical education and we developed a certain kind of closeness. When my uncle came here in 1941 he was still interested in working as an electrical engineer. He got a job repairing electric motors. He and I were quite friendly in those days and he used to tell me about his reactions.

[But at the time of the election] they organized bands of hooligans. They came twice when my father and I were davening and took away our *Sefer* [Torah scroll]. I was trying to negotiate the situation and I told my uncle that in light of the way he was behaving I could not support him. Since then he has tried to make life miserable for me.   (BG)

The competition also created strains between the two sisters and the two brothers-in-law.

My father did not take it all very well at first. He looked at his options. He wanted to stay with the yeshivah he had built up, and he swallowed his pride. He did the best he could.   (BG)[5]

No one seemed to have suffered more than Reb Samarious's son Barry, who became estranged from the Lubavitcher movement.

The Missing Books

According to Barry Gourary's account, he had received the permission of his aunt, Chaya Schneerson, to take whatever books he wanted from the library.

In 1984 my mother and my aunt had reached an accommodation on the library. They were the two heirs. My aunt had been depressed by grandfather's death. She said: "I'm not going to read those books. Why don't you take what you want."   (BG)

He then proceeded "quietly" to remove some of the books. A hidden video camera, however, recorded his actions, and the indignant outcry reverberated from Kingston Avenue to the Federal Courthouse in downtown Brooklyn.

Barry Gourary tried to treat the affair matter-of-factly.

I took the things that had no emotional value for the movement to sell them. I took about seven hundred volumes. I made a catalogue, and computerized it to talk to various buyers. I sold about a hundred volumes, some of the older volumes, obviously. I got a total of $186,000 for it.   (BG)

Rabbi Yehuda Krinsky, a Lubavitcher spokesman, observed in anger: "These books were not taken for sentimental reasons, but because he wanted money. Some people rob banks, and some steal books. He's a thief, an outright thief." [6]

Barry Gourary expressed surprise at the sudden outburst of anger stemming from the appropriation and sale of the books.

> About May 7, 1985, my uncle [the Lubavitcher Rebbe] was informed about it. At that point he decided that he wanted to make some trouble. He called my father and said he wanted the sales stopped, the books returned, and the money returned. He said he would pay $25,000 to each of the two heirs. I told my father to tell him let's get together to discuss it. He replied: "I've already said what is to be done. What is there to talk about?" And he said, "If not, I'm going to go public about it." (BG)

The Lubavitcher community then took extraordinary action. Rather than go to a rabbinical court to seek a judgment, they went to civil court and filed for a restraining order blocking further sales, something that a rabbinical court could order but not enforce. It marked, however, reliance on the secular courts to resolve an internal Hasidic problem, a point not overlooked by opponents of Lubavitch such as Jacob Cohen.

> Lubavitcher Hasidim don't want to go to a *dintoyre* [bring a dispute to a religious court]. They just want to go to [secular] court. Which is a desecration. Well, if rabbis don't want to go to a dintoyre, who's the dintoyre made for? But Lubavitchers have their own way of thinking. Anybody who goes to a non-Jewish court for Jewish matters is desecrating God's name. (JC)

As we have seen earlier, the Code of Jewish Law (the Shulhan Arukh) provides a rationale both for avoiding and for utilizing secular courts. While use of the secular court is frowned on, when there is evidence that one of the parties to the suit would not abide by the decision of the religious court it is considered imperative to bring the suit to a secular court. In deciding where to bring their complaint Lubavitch leaders considered two questions: First, would Barry Gourary heed the instruction of a rabbinical court? Since the religious court has no power of enforcement it is incumbent on the parties to the suit to recognize its authority. Lubavitch contended that Barry Gourary was not an observant Jew and therefore was not likely to accede to a religious authority. Second, how could they constrain Barry Gourary from continuing to sell other books from the library still in his possession? To wait for him to decide to accept the decision of a religious court would make the case moot. Lubavitch determined that they needed an immediate restraining order with the enforcement power of the civil court.

The Rebbe's talks at Lubavitch farbrengens were scorched with references to the missing books: "On one occasion he called them 'bombs' that would explode unless they were returned to 770 Eastern Parkway and on another referred to them as 'sparks of holiness' that had actually become parts of his predecessor." [7] Barry Gourary claimed that the Rebbe so inflamed his followers that some took action against Gourary and his family. He contended that following a farbrengen on July 13, 1985, one of the Rebbe's followers broke into his parents' apartment on the third floor of 770 Eastern Parkway and came close to killing his mother. Her hand, nose, and palate were fractured in the attack. The Lubavitcher Hasidim maintained variously that they did not know the identity of the perpetrator, that the man was deranged, and that he had fled to Israel and could not be located.

> He [the Rebbe] made speeches about it in the besmedresh and on the radio. As a result of those speeches, a car tried to run my daughter off the road. A week later, making one of those inflammatory speeches, one of his followers beat my mother about the head with an iron bar and left her for dead. He told her: "Stop doing things which annoy the Rebbe."
> We believe we know who it is but he has never been identified. Chabad said the person was not completely sane and had left for Israel. The police investigated but the community did not cooperate. My uncle never said anything about it, and they took this as a sign of approval. Three weeks later they started the case against us.   (BG)

Ownership

It has always been an open question what a Rebbe and his family possess in their own right. A great deal depends on the particular relationship that develops during the years of the Rebbe's tenure, on the contractual agreements that transpire, and on the gifts that may be exchanged. To protect and honor their Rebbe, the community corporation might put the Rebbe's name on community property such as the Rebbe's residence, and some Hasidic courts also assign to the Rebbe rights to the besmedresh, the mikvah, a summer camp, or the library. Or the Rebbe might not have his name on any community property whatsoever. In the Lubavitcher community, the building at 770 Eastern Parkway was mortgaged to the Rebbe.[8]

If the library had been purchased specifically for the Rebbe, did it now belong by right of inheritance to his family? If the Rebbe owned the library, had he assigned those rights to his Hasidim?

Why did this case create such a high level of excitement? The library itself, while of great value, does not appear to have played a vital role in Lubavitch life. In point of fact the library was seldom used, and, according to most accounts, was poorly cared for. Scholars from the outside world had difficulty using the facilities for study or research (a charge denied by Lubavitch). As one scholar in Judaic studies recounted: "One needed permission to use the library as though it were the Vatican. Perhaps that's because the library contains chapbooks—'The Romance of the Yeshivah Bokher [boy]' " (AI).

Barry Gourary argued that the books he had taken were not sacred.

> About one-third of my grandfather's books were extremely secular—Bialik [a modern Hebrew poet], for example. Grandfather was a collector and he enjoyed collecting. Some were sacred and some were not. Books that I had taken were far from sacred in the Jewish sense—the Old Testament printed by missionaries, with notes by priests in beautiful handwriting. (BG)

Sacred or not, some of the works Barry Gourary had appropriated were of considerable value. These included incunabula printed before 1500, a fifteenth-century illustrated Haggadah, and rare works on Jewish mysticism.

Of more import was the psychological disruption to the community. With the library in danger so too was the commitment to preserving essential elements of Lubavitch for future generations. Barry Gourary's contention that half the library was his mother's by right of inheritance appeared to strike at the integrity of Chabad and the authority of the present Rebbe. It was as though the Rebbe's then tenure of thirty-five years had been swept away and his power as Rebbe challenged. In point of fact, Gourary had a more direct link to the previous Rebbe (through his mother) than did the present Lubavitcher Rebbe, a distant relative of the previous Rebbe's whose main source of power had come through his marriage. However, the present Rebbe's accomplishments had raised his position to a completely new level, far exceeding the authority of anyone in the family. Since Barry Gourary was estranged from the community, his lineage could be seen as a kind of negative power, the antithesis of the Rebbe's positive power. Gourary's contention of familial rights was a poisonous thorn threatening the Rebbe and the well-being of the community.

Consider the consequences of a negative decision in the American court. At the very least it would mean the diminution and possible total loss of a precious (if little used) archive. Gourary's actions could undermine Chabad and retard the spread of Yiddishkayt. Consider too the deep wound the Rebbe's symbolic authority would suffer. A public humiliation in an American court would undermine the Rebbe's reputation—hardly a miracle tale worthy of recording. The unknown elements loomed far greater than the certainties of justice.

Barry Gourary had added to the stakes by attacking the direction Lubavitch had taken under the leadership of his uncle. Soon after he was called to account for the books, he complained publicly that the Lubavitcher movement "had acquired many characteristics of a cult, in which people have stopped thinking for themselves." [9]

> Chabad started out as a spiritual and philosophical movement. Nowadays ChaBaD stands for charisma, blessings, and dollars, especially dollars. It's a different kind of thing. I'm not interested in money. It's a means to an end.
>
> At one time Chabad was concerned with joyful worship of God. Nowadays the group is primarily interested in proselytizing. My uncle organized the outreach movements, and some of this is now good and some is bad. He became power hungry. He began to measure his achievements. After a while he began to encourage anyone who would treat him as the Messiah.
>
> It's been thirty-nine years since he became Rebbe. It took him a long time to take this particular group and turn it into a money-mad organization. It specializes in power, money, and organization. It would take a long time to turn it around to a spiritual organization.
>
> My grandfather considered himself bound by Jewish law. My uncle is an innovator. The Hasidim often say the Rebbe is the Shulhan Arukh. The Rebbe is the law. That is the major change.
>
> Lubavitch is a huge moneymaking machine, a cash cow. It could die if my uncle dies. Those in the bureaucracy are trying to build a shrine at 770. They've built a replica of 770 in Israel. Some are trying to insure their livelihood. The library and 770 are parts of the shrine to keep the money rolling in. They need the library. They need a shrine that can be pursued properly. What if the Messiah departs without taking the Jews to Israel? They could still stay in power and continue to milk it.   (BG)

The Trial

Throughout the trial the Hasidim held lotteries to determine who would go to the courthouse each day, and the lucky winners were transported back and forth by a school bus. Seating in the courtroom itself followed the rules of the shul: a hundred or so men occupied the seats in the forward section, while women sat separated from them in the back rows. The defendant felt under siege, and the defense attorney, Alvin Hellerstein, worried that the presence of so many Hasidim would serve to intimidate defense witnesses. The community, however, was as insecure as the defendant. Each night when they returned from the federal courthouse, the Hasidim celebrated the day's events as if to confound despair with joy.

In the course of the trial two types of holdings in the library were carefully distinguished: on the one hand the books and manuscripts in the collection, and on the other the ksovim, the personal writings of the Rebbes that were held in special regard. Judge Sifton would describe the ksovim as "property, regarded within the community as a community asset to be used by the community's leader, [which] was nevertheless treated as personal property within the Rebbe's family." [10] In the case before him, Judge Sifton's major focus concerned the books in the library and not the ksovim.

There was some crucial testimony to consider. In contradiction of Barry Gourary's testimony that his aunt, Chaya Schneerson, had given him permission to take the books, Chaya Schneerson maintained that "I think they belonged to the Hasidim, because my father belonged to the Hasidim." [11]

One of Barry Gourary's key witnesses was ninety-three-year-old Rabbi Chaim Liberman, who for decades had been a fixture in the front office as the Rebbe's personal secretary and Lubavitch librarian. Letters of solicitation from Liberman had in fact sought gifts not as a personal offering to the Rebbe, but "'in the name of the library,' 'for us,' or for 'our library,' 'the library,' or for 'the Lubavitch Library' from 'whoever knows and honors the name of Lubavitch.'" Nonetheless, he now appeared in support of the defendant's claim. Under cross-examination by Nathan Lewin, representing the plaintiff, Chaim Liberman conceded his close ties to the defendant: that he took his meals with Barry Gourary's mother, and that he had made Barry Gourary his beneficiary. He also admitted his anger at being denied entrance to the library after the many years he had dedicated to its development. His final devaluation as a witness came with his admission that he had burned papers relevant to the case. [12]

Some of the plaintiff's points too were given little accord. The plaintiff argued that the library was "trust property or property belonging to the community" since it had been acquired with religious contributions (ma'amad). Judge Sifton ultimately disallowed this argument, although he noted that "it does serve to emphasize the religious purpose for which the library was put together." [13]

The contradictions in the oral testimony and the dismissal of many of the plaintiff's arguments made the letters from the sixth Rebbe all the more critical in shaping Judge Sifton's opinion. Three letters formed the primary written evidence as to the Rebbe's intentions. It was to these letters that Judge Sifton turned his primary attention.

In 1939, while he was still in Warsaw, the Rebbe had sent a letter to Rabbi Chaim Liberman, who had been instrumental in obtaining and organizing the library:

> I have no apartment, and I find myself living with friends with my entire family in one room; consequently, I have no space for the books which Agudas Chabad loaned me for study. I would be pleased if Agudas Chabad were to take these books back. [14]

From Riga in 1940, before his departure to the United States, the Rebbe had also written to Rabbi Israel Jacobson in Brooklyn concerning the library:

Surely I will receive within a few days a detailed letter about all that has been done for the saving of my library and about taking it out from there . . . There are about a hundred and twenty boxes of books and three boxes of manuscripts of our revered and holy parents; the saintly Rabbis . . . and you will surely do all you can to bring them to your country . . . Please write, or better still, telegraph to the American Consul in Berlin that he inform the Consul at Warsaw that he take over the library of Agudas Chabad (of the U.S.) and of Rabbi Schneersohn—for I have told them that a part of the library is mine, and that it is located in Otwock, near Warsaw, in 7 Nalevka Street, Apartment 16. There are also three cases of sacred manuscripts which are the property of Agudas Chabad of the U.S. and that they send everything direct to New York.[15]

In 1946 he wrote to Dr. Alexander Marks to enlist his aid:

In order that the State Department should work energetically to locate these manuscripts and books in order to return them to their owners, the State Department needs to understand that these manuscripts and books are great religious treasures, a possession of the nation, which have historical and scientific value.

Therefore, I turn to you with a great request, that as a renowned authority on the subject, you should please write a letter to the State Department to testify on the great value of these manuscripts and books for the Jewish people in general and particularly for the Jewish community of the United States to whom this great possession belongs.[16]

In the 1939 letter the Rebbe had laid the basis for community ownership when he noted that there are "books which Agudas Chabad loaned me for study" which he would be pleased to return. Other comments supported that contention, even if at times an element of ambiguity entered into the correspondence. A year later, writing from Riga to Rabbi Jacobson, the Rebbe noted: "the saving of my library" and that "a part of the library is mine." This was understood at the time by the State Department to mean that the library was the property of Agudas Chabad, and in the course of correspondence they requested "an affidavit in triplicate proving that the library is American property and showing how title was acquired and when." In the letter written at the same time from Latvia to Rabbi Jacobson, the Rebbe again said that a part of the library was the property of Agudas Chabad of New York and a part his.[17] The rescue attempts failed, and further efforts had to wait until the end of the war.

Six years later, in 1946, when the Rebbe was in the United States and anxious to accomplish the release of the library from Poland, he emphasized the library's importance to the community in writing to Alexander Marks. Barry Gourary countered that this letter was a deliberate lie which circumstances required to obtain the release of the library. Judge Sifton felt to the contrary: "Not only does the letter, even in translation, ring with feeling and sincerity, it does not make much sense that a man of the character of the sixth Rebbe would, in the circumstances, mean something different than what he says, that the library was to be delivered to plaintiff for the benefit of the community." He reasoned that the letter answers the question "who the real or beneficial owner is. The letter makes that patently clear. It is 'the Jewish people in general and particularly the Jewish community of the United States to whom this great possession belongs.'"[18]

On January 6, 1987, the decision of Judge Charles P. Sifton of the Eastern District was handed down in Brooklyn. The court awarded the forty thousand books and manuscripts to the Lubavitcher community and rejected the claim of Barry S. Gourary, the grandson of the sixth Lubavitcher Rebbe, that the library had passed into his hands. The twenty-nine-page report was carried to the Lubavitcher Rebbe by Rabbi Krinsky that morning. Although Gourary had already taken four hundred of the works and had pocketed $186,000 in sales to rare book dealers in Europe before being enjoined from further sales, Judge Sifton's decision ensured that the collection was safely in the hands of the community. Judge Sifton wrote: "The conclusion is inescapable that the library was not held by the sixth Rebbe at his death as his personal property, but had been delivered to plaintiff to be held in trust for the benefit of the religious community of Chabad Chasidism."[19]

At the outset of the trial Judge Sifton had invited the lawyers for both sides to his chambers and explained that until his divorce he had been the son-in-law of the Protestant theologian Reinhold Niebuhr. He assured all parties to the dispute that this fact would have no effect on his judgment.

Barry Gourary attempted to maintain that his defeat in court turned on the influence Reinhold Niebuhr had had on Judge Sifton.

> Judge Sifton is the former son-in-law of Reinhold Niebuhr. He is since divorced. He was of the tradition that the church owned the property and not the priest. Because of the numbers they sent [every day to the courthouse], he saw this as a case of the Jewish population against Barry Gourary. Only later Satmar [that is, Jacob Cohen] entered the case [on my side]. (BG)

Throughout the trial there had been a considerable unknown: the investigation, analysis, and judgment—in short, the entire legal and moral decisionmaking apparatus—had been surrendered by the Jewish community to a civil court under the authority of a non-Jewish judge. Could such a court understand the implications and the issues involved?

Judge Sifton had met every challenge with perception of the Jewish way of life and of the changing course of history.

> The problems of conveying this community asset from generation to generation of Rebbes might have remained, as it had in the past, one to be sorted

out among members of the Rebbe's family through the laws relating to private transactions, including those of inheritance and sale, had it not been for the holocaust. The effects of the holocaust included, among others, a necessity for the Rebbe, during his life and not simply in contemplation of his demise, to define for the outside world the relationship between himself, the community he served, and the property he possessed.[20]

Celebration

The news that noon was electrifying. It heralded a day of extraordinary communal joy in the Lubavitch community. The celebration began on the instant. A class of schoolboys, eleven- and twelve-year-olds, hurried with their teacher to the end of the block to set up trash cans to block off the side island of Eastern Parkway. Traffic would continue to speed down the broad six-lane center drive of the avenue, but the side drive would belong to the Hasidim for celebrating. At the same time, in front of Lubavitcher headquarters at 770 Eastern Parkway, the music began. A tape of a Lubavitcher choral recording began to blare "Didan notzakh" (We are victorious).[21] Yeshivah students streamed from the building and began a tight circle dance, eight or ten bodies wide, in front of the building. The dancers ran forward toward the center, shouting and embracing, with their hands on the shoulders of the next dancer. The music grew still louder when a guitarist plugged in his amplified instrument and led the music. The dancers swept by in an exuberant circle, hugging and kissing one another.

Cases of half-gallon jugs of vodka were carried out to the street. Bottles of soda were set on cars and on a makeshift table. The celebrants began to drink.

The dancers didn't stop. From time to time they paused momentarily when one or another of their number, perched on someone's shoulders, frantically waving, brought the swirling crowd to a halt in order to proclaim a blessing in the name of the Almighty. Then with a pious roar the throng would be released to reach a new, still stronger wave of the dance.

Those who came to seek charity in front of the besmedresh that day felt the generous outpouring of tzedakah. The face of one tiny, elderly lady, half hidden in the crowd bordering the dancers, burned with excitement as she giddily accepted bills from one celebrant after another. What a happy day!

The song from Eastern Parkway carried up the street and around the corner to Kingston Avenue. The music was picked up by a tape blaring from the Lubavitcher photocopy store, and then again from a store on the following block: "We are victorious." As the song piped up the avenue, the Hasidim living on the surrounding streets, many already alerted by telephone, hurried down to Eastern Parkway. By now the entire neighborhood had heard the news of the decision. The older men, abandoning work and business, appeared at the headquarters, standing on the street or slipping inside the besmedresh at 770 to share the great good news. Inside there were vodka and paper cups for those at prayer or study to toast the decision.

Outside the crowd grew as mothers and their small children, many bundled in strollers, came to watch the festivities. As the crowd increased, additional police arrived. Four policemen kept the curious traffic spinning past the corner. At the far end of the block officers moved in, removed the trash cans, and controlled the lane by parking their patrol car there instead. The automobiles of Hasidim arriving from other neighborhoods as men hurried back from work were now parked helter-skelter, and illegally, on the walkway and would soon be ticketed. The officer in charge, Sergeant Costello, moved inside the besmedresh and strolled quietly among the indoor celebrants who had broken off from the circle dance and were passing out cups of vodka. There was nothing for the sergeant to do with such a peacefully exuberant crowd. The sergeant was no cossack, and so for their part the Hasidim took no notice of his presence.

At two in the afternoon, after two hours of continual dancing, the enthusiasm and spirit of the dancers appeared undiminished. The participants flew at times with electrifying speed; but by now some of the younger and less experienced drinkers were reeling from the effects of the vodka. On the edges of the circle, some dancers going met others coming. When they met they hugged and kissed and exchanged greetings: "This is the happiest day in a year!"

Some of the young dancers broke away from the dance to confide their thoughts:

The reason the Messiah hasn't come is we all want him—but not at this moment. We're busy and that's why he doesn't come. If we all wanted him, he would come. Look at my [crushed] hat! I'm crazy.   (IB)

The dancers swept by the onlookers, the older Hasidim, and the younger wives with baby strollers. The January air was pleasant and the slight chill in the air seemed to be warmed by the enthusiastic crowd.

A young dancer broke from the crowd to confide a miracle said to have occurred ten years earlier.

The Rebbe was very sick. He had had a heart attack.[22] He was in bed but he had to give a *ma'amar* [discourse]. So he was wired up to his medical monitoring equipment. The doctor stayed in the house monitoring the equipment and the Rebbe was in his office speaking to the people. The doctors were sending notes to the Rebbe trying to protect him and keep him from getting overexcited and damaging his heart.

When the Rebbe started his ma'amar the equipment stopped registering. They examined it and discovered it wasn't broken. This is because it was God speaking through the Rebbe. That's why there was no effect shown on the equipment. One of the old men who sits behind the Rebbe told this to me. (IB)

The scraggly patch of lawn and the adjacent sidewalk showed the strenuous efforts of the dancers. Some coats lay in the dirt, tossed aside or abandoned. Scattered nearby were crushed plastic cups and some broken vodka bottles. A few of the dancers, beyond their depth, were being helped homeward up Kingston Avenue. But the circle dance never thinned out as other dancers came to take their places. More family members filled in the edges of the crowd.

Word spread that at four o'clock the Rebbe would daven in the large downstairs besmedresh. This was a departure from his customary practice of davening in the smaller shul upstairs, and so it was clear that the Rebbe would report on the good news. By four o'clock the majority of the older men had arrived from work and business in other parts of the city to join in the afternoon prayer. They skipped the dancing in front of the building and celebrated inside the besmedresh until it was time for prayer and the Rebbe's message.

When the Rebbe strode into the room it was clear that he too was ignited by the news. He told the assembled Hasidim that they had gone through a difficult time, but that God did not want them to suffer. He compared the recovery of the library to the release of Rabbi Shneur Zalman from tsarist prison on the nineteenth of Kislev in the year 5559 (1798). The Misnagdim had accused the Rebbe of supporting the Turks against the Russians.[23] When he was freed Rabbi Shneur Zalman intensified his efforts. The protests of his opponents encouraged him to new efforts. He taught even more. Previously he had utilized the kabbala to teach Hasidic philosophy at an advanced level. Now he would teach it in a more practical way so that everyone could learn the philosophy of Chabad. The movement would broaden and spread among the populace with new vigor.

The Rebbe then brought his theme to the present. He explained that in the present day some wanted to take the ksovim, the previous Rebbe's manuscripts, and sell them. They said that no one used them. "Now," he said, "we will spread more Yiddishkayt. We will publish these writings and we will start more Chabad houses." The Rebbe's enthusiasm embraced still another idea: everyone should have a Chabad house. In each home the children's room should become a special room with a charity box (pushke), a prayer book, and a Bible. These would radiate out from the children's room throughout the whole house. "The obstacles we have faced have been overcome. They are no longer obstacles. They show us how far we can go in our devotion. They show us how hard we must work."

The holiday atmosphere of the room had already hardened into resolve. The older men soaked in the Rebbe's words. It was time for joy, for a new and still stronger mandate. The men nodded in agreement as the Rebbe spoke.

But action would have to wait until that day had passed. Those who had had too much to drink slowly wilted in the indoor temperature of the besmedresh. Some in the crowd below slumped forward to sleep. An occasional figure, cheek pressed against a table, leaked vodka or cola from his half-open mouth onto the table and the floor.

As the prayers were ending inside the besmedresh, there was a flurry of activity in the windows of 784 Eastern Parkway, the headquarters of the Lubavitcher education center adjacent to 770. A banner was strung across the face of the building from the second floor: "God has given us a happy day!" "Me kamokha?" (Who is like unto Thee [O Lord among the mighty]?).[24]

There were accompanying shouts and waves from above and below. It was as though a rebel force had taken over the building and was proclaiming its slogans.

The chill air had stiffened backs, and the dancing resumed. The circle dance grew wild, now stirred by a small band that moved out onto the lawn—a fierce drummer, a determined guitarist, and an enthusiastic flautist, keeping tempo for the dancing which was startling homebound traffic on Eastern Parkway. A lone dancer began spinning on the small lawn that rose above the crowd—a whirling fiddler on the roof.

When night finally came the dancing continued inside the besmedresh. A band played in the besmedresh during the long, happy night until seven in the morning.

The passage of time did not stop new arrivals from joining the celebration. The following day Hasidim arrived from all over the country; forty Lubavitcher Hasidim arrived on a flight from Paris to participate in those happy, happy days. It was extraordinary not only to observers but to the Hasidim themselves. Few had ever reached such an intense level of collective joy. From their vantage point God had seen the Hasidim and their Rebbe through the ordeal and through the American system of justice. Lubavitch had emerged stronger than when they entered the struggle, with renewed vigor and intensity. God had provided a happy day—one of the happiest in the history of the Lubavitcher movement.

Aftermath

Barry Gourary appealed the decision of the Federal District Court, but he was denied relief in the U.S. Court of Appeals. The books were returned in an armored truck sent by Chabad. The Rebbe decided that the best way to celebrate the victory would be to intensify the study of Torah. As a sign the Rebbe chose one of the volumes from the returned collection to be reprinted: Rabbi Meir ibn Gabbai's *Derekh Emunah* (The Way of Truth), a kabbalistic work from the sixteenth century.

> The books have all been returned. He has not yet returned the money. He says he spent it. There are still some little things pending.
>
> He took the most valuable books. We paid those who had purchased the books the money they had paid. The booksellers didn't lose any money; they even kept their commissions. The only restriction was that the purchasers could not profit.[25] The case is finished.   (YK)

The case did not quite end at that point. Still at issue was the recovery of the monies from Barry Gourary for the sale of the books. Negotiations were stalled by a countersuit for ten million dollars against Lubavitch by Barry Gourary for the injuries suffered by his mother.

> Somebody beat up Barry's mother. He did a terrible thing. Different people come in and out of the building. Somebody came upstairs and opened the door. The Rebbe has also been threatened. That's why he always has protection. They have a countersuit that because the Rebbe is against them the assault took place. They are looking for ways to embarrass Lubavitch. Lubavitch is suing for the half million dollars for which the books were sold. They have a countersuit for ten million dollars for the injuries to her face because it happened in the Lubavitcher's house.   (MS)

Gourary's lawyers subpoenaed the Rebbe to appear in court, but the Rebbe's lawyers countered that he was too ill to appear. The negotiations and the defamatory charges continued for a time until the parties came to an agreement out of court. The details of the settlement have been sealed by court order.

The major legal and moral issues were settled earlier by Judge Sifton's ruling on the disposition of the books taken from the library. The most damaging underlying argument against Barry Gourary was that he sought to dissemble actions undertaken for personal profit. In so doing, he undermined the efforts of all the Lubavitcher Rebbes and the thousands of Hasidim who had contributed to the purchase and preservation of the library. One other result of the trial, which may prove increasingly significant in years to come, established that the collective rights of a Hasidic dynastic court had been authenticated by the ruling of an American judge.

In the end the Hasidim used the threat to the library as inspiration to continue their mission and to utilize the library more intensively. New publications were planned from the storehouse of material. The physical setting of the library in the building adjacent to 770 was also bound more closely to the central structure. In the expansion of the besmedresh, the basements of the two buildings were joined, and though an alley still separates them on the surface (where each year a sukkah is constructed), there are now passageways connecting the two buildings on the second and third floors. This renovation now seemed blessed by news from representatives of Lubavitch who had traveled to the Soviet Union to negotiate for the return of the library seized by the Soviet government seventy-five years earlier. During a summit meeting President Bush had raised the issue with Soviet President Gorbachev, and the matter had moved to the Soviet courts. In October 1991 a three-judge panel of the State Arbitration Tribunal of the Soviet Union ordered the Lenin Library in Moscow to release the 14,000-volume library to Chabad-Lubavitch. The two libraries of the Lubavitcher Rebbes would soon be united at 770 Eastern Parkway.

· 25 ·

Satmar:
Litigation and Leaflets

Bedford Rehabs

During the 1980s, when funds for public housing became unavailable, the Satmar community sought opportunities to construct housing for middle-income families who could afford to purchase an apartment or condominium. The plan to develop private housing in the Hasidic community was undertaken with the best of intentions, perhaps with the same good spirit with which the Tower of Babel was begun.

In 1982 the Bedford Rehabilitation Corporation was formed by the Jewish community in Williamsburg to rehabilitate four abandoned apartment houses provided by the city. The buildings, on Bedford Avenue between Ross and Rodney Streets, were to be renovated into sixty co-op apartments. Each apartment was to be designed with Hasidic needs in mind: there would be several bedrooms and an ample kitchen area as befitting a large family. The cost for an average apartment was initially estimated at fifty thousand dollars, a bargain on the expensive and limited New York real estate market. A low-cost loan in the neighborhood of five million dollars was arranged. The Sunset Construction Company, which undertook to develop the project, was advanced building materials by Certified Lumber, a company owned by two Satmar Hasidim, Isaac and Abe Rosenberg.

Interest in Bedford Rehabs was so intense in the Hasidic community that as construction got under way in 1984 a lottery was required to assign the apartments. Present at the drawing of the winning numbers were Hasidim from Satmar, Pupa, Vizhnitz, Tselem, and Devina, as well as members of other courts and congregations, most of whom had representatives on the Executive Board of the United Jewish Organizations of Williamsburg.

> Several hundred people were there. There was a stage and they picked out envelopes. There were cries of joy and cries of pain. I was number 41. (FR)

In return for providing the building shells, the city had insisted that five of the apartments be earmarked for low-income families. These apartments would sell at the base price of twenty-five thousand dollars. When the names of those fortunate families selected were made public, the choices proved to be controversial. Criteria other than economic ones appeared to have weighed heavily in determining the winners, and the charge was made that the city's mandate was being compromised. There were some questionable nominations.[1]

> We had the authority and we were so generous about it that we didn't take the five apartments for Satmar. We gave one apartment to B., a family from a small congregation here, because his son is not so well. One apartment went to one of the heads of our yeshivot. He had a big family. He wanted to move out to Monroe because he had no apartment and so we promised him that he'll get one of these five. He's a poor man. Another went to F. His wife died. He had ten children and he had no apartment. He had to pay sixty to seventy thousand because the price went up. All of them were destitute people. F. is a destitute person. Now he is a board member; we elected him. At that time he had nothing. It was all done with a sense of pity. All of the five are so poor that they cannot be poorer. (RH)

Some of the selections could no doubt be defended, but not even a friendly jury could justify the startling choice of one newly married couple: the grandson of the Satmar Rebbe and his new bride, his first cousin, a granddaughter of the Vizhnitzer Rebbe and of the Satmar Rebbe.

> One of the apartments went to the Rebbe's grandchild who is also a poor young man. Sure he's a poor man. From what is he making a living? The Rebbe himself has his livelihood. His son has his livelihood, and he has nine children and each one sits and learns and he has to maintain them. (RH)

Whether or not the Rebbe's grandson was financially independent at the time of his marriage, the family position and connections provided him with distinct advantages over other newlyweds. (One could argue that the wedding gifts alone were a good hedge for the future.) The outrage of the other investors was soon heard throughout the community. Idle rumors exaggerated what had actually taken place: one account told that the Rebbe's two newly married grandchildren had each received an apartment; another still more outlandish report said that all five apartments had gone to grandchildren of the Rebbe. The truth was bad enough. To many it seemed that the leadership had doled out the apartments as spoils in much the same manner as would the local Democratic Club.

Rumors of bad faith soon became intertwined with the financial woes of the project. Inflationary costs pushed up the price of each apartment.

Isaac Rosenberg, who as president of Certified Lumber was supplying the construction materials, saw the financial crisis deepen as the result of bad management.

> Sunset, the construction company, misled us. They underestimated the cost. They didn't perform and they were kicked out. It's in the courts.   (IR)

The failure of the construction company left a shortfall of two and a half million dollars. The construction company was bankrupt, and the bankruptcy court placed Isaac Rosenberg of Certified Lumber in charge of completing Bedford Rehabs. Having advanced the materials, Rosenberg had no choice but to manage the project in order to protect his investment.

No matter who was in charge, the cash deficit had to be made up by the co-op owners. The price of each apartment crept up to an average of between $80,000 and $150,000, depending on the number of rooms. In order to bring the project to completion at a reasonable cost, the organizers decided to put up six additional apartments, to be accomplished by purchasing an adjacent parcel of land and by eliminating the project's large backyard. The city, in turn, charged $150,000 for the lot to be utilized and required that two of six apartments be held for low-income families.

As the project headed toward completion in 1987, the apartments had almost tripled in price. Frustrated and angry over the delays and by the repeated demands for additional funds, the tenants took the dispute to the bet din, the rabbinical court. The co-op owners argued that they should be charged only a 10 percent increase over the original purchase price. Many of the apartments were ready for occupancy; however, Rosenberg denied entrance to the apartments until all financial obligations were settled.

In the finding of the judge of the bet din, the apartment owners won the right to move into their apartments while the other matters were being resolved. The decision weakened the position of the contractor, and the Rebbe expressed his disagreement with the legal interpretation. According to the Rebbe, under Talmudic law the contractor could not be forced to accept a loss, and the Rebbe's view had the effect of overruling the decision of the bet din.

> But it can never be accused that the Rebbe said, "Don't listen to what the rabbinical court is saying." The Rebbe said that the contractor is not bound to lose money. According to the Jewish law if a contractor makes an agreement with you to build you a house for $125,000 and it turns out that the house costs $25,000 more, the contractor does not have to lose the money. That is the Jewish law.   (RH)

Although the parties had agreed to abide by the decision, the religious court lacked the power to compel the litigants to comply, particularly in the face of the Rebbe's disagreement.

> It's an embarrassment. The Satmar Hasidim can say to the Lubavitcher Hasidim: "You shouldn't go to a civil court. Go to the bet din, the religious court." The Lubavitchers can answer: "But your Rebbe doesn't obey the decision of the bet din." (TP)

It was clear that by commenting on the dispute the Rebbe had lost the high ground. The householders now included the actions of the Rebbe in their litany of complaints.

> The Rosenbergs give money to the Rebbe so the Rebbe is good to him. The Rebbe should be good to people who do right, not the rich who take advantage. (FR)

One particularly litigious householder took the case to civil court; however, he not only lost the case but his actions so offended Rosenberg that he was banned from the project altogether.

For a time the tenants continued to be excluded from their apartments. Some moved in and paid a monthly rent, but they did not receive the title to their apartments. The stalemate left a residue of disappointment and bad feelings.

> Now the people live there without title and pay $700 a month for their own apartments. They keep saying they'll get title. The heat is not worth a penny. They need a different heating system which could cost another ten thousand dollars. There is a lot of resentment against the community. There are vacant lots and nothing is done. The city gave three million for the community they should build better apartments. What happened to the money? What did they do? The resentment is directed against the leaders and the Rebbe too. If the Rebbe opposed them they wouldn't be able to get away with it. If the old Rebbe were here there wouldn't be so much corruption. I respect the Rebbe but I'm talking against him because I feel cheated. (FR)

While to most loyal followers the accusations of manipulation and profiteering seemed exaggerated, it was evident that matters had been mishandled. The growing number of rumors reflected the tension and suspicion in the community. Most Satmar Hasidim continued to speak of the new Rebbe with deference. Everyone acknowledged, however, that a new, more rancorous day had dawned.

> There was resentment and this cost us very hard in the congregation. We're very hurt about this. But it's not a private fight between a group of people with contractors. The Rebbe was involved because he had to manage both sides. The people came to him for advice. The builders said that they cannot afford to lose money for the project. They didn't take it on to lose money. So

he was caught between two sides. At that time I negotiated many times with the Rebbe and I told him, "Why is the Rebbe going to be mixed in a thing which will only be to his disadvantage?" But he said, "What can I do? I want to straighten out this matter." (RH)

The events of the year had delineated the problems of developing housing for the middle class: the co-op owners had seen their costs tripled; they had been to religious court and to civil court; they had battled with the architect, the construction company, and the receiver named by the bank, and were even at odds with the Rebbe himself. However meritorious the Rebbe's motivations might have been, the disruptions that were becoming commonplace under his reign contrasted sharply with the order that had been maintained under his predecessor.

By the following year, however, matters concerning the funding and tenancy were resolved. Despite the delays, the added costs, and the disputes, it could be argued that Bedford Rehabs was a qualified success. The project was completed. Tenants settled in their apartments, and they happily compared the luxurious new space to their previously cramped quarters. The atmosphere was so improved that when Rosenberg, the president of Certified Lumber, married off his son, some of the tenants took out an ad in *Der Yid,* in the name of all the co-op owners, congratulating the new couple and their families and wishing them luck. The controversy appeared to have died with the weeds that each summer snarl the empty lots of the neighborhood.

"Poshkeviln" (Anonymous Leaflets)

Until the construction of the Bedford Rehab co-ops, no one realized what Williamsburg residents were willing to endure to have a decent apartment. A new plan to provide middle-income housing was soon under discussion. The leaders of the new plan were men respected and well placed in the hierarchy of the community, and everyone was immediately elated by the news. Hopes for this new proposal, however, were dashed when it was learned that the price of an apartment contained a substantial hidden cost. It was said that a significant sum required of the investors was to be redirected to the development of a Satmar school in Israel. There was an immediate outcry against the possible exploitation of people desperate for new housing.

As usual few facts were known and rumors served in their place. It was inevitable that the Rebbe be named by some as one of the principals whether there was evidence for it or not.

C. suggested adding fifty thousand dollars to the cost of an apartment. And they say that he presented the idea in the name of the Satmar Rov, although some people say it's not true. I don't know. (AI)

The Rebbe's name had once again been brought into an unsavory situation.

> I don't know anything about the discussions. I wasn't involved in that. But I know for sure that the Rebbe was not involved at all and never had anything to do with it. This was one of the accusations against the Rebbe which hurt him very much, and he couldn't help himself. The Rebbe told me this even before that he didn't want to hear anything about donations concerning the apartments for public purposes, for yeshivah purposes, even for holy purposes. He didn't want to take it.   (RH)

The details of the discussions were quickly disseminated in the besmedresh and in the street. One of the participants was said to have secretly taped the proceedings.

> One of the listeners in the conference was Abraham Ableson.[2] It's a big family. He's a wealthy man himself, a millionaire. And he was quite upset about it because he was on the committee and he felt they tried to push him out. He taped the conversation and he gave it out.   (AI)

Mischief ran in the Ableson family. Abraham Ableson's son, Yosel, a young man of twenty-four with a reputation as a prankster, decided to add his own spice to the mix. He contrived to send out a prank letter ridiculing the plan with a pretended open solicitation. Since it was a prank he felt no qualms about using the organization's letterhead and affixing a false signature.

> Ableson's son Yosel sent out a little paper on the letterhead of Yeshivah Mesifta. It was a little form letter that said it was agreed according to the suggestion of the Rebbe that everybody should add an additional $50,000 and this would go for a very good purpose and whoever wants information and applications should call these numbers. And he gave the personal numbers of these leaders, and signed it, you know, on everyone's behalf. He can deny it but they say this Yosel Ableson printed these letters.   (AI)

The Rebbe and the board were embarrassed, and they reacted with a heavy hand. Using a real letterhead, they announced that the Ablesons, father and son, were no longer allowed to enter the besmedresh.

The younger Ableson tried to assume all of the responsibility for the prank.

> Yosel Ableson called up these people and he told the Rebbe's spokesman, "You know, my father had nothing to do with it. This was my prank, leave him out of it. I wanted to send out letters. I did something, fine. Kick me out. But what have you got against my father?" He also said, "I would appreciate it if you at least hear my point of view. You know I also have something to say."
>
> Yosel Ableson knew they were going to hang up this announcement in the shul. He warned the Rebbe's spokesman, Aaron Lichten: "I know you can

do something about it. If you're going to put it up there there's going to be bloodshed."

But they didn't agree to hear his side of the story. They posted these announcements out in the shul that he can't come in. Of course he wasn't so scared, but . . . the children, his sons and the daughters, were also automatically out of school. It's automatic, everyone is expelled. It's something like they don't belong in here anymore.

Probably if they would come and apologize it could have been corrected. If they would come apologize with a little check it would be accepted, but the next day the next thing happened.   (AI)

The official announcement of the ban was posted in the Satmar besmedresh on Rodney Street. It was a large poster and the wording left nothing in doubt. The Ablesons, father and son, were banished from the shul; their children were excluded from the yeshivah.

While the entire board had voted on the ban, the individual on the firing line was the Rebbe's representative Aaron Lichten.

The Rebbe's spokesman Aaron Lichten put up the announcement at the shul that they're out of the community. And probably this Aaron Lichten was the primary pusher for this note. The Satmar is a kind of a nervous guy, and he agrees with whoever has the last word. He's the kind of a guy who doesn't think too much. He's nervous. That's why Yosel told Aaron, "I know you can do something about it. I know if you talk to him . . . You can convince him. I don't want you to put up that announcement."   (AI)

The appearance of the notice and its unyielding tenor seemed to signal a still stronger reaction from Yosel Ableson. Unfortunately, he had used up his store of wit. Whereas before he had mocked his adversaries, now he took direct action.

This Yosel Ableson just waited. The following day, Friday, Yosel waited for Aaron to come back from mikvah. It was Friday afternoon. He waited in front of his house with his nice little rented car. He didn't want to smash up his Lincoln Continental. He waited there and he just went zoom—he backed up—and Aaron fell down. Aaron stood up, and Yosel saw that he stood up, and he did it a second time. And the second time he did a good job.   (AI)

Opinion was divided as to whether or not the "accident" was planned.

I don't believe that he hit him deliberately. I would say he was involved in a teasing situation with him, like driving with his car back and forth, threatening, that kind of thing, but actually hitting him . . .? He hit him but I don't think he meant to hit him. But he did hit him.   (AI)

Yosel Ableson immediately fled from the scene. He drove from Williamsburg back to Borough Park, where he lived. Perhaps he thought he would be more welcome in the shul where he davened. The ban against him, however, was community wide. When he arrived it was close to Shabbes and people were gathering for prayer.

Yosel Ableson went into the Satmar shul and they said: "You know, you're not supposed to be here."

"I don't care whether I'm not supposed to, I'm here."

The gabbai of the shul in Borough Park felt that he would be blamed by the rov that you didn't follow my orders or something like that. So he stopped [praying] in the middle of the line of the Torah and he turned around. "We're not continuing because he's not supposed to be in here." He wanted to save his skin.

The people went to a different shul and they started the service over there and Yosel went home. (AI)

Both sides were frightened by what had been set in motion. For a time Aaron Lichten was in critical condition. Fortunately he recovered, but he was forced to use crutches.

The question in everyone's mind was the degree to which Ableson's actions represented the community's perceptions. Although he is a prankster, Yosel Ableson is not an outsider who could be dismissed out of hand. The Rebbe's first task appeared to be to win the community over to his side. He accomplished this in a talk in which he considered the events in the perspective of Talmudic tradition.

What the Rebbe did was he made everybody come to the shul and he referred to the commentary on the reading of the week. The same thing had taken place. Esau's son received money to kill Jacob, but because he was a grandchild of Isaac he couldn't do it. His grandfather was still Isaac. That held him back. That's what the Midrash said. So the Rebbe said, "Because his grandfather was decent that at least should have prevented him from doing this, but it didn't."

It fit the situation very well. He cried in a way: "How can a person be like this? How can a person do a thing like this to another person?" He gained some sympathy from the people I can say. I mean, after all, it's a ridiculous thing to run over someone. (AI)

The underlying issues, however, could not be completely ignored. Yosel Ableson's protest had concerned housing, profits, and misleading fundraising.

It was a very embarrassing situation, the whole thing. The father of Yosel Ableson was trying to make up. They say there was a settlement for $200,000 to pay off Aaron Lichten and the case would be closed. (AI)

With Yosel Ableson's flight, reportedly to South America, and the payment of a settlement for damages, the matter quieted down and the community had time to reflect on what had happened. The posters and leaflets, real and counterfeit, that began the controversy had papered over the community's conflicting emotions concerning their new Rebbe. While everyone acknowledged that the new Rebbe could not match the older Satmar Rebbe in intellect or in character, unsubstantiated gossip over the Rebbe's concern with business matters had not improved his image.

The worsening housing shortage in Williamsburg had helped to keep the community seething. The failure to satisfy community needs was contrasted sharply with the effort taken to make the Rebbe comfortable. The Rebbe's mansion sat in solitary splendor on the site planned for public housing, making it an eyesore rather than a landmark. The co-op apartment owners believed themselves to be exploited, and the Rebbe appeared to side with the contractors by ignoring the findings of the bet din. A new scheme to raise prices for housing had been uncovered, increasing intracommunity squabbling. The automobile "accident" had caused the controversy to boil over. For the moment the fire was dampened by an agreement between the aggrieved parties, but the controversy was far from being resolved.

A Door to the Past

A sudden downdraft brought the smoldering embers of the dispute back to life. Yosel Ableson, tired of his exile, returned to the community and was promptly arrested as a fugitive from justice.

> After half a year this Yosel Ableson decided, "Let me come back to New York. How long is this to last with us? It's enough." So he came back and they arrested him. They arrested him just as they do the biggest criminals: he maliciously intended to kill a person on two occasions. He was treated very badly in jail. He was beaten up by the police and so on.   (AI)

In his stay abroad Yosel Ableson had not lost any of his audacity.

> I heard when he was arrested, Isaac Ableson, who is related to him and is a very important figure here, went to visit him in jail. Yosel told him, "I have this message to give to the rabbi."
> He asked, "What is this message?"
> "Tell him if I'm sitting here twelve hours more, he will be here to pray during all the holidays, for Rosh Hashanah, Yom Kippur, and Sukkot, and he will be kept company by twenty of the nicest people of Satmar who will be here sitting here in this jail." He claimed that he knows enough stories on the leaders that he can have all of them arrested.   (AI)

The threats from the jail were echoed by others in the Ableson family. Much of their ire was directed at the dayyan, the rabbinical judge who had negotiated the $200,000 settlement.

> The mother of this Yosel Ableson came to shul yelling that there was an agreement: "$200,000 we gave and while you're sitting here and learning

you're not keeping your word." And this and that. She said this to the
dayyan. (AI)

The Rebbe's son Aaron, the rov and leader of the Kiryas Joel community and the Rebbe's heir apparent, proceeded to thicken the controversy
with a few ill-chosen words of insult and innuendo. On this occasion a
new virulent element was injected into the situation: two strains of gossip
from different ages were suddenly linked by an ill-timed reference to an
old legend.

Then a different thing happened altogether. The Satmar Rebbe's son, the
oldest son, Aaron, he has sometimes a big mouth.

Aaron, the Rebbe's son, gave a speech and he called Ableson's mother a
hatzufah [impudent woman]. "This Ableson's mother—that impudent
woman with her *tsiganer* [gypsy] family—came to the shul and starts yelling." You know, with that phrase he was trying to bring up an old pain.

There is an old story about the Ableson family, given only from mouth to
ear, about the quality of their family. There were some rumors about a hundred years ago about the Ableson family, that it's not so spotless. A woman
in the family had a relationship with some demon or something and that's
how the branch of the family got started. This is a sensitive issue in which a
lot of families are involved and you don't talk about it in public because
somebody from the family might be around. This is something which you
only talk about quietly when you know everyone is clear from around here.

Nobody knows how she became pregnant. She went away to a different
town and she came back pregnant and she didn't have any love affair. She
was a virgin. She was still a virgin. That was the main issue.

She married later, but this child was from that pregnancy. She had a girl.
That girl's name was Yita. They call her the *baba* [grandmother]. When they
want to make a little joke in the family they say, "Yeah, that's what the Baba
Yita wanted." And they all say, "Yeah we all come from the Baba Yita." In
the family it's a joke to them, but outside you have to shut up. It's a sensitive
issue which you don't bring up.

It's written in a lot of books at that time. The Kotsker, one of the big
rabbis, said that one of their ancestors was made pregnant by a demon.[3]

This goes back six generations. The family is spread out and the descendants feel a little guilty. They try to behave, you know, so that nobody should
throw it back at them. The family is so widespread because they're so rich.
They've gotten into every family. They're very aggressive people, probably
because they come from the devil. For a joke it's okay to say that. There are
plenty of very rich Ablesons and there are a lot of other families involved.

Even today when somebody is making a marriage arrangement he wants
to find out if the family is not from the witches. I know that my mother and
my father when they made a marriage arrangement, it was a day before they
left the country, they found out if there's a witch or not. There are clean
Ablesons also. I don't know all the families and I don't care to know. If I
would have to find a girl for my boy I would find that out. (AI)

Reb Aaron had not retold the story, but his caustic reference to the character of Yosel Ableson's mother summoned up bitter memories of the legend of the Ableson ancestry. The words were no sooner out of his mouth than he regretted them.

> He mentioned this thing and then he corrected himself, that he respects them. His closest people are the Ablesons. And not only now, but for tens of years and a hundred and two hundred years they've been the loyal people of the Sziget and Satmar families. (AI)

But those present remembered the charges and paid little attention to the explanation that followed.

> This Aaron, the Rebbe's son, gave a speech and he reminded everyone of the story when he called this woman a *hatzufah*—"that impudent woman with her gypsy family." All the people heard it. And they felt very hurt about this—that a rabbi should come out in public and label the family. Rabbis a hundred years ago were very careful about this issue because it touched so many decent families.
>
> He really got back at the Ablesons with that. I mean he paid them back. He paid them back and he paid it good. But the thing is, all the money comes in from this family. Seventy percent of the millionaires in Satmar are from the Ableson family—Ableson and the families related to the Ablesons. The family is about five hundred or a thousand families. (AI)

The legendary gossip had stirred up more animosity and sharpened differences between major elements in the community. Moreover, by involving the Rebbe in the controversy, it undermined his unique status and made it easier to attack him and his representatives.

> Everything fell apart. The housing didn't come through, nothing, nothing. Both of them lost. Nobody wins in this case. I mean it just busted the whole thing. But you know people don't want to remember all the time. You know how it is in politics. You know something happens sometimes and then it passes.
>
> The ban is forgotten already. It was good for two days until the accident. The Lichtens didn't press charges. It was settled and finished.
>
> You know, it's an interesting experience. They all lost a little bit on it. Lichten the spokesman lost his health, and the Rebbe lost a little of his prestige. Ableson lost $200,000, plus there was jail, he was beaten up a little bit, and they were called gypsies. The family's prestige has been lowered because of that phrase. (AI)

The diminution of the prestige of the central leadership had led to wider swings of opinion and to a sense of social disequilibrium. Rumor and gossip had increased. The signs of increasing turmoil threatened surprising new schisms in Williamsburg and in Kiryas Joel.

· 26 ·

Kiryas Joel:
In Court and Out

Problems and Promise

The religious environment of Kiryas Joel initially proved to be as promising as the first settlers had hoped. The village was a marriage of shtetl and suburb, a contemporary rural community strengthened by its ties to the past. Soon after the death of the old Rebbe in August 1979, however, the bonds holding the community together began to fray as the new leadership was questioned and disputes threatened the traditional order.

Kiryas Joel contained ideas both old and new. Almost everyone was soon forced to take sides on a variety of issues concerning the powers of the Rebbe and the rov, methods of education, and the rights of villagers to go their own way and manage their own affairs. Some who had children who were physically or mentally impaired were eager to push ahead into a world of new ideas to improve their children's education and ability to socialize. They presented plans and waited eagerly for words of encouragement. Others, anxious to revitalize the community, considered a return to an idealized past preferable to what to them had become a tame religious order quenched of its anti-Zionist zeal. They found the new leadership wanting in terms of charity and generosity of spirit in comparison with their memories of Reb Joel. Some tightened their ties to the old rebbetsn. They recalled the old Rebbe's warnings: beware of false prophets; measure every action against the words of the Torah.

The community expected order and continuity. A few also hoped for wisdom and understanding. For their part Reb Moshe, the new Rebbe, and his son Reb Aaron, the chief rabbi of Kiryas Joel and dean of the yeshivah, reacted harshly to any presumed threat to their authority, no matter how small the matter. In their eyes it seemed that dissenters to authority should suffer the same fate as Korah, the rebel in the desert who opposed Moses and who together with his followers and their households were swallowed up and went down to Sheol.[1] This would prove to be unsettling as the community faced a series of encounters with the outside world that required their united strength to overcome. More turmoil and transformation lay ahead.

The Monroe-Woodbury School District

Families in Kiryas Joel with children who suffered from physical and mental disabilities were now aware of advances in educational, vocational, and therapeutic services. Their primary goals were to break the cycle of isolation and shame and to bring normal and handicapped children to play together. In 1983 in Kiryas Joel families formed a special school for handicapped children. The school, called Sha'arei Hemlah (Gates of Compassion), met in an annex to Bais Rachel, the girls' school. Special education classes were offered by public school teachers. Some fifty handicapped Hasidic children under the age of five were brought to Bais Rachel each day from suburban settlements in New Square, Monsey, and Monroe. The major force behind the school was Reb Wolf Lefkowitz.

> Rabbi Wolf Lefkowitz founded the school. He has a Down's syndrome child. They used to put such children in the closet. He found out how it was possible to work with them. He's a rich person and he got donations. He hired teachers. In other schools the children felt different. In this school they felt like the rest of the children. They worked that the children shouldn't feel different. They had to know how to pray, to observe the holidays. It had a psychological effect on the children. Before the effect on them had been bitter. Now they were in the same building with the rest of the kids and that encouraged other kids to come in during lunch time to play with them. They were made part of the school. It had a beneficial effect on these kids. You could feel them, touch them, push their wheel chairs, play with them. The handicapped children mingled with the rest of the kids.   (JW)

The classes continued until the close of the 1984–1985 school year. At that time the Monroe-Woodbury school district suspended its special services to Kiryas Joel in response to a recent ruling by the Supreme Court that public school teachers are not permitted to work on the grounds of a parochial school. The district school board took the ruling one step further by relying on the Education Law of New York State which required seriously handicapped children who do not attend public schools to be provided for in facilities not separate from public school students. Ironically, the intent of the New York State law was to ensure that such students would not be treated in an inferior way; however, in this situation it ensured that no aid at all would be provided.

To receive the assistance of public school teachers, the superintendent and the district school board determined, the Hasidic children would have to attend the public school.[2]

The offer to provide services for handicapped children in the public schools was refused by the Hasidim. From the Hasidic point of view busing the children to the public school presented impossible hurdles for a religious community: classes were not separated by sex, there were linguistic and cultural barriers, and the danger existed that the children would absorb secular knowledge that would conflict with community values. There were social ills as well: the children attending a secular school would suffer humiliation at the school because of their dress, sidecurls, and customs, and they would be stigmatized at home in the village for having been contaminated by secular contacts.

The community asked that special services for the handicapped be provided at a neutral site, such as the mobile vans used to provide remedial educational services, an option which had been accepted by the federal courts for remedial education programs that are federally funded. Their request was denied by the school board, however, as being inconsistent with the Education Law of New York State. The board maintained that since no federal funds were involved and only state funds were used, only state education laws were applicable. The precedent established by the Supreme Court was ignored. In April 1986 five parents sued the school district. Abraham Wieder, a spokesman for the group and the parent of a hearing-impaired daughter, stated their goals: "All we want is what the state says the School District can provide and what federal law permits." [3]

The issue seemed momentarily settled when State Supreme Court Justice Irving A. Green ruled in favor of the parents that a neutral site could be used as a classroom. For a few months, between December 1987 and February 1988, the school district offered classes for six children in the basement of a senior citizens' housing complex located in the village. This ended in 1987 when the Appellate Division reversed the lower court's ruling as a violation of the separation of church and state in that it accommodated the Hasidim's religion and culture. The next step up the legal ladder was the Court of Appeals.

The superintendent of the school district, Daniel D. Alexander, had been in his post since 1978. During that time he had had experience with the Hasidic communities in New Square and Monsey in Rockland County, just south of Orange County. They had served as subjects for his Ph.D. dissertation, "The Political Influence of the Resident Hasidic Community on the East Ramapo Central School District." In his dissertation he maintained that school administrators should examine the ways in which the Hasidim achieve and wield political influence. In Rockland County Superintendent Alexander had found that Hasidic political influence was ineffective and ambivalent and that "there appears to be a large gap between real political influence and that perceived by many in the community." [4] He noted the unchanging attitude of school boards (to which he owed allegiance) concerning the need to maintain the separation of church and state. In Rockland County, community clashes on the budget primarily concerned capping the funds available for transportation and athletics, items of relatively little interest to the Hasidim and of primary concern to the general community. Hasidic negative views on these matters were usually smothered by a still stronger counter-reaction from the majority of the population.[5]

There were sharp differences, however, between circumstances in Rockland County and the situation facing Alexander twenty miles away in his post in Monroe Township in Orange County. The Satmar Hasidim in Kiryas Joel were more numerous and more affluent than their counterparts in New Square and Monsey. They were also tightly organized and accustomed to controversy. Moreover, the question of receiving therapy and training from state personnel was a critical issue. For those families involved it was a matter of their children's survival, and it aroused them to take direct action on their own. They would not back down nor compromise.

The parents reiterated that what they were requesting was within the federal and state legal framework of aid to students in parochial schools. Why weren't the education administrators capable of setting aside their doubts in favor of helping handicapped children? Superintendent Alexander was cooperative up to but not beyond the letter of the law as he understood it. Both he and the school board felt secure that their perception of the state law and the need to maintain the separation of church and state would be upheld in the courts.

By 1988 the children had been without needed services for three years, a loss of time and training especially critical for those with physical and mental disabilities. The July 1988 ruling of the New York State Court of Appeals was then published. The ruling struck at both sides in the dispute. While the court noted the justice of the Hasidic cause to receive services, their "statutory entitlement to special services does not carry with it a constitutional right to dictate where they must be offered."[6] With regard to the school district's argument, the court summarily dismissed their plea that it was necessary to hew to the literal letter of the law in providing services to educate handicapped children only in public school classrooms. The court found that the legislature indeed intended to provide these benefits for students in religious schools. The court asked for the development of programs designed for individuals and for the programs to be delivered in homes, hospitals, and other institutions as well as classrooms. While the court specifically avoided ruling on the constitutionality of using neutral sites, its noting it as a possible option was a clear indication of the court's view of the subject. It ruled that the district was empowered to provide programs at a neutral location, including mobile vans, but the court could not force the district to act. The court pointed the way out of the dilemma but it would not provide an unequivocal practical remedy.

District Superintendent Alexander was scarcely fazed by the ruling. He asserted that all the options cited by the court were already employed, and he returned to his essential argument: "We cannot segregate children on the basis of religion or anything else when we recommend a program for them." Despite the court's plea for flexibility and its permission to utilize a neutral site, the superintendent could not foresee changes in the program.[7] The superintendent and the school board had reached the limits of their imagination.

The Hasidim took the court at its word. At the end of the summer they asked the school district to prepare individual education programs for the Hasidic children, whose number had now reached approximately one hundred. Alexander maintained his position in the face of this new deluge: "We're handling each application on an individual basis as we do every application. However, we're not going to serve them in a segregated setting."[8]

The case had struggled through the court system but it appeared that little had been accomplished. It seemed inevitable that the case be passed upward to the Supreme Court to be decided; however, the matter would soon take a radical turn.

B'nai Joel

While the case concerning services for the handicapped was going through the courts, another school problem arose which divided rather than united the Kiryas Joel community. Parents with children within the normal range of intelligence and physical activity were also disturbed about the educational program of the schools at Kiryas Joel. In 1988 a half-dozen families whose sons were having difficulty mastering the intricacies of a page of Talmud expressed dissatisfaction with the size of the classes and complained of the failings of a particular teacher. They went to the principal of the yeshivah and sought a change; he sent them to the governing board, who in turn referred them back to the principal. Their frustration with the yeshivah administrators led the parents to form a small school of their own so that their sons could catch up with their peers.[9] The new school was named B'nai Joel, in honor of the old Rebbe. The very name signified their loyalty to the past and sent a challenge to the present leaders.

The group of parents involved now faced a direct and angry response from Reb Moshe, the Rebbe, and from his son Reb Aaron, the rov and rosh yeshivah, who would not tolerate a competing school. Any such venture was seen as an affront to their authority and to the unity of the community. Since the families would not disband the school, punishment was meted out to bring them back into line and to discourage others from joining them.

Six families were banned from the principal congregation, Yeter Lev. They could not daven in the besmedresh, hold a wedding ceremony, or bury a family member in the cemetery. The place of the children too became part of the censure: if one child in the family was enrolled in B'nai Joel, his brothers and sisters were invited to leave the United Talmudic Academy, the community school. Those in opposition to the Rebbe and the rov were thus effectively banned from participating in community life: the parents were thrown out of the synagogue and the children along with their brothers and sisters were expelled from the yeshivah.

Ironically, the expulsions served to strengthen the new school, which expanded to handle the new students forced to leave the yeshivah. B'nai Joel soon numbered over a hundred students. The parents' complaint about the level of learning and their punishment were discussed in the besmedresh and in every household. (Although in some households the women were advised not to listen to or participate in political discussions.) Leaflets were posted and passed out in the street.

> The school started with six boys and they wanted to stop it right away. They expelled other children in the same families. The result was that the other school became bigger. There was a nasty fight. There were leaflets on the streets. A couple of men were told formally not to daven in the besmedresh. Some had their kids knocked out of school. (YA)

Community battle lines were drawn still more sharply the following year, in March 1989, when in his weekly talk in Williamsburg the Rebbe made a decisive statement attacking the dissidents: "If troublemakers come into the synagogue, don't have anything to do with them. They don't belong in our synagogue if they want to sabotage our institutions." Others recalled still harsher language: "Whenever you see any of those people do not speak to them. Do not go to their homes. Do not invite them into your homes. Treat them as though they were gentiles." His listeners were urged to shout *Sheygetz aroys!* (Hooligans get out!) at the disloyal villagers.[10]

The Rebbe's supporters saw the rebellious families as troublemakers unwilling to accept his rule.

> It's simple. They don't want to obey the boss, the government. They were warned and told to stop. They can leave. They can open the school outside the boundaries. They have persisted because they want to show that they are not under the Rebbe's jurisdiction. (JI)

The protective parents had become rebels and were cut off from the community around them.

> We were frightened but we had expected it. The only thing they could still do to us is not bury us in the cemetery and not allow us to visit the older Rebbe's grave. (JH)

The community ban encouraged some of the most zealous supporters of authority and conformity to harass the renegade families. Telephone threats were made to the dissidents; automobile tires were slashed; and on occasion rocks were hurled through the window of a shul or household. In a move made apparently to please their elders, some of the older yeshivah boys went to B'nai Joel and disrupted the class. They sent the children home and turned the tables over. One account related that they shoved the teacher around as well. What made matters worse was that the perpetrators, whether they were extremists or undisciplined yeshivah students, could act without fear of punishment from the community. For protection the threatened Hasidim had to call the New York State Police.

Despite these difficulties B'nai Joel did not fold. The ban divided the community but it did not defeat the dissidents. Initially classes were offered in various homes, such as that of Nathan Brach, who lived most of the time in the city and whose house in Kiryas Joel stood empty. (Brach, himself an unrepentant disciple of the old Rebbe who maintained his loyalty to the rebbetsn, was struck on the head in 1984 by a student whom he had confronted removing a plaque honoring the old Rebbe. It took fifteen stitches to close the wound.[11] Of the incident Brach later said: "Until that time I knew nothing. They opened my head and my brains started working.") Eventually, as the school grew in size, they rented a building previously used as a Catholic school in nearby Harriman. The Rebbe and his supporters apparently had not realized that the opposition was so entrenched and so stubborn. Nor had they considered that so many would ignore Reb Moshe's commands.

> If everyone accepted the ban no one would associate with them. After a couple of days it was clear that the *herem* [ban] didn't have any lasting effect: don't do business with them, don't intermarry with them, don't play with them. People realized that they're not so bad and ignored the ban. (TP)

The dissidents had their own standards to adhere to.

> They [in B'nai Joel] are willing to accept the authority of the rov and even turn over their school. But they want to make sure that the school keeps true to the preachings of the old Rebbe. (TP)

A New Public School District

District Superintendent Alexander and the school board remained as insurmountable obstacles in the way of obtaining services that both court and conscience dictated that handicapped children should have. The parents proposed to resolve the issue by carving out their own school district.[12] A new school district would enable the Hasidim to request funds from the state for tutors, therapists, and equipment needed to educate handicapped children, now estimated to have reached two hundred in number. Funds would be sought for those children only. In conformity with state law the classrooms would be coeducational and be kept free of signs of religion.

The tentative solution won immediate widespread support. In the State Legislature Assemblyman Joseph Lentol from Brooklyn sponsored a bill proposing the new school district. If the Hasidim were eager to leave the Monroe-Woodbury school district, the school board was just as eager to have them out. Frayed by the lengthy struggle, the board voted in favor of a resolution supporting the creation of the new district. Superintendent Alexander was among the bill's vocal supporters: "In practical terms it means they will be able to run a public school system for special-education children. There is no intent on the village's part to run a public school system for anything else."[13] The bill carried unanimously in the State Legislature, and Governor Mario Cuomo, seizing this opportunity to satisfy all parties to the dispute, signed the bill into law on July 25, 1989. (A month later, in August 1989, Superintendent Alexander retired, and Terrence L. Olivo was named to replace him.)

The creation of the new school district was not without its detractors. The state Education Department and the New York State School Boards Association had opposed it, as well as civil liberties groups including the New York Civil Liberties Union and the American Jewish Congress. The major concern of civil libertarians was that the new district was a violation of the First Amendment of the Constitution prohibiting the government from making any law providing for the establishment of religion. Donna Lieberman of the New York Civil Liberties Union warned: "We strongly suspect that both the purpose and the primary effect of creating a separate school district for the village of Kiryas Joel is the promotion of religion in violation of the establishment clause [of the Constitution.]"[14] The Anti-Defamation League of B'nai B'rith also registered its opposition to permitting the village to be organized as a separate school district, arguing that "the creation of a state-sanctioned, tax supported school district specifically for the Hasidic community would violate the First Amendment separation of church and state."[15] It was left to the New

York State School Boards Association, however, to file a legal challenge to the constitutionality of the statute in the State Supreme Court in Albany.

The Election of the School Board

While the question of the legality of the new school district made its way through the courts, the bill made it possible to transform Sha'arei Hemlah, the special school for handicapped children, into the centerpiece of the new school district. Now able to receive state funds for handicapped children, the school had become a community-wide concern. The next order of business was to hold elections for the members of the school board of the new district.

The election of school board members was held in January 1990. Seven candidates ran for office with the approval of Reb Aaron. Some candidates, including those who had first created Sha'arei Hemlah, declined to run unless they could present their own slate, but this action did not win the approval of the rov.[16]

The name of only one independent candidate, Joseph Waldman, appeared on the ballot. Waldman asserted that an independent candidate was needed since the district had been created for the well-being of the entire village. Known for his unswerving support of the old Rebbe and for his opposition to the new leaders, Waldman had become an increasingly outspoken presence in the community. At the time he asserted that "90 percent of the people are in the opposition but 85 percent of them are afraid to say so." In 1988 Waldman had run afoul of the Rebbe and Reb Aaron by supporting the organizers of B'nai Joel and opposing actions taken to force the dissidents out of the community. Waldman had been expelled from the congregation Yeter Lev in October 1989 for allegedly distributing unsigned derogatory leaflets.[17] In response Waldman had organized his own shul. In August 1990 he promised to become even more vocal when he started his own monthly newspaper, the *Jewish Tribune of Upstate New York,* which printed world news of Jewish interest. Although some newsstands reportedly refused to handle the monthly, Waldman established a mailing list and claimed a readership of 8,000 in Kiryas Joel, Spring Valley, and Monsey.

Waldman did not win a seat on the school board, but in losing he received a surprising 673 votes, roughly 40 percent of the electorate. Waldman claimed that if the yeshivah students of voting age had been excluded he would have won a seat on the school board, a contention disputed by the Rebbe's followers.[18] Waldman's popularity demonstrated that there was more substantial opposition in Kiryas Joel than had been admitted earlier. There was also evidence that people felt intimidated by groups of the Rebbe's supporters outside the polls and were fearful that their votes were not confidential.[19]

Some weeks after the election results were known, in March 1990, Waldman's six children were dismissed from school.

> They held another meeting and wrote me a letter saying I had brought shame in front of the goyim because I ran for office and because of this they are throwing out my kids. They are giving me a week till Rosh Hodesh [the new month], which was the week before Passover, to ask for forgiveness. I should come down to the congregation and repent and do whatever they tell me and they'll see what they'll do.   (JW)

Waldman's resolve, however, could not be shaken: "We live in a free country."

> I wrote four letters: one to the Satmar congregation, one to Rabbi Aaron's house, one to the rabbinical court in Williamsburg, and one to the rabbinical court in Monroe. I said, "If you have anything against me I'm ready to go to a dintoyre [hearing], and I will accept what they have to say." What do my kids have to do with what I did? In the letter I said, "Even in Russia when someone is accused you can defend yourself and have a lawyer. How could you send me out and call me names and dismiss my children before listening to me? I'm in Monroe. How is it that the Williamsburg rabbinical court is making decisions? If this is not brought to a dintoyre I'm going to a [secular] court of law.
>
> The members of the court are afraid themselves. We are prisoners ourselves.   (JW)

Unable to find a satisfactory remedy within the community legal system, Waldman then brought suit in the secular court to force the school to readmit his children. State Supreme Court Justice Peter C. Patsalos took Waldman's request to have his children reinstated under advisement. In the meantime he issued a temporary order reinstating the children. The yeshivah, however, refused to accept the children back and asked the judge to dismiss his findings. Judge Patsalos ordered Reb Aaron to appear in court to answer to contempt charges.

Waldman's appeal to a secular court brought him still greater notoriety. It was considered by many loyalists to be an added insult to the authority of the Rebbe and the rov. To others Waldman was a hero. His action had the effect of cutting the rov down to size. Reb Aaron now had to explain his actions to a higher authority other than his own father.

> It was humiliating what they did to my kids. God gave me somehow the courage [to resist]. I would never have believed I would survive it. I felt I had some external courage that gave me that power.   (JW)

The New School District

In January 1990 the New York State School Boards Association mounted a legal challenge to the new school district as a violation of the First Amendment separation of church and state.[20] This new threat to the governance of the community once again required the services of Nathan Lewin, the Washington-based attorney who has handled every case for the Hasidim (both Satmar and Lubavitch) involving constitutional law.

Lewin soon found he had a surprising new ally: the Monroe-Woodbury School Board. The new superintendent of schools, Terrence L. Olivo, and the school board joined in support of the new law. It was clear that if the statute was found to be unconstitutional they would be back in the same difficult situation as before—either unable to satisfy the requirements of the state law or denying the needs of the Hasidic handicapped children. The school board asked to be named as a defendant in the suit. The board argued that the legislative act of forming the school district was cut from the same cloth as the creation of the village itself. Denial of the new district would lead to an untenable consequence: consideration of the possibility that the village itself was unconstitutionally created. From their point of view that would fly in the face of American history and tradition.

The target date for opening the new school was September 1990. In spite of the legal threat to its existence, the newly elected school board began to hold meetings. As soon as the fiscal year began in July the board took action. A building was leased. They hired as school superintendent Dr. Steven Benardo, a forty-two-year-old specialist in bilingual education who was then employed as superintendent of special education in the public school system in the Bronx. Dr. Benardo said he was challenged by the need to initiate and administer a completely new program.

The Kiryas Joel Village Union Free School District began holding classes for disabled students in September 1990. As a measure of the need for the school, the parents and the community adhered to all the demands of the secular law. As a public institution the school followed the customary legal guidelines: boys and girls were seated in the same classrooms; physical education was a requirement; the secular calendar measured the year and the holidays observed (including Thanksgiving and Martin Luther King Day); school was closed on Christmas as well as on Yom Kippur; there were no mezuzot on the doorposts and no siddur (prayer book) at hand. Of course not every Hasid was happy with the limitations set on Yiddishkayt, but the leadership knew the rules and were determined to abide by them. Benardo, the superintendent, was easily identifiable: he had no beard, he wore no yarmulke, and he spoke no Yiddish.[21] These differences did not seem to affect Benardo's style as an administrator. To judge by his account of invitations to attend family celebrations, he was welcomed to village affairs.

In the first year the school enrolled 52 full-time students and 160 on a part-time basis. The ages of the students spanned from three to twenty-one. More than half of the students were from New Square and Monsey. In addition to the superintendent there were ten teachers in special education and two in remedial reading.[22] The new school was a victory for the parents and the children involved. For the moment everyone preferred to ignore the challenge to the formation of the school district that was under consideration in the court.

Vacation in Williamsburg

In the spring of 1990 the focus of the struggle between supporters of the new Rebbe and those who continued to revere the old Rebbe shifted to Williamsburg. The older Rebbe's one-story residence on Bedford Avenue was a stately pillared house, its compressed classical lines at odds with the neighborhood's leaner urban brownstones. Since the rebbetsn rarely visited there, one section of the building had been used as a shul for a small congregation of approximately fifty persons who remained attached to the rebbetsn and their memory of the old Rebbe. The one hundred foot building lot on which the house stood was particularly valuable because it was four times the size of the street's standard lot and took up roughly half the block on Bedford Avenue. The property had been in the name of the congregation of the older Rebbe who had prayed there. Since the Rebbe's death the deed had been transferred to the congregation of the rebbetsn and it was intended that she have the right to live there for the remainder of her life.[23] The house was directly across the street from the new Rebbe's larger but less regal home.

In 1989 the older rebbetsn had decided to sell the property to Nathan Brach, a successful importer and exporter of electronic components. Brach had been a devout follower of the old Rebbe and remained a strong supporter of the rebbetsn. He had a home in Williamsburg and another in Kiryas Joel (which for a time he loaned for the use of the school B'nai Joel). It was said that he paid three and a half million dollars for the Rebbe's house. Brach's plan was to extend the synagogue and build a mikvah and some additional apartments on the property. Most believed that his intent was to use the property as a shrine to the old Rebbe and to maintain it as a dissident congregation. The end result would establish the house as the headquarters of the opposition and lay the groundwork for a separate community.[24] The plan offended Reb Moshe. It provided a base for his enemy in the sacred and resplendent home identified with the old Rebbe. To add insult to injury it was just opposite his own home.

What Brach means to say is that Rabbi Joel was my Rebbe and though he's dead he is still going to be my Rebbe. He wants to maintain his independence from the new Rebbe. He doesn't want all the institutions to be under the jurisdiction of the new Rebbe. The main purpose is to keep the house as it is so it would always belong to the old Satmar Rebbe and it would not be intermingled in the affairs of the new Rebbe. It would always be the house of the old Rebbe. (AG)

Reb Moshe and his followers contended that the property belonged to the community rather than to the rebbetsn. (The situation was somewhat similar in principle to the case contesting the ownership of the Lubavitcher library.) The Satmar leaders opposed the transfer of the deed, arguing that the house was meant for the rebbetsn's use in her lifetime and was not transferable for profit (although it was assumed that the money would be used for charitable purposes).

During Passover week in April 1990 the yeshivah boys were home on vacation from their studies in Kiryas Joel and needed little encouragement to search out an enemy of the Rebbe. Early in the week they gathered by the house to harass Nathan Brach. In retaliation Brach closed down the shul located in the house and put up a heavy metal gate to prevent anyone from entering. He also took the precaution of notifying the police, and a patrol car was dispatched to watch the gate. A crowd of some two hundred young protesters arrived and the gate was torn down. Some say the police present thought it wiser to close their eyes to what was happening. The broken gate whetted the appetite of the enthusiastic crowd, and, unfortunately, at that moment three of Brach's associates, with their own histories of opposition to the current leadership of Satmar, arrived at the scene in their car. The crowd pulled the men out of the car, but the police broke through and drove off with the men in their patrol car. The car they had been forced to abandon was then set on fire. It is said that Nathan Brach was so furious at what had taken place that he threatened to sue the police for failing to do their duty.

At this writing, the determination of the ownership of the old Rebbe's house lies with the civil court. Both sides agreed that it would be preferable to have an out of court settlement, and both expressed willingness to go to a rabbinical court.

Attempts at Reconciliation

Although Joseph Waldman lost the election for the school board, he had established that he was a popular figure in the community. His courage was clear and he was prepared to use the secular courts to support his position. Waldman still had cause to protest: "In one of his talks the

Rebbe said that anyone who voted for me should go to the dayyan and repent."

More and more Hasidim in the community had come to realize that matters could not remain in such continual turmoil. The rov and his advisers were anxious to quiet matters down and to come to terms with Waldman. They had already been humiliated in court and did not care to return their difficulties to its jurisdiction.

> They called down my father, my brother, and my brother-in-law. They wanted to make peace. They complained that the Rebbe just wants peace. I should get out of it and not be in the newspapers. The dayyan came to me and my brother came to me and said they're willing to forgive. I said how do I know they're not going to change their minds? The dayyan said the bet din is going to give me something in writing. Every day I was under pressure. I was threatened with assassination. I had to keep my wife and kids strong. My own brothers and mother were pressuring me to end it.   (JW)

The two sides agreed to sit down before a rabbinical court to iron out their differences. Three Satmar rabbis were selected to judge the case: one rabbi was from Monroe, a second was from Williamsburg, and a third came down from Montreal. (An additional rabbi from Monroe also sat in on the case.) After hearing from both sides the court proposed the following settlement: Waldman would offer an apology to Reb Aaron for his actions and for bringing the matter to a secular court, end his lawsuit contending that Reb Aaron had no basis for being involved in secular school matters, surrender the fines collected, stop attacking the Satmar leadership in the press, and close his shul. In return the community would accept Waldman's children back in the yeshivah and would reinstate him in the congregation. They were to respect him and not talk about past sins. Both sides accepted the recommendations of the rabbinical court. They signed an agreement and concluded matters with a ceremonial tumbler of whisky and piece of cake.

In the account of the agreement in the local press Waldman appeared cautious and contrite. "I apologized for any hardship I caused them. I should have tried harder to solve it within the community. I'm remorseful for that." He would say no more since he had agreed not to talk to the press.

There was still a touch of pique in Reb Aaron's response: "Mr. Waldman recognized his guilt and therefore he apologized." Referring to the claims and counterclaims, Reb Aaron said, "The lies started to fall apart." He explained that the children had been excluded from the school as a result of the religious sins of their father, which included publicizing the case in the press and seeking a resolution in a secular rather than a religious court. In a final swipe at the secular court, Reb Aaron concluded: "Judge Patsalos had no right to come in our schools." [25]

A few days later during Shabbes the two men passed each other and exchanged greetings for a good Shabbes.[26] The ceremonial good relations were short lived, however. Within a few weeks Reb Aaron found fault with an article in Waldman's newspaper concerning the dismissal of the village clerk.

> I was stopped. They threw out my kids again. I agreed to close the newspaper. I didn't want to start up again. The kids were enrolled but the school season hadn't started yet. It wasn't in the middle of the year when I could get help from the [secular] courts. My wife is sick and tired of it. I thought it better not to start it up again. They said they bought me out but they closed it. They made a commotion that they paid but it's completely untrue. Some said I was paid $100,000 and some said $50,000. I was happy not to look like a fool. Now I'm doing something else—a business directory. They're strengthening the pressure on people. People are threatened. If they pursue the case in court they will be thrown out.   (JW)

The New School District Is Dissolved

On January 22, 1992, a year after the suit was filed against the new district by the New York State School Boards Association, Justice Lawrence E. Kahn of Albany County ruled that the Kiryas Joel Village Union Free School District should be annulled.[27] Justice Kahn used three basic criteria established in earlier cases concerning the separation of church and state on which to base his decision: "if it has a secular purpose, has the principal or primary effect of neither advancing nor inhibiting religion, and does not foster an excessive entanglement with religion." [28] The statute creating the new school district, the Justice found, transgressed all three criteria, having a religious rather than a secular intent. It served religious needs, and had "the effect of advancing, protecting and fostering the religious beliefs of the inhabitants of the school district." He found that the creation of the school district constituted "a most direct affront to the establishment clause. The legislation is an attempt to camouflage, with secular garments, a religious community as a public school district."

Justice Kahn's ruling struck down a political compromise undertaken to reconcile differences among the religious community, the local school board, and the demands of state and federal law. While he expressed a rueful sympathy for the efforts made on behalf of the Satmar Hasidim, Justice Kahn was not unmindful of the harm that such good intentions could bring about:

> The Satmar Hasidic sect enjoys religious freedom as guaranteed by the very First Amendment that they are now seeking to circumvent. This short range accomplishment could in the long run, jeopardize the very religious freedom that they now enjoy.

The strength of our democracy is that a multitude of religious, ethnic, and racial groups can live side by side with respect for each other. The uniqueness of religious values, as observed by the Satmar Sect, is especially to be admired as non-conformity becomes increasingly more difficult to sustain, however, laws cannot be enacted to advance and endorse such parochial needs in violation of our deep-rooted principle of separation of Church and State.[29]

Not unexpectedly, attorney Nathan Lewin was pained by the decision and promised to enter a plea in the New York State Appellate Court. He predicted that the case might proceed to the U.S. Supreme Court. Governor Cuomo instructed the State Attorney General to appeal the case; the Monroe-Woodbury school board also voted to join in the appeal. Meanwhile, pending the outcome of the appeals, the handicapped students, whose numbers had grown to 138 full-time and 200 part-time, continued to attend classes.

Not everyone in Kiryas Joel was upset by the decision. Some welcomed Justice Kahn's ruling: "The truth is as the judge says. I said so from the beginning. By creating the school district we are undermining the system that has served so well to protect us" (MR).

The Future of Satmar

While the struggles within the court had revealed the diversity and the animosity that existed in the village, the fighting may have strengthened the hand of Reb Moshe, the Rebbe. Most of the Hasidim now realized that for better or worse he was the Rebbe and there was no alternative but to accept him as their leader. Most Hasidim decided either to support the central authority and repress the opposition or to refrain from entering the struggle. For most acquiescence seemed the only way to maintain the institutions of the community, the yeshivah and the besmedresh. Some of those who had earlier complained about the Rebbe and the rov became extremely cautious after witnessing the trials of the Rebbe's opponents.

> I refuse to choose between the sides. There is some justification in both camps. If it came down to it I would have to side with the leadership. I would never do anything to hurt any of the others. But when you realize that there are 4,500 children in the school here you have to favor the leadership. (MR)

Not everyone was reconciled. The fifty to sixty families that continued to operate B'nai Joel, the independent school, were still not allowed in the shul. Although they lived in Kiryas Joel, their religious and educational institutions were completely separate from those of the rest of the community. They had their own school and ran their own school bus. B'nai Joel rented two buildings for its classrooms at a reported cost of

$10,000 a month, an indication of the dissidents' commitment and the level of their financial support. (After being harassed and photographed at a melave-malke they held to raise funds, they began to solicit aid through the mail.)

The families davened at shuls they often had organized themselves, and they went to their own mikvah. Although some of the established community leaders might have liked to put the families under a total ban and order everyone to avoid them, this was not possible. Nor were the leading rabbis in the community united in wanting to be so severe with their fellow townsmen. Some families in the village did not have anything to do with them, while others continued to talk to them. There were many in the community who were sympathetic with the rebels, but they were also aware of the problems they could create for themselves and their families if they joined in any protest against the established leadership.

It did not appear to be likely that the families running B'nai Joel would sit with the rov before a rabbinical court for judgment. It was said that they feared that any rabbinical court would be reluctant to rule against Reb Aaron. Although they were often frightened by events, the families remained unwilling to apologize and surrender their school. They had shown that if need be they were prepared to face down the thousand other families in the community.

The antagonism between supporters and detractors of the present Rebbe, Reb Moshe, had hardened. The stakes were high because it was generally accepted that Reb Aaron would one day succeed Reb Moshe, and Reb Aaron's opponents believed they were already well acquainted with his failings. A number of the settlers in Kiryas Joel continued to resent the arbitrary rule over them, and their initial resentment had blossomed into enduring anger.

For a time the turmoil and dissatisfaction in Satmar suggested that the absence of one of Hasidim's greatest strengths—unanimous devotion and loyalty to the Rebbe—might augur the breakup of the most powerful and populous American Hasidic court. The nagging underlying question was usually unspoken: Why not leave the Satmar Rebbe? For some this was an impossible paradox. "Leave the Satmar Rebbe? Where would we go?" (AI).

Others saw change taking place slowly.

I don't think it's a case of people going [anywhere]. Everyone would stay put where they are. There would just be more diversity. No one would leave the community physically. For example, during the tish on Friday night, when the Rebbe eats his meal, the tradition in the community is that everyone goes over to the shul and spends time with him there during the meal. If his father had two hundred people, he may end up having only twenty people with him any given Friday night, whereas the late Rebbe may have had three hundred or five hundred people. So it's not that people leave, they just don't participate actively as they would if they were totally satisfied with him. But then again who knows? I can't foresee the future. He may wind up being the most successful Rebbe in history. (MR)

For a small number of Satmar Hasidim the search for the successor of Joel Teitelbaum, the old Rebbe, was still under way.

> I daven in the Satmar shtibl in Borough Park, and my children go to Satmar. Basically I stay with the community and make the best of it. [But if you want a blessing?] Well, you look, you search. I would go to the Vizhnitzer Rebbe in Monsey, New York. (AI)

Some like Nathan Brach who had endured the tremendous emotional upheaval of the past decade, from the death of Rabbi Joel Teitelbaum to the present struggles, were now as cynical concerning Rebbes and rabbis as were the intellectuals who abandoned Orthodoxy before the war. Some not only worried over what had become of their community, they seemed to have lost faith in the institution of the Rebbe itself.

> We have no Rebbe. The old Rebbe was a holy man. The new Rebbe has nothing to sell. Some people didn't believe in him and didn't trust him. He became Rebbe just because his uncle was a big man. We don't believe in Rebbes. We see they're not honest.
>
> We don't believe in Satmar as a sect. We've become like the Litvaks [Orthodox Lithuanian Jews who were opposed to the Hasidic Rebbes]. We follow the Torah. We don't need any middlemen any more. We pray ourselves. (NB)

For the first time, within the lifetime of the living Rebbe people discussed the possibilities of future succession. No one expected the present hierarchy to receive the Messiah.

There were still many who had been born as Satmar Hasidim who be-'ieved they had greater rights to identify as members of the community than the current Rebbe and his son. Perhaps there was justification for believing that the tradition concerning the dynasty of sovereign kings was applicable. Reb Moshe would always face some opposition because he had come to power through election after the death of the old Rebbe. After maintaining his power through his lifetime, however, Reb Moshe would be able to pass his authority directly to his son. Despite the present opposition there was reason to believe that when Reb Aaron became the Rebbe through inheritance the matter of his power over the community would be sealed.

Whatever happens, Joseph Waldman cannot consider leaving Satmar. Since recanting his opposition Waldman has been forced to remain silent. His essential loyalty to Satmar, however, is incontrovertible.

This is what I told them in court: "Who is this principal, just appointed, to throw my children out of school? When I was eight days old I was in the older Rebbe's lap. I never davened any place other than Satmar. For five generations my family has been with Satmar. If you cut one of my arteries the blood that will flow is from Satmar."

· 27 ·

Rumor and Riot in Crown Heights

Complaints Real and Imaginary

During the decade of the 1980s South Crown Heights once again became a desirable neighborhood for Hasidic Jews, but despite its apparent attractiveness Crown Heights was clouded by racial tension. During the previous three decades the neighborhood had seen an overall shift in the population from white to black. The black population in North and South Crown Heights had increased from 20 percent in the 1960s to 80 percent by 1980. There were tensions because of the high crime rate and the scramble for housing. A key area of contention concerned perceptions as to who was benefiting from government aid and police protection. There were accusations of preferential treatment for the Hasidim.

The community continued to struggle with problems of neighborhood redevelopment. Blacks and whites were in need of additional housing, but redlining by banks and insurance companies limited the funds available for mortgages and renovation. The funds disbursed under the poverty programs paled before the larger sums of money needed for mortgages, which were under the control of private banks. Local banks failed to utilize local savings for the good of the neighborhood and preferred to invest their funds elsewhere.[1] In fact, Crown Heights saw the closing of two bank branches between 1977 and 1986; a third closing soon followed. In great measure the closings were in keeping with a nationwide trend to shut down banks in urban areas in favor of opening new branches in suburbia.

Most black homeowners in Crown Heights had purchased their homes twenty years before from Jewish families fleeing the area. Now the balance steadied as the children of the earlier Hasidic settlers married and had families of their own. Since the continuance of Hasidic life depends on close proximity to one another and to the primary centers of court life—the besmedresh, the schools, and the kosher food shops—the new generation intended to live close by. Other Hasidim also wanted to move in and enjoy the benefits of a now stable religious community. There was impetus to renovate older housing and to search out every possible apartment and house that might become available close by. In the renovation and expansion of the synagogue and educational institutions, as well as their investments in new housing, the Lubavitcher Hasidim had staked their future on remaining in Crown Heights.

As the Hasidic community grew from within and as a small number of Russian immigrants arrived from abroad, some black residents expressed resentment about the influx of new Hasidic families and charged that the Hasidim were "taking over the neighborhood." From the Hasidic point of view it was not unreasonable to assume that their community could grow without prejudice to blacks, and that the balance of whites and blacks could continue to shift as it had over the previous three decades.

Hasidic efforts to obtain additional housing were concentrated in the blocks close to their religious and educational center at 770 Eastern Parkway and down both sides of Kingston Avenue to Empire Boulevard. Blacks close to the Lubavitch religious and shopping area felt harassed by frequent offers to buy their homes. From the Hasidic point of view the request was legitimate: they offered a good price, usually higher than the normal market would allow, and the offer could be easily and quickly declined. A 1987 survey of homeowners by the city's Human Rights Commission uncovered no signs of blockbusting; however, more than half of the black homeowners had been asked if their homes were for sale. Mayor Koch thereupon penned a letter warning that "this type of persistent and unwelcome solicitation of homeowners . . . constitutes a form of harassment that can only lead to increased tensions within that community. Neither the need for housing nor the need for proximity can justify harassment of the type documented by this report." [2]

Blacks also accused the police of providing preferential treatment to the Hasidim and of ignoring the needs of the black community. An occasional charge of police brutality, as in the case of Arthur Miller, a black man who died while being arrested by the police, had nothing to do with the Hasidim but stoked the fires of black resentment. Recalling the Hasidic invasion of precinct houses in Borough Park and Williamsburg, some blacks complained: "Could you imagine if black people had stormed the precinct? We would have been carried out in body bags." [3] Blacks questioned the need for police protection for the Lubavitcher Rebbe and the presence of a patrol car stationed outside Lubavitcher headquarters during services. This had largely been an issue in the past rather than the present, since Mayor Edward Koch had had the patrol car withdrawn soon after taking office in 1978. Mayor Koch had also discontinued the blocking of the service road in front of 770 Eastern Parkway during the Sabbath, which had proved irksome to neighbors on the block.

The mayor did offer protection to the Rebbe, particularly in view of his international prominence: when death threats were made on the Rebbe's life in 1981, Koch assigned an unmarked patrol car to accompany the Rebbe twice a week to the Old Montefiore Cemetery in Queens to visit the grave of the former Rebbe. Nonetheless, the perception of special treatment and round-the-clock surveillance persisted.

A few black neighbors complained about the presence of police cars when Hasidic religious services were in session. On the Sabbath when 2,000 people attended services (the number increased to between 5,000 and 10,000 on holidays) one or two patrol cars would remain near the besmedresh to channel the traffic and ensure order. Some blacks found the protection to be excessive. The police policy, however, was to try to be present wherever there were large crowds and heavy traffic; police cars also appeared when church services for the major Christian congregations let out and even when audiences exited the movies at night. On Sundays after prayer services there were police cars stationed outside Rev. Heron Sam's St. Mark's Episcopal Church on Union Street and Rev. Clarence Norman's First Baptist Church on Rogers Avenue. Assemblyman Norman, the son of Rev. Norman, recognized the need for police at such times, but he wanted to reduce the number of patrol cars for the Hasidim from two to one.[4]

Still more serious were allegations of favoritism in the allocation of funds. In 1987 Lydia Chavez of the *New York Times* described the breakdown of Community Development Agency funds, which were recommended by a policy board composed of ten blacks and eleven whites. The development funds that year totaled $295,138—of which 59 percent went to organizations run by Jews (45 percent to the Crown Heights Jewish Community Council and 14 percent to a Jewish day school) and 41 percent to black organizations (14 percent to the Crown Heights Youth Collective, 13 percent to the radio station of Medgar Evers College, and 14 percent to a black organization that subsequently could not comply with the financial regulations). It should be pointed out that the Jewish Community Council serves all races, so that blacks actually received approximately 38 percent of funding administered by the Hasidim, while whites received 47 percent, Asians 11 percent, and Hispanics 3 percent. Nonetheless, there was an obvious discrepancy between overall population and involvement in political and financial control of the neighborhood development fund. The whites, who constituted only 9.3 percent of the population, handled 33 percent of the funds, while the blacks, who made up 78 percent of the population, managed 60 percent. (A similar inversion was true for Hispanics and Asians: the Asians, who represented 1.2 percent of the population, received 4.5 percent of the grant funds; Hispanics, 9.5 percent of the population, took in only 2.2 percent.)[5]

The Hasidim contended that it was difficult to discuss dividing funding equally since divergent elements such as need and merit played a part depending on the type and source of funding involved.

> Equality of funds? If there are 5,000 blacks who need welfare and only 300 Hasidim, should we divide the welfare funds equally? That's based on need. Funds for projects should be awarded on merit. If you have a better project or are more active than I am then you deserve the funds. We do well because we care about our community. There hasn't been any housing funding since Reagan came into office. The only housing that went up seven or eight years ago was built by Section 8 and it got started before Reagan got into office in 1980. They built some 3,000 units and we received between 500 and 600 units. (MS)[6]

The school board was another area of friction. The Hasidim usually managed to win two seats in the elections for the nine-person local school board. They explained their success by the low voter turnout of other ethnic groups at election time.

The perception on the part of many blacks of being disenfranchised persists in the face of considerable gains in political representation by blacks. Blacks have steadily garnered local and citywide offices. Crown Heights voters choose two Council members, four Assembly members, and two State Senators. With the exception of State Senator Marty Markowitz (who represents a Caribbean constituency), since 1978 all of the elected officials have been black. The Congressman from the district, Major Owens, is black.[7] Since the 1990 election both the Mayor and the Chief of Police are black, as is the Democratic County Leader. (During Mayor Koch's tenure, too, the police chief was black.) Since the last election the Area Policy Board, which allocates monies for social services, has been dominated by blacks who won elections to their posts.

Riot

On August 19, 1991, a confrontation between Hasidim and blacks was triggered by a tragic accident in which an automobile driven by a young Hasid struck and killed a black child and critically injured another child. The accident took place at the corner of Utica Avenue and President Street, on the periphery of the Crown Heights Hasidic community where the vast majority of the population is black. It occurred at about 8:20 P.M. on a Monday night, and it set off clashes, lootings, and marches that lasted through the remainder of the week.[8] Reactions to the accident provoked blacks to express a range of grievances against American society in general and the Hasidic community in particular. The fast-moving events would strain black-white relations at the local level and ultimately test the justice system's immunity to the threat of racial violence.

The incident began when the Lubavitcher Rebbe and an entourage of three cars were returning from the cemetery where the Rebbe had been visiting his wife's grave. The lead automobile was an unmarked police car with two policemen; the last of the three was a station wagon driven by Yosef Lifsh, a twenty-two-year-old Hasid, who was accompanied by two other young followers of the Rebbe. Lifsh's car had strayed behind the others in Brooklyn traffic and witnesses said that in trying to catch up Lifsh ran a red light, a contention that Lifsh denied. The station wagon collided with another car (or swerved to avoid a car) and skidded onto the sidewalk, where it struck two seven-year-old children. Gavin Cato, who had stopped to fix the chain of his bicycle, was crushed against a window grating and was killed; his cousin Angela Cato was critically injured. The children had arrived with their parents as immigrants from Guyana the year before.

A crowd gathered, its numbers soon swelled by hundreds of young blacks exiting from a B. B. King concert. As the shaken occupants of the station wagon got out they were surrounded by angry young blacks, who began to beat them. There was a cry of "Kill the Jews." An ambulance from Hatzolah, the Jewish volunteer ambulance service, answered the alarm and reached the scene of the accident either shortly before or simultaneously with three ambulances from the city Emergency Medical Services (EMS). A policewoman told the Jewish volunteer paramedics that they should leave at once with the three injured Hasidim; the children could be treated by the paramedics from the EMS.[9]

In an account that came to light later through interviews by Stewart Ain of the *Jewish Week,* the Hatzolah attendants reported:

> When we arrived there were 100 to 150 black people screaming and crying. We got out and ran through the crowd calling, "Where's the patient? Where's the patient?" A policewoman and a black man came over and said, "Go over there and get that man out of here. They're going to kill him." The attendant . . . was told that the patient was "being taken care of" . . . Three or four black people were trying to get him [Lifsh] out and were beating him. He was in the station wagon—halfway in—and he was bleeding from the face and head. The policewoman said, "Please get this man out of here and get yourself out of here" . . . The attendant said Lifsh was also "robbed of his wallet and all of his money and of a cellular phone he had in his car."[10]

Another Hatzolah attendant told reporter Ain that he arrived in his own car at the scene of the accident. The city EMS attendants were administering CPR to Gavin Cato as he was taken to the ambulance on a stretcher. The Hatzolah ambulance was parked off to one side. In his efforts to assist the EMS technician tending to Angela Cato the Jewish paramedic brought him an airway that was needed. A backboard was requested but when he went to pass on the message a policeman said he would take care of it and then told him, "Get your bag, get in your car and get out of here." None of the Hatzolah paramedics was injured.

The departure of the Hatzolah ambulance quickly became a cause célèbre. The rumor spread through the crowd that the attendants had given medical treatment to the Hasidic men only and had ignored the black children. Mary Pinkett, the black Councilwoman of Crown Heights, summed up the version of events that became current in the black community:

> Some say the ambulances came at the same time. The Hasidim appear to have been there first. When an ambulance arrives it should treat the most seriously injured first. The child was still pinned under the car. After the ambulance left they lifted the car. So it appeared to the crowd that to them the lives of the children didn't matter. (MP)

An editorial in Wednesday's edition of the *New York Times* dealt directly with the inflammatory rumor concerning the ambulances:

> the complaint about the Jewish paramedics' conduct seems off base; an ambulance from the city Emergency Medical Services arrived almost simultaneously [with the ambulance from Hatzolah]. When the E.M.S. began first aid for the injured children, police instructed the Jewish paramedics to remove the Hasidic men in order to protect them from the angry crowd. But by then it was too late. The rumor blazed: a Jewish ambulance crew had supposedly whisked away lightly injured Hasidic men while the black children lay grievously wounded in the street. As the rumor spread, other incidents followed.[11]

The crowd's anger quickly exploded into violence. John Kifner reported in the *New York Times:*

> hundreds of black youths began running through the streets, smashing windows and shouting "Jew! Jew!"
>
> Racing along President Street, a group of black youths surrounded Yankel Rosenbaum, a 29-year-old scholar from Australia, and they stabbed him at about 11:25 P.M., the police said. He died about an hour later at Kings County Hospital.

Yankel Rosenbaum was stabbed to death three hours after the accident that resulted in the death of Gavin Cato. A Lubavitcher Hasid later told James Barron, a *New York Times* reporter: "He was killed for no other reason than he was Jewish and white and for vengeance, vengeance for an incident that was an accident and there was no reason for vengeance."[12]

Two teenagers were arrested and shortly afterward one was identified by Yankel Rosenbaum, still conscious and waiting on the street for the ambulance to arrive. A sixteen-year-old boy was subsequently charged and indicted for murder in the second degree. Some Hasidim, however, complained that the quick capture of the assailant was due to the fact that the police had witnessed the attack but had done nothing to stop it. Later that night Mayor David Dinkins and Police Commissioner Lee Brown, both black, went to Crown Heights to try to clarify misleading rumors and calm the situation, but their presence had little effect on the gangs of young blacks roaming the streets.

The following day, Tuesday, August 20, Deputy Mayor Bill Lynch, who is also black, met with members of the community in a nearby school and heard complaints accusing the police in the 71st Precinct of giving the Hasidim preferential treatment.[13] Four black political activists also arrived in Crown Heights in the early evening in the person of Rev. Al Sharpton, Alton C. Maddox, Sonny Carson, and C. Vernon Mason. Rev. Sharpton called for the arrest of the driver of the station wagon and attacked the Hatzolah as "an apartheid ambulance service." The rioting attracted young toughs from other neighborhoods. The militants called for a march the following day.

That night the marauding gangs moved through the neighborhood with little restraint. There were few arrests even though cars were set on fire, people were beaten, houses were stoned, and stores were looted. The most serious damage was done near where the accident had occurred, in the predominantly black area of the neighborhood. On Utica Avenue the Sneaker King, a store owned by Korean immigrants which sold athletic footwear, was emptied of its contents; the restaurant N.Y. Chicken was raided; and the Utica Gold Exchange was also looted and burned down. Storeowners complained that the police stood by and watched the rioters break into the stores and carry off their loot. The Hasidic community also reported eighteen injuries, the destruction of a "Mitzvah tank," and damage to fifty cars and sixty homes.[14] The roving gangs had identified Jewish homes by the mezuzah tacked on the right doorpost.[15]

On Wednesday morning a funeral service was held for Yankel Rosenbaum. That afternoon hundreds of young blacks, many from other neighborhoods, joined a march that had been planned by the black activists. The leaders, however, quickly lost control of the crowd. Roving bands threw bottles and rocks at passersby. Jews walking alone were in danger of being punched and kicked. Rioters approached the barricade set up in front of 770 Eastern Parkway. They shouted "Heil Hitler!" and tore and set fire to a crude copy of an Israeli flag.

Mayor Dinkins's attempts to calm the situation were booed. When he visited the apartment of the grieving Cato family he was forced to remain inside as bottles and rocks rained on the building. The police commissioner's car took a pounding. Police cars were tipped over. Ten police officers were hit by bricks and a Molotov cocktail hurled from a rooftop.

Eight other officers were struck by shotgun pellets, and several reporters were injured.

The riot in Crown Heights was covered on television, but it was overshadowed by the attempted coup in the Soviet Union. The events overseas also drove the riot from the front pages of the *New York Times*. The editorial in the Wednesday edition dealt directly with the question of the ambulances, but it appeared too late to counter the inflammatory rumor. As Mary Pinkett observed:

> There was the perception that if the Jewish ambulance had taken them the kids would have lived. When they left the child was still pinned under the car. (MP)

Despite the denials by the Hatzolah and by city officials, a week after the riots began most blacks continued to believe the rumor that the children had been ignored by the Jewish paramedics.[16]

On Wednesday evening, while the rioting continued, the Lubavitcher Rebbe spoke after prayers. Without saying anything directly about what their response to the riot should be the Rebbe referred to the weekly portion of the readings: "When you take the field against your enemies, and the Lord your God delivers them into your power and you take some of them captive . . ." (Deut. 21:10). The Rebbe pointed out that "When you take to the field" could also be translated as "*If* you take to the field." His remarks were interpreted to mean that it was inappropriate for Jews to go to war. Rather than commit violence Jews must use restraint and do battle with Torah and mitzvot.

The policemen on the beat, apparently under strict orders to use restraint, were even more frustrated than the Hasidim.[17] Faced with increasing chaos and sagging morale, Chief of Patrol Mario A. Selvaggi devised tougher new tactics for dealing with the rioters. On Thursday more police were sent out on the street and ordered to deal swiftly with any violence. Motorcycle patrols kept pace with the marchers, and arrests became more frequent.

That same day Borough President Golden held a meeting at Borough Hall of twenty-five or so community leaders, among them two black women, Joan Gil, the former Democratic district leader of Crown Heights, and Mary Pinkett, City Councilwoman from Crown Heights. Both women knew that something had to be done quickly.

> Community people have been hurt. Property has been destroyed. The other night a thirty-year-old black man was shot. People are concerned about these agitators. They're afraid that their children are going to get caught up in it. The older people in the black community are worried. Everyone feels that the Hasidim get preferential treatment but they did not expect the vio-

lence. Even Clarence Norman agreed. I can't believe I'm talking to the same Clarence Norman. Everybody wants peace. It got out of hand. Tuesday night at a meeting at Public School 167 the teenagers denounced me for urging restraint. They even booed Norman.

We pledged that we would come up with a solution. We only come together in an emergency. We all agreed something good will come out of this. (JG)

Mary Pinkett was eager to bring blacks together with Jews in the district.

At the meeting at the Borough President's office someone said, "They must apologize. I have heard no expression of sorrow." That was an inappropriate comment. As they talked a young woman from the Jewish community said she has a child who was hit by a car and she knows how they feel. She said a child from the Lubavitcher community was killed by a car driven by a black driver from Crown Heights. They did not loot, they did not burn. They cried for their child. People did not know this. What has to happen is this kind of communication.

What has to happen is that the Hasidic community has to show they care about our children. I know they care about children. They must declare it. They did declare their sorrow, probably on Wednesday. They said they wanted to go to the family but were afraid. That's the kind of paralysis that mob rule brings to a community. People on both sides are afraid.

What has to come out of this is that both sides have to sit down together. What has to come first is the response to the facts. The Grand Jury is supposed to be impaneled. An expert is said to testify what happened. He has to determine how the accident occurred. (MP)

When newspaper reporters interviewed young blacks in the neighborhood they heard of deep-seated complaints of broken homes, unemployment, and lack of opportunity. It appeared from the comments of the neighborhood residents that many of the marchers and rioters were not from the community. In searching the faces of the marchers Councilwoman Mary Pinkett could not find any of her constituents among those roaming the streets.

There are people who are using this tragic incident for their political purposes. I saw the marchers in the street and I didn't recognize any of them. As I rode through the neighborhood the community people were sitting in front of their houses. They wanted their children home. They were not milling around in crowds waiting for something to happen. (MP)

There was a meeting of community leaders in the 71st Precinct house on Friday afternoon. Their number included Al Sharpton, who was urged to cancel any further marches. The grand jury was then in session listening to testimony. Sharpton considered the request but subsequently ordered the march to be carried out.

Friday night was quiet. The Hasidim were in the besmedresh with prayers welcoming the Shabbes. Police remained on high alert until 11:00 P.M., when the Hasidim would have returned to their homes. The riot seemed to be at an end, but no sooner did the police withdraw than the roving bands took over the streets looking for stragglers.

On Saturday three busloads of marchers were brought in from other neighborhoods to support Rev. Sharpton. They joined two hundred others in a walk through Crown Heights to a Bedford-Stuyvesant junior high school. It was a paltry showing and offered the best evidence that the local community had not turned out. The 2,000 police mustered that day far outnumbered the 400 or so protesters who marched between ranks of policemen.

Even at the early stages of the events the community had begun searching for answers as to why this had taken place in Crown Heights, a well-organized and generally peaceful middle-class neighborhood. Mary Pinkett summed up what she believed to be the view of most blacks in the area.

> The incident was the culmination of anger. The complaint the blacks have is the racism of American society. When you bring that conflict together with the situation that happened the other night—a child is killed and another critically injured, an ambulance arrives and the crowd is menacing the occupants of the car and the police telling them to go ("Take your people and go") without evaluating the crowd or the injured youngsters—to the crowd it says they did not care about our children. They did not care about us. With this in mind all the anger is taken out on the driver of the ambulance.
>
> There are those who want to make it a deliberate act against us. I don't believe it was deliberate. If a pattern of preference is already there and once a situation occurs that people can see it they say, "See, this is what I've been telling you all along." (MP)

At the core of black sentiment was the sense that blacks did not receive equal treatment in police protection, in housing, and in economic advancement. The Hasidim, whose aloofness had irritated some blacks, were quickly identified as a target, and they served as a ready scapegoat for a host of social ills. The riots expressed the feelings of the most frustrated elements of the black populace—teenagers unemployed and restless after a long hot summer, the unemployed underclass, as well as militant activists and opportunistic agitators.

Senator Daniel Patrick Moynihan, viewing events from the perspective of American history, characterized the murder of Yankel Rosenbaum as "a lynching."[18] The Hasidim saw the riots in the context of their experience: this was a pogrom. Rabbi Shmuel Butman, the director of the Lubavitch Youth Organization, viewed it as expressing deep-rooted anti-white and anti-Semitic feelings.

Unfortunately we saw a pogrom in 1991. We saw and we heard things: Heil Hitler! Kill the Jews! This is not Berlin 1930 but New York 1991. (SB)

The Hasidim were also concerned about the long-term effects of the riot. Would they be able to walk the streets in safety in the future? Would blacks continue to use the tragic accident as an excuse to harass them?[19] There was also an attempt to influence the findings of the grand jury when black protesters demanded that the driver of the car be arrested and charged with manslaughter. Earlier in the week marchers had responded to Mayor Dinkins's pleas for calm with "No justice, no peace!" and "Arrest the Jews!"

On Sunday Mayor Dinkins was accorded a welcome in the First Baptist Church of Crown Heights, the church of the late Rev. Clarence Norman, Sr., the father of the Assemblyman and local Democratic leader. Dinkins tried to balance his comments.

"There will not be one brand of justice for one community and another for another community," Mr. Dinkins told a clapping congregation . . .

But even as he pledged to try to resolve conflicting claims of preferential treatment by both the black and Jewish communities in Crown Heights, Mayor Dinkins repeated that no grievances justified further violence. And he drew a sharp distinction between the killing of a black child by a car driven by a Hasid and the stabbing death hours later of a rabbinical student by blacks in apparent retaliation.[20]

On Sunday afternoon Hasidim who lived close by ignored the earlier threats and visited the grieving Cato family to express their sorrow. That afternoon the mayor visited the Lubavitcher Rebbe, Menachem M. Schneerson, who gave the mayor two one dollar bills, as is his custom, to encourage the giving of charity, and the Rebbe blessed the mayor.

"You have blessed me in the past and your prayers have helped," Mr. Dinkins said.

The rabbi responded that he hoped the Mayor would be able to bring peace to the city.

"Both sides," Mr. Dinkins said.

"We are not two sides," the rabbi replied. "We are one side. We are one people living in one city under one administration and under one God. May God protect the police and all the people of the city."[21]

Some orators at the funeral held the next day at St. Anthony's Baptist Church rejected the path of reconciliation and intensified their violent rhetoric as they warned of "the fire next time." In a booming voice Rev. Al Sharpton sought to tie the unfortunate accident that had cost Gavin Cato his life with the 1963 segregationist fire-bombing of a church in Birmingham, Alabama, which had taken the lives of four little black girls.[22]

In the week that followed Brooklyn District Attorney Charles J. Hynes brought the case of the accident to the grand jury to determine if there would be a criminal indictment. Rev. Sharpton, who had already demanded an indictment, now insisted that a special prosecutor be appointed. (In the Howard Beach case Rev. Sharpton had urged that the very same Charles Hynes be appointed as special prosecutor. Hynes then went on to win election as Brooklyn District Attorney.) Kings County Democratic Leader Clarence Norman, Jr., went on local radio to express confidence in Charles Hynes. He promised his constituents to introduce legislation to make certain that blacks would receive an equal share of all funds coming into the district.

Hasidim were scornful of the calls for calm.

Now they're calling for cooler heads to prevail. Who contributed to all this anger? Clarence Norman. He tried to polarize the neighborhood as much as possible. (AF)

Hasidim were equally skeptical that something could be done to avoid similar problems in the future.

Impossible. As long as we have somebody like Sharpton around we cannot avoid it. An accident happens and he's looking for opportunities to create issues. As long as there are accidents and lawyers there are going to be ambulance chasers looking to make something of it. Ninety-nine percent of the trouble came from outsiders. If I were a black from Crown Heights I'd feel ashamed that these people came here to beat people and cause trouble. (MS)

On Labor Day, September 2, 1991, the West Indian–American Day Parade was scheduled to march along Eastern Parkway. The Hasidim were alarmed that the parade, which would pass by their front door, could be used to arouse tempers and could result in renewed violence. Some suggested requesting an injunction, but after further consultation and discussions with city and state leaders the Hasidim agreed not only to accept the parade but to send representatives to march alongside Mayor Dinkins. On the eve of the parade, David Gonzalez, a reporter for the *New York Times,* found the black residents calm about forthcoming events.

"We're in full control of this area. We don't want any of the outrage . . . Most of that came from people from different parts of Brooklyn."

He said the rioters were youths who were misled by organizers capitalizing on the dearth of viable local leaders they could relate to. "We need a strong black image to make names like Sharpton and Maddox dinosaurs," he said.[23]

On Labor Day the parade of colorful dancers, steel drum bands, and flatbed trucks stretched out for three miles along Eastern Parkway. The mayor was grand marshal of the parade and at his side were six Luba-vitcher Hasidim, who were fitted out with bulletproof vests beneath their black jackets. At the reviewing stand by the Brooklyn Museum the mayor was applauded for his call for mutual respect in the community, and Rabbi Shmuel Butman was cheered when he told the crowd that he had joined the march in the spirit of "brotherhood, camaraderie, friendship, and peace."[24]

In joining the West Indian parade Rabbi Butman and other Hasidim had tried to demonstrate their openheartedness toward other groups. They took a tougher line, however, to complaints that they were aloof and unfriendly in daily life. Reference to social style was no excuse for the riot that had taken place.

> There is an undercurrent of deep-rooted anti-Semitism—anti-white and anti-Semitic. There can be no excuse for rioting. We're fine. We're friendly to the blacks. We're a peaceloving community. No one is afraid they're going to be attacked by us. No one walking on the street has to say, "Watch out. There are two Hasidim behind you." We mind our own business. What does that have to do with murder and riot? There is no justification whatso-ever for lawlessness. In September 1989 a black driver was speeding on Kingston Avenue and Crown Street and he killed a three-year-old Jewish boy. Did the Jewish community take to the streets? Or put 158 cops in the hospital? Did the Jewish community turn a community into a battle-field? (SB)

Concerning the criticism that the Jewish community did not commu-nicate with the Cato family, Rabbi Butman was adamant.

> We reached out. We sent representatives to the family. We sent them a letter and flowers. Over the past twenty years there have been thirteen cases of murder of members of the Jewish community. Never did a black representa-tive come to a Jewish funeral, not of a Jewish child, nor of Israel Rosen. No one even said "We're sorry, we wish you well." (SB)

On Thursday, September 5, 1991, the grand jury declined to bring criminal charges against Yosef Lifsh. The grand jury, which was 50 per-cent black, 36 percent white, and 14 percent Latino, decided that the death of Gavin Cato, age seven, had been a tragic accident. In a public statement approximating his testimony before the grand jury Yosef Lifsh related how he had tried to avoid striking the children and had steered his car into the wall.

> Unfortunately, the car did not come to a full stop upon impact with the building but rather slid to the left along the wall until it reached the children . . . the first thing I did was try and lift the car [to release the two children pinned underneath].

He told how the crowd had beaten and robbed him.

From the moment this tragedy befell the Cato family, I have wanted to personally extend my condolences and deep regrets to them. I have been told not to do this—that it is unsafe to do this.[25]

In the aftermath of the riot the newspaper *New York Newsday* undertook to investigate whether the perception of favoritism to Hasidic Jews was supported by facts.

A *New York Newsday* analysis, based on dozens of interviews and an examination of city and state budget documents and contracts, found little evidence of overt government favoritism in terms of dollars for the Crown Heights Lubavitch Jewish community—whether the field is subsidized housing, street repaving, economic revitalization or youth and social programs.[26]

The article continued that the charge trumpeted by Rev. Herbert Daughtry and other black activists of a Hasidic community "abusing their power in collusion with city officials" still persisted, "but an analysis of spending in the areas of Community Boards 8 and 9 shows that accusations of preferential treatment in terms of dollars for the Crown Heights Lubavitch Jewish community are hard to sustain."

The *Newsday* report did assert that in the past the Hasidim had had more political influence, and it cited contemporary irritants such as temporary street closings, double parking by 770 Eastern Parkway, and the wailing siren sounded to signal the beginning of the Shabbes. At the same time the article offered considerable evidence to support the view that the black community was reaping most of the rewards offered by city, state, and federal agencies in correspondence to the size of its needy population. Of the 823 city-subsidized housing units built in Crown Heights between 1986 and 1991, 87.1 percent had gone to blacks and only 5.7 percent to whites. In South Crown Heights, where the Hasidim are concentrated, out of a total of 300 apartments only 43 went to whites. Of the fifteen job training programs located in Crown Heights and Fort Green, fourteen were in minority areas and only one was organized by Orthodox Jews. Similarly, there were six senior citizen centers for blacks and Latinos and only one for the Jewish elderly. *New York Newsday* also noted that virtually all of the youth programs in the area were for black and Latino young people.

As it turned out, Lemrick Nelson, Jr., the sixteen-year-old identified by the dying Yankel Rosenbaum as his attacker, had not been out to avenge Gavin Cato. It was reported in the *New York Post* that young Nelson nursed a grievance against the Jewish landlord of the apartment house on Linden Boulevard in East Flatbush where he lived with his father. Lemrick Nelson, Sr., was reputed to be a strict disciplinarian. Other tenants in the house had complained to the landlord of continual loud music played by Lemrick and his friends in the Nelson apartment. The landlord had carried the complaints to Lemrick's father, who had then laid down the law to his son. Lemrick blamed the landlord for getting him in trouble with his father, and the day after the confrontation he drew a Star of David on the wall of the vestibule and in the center he inscribed his initials. On August 19 Lemrick Nelson, Jr., was visiting a girlfriend who lived in South Crown Heights. As he was leaving his girlfriend's house he saw a gang of blacks chasing a religious Jew. He joined in the chase and, being a high school athlete, he was among the first to reach Yankel Rosenbaum. He heard Rosenbaum speak in a strange Australian accent to those who confronted him. Lemrick Nelson struck Rosenbaum again and again with the four-inch folding knife that he carried.[27]

For the general public the most enduring symbol of the Crown Heights riot was a photograph of a Hasidic man lying on the ground after being hit by a brick and then beaten by a gang of youths. His legs appear crumpled under him and his hat lies at his feet on a sidewalk littered with cans and stones. Crouched next to the man is his terrified, weeping twelve-year-old son. His father had fallen on him to protect him from the blows of the gang. Less well known is the fact that the injured Hasid attributed his survival to three local black men, who whispered to him to lie still while they deceived the gang of youths and urged them to run on.[28]

It is a given that for Hasidim events involving the community as a whole are seen as part of the grand epic of judgment and redemption.

> Everything that is happening now in this epoch has to be connected with the Messiah. Everything that happens leads one closer to the Messiah. The violence points toward the final battles, when the greatest darkness precedes the greatest light.   (SB)

For most Hasidim, however, the tragic death of Gavin Cato was an accident without specific supernatural cause or explanation. The child from Guyana had no tie to the Jewish past or to questions in Jewish theology. The aftermath of the accident, including the murder of Yankel Rosenbaum, was seen by the Hasidim as a social fact which repeated the tragic history of Jews lost in pogroms to mob rage and unreason.

Community and City Actions

Despite the predisposition of Hasidim to supernatural concerns, members of the community, black and white, immediately took some practical steps to reduce tensions and improve social relations. Rabbi Jacob Goldstein, the chairman of the local Community Board, named fifteen people to a Committee for Racial and Religious Harmony. The committee designed a poster of a white and black handshake with the message "Say Hello to Your Neighbor." Con Edison paid for the printing, and the poster was tacked up in stores throughout the neighborhood. The local public school initiated classes in intercultural studies. At the adult level Hasidic women were invited to join in an ongoing series of meetings in the Brooklyn Museum between black and Jewish women which were sponsored by the National Conference of Christians and Jews and the NAACP. The Hasidic women had mixed feelings about facing more black frustration and anger, particularly since the riots had left them with a sense of bitterness of their own. Nonetheless, they began a dialogue with a sense of optimism that at last a door between the two groups had opened. As one of the participants hopefully observed: "Maybe if I keep showing them that I'm a mensh [human being] . . ."

The Hasidim named an Emergency Committee to generate ideas and coordinate activities. The committee accepted a plan to bring black and Hasidic youth together on the basketball court, an idea initiated by David Lazerson, a Lubavitcher in special education, and Richard Green, the black director of the Crown Heights Youth Collective, a youth center and school. The two men, who were already friends themselves, proposed to improve rapport between the two groups through sports and discussion. By November a series of games and dialogues had begun, usually at Medgar Evers College on Bedford Avenue. The teams were integrated so that Hasidim and blacks played with as well as against each other. Although few Hasidim can play basketball, the games had symbolic value and illustrated the willingness on the part of Hasidim and blacks to get to know each other. The plan found favor with Mayor Dinkins, who tossed out the ball to start one game which was refereed by Deputy Mayor Bill Lynch. The participants reported that the camaraderie established carried over into the streets. As a result of their success Lazerson and Green planned other projects designed to create a spirit of harmony in the neighborhood.

Few expected wholesale changes in attitude. Not every Hasid or every black was in accord with these attempts to heal the breach between the two communities. Rabbi Joseph Spielman, the chairman of the Jewish Community Council, complained:

> All we're saying is let us live in peace. We have our own way of life and leave us alone. It hasn't stopped since the riots. Last night we had car windows smashed. Last week BB guns were shot. They tell us you're too closed. You have to have a relationship with the blacks. I don't have to have a relationship with them. These basketball games are window dressing to calm things down. It's not something we really want. We don't have to answer the question "Why are you so reclusive?" Because I choose to be. No one has the right to touch anyone else. (JZ)

At the same time black complaints about special privileges enjoyed by the Hasidim continued, Hasidic and official denials notwithstanding. To avoid any hint of favoritism, the city police clipped the wings of Rabbi Shmuel Butman, director of the Lubavitch Youth Organization, who had planned to light the giant menorah at Fifth Avenue and 59th Street in Manhattan on Hanukkah eve, Friday, and then fly to Brooklyn in a private helicopter before the setting sun ushered in the Shabbes. Pointing to the tragic accident that had occurred on August 19, the police declined to provide Rabbi Butman with the police escort needed to speed him to the heliport. The police suggested that a Lubavitcher Hasid in Manhattan could light the menorah and return home well before the lighting of the Shabbes candles. Butman was outraged by what he considered to be an insult to the Jewish community and possibly to himself; however, many Lubavitcher Hasidim agreed with the police. A Lubavitcher in Manhattan could indeed light the menorah and also avoid the unnecessary cost of using a private helicopter. It was an unnecessary conflict and Butman was criticized in the Hasidic community for exaggerating its effect.

In November 1991, facing cuts in funding in the Home Energy Assistance Program (HEAP), the city's Community Development Agency reduced the number of outreach centers which received applications from the working poor from seventeen to eleven. The outreach program provides grants of from $85 to $195 to help poor working families meet their winter utility bills. Hardest hit in the reduction were Jewish agencies. Six of seven Jewish community organizations were eliminated from the program. Included in the cuts were the Crown Heights Jewish Community Council and the United Jewish Organizations of Williamsburg. Their responsibilities in the HEAP program were turned over to a black agency in Crown Heights and a Hispanic organization in Williamsburg. The shifts moved the HEAP offices from streets with Jewish populations to streets with heavy concentrations of blacks and Latinos.

Sixteen City Council members, both blacks and whites, who represented the areas hit by the changes, sent a letter of protest to the mayor's office on December 16, 1991. They pointed out that "The only remaining office located in a Jewish community area is the HEAP office in Boro Park." Mary Pinkett, the black councilwoman from Crown Heights, said, "I hate to think that being Jewish means you can't get service." [29] After observing that as usual the most deprived ethnic groups were fighting each other for dwindling resources, Joan Gil voiced her protest: "Why take away services we already have? The idea should be to add to what we have in the community. Why not do more?"

The Metropolitan New York Council on Jewish Poverty and the local Jewish agencies felt the sting of being dismissed from a program that they had helped to initiate and administer. Rabbi Joseph Spielman, the chairman of the Jewish Community Council of Crown Heights, recalled that the Council on Jewish poverty had brought the federal program to the attention of the Koch administration around 1980: "At the time this program began this Jewish organization was the only grassroots organization here" (JZ).

To justify the changes, Commissioner Gladys Carrion argued that Jewish clients had been "accessing the program far in excess to their percentage of the poverty level. At the same time other segments of the population were not accessing the program [at] their rates of eligibility." [30] Claiming that applicants to the Jewish offices in Crown Heights and in Williamsburg were mostly whites, she observed that in a Jewish senior citizens' center in Williamsburg white families (who constituted 46 percent of the population) received 71 percent of the grants while Latinos (43.5 percent of the population) received but 25 percent. In Crown Heights, however, the city's arithmetic did not hold up: there 73 percent of the applicants who received aid were black, while 26 percent were white, and 1 percent were Latino. [31]

In a press conference on December 27 Mayor Dinkins defended the changes: "I don't think it is the commissioner's desire to decrease the number of Jewish applicants but rather to increase the number of others." [32] The mayor and the commissioner also claimed that the granting agencies in Brooklyn were now equitably balanced with four offices, one central office and one representing each of the major ethnic groups: one for the black community in Crown Heights; one for Latinos in Williamsburg; and a third for the Jewish population of Borough Park, the only neighborhood which still had a Jewish agency administering the HEAP program. [33]

To some observers, however, there appeared to be a strong political component to the actions taken, not only to please blacks and Latinos but also to strengthen the hand of some local politicians. The HEAP office previously in the Jewish Community Council office on Kingston Avenue was moved a few blocks away to the Crown Heights Service Center at 786 Nostrand Avenue, in a black neighborhood and near the office of Assemblyman Clarence Norman, the Democratic party leader of Kings County. To Joan Gil the change in the address was "a reward for the other side."

Rabbi Spielman's greatest concern was that other possible actions by city agencies would be still more threatening to the well-being of the community:

This is just the first shot in the question of area policy boards. If they should remove those funds the community councils will have to close up shop. This is a preview of what's going to happen to other programs that are also supervised by the Community Development Agency. The Area Policy Board allots $250,000 to the area and the Jewish Community Council gets about a third of the money. A cut will in effect close my agency.   (JZ)

A Murder in the Neighborhood

Violence brought anguish to Crown Heights once more on Thursday afternoon, February 6, 1992, when Phyllis Lapine, a Lubavitcher mother of four children, was slain. Mrs. Lapine was stabbed to death as she carried groceries into her ground-floor apartment on Lefferts Avenue.

When word of the murder circulated through the neighborhood many Hasidim gathered in the streets. Phyllis and her husband, Dennis Lapine, were baltshuves, relative newcomers to Orthodox Judaism. They had moved from Texas to Crown Heights in 1985 to be near the Rebbe and be part of the Lubavitcher community. Distress over the murder was sharpened by the knowledge that the renewal of Orthodox ties had had such tragic consequences. There was also fear that the killer would soon strike again. "Some Hasidim marched through the streets, chanting: 'No more welfare! Go back to Africa!'"[34]

The next day, Friday, there was a funeral procession to the Lapine home. A dense crowd of mourners gathered to register their sorrow and demand police protection. The crowd spilled down to the corner, where there were apartment houses with large numbers of black tenants. There the mourners were met with a barrage of bottles and rocks that increased their anger. A few news photographers, thought to be out of place in a crowd mourning a loss, were jostled. The Hasidim, some continuing to chant insults, marched several blocks to the 71st Precinct police station, where Reb Sholem Ber Hecht, chairman of the Crown Heights Emergency Committee, and others addressed the crowd, demanding police action to find the guilty party and to protect the community. The police had failed to find the subway killers of Israel Rosen in 1986, and while they had captured the murderer of Yankel Rosenbaum at the time of the riots, no other member of the mob involved in the slaying had ever been arrested.

The protest meetings at the police station were suspended for Friday night, but on Saturday and Sunday nights the Hasidim assembled again to voice their demands. On Monday an arrest was made. The police charged a twenty-three-year-old unemployed black man, Romane LaFond, with the murder of Phyllis Lapine. Mr. LaFond, a resident of Crown Heights, was identified by others in the neighborhood as someone who pretended to be a handyman in order to gain access to apartments. Since his release in October 1991 from a six-year sentence for robbery he had reportedly broken into several homes and assaulted women.[35] He was already under arrest on a charge of sexual abuse when police tied him to the murder of Phyllis Lapine.

The arrest had a calming effect on the neighborhood, although the charges would have to be proven in a court of law. The local residents, black and white, noted that without the intrusion of outsiders there had been little racial antagonism. Aside from a few individuals on both sides who exchanged insults, the Hasidim did not use the crime as an excuse to attack or demean blacks. No one labeled the murder of Phyllis Lapine an anti-Semitic incident. She had not been killed as a Jew but because she had accidentally confronted a murderer. The Hasidim focused their attention on insisting that the murderer be found and that police protection be increased. The murder had sent a chill through a neighborhood already traumatized by the summer's riots. "People could have faith in God but we're living in a harsh, brutal world" (AI).

· 28 ·

Lubavitch:
The Messiah Issue

The Messiah and the Rebbes

In each generation Orthodox Jews impatiently await the coming of the direct descendant of the House of David who will defeat the oppressor, rebuild the Temple, and reign in Jerusalem. They anticipate as well the war of Gog and Magog that will mark the coming of the messianic era. These beliefs are cornerstones of Orthodox Judaism.[1] Not even the Holocaust has broken the messianic faith of most Hasidic survivors.

Concepts differ on how the arrival of the Messiah can be hastened. One view asserts that when everyone in the community adheres to the Mosaic laws the Messiah will appear; another maintains that the Messiah will come when there is a complete breakdown of social control. The two ideas are not mutually exclusive. They exist side by side, one taking precedence over the other according to social conditions. In the Hasidic community, punctilious fulfillment of the commandments is based in part on the assumption that adherence to the laws will promote the coming of the Messiah and the end of the exile. Messianic fervor, however, has never gripped the entire Hasidic community as it had seventeenth-century Jewry, when Sabbatai Zevi's claims led to a collective frenzy of hope followed swiftly by disillusionment and despair. In fact Gershom Scholem argued that in early Hasidism messianic hopes were for a time neutralized. With messianism removed from the center of religious thought, greater emphasis was placed on serving God in exile.[2]

While Hasidism may have initially reduced the level of "high Messianic tension," nonetheless, the messianic ideal persisted in Hasidism in sustainable proportions from its inception.[3] A Messiah is said to be born in every generation, and from time to time some Hasidim have professed to know the identity of the Messiah. A number of the Baal Shem Tov's followers apparently regarded him as the Messiah, although the founder of Hasidism had no such illusions himself.[4] Among the early tzaddikim, Rabbi Nahman of Bratslav is said to have thought that he possessed the

soul of the Messiah.[5] The Rizhiner Rebbe too was closely identified with
the Messiah.[6]

> There is a Rizhin tradition that when the Messiah comes he will be from the
> house of Rizhin, because Rizhin is said to be descended from the House of
> David. The Rizhiner Rebbe had a *yikhes brief* [family tree] which traced his
> ancestry to Rashi [1040–1105], and Rashi is supposed to be a direct de-
> scendant of King David. There was a fire and that yikhes brief was burned.
> The Rizhiner, to pacify his family, said: "From now on the yikhes will come
> from me."   (IF)

European wars were frequently identified with the war of Gog and Magog which would herald the end of days and the beginning of the Messianic era. In the early nineteenth century Napoleon was identified by
many of the pious as the leader of the final battles before the appearance
of the Messiah.[7] In more recent times Hitler's death camps seemed certain
to bring on the end of the old order of the world, but the wave of death
washed up and then withdrew, leaving no trace of redemption and reward.

Accounts of Rebbes who fled to America tell of their waiting in hope
and despair for the appearance of the Messiah. Until the end of his life
the Stoliner Rebbe waited impatiently in Brooklyn for the Messiah to arrive.[8] Stoliner Hasidim, however, maintained that their Rebbe *was* the
Messiah but that God did not permit him to reveal it. Tradition also
linked the fate of the Rebbes to the appearance of the Messiah: the Sandz-
er Rov (1793–1876) had forecast that when the Rebbes die out it is a sign
that the Messiah will appear. When the sixth Lubavitcher Rebbe, Rabbi
Joseph Isaac Schneersohn, passed away in 1950 his followers were in
shock that their Rebbe had died without bringing the Messiah.

Present-day Lubavitcher Hasidim are not to be outdone by their predecessors, and they have prepared the next generation to continue the vigil.

> The coming of the Messiah is not a far-off thing. Our children talk about the
> Messiah all the time. They sing, "Let the Messiah come now." If something
> is scheduled for three weeks away, they say, "God forbid the Messiah isn't
> here by then."   (AF)

The Seventh Lubavitcher Rebbe

Rabbi Menachem Mendel Schneerson, the Lubavitcher Rebbe, is a man
of quiet intensity. In public, his followers can see the passion he has for
his mission to increase Yiddishkayt; in private, visitors sense his inner
repose. The desk at which he receives visitors is bare. There is nothing to
distract the Rebbe's will to provide help and direction.

In recent years the public and private images appear to have merged.
Until a decade ago the Rebbe maintained the practice of sitting up all

night several nights a week in order to meet with petitioners individually. Since then his strength has been husbanded for public appearances, and for the most part he responds to questions from his followers in writing only. His Hasidim rarely see him alone. Nonetheless, the Rebbe's energy to speak in public for hours at a time seems undiminished. His physical movements are contained, but a sharp half-stroke of his arm starts his followers into exuberant song, just as a brief word sends his youthful disciples off to reinvigorate religious practice and belief on the streets of New York and a hundred other places around the world.

The Rebbe has also altered the times and frequency of public meetings. A farbrengen is now held every Shabbes rather than only on selected Saturdays as was the custom in the past. Full-scale farbrengens have been discontinued during weekdays except for holidays; however, on occasional evenings after prayers the Rebbe offers a single *sicha* (talk) at a relatively short meeting.[9]

The Shabbes and midweek meetings are different in scope and detail. On Shabbes the Rebbe is seated with distinguished rabbis, elders, and guests at a long wooden table that stretches along one side of the besmedresh; during the week the Rebbe remains standing at his podium at his customary place of prayer in the southeast corner of the besmedresh. At the Shabbes farbrengen the Rebbe gives several short sichas interspersed with singing and toasts *(l'chaim)* offered to him by his followers over a glass of wine. During the week the Rebbe offers only one sicha; there are no toasts; and the long table remains cluttered with books. On the profane weekdays the Rebbe's words are carried over a microphone, and since the Shabbes laws concerning handling money are in abeyance, following his talk the Rebbe distributes single dollar bills for charity to each follower who passes before him. The midweek talks are carried by telephone satellite all over the world. One might expect that the most compelling talks would be offered on Shabbes, but that is not always the case. The impromptu midweek meetings sometimes carry the excitement of a specific event that moved the Rebbe to speak.

As the Rebbe enters into his nineties (he was born in 1902), in Lubavitcher circles the sensitive issue of who eventually will succeed him is considered an unseemly subject for discussion. The Rebbe is seen as a beloved father and not as a political figure elected for a term of office. It is unthinkable to ask who will be your father after your father dies—no one can take his place.

A Jew said to me—he is religious and of Hasidic background but with a secular education: "What I can't stand about Lubavitch is that other groups will readily admit that their current leader is not of the same stature as their predecessors of a hundred years ago or even of fifty years ago."

All right, we [at Lubavitch] recognize the deterioration of the generations.

But as the Rebbe says, even a dwarf can see farther if he stands on the shoulders of a giant, and if he's also a great man he can see farther still. And besides, the men of the past were great but they failed to bring the Messiah, but our Rebbe will bring him.   (AF)

The continuity of Lubavitch is pointedly threatened by the thought of a successor to their Rebbe. There is no candidate at hand. The present Rebbe is childless. His nephew, Barry Gourary, the previous Rebbe's grandson, is unacceptable to the Hasidim as a potential leader. He not only stands outside the movement, but he is an antagonist of the Rebbe and the court. In Lubavitch, as in all Hasidic courts, any thought of the Rebbe's demise is pushed aside with the hope that the arrival of the Messiah will precede the death of the Rebbe.

Present Hopes

There is always a crowd around 770 Eastern Parkway each fall during the month of Tishrei, the beginning of the New Year, when Rosh Hashanah, Yom Kippur, and Sukkot are celebrated.[10] The holidays bring the Lubavitcher Hasidim to their Rebbe in Crown Heights from all over the world. The Rebbe in turn uses the opportunity to gather his people, inspire them, and send them back to their assignments reinvigorated. Often the Rebbe uses the holidays to initiate a new program or present an inspired new idea. In 1989 the Lubavitcher Rebbe assured his followers that the coming of the Messiah was close at hand and only the community's lack of repentance delayed his arrival. It was not a new message, but there was a special earnestness and intensity in his appeal to their faith.

Not only do we have the capacity to permeate our lives with light, we also have the ability to transform the darkness of Golus [exile] into light.
This ability to transform darkness into light is especially pertinent in this year, 5749 [1989].
The kabbala states that each of the six days of creation correspond to one thousand years of the world's existence. We are currently almost at the end of 749 years in the sixth millennium. Furthermore, the year 5750 has been coded in Jewish writings as a predestined date of redemption. Ostensibly we are in the final moments of exile; the coming of the Messiah is not only imminent, it is actually due now. The Talmud states that the redemption is dependent on Teshuvah [repentance].[11] This may also be interpreted to mean that, in essence, the Messiah is here for our work has been done. We lack only Teshuvah for *HaShem* to *return* us to Eretz Yisroel.[12]

The Rebbe's followers are swept up by the Rebbe's enthusiasm for the coming of the Messiah.

The Rebbe says, "Let's go greet the Messiah. May we merit the day when he arrives. The clouds should come and take us to Israel. Great leaders should be resurrected. Every day he urges us—for thirty-five years, every day. We're overwhelmed with the Messiah because the Rebbe keeps us going in this messianic inspiration. He has given us the most hope that anyone has given us. You have to believe in the Messiah in your days and it's a possible thing to happen. Many Jews don't believe it to be realistic. The Rebbe has made it seem realistic. (BJ)

The actual coming of the Messiah, however, is perceived differently within the community.

In Lubavitch many think it's a miracle going to happen in a moment, but it's a process and not a moment. It's a war: light over darkness, purity over impurity. It's a process of understanding. The Rebbe is definitely a link. All agree that the Rebbe is a link, but so is every tzaddik, and every Jew. Every Jew has the spirit of the Messiah, every Jew is going to reveal the spirit of the Messiah. Each Jew has a spark. The Rebbe asks, "Why do we want to gather so many Jews together? Because with many sparks it is easier to start the flame." (BJ)

The messianic concern of the Satmar Rebbe made the State of Israel the focus of his talks and the target of his anger. As the State of Israel became stronger the restoration of the Jews in Orthodox terms seemed further and further away. In contrast, the Lubavitcher Rebbe restored to Hasidism what Scholem called "acute Messianism or high Messianic tension." [13] In the Lubavitcher Rebbe's talks the Messiah is virtually present but is just out of sight. His arrival is expected momentarily, and the vital tension is maintained.

The Rebbe doesn't permit a let-up. On the first day he became Rebbe he said that the goal of our generation is to bring the Messiah. If you ask, has the Rebbe spoken about the Messiah more than other Rebbes, the answer is yes. (AF)

The Rebbe, the Messiah

It was inevitable that some zealous yeshivah students of Lubavitch, like other students of honored tzaddikim, would fervently believe that the Lubavitcher Rebbe *is* the Messiah.

The Talmud says in Sanhedrin that various schools and students were asked, "What is the name of the Messiah? And each one gave the name of his Rebbe as the Messiah. The Hasidim of the Baal Shem Tov were hopeful that the Baal Shem Tov was the Messiah. What does this mean? The Messiah is not someone who is going to come like Superman and fly from out of nowhere. This is not a messianic movement. We all hope the Rebbe is the Messiah and we're optimistic. There really is no issue. Others with other Rebbes would say, "I hope not!" They don't have the strong faith and love and reverence. The Messiah is the perfect person, wiser than King Solomon. The only thing he cannot do is prophesy with Moses.   (AF)

Believing you know who the Messiah is makes it easier. Why should he come suddenly? Why are they still loyal to that belief? It gives us a lot of inspiration. It's like a horizon. You can see it but you can't touch it.   (BJ)

Some of the Lubavitchers guard against exaggerating their faith in the Rebbe:

We hope it's him. We hope it's anybody. Being a follower of his and knowing his righteousness he might be a candidate. He's one of the few candidates around. That's not the same thing as saying that it's him.

The Rebbe is preparing us for the Messiah, whether the Rebbe is or is not the Messiah. I don't preach to my children that the Rebbe is the Messiah. The Rebbe gives us insight and keeps us hoping for *Mashiah*. If HaShem had wanted us to know he would have told us. Asking who is the Messiah is an irrelevant question. The Rambam [Maimonides] said we cannot be carried away with prophecy. You have to carry out what you have to do.   (BJ)

Rabbi Yehuda Krinsky, the leader of the Lubavitcher educational programs and a frequent Lubavitcher spokesman, considers the enthusiasm of the students to be expected:

What's the issue? So what if the students think the Rebbe is the Messiah? What are they [outside critics] worried about? Yeshivah students have always thought that their Rebbe was the Messiah. Some students say that the Rebbe is the Messiah. There are people who don't believe. But we believe. And the Rebbe could be the Messiah.   (YK)

It is clear that Lubavitch is not a monolithic movement, and there are differing perspectives and interpretations, particularly on a subject so controversial as the coming of the Messiah. The faithful are ranged at different levels of knowledge and understanding, and there is a sense that the debate will continue without resolution. Many Lubavitcher Hasidim profess the belief that their Rebbe is the Messiah, and others hope but are less than certain about the matter. One Lubavitcher Hasid provided his own rough estimate of the range of opinion within the Lubavitcher community.

I would say that 35 percent would say that the Rebbe is the Messiah, and that 35 percent believe inside that the Rebbe is the Messiah but wouldn't say it. And 20 percent believe that it's not the person but the idea [that's important]. It could be the Rebbe but not necessarily. The third group are we here who work with the Rebbe. We have an intuition about the Rebbe, an inner feeling, deep within. We don't discuss it. It's not the same issue as with the other two groups. The issue is, what have I done today to bring the Messiah? How many people have I educated on the subject? That's much more practical. The theoretical issue is not going to help me.

We have one extremist in Israel who asserted that the Rebbe is the Messiah. He wrote a book and a song. The Rebbe told him to stop. "Think it if you must, but don't write it, and don't say it." The Rebbe warned him, "You're fighting me, you're fighting all the Lubavitcher Rebbes, and you're fighting the Messiah." Instead of working for the cause, he's fighting the cause.

The Rebbe doesn't think it's an issue. The Rebbe doesn't want to help you think. People came to these conclusions; they have to get out of it on their own. In Lubavitch people don't think about it. They go on with their lives. (BJ)

Criticism

In the Hasidic community at large the argument begins rather than ends there. Lubavitch activities have already aroused resentments that feed into any new controversy. Conflict concerning messianic pretensions is particularly explosive. Critics of Lubavitch in the Hasidic world complain that Lubavitch is promoting a "cult of personality." They scorn the ubiquitous photographs of the Lubavitcher Rebbe that appear on living room walls, in offices and stores, and in advertisements in the press for a televised farbrengen. Nonetheless, there is a steady sale of large framed photographs and paintings of the Rebbe in stores on Kingston Avenue and at other centers of Lubavitch activities around the world. The visual record now includes videos of the Rebbe's talks at farbrengens and at other activities.

Satmar Hasidim, whose beloved Rebbe died in 1979, point to their own relative moderation on the question of redemption:

We never claimed our Rebbe was the Messiah. We believed he was going to live to see Mashiah. We couldn't believe that he wouldn't live to see Mashiah. When the rebbetsn built the new house she said she built a room so that the Rebbe could invite the Messiah in. But the Lubavitchers say "The Messiah is here." (MR)

Extremist opponents of Lubavitch have distributed circulars with the bitter legend: "Who will be the next Rebbe when your Messiah Rebbe dies?"

Do these fervently expressed dreams and the beliefs swirling around the seventh Lubavitcher Rebbe represent a new messianic delusion? The issue was raised to the general public by a 1988 interview in *New York Newsday* provocatively headlined "Is There a Messiah in Crown Heights?" In an interview, Rabbi Krinsky was asked: "Is it true that many of [Rabbi Schneerson's] followers believe he is the Messiah?" Rabbi Krinsky answered: "Our sages teach us that the Messiah will be a human being who lives among us. We believe that in every generation there is a person who has the qualifications to be the Messiah of the Jewish people. I don't know of anyone around now more suitable to fill the shoes of the Messiah than the Rebbe." [14]

Rabbi Krinsky's comments were for the most part the litany of Orthodox Judaism, with the addition of special praise for his Rebbe. Two weeks later, however, an article in the *Jewish Week* laid out the threads of an argument based largely on the accusations and speculations of persons critical of Lubavitch. The article cited unnamed leaders of unspecified Orthodox organizations: "Officials of some Orthodox organizations said they interpreted Krinsky's statement to *Newsday* as a tantamount declaration that Schneerson *is* viewed as the Messiah, a feeling they see echoed by Lubavitcher Hasidim with increasing openness. 'This is the final proof that what we've suspected all along is true,' one leader said." The article argued that "Some Orthodox officials, from the 'modern' wing to the 'right-wing' and Hasidic, say a growing number of followers of Rabbi Menachem Mendel Schneerson identify the [then] 86-year-old Lubavitcher rebbe as *Mashiah,* the anointed leader whose appearance will herald the world's final salvation." [15]

The article listed signs and portents taken as evidence: (1) a belief that the seventh Rebbe in the line will presage the messianic redemption of the Jews; (2) the belief that Schneerson's genealogical line extends back to King David; (3) the fact that the Rebbe is childless; (4) the fact that no successor has been designated; (5) consternation over the construction of an exact replica of 770 Eastern Parkway in Kfar Chabad, the major Lubavitch settlement in Israel, as if it were a sacred shrine. Two other citations are of significant interest. One concerns a book published in Kfar Chabad to celebrate the Rebbe's eightieth birthday: "Entitled *The Anointed King and Complete Redemption,* the publication referred to the rebbe as 'chosen by *Hakodesh Boruch Hu* [the Holy One, blessed be He], as His anointed and the redeemer of His people.'" The last piece in this kabbalistic puzzle concerns the addition of the word *mamosh* (actuality) to the prayers for the coming of the Messiah in our time, which commonly conclude the Rebbe's talks: "Observers note that the apparently superfluous word in its Hebrew spelling (MMS) is the acronym for the rebbe's name, Menachem Mendel Schneerson, and is thus a Lubavitch code for identifying the Messiah." [16]

The Lubavitchers expressed surprise at the "evidence" collected. To them the construction of a building in Israel identical to the one in Brooklyn that has been the home of the court for forty-eight years is a sign of identification but not messianism. As for the Hebrew word *mamosh* and the supposed acronym MMS of the Rebbe's name, they point out that the word *mamosh* appears frequently in the *Tanya* of Rabbi Shneur Zalman of Ladi, the first Lubavitcher Rebbe: "They make a fuss that it is an acronym of the Rebbe's name, a code word. It's ridiculous. The Rebbe ends all his talks with the fervent wish that the Messiah will appear soon—*mamosh*—tangibly soon" (AF). The use of evidence based on signs and intuitions usually comes into play when the major figures and witnesses have passed away and little concrete evidence remains. That is not the case today. Besides, it is not necessary to resort to interpreting signs. Lubavitcher Hasidim are pleased to discuss the matter and willingly respond to a direct question.

Some Bumps in the Road

The year 1989 marked the fourth decade of Menachem Mendel Schneerson's leadership of the Lubavitcher dynasty. To celebrate the occasion, on April 13, 1989, a few days before the Lubavitcher Rebbe's eighty-seventh birthday, a caravan of forty "mitzvah tanks" (in this instance Winnebago Motor Homes), moved out from 770 Eastern Parkway in Brooklyn to spread instruction concerning the forthcoming festival of Passover. Each "tank" was outfitted with tables, books, candles, wine, cakes, and tefillin. Led by a police escort, the line of vans crossed over into Manhattan and drove up Sixth Avenue to Central Park South; after circling Columbus Circle the caravan headed south on Fifth Avenue and soon after broke up. Each camper headed off to park at a specified site around the area to contact Jewish passersby, provide them with literature, and point the way to fulfillment of the mitzvot. At the end of the day the yeshivah students who manned the tanks would do a report recording how many people had been contacted, the number of books and candles given out, and the kinds of questions they had answered. The students had been on other missionary excursions before, but this was a special occasion—the commemoration of a joyful feast celebrating the flight from Egypt, and a celebration of forty years of historic leadership. Some speculated that perhaps the time of the redemption was close at hand. There had been a special printing of 13,000 copies of the *Tanya* of Rabbi Shneur Zalman, and the Lubavitcher Rebbe personally handed out 10,400 copies, along with dollar bills to encourage the giving of charity, to each adult and child who passed before him. Later the Rebbe explained: "The reason we called even children to give the booklet and the dollar is because we're giving them the opportunity to grow up in an atmosphere that they can always cherish—the sweet cake, the sweet discourse, and the sweet dollar to make someone happy."

While the Rebbe's spirit and good will are much admired, his place in the world of politics has been questioned. In 1988 the Rebbe's image in the secular world of a tolerant and benign paterfamilias was shredded with his entrance into Israeli politics. In the Israeli elections in the fall of the year the Lubavitcher Hasidim endorsed the Agudat Israel party, which won five seats in the Knesset. Lubavitch also championed the movement to change Israel's Law of Return, which centered on the question of conversion to Judaism. If the campaign of the Lubavitchers and other ultra-Orthodox Jews were to succeed, the only converts in Israel to be considered Jews and automatically receive Israeli citizenship would be those who had undergone an Orthodox conversion. The campaign to change the Law of Return was particularly offensive to members of the American Reform and Conservative movements, who regarded it as a deliberate affront. The majority of Jews in Israel and in America were suspicious of this sudden grab for power and authority.

The issue of "Who is a Jew?" divided Jewry worldwide and split the political parties in Israel, with Likud supporting the ultra-Orthodox proposal (at least for the practical purpose of keeping a majority in parliament), and the Labor party maintaining strong opposition. Many of the leaders of the Modern Orthodox movement, believing that it was not possible to win this argument, advised a tactical retreat. Some placed the blame directly on the Lubavitcher Rebbe for fostering a growing split between Orthodox and non-Orthodox Jews. For their part, the Lubavitchers continued to see the issue as having great "magnitude."

The Rebbe had always drawn substantial financial and moral support from the community of secular Jewry who found Lubavitch a safe harbor of fellowship. This image had been abruptly jarred by the championing of the movement to change Israel's Law of Return. The leadership at Lubavitch soon became aware that contributions had fallen off sharply, workers in the Chabad centers were becoming embroiled in argument, and other educational programs were suddenly in jeopardy.

At a farbrengen on the first of the year 1989 the Rebbe addressed his emissaries *(shlikhim)* in the United States and in Israel directly:

> [It] is not the role of the shlikhim to be involved in these matters . . . Tell them it is their holy task to be involved solely in their role of spreading Yiddishkayt, to make the world civilized and a place for Godliness, in that to prepare the world for [the] Messiah. Do not get involved in matters not directly related to this work no matter how good and important they may be, and definitely do not get involved in debates or controversial argumentation.

Some in Lubavitch used the Rebbe's remarks as the cue to cut their losses, remove themselves from Israeli politics, and get on with the business of raising funds and spreading Yiddishkayt. In a short time, however, the Rebbe again became enmeshed in Israeli politics. In March 1990, Prime Minister Yitzhak Shamir's government fell after a parliamentary vote of no confidence. The coalition government of the Labor

Party and the Likud Party fell over the issue of terms for establishing peace talks between the Jews and the Arabs. The Labor Party expressed a willingness to trade land for peace, and the Likud Party refused to accept this premise. The following month the Labor Party failed to form a government when two members of the Labor coalition withdrew (with their resignation the Labor Party and the Likud Party each had sixty votes). The two members of the Orthodox Agudat Israel Party, Avraham Verdiger and Eliezer Mizrrachi, who had initially agreed to join with the Labor Party in a vote of confidence to form a government, withdrew their support after telephoning Lubavitcher headquarters in Brooklyn. Rabbi Krinsky was adamant that the Rebbe had issued no orders and had not spoken with the men. He related that before the parliamentary session Verdiger had called to inquire if the Rebbe's position against surrendering land had changed; after being informed that it had not, the two men dropped from the coalition.

The voting debacle drew hostile cries in both Israel and the United States. An editorial in the Israeli newspaper *Yediot Aharonot* expressed the general sentiment of the opposition to the Rebbe, bemoaning the fate of a nation that is "in the hands of a rabbi who lives in Brooklyn, who has never set foot in Israel." [17]

A New Direction

Events in the site of the ancient world brought new evidence of the final battles that would occur before the arrival of the Messiah. The summer months in 1990 saw real war come to the Middle East. On August 2 Saddam Hussein sent Iraqi Army divisions into Kuwait. To protect its threatened borders the government of Saudi Arabia gave permission for elements of the United States military to enter the country and mobilize the forces of an international coalition against Saddam Hussein. Israel also was now under direct threat and quickened its readiness. In the upper levels of the Israeli government there was a quarrel over the lagging distribution of gas masks. While Foreign Minister David Levy pressed for immediate distribution of the masks, defense department officials found that "panicky reactions were unjustified." The Lubavitcher Rebbe also urged calm. Readers of the *Jerusalem Post* in Israel learned that at his weekly farbrengen in Brooklyn the Rebbe advised his followers that "the events do not have to disturb the spiritual and physical peace of a single Jew because they are a preparation and preface for the actual coming of the Messiah." [18]

> The entire world is gripped with pregnant anticipation of the future. Our sages spoke clearly of such an era. To quote *Yalkut Shim'oni:* "In the year that *Mashiach* will be revealed, nations will challenge one another. The King

of *Paras* will challenge an Arab king . . . and the entire world will panic and will be stricken with consternation . . . Israel will also panic and will be confounded . . . [G-d] will tell them: 'My children, have no fear. Whatever I have done, I have done only for your sake. Why are you afraid? Have no fear; the time for your redemption has arrived!' Mashiach will stand on the roof of the *Beis HaMikdash* [Temple] and proclaim, 'Humble ones: The time for your redemption has arrived!'" [19]

After a long and careful buildup of arms, on January 16 the forces of the international coalition led by the United States launched their first air attacks against Iraqi forces in Iraq and Kuwait.

Families with children in Israel besieged the Rebbe for advice. Should they call their children home? Should people flee Israel? The Rebbe assured the families that their children would be safe. The Lubavitcher urged everyone not to flee. (Similarly, the Boyaner Rebbe was reported to have said that those who left Israel would hear of miracles but those who remained would *see* them.) Should they put on gas masks? The Lubavitcher Rebbe said that it was not necessary, as there was no danger, but that they should do so in deference to the authority of the government.

> The Rebbe says nothing will happen. There is nothing to fear. Other Rebbes are condemning the Rebbe for sending Jews to Israel. (BJ)

Three months later, on April 6, 1991, the war ended with Iraq's acceptance of cease-fire terms. The Rebbe's fame as prophet and seer had never been higher. The time for the Messiah to arrive seemed ever closer.

> Since August 1990 the Rebbe has been speaking of this. After the war with Iraq and after worldwide war the Temple will be rebuilt and the Messiah will stand on the roof of the Temple to summon home the Jews scattered around the world: the time of the exile is at an end. One half of the Midrash [*Yalkut Shim'oni*] has been accomplished—the war between the United States and Iraq. The second half of the Midrash is not accomplished yet— the rebuilding of the Temple and appearance of the Messiah. (BJ)

On Thursday, April 11, 1991, the Rebbe spent the afternoon at the gravesite of Rabbi Joseph I. Schneersohn, the previous Rebbe, and then returned to 770. In the evening, with prayers ended, the Rebbe remained standing at his usual place by the eastern wall. A sea of Hasidim watched him and listened intently as he began his sicha. They were soon startled by the words of the Rebbe: "With all the work that I've done I can't find even ten people who really want Mashiah. I'm speaking about this in public because hopefully if I talk about it maybe it will affect one, two, or three Jews who will be stubborn and will not agree to any substitutions other than Mashiah." Declaring that he had done all that was possible to bring the Messiah, he said his work had carried him to "futility and emptiness" *(hevel verik)*. It was now up to his followers to take up the task.

What more can I do?! I have done all I can to bring the Jewish people to truly demand and clamor for the redemption. Yet we are still in exile and, more importantly, an internal exile of distorted priorities.

I leave it to *you*. It is not sufficient to mouth slogans. It is in your hands of each of *you* to bring the ultimate redemption with your actions. Through your study and observance of Torah you can bring about the peaceful world of Mashiah.[20]

When he finished speaking a chant broke out in the crowd: "*Ad mosai?*" (Until when [will we remain in exile]?). The rhythmic chanting, customary when the Rebbe speaks of the Messiah, was heightened by an awareness of a new tone in the Rebbe's remarks and his call for a higher level of commitment. The failure to bring the Messiah was on their shoulders.

He never demanded so much from us as he did in this speech. In effect he said, "I'm finished and it's up to you." Each one of us has to work in this direction.   (AF)

The following Shabbes afternoon, two days after the Rebbe's evening talk, the Rebbe spoke at a full-scale farbrengen. As is customary there were toasts by individuals who raised their glasses to him and accepted his toast, "l'chaim," in return. It is an exciting moment for each Hasid in the crowd whose eyes meet those of the Rebbe. One of those so singled out with a toast suddenly shouted out that the Rebbe should reveal himself as the Messiah, but the Rebbe ignored his words. The Rebbe's gaze passed to another Hasid who jumped to his feet and shouted out a further challenge: "'A tzaddik decrees and God fulfills!' We ask the Rebbe to decree that the Messiah should come." This time instead of ignoring the uproar the Rebbe turned toward the Hasid who had shouted. "I know what my work is. Don't give me new assignments. I already said what work you have to do."

The Torah reading for the week pointed to "imminence of *Mashiah's* coming."

Parshas Tazria [Lev. 12–15] begins with the mention of a woman giving birth to a son. This is an allusion to the coming of the future redemption which is often described using the metaphor of birth. In particular, the birth of a son can be interpreted as a reference to the strength and permanence that will characterize the ultimate redemption, for this redemption will not be followed by an exile. In this context, the woman is an allusion to the Jewish people whose service will ultimately bear fruit in the advent of the era of Redemption.[21]

The Rebbe then suggested the practical steps needed to hasten the coming of the Messiah: intensify Torah study programs throughout the world, concentrating on redemption and the Messiah; carry out the mitzvot "in a beautiful and conscientious manner," particularly the giving of charity.

In the days and weeks that followed there were printed directives to give order and form to the new drive.[22] It seemed to be a repetition of the Rebbe's messages through the years, but clearly his followers felt that the words had been newly cast from a fiery furnace. Although Chabad's educational and religious goals were already carefully charted, many of the students and followers felt that for the first time their duties were clearly spelled out for them.

> Some of us now feel it stronger than ever once the issue is brought out. For some people when they are pushed the easy way out is to call for the Rebbe to reveal himself.
>
> Now we know what to do. The Rebbe wants to see massive action to bring the Messiah: charity, learning, and getting people's attention concerning the Messiah. They should demand it, want it. Everyone should talk about it. (AF)

There was support for the Rebbe's statement from other Hasidic courts as well as from the general Orthodox community. Some two weeks after the Rebbe's initial pronouncement, "An Urgent Message" signed by rabbis and representatives of a number of Hasidic courts (including Belz, Ger, Skver, Vizhnitz, Klausenberg, and Lubavitch), as well as other Orthodox organizations, was advertised in the Jewish press. The suggestions in the message too were the traditional counsel to hasten the coming of the Messiah: pray for the Messiah, demand his coming, increase public study of Torah especially concerning the Messiah, and perform good deeds, particularly the giving of charity.

There was other speculation in the outside community concerning the meaning of the Rebbe's talk. Did the Rebbe's message and his cooperation with a range of other Hasidic courts signal a renunciation of a messianic role long attributed to him by his followers? Jonathan Mark of the *Jewish Week* found that the Rebbe had initiated a "new Lubavitcher world view," explaining that this is "the rebbe's most explicit refutation of those who say he is the unrevealed Messiah." His exhortation is to be "interpreted as the bluntest possible declaration that he has physical and mystical limitations and should not be 'bowed down to.'"[23] As proof Mark cited a rumor (circulated on the Sunday following the talk) that privately the Rebbe had expressed his opposition to talk promoting him as the Messiah and said it should be stopped. No public statement on the issue was forthcoming from the Rebbe.

There were other speculations. In his talk was the Rebbe responding to his critics or was he listening to another voice—that of his predecessor or perhaps his own inner voice? As he approached his ninetieth year, sensing perhaps that his mission was beyond his reach, had he contemplated a new approach, one long in gestation, to rouse his followers and ensure a measure of success? Nine days after his first talk, on April 20, 1991, the Rebbe saluted the United States, "this generous country" which helps Jews to observe the laws of the Torah and thereby enables them "to leave their inner exile, even before the redemption from the exile in the world at large." [24] Recognition of an inner awakening, as opposed to being a witness to a public event, would mark a revolution that would carry Hasidism to a new and broader shore. For the Rebbe the end of an inner exile surely meant the transformation of daily life so that Torah and charity are paramount for every Jew no matter in what land he resides: "the world of Mashiah is not a negation of what we are now. Rather, it is the perfection and enhancement of the very same elements which make up our lives today." [25]

That is precisely the role of a revitalized faith—to renew and uplift traditional belief. After the Rebbe's first talk there was a sense of heightened expectation and an onrush of activity. Whether or not the Rebbe's words had quieted the imagination of his followers concerning his future role remained to be seen. Increased discretion was no indication of any deep change, and thus far there had been no evidence of diminished hope that the Rebbe would emerge as the anointed leader.

> Beyond the renewed effort nothing has changed. Outside the community there are those who react critically and label us a messianic movement. We proclaim that the arrival of the Messiah is imminent and our critics object. What the Rebbe said was not a refutation. The Rebbe never said who is or who is not the Messiah. He does not want public speculation as to who is the Messiah. (AF)

The messianic preoccupations of Lubavitch and some other Hasidic courts seemed juxtaposed with ongoing events. As much as the war in Iraq, the ingathering of Jews to Israel from every part of the world, including the seemingly miraculous release and return of Jews in large numbers from the Soviet Union and Ethiopia, lent credence to the ancient prophecies. As a result, this concentration on the mythic idea of messianic redemption seemed less far-fetched than it would have in ordinary times. It did not seem to have hindered the Rebbe's rapport with returnees to Orthodoxy who had had a modern upbringing. Lubavitch still had the reputation of being the most modern and rational of the Hasidic courts.

There was another stir in the community when the coup in the Soviet Union began on August 19, 1991. Chabad Lubavitch had just sent over a contingent of young emissaries (and there was a sensitive dispute under way concerning the possible return of the Rebbe's library that had been confiscated seventy-five years earlier). Should their young people be recalled? As he had during the Gulf War, the Rebbe urged calm. He assured everyone that they would be safe. His followers were amazed when the coup ended on August 21 and Gorbachev returned to Moscow the following day.

> If you would live in Crown Heights you would see—the war in Iraq, the coup in Russia—and the Rebbe says nothing will happen, there is nothing to fear. The Rebbe called it a year of wonders, a year of miracles. (MA)

> The way the Rebbe speaks it's as though the Messiah will be here instantly. It's right here and now. It's literal. It will be in the middle of our talk. The Messiah will appear on the roof of the Temple in Jerusalem and summon back all the Jews. Of course the Temple isn't rebuilt yet. But the Gemara tells us that in the exile all the houses of worship and other holy houses are like the Temple in Jerusalem.[26] It's possible for the Messiah to appear at 770 first to gather the Jews there and other places before he goes to Jerusalem. (SV)

The year of miracles, 5751 (September 19, 1990, to September 7, 1991), called the year of revealed wonders, ended without the appearance of the Messiah. Rosh Hashanah, the celebration of the Jewish New Year, fell on September 8–10, 1991. Like a man surprised before a locked gate and fumbling for the latch, the Rebbe ran a series of familiar keys through his fingers. Utilizing acronyms, Hebrew grammar, and gematria (in which the letters of the alphabet are assigned numerical values and these values are used to find cryptographic meanings—which often are prayers for the Messiah) the Rebbe pointed to a range of juxtapositions that had mystical meaning. In the first sicha of the farbrengen he said:

> The beis in the letters of the year's Hebrew date also refers to the word Binah, "understanding." The previous year, a year when "I will show you wonders," shared a connection with the power of Chochmah [wisdom] (for sight is associated with that potential). This year complements that potential, drawing this influence into Binah. Thus, we will soon merit the revelation of the Third Beis HaMikdash [Temple]. And from the Beis HaMikdash, we will return to our homes, "every man under his vine and every man under his fig tree."
>
> There is also an allusion to the imminence of the Redemption in the two days of Rosh Hashanah. There two days are referred to as "one long day." Similarly, in regard to the exile, although it is extremely prolonged, in the very near future, it will be revealed how it was all merely one day.
>
> ... May it be G-d's will that together ... we continue this gathering at the ultimate feast to be served at the coming of Mashiah. And then we will "bless G-d for the good land which He has granted us," for Eretz Yisrael, as it will exist in a complete state. At that time, we will have the opportunity to observe the Yovel [jubilee] and all the other mitzvot that are dependent on Eretz Yisrael.

The closing of the first sicha, in which the Rebbe modestly deferred to the leadership of his predecessor, swept away notions, at least for the moment, that the Rebbe saw himself as the annointed redeemer: "And with the Previous Rebbe at our head we will proceed immediately to the Future Redemption." [27]

Melave-Malke

The women of Lubavitch organized a melave-malke to conclude the weekly Shabbes on Saturday night, January 4, 1992. A melave-malke is a time of tale telling and good humor. This celebration was to testify to the solidarity of the faith of Lubavitcher women in the coming of the Messiah. In tradition the exodus from Egypt was due to the righteousness of Jewish women.[28] From the Lubavitcher point of view, the generations, past and present, are linked, and the merit of women today can bring about the release of the Jews from exile and the redemption of the whole world.

Messianic expectations had continued to climb higher in the past year. In kabbalistic terms if each millennium since creation were considered to be a day, the calendar would be at the sixth day, Friday. This year was 5752, and only 248 years remained to reach the year 6000, considered to be Shabbes, when humanity would be expected to arrive at the golden age. The Rebbe had foretold that during the year 5752 miracles would be found everywhere. Seen in those terms the arrival of the Messiah appeared to be imminent.

The Rebbe was not present at the melave-malke, and other rabbis addressed the crowd. Rabbi Yoel Kahan, regarded as one of the geniuses of Lubavitch, was one of the speakers present. He was called the *Khoyzer* (the repeater) because for the last forty years he had memorized the Rebbe's Shabbes talks and repeated them verbatim at a later date when the words could be discussed or written down. Rabbi Kahan told of a Jew who rented an inn from his Polish landlord for thirty rubles a year. Once he sent his son to pay the rent. On his return the young man triumphantly announced the bargain he had arranged—three years for fifty rubles. "Fool!" his father retorted, "the Messiah is coming next year."

The Hasidim recognize the irony of the tale—after all, the Messiah did not come to Poland. They know that they must not fear being disappointed. They must not mind that their mystical ideas are often mocked as being naive. From a Hasidic perspective maintaining devout faith is more significant than having a sense of what the secular world terms reality.

Afterword

Some visitors to mid-Manhattan consider all Hasidim to be well-to-do retailers and diamond merchants, a view supported by press photos of opulent weddings depicting marriages between the children of Rebbes. There are indeed a number of successful businessmen who have become wealthy through real estate, retail and wholesale businesses, and manufacturing; however, most Hasidim earn modest incomes as skilled workers, bookkeepers, clerks, or computer operators, or are employed in the yeshivah system as teachers or bus drivers, or work in the kosher food industry. Each court has its elderly poor and families struck hard by illness and misfortune who are unemployable. Hasidim are severely restricted in the jobs open to them because of their exotic appearance and the demands of their religion (for example, the need to be home before sundown on Friday and to pray and rest on the Shabbes). Many lower- and middle-class wage earners have difficulty paying yeshivah tuition fees and are concerned about rent, food, and transportation costs. When there is a slump in an industry in New York City (such as the diamond or clothing industry) the Hasidim are among the first to feel the effects. Some families must rely on scholarships, charity, and hand-me-down clothing for their children. Despite this, rich and poor live together in close proximity without apparent rancor regarding wealth, in great measure because good fortune is considered to be a gift of the deity, and one that must be returned in the form of charity to needy individuals and support of the court's major institutions.

The Hasidim have to contend with other misunderstandings, such as the sentimentalization of Hasidism and the inability of outsiders to recognize their basic tenets: belief in the absolute authority of religious law, in the covenant between Israelites and God, and in the certainty of messianic redemption. Just as troubling are the views of those less sympathetic to Hasidism, Jews and non-Jews, who hold pietists to a higher standard than other men and fail to recognize that every community has its fools and wise men, its saints and charlatans.

Discord is an inevitable fact of life among true believers. Factional strife within courts, as has occurred in Satmar, is most common following the death of a Rebbe, when partisans of old and new ways may come into conflict. The various courts of devout pietists are frequently entangled in argument and dispute with one another, some of it deeply acrimonious and long-lived. Efforts of one court to control the direction of the Hasidic movement frequently engender hostility between courts. The arguments take both political and ideological directions: contention over rabbinical supervision of kashrut, control of the bet din, promotion of a particular philosophy, and the quest for disciples. Disagreement over the State of Israel has in recent years been the major stumbling block to the improvement of relationships between courts. With the death in 1979 of Rabbi Joel Teitelbaum, the older Satmar Rebbe, those Hasidim opposed to the new State lost their greatest champion. While pockets of opposition remain strong, particularly among some Satmar and M'lochim Hasidim, the din of dispute concerning Israel has been reduced along with a sense of impending crisis. The elder Satmar Rebbe passed away, the Messiah has not come, and life goes on.

Orthodox law and established religious myth support the concept of a redeemer who will rescue and restore the Jews from exile. Orthodox Jews believe with full faith in the coming of the Messiah. Conditions, however, are not conducive to a mass delusion, and the Orthodox maintain a quotient of logic, skepticism, and disbelief that enables them to live with the contradictions and ambiguities of the real and mythic worlds. The Gulf War in 1991 raised hopes that the final days were at hand, but passions soon cooled. While most Orthodox insist they expect the Messiah to arrive momentarily, if someone ran through the streets claiming that the Messiah was at the gates he would surely be regarded with pity or scorn. And if one Rebbe is acclaimed as the Messiah by his followers, most others outside that particular court are irked at the gall and the egotism of this pretension. Moreover, the Hasidic people are eminently practical. The salvation of the present generation is their primary responsibility. While they are waiting for supernatural redemption they have to provide milk for their children, food and housing, mikvot, schools, and centers for prayer and learning. Remedies for social problems demand continual attention; the expectation of immediate messianic redemption rises and falls with historical regularity and in response to crises.

The unexpected whirlwinds that have swept through the world during the past sixty years testify to the futility of trying to predict circumstances to come. Like the rest of humanity the Hasidim are beset by a variety of natural and social forces that will shape their future. Not the least of these problems is the population explosion that is straining the resources of the community. The rapid growth of the Hasidic population is due in good measure to their adherence to religious law concerning procreation and their faith in the Almighty's power to provide for them, as well as to advances in public health and medical care. Now and in the foreseeable future the Hasidim will struggle with other ethnic groups to find space, jobs, and economic opportunities for their growing numbers.

Isolated in the center of a metropolis, many Hasidim consider themselves to be soldiers struggling to defend a beleaguered fortress. Most frown on television, secular education, and liberties for women such as the right to drive cars, all of which are seen to encourage social mobility and independence and threaten to alter the balance of the family. Nonetheless, conceptual changes have taken place in the Hasidic world. Despite attempts to bar external influences, the American democratic system of individual freedom has had its effect in the general Hasidic community so that some individuals have gained courage to challenge authority. More grievances are being redressed in a civil rather than a religious court than ever before. Families who had endured in private the trials of raising a child who was physically or mentally disabled now openly seek help and join with others in similar circumstances to effect rehabilitation and education. In spite of long-lived prejudices, more mature women are completing secular studies and playing more active roles in the community. In these and in other ways there is a sense of dramatic change taking place among Hasidic people.

The number of those who have left the community since the Second World War is infinitesimally small, but some of the pious fear the possibility of negative change from those who should leave but remain, who wear Hasidic garb but whose lifestyle has changed and who no longer abide by the strict religious proscriptions. Some of the more curious and adventurous have had contact with forbidden pleasures. It remains to be seen whether or not in time a greater number of Hasidim will slowly cast off their ties and slip into a less demanding Jewish environment, much as did an earlier generation of immigrants. Equally unknown is whether Hasidism will continue to influence the religious life of the general Jewish community to the extent that it does today. Less likely is the possibility that the core of Hasidic belief and behavior will be tempered and lead its followers to become a moderate sect.

The behavior of their fellow Jews, religious and nonreligious, is of vital concern to the Hasidim, since punishment or redemption of the community hinges on the efforts of everyone. For most Hasidim this calls for greater insularity from the outside; for others, such as the Lubavitchers, it calls for dedication to reeducating the less religious. Secular-minded Jews will be misled if they expect an accommodation of views short of surrender to absolute Orthodoxy. And this is as true of the proselytising Lubavitchers as it is of the most adamant Satmar Hasidim. Nonetheless it is tempting for some to speculate that if tempers could be curbed on such explosive issues as Israel, a reconciliation could be effected between the Hasidim and less Orthodox communities.

In the spring of 1990 one of the leading elders of the Hasidim, Menachem M. Brayer, was invited to present a talk on the essence of Hasidism at the Fifth Avenue Synagogue, a modern Orthodox synagogue on East 62nd Street in Manhattan which is marked by an imposing stone seven-branched menorah near the entrance. An elevator took visitors to a small ballroom on the fourth floor. Inside, upholstered chairs had been arranged in rows to accommodate a hundred guests. The carpeted floor and the walls covered with embossed foil wallpaper provided a sharp contrast to the rough wooden benches, tables, and bookcases in a typical Hasidic shtibl. The audience was of course unlike one the speaker was accustomed to address at a Hasidic gathering: the men were clean shaven and unused to wearing yarmulkes outside of the synagogue. They wore well-tailored suits rather than black kaftans. Since this was not a prayer service, men and women were seated together.

The talk was spiced with Hasidic wisdom that seemed to dispel petty differences among men. It ended with the retelling of a well-known legend of the Mezritch and Rizhin dynasty. The tale is employed to bring to a close Gershom Scholem's chapter on "Hasidism: The Latest Phase," which concludes his great work on Jewish mysticism.[1] In the tale Israel of Rizhin recounts how in times of need the Baal Shem Tov "would go to a certain place in the woods, light a fire and meditate in prayer—and what he had set out to perform was done." In similar moments the Maggid of Mezritch, the Baal Shem Tov's disciple, would also go to that spot in the forest, and he would say: "We can no longer light the fire, but we can still speak the prayers—and what he wanted done became reality." In the succeeding generation Reb Moshe Leib of Sassov performed the same rite but with diminished certainty: he could not light the fire, nor did he recall the meditations, but the fact that he knew the woods was enough. Following him a generation later Rabbi Israel of Rizhin confessed: "We cannot light the fire, we cannot speak the prayers, we do not know the place, but we can tell the story of how it was done. And the storyteller adds, the story which he told had the same effect as the actions of the other three." In a concluding paragraph Scholem notes that the tale may signify decay to some and be a sign of transformation to others.[2]

One of the listeners in the meeting room later recalled a visit he had made to a small town in West Virginia, in the heart of the Appalachian coal mining region, where he was invited to spend Friday night, Shabbes eve, with the men of the minuscule Jewish community who lived there. The men, shopkeepers all, seemed to have settled in the narrow valley like trail-weary peddlers grateful to find customers in sufficient numbers. As if to restore an ancient balance, an Arab family also settled there and opened a restaurant and poolroom. They were far from New York or Cincinnati, let alone Warsaw, Vienna, or Jerusalem, but this handful of men had built a small synagogue where they had a minyan every Friday night and tried to maintain a sense of community.

The few Jews in the mining community also remembered their duty to give charity and do acts of lovingkindness. One good deed was to bring over a survivor of the concentration camps, the members contributing sufficient money to enable the newcomer to open a pawnshop, a small business of buying and trading that they understood and one that suited the haphazard economy of the valley.

Attending the synagogue in the mining town that Friday night, the visitor discovered that the men met in their little synagogue every Shabbes not to pray but to play poker. Their great transgression, however, had to be measured against their charitable works and community service. They carried out their duties as well as they remembered and as best they could. Like the tzaddikim in the tale, they had forgotten the full score of the rites and rituals required, but whatever they did continued to keep them together as a community. That was the way the visitor identified the tale with his own perceptions and with the varieties of the American Jewish experience.

Others in the audience at the Fifth Avenue Synagogue, struck by the spirit of the account of the Rizhiner Rebbe, were reminded of social adjustments and good deeds accomplished during their immigrant experience and that of their parents. To many in the meeting hall the Hasidic speaker, an elder scholar with a distinguished lineage of his own, appeared able to bridge intellectual and religious differences in contemporary Judaism. In fact the whole tone of the talk was so ecumenical in spirit that an older man in the audience asked the speaker for his view on the possible accommodation among the diverse wings of Judaism—Hasidic, Orthodox, modern Orthodox, Conservative, Reform, Reconstructionist, and secular. "How can we Jews get together?" he asked innocently.

The audience had warmed to the presentation of Hasidic wit and legend, and they hoped that the icy distance between the groups could be melted. The speaker's response therefore cut as sharply as a winter wind: "We will come together when *you* return to Orthodoxy," he said. "It is not up to us to moderate our views. You left us and when you return we shall be together once more."

Notes

Introduction

1. The three principles on which the world is based as expressed by Simeon the Just in the *Pirke Avot* (Ethics of the Fathers), 1:2. They serve as the guiding principles of every Orthodox Jew.

2. *Gemilut hasidim* refers to any act of lovingkindness which is done without thought of reward; *tzedakah* specifically refers to acts of charity.

3. A large percentage of yeshivah students earn rabbinical degrees; however, very few actually serve as rabbis in the community or have any religious or ritual responsibility. A diamond setter, sewing machine operator, salesman, or computer programmer may be addressed with the general title *rabbi* or *reb* as an equivalent of *mister*. It is even more common to use the title in greeting those who have religious duties—a teacher of advanced students, a *mashgiah* (overseer of food preparation), or a *mohel* (circumciser).

4. *Babylonian Talmud (B.T.)*, general ed. Isidore Epstein (London: Soncino Press, 1935–52), Moed Katan 16b. Support for this principle lies in Gen. 18: 20ff and Exod. 23: 7–14.

5. These powerful elements of Hasidic devotion are expressed in the doctrines of *kavvanah* (mystical intention or concentration toward God), *devekut* (devotion or communion with God), and *hitlahavut* (ecstasy). See Gershom Scholem, *Major Trends in Jewish Mysticism* (London: Thames and Hudson, 1955), pp. 335–336.

6. Samuel C. Heilman and Steven M. Cohen, "Ritual Variation among Modern Orthodox Jews in the United States," in *Studies in Contemporary Jewry*, ed. Peter Y. Medding, vol. 2 (Bloomington: Indiana University Press, 1986), p. 167.

7. When quoted in the text, informants are identified by initials. Full names or descriptions appear in the list of Informants Cited. Real names and initials are employed whenever possible, but for informants who requested anonymity, pseudonyms or the initials AI are substituted.

8. Martin Buber termed the Hasidic tale "a valid form of literature, which I call legendary anecdote." Martin Buber, *Hasidism and Modern Man*, ed. Maurice Friedman (New York: Horizon Press, 1958), p. 25.

9. See *Code of Jewish Law* (Kitzur Schulchan Aruch), ed. Rabbi Solomon Ganzfried, tr. Hyman E. Goldin, rev. ed. (New York: Hebrew Publishing Co., 1927), vol. 1, ch. 30, pp. 97–100.

1. The Dynasty of Reb Dov Ber: From Mezritch to East Broadway

1. Solomon Maimon, *An Autobiography*, tr. J. C. Murray (1888), ed. Moses Hadas (New York: Schocken Books, 1947), p. 54.
2. See Samuel H. Dresner, *The Zaddik* (1960; New York: Schocken Books, 1974), pp. 75–112.
3. Gershom Scholem writes: "The whole development centers round the personality of the Hasidic saint; this is something new. *Personality* takes the place of *doctrine.*" *Major Trends in Jewish Mysticism* (London: Thames and Hudson, 1955), pp. 344, 349.
4. See Jerome R. Mintz, *Legends of the Hasidim: An Introduction to Hasidic Culture and Oral Tradition in the New World* (Chicago: University of Chicago Press, 1968), pp. 189–191.
5. See Itzhak Alfassi, "Ruzhin, Israel," *Encyclopaedia Judaica* (New York: Macmillan, 1971), vol. 14, p. 532. Gershom Scholem rendered a stern appraisal: "the greatest and most impressive figure of classical Zaddikism, Israel of Rizhin, the so-called Rabbi of Sadagora, is to put it bluntly, nothing but another Jacob Frank who has achieved the miracle of remaining an orthodox Jew. All the mysteries of the Torah have disappeared, or rather they are overshadowed and absorbed by the magnificent gesture of the born ruler. He is still witty and quick at repartee, but the secret of his power is the mystery of the magnetic and dominant personality and not that of the fascinating teacher." *Major Trends in Jewish Mysticism*, p. 337.
6. In a tale of Rabbi Levi Yitshok of Berdichev, the Rebbe found that on Passover eve he could easily obtain contraband silk but not bread, since leaven is forbidden: "God in Heaven, look at Your children. Silk that the Tsar forbids, that soldiers search for and with guards at every post, can be obtained in unmeasurable quantity, but bread which is forbidden by Your commandments alone cannot be obtained." Mintz, *Legends of the Hasidim*, pp. 10–12, 242.
7. For examples in Hasidic tales, ibid., pp. 10–13.
8. See Joseph Dan, ed., *The Teachings of Hasidism* (New York: Behrman House, 1983), p. 63.
9. The Immigration and Nationality Act of 1924.
10. The province of Bukovina was returned to Romania after World War I, and was part of the Soviet Union after World War II.
11. Agudat Israel is the Orthodox association established in 1912 to oppose assimilation, Reform movements, and Zionism.
12. "It happened eventually during the Holocaust we sent dozens and dozens of affidavits to save some of them." (IF).
13. Ps. 105:27; 106:22.
14. The Council dealt with a range of problems, often unprecedented, sometimes

of a political nature, and tried to resolve them in accordance with religious law.

15. "It was only later on, much later on after World War II, when the influx of immigrants came and we had pride in Israel, that one felt at ease to wear Hasidic garb, to put on a yarmulke in the street, to even think of wearing a yarmulke when studying and going to school and college, or working with a computer or as a scientist at IBM or for a fancy law firm" (IF).

2. The M'lochim

1. Bernard Sobel, who did field research among the M'lochim in the 1950s, states that the Malach arrived in America in 1914; however, M'lochim interviewed more recently assert that the year was 1923, and the later date appears to be in accord with other evidence. See Bernard Sobel, "The M'lochim: A Study of a Religious Community" (M.A. thesis, New School for Social Research, 1956), p. 54. The different dates may be the result of confusing the arrival time of the Malach with that of his son, Zalman. Some explain that Zalman had to escape being conscripted into the Russian army (probably in 1914). It is also said that Zalman had left for America before his father, and that the Malach came to America when he heard that his son had become assimilated.

2. Letter from the Malach, ibid., p. 84.

3. Ibid., p. 81.

4. Gilbert Rosenthal, *Contemporary Judaism, Patterns of Survival* (New York: Human Sciences Press, 1986), pp. 27, 46–47. See also Alexander S. Gross and Joseph Kaminetsky, "Shraga Feivel Mendlowitz," in *Men of the Spirit*, ed. Leo Jung (New York: Kymson Publishing Co., 1964), pp. 553–569.

5. The actual title of Shneur Zalman's book is *Likkutei Amarim* (Collected Sayings), but it is generally referred to by the first word in the work, *Tanya* (It has been taught). The work, which first appeared in 1797, is the primary source for the Chabad movement. Concerning Rabbi Mendlowitz see Gross and Kaminetsky, "Shraga Feivel Mendlowitz," pp. 558, 566.

6. Sobel's analysis of the Malach's correspondence underlines the focus of his concerns: "In his letters . . . the Rabbi seems terribly concerned with two things: (1) his physical health, and (2) his sinfulness . . . most of the letters are dominated by these preoccupations . . . in many of the letters, there are references to secularism and what seems to be an equating of this concept with sensuality . . . there is constant and repeated reference to prostitution and sensuality. I believe these references, however, to be more an indication of the Rabbi's desire to draw sharp distinctions rather than of a personal preoccupation with sex" (Sobel, "The M'lochim," pp. 81–82). In letters 2, 3, and 4 in the appendix of Sobel's work there are ready examples of these points: "in reference to my health, which is a punishment for my sins, it is still the way I expected it would be, but I hope that G-d will heal me soon, both my sickness and that of the Jewish nation . . . If I were really worthy of ever reaching even a particle of truth, I would not have to request anything except atonement for my sins . . . To those who fulfill the Commandments

(mitzvot) of the Lord's Torah, the Lord shows His grace. His guidance is revealed in many ways. Those who have repented of the sins of their childhood are called *keepers of the covenant* and it is as if they had never committed any sensual sin at all: their hands are clean of blood" (pp. 85–86).

7. Ibid., p. 54.
8. Gross and Kaminetsky, "Shraga Feivel Mendlowitz," pp. 560, 568.
9. Sobel, "The M'lochim," p. 80. Today the M'lochim study the works of the first, second, and third Lubavitcher Rebbes. They ignore Lubavitcher materials beginning with the fourth Rebbe (Rabbi Shmuel, 1834–1882), since he was the father of Rabbi Sholom Dovber, who expelled the Malach.
10. After the death of Rabbi Schor in 1982, Rabbi Weberman continued to act as chief rabbi of the M'lochim.

3. Satmar in America

1. Lucy S. Dawidowicz, *The War Against the Jews, 1933–1945* (1975; New York: Seth Press, 1985), pp. 382–383.
2. Many of these were in the army, or in hiding, or had fled to the Soviet Union. See Dawidowicz, *The War Against the Jews,* p. 397.
3. Nisson Wolpin, "My Neighbor, My Father, the Rebbe," *Jewish Observer* 14, no. 4, Nov. 1979, p. 9.
4. Reb Jekuthiel Judah perished at Auschwitz in 1944.
5. The prohibition is based on law and folk belief. "Before his hand-washing one must not touch one's mouth, nose, eyes, ears, anus, nor any kind of food, neither in the place where a vein is open, because the evil spirit that rests upon the hands before washing is injurious to such places and things." See *Code of Jewish Law,* vol. 1, ch. 2, no. 4, p. 4.
6. Wolpin, "My Neighbor, My Father, the Rebbe," pp. 8–12.
7. See Mintz, *Legends of the Hasidim,* pp. 90–91, 126–127.
8. Other subsidiary organizations came into being. The summer camp Camp Rav Tov was initiated to continue work with the children during the summer months.
9. See David Rosenthal, "The Orthodox Approach," *Manhattan. Inc.* 2, no. 12, Dec. 1985, pp. 114–122. In January 1992, 47th Street Photo defaulted in its payments to Transamerica Commercial Finance Corporation and filed for bankruptcy protection. The company's financial situation had been weakened by a 21 percent fall in sales during 1991–1992 and by investments in real estate that had dropped in value during the recession. At that time the company was reported to have assets of $30 million and debts totaling $57 million. It had decreased its sales force by 20 percent to about three hundred. During this period of turmoil the company's stores remained open and conducted business as usual. The company intended to contest the judgment against it. See Stephanie Strom, "47th St. Photo Files for Bankruptcy," *New York Times,* Jan. 22, 1992.
10. See Stephen Charles Price, "The Effect of Federal Anti-Poverty Programs and Policies on the Hasidic and Puerto Rican Communities of Williamsburg" (Ph.D. diss., Brandeis University, 1979), p. 162; Bernard Weinberger, "Con-

fessions of an Orthodox Rabbi or A Tale of Three Bridges," *Jewish Life*, Sept.–Oct. 1975, pp. 18–19.

11. The war years had forced young people to function in extraordinary situations. In the postwar displaced persons camps some had acquired enough English to serve as translators. Others had organized classes, helped to establish kosher kitchens, or worked to locate children orphaned by the war. They were generally energetic and community-minded people, who once in America again adapted quickly to their new circumstances.

12. One leader noted: "I've lived outside the community for most of my life. That maybe has given me the background. My father is a Hasidic rabbi. It's just that I had no associates. I had no friends where I grew up. I went to school in the Hasidic community, but when I came home I had no one to talk to. So I associated with kids in the neighborhood." (ES)

13. In 1988 another weekly, *Der Zeitung*, privately owned by its editor and publisher, Albert Friedman, was successfully launched. It deals primarily with international and national affairs.

14. It was a requirement in past times for the Jewish community to act in concert to pay a fine, provide back taxes, rents, or fees, or ransom a Jew from military service, a child from a forced conversion, or a family from pirates or kidnappers. Even in recent times, the community was forced to pay exorbitant sums to avoid government crackdown in a Nazi satellite, or to win the freedom of Jews awaiting arrest or even already in concentration camps. In World War II, government officials in Romania and Hungary were reported to have received extensive payments, and even the Nazi SS demanded and received goods in exchange for Jewish prisoners.

15. For their part, federal and state authorities find some demands to be impossible to fulfill, if only for the reason that similar actions would be required for the entire prison population.

16. See "Agudat Israel," *Encyclopaedia Judaica*, vol. 1, pp. 421–426.

17. The criteria for recognizing the Messiah when he appears were listed by Maimonides: "If there arise a king from the House of David who meditates on the Torah, occupies himself with the commandments, as did his ancestor David, observes the precepts prescribed in the Written and Oral Law, prevails upon Israel to walk in the way of the Torah and to repair its breaches, and fights the battles of the Lord it may be assumed that he is the Messiah. If he does these things and succeeds, rebuilds the sanctuary on its site, and gathers the dispersed of Israel, he is beyond all doubt the Messiah." *The Code of Maimonides*, tr. Abraham M. Hershman (New Haven: Yale University Press, 1949), vol. 14, Judges, treatise 5, Kings and Wars, ch. 11, p. 240.

18. *Vayoel Moshe* (Brooklyn: Deutsch Printing, 1961), pp. 9, 47–49, 62.

19. Among them, Shimon Peres, then the Israeli premier, Israeli President Chaim Herzog, and the mayor of Jerusalem, Teddy Kollek. See for example; *New York Times*, April 25, 1958; Nov. 5, 1963.

4. Lubavitch

1. According to traditional thought a Jew always remains a Jew (with a Jewish soul) notwithstanding his level of identification and commitment. Lubavitch

seeks to awaken that "Jewish spark" *(pintele yid)* that is thought to exist in every Jew. The Lubavitcher Hasidim do not seek converts from Christianity.

2. The mansion was purchased in 1940 from a doctor who had used it both for his residence and as a private clinic.

3. Eastern Parkway, which was built in the 1870s, was designed by Frederick Law Olmsted, the landscape architect and writer who also planned Central Park in Manhattan. At present the city is struggling to restore the once world famous boulevard to its earlier elegance.

4. According to Shneur Zalman, these three faculties are said to comprise the intellect. In kabbalistic symbolism, they are the three highest of the ten *sefirot* (emanations of the deity).

5. The first Chabad Rebbe to live in Lubavitch was actually Rabbi Shneur Zalman's son and successor, Rabbi Dovber, who moved there in 1813–1814. Joseph I. Schneersohn, *Lubavitcher Rabbi's Memoirs,* tr. Nissan Mindel (Brooklyn: Otzar Hachassidim, 1956), pp. 1–5.

6. "Sicha of the Lubavitcher Rebbe," free translation, Blessings, 5747 [1987], pp. 13–14.

7. Military imagery is not unusual for devotees of Torah study. When Rabbi Shraga Mendlowitz of Torah Vadaat founded a yeshivah an hour's drive from the city in Spring Valley (Rockland County) in 1941, he tagged his dedicated and valiant students as "Torah-paratroopers." Gross and Kaminetsky, "Shraga Feivel Mendlowitz," p. 563.

8. Deut. 28:10, *B.T.,* Berakhot 6A.

9. *Pirke Avot* (Ethics of the Fathers), 4:2.

10. The Rebbe emphasized that every Jew should have some knowledge of Torah. Classes were set up for a great variety of people, students and adults. Stories, laws, and verses were recorded in various languages and made available for listening by telephone.

11. The mezuzah contains two protective biblical judgments: Deut. 6:4–9 and 11:13–21.

12. There are several costs incurred in making a home kosher. A blowtorch is used to cleanse the oven, while dishes and pots have to be boiled or purchased anew.

13. Lev. 19:18.

14. There are still other campaigns. In 1984 Chabad initiated publication of the *Mishneh Torah* (The Code of Maimonides), which includes the laws of the Torah in fourteen sections, so that every Jew would be able to follow the injunction to learn the Torah. The book can be finished within a single year if one studies three chapters a day. In a similar vein, the Rebbe is adamant that the elderly continue Torah study. He established a *kolel,* a study center, for retired men, and a "house of the wisdom of women" for the women. Just as young married men are paid to continue to study at a kolel, so too does the Rebbe ask that retirees receive payment for continuing their learning.

15. Ps. 140:14.

16. A cable television channel and videotapes enabled the Rebbe to reach a still wider audience until 1984 when broadcasts were discontinued. This use of

television is in contrast to other Hasidic courts who regard television as a source of dangerous sacrilegious behavior. While the Lubavitcher Hasidim do not normally watch television because of the shabby content of the programs, they maintain that modern technology provides important communicative tools. Television and other forms of communication are seen as the equivalent of using printed books instead of scrolls in the Middle Ages. They are able to reach a wider audience of Jews. In recent years the Rebbe's far-flung followers have been able to keep in touch with the Rebbe's talks through radio and telephonic communications.

17. A stronger drink is frequently imbibed by some at the end of the farbrengen. Every Shabbes those who are celebrating the dedication of a Chabad center or the promotion of a course of study leave a bottle of vodka or schnapps (brandy) before the farbrengen with the *gabbai*, the Rebbe's aide. The gabbai arranges the twenty or thirty bottles on a table in the besmedresh; toward the conclusion of the farbrengen he puts a little vodka or schnapps in cups for the petitioners so that they can toast the Rebbe.

18. This is particularly important if the farbrengen is held on a Shabbes or holy day when electrical recordings are forbidden and the court's remembrance depends on the remarkable memories of one or two men.

19. See Rabbi Yosef Y. Schneersohn and Rabbi Menachem M. Schneerson, *Basi LeGani*, ed. Uri Kaploun (Brooklyn: Kehot Publication Society, 1990).

20. "Synopsis of the Talks of the Lubavitcher Rebbe, Shlita, Shabbos Parshas Emor, 8 Iyar, 5749," Vaad Hanochos Hatmimim.

5. Satmar, M'lochim, Lubavitch: The Struggles between the Courts

1. Speaking at a farbrengen Schneerson added that "Any attempt to cast blame, for whatever reason, upon those who perished is shocking." This, Schneerson's most recent defense of the Jews who perished, was in response to the views of another long-time opponent, Rabbi Eliezer Schach, dean of the Ponevezh Yeshivah in Bnei Brak, Israel. Schach has maintained that the Holocaust was the result of God's anger toward the Jews for their failure to abide by the mitzvot and their falling under the spell of Zionism and the enlightenment. See "Schneerson Assails Claim That Holocaust Was God's 'Punishment,'" *Jewish Week*, Jan. 4, 1991.

2. One of the first antagonists of the Satmar Rebbe in the United States was the Klausenberger Rebbe, who openly supported the government of Israel. The dispute between the two courts dissipated when in 1959 the Klausenberger together with fifteen families left for Israel, where he founded a village and a hospital. He subsequently moved to Union City, New Jersey, where he established a yeshivah. Thereafter he spent comparatively little time in Williamsburg.

3. The Lubavitcher Rebbe's viewpoint concerning territorial rights is based on a Talmudic law concerning the Shabbes. If a Jewish border settlement appears to be threatened by its neighbors it is permitted to desecrate the Shabbes and take up arms in its defense. See *B.T.*, 'Erubin 45a. "Go and smite the Philistines, and save Keilah" (1 Sam. 23:4).

4. Sobel, "The M'lochim," p. 1, n. 1.

5. Lubavitcher Hasidim deny engaging in this kind of activity. They assert that they would attend Talmudic discussions and present their own point of view on the subject at hand.

6. Sobel, "The M'lochim," pp. 19, 43.

7. Ibid., p. 47. It should be noted that the M'lochim take umbrage at Sobel's description of feminine dissent within their families, as Rabbi Meyer Weberman notes: "A M'lochim woman never wanted to buy a newspaper and so that couldn't be true."

8. There are ten days of repentance at the beginning of the calendar from Rosh Hashanah to Yom Kippur.

9. Three passengers were killed; one passenger had been removed to a hospital earlier and is presumed dead; the leader of the assault, Lt. Col. Yehonathan Nethanyahu, age thirty, also perished. Thirty Ugandan troops were killed in the fighting, thirty-two others were wounded, and eleven Soviet MiGs were destroyed along with the terminal building.

10. Exod. 14:14. When the Israelites fleeing Egypt saw the Egyptians gaining on them they lost heart and were admonished by Moses: "Have no fear! Stand by, and witness the deliverance which the Lord will work for you today; for the Egyptians whom you see today you will never see again. The Lord will battle for you; you hold your peace!"

6. Families

1. In the previous century early marriage was often necessary in order to avoid the onerous military conscription. In the first half of the nineteenth century, the conscription laws of the tsars often meant twenty-five to thirty years of military service. Marriages between thirteen- and fourteen-year-olds were commonplace.

2. Samuel Heilman discusses the preparation for the nuptial encounter in "The Social and Psychological Underpinnings of the Hasidic Life" (paper presented at the Messorah Symposium on the Treatment of Hasidim, Meeting of the American Psychiatric Association, New York, May 1990). Heilman's research concerns the Haredim, the extreme pietists in Israel, but his observations hold true for the Hasidim in the United States: "The kind of guidance they give is couched in all kinds of homilies, biblical references . . . 'You don't need to worry,' the male would be told. 'It is something others have done before you. Abraham did it. Isaac did it. Jacob did it. Your father did it. I do it. Even the Rebbe does it.' If the Rebbe does it then once that is told that sort of demystifies it . . . What needs to be kept in mind . . . is that the physical is only secondary to the spiritual and religious character of the event."

3. "The daughters of Israel imposed spontaneously upon themselves the restriction that if they saw [on their garments] a spot of blood no bigger than a mustard seed, they waited for seven days without issue [before taking a ritual bath]. (Whereas the law demanded this only if an issue was observed three days running, during the eleven days between the menses.)" B.T., Megillah 29a.

4. Covering the hair of a married woman has foundation in rabbinic law. To

conceal a woman's hair, the crown of her beauty and erotic sexuality, is one way of mastering the *Yetser haRa*, the evil inclination, which the Orthodox believe exists in all human beings. There is nothing in religious law, however, requiring a woman to shave her head, a custom which goes beyond the edicts of the rabbis, or, for that matter, to wear a wig, a custom which came into vogue in relatively modern times.

There is, moreover, some ambivalence concerning the stringency of the law. Biblical verses refer to the beauty of woman's hair (Song of Songs 4:1) and to women dressing their hair (2 Kings 9:30); at the same time shaving a woman's hair was considered a heathen practice carried out to mourn the dead (Deut. 4:1; Lev. 21:5). See "Hair" in *The Jewish Encyclopedia* (1904), vol. 5, pp. 157–158.

Proscriptions concerning modesty are frequently tied to questions of male dominance and on occasion to matters concerning one's treasure. In the Talmud the causes for women to be divorced ("without receiving their kethubah," that is, without receiving the sum stipulated in the marriage contract), include a woman "going out with uncovered head" (a proposition derived from the ancient Babylonian Code of Hammurabi). However, "uncovered" can also be interpreted as "with hair loose or unbound"; see *B.T.*, Kethuboth II, 72a and n. 6; see also *The Code of Maimonides*, bk. 4, The Book of Women, treatise 1: Marriage, ch. 24, no. 12, tr. Isaac Klein (New Haven and London: Yale University Press, 1972), p. 155.

In past times in Eastern Europe married women wore kerchiefs or ornate bands to conceal their hair; wigs came into fashion in the late Middle Ages. The Hasidim follow the strict interpretations found in the mystical writings of the Zohar. There R. Hizkiah said: "Cursed be the man who allows his wife to let the hair of her head be seen." And R. Judah added: "The hair of the head [126a] of a woman being exposed leads to Hair of another kind being exposed and impaired. Hence a woman should not let her hair be seen, even by the beams of her house, much less in the open." In a reference to the abstemious customs of the Nazirite it is added: ". . . the grapes grow no hair nor beard, symbolic as it were, of the female, who has to remove her hair before having relations with the male, and who is by nature beardless." *The Zohar,* tr. Maurice Simon and Harry Sperling, 5 vols., vol. 5 (London and Bournemouth: Soncino Press, 1949), pp. 183, 184, 189.

There are sufficient ambiguities in customs surrounding the law so that today most modern Orthodox married women keep their hair and do not wear either wigs or kerchiefs.

5. The women of Lubavitch appear to have more standing and greater authority than those in most other courts.

6. On this point a Lubavitcher comments: "In Lubavitch the dictum 'separate but equal' would be more operative."

7. Boyan and Kapitshinitz: The Sons of the Rebbes

1. When the Torah scroll is raised at the end of each reading, it is encircled by a cloth which binds together the two sections of the scroll and prevents them from tearing. Here the tzaddik is seen as the living Torah.

2. Rabbi Israel is employed as a bookkeeper in an accounting firm.
3. Tearing one's clothing as a sign of grief.
4. The Rizhiner dynasty has two yeshivot in Israel, one in Jerusalem and another in Bnei Brak, with a total student population close to one thousand as of 1989.
5. There are other Rebbes of the Rizhin dynasty in Israel in addition to the Boyaner: the Buhusher, the Sadagerer, and the Vasloyer.

8. The Declining Years of the Satmar Rebbe

1. "The origin of this custom is not known and interpretations of its meaning vary. Many Hasidim see the *remains* as a opportunity to partake of something which the Rebbe had made holy and potent. Others hold the subtle view that the Rebbe takes from the food that aspect of it on which he subsists—its spiritual content (it is apparent to the Hasidim that the Rebbe scarcely touches the food and takes little interest in savoring its taste). What the Rebbe leaves intact in the food is its material content." To share in the remains represents the promise of increased material benefits, a better livelihood. Mintz, *Legends of the Hasidim*, pp. 96–97.

9. Lubavitch: Redeeming Fellow Jews

1. In addition, most Chabad houses have a free loan society which provides small loans to be repaid without interest.
2. The founder of the Chabad center in Irvine, California, expanded its program to include running a small shul and a preschool. Unfortunately, loans cosigned by local members were required to pay the rent and meet the payroll. After more than a decade of expansion supported by spiraling debts, the director of the center was forced to resign. He left behind debts estimated to be close to a million dollars and a number of disillusioned center members and creditors. The disappointed director explained, "To be honest with you, we were expecting a couple of miracles." Tom Tugend, "Chabad Emissary Quits under Cloud," *Jewish Week*, Aug. 30–Sept. 5, 1991.
3. See Rabbi Menachem M. Schneerson, *Likutei Sichos*, vol. 6 (Heb.) (Brooklyn: Kehot Publication Society, 1972), p. 276.
4. See Lis Harris's account of a baltshuve, "A Reporter at Large, Lubavitcher Hasidim," *New Yorker*, Sept. 16, 23, 30, 1985; later republished as *Holy Days* (New York: Collier Books, 1986).
5. *Wellsprings*, Oct.–Nov. 1986.
6. "Sicha of the Lubavitcher Rebbe," Rosh Chodesh Shevat, 5746 [1986], p. 19.
7. "Synopsis of the Shabbes Mattos-Massei Farbrengen, 2 Menachem Av, 5748, Year of Hakehel/Tismach," Vaad Hanochos Hatmimim.
8. The blech is a tin sheet placed over the oven burners to retain heat and keep food warm on Shabbes. Just before sundown on Friday the blech is placed over the stove top. The burners are turned on low and kept burning throughout the Shabbes, turning the blech into a hotplate. Food prepared just before

Shabbes is kept warm on the blech, thereby avoiding the necessity of lighting a fire.

9. Exod. 9:1.

10. Borough Park

1. See Egon Mayer, *From Suburb to Shtetl, The Jews of Boro Park* (Philadelphia: Temple University Press, 1979), p. 31.
2. Mayer, *From Suburb to Shtetl,* pp. 100, 158. Marvin Schick, "Borough Park: A Jewish Settlement," *Jewish Life,* Winter 1979, p. 186.
3. Egon Mayer, "The Boro Park Community Survey, 1982–1983," Council of Jewish Organizations of Boro Park, p. 6.
4. In 1978, according to a study by the Community Council of New York, 44 percent of the Jews in Borough Park earned less than $10,000 a year, while 20 percent, many of them elderly retirees, earned less than $4,000 yearly.
5. These dovetailed with other long-standing voluntary charities. Meals for the hospitalized and homebound are prepared and delivered daily; food is collected from stores, bakeries, and homes during the week, bagged on Thursday evenings, and then delivered anonymously to needy families for the Shabbes. A free first-aid and ambulance service was started by Hasidic men; a women's organization established aid for medical expenses and for necessary clothing and furniture.
6. See Robert D. McFadden, "70 Are Hurt . . .," *New York Times,* Dec. 3, 1978.
7. See article by Andy Edelstein, *Jewish Press,* Dec. 16, 1979.
8. Bob Kappstatter, "Order End of Sabbath Store Picketing," *Jewish Press,* April 1980.
9. Brian Lipsitz, "Boro Park Reacts to Attacks on Jews," *Jewish World,* June 13, 1980; James Harney, "Hasidim Told: Fight Back," *New York Daily News,* May 19, 1980.

11. Two Courts in Borough Park: Bobov and Stolin

1. He was called the Frankfurter because he had died in Frankfurt in 1923.
2. See Mintz, *Legends of the Hasidim,* pp. 204–211, 310–321.
3. First-cousin marriage is illegal in many states, but among the Hasidim it is considered to be a mitzvah, an act very much in keeping with the tradition initiated by the patriarch Abraham.
4. *New York Times,* March 12, 1977.
5. There was good reason for the move to Israel since the Stolin community there is more populous and active than its American counterpart. The court's printing facilities are in Israel; in addition to rare texts they produce a bimonthly pamphlet concerning historical writings and commentary.
6. The Stoliner Rebbe's new bride was Chaya Miriam Steinwurzel, the daughter of Rabbi Moshe David Steinwurzel, the rosh yeshivah of Bobov. Rabbi Moshe, however, was a follower of the Boyaner Rebbe, Rabbi Mordchei Shlomo Friedman (d. 1971) rather than either the Stoliner or Bobover dynas-

ties. When Reb Moshe died suddenly at age fifty-eight in December 1991 his body was taken to Israel and buried near the grave of the Boyaner Rebbe.

7. The Rebbe has tried to put to rest present and past disputes. A student in the Bobov yeshivah who wanted to publish a study on the conflict in the previous century between Sandz (the Bobover Rebbe's forebears) and Rizhin was reportedly invited to leave the yeshivah.

8. See H. W. Bomzer, *The Kolel in America* (New York: Shengold Publishers, 1985), pp. 73–79.

9. Bobov has not sought to duplicate all of the social services, mental health programs, and the prenatal and postnatal care developed by Satmar in Williamsburg. For social and psychological services, Bobov Hasidim rely on the facilities of the Council of Jewish Organizations of Boro Park, on OHEL Children's Home and Family Services, and on other agencies. Nonetheless, the Bobover Hasidim operate a wide range of traditional community programs for their own congregation—a free loan society, visiting the sick, a medical fund, and federally funded training programs. The range of activities is fairly typical: "We have a free loan society. Businessmen loan the money. They put in $5,000 to $10,000 and then collect donations. No interest is charged. The loan is usually carried for ten to twelve months. The average loan is $1,000 to $1,500. If someone needs a few thousand dollars it's usually for a short term for two months. Small loans are more common. No one ever asks for $5,000.

   "We have other kehillah organization activities such as visiting the sick. We also have a fund to pay for doctors and to help you get a doctor or special equipment and run it. We have summer camps in the Catskills for the summer. We run a Job Training Program, Career Development for Youth, funded by the U.S. government, where we teach computer programming. Before we had a program for diamond setting and watchmaking but there's no market for it. The job market has changed and people have worked in everything from lumber yards to plastics to knitting goods" (JF).

10. Rabbi Yonasan Goldberger, one of the Rebbe's sons-in-law, is head of the kolel for married students, while his wife, Devorah, the Rebbe's daughter, is responsible for the girls' school. Another younger son-in-law, Jacob Meisels, is the chief rabbi and leader of the Bobover Hasidim in Israel. Benzion Blum, another son-in-law, is the dayyan in London, and directs the Bobov institutions there. Barisch Horowitz, another son-in-law, at present is studying in the kolel. The Rebbe's younger son, Benzion, teaches advanced students in the Bobov high school and is being groomed to take on greater responsibilities.

12. The Succession in Satmar

1. Only three hundred Bratslaver Hasidim are to be found in the United States and Canada. A World Bratslav Organization, however, claims a worldwide membership of over three thousand, largely in Israel. One of the benefits of the Russian glasnost was to allow the Bratslaver Hasidim to pray at the grave of their leader on Rosh Hashanah, the Jewish New Year, as their Rebbe had

requested. In September 1989 it was reported that one thousand Bratslaver Hasidim planned to make the trip to Uman in the Ukraine. Lieb Berger, executive director of the Bratslav Organization, observed: "They call us 'the dead,' but we are alive and well. And with us lives Rav Nachman, whose writings and teachings we follow always." Ari I. Goldman, "Rosh ha-Shanah Journey to Hasidic Master's Tomb," *New York Times,* Sept. 27, 1989. See also Arthur Green, *Tormented Master: A Life of Rabbi Nahman of Bratslav* (1979; New York: Schocken Books, 1981).

2. These accounts were sometimes told in the form of dramatic dialogue between the protagonists. Of course it is not known how accurate these accounts might be, or even if such dialogues took place at all, but they focus on human issues and encapsulate the notions current in the community concerning the old rebbetsn and the new Rebbe: "After the Satmar Rebbe passed away there were certain conversations between the Szigetter Rov and the old rebbetsn. The old rebbetsn mentioned: 'Did you send somebody that the Rebbe should divorce me?' And also she mentioned: 'All the time the Rebbe was alive you waited to be his successor.' So he told her: 'If I wanted that the Rebbe should have a son, obviously I didn't really think about being his successor'" (YA).

3. One of the leaders of the community (RH) takes credit for inadvertently beginning this tale. He recalls that someone came to him with the story that Meisels had said the old Rebbe had given him the keys to the school. After listening to the account he then supplied the ending of changing the locks, a riposte which was now attributed to the Rebbe.

   In any event many regarded the account with skepticism: "I don't believe such an exchange ever took place. Nussen Yosef Meisels would never tell something like that to the Rov. It doesn't work that way. Because as soon as the Rebbe becomes Rebbe he has to be like a subordinate and he cannot speak to him in that way. If he would speak to him that way he wouldn't be able to become rov of the *kehillah* [community] in London. That's nonsense. It would be a kind of *hutzpah* to speak in that tone" (AG).

   Most people saw Meisels's posting to England not as a punishment but simply as a convenient way of dealing with an awkward situation. "Since they were always searching to find a rov for the kehillah in England, this was a perfect opportunity" (AG).

4. This was the case with the older Rebbe, so the rebbetsn still holds the deed for their home.

5. The *Algemeiner Zeitung* is an independent Yiddish newspaper with ideological ties to Lubavitch.

6. In 1956 during the Sinai campaign, it was said, the Belzer Rebbe fasted and prayed for three days in support of the Israeli army. Reb Aaron died the following year, and opponents in other courts blamed not the Rebbe but those around him for stage-managing Belz's rapprochement with the secular state. Nine years later, in 1966, Reb Aaron's nephew, Rabbi Issahar Dov Rokeah, then only eighteen years old, became the new Belzer Rebbe. Reb Issahar and his followers continued to cooperate with the Israeli government and to utilize government funds to support their yeshivot.

7. See Ari L. Goldman, "Behind the Fight of Hasidic Sects in Williamsburg," *New York Times,* Oct. 30, 1979. These accusations are vehemently denied by the Satmar leadership. See also Allan N. Nadler, "Piety and Politics: The Case of the Satmar Rebbe," *Judaism* 31, no. 2 (Spring 1982), pp. 135–152.

8. See Ari L. Goldman, "Police to Guard Israel Rabbi Due in New York Today," *New York Times,* March 3, 1981. The *Times* printed a photograph of the caricature mentioned.

   The public curses were matched by covert threats against those who extended a courteous welcome to the Belzer Rebbe. One example illustrates the kind of pressure applied. "When the Belzer Rebbe came to America my brother got a telephone call. In this building we have a man, Mr. K, who is a former President of the Union of Orthodox Congregations, and a rather rich man. He is not a Belzer hasid, but his brother-in-law is a very close friend of the Belzer Rebbe. And they asked this Mr. K to make a reception for the Belzer Rebbe in this building, and he agreed. So somebody called up my brother, and at first, very politely said, 'After all, you knew your father saw the Satmar Rebbe on many occasions. How do you allow the Belzer Rebbe, who is such an enemy of the Satmar Rebbe, to come to your building and to your shtibl?' At first my brother said, 'First of all he's not coming to our shtibl. And I have no control over what Mr. K does in his own private home. It's a free country. If Mr. K wants to invite Mr. X and Mr. Y he's free to do that. And although I and my brother might have something to say about our shtibl, I certainly wouldn't have any objection against the Belzer Rebbe coming.' It was sort of a decent, civilized conversation. When this man, however, realized that he wasn't getting anywhere, somebody else took over and more or less openly threatened my brother that something might happen to this house if the Belzer Rebbe would be allowed to come. Subsequently it developed that Mr. K didn't agree to have a reception. And that was repeated many, many times" (BP).

9. The Rebbe's third son, Leibish, is employed in the Satmar office, but he has no religious functions to perform. In past times he had been in the diamond industry. The Rebbe's youngest son, Sholem Lazer, was named as rabbi in the Satmar shul on 15th Avenue in Borough Park. Since it is a small congregation of about seventy members, it provides only a modest livelihood.

   The Rebbe has three married daughters. The eldest son-in-law, Reb Berish, was named by the Rebbe to be the rov of a Satmar shul in Borough Park. The Rebbe's second son-in-law was named to be chief rabbi of Satmar in Montreal, Canada, where he is in charge of all Satmar institutions. The third son-in-law settled in Monsey and at this time has not yet received any rabbinical post.

13. Politics and Race in Crown Heights

1. In the 1950s 90 percent of the 2.7 million persons in Brooklyn were white; the remainder were black and Puerto Rican. Twenty years later, in the mid-1970s, the white population had fallen to 60 percent, with the promise of the continued departure of whites in the decade to come. See Toby Sanchez, *The*

Crown Heights Neighborhood Profile (Brooklyn: Brooklyn in Touch Information Center, 1987), pp. 3–7, 27–29.

2. *New York Times,* Sept. 28, 1975. The murder of Israel Turner was quickly solved when a twenty-three-year-old black man was apprehended with the murder weapon in his possession.

3. *New York Times,* Sept. 30, 1975, p. 41. In its coverage of the incidents the *Times* had noted the dramatic shift in the racial makeup of the neighborhood during the decade of the sixties. Mendel Shemtov, the leader of the Jewish Community Council, however, minimized the statistics: "The racial change is not the problem. Basically we coexist in peace. But we definitely need more police protection." *New York Times,* Oct. 2, 1975, p. 43.

4. *New York Times,* Oct. 2, 1975.

5. The overall population of Crown Heights in 1970 was 222,868. By 1970 68 percent of the residents were black, 27 percent white, and 5 percent Hispanic. Ten years earlier, in 1960, the population percentages had been reversed: 71 percent white, 27 percent black, and 2 percent Hispanic.

6. Population statistics are taken from Sanchez, *Crown Heights Neighborhood Profile,* pp. 27–29.

7. Cited by Dorothy Rabinowitz in "Blacks, Jews, and New York Politics," *Commentary* 66, no. 5, Nov. 1978, p. 45.

8. Ibid.

9. Rev. Daughtry himself lived in New Jersey, where earlier he had been sentenced to jail for robbery and forgery.

10. *New York Times,* June 21, 1978.

11. *New York Times,* June 18, 1979, p. B6; Rabinowitz, "Blacks, Jews, and New York Politics," pp. 44–45.

12. At its inaugural three hundred black men, dressed alike in green jackets, became members of the Front by "snuffing out candles with their bare fingers and mingling blood in an oath-taking ceremony." Rabinowitz, "Blacks, Jews, and New York Politics," p. 46.

13. At the same time the Patrolmen's Benevolent Association held a ceremony nearby to honor policemen slain in the line of duty and to underline contract demands. They marched to the blacks' rally, where curses and insults were traded between the patrolmen and blacks.

14. George Vecsey, "In Crown Heights, an Uncertain Alliance Is Put to the Test," *New York Times,* July 24, 1978.

15. Rabinowitz, "Blacks, Jews, and New York Politics," p. 47.

16. Concerning Chevra see "City Council Report on Chevra Machazikei Hashcunah, Inc., 1978." The report, NNY-0696, was issued by City Council President Carol Bellamy. It is available on microfiche, Greenwood Publisher's Group, Westport, Conn. Funds for security guards came from the Law Enforcement Assistance Administration (LEAA), whose purpose was to reduce crime and whose funds were disbursed through the Criminal Justice Coordinating Council (CJCC), a local agency. The CETA programs were from Titles I and VI. Section 8 is part of the Housing Act of 1937 and the 1974 Housing and Community Development Act.

17. The Bellamy report stated: "More than 50% of Title VI work sites are owned

by Chevra board members, other private individuals, or corporations, in direct violation of the contract which calls for the rehabilitation of 'Chevra-owned work sites.' Thus, CETA funded enrollees are used to improve privately owned sites contrary to: the contract, regulations, and Chevra's own representations made when applying for these grants" (p. 6).

18. Maurice Carroll, "Black Supplants Rabbi as Crown Heights Chief," *New York Times*, Feb. 1, 1979.

19. Sheila Rule, "Crown Heights Gets 'Hot Line' to Avert Crises," *New York Times*, May 10, 1979. See also Sheila Rule, "Some Blacks and Jews Reach Pact on End to Crown Tension," *New York Times*, May 9, 1979.

20. See Sheila Rule, "An Air of Aloofness Covers Tensions in Crown Heights," *New York Times*, June 18, 1979.

21. Ibid.

22. Peter Kihss, "Two Rabbis Protest 'Smearing' at Trial," *New York Times*, Feb. 29, 1980.

23. Bellamy had previously cut Chevra from two federal programs for failure to respond to her questions and for "potential fiscal irresponsibility." *New York Times*, Dec. 11, 1978. The summer lunch program was not renewed.

24. See Tom Robbins, "Tales of Crown Heights: The Fruits of Harassment," *City Limits*, Dec. 1981, p. 14; Michael Power and Jennifer Preston, "Little Proof Inequity Persists," *New York Newsday*, Sept. 3, 1991, pp. 13–14.

25. Toby Sanchez, while carefully relegating some charges to the realm of rumor, noted their ill effects nonetheless: "For years rumors have circulated that Chevra harasses black tenants out in order to do a renovation and afterwards rents to only a token few black families. Such beliefs, whether true or not, add to the tensions in Crown Heights." *Crown Heights Neighborhood Profile*, p. 15.

14. Satmar and Lubavitch in Conflict

1. The break between Satmar and Lubavitch did not begin until the sixth generation of Lubavitch, with Rabbi Joseph I. Schneersohn (d. 1950), and the present seventh generation of Rabbi Menachem M. Schneerson. Their leadership occurred during the period of Hasidic immigration to the United States and the development of relations with the State of Israel.

2. *Al HaGe'ulah V'al HaTeMurah* (On the Redemption and Exchange) (Brooklyn: Deitsch Printing, 1967). The title is derived from the Book of Ruth 4:7.

3. Most accounts exaggerate the responses of the families. Jacob Cohen provided the most negative version: "They are Lubavitch and their parents are Satmar. Some of them put a *herem* [ban] on those boys and some of them didn't. It had to do with one reason: did they want to make trouble in the family, try to spread the word. That's what it boiled down to. Some of them had to break off completely. Some of them didn't. It depended on the behavior of the person. Some of the families disassociated completely with them and have nothing to do with them. Most of them sat shivah for them. Some are still on talking terms and some of them aren't. It boils down to if they are

trying to make trouble for their sisters and brothers, trying to influence them. That's the only breaking point in talking to them."

4. See Rabbi Shneur Zalman, *Likutei Amarim, Tanya* (Brooklyn: Kehot Publication Society, 1984), bilingual ed., pt. 2, chs. 1–3, pp. 283–295.

5. Lev. 19:27: "You shall not round off the side-growth on your head, or destroy the side-growth of your beard."

6. See the account of events by Lis Harris, "Lubavitcher Hasidim—Part III," *New Yorker*, Sept. 30, 1985, pp. 83–86.

7. *Daily News*, May 31, 1983.

8. In the press a Satmar spokesman made it clear that the leadership disapproved of the attack: "If the people who did this are identified as Satmars, we will deal with them in a manner far harsher than the penal code. Beard cutting is an abomination. It makes us all shudder." *Daily News*, May 31, 1983.

9. *New York Times*, June 22, 1983.

10. Mike Santangelo, "'Holy War' May Be Resolved," *Daily News*, July 6, 1983.

15. The Struggles between the Courts Continue

1. *Habina, Voice of Cult Anonymous.*

2. Jacob Cohen was born in Brooklyn in 1954 and spent a good portion of his early life in Crown Heights. According to Cohen, his father, who had immigrated to the United States from Hungary, first sent him to study in Lubavitch but subsequently sent him to the Yeshivah Torah Vadaat—the Orthodox yeshivah from which the M'lochim had been expelled four decades earlier.

3. See Exod. 20:4, 34:17; Deut. 5:8. The M'lochim in particular eschew even the decorative symbols that customarily adorn the cloth covering of the holy ark in the shtibl. The Lubavitcher Hasidim, however, argue that the face of one's teacher is a source of strength and inspiration. They cite Isaiah 30:20: "My Lord will provide for you meager bread and scant water. Then your Guide will no more be ignored but your eyes will watch your Guide; and, whenever you deviate to the right or to the left, your ears will heed the command from behind you: 'This is the road; follow it!'" They also cite the collection of photographs of many other Rebbes and rabbis in any religious bookshop and the now commonplace practice among young students of collecting and trading the photos of Rebbes much in the manner of baseball cards. "So why pick on Lubavitch?" they ask.

4. For example, of the Bobover Rebbe's move from Crown Heights to Borough Park, Cohen says: "The Bobover left because the Lubavitcher is there. They did missionary work with him and he didn't want to fight with them and so he left." There seems to be little to substantiate this account of the Bobover's move to Borough Park. There is much more support for the view that the Bobover Hasidim left Crown Heights because of the increasing crime in the area.

5. "Lubavitch: The Everlasting Court of the True Messiah, or a Troubled Empire About to Self-destruct?" *Habina, Voice of Cult Anonymous*, n.d.

6. The Lubavitcher Rebbe refrains from shaking hands with women, as do

most Hasidic and Orthodox rabbis. There is, however, no law that prohibits shaking hands. Refraining from doing so is regarded simply as a means of avoiding illicit thoughts and maintaining a state of holiness. A recent opinion on the subject by Rabbi J. Simcha Cohen was published in the *Jewish Press*, June 2, 1989: "The Midrash states that the imposition of safeguards (fences) to hinder illicit sex generates a degree of *Kedusha* [holiness]. (See Leviticus Raba 24 also Rashi Leviticus 19:1) As such, some may assume a stringency to prohibit any and all forms of physical contact between men and women. It would be in the realm of a safeguard to promote kedusha.

"Accordingly, since the very act of shaking hands is permitted by Halacha, and physical contact with women curtailed only as a safeguard, then, perhaps, so as not to shame or humiliate anyone, it would be permissible to respond to another's action [if a woman innocently proffers her hand]. What is evident is, that those who do shake hands with women should under no circumstances be presumed to violate Halacha."

7. Cohen says: "Today he [the Lubavitcher Rebbe] met with the ladies and spoke with them for three or four hours, and the other day he met with Shazar. Do you know what Shazar was before he was the President of Israel? He was the Minister of Immigration. The Jews came up to Israel through him and became irreligious. This man was involved with assimilating more Jews than the Spanish Inquisition. And he [the Lubavitcher Rebbe] kissed that person. Do you want to tell me that he cares for extending the Orthodox population when he can kiss such a person. The Lubavitcher Rebbe kissed Shazar."

8. Chaya Schneerson was the daughter of the sixth Lubavitcher Rebbe, Joseph Isaac Schneersohn; however, she was seldom seen in court circles. It was said that she was more worldly than most Hasidic women and had friends outside of the court. Cohen makes much of what was purported to be common knowledge—that the rebbetsn refused to wear a sheytl—although such matters were not discussed openly. Lubavitcher Hasidim have honored the memory of the rebbetsn since her death in 1988. Frequently cited qualities were her erudition and intellect. While recognizing her independent turn of mind they also noted her readiness to honor her husband and have his views take precedence over hers.

9. Cohen adds: "I had another catch—the Vizhnitzer. This was many years ago. The Vizhnitzer didn't want to look at the pictures. His wife looked at them. This was many years ago, eight or ten. He was totally opposed."

10. Irving C., an attorney: "During a break in the trial I started talking with one of the Hasidic kids. I said, 'Since when do the ends justify the means?' He smiled at me with gloating arrogance. 'Yeah, but they won't send a Lubavitcher to teach in our area any more. That'll teach them a lesson.' 'Since when does the Torah justify violence?' He gave me a gloating smile and he went off smoking a cigarette."

11. Joseph Caro, *Code of Hebrew Law, Shulhan 'Aruk*, Hoshen Hamishpat, Treating of the Laws of Judges, tr. Chaim N. Denburg (Montreal: Jurisprudence Press, 1955), vol. 2, ch. 26, 1, 2, pp. 330–334.

12. Despite the quarrels among their followers, the leaders of the Hasidic courts

from Borough Park, Williamsburg, and Crown Heights jointly visited Mayor Koch to ask for his aid after his election, as a Lubavitcher spokesman reports: "We worked together even after the big fight. We had demonstrations. We went to see the Mayor. We asked for housing, police protection—our needs are the same. But the doors are closed with Koch and with the administration. It would work but we didn't have any common thing to do together because Koch threw us out all together. There was no pie to share" (MS).

13. The Pupa Hasidim are a significant Hasidic group who came from Pupa, Hungary, and established settlements in Williamsburg and Borough Park, as well as Monsey, Jerusalem, and Montreal. At the time of his death at age eighty-two in 1984, Rabbi Yosef Grunwald, the Pupa Rebbe responsible for rebuilding the Pupa dynasty after World War II, was said to have approximately 10,000 followers. Rabbi Yaakov Yechezkhal, one of Reb Yosef's three sons, succeeded his father as the new Rebbe.

16. Family Problems

1. Women are required to wear heavy-gauge rather than sheer stockings.
2. See note 4 to Chapter 6. In Eastern Europe, in accord with rabbinic traditions, married women covered their hair; however, wigs were not employed until the late Middle Ages. Wigs were opposed by the early Hasidim for appearing too much like one's own hair. See Israel Abrahams, *Jewish Life in the Middle Ages* (Cleveland and New York: Meridian Books, 1958), pp. 281–282. See also Samuel Rappaport, "Wig," *Universal Jewish Encyclopedia* (1984), vol. 10; "Wig," *Jewish Encyclopedia* (1904), vol. 6.

   The negative power unloosed by failing to exercise modesty in covering one's hair can be seen in the Zohar. R. Judah advised: "Consider the harm a woman's hair brings about. It brings a curse on her husband, it causes poverty, it causes something besides to happen to her household, it causes the inferiority of her children. May the Merciful One deliver us from their impudence!" In contrast, for the wife who covers her hair "her children will excel all other children; her husband, moreover, will receive blessings from above and from below, will be blessed with riches, with children and children's children." *The Zohar*, tr. Simon and Sperling, vol. 5, 125b, 126a, pp. 183–184.

   Concerning magical and demonic power associated with hair, see Joshua Trachtenberg, *Jewish Magic and Superstition: A Study in Folk Religion* (New York: Behrman's Jewish Book House, 1939), pp. 31–32, 40–42, 196–197.
3. With the exception of a rare rebel, belief in the supernatural precepts is usually uncontested: "When I was young I lived at my uncle's house for a year. I must have been eight. Shabbes was the biggest bother because you couldn't do anything. If the other kids were bothered they didn't express it. They told all these stories of dybbuks and devils. I never believed in the miracles. That was always weird. As a child I used to think, 'Are they nuts or am I nuts?'" (AI).
4. Most Hasidim would not have a television set. This may say something about more liberal attitudes concerning television among the Lubavitcher Hasidim

One can also take a more indulgent view of those who have been away from the faith.

5. It is difficult to collect accurate statistics on divorce among the Orthodox because there are many independent courts granting divorces, and they do not maintain public records. A sample from the Rabbinical Council of the Modern Orthodox illustrates the rise in the number of divorces sought between 1969 and 1987: 219 (1969), 337 (1973), 459 (1975). With the exception of the years 1981 and 1984, divorce requests since 1977 have averaged over 500 a year. A little under three-fourths of the divorces requested are completed. These figures of course represent only one rabbinic court, but they do illustrate that at least in this court the number of divorces has doubled over the past twenty years. Of course this may simply be a reflection of the increasing Hasidic population; however, those closely involved in the process believe that other factors have accelerated requests for divorce.

6. It is estimated that the general American divorce rate for marriages made between 1970 and 1985 is 50 percent. Rates of divorce among American Jews are somewhat lower, with approximately one of every three or four marriages predicted to end in divorce. The percentages scale downward depending on degree of religiousness, with close to 50 percent predicted for the general Jewish population in most urban centers, while a quarter of modern Orthodox marriages are destined for failure, and divorces among the ultra-Orthodox will hover at over 10 percent. All the rates for divorce are the highest in the history of Judaism. See Nathalie Friedman and Theresa F. Rogers, *The Divorced Parent and the Jewish Community* (New York: American Jewish Committee, 1985); Jay Y. Brodbar-Nemzer, "Divorce and Group Commitment: The Case of the Jews," *Journal of Marriage and the Family* 48, May 1986, pp. 329–340; Greer Fay Cashman, "Making Marriage Work," *Jerusalem Post*, July 17, 1985.

7. According to Orthodox standards, a woman who does not receive an Orthodox *get* (divorce decree) from her husband is not considered to be divorced. Any children she might bear in the future, even if sanctioned by a new marriage in a civil court, would be considered illegitimate. Moreover, her line cannot marry into the Jewish community for ten generations. Since only the man is able to grant his wife a divorce, an embittered husband can refuse to accede to a religious divorce. This effectively prevents his wife from remarrying and having legitimate children in a new marriage sanctioned by Orthodox law. In some instances husbands have demanded a financial settlement in payment for a religious divorce. In Israel the rabbinical court can order a husband to grant a *get*. In the United States rabbinical courts have no such authority. On occasion some families have taken matters into their own hands. Five Hasidim were indicted for kidnapping and beating a fellow Hasid who had refused to grant his wife a divorce (*New York Times,* May 16, 1973). It is estimated that there are some 15,000 women who have obtained civil divorces but are unable to obtain a religious *get*. To help women obtain religious divorces a new organization was formed: GET, Getting Equitable Treatment. The organization promotes education on the problem and investigates cases brought to its attention. Its major weapon is public shame,

and on occasion its members have picketed the home of the recalcitrant husband to force him to take action. A bill passed in the New York State Legislature in 1987 established that the party suing for the annulment or divorce must remove all barriers to prevent the other person from remarrying. This does not resolve the matter, however, when the husband is the defendant. In New Jersey in 1988 a trial court ruled against a husband who had refused to give his ex-wife a *get* on First Amendment grounds. The former husband had demanded that his ex-wife establish a $25,000 trust fund in his daughter's name as a prerequisite to his securing a *get*. The court found that the husband's actions were bound by their written marriage contract, the *ketubbah,* and the Mosaic law. "Accordingly, it says, where the parties have divorced under civil law and the husband has remarried in a civil service, he must take steps to release his former wife from the ketubbah." *Family Law Reporter,* April 5, 1988, pp. 14, 22.

17. Before the Supreme Court

1. Both Satmar and Lubavitch were represented by Nathan Lewin of the Washington, D.C., firm of Miller Cassidy Larroca & Lewin. Nathan Lewin is himself an Orthodox Jew and a graduate of Yeshivah University. He handled the voting rights case without charge.

2. In 1968, when redistricting brought Williamsburg into the same congressional district as Brooklyn Heights, reformers in the Democratic party saw an opportunity to unseat Rooney. The Democratic candidate, Frederick W. Richmond, made the mistake of promoting his Jewishness by passing out prayer books. The notion that they could be bought by a chauvinist appeal cost him support in the Hasidic community. Nor did Richmond's religious activity square with other aspects of his life. A few days before the primary election the political professionals at the Seneca Club circulated a wedding photograph showing Richmond and his gentile bride leaving church. Hasidic support brought Rooney a narrow victory at the polls. See Price, "The Effect of Federal Anti-Poverty Programs and Policies on the Hasidic and Puerto Rican Communities of Williamsburg," pp. 104, 107, 110–111, 170–178.

3. Lowenstein had lost his seat in Congress when Republican state leaders gerrymandered his Long Island district out of existence.

4. Price "Effect of Federal Programs," pp. 188–197; *New York Times,* Oct. 8, 1972.

5. Price, p. 110.

6. *The United States Law Week,* extra ed. no. 1, Supreme Court Opinions, vol. 45, no. 33, March 1, 1977, pp. 4228–4229.

7. *New York Times,* March 2, 1977.

8. Liepa Friedman had died five years earlier in 1972.

9. Menachem M. Schneerson, "Chanukah, Growing Older and Wiser," *Wellsprings* no. 14 (vol. 3, no. 2), Dec.–Jan. 1986/87, p. 3.

10. See Linda Greenhouse, "Religious Displays," and "Court Opinions on Religious Displays," *New York Times,* July 4, 1989.

11. In contrast to Blackmun's view, Justice Brennan found that "The city's erec-

tion alongside the Christmas tree of the symbol of a relatively minor Jewish religious holiday, far from conveying the city's secular recognition of different traditions for celebrating the winter holiday season or a message of pluralism and freedom of belief, has the effect of promoting a Christianized version of Judaism." Greenhouse, "Court Opinions on Religious Displays."

12. These include the American Jewish Congress, the American Jewish Committee, the Union of American Hebrew Congregations, and the Anti-Defamation League of B'nai Brith.

13. *New York Times,* Dec. 30, 1989.

14. Susan Birnbaum, "Lubavitch Menorah Placement Faces Supreme Court Challenge," *Jewish Week,* Dec. 30, 1988, p. 18.

15. David Friedman, "Jewish Groups Hail Ban on Menorah in Public Park," *Jewish Week,* June 22, 1990.

16. Nathan Lewin, "The Case for Menorahs on Public Property," *Jewish Week,* Nov. 29–Dec. 5, 1991, p. 28.

17. Allan Nadler, "Lubavitchers Setting Fire to Wall of Separation," *Jewish Week,* Nov. 29–Dec. 5, 1991, pp. 47, 28. On earlier occasions Nadler criticized the Lubavitcher Rebbe for hewing to the belief that the return of any portion of conquered territory to the Arabs is contrary to rabbinic law (thereby preventing the formation of a Labor government), and for his insistence on Orthodox prerogatives concerning Israel's Law of Return. See Allan Nadler, "From Zion, Not from Brooklyn," *New York Times,* April 14, 1990. At the time Nadler was the rabbi of a congregation in Montreal and taught courses in Jewish studies at McGill University. He recounted the critical responses that followed in "The Demise of Modern Orthodoxy," *Baltimore Jewish Times,* July 20, 1990, pp. 8–10.

18. Nadler, "Wall of Separation," p. 28.

19. Ibid., p. 47.

18. New Square: Shtetl and Suburb

1. Skver (or Skvira) is a town near Kiev in the Ukraine.

2. See Richard Laudor, "In New Square, Tradition Reigns," *Journal News* (Rockland County, N.Y.), Aug. 1, 1982. Rumors concerning the Hasidim expressed fear that they would be dirty and unkempt and would not care for their community. At the hearing "Judge Kelly said he had visited the area and any group which would name their streets after the Presidents [Roosevelt, Adams, Washington, Lincoln, Cleveland, Harrison, Taft, Jefferson, Truman, Eisenhower, Wilson] are patriotic Americans." See also Daniel D. Alexander, "Political Influence of the Resident Hasidic Community on the East Ramapo Central School District" (Ph.D. diss., New York University, 1982), p. 48.

3. See Mintz, *Legends of the Hasidim,* pp. 43–47; James Feron, "New Square: Poorest, but Its Hasidim Do Not Live by Bread Alone," *New York Times,* July 18, 1975.

4. "County Still Picking up the Tab for 1969 New Square Tax Bill," *Journal News,* Dec. 10, 1979.

5. See articles by Kevin Coupe and Thomas Maier in the *Journal News,* Dec.

10, 12, 26, 1979; Jan. 11, 16, 21, 1980. The price paid by the original operators to regain the property was $110,000. The $30,000 collected in rent
money was said to be included in the total fee.

6. Alexander, "Political Influence," pp. 157–180.

7. Beginning in 1979 the village received grants from the federal Small Cities
program and Community Development Program to encourage the growth of
industry and employment. The Department of Housing and Urban Development provided funds for low-interest loans to finance a professional building
on Highway 45 and a hotel-motel inside the village. With a loan from the
state Housing Finance Agency, New Square built a 45-unit low-cost housing
complex for newly married couples, and, with aid from HUD, a community
center adjacent to the low-cost housing. See David Colton, "New Square
Gets Fed Grant to Build Offices, Motel-Hotel," *Journal News,* Aug. 10,
1980. See "New Square Gets Funds for Own Community Center," ibid.,
March 2, 1984.

8. Over the past several years the birth rate has averaged 50 boys and 50 girls
each year.

9. In 1986 the yeshivah had an enrollment of over 1,000, including 250 children bused in from Monsey.

10. According to the 1970 census the per capita income in New Square was
$962 a year. This statistic is influenced by the high number of children in
each family. See Feron, "New Square: Poorest, but Its Hasidim Do Not Live
by Bread Alone."

11. See Kevin McCoy, "Little Changes in New Square, Per Capita Remains
State's Lowest," *Journal News,* March 13, 1983. In 1984 President Reagan
designated the Hasidic Jews of Rockland County a disadvantaged minority.
This made them eligible to participate in programs encouraging minority
businesses. "Hasidim Labeled as Disadvantaged," *Journal News,* June 28,
1984.

12. Divorce rates are consistently low. In 1984, too, only one couple divorced.
They had been married for nine years and had three children.

13. Even before the introduction of the kolel a few married men had extended
their studies. In 1963 there were three newly married men and two *batlonim,*
adults who receive outside support.

14. Community rules and customs were also applied when a satellite branch of
Rockland Community College offered courses in Jewish studies at New
Square. The coordinator of another Judaic Studies program in the SUNY
system charged that at New Square "procedures . . . unfairly limit employment and access to courses to those who follow Jewish customs." Cited were
the separation of male and female students (as well as the separation of male
students and female instructors) and prerequisites which required knowledge of Hebrew, Yiddish, and Aramaic. The constitutionality of permitting
religious customs to determine college programs was questioned. SUNY officials, however, supported the existing program, arguing that "limited enrollment is fine if the same courses are offered elsewhere." They pointed out
similar adaptations made in other programs (such as use of the Spanish language in areas with large Latino populations). "Those modifications . . . are

a means to a more important end—providing education." Kim Fararo, "Professor Critical of RCC Satellite at New Square," *Journal News*, Aug. 11, 1986.

19. Satmar's Kiryas Joel

1. A number of Satmar Hasidim were already employed at Crystal Clear Industries, the company owned by Leibush Lefkowitz, the president of Satmar, which was located in an industrial park in Dutchess County. This cut in half the distance to drive to work in the city.
2. George Dugan, "Jewish Sect to Go to Orange County," *New York Times,* July 21, 1974.
3. *New York Times,* Oct. 17, 31, 1976.
4. In 1979 the per capita income was $1,535, a little higher than that of residents of New Square. See Michael Batutis, *American Demographics* 8, Sept. 1986, pp. 54–55.
5. The population is still greater if the Satmar families living just outside the legal territorial limits of Kiryas Joel are included.
6. Often a worshiper in an expansive mood (on the morning of a family wedding or the yortsayt of a close relative) will cover the cost of the day's expenses.
7. See Edward Hudson, "For Hasidim, School Buses Stir a Dispute," *New York Times,* Sept. 4, 1986.
8. See Judy Rife, "Broad Appeal," *Sunday Times Herald Record* (Middletown, N.Y.), May 29, 1988.

20. Family Problems: Views of the Therapists

1. As Rabbi Stauber, one of the early proponents of providing mental health facilities in the community, noted: "those in this community seemed to stigmatize mentally retarded, developmentally disabled or the emotionally disturbed more than most people." Jeff Meer, "An Open Door," *Psychology Today* 21, no. 4, April 1987, p. 17.
2. *B.T., Shabbat* 55a. Rabbi Chaninah ben Dosa similarly advised: "It is not the poisonous snake which kills, but our sins which cause Divine retribution." *B.T., Berakhot* 33a.
3. Yehuda Nir, "Psychiatric Treatment of a Subgroup among Orthodox Jewish Patients (Satmar Hasidim)" (paper presented at the Messorah Symposium on the Treatment of Hasidim, American Psychiatric Association, May 1990, New York City). Quotations from this symposium are from a taped account of the meetings.
4. Harvey N. Kranzler, "Treatment of the Hasidic Child and Adolescent" (paper presented at the Messorah Symposium on the Treatment of Hasidim).
5. Mintz, *Legends of the Hasidim,* pp. 411–412.
6. Allen Manovitz, "The Psychiatric Treatment of the Hasidic Patient in the Acute Psychiatric Inpatient Service" (paper presented at the Messorah Symposium on the Treatment of Hasidim).

7. Prov. 10:2. See *B.T.*, Shabbat 156b, for an account of how on the day of her marriage a good deed saved Rabbi Akiba's daughter from a death foretold by astrologers.

8. Meer, "An Open Door," p. 17.

9. Manovitz, "The Psychiatric Treatment of the Hasidic Patient."

10. Kranzler, "Treatment of the Hasidic Child and Adolescent."

11. Nir, "Psychiatric Treatment of a Subgroup."

12. Manovitz, "The Psychiatric Treatment of the Hasidic Patient."

13. Nir, "Psychiatric Treatment of a Subgroup."

14. By all accounts there are few very drug addicts in the Hasidic community. The death of a young Hasid by an overdose of drugs was reported in the press as "the first in Williamsburg." See article by Douglas Martin, *New York Times*, March 8, 1989. The extremely low incidence of drug use is supported by interview data: "I was one of the first Hasidim to do drugs, literally. It's not a major problem [in the Hasidic world]. It's definitely increased but it's much less than in general society. If 15 percent of American youth do drugs, among the Hasidim it's one-tenth of one percent. Very, very, very few Hasidim have taken to drugs. There are fifteen to twenty men in their twenties and thirties, businessmen, working men. It's not a major epidemic. I'm still the first one that will talk about the problem. It's taken the people seven to ten years to talk about it. That has happened through a guy named Twerski who runs a program in Pittsburgh. He's helped them come out of their shell" (AI). Abraham Twerski, a Bobover Hasid, founded Gateway, a rehabilitation center in Pennsylvania. See Nancy Hass, "Hooked Hasidim," *New York Magazine*, Jan. 28, 1991, pp. 32–37.

15. Kranzler, "Treatment of the Hasidic Child and Adolescent."

16. The first national conference of Orthodox Jewish psychotherapists was held at the Yeshiva University Ferkauf Graduate School of Psychology on April 24, 1988, with roughly 175 in attendance. One participant reported that the number of Orthodox psychotherapists was now 500, as opposed to only 50 twenty years earlier. Steven Erlanger, "Orthodox Jewish Psychotherapists Face Conflicts," *New York Times*, April 26, 1988.

17. One psychotherapist at the national conference of Orthodox Psychotherapists reported on the Orthodox fear of "libertine behavior" that "people heard him [Freud] to say that the answer to many problems is a release from repressions and inhibitions, and as any religion does, Orthodoxy imposes strict inhibitions . . . So there has been a fear that Orthodox patients will throw off all their religion. There has been a great deal of hostility toward us, and we're still dealing with that." Ibid.

18. The morning hours are 8 A.M. to 12 noon Monday through Friday, 9 to 11 A.M. Sunday; and the evening hours are 8 to 11 P.M. Monday through Thursday, 9 to 11 P.M. Sunday.

19. Manovitz, "The Psychiatric Treatment of the Hasidic Patient."

20. Ibid.

21. Kranzler, "Treatment of the Hasidic Child and Adolescent."

22. Dr. Kranzler added: "In my own private practice I typically see young Hasidic adolescent males with psychosis, affective disorders, often with psychotic

symptoms, occasionally children with severe attention deficit hyperactive disorders that can't be maintained in the classroom setting and obsessive compulsive disorders that have overt symptoms that are disruptive. I have rarely evaluated a Hasidic child who had a pure conduct disorder, a generalized anxiety disorder or gender identity disorder, even though my assumption is that they do exist."

23. Nir, "Psychiatric Treatment of a Subgroup."
24. Manovitz, "The Psychiatric Treatment of the Hasidic Patient."
25. Ibid.
26. Orthodox society has permissive as well as prohibitive points of view. Of course all actions must be within the confines of the law. Every Orthodox Jew is familiar with the strictures concerning types of forbidden intercourse (e.g., incestuous, homosexual, adulterous, and animal) as well as forbidden times and circumstances (e.g., during menstruation, while intoxicated or angry, while one partner is asleep, during daylight, or by the light of a lamp); at the same time they are also aware of the freedom regarding the sexual act between married couples. Maimonides wrote: "Since a man's wife is permitted to him, he may act with her in any manner whatsoever. He may have intercourse with her whenever he so desires, and kiss any organ of her body he wishes, and he may have intercourse with her naturally or unnaturally, provided that he does not expend semen to no purpose." *The Code of Maimonides,* bk. 5, The Book of Holiness, tr. Louis I. Rabinowitz and Philip Grossman (New Haven and London: Yale University Press, 1965), p. 135.

21. Political Change in Crown Heights

1. This discussion concerns local politics. In the national election the majority of the Hasidim voted for Republican candidates. The Hasidim were more in sympathy with Republican national candidates who espoused the so-called family values: an aggressive stand on crime, opposition to abortion, and conservative economic policies. On the local level they remained good Democrats and were deeply concerned with reform.
2. Joan Gil: "There is insufficient housing for blacks and whites. The Lubavitchers have put up two buildings on Crown and Albany and one on Carroll and Kingston. The latter is a co-op. I sent some people to them but due to the size of Hasidic families the apartments are large and expensive. The family I sent could afford the $100,000 but they declined. He had the opportunity but he declined."
3. The seven Noahchide commandments appear in the *Tosefta*, the supplement to the *Mishnah* (ca. 200 C.E.) and are discussed by Maimonides in *The Code of Maimonides,* vol. 14, treatise 5, chs. 9–10, pp. 230–238. The laws are also listed in the Lubavitcher publication *Wellsprings,* June–July 1987, p. 14.
4. Preoccupation with obtaining publicity for the laws of Noah led some of the Rebbe's followers to invite the Chilean dictator General Augusto Pinochet to be seventh signer of an International Scroll of Honor commemorating the Lubavitcher Rebbe's eighty-fifth birthday in 1987. Pinochet used the occasion to praise the principles of his own authoritarian regime; and he was in

turn praised by the lay president of Chabad in Chile, David Feurstein. The originator of the proclamation, Rabbi Abraham Shemtov, director of the Chabad House of Philadelphia, was surprised by the firestorm of protest raised by opponents of the dictator's regime in Chile. Ethical and moral problems in contemporary politics seemed beyond the narrow focus of Lubavitch concerns. Shemtov explained that he does not understand Spanish or politics: "Political science and current political goings-on in all parts of the world are not really my field." J. J. Goldberg, "Chilean Dictator Signs . . ." *Jewish Week,* Jan. 15, 1988.

Ironically, the Rebbe's point of view concerning the Noahchide laws found support in Washington, where the leadership appeared eager to accommodate a religious constituency, even if it meant praising a campaign that could be said to underrate their own moral capabilities and their place in the Almighty's scheme. A proclamation was issued in the spring of 1986 by President Reagan affirming the duty of mankind to obey the seven Noahchide laws. See "Guaranteeing Morality, The Seven Noahchide Commandments," *Wellsprings,* June–July 1987, p. 14.

5. This represented only a small part of the renovations taking place throughout Community Boards 8 and 9. From 1979 to 1986 there were 9,571 housing units renovated. Most of the housing lost was in North Crown Heights, Community Board 8. See Sanchez, *Crown Heights Neighborhood Profile,* p. 7.

6. The hotel opened in September 1984, but renovations were still under way. Plans called for sixty rooms, a kosher restaurant, and various Orthodox amenities, such as sinks for ritual hand-washing outside the bathrooms and a mezuzah posted on every door. See *New York Times,* Jan. 28, 1985.

7. Conference on Interethnic Concerns, organized by the Jewish Community Council of Crown Heights, March 3, 1987.

8. Joan Gil is also unpopular with Rev. Sam: "I don't work with anyone who represents the Hasidic community. She is sponsored by the Jewish Community. You can't expect us to be in love with her. Politically we don't get involved. She doesn't represent us, even in the coalition. You have to have your interest first. You come to the bargaining table as equal partners."

9. Mendel Shemtov's two sons and his brother were already working for Chabad. To aid the movement he purchased a house on Eastern Parkway and refurbished it as a home office with conference rooms and living quarters for Chabad leaders when they returned to 770 for meetings and discussion.

10. "New York City Police Dept. Crime Comparison Report, 1985," *New York Times,* April 5, 1986; March 24, 1987. Reprinted in Sanchez, *Crown Heights Neighborhood Profile,* pp. 55–56. In Precinct 77 in North Crown Heights the numbers were generally somewhat higher: 2,594 and 2,537 burglaries, 1,897 and 2,144 robberies, 629 and 774 auto thefts, 109 and 75 rapes, and 38 and 41 crimes of murder and manslaughter.

11. *Jewish Week,* Feb. 27, 1987.

12. Peter Noel and Charles Baillou, "Koch Employs Apartheid Game Plan on Protestors," *Amsterdam News,* April 18, 1987.

13. Ibid.

14. A favorite target, however, was no longer available since Mayor Koch had removed the police stationed in front of 770. As a result the newspaper was reduced to complaining that the Hasidic headquarters "have until very recently received constant police protection."

15. Todd S. Purdum, "Brooklyn Groups Agree to Black-Hasidic Patrol," *New York Times*, May 23, 1987.

16. The neighboring building, 784–788 Eastern Parkway, which housed the printing, editorial, and education offices, was to be demolished to make room for the new structure. In addition, Lubavitcher building plans included a new girls' school on Brooklyn Avenue and a boys' school on Albany Avenue. These represented an enormous financial investment for the community, totaling $37 million: $20 million for the new addition, $12 million for the girls' school, and $5 million for the boys' school. Financial aid for the projects came from outside the Hasidic community. See also Ari L. Goldman, "Hasidic Group Expands Amid Debate on Future," *New York Times*, Sept. 5, 1988.

17. Rabbi Shmuel M. Butman, "Challenge," *Jewish Press*, Sept. 30, 1988.

18. According to Lubavitch sources, the court was spending $200 million dollars in building educational institutions all over the world.

19. See Arnold Fine, "Fears and Tension in Wake of Crown Heights Mugging," *Jewish Press*, March 10–16, 1989.

22. The Housing Labyrinth in Williamsburg

1. See George Kranzler, *Williamsburg, A Jewish Community in Transition* (New York: Philipp Feldheim, Inc., 1961), pp. 16–20.

2. See Price, "The Effect of Federal Anti-Poverty Programs and Policies on the Hasidic and Puerto Rican Communities of Williamsburg," pp. 10, 19–21.

3. Emanuel Perlmutter, "Priest Charges . . ." *New York Times*, May 3, 1973.

4. See Price, "Effect of Federal Programs," p. 120. In this regard Price also refers to Arthur M. Klebanoff, "The Demographics of Politics: Legislative Constituencies and the Borough of Brooklyn, 1950–1965" (senior honors thesis, Yale University, 1969).

5. Price, p. 103.

6. Quoted in ibid., pp. 147–148.

7. Ibid., p. 147. Rabbi Bernard Weinberger of Young Israel was a leader of the Orthodox community; Rabbi Liepa Friedman was the leader of the Satmar community.

8. Ibid., pp. 99, 118–121, 184–187. Price cites the *New York Times*, Dec. 9, 1965. Even so, Klebanoff's study of voter registration in New York City ("The Demographics of Politics") showed that blacks and Latinos did not reach a registration level of 35 percent (in comparison with white sections which were higher than 65 percent). Moreover, the turnout levels were only a small percentage of the registration figures. See Steven R. Weisman, "New York City, Mississippi: Surprising Pair," *New York Times*, Jan. 13, 1974, sec. 4, p. 4.

9. VISTA (Volunteers in Service to America) was founded in 1964 to enlist "in-

dividuals committed to improving the self-sufficiency of low income communities."

10. Letter to author, Nov. 5, 1990.
11. Price, pp. 225–226.
12. The defendants included the New York City Housing Authority and the United Jewish Organizations of Williamsburg (UJO), among others.
13. U.S. District Court, Southern District of New York, 76 Civ. 2125 (CHT).
14. The 92nd Precinct building at the corner of Lee Avenue and Clymer Street, vacated by the police, was rented to the Hasidim for a modest fee and turned into a synagogue; a long-term lease was also given to the Hasidim for the former Eastern District High School at Division Avenue and Keap Street, which they used as a yeshivah for girls. (Boricua College, a Latino institution, had also been interested in the high school site.)
15. WIC is funded by the Department of Agriculture and organized by the State of New York. By 1985 Satmar's ODA administered $375,000 for 8,950 people in the WIC program each month in Williamsburg. ODA also administered the home attendant care program, which provided aid for the elderly on Medicaid and arranged services for brain-damaged children and adults, people with MS and neurological illnesses, and the retarded. The program then (1985) managed 1,000 people working to take care of 700 clients. Funds to support this program came from the federal government, the state, and the city. Care was provided without regard to race, religion, or the ability to pay. Seventy to 80 percent of the patients treated were Hasidic and the remainder Latino and black. The sole criterion for accepting new patients was that they live in the South Williamsburg community. During that same period, the medical center's doctors, most of whom were Jewish but none of whom were Hasidic, handled approximately 400 deliveries, and provided prenatal and postnatal care to over 2,000 patients a month. The staff also included doctors with various specialties, including dentists, obstetricians, internists, and pediatricians, as well as paramedics. There was a mix of various ethnic groups among the staff as well as the patients. ODA also managed the weatherization program (refitting older houses) for the Williamsburg area, and it initiated the Human Development Association, which includes a homemakers' program.
16. Under the aegis of its nonprofit community organization, the ODA was able to train Hasidim as mechanics, machine repairmen, computer programmers, bookkeepers, and secretaries; it also established an English-language training program for children whose first language is Yiddish.
17. The secular arm of the Satmar community has achieved a remarkable record of success. In establishing programs for health and natal care, vocational training, and business loans they have helped to ensure the continued vitality and well-being of their community. Thanks to the organizational skills of the Satmar managers, Hasidic enterprises have often been cited as model programs using government funding.

   The major funding sources for the ODA have been the Minority Business Development Agency of the U.S. Department of Commerce, the U.S. Department of Health and Human Services, and the Small Business Administration.

For a listing of U.S. government agencies tapped, and programs offered by New York State and New York City, see Roy Betts and Lewis Giles, Jr., "Kestenbaum Discusses the Opportunity Development Association's Assistance in the Hasidic Community," *Minority Business Today,* U.S. Department of Commerce, Minority Business Development Agency (May 1985), vol. 4, no. 2, pp. 13–15.

18. Under the headline "The City Builds a Brooklyn Holyland," Wayne Barrett wrote in the *Village Voice,* May 10, 1983: "The Board of Estimate's unanimous approval of the sale of a Williamsburg urban renewal site to a Hasidic developer last Thursday was the latest in an extraordinary series of city favors for the dominant Satmar sect in that neighborhood, circumventing city law, the federally approved objectives for the renewal area, and the constitutional line between church and state. The scandal of the planned and already publicly subsidized conversion of the renewal area into a new Satmar holyland—with yeshivas, chapels, seminaries, and dormitories, a luxurious residence for the grand rebbe, and six-figure condos for the Satmar rich—is not just the scandal of the Koch administration. Brooklyn borough president Howard Golden and the rest of the Board members have routinely rubberstamped the cynical deals proposed by the city's Housing Preservation and Development Agency."

19. The fund had the approval of the City's Department of Housing Preservation and Development (HPD). The agreement was amended a year later in 1986. Since that time other negotiators for both sides have entered the picture with more acrimonious results.

20. Brooklyn Villas is a private limited partnership. It is a profitmaking organization and has only a tenuous affiliation with Satmar and with other Hasidic groups.

21. Each unit was estimated to sell at between $135,000 and $185,000. A city requirement stipulates that 20 percent of these units be sold for $81,000 and $87,000 to families earning less than $48,000 a year, the standard figure in New York for a moderate income. The cost of the land to the Hasidic developers was $3,500,000.

22. Latino interests center on housing for low-income families earning between $24,000 and $45,000. Each unit was to be constructed at a cost of $100,000 and would be subsidized in far greater measure than is customary for city and state housing because of the cross-subsidy money.

23. See Jane Perlez, "U.S. Court Bars School Partition for Hasidic Girls," *New York Times,* Oct. 4, 1986.

24. Kathy Dobie, "Sex Crimes and Prejudice," *Village Voice,* Feb. 12, 1991.

25. *New York Post,* Nov. 1, 1990. Harassment charges against the woman and her family had previously been filed by Jews and by blacks. Marc Schneir, *Jewish Week,* Nov. 23, 1990.

26. From the reports it appears that the injuries were minor.

27. Officer Ariza was again in the news because of his arrest of a Hasidic man whom he charged with assaulting him. The Hasid in turn accused Ariza of having arrested him without provocation. Ariza was subsequently transferred from the 90th Precinct for ninety days pending an investigation of his

alleged assault on a motorist after both were involved in a collision while the officer was off duty. He later returned to the 90th Precinct.

28. Catherine Crocker, "No Favoritism toward Hasidim," *Jewish Week,* Dec. 28, 1990.

29. "Housing Update," *El Pitirre* (P.O. Box 11-0159, Williamsburg Station, Brooklyn, NY 11211) 2, no. 3, June 1991.

30. The litigation actually included a new lawsuit and a motion for contempt relating to the failure to abide by the terms of the 1978 Consent Decree. This was the same legal team that had brought suit in the 1976 housing case and in the suit opposing the use of a separate wing for Hasidic girls in a public school. The defendants in the housing case were the City of New York, the U.S. Department of Housing and Urban Development, the United Jewish Organizations of Williamsburg, and the Epiphany Church, as well as the Ross Rodney Housing Corporation, United Talmudic Academy, Kraus Management, Inc., and Brooklyn Villas, Inc.

31. See Robert Fleming, "Housing Furor in Williamsburg," *Daily News,* Nov. 5, 1989.

32. Because *Der Zeitung* is privately owned (by a Satmar Hasid), as opposed to *Der Yid,* which is owned by the Satmar community, the Brooklyn developers argued that their choice demonstrated that they wanted to expand the potential readership beyond the Satmar community.

33. U.S. District Court, Eastern District of New York, 90 Civ. 31 (EHN). Verified Complaint.

34. Informal transfer of apartments among relatives and friends cannot of course be regulated. There is a concern among the Latinos that even the new agreement will be frustrated by these informal transfers of apartments from Hasidim to other Hasidim.

35. Douglas Martin, "About New York," *New York Times,* Sept. 29, 1990. The article noted that there are approximately 3,000 homeless Jews in New York, belying the common notion of all Jews as well-to-do.

36. Ibid. Rabbi Stauber reported receiving requests from sixty homeless families following an article in a Yiddish publication.

37. U.S. District Court, Eastern District of New York, 90 Civ. 31 (EHN). Verified Complaint, num. 177, p. 44.

38. The U.S. Court of Appeals for the Second Circuit, no. 1251, Aug. term 1990, argued Feb. 20, 1991, decided March 26, 1991. Docket no. 91-7045. Concerning the sale of lands for religious use, see p. 7.

23. A New Boyaner Rebbe Is Named

1. Israel Friedman: "Today in New York City real Boyaner Hasidim number 200 to 250. In Israel I would say between 750 and 1,000. The average tish in Israel is attended by 700 to 800 people. There are Hasidim in Bnei Brak and there are Hasidim in Tel Aviv, and there are Hasidim in other sections. Not everybody can come.

"Why do we have so many Hasidim now? Because our Rizhin yeshivah produced them. Forty or fifty years ago I would say that 90 percent of the children of the then Hasidim turned away from Orthodox Judaism. Now the youngsters, the children of the Hasidim, are more religious and more observant and more extreme than the parents. So almost every one of our Hasidim now has children and grandchildren who went to our yeshivah."

2. The third meal is especially sacred to the Hasidim. The Rebbe offers his oration at dusk as the final moments of the Shabbes slip away. See Chapter 3 for a description of the same scene in the Satmar besmedresh.

3. Lag ba-Omer is the thirty-third day from the offering of the first sheaf of barley (the omer). The festival is associated with Rabbi Shimon ben Yohai, but it has its roots in a more ancient seasonal ceremony.

24. Lubavitch: Days of Trial, Days of Celebration

1. Agudas Chassidei Chabad of the United States is the religious corporation that administers the synagogue and other communal affairs for the world Lubavitch community.

2. Hanna Gourary testified in court that the library had been seized in 1920; Rabbi Y. Krinsky placed the date in 1916.

3. U.S. District Court, Eastern District of New York, Agudas Chassidei Chabad of the United States, Plaintiff, CV-85-2909, Memorandum Decision and Order, against Barry S. Gourary, Defendant, and Hanna Gourary, Defendant-Intervenor, Jan. 6, 1987, p. 10, n. 4. Other books were presented as gifts, these often being solicited by advertisements placed in American and European journals. The library purchased had belonged to Shmuel Wiener, the former head of the Asiatic Museum in Leningrad. The library included not only sacred texts and scholarly studies but also works of a heretical nature, anti-Semitic tracts, and some scatological books not ordinarily found in the personal library of a learned rabbi.

4. U.S. District Court, Memorandum Decision and Order, p. 7.

5. Samarious Gourary remained loyal to the cause of Lubavitch in the contention over the library as well, despite the great pain he must have felt. In opposition to both his son and his wife (who was also involved as the defendant-intervenor), he asked his son to restore the books and return the money. Rabbi Samarious Gourary died in February 1989, at the age of ninety-one.

6. The same statement (with two words changed) also appeared in David Margolick, "Suit on Books Gives Look at Hasidim," *New York Times*, Dec. 18, 1985.

7. Ibid.

8. This provides the Rebbe with "a formal legally binding claim on the building of which his heirs thereafter availed themselves. Tax exemption was obtained from the State of New York for those portions of the building that remained in the possession of plaintiff [Chabad] and where the library was located." U.S. District Court, Memorandum Decision and Order, p. 20.

9. *New York Times*, Dec. 18, 1985.

10. U.S. District Court, Memorandum Decision and Order, p. 14.

11. Margolick, "Suit on Books Gives Look at Hasidim," *New York Times*, Dec.

18, 1985. Rebbetsn Chaya Moussia Schneerson died in 1988 at the age of eighty-seven.

12. Ibid.

13. U.S. District Court, Memorandum Decision and Order, p. 10.

14. Ibid., p. 15.

15. Ibid., p. 17.

16. Ibid., p. 22.

17. Another letter, however, handled by a German attorney, written in German, and passed through the German Consulate, states in the first person that the issue concerns "my library."

18. U.S. District Court, Memorandum Decision and Order, pp. 22, 28n13.

19. Ibid., p. 24.

20. Ibid., pp. 14–15.

21. Midrash Rabbah 30:2. Leviticus (Emor).

22. Rabbi Schneerson suffered a heart attack on the eve of Shemini Azeret in October 1977. The Rebbe instructed his followers to continue with the celebration as if he were there. He refused to go to a hospital, and a well-equipped emergency Internal Cardiac Unit was established in his office. At midnight on the night following the holiday the Rebbe spoke to his followers for twenty minutes on the radio through a hookup to his room.

23. Rabbi Shneur Zalman had established a charity to help impoverished Jews who had settled in Palestine. Russia was then at war with Turkey. At his trial the Rebbe was found innocent of the charge that he was helping the Turkish cause.

24. The eleventh line of the hymn of praise following the miraculous destruction of the Egyptian forces in the Red Sea. Exod. 15:11.

25. Some dealers retained the profit from the resale of the books. One dealer paid $69,000 for a fifteenth-century Haggadah and then sold it to a collector for $149,000, the price Lubavitch had to pay to regain the work. The dealer retained his profit—the difference between the payment and sale price. See Margolick, "Suit on Books Gives Look at Hasidim."

25. Satmar: Litigation and Leaflets

1. Some apartment owners say that those named to receive low-income apartments were chosen by all the courts, including Satmar, Tselem, Devina, and Pupa. A Satmar leader, on the other hand, recalled that Leibish Lefkowitz, the president of the Satmar community, himself decided on the lucky recipients. Not everyone selected in the lottery or designated as a poor family decided to move into the apartments; some sold their rights to other families at a profit.

2. In this account the names of the people involved have been changed.

3. Menahem Mendel Morgenstern, the idiosyncratic Rebbe of Kotsk (1787–1859).

26. Kiryas Joel: In Court and Out

1. Num. 16:1–36.

2. Justice William Brennan "held that school district's shared time and community education programs, which provided the classes to nonpublic school students at public expense in classrooms located in and leased from nonpublic schools had the 'primary or principal' effect of advancing religion and therefore violated dictates of the establishment clause of the First Amendment." School Dist. of City of Grand Rapids vs. Ball, 105 S.Ct. 3216 (1985). The state ruling cited by the Monroe-Woodbury School District is Section 3602-C 9 of the New York State Education Law.

3. Ruth Boice, "Parents Sue over Special Ed," *Times Herald Record,* Middletown, N.Y., April 2, 1986.

4. Daniel D. Alexander, "The Political Influence of the Resident Hasidic Community on the East Ramapo Central School District" (Ph.D. diss., School of Education, Health, Nursing, and Arts Professions, New York University, 1982), p. 201. He pointed to the ballot box as a more certain indicator of future social change.

5. At times of school closings forced by budgetary constraints anger was at times mistakenly directed toward the Hasidim when it more properly should have been directed against the school board.

6. See Judy Rife, "Ruling Fails to Resolve Hasidim Dispute," *Times Herald Record,* July 13, 1988.

7. Judy Rife, "M-W Superintendent Applauds Court Decision," *Times Herald Record,* July 19, 1988.

8. Judy Rife, "Hasidim to Ask M-W for Special Programs," *Times Herald Record,* Sept. 15, 1988.

9. Parents also were dissatisfied with the quality of education received by the general population of children in the lower grades. Their complaints were corroborated by a 1988 State Education Department report, at least so far as the English language was concerned. The report revealed that only 19 percent of the third-grade girls at Bais Rachel in Kiryas Joel passed the reading test, and the school was listed as one of two schools from Orange, Sullivan, and Ulster Counties on the department's list of low-achieving schools. A spokeswoman at the school argued that the low reading scores were due to the cultural bias of the test and the community's emphasis on Yiddish rather than English. She expressed assurance that the children would catch up to their level in a year or two. Nonetheless, the news supported the parents' concerns about the quality of the education program. See Sylvia Saunders, "Poor Reading Skills Found in Two Orange Schools," *Times Herald Record,* April 21, 1988.

10. See William Berezansky's report "The Untold Rebellion," *Times Herald Record Sunday Magazine,* March 25, 1990, p. 5.

11. Ibid.

12. In an article in the *Times Herald Record,* Laura Shaham pointed out the similarity of the solution to the action taken to incorporate Kiryas Joel as a village in order to bypass housing and zoning constraints imposed by the town. "Hasidim Hope School Split Benefits All," June 29, 1989.

13. J. J. Goldberg, "ADL May Fight Separate Chasidic School District," *Jewish Week,* Aug. 4, 1989, p. 4.

14. Elizabeth Kolbert, "Hasidic Village in New York Wants Own Public School District," *New York Times*, July 21, 1989.

15. Goldberg, "ADL May Fight Separate Chasidic School District."

16. At the time it was reported that four other persons affiliated with Sha'arei Hemlah had indicated that they would run but then had dropped out at the last moment. It was alleged that they had received telephone calls warning them to drop their petition and remove their names from the slate. It was said that the four considered their situation to be untenable: until the new school board could be seated the four would receive funding from the United Talmudical Academy, after which they would again be under the aegis of Reb Aaron and his designees. They therefore decided to surrender their authority over the school they had worked so hard to develop. According to one account they confronted Reb Aaron and gave him the keys to the school building. When Reb Aaron suggested that they remain in charge of the school, one of the group reportedly replied: "No. Am I stupid? You're going to run the school and I'll just be a *shames* [beadle]?" (MR).

17. Waldman contends that soon after attending a fundraising dinner for the new school in Borough Park, he found himself in trouble with the leadership of the village and was expelled from the synagogue.

18. Although they are not year-round residents of the community, because they live in the yeshivah dormitory students over the age of eighteen have a legal right to vote there. While the students clearly influenced the results of the election, according to the Rebbe's supporters they constituted approximately 200 votes, which would still have left Waldman 200 votes shy of victory.

19. William Berezansky, "Maverick Loses Kiryas Joel Bid," *Times Herald Record*, Jan. 18, 1990, pp. 3, 21. Aside from the men possibly taking notes outside the polling places, Waldman claimed that there were too few poll watchers, and even that television cameras had been set in the ceiling in one site so that each vote could be recorded along with the identity of the voter.

20. Louis Grumet, executive director of the Association, summarized the Association's position: "We believe the establishment of a school district for a religion is not permitted under the Constitution," adding that the district had been created for the Satmar Hasidim to "isolate their children from the larger diverse outside society." Grumet also noted that the law mandates that handicapped and nonhandicapped students be integrated and that the proposed program could not legally be carried out. If such a legal precedent were to be established other groups could attempt to follow the same course. See William Berezansky, "School District Violates Constitution, Suit Claims," *Times Herald Record*, Jan. 19, 1990, p. 3.

21. Dr. Benardo is a Sephardic Jew and is fluent in Spanish.

22. The budget for its second year of operation, the fiscal year 1992, was estimated at approximately $3 million. The real estate tax base funded the school and each year the funds had to be approved by the voters in the school district. The gender of the school bus drivers was no longer a problem since the handicapped boys were exempted by the rabbis from the religious

requirements concerning separation of the sexes. In any case the problem was moot since unlike the Monroe-Woodbury school district, which owned and operated its own buses, the new school district contracted for bus service. There was no obligation for the contractor to employ union drivers. The students were few in number and arrangements far more flexible than had existed in the former public school district were possible. Bus transportation for the 3,500 to 4,000 students attending the private yeshivah continued as before. The only students who had been affected by the previous ban on female bus drivers were the children of the 100 to 125 Hasidic families who resided outside the boundaries of Kiryas Joel. There the luck of the draw prevailed: if the driver assigned to the route was a man the boys boarded the bus; if the driver was a woman other transportation was provided.

23. The property was deeded to the congregation of the rebbetsn to help her secure a loan to build her home in Kiryas Joel.

24. The new Rebbe particularly objected to the sale to Nathan Brach, who two years earlier had built a girls' school at 31 Division Avenue, and who had sided with the Rebbe's opponents at Kiryas Joel. Despite the Rebbe's opposition, and the banning of some families, the school had an enrollment of over one hundred girls.

25. William Berezansky, "Kiryas Joel Factions Make Peace," *Times Herald Record*, May 18, 1990, p. 4.

26. William Berezansky, "Truce Holds in Kiryas Joel," *Times Herald Record*, May 25, 1990, p. 21.

27. *Grumet vs. New York State Education Dept.*, RJI 0190 021649 (State of New York, Supreme Court, Jan. 22, 1992). See also William Berezansky, "Kiryas School Ruled Unconstitutional," *Times Herald Record*, Jan. 23, 1992, p. 1.

28. *Lemon v. Kurtaman*, 403 US 602, 91 S.Ct. 2105, 29 L.Ed. 2d 745.

29. *Grumet vs. New York State Education Dept.*

27. Rumor and Riot in Crown Heights

1. Sanchez, *Crown Heights Neighborhood Profile*, p. 49.

2. See Michael Powell and Jennifer Preston, "Little Proof Inequity Persists," *New York Newsday*, Sept. 3, 1991. The letter indicated that 59.8 percent of black residents had been approached and over three-fourths of the solicitors were Jewish or Hasidic.

3. Mitch Gelman and Pamela Newkirk, "Favoritism Is the Perception," *New York Newsday*, Sept. 3, 1991, p. 23.

4. Until repairs were begun on the nearby section of Eastern Parkway in 1989 and the road was closed, the only other privileges of importance to the Hasidim concerned limiting traffic on the service road that passes in front of 770 on Jewish holy days, and ignoring parking violations on the Sabbath because Orthodox Jews are not permitted to drive until nightfall.

5. See Lydia Chavez, "Racial Tensions Persist in Crown Heights," *New York Times*, April 10, 1987. The presence of the Hasidim in neighborhood com-

mittees can be a positive force in generating and distributing funds. Their presence is one way to account for the success of Community Board 9 during the years 1979–1986, when the Board succeeded in administering 2,982 small loans ($3,000 to $5,000) for apartment house repairs for property owners, three times as many as were available under Community Board 8. (See "Crown Heights Neighborhood Preservation Area, Publicly Assisted Housing Rehabilitation & Construction, 1979–86," HPD Crown Heights Neighborhood Preservation Office, rpt. in Sanchez, *Crown Heights Neighborhood Profile,* pp. 43–44.) These small loans at 3 percent interest for apartment house repairs averaged less than a million dollars a year in government funds for Community Board 9. After the riots on Utica Avenue following the 1977 blackout, Rabbi Rosenfeld was able to obtain loans for merchants of Utica Avenue who were members of minorities from the Small Business Administration, and he brought in a jobs program for seventy mostly black and Hispanic teenagers to help clean up the debris left by the rioting.

6. In an interview in *New York Newsday* in 1987 Rabbi Rosenfeld observed that "since 1979 the Jewish Community Council has handled no government funds for housing. Before that, the council bought 'a few buildings, some partially occupied, some vacant, some shells,' he said, and used federal funds to rehabilitate them. Any buildings acquired after 1979 were bought with private funds, he said." See Merle English, *New York Newsday,* July 19, 1987.

7. Sanchez, *Crown Heights Neighborhood Profile,* pp. 56–57.

8. The basic facts in this account are drawn for the most part from articles by John Kifner, James Barron, Felicia R. Lee, Ari L. Goldman, Seth Faison, Jr., Sara Rimer, Todd S. Purdum, and David Gonzalez (as well as unsigned editorials) that appeared in the *New York Times,* Aug. 21–27, 1991.

9. The police account reported in the *New York Times* stated: "The Hatzolah ambulance driver said he arrived simultaneously to EMS and observed one of the children already receiving treatment . . . [he was] instructed by the police to leave the scene with Yoseph Lisef because of the hostilities directed toward him by the crowd." A spokeswoman for EMS placed the Hatzolah ambulance as the first at the accident. Within minutes the EMS ambulances arrived: "Once on the scene, the first EMS ambulance began treating Gavin; the second one took him to Kings County Hospital. The technicians from the first ambulance had also been treating Angela, and took her to the hospital." The spokeswoman added: "They followed procedure and in fact it worked the way it was supposed to." Evelyn Nieves, "The Accident That Started It All: The Focus of Protesters and a Grand Jury," *New York Times,* Aug. 23, 1991. See also Jonathan Mark, "Crown Heights: A Deadly Confrontation," *Jewish Week,* Aug. 23–29, 1991, p. 7.

10. Stewart Ain, "Paramedic from Jewish Service Aided Black Child," *Jewish Week,* Aug. 30–Sept. 5, 1991, p. 4.

11. Other reports of actions by police at the scene also played a part in building a picture of callousness and insensitivity toward blacks: "Then a man was bent over the body of the fallen child. It was the boy's father. A police officer

pulled the father of the child away without knowing who he was, without asking. In their eyes the crowd saw this as they not having any compassion or concern about the father" (MP).

12. Yankel Rosenbaum was a lecturer at Melbourne University in Australia who was in New York to do research at YIVO Institute for Jewish Research in Manhattan on the Holocaust. He was the son of Holocaust survivors who had settled in Australia. His studies in New York were almost completed, and he had planned to return home within the month.

13. The four other deputy mayors are white.

14. Reported by the Crown Heights Jewish Community Relations Council. Jonathan Mark, "Crown Heights," p. 7.

15. John Kifner, "Youth Indicted in Racial Slaying That Followed Automobile Death," *New York Times,* Aug. 27, 1991.

16. Felicia R. Lee, "A Bitter Funeral for Crown Heights Car Victim, 7," *New York Times,* Aug. 27, 1991. Hatzolah's response to the rumors had appeared in the *New York Times* a few days earlier: "Some blacks accused Hatzolah of treating the Hasidim and ignoring the critically injured children. Hatzolah officials, backed by city officials, have denied the allegation, contending that the police instructed Hatzolah to treat the Jewish victims while paramedics from an Emergency Medical Service ambulance tried to save the youngster's life." James Barron, "Fear, Anger and Loss Haunt Torn Brooklyn Neighborhood," *New York Times,* Aug. 22, 1991. It was also learned that Yosef Lifsh, the driver of the station wagon, had been awarded a police department commendation for bravery in 1990 for climbing a fire escape and rescuing two black children from a cleaning store fire that claimed four lives.

17. Phil Caruso, the head of the police union, had a memo posted in the precinct station houses: "Over the last three nights, New York's Finest have been transformed into New York's 'Lamest.' Lamed—not only because of the severe nature of the injuries sustained—but because of the relatively lethargic, virtually inert response that police officers under an actual state of siege have been allowed to put forth. Restraint in the face of danger is admirable, but too much restraint has a tendency to be deadly. We don't want any dead cops out there." John Kifner, "Dinkins Vows Police Crackdown in Racial Strife," *New York Times,* Aug. 23, 1991.

18. Mayor Dinkins echoed Senator Moynihan's charge and as a result Elombe Brath, a black militant, argued that the mayor "does not seem to distinguish premeditated murder from retaliatory murder." Andy Logan, "Around City Hall," *New Yorker,* Sept. 23, 1991, p. 108.

19. In the three weeks following the riots the bias unit of the police department reported two dozen incidents of an anti-Semitic nature in the various boroughs of the city. See Stewart Ain, "Bias Crimes," *Jewish Week,* Sept. 13–19, 1991, p. 4. In several instances attacking blacks made reference to Crown Heights.

20. Todd S. Purdum, "Dinkins Bids Crown Heights Find Healing in 2 Tragedies," *New York Times,* Aug. 26, 1991.

21. Ibid.

22. Lee, "A Bitter Funeral."

23. David Gonzalez, "Hasids Agree to Take Part in Annual West Indian Day Parade in Brooklyn," *New York Times*, Sept. 2, 1991.

24. John Kifner, "Steel Drums, Reggae, Song and Crown Heights Truce," *New York Times*, Sept. 3, 1991.

25. Steven Lee Myers, "Judge Bars Release of Crown Heights Jury Record," *New York Times*, Sept. 7, 1991.

26. Powell and Preston, "Little Proof Inequality Persists," p. 6.

27. See Mike McAlary, "Portrait of Teen in Hasid's Killing," *New York Post*, Sept. 11, 1991, pp. 4, 18.

28. This incident is cited as another example of the failure of the police to deal with mob actions during the first days of the riots. No one involved was arrested. See Stewart Ain, "Chasid 'Still Recovering' from Beating," *Jewish Week*, Sept. 6–12, 1991.

29. Bob Liff, "Dinkins Shifts Grant Program Administration," *New York Newsday*, Dec. 28, 1991. James C. McKinley, Jr., "New York Shifts Heating Subsidies," *New York Times*, Dec. 28, 1991.

30. David Seifman, "Pols: Were Jewish Groups Excluded from City Program," *New York Post*, Dec. 27, 1991.

31. The figures for Williamsburg were cited in the *New York Times*, Dec. 28, 1991; the contradictory statistics concerning Crown Heights appeared on the same date in *New York Newsday*.

32. *New York Times*, Dec. 28, 1991.

33. In an effort to mollify critics, Commissioner Carrion announced that past grantees would receive postcards informing them of their eligibility and the location of the new offices where applications could be obtained. In addition, two mobile three-person teams (one with a speaker fluent in Yiddish and Russian) would schedule visits to any agency that requested them and thereby eliminate the need for applicants to travel to a different and possibly intimidating location. *Jewish Week*, Jan. 10–16, 1992.

34. See James Barron, "Suspect Arrested in Woman's Death," *New York Times*, Feb. 11, 1992. See also N. R. Kleinfield, "A Journey of Love and Religion Ends Sadly in Crown Heights," *New York Times*, Feb. 9, 1992.

35. "Suspect in Stabbing Death Finished Term in October," *New York Times*, Feb. 12, 1992.

28. Lubavitch: The Messiah Issue

1. See *The Code of Maimonides*, vol. 14, Judges, treatise 5, Kings and Wars, ch. 11, p. 238: "King Messiah will arise and restore the kingdom of David to its former state and original sovereignty . . . rebuild the sanctuary and gather the dispersed of Israel."

2. See Gershom Scholem, *Major Trends in Jewish Mysticism*, pp. 329–330.

3. See Gershom Scholem, "The Neutralization of the Messianic Element in Early Hasidism," in *The Messianic Idea in Judaism* (New York: Schocken Books, 1971), p. 184.

4. Evidence from the *Shivhei ha-Besht*, the first account of his life based on

legends, and from an extant letter indicate that the Baal Shem Tov looked to someone other than himself to be the anointed one. In one tale, for example, the Baal Shem Tov goes to the palace of the Messiah, where the Messiah speaks to him. *In Praise of the Baal Shem Tov* [*Shivhei ha-Besht*], tr. and ed. Dan Ben-Amos and Jerome R. Mintz (1970; New York: Schocken Books, 1984), esp. pp. xxx, 6, 57–58. In a letter written by the Baal Shem Tov to his brother-in-law Rabbi Gershon around 1752 the founder of Hasidism describes an earlier visionary experience when he ascended to heaven and asked the Messiah when he would come. See Scholem, "The Neutralization of the Messianic Element in Early Hasidism," p. 182. Scholem cites another version of the letter, which is printed in full in Simon Dubnow, *Geschichte des Chassidismus* (Berlin, 1931), I, p. 106.

5. See J. G. Weiss, "Contemplative Mysticism and 'Faith' in Hasidic Piety," *Journal of Jewish Studies* 4, 1953, p. 28.

6. See Gershom Scholem, "Toward an Understanding of the Messianic Idea," in *The Messianic Idea in Judaism*, pp. 34–35, 179.

7. Other Hasidim saw Napoleon in even more threatening terms as the bearer of Western enlightenment who would set the religious community free from necessary constraints.

8. In the final months of his life the Stoliner Rebbe lay ill in a paralytic state. One Shabbes his gabbai came into his room, and the Rebbe asked: "Are they talking about the Messiah on the streets?" When the gabbai informed him that the Rebbe knew that the Messiah won't appear on the Shabbes, the impatient Rebbe replied: "He could come on Saturday night." See Mintz, *Legends of the Hasidim*, pp. 95, 201, 209–210.

9. See Chapter 4 for a description of the types of talks given by the Rebbe.

10. The month of Tishrei falls between mid-September and mid-October.

11. B.T., Sanhedrin 97b.

12. "Synopsis of the Talks of the Lubavitcher Rebbe, Shlita, Shabbos Parshas Bechukosai, 22 Iyar, 5749," Vaad Hanochos Hatmimim.

13. Scholem, "The Neutralization of the Messianic Element in Early Hasidism," p. 184.

14. Jon Calish, "Interview with Rabbi Yehuda Krinsky: Is There a Messiah in Crown Heights," *New York Newsday*, June 1, 1988.

15. Steve Lipman, "The Messiah Issue," *Jewish Week*, June 17, 1988.

16. Ibid.

17. See Joel Brinkley, "Israeli Coalition Cracks at Last Minute," *New York Times*, April 12, 1990; Ari L. Goldman, "One Brooklyn Rabbi's Long Shadow," *New York Times*, April 13, 1990; Allison Kaplan, "Schneerson Assailed for Involvement in Internal Israeli Politics," *Jewish Week*, April 20, 1990.

18. "Schneerson: 'Have No Fear, Gulf Crisis Heralds the Messiah,'" *Jerusalem Post*, Aug. 20, 1990.

19. From "I Will Show You Wonders: Public Statements of the Lubavitcher Rebbe, Rabbi Menachem M. Schneerson, before and during the Gulf Crisis," Sichos in English, April 21, 1991, pp. 8, 33, 35. The Rebbe was quoting the *Yalkut Shim'oni*, 2 vols. (New York: Pardes, 1944, rpt. of Warsaw ed. 1877),

vol. 2, interpreting Yeshayahu (Isaiah) 60:1. The *Yalkut Shim'oni* ("The Compilation of Simeon") is a collection of Midrashim (interpretations of passages from the Scriptures). It is attributed to R. Simeon of Frankfurt, who composed it in the early part of the thirteenth century. Others believe the compiler was Rabbi Simeon Kara, who lived in the time of Rashi in the eleventh century.

20. "The Week in Review, from the Talks of the Lubavitcher Rebbe Shlita," vol. II, no. 30, April 9–15, 1991.

21. "Shabbos Parshas Tazria-Metzora, 6th Day of Iyar [May 20, 1991]." Sichos in English, p. 3.

22. Torah study classes were advised, in addition to one's own in-depth reading, and it was suggested that "An added commitment to the mitzvah of Charity also hastens the redemption." "The Week in Review from the Talks of the Lubavitcher Rebbe Shlita," vol. II, no. 31, April 16–22, 1991.

23. Jonathan Mark, "Messianism 'Crescendo,'" *Jewish Week*, May 10–16, 1991.

24. Quoted in ibid.

25. "The Week in Review, from the Talks of the Lubavitcher Rebbe Shlita," vol. II, no. 32, April 23–28, 1991.

26. *B.T.*, Megillah 19a.

27. "A Digest of the Farbrengen of the Lubavitcher Rebbe Shlita, Rosh Hashanah, 5752," Sichos in English.

28. *B.T.*, Sotah 11b.

Afterword

1. Scholem, *Major Trends in Jewish Mysticism*, pp. 349–350.

2. Elie Wiesel utilizes the tale as a preamble to his novel *The Gates of the Forest* (New York: Holt, Rinehart and Winston, 1966). He retells the story in *Souls on Fire*, but he concludes on a somber note. Retelling the tale is not enough to ward off danger threatening the Jews. "It no longer is. The proof is that the threat has not been averted. Perhaps we are no longer able to tell the story. Could all of us be guilty? Especially the survivors?" *Souls on Fire: Portraits and Legends of Hasidic Masters* (New York: Random House, 1972), pp. 167–168. Wiesel's point of view seen through his use of the tale is discussed in Michael Berenbaum, *The Vision of the World: Theological Reflections on the Works of Elie Wiesel* (Middletown, Conn.: Wesleyan University Press, 1979), pp. 88–90. See the discussion preceding the tale, esp. pp. 14–21.

Informants Cited

AI   Informants who chose to remain completely anonymous

AF   Avrom Flint, Lubavitcher Hasid, member Crown Heights Jewish Community Council and Community School Board 17, and housing advisor in office of Community Council

AFF   Albert Friedman, Satmar Hasid, former reporter for *Der Yid,* present publisher and editor of *Der Zeitung;* son of Lipa Friedman, former head of the Satmar community

AG   Aaron Green, Satmar Hasid, Williamsburg

AH   Abraham Hecht, rabbi, Lubavitch

AR   Aaron Raskin, Lubavitcher Hasid, high school teacher, on research staff at Chabad

AS   Satmar Hasid, businessman

BF   Williamsburg Hasid

BG   Barry Gourary, nephew of the Lubavitcher Rebbe

BH   Orthodox woman therapist

BI   Borough Park counselor

BJ   Barukh Jacobson, Lubavitcher Hasid, employed in translation section of Lubavitch education program

BM   Barukh Meir Yaakov Sochet, the present Stoliner Rebbe

BP   Borough Park Hasid

CL   Nineteen-year-old engaged girl from Monsey, unaffiliated

CN   Clarence Norman, Jr., Democratic Assemblyman and District Leader from Crown Heights

CS   Chaim Stauber, Satmar leader, founder and director of Pesach Tikvah, a mental health center

DH   Dov Hikind, Democratic Assemblyman

EA   Female social worker and family therapist

EB   Williamsburg housewife

EM   Williamsburg housewife

EES   Edwin Svigals, once a participant in the Lubavitch baltshuve program

EKT   Lubavitcher Hasid, artist, baltshuve

ES   Efroim Stein, former Satmar community leader, business entrepreneur

ET	Satmar Hasid, Borough Park
EZ	Ezra Sochet, father of the present Stoliner Rebbe
FH	Frieda H., Bobover Hasid, married to MH
FP	Young housewife in New Square
FR	Young Williamsburg housewife, Satmar, householder in a building reconstructed under Satmar auspices
HS	Rev. Heron A. Sam, rector of St. Mark's Episcopal Church
IA	Rizhin Hasid
IB	Young Lubavitcher Hasid
IF	Israel Friedman, the uncle of the present Boyaner Rebbe, son of the previous Boyaner Rebbe, president of the American Committee for the Rizhin Yeshivah
IP	Williamsburg Hasid
IR	Isaac Rosenberg, Satmar Hasid, president of Certified Lumber
IS	Israel Shemtov, Lubavitcher secular leader, owner of a retail clothing store
JA	Female psychotherapist, non-Jewish
JC	Jacob Cohen, one of the M'lochim and a bitter opponent of Lubavitch
JF	Bobover Hasid, court financial officer
JG	Joan Gil, former Democratic District Leader
JH	Resident in Kiryas Joel
JI	Satmar Hasid, storekeeper in Williamsburg
JM	Bobover Hasid
JS	Joel Schwartz, Modern Orthodox, public relations administrator of Community Organization of Borough Park
JW	Joseph Waldman, Satmar Hasid, member of the opposition in Kiryas Joel
JZ	Joseph Spielman, chairman of the Crown Heights Jewish Community Council
KA	Young man, potential baltshuve at Lubavitch
KG	Young housewife and mother, New Square
LA	Satmar Hasid
LL	Satmar Hasid
LO	Wife of a Hasid who moved from Satmar to Lubavitch
LV	Lubavitcher woman, formerly of Satmar, married to SV
MA	Mendel Azimov, a Lubavitcher Hasid
MB	Woman member of a Conservative synagogue in Flatbush (close to Borough Park)
MF	Williamsburg woman, unaffiliated
MH	Bobover Hasid, married to FH
MMB	Menachem M. Brayer, father of present Boyaner Rebbe, psychologist, professor at Yeshiva University
MN	Martin Needelman, attorney, director and chief counsel for Brooklyn Legal Services Corporation A
MP	Mary Pinkett, elected Democratic Councilwoman of Crown Heights
MR	Satmar Hasid

MS   Mendel Shemtov, Lubavitch, businessman and lay leader, formerly on Jewish Community Council and on Community Board

MSS   Rabbi Morris Shmidman, director of COJO (Council of Jewish Organizations of Borough Park), rabbi and attorney

MW   Rabbi Meyer Weberman, Chief Rabbi of the M'lochim, disciple of the Malach

NB   Satmar Hasid

ND   Reb Nahum Dov, the Boyaner Rebbe, presently living in Israel

PK   Pinchas Korf, Lubavitcher teacher known for his knowledge and charitable nature

PM   Satmar Hasid

PR   Stoliner Hasid in Borough Park

PS   Newlywed Hasidic woman from Israel, unaffiliated

RA   Housewife, activist, Lubavitch

RB   Williamsburg Hasid

RH   A leader of the Satmar community

RM   Williamsburg housewife

RP   Bobover Hasid

RS   Rashi Schapiro, Ph.D., psychologist with wide experience with clients in several Hasidic communities

SA   Young married woman, affiliated with Skvir

SB   Rabbi Shmuel Butman, director of the Lubavitch Youth Organization

SJ   Simon Jacobson, editor and translator of Lubavitcher Rebbe's talks, leader of a small seminar in Lubavitch hasides

SH   Syshe Heschel, son and brother of the Kapitshinitzer Rebbes, father-in-law of present Boyaner Rebbe

SL   Hasidic woman from Monsey, unaffiliated

SN   Young Hasidic housewife, Lubavitch

SP   Williamsburg housewife

SV   Lubavitcher Hasid who broke with Satmar after studying with Mendel Wechter

TP   Williamsburg Hasid with ties to Satmar

YA   Williamsburg Hasid with ties to Satmar

YK   Yehuda Krinsky, Lubavitcher spokesman, responsible for the educational arm of Chabad Lubavitch

ZR   Young Hasidic woman, Lubavitch

ZS   Satmar Hasid

Major Rebbes Discussed

Rebbes are usually identified by association with their towns, and "er" is appended to the town's name. The exception is the Satmar, where a final "er" would make pronounciation awkward. The village of New Square is spelled as it appears on the New York State map; however, the Rebbe is referred to as the Skverer in accord with past ties and present pronunciation.

Apter, the
> Abraham Joshua Heschel (1765–1835)

Baal Shem Tov
> Rabbi Israel ben Eliezer (1700–1760), the founder of Hasidism

Belzer, the
> Aaron Rokeah (d. 1957)
> Issahar Dov Rokeah (b. 1948), the nephew of Aaron

Bobover, the
> Shlomo Halberstamm (1905–) present Bobover Rebbe

Boyaner, the
> Mordchei Shlomo Friedman (1890–1971), son of Yitshok, scion of the Rizhin dynasty
> Nahum Dov Brayer (b. 1959), grandson of Mordchei Shlomo, named Rebbe in 1985

Dov Ber, the Maggid of Mezritch (1704–1772)
> Disciple of the Baal Shem Tov, leader of the Hasidic movement, progenitor of the Rizhin dynasty through the present Boyan dynasty

Kapitshinitzer, the
> Abraham Joshua Heschel (1887–1966)
> Moshe Heschel (1927–1975)

Lubavitcher, the
> Shneur Zalman of Ladi (1745–1813), the first Lubavitcher Rebbe
> Joseph Isaac Schneersohn (1880–1950), the sixth Lubavitcher Rebbe

Menachem Mendel Schneerson (1902–), the seventh Lubavitcher Rebbe, son-in-law of Joseph Isaac Schneersohn

Rizhiner, the

Israel Friedman (1798–1850), great-grandson of Dov Ber of Mezritch, great-great-grandfather of the present Boyaner Rebbe

Satmar, the

Joel Teitelbaum (1886–1979)

Moshe Teitelbaum (b. 1913), nephew of Joel, formerly the Szigetter Rov

Skverer, the (of New Square)

Yaakov Yosef Twersky (1900–1968)

David Twersky (b. 1940), son of Yaakov

Stoliner, the (Stolin-Karlin)

Yohanan Perlow (1900–1955)

Barukh Meir Yaakov Sochet (b. 1954), grandson of Yohanan Perlow

Glossary

All of the words included in the glossary are used in the Yiddish language. Hebrew derivations are noted. Plural forms are provided when they appear in the text.

The primary consideration is to present in English the most recognizable forms of Yiddish and Hebrew words. Spellings of Yiddish words (and of Hebrew words found commonly in Yiddish) use as a guide the YIVO transcription rules for spoken Yiddish; however, there are frequent exceptions to the YIVO rules since the most commonly used words already have established and recognizable forms. The transcription rules are described in Uriel Weinreich's *Modern English-Yiddish Yiddish-English Dictionary* (New York: YIVO Institute for Jewish Research, McGraw-Hill Book Company, 1968). Hebrew words generally follow a simplified form of standard Hebrew orthography as described in the *Encyclopaedia Judaica*, vol. 1 (New York: Macmillan, 1971). A few standard English spellings are employed (such as Rosh Hashanah). Some variant spellings may appear in proper names and in material quoted from other sources.

alter: elder, older
atorah (Heb.): crowning (naming the Rebbe)
baltshuve, baltshuves (Heb. *ba'al teshuvah, ba'alei teshuvah*): repentant sinner; returnee to Orthodox faith and practice
bar mitzvah (Heb.): confirmation for boys at age thirteen
besmedresh (Heb. *bet ha-midrash*): house of study; synagogue
bet din (Heb.): rabbinical court; the judges who conduct the hearing
bris, brisn (Heb. *brit*): religious ceremony of circumcision
Chabad (Habad): acronym of *hokhmah* (wisdom) *binah* (understanding), *da'at* (knowledge); the Lubavitcher movement founded by Rabbi Shneur Zalman
challah (Heb. *hallah*): festive Sabbath loaf
daven: to pray, usually with a slight rocking motion
dayyan (Heb.): judge in a rabbinical court
didan notzakh (Aramaic): we are victorious

dintoyre (Heb. *din Torah*):   the trial or hearing in a rabbinical court

dybbuk (Heb.):   soul of a dead person that returns to inhabit the body of a living person

erev (Heb.):   evening, the eve of

Eretz Yisroel (Heb.):   the Land of Israel

farbrengen: Lubavitcher gathering (*farbreng:* to spend time, to enjoy)

gabbai, gabbaim (Heb.):   major-domo of the Rebbe's court; Rebbe's secretary

gartl: a silk belt which serves to separate the upper (higher) body (heart and brains) from the lower (profane) half where the excretory and sexual organs are located

Gemara (Heb.):   the portion of the Talmud which discusses the laws in the Mishnah

gemilut hasidim (Heb.):   acts of lovingkindness

glat kosher: unquestionably kosher, the most extreme standards of kashrut

golus (Heb. *galut*):   exile, diaspora

goy, goyim (Heb.):   gentile

halakhah, halakhot (Heb.):   the law, the portion of the Talmud concerned with the Law; a rabbinic legal decision

Hanukkah (Heb.):   festival of eight days celebrating the victory of the Maccabees in the year 161 B.C.E.

HaShem (Heb.):   God, the Lord, the Name

hasides (Heb. *hasidut*):   Hasidic teachings, philosophical exposition

hasidishe (Heb. *hasidi*):   Hasidic

Haskalah (Heb.):   "Enlightenment"; the movement promoting secularism and modern European culture among the Jews in the eighteenth and nineteenth centuries

hatzufah (Heb.):   an impudent woman

havdalah (Heb.):   the ceremony marking the close of the holy Shabbes and the beginning of the secular week

hazan (Heb.):   cantor, leader of prayers

hekhsher, hekhsheyrim (Heb. *hekhsherim*):   permit of ritual fitness issued by a rabbi

herem (Heb.):   ban

hoyf, hoyfn: the dynastic court of the Rebbes; the courtyard in the European shtetl where the community's major institutions (the besmedresh, yeshivah, bet din, and mikvah) and the Rebbe's house were located

hutzpah (Heb.):   impudence, nerve, gall

kabbala (Heb.):   corpus of mystical writings; Jewish mystical tradition

kaftan (Polish):   long coat

kashrut (Heb.):   the dietary laws

kehillah (Heb.):   community, the community council

keri'ah (Heb.):   to tear one's clothing as a sign of mourning

kiddush (Heb.):   benediction over wine

kolel (Heb.):   yeshivah for married men to continue their Torah studies

kosher (Heb. *kasher*):   food ritually permissible to eat

ktav hiskashrut (Heb.):   a letter binding together Hasidim and new Rebbe, signed by the Hasidim and sent to the Rebbe *kvitl, kvitlekh:* petition presented to Rebbe containing the request, the names to be blessed, and the name of the petitioner's mother

l'chaim (Heb. *lehaim*): a toast: to your health, to life

loshon horah (Heb. *lashon harah*): gossip, evil speech

lulav (Heb.): palm branch used to celebrate the holiday of Sukkot

ma'amar (Heb.): esoteric discourse at a farbrengen; the most mystical portion of the Rebbe's discourse

ma'ariv (Heb.; Yid. *mayrev*): evening prayer

maggid, maggidim (Heb.): itinerant preacher

mashgiah (Heb.): overseer in the preparation of kosher food

mashiah (Heb.) (also *moshiach*): messiah, the anointed one

matzah, matzot (Heb.): unleavened bread eaten particularly during Passover

mazl tov (Heb. *mazal tov*): congratulations, good luck

me kamokha (Heb.): Who is like unto Thee [O Lord]?

melave-malke (Heb. *malkah*): literally, "escorting the Queen," the meal which takes place after the Shabbes is ended; it is a time treasured for storytelling

Melekh Olam (Heb.): King of the Universe

menorah (Heb.): seven-branched candelabra used in antiquity; Hanukkah menorah: eight-branched candelabra lit during the holiday of Hanukkah

menshlekhkayt: humaneness, being civilized and considerate of others

mezuzah, mezuzot (Heb.): small scroll with written inscriptions from Deut. 6:4–9; 11:13–21 placed in container and attached to doorpost

Midrash (Heb.): an interpretation of scripture using legal discussion, stories, and homiletics; a collection of such interpretations

mikvah, mikvot: ritual bath

minhah (Heb.): afternoon prayer

minyan, minyanim (Heb.): quorum of ten Jewish men (over age thirteen) required for public prayer

Mishnah (Heb.): codex of laws compiled by Rabbi Yehuda ha-Nasi about 200 C.E.

Misnagid, Misnagdim (Heb. *mitnaged, mitnagdim*): opponents of the Hasidim

mitzvah, mitzvot (Heb.; Yid. *mitzve, mitzves*): commandment, good deed

mitzvot kalot (Heb.): the lighter, lesser commandments

mohel (Heb.): circumciser

nigun (Heb.): song, melody

parnose (Heb. *parnasah*): livelihood

Pesach (Heb. *Pesah*): Passover

peyes (Heb. *pe'ot*): earlocks

pidyen (Heb. *pidyon*): gift of money attached to the kvitl and presented to the Rebbe at the time of a visit; literally, "redemption"

pushke (Heb. *pahit*): tin can used to collect coins for charity

rabbi, rabbis (Heb. *rav, rabbanim*): title for one qualified to render decisions on matters of Jewish law; leader of a congregation; Chief Rabbi of a community; a teacher; literally, my teacher

Rebbe, rabbeim (Heb. *rabbi*): the leader of a Hasidic court; tsaddik; my teacher and master

rebbetsn: Rebbe's wife

Rosh Hashanah (Heb.): Jewish New Year

Rosh Hodesh (Heb.): the new moon; the beginning of the Jewish month

rosh yeshivah, rashe yeshivot (Heb.): head (or dean) of a yeshivah; master teacher

rov, robbonim (Heb. *rav, rabbanim*): rabbi, chief rabbinical authority of a community

schnapps: brandy

Sefer Torah (Heb.): Torah scroll

Shabbes, Shabbosim (Heb. *Shabbat*): Sabbath

shadkhan, shadkhanim (Heb.): matchmaker

shaharit (Heb.): morning prayer

shaleshudes (Heb. *se'udah shelishit*): the third meal of the Shabbes and the setting for the Rebbe's mystical discourse

shames (Heb. *shammash*): beadle

sheygetz (Heb. *sheketz, shekatzim*): pejorative reference to a gentile man; a hooligan; also used pejoratively to characterize an errant Jew, an extremist, an impudent prankster

sheytl: wig worn by women after marriage

shidukh (Heb.): matrimonial match

shirayim (Heb.): the remains of the Rebbe's meal, which are shared by his followers

shi'ur (Heb.): learning

shivah (Heb.): the seven days of mourning

shlikhim (Heb.): emissaries

shohet, shohatim (Heb.): ritual slaughterer

sholom aleykhem (Heb. *shalom aleikhem*): hello, peace be with you

shtetl: town

shtibl, shtiblekh: small house of prayer of Hasidim, usually consisting of one room

shtrayml, shtraymlen: fur cap worn on the Shabbes, holidays, and at weddings of relatives

shul, shuln: synagogue

Shulhan Arukh (Heb.): code of Jewish law; compendium of Jewish law prepared by Joseph Caro in the sixteenth century

sicha, sichot (Heb.): discourse, talk, lecture

siddur, sidurim (Heb.): prayer book

Simhat Torah (Heb.): Festival of the Law; the day when the yearly cycle of reading the Torah is completed

sukkah (Heb.): booth; wooden hut covered with branches in which all meals are taken during the holiday of Sukkot

Sukkot (Heb.): Feast of Tabernacles which begins four days after Yom Kippur

talmid khokhem, talmidim khakhomim (Heb. *hakham*): scholar, learned man

Talmud (Heb.): the oral law; it includes the Mishnah (in Hebrew) and the Gemara (in Aramaic), commentaries on the Mishnah

Tanya (Aramaic): the first word (*It has been taught*) of Shneur Zalman's work *Likkutei Amarim,* by which the book is known

tefillin (Heb.): phylacteries; leather cases that are bound to the forehead and

the left arm during morning prayer, containing parchment on which are written the following lines from the Hebrew Bible: Exod. 3:1–10, 11–16; Deut.
6:4–9, 9:13–21

tehilim (Heb.):   psalms

teshuvah (Heb.):   return, repentance

tish, tishn: table; a communal meal at the Rebbe's table

Tishah be-Av (Heb.):   the ninth day of the Jewish month of Av; day of mourning of the destruction of the Temple and Jerusalem in 586 B.C.E and 70 C.E.

Torah: the Pentateuch

Torah Vadaat: an Orthodox yeshivah once located in Williamsburg and now
in Flatbush

toyre (Heb. *torah*):   Rebbe's teachings, usually given at a Shabbes meal

treyf (Heb. *taref*):   food considered impure (unkosher); not permissible to eat;
not prepared according to the ritual law or found to contain some defect

tzaddik, tzaddikim (Heb.):   a righteous man; the leader of a Hasidic court;
synonymous with Rebbe

tzaddikism: a period of the Hasidic movement which saw the proliferation of
Hasidic courts; at that time major emphasis was placed on the miraculous
powers of the tzaddikim

tzedakah (Heb.):   charity

tzigayner: gypsy

tzitzit (Heb.):   fringes sewn at the four corners of the prayer shawl and the *talit
katan* (Yid. *talis koten,* fringed undershirt) as reminders of God's commandment (see Deut. 22:12; Num. 15:37–41)

Tzivos HaShem (Heb.):   army of God, the organization of the younger students
of Lubavitch

yarmulke: skullcap

yeshivah, yeshivot (Heb.; Yid. *yeshive, yeshives*):   school for advanced talmudic
and rabbinic studies

Yetser ha-Ra (Heb.):   the evil inclination, the evil urge

Yetser ha-Tov (Heb.):   the good intentions in man

Yiddishkayt: the essence of Orthodox life—the observance of mitzvot and the
furtherance of Torah learning

yikhes (Heb. *yihus*):   lineage; status based on lineage

Yom Kippur (Heb.):   Day of Atonement

yortsayt, yortsaytn: anniversary of a death

Index

Index

Index

Index